TREASURES TO HOLD

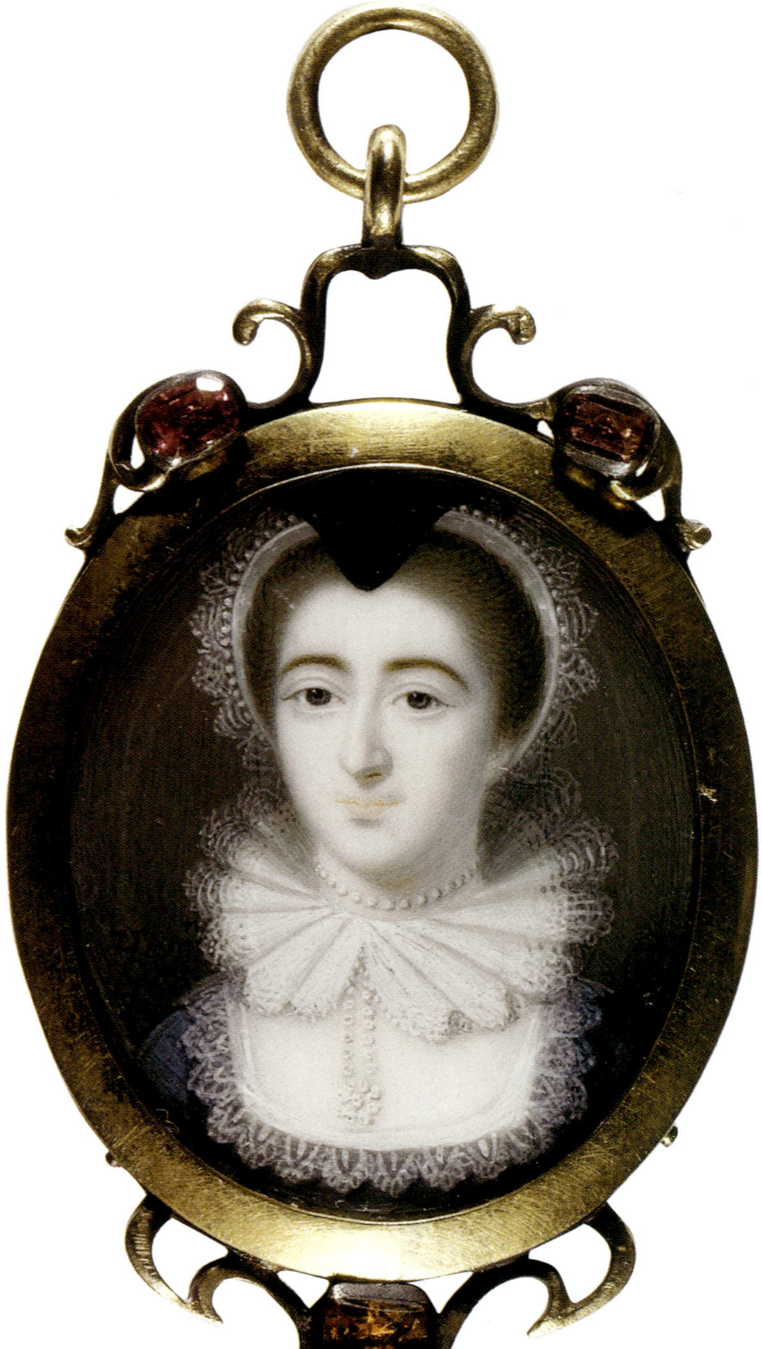

TREASURES TO HOLD

Irish and English Miniatures 1650–1850

FROM THE NATIONAL GALLERY OF IRELAND COLLECTION

Paul Caffrey

NATIONAL GALLERY OF IRELAND 2000

This book accompanies the exhibition

Treasures to Hold:
Irish and English Miniatures 1650–1850
from the National Gallery of Ireland Collection

At the National Gallery of Ireland, Dublin
25 October – 10 December, 2000

Sponsored by Wellington Ophthalmic Laser Clinic
www.well-eyeclinic.com

Wellington Ophthalmic
Laser Clinic

Hardback ISBN 09 0316 280 6
Paperback ISBN 09 0316 275 X

Edited by Adrian Le Harivel
Photography by Roy Hewson
Design by Jason Ellams
Typeset in Sabon
Printed by Inkspot, Dublin

Illus. 26 by Seán O'Sullivan © The Artist's Estate

Front cover: *Sarah Siddons*, 1784 and *Self-Portrait*, c.1785, by Horace Hone (1754/56–1825/27), *Portrait of a lady*, by Lucius Barber (1720–1767) and *Captain Robert Bransby*, c.1670 by Thomas Flatman (1635–1688)

Spine: *Portraits of a man and a lady*, 1761, by Thomas Frye (c.1710–1762)

Back cover: *Romeo and Juliet*, 1783, by William Birch (1755–1834)

Frontispiece: *Portrait of a Lady in Elizabethan costume*, 1764, by Gustavus Hamilton (c. 1739–1775), substantially enlarged

Endpapers (hardback only): Irish 19th century paper from book of engraved Antique tombs (NGI 20706) rebound by T. Connolly, Dublin.

Contents

Preface

The Wellington Ophthalmic Laser Clinic is honoured to be associated with the Treasures to Hold exhibition of *Irish and English miniatures* which opens at the National Gallery of Ireland on the 25th of October 2000.

Miniatures are a micro art form full of nuances; fine details of the artist's treatment of lace, jewellery, face and eyes. The brushstrokes will often denote who the artist is. To observe this fine detail, magnification is required. Through the gift of modern technology, in the form of microscopes and lasers, details of the eye are revealed to the eyes of the eye surgeon as never before, enabling us to perform fine microsurgery that was unthinkable in the past. Given this common bond with fine detail and microscopes, we are delighted to assist in revealing this wonderful collection, so that art lovers can admire the artistic work of these masters of the art of miniature painting.

Frank L Lavery F.R.C.S.
Arthur B Cummings F.R.C.S.
The Wellington Ophthalmic Laser Clinic, Dublin.

Foreword

Although the National Gallery of Ireland is best known for its splendid Old Master and Irish paintings, it is also the repository of an exceptional collection of miniatures, which are generally viewed by individuals in the Print Room. Whilst there are fine examples of the work of many distinguished continental masters, the true glory rests in a comprehensive array of examples by Irish and English painters. The present exhibition sets out to provide the public with the most comprehensive presentation to date of this remarkable, though little known, element of the Gallery's holdings, by putting on view some 130 works from the collection.

In his text Dr Paul Caffrey provides an illuminating survey of the origins and development of the art of miniature and particularly of its flourishing in these Islands, where it was practised with particular distinction, becoming an object of special interest, providing patrons with a vehicle in which to express their romantic and familial relationships as well as their good taste. The textual commentary on the exhibits provides a detailed account of the authorship of each piece, its technical characteristics and subject matter, which in most instances will constitute the most comprehensive account to date.

The Gallery is immensely grateful to Paul Caffrey for his research into the collection and for his personal commitment to the project, within a tight timeframe. This scholarship, however, might never have reached the public domain, were it not for the generosity of Wellington Ophthalmic Laser Clinic, which has most generously sponsored this exhibition. Adrian Le Harivel has worked closely with Paul Caffrey in its preparation and edited the catalogue. The project was coordinated by Fionnuala Croke, Head of Exhibitions. Exhibits were prepared for display by Niamh McGuinne and Zoë Reid and photographed by Roy Hewson.

Raymond Keaveney
Director, National Gallery of Ireland

A good painter hath tender senses, quiet and apt; and the colours themselves may not endure some airs, especially in the sulphurous air of seacoal, and the gilding of goldsmiths. Sweet odours comfort the brain, and open the understanding, augmenting the delight in limning. Discreet talk or reading, quiet mirth or music, offend not, but shorten the time and quicken the spirit, both in the drawer and he which is drawn.

Nicholas Hilliard (c.1547-1619)
The Arte of Limning, c.1600

Horace Hone called & talked of the badness of the times, of having much employ in his Professional Capacity only during a part of the year.

Bone called after dinner... We talked about Enamelling. He said, that with the assistance of three of his sons he was proceeding to make a complete collection of Enamel pictures of the remarkable characters of the reign of Queen Elizabeth, that many of them were finished, and that he had pictures lent him for this purpose by the Duke of Bedford & many others of the first families in the Kingdom.

The Diary of Joseph Farington,
1 September 1807 and 8 February 1813

Acknowledgements

The author acknowledges with sincere thanks the assistance of the following in the preparation of this work: Raymond Keaveney, Director of the National Gallery of Ireland; Adrian Le Harivel, Curator of British and Dutch Paintings, to whose scholarship and knowledge of the collections I am greatly indebted; my friend and colleague at N.C.A.D, Hilary O'Kelly, who most generously allowed me to call on her encyclopaedic knowledge of dress history; Dr Frank Linton Lavery; James and Thérèse Gorry of the Gorry Gallery; Dr Maureen Dillon; John and Fiona Bellingam; Liz Davies; Dr Joan Buchanan; Dr Claire Donovan; Professor Colin Platt; Una Barry and Dr David Tomkin. At the National Gallery of Ireland, Fionnuala Croke, Head of Exhibitions; Jane MacAvock, Curator of Prints and Drawings; Niamh McGuinne and Zoë Reid (Paper Conservators); Elline von Monschaw (Paintings Conservator); Roy Hewson (Photographer); Celeste Augé (Library Assistant) and Jason Ellams (Designer).

In particular, the author wishes to acknowledge the assistance of the staffs of the National Gallery of Ireland Library; the Library of the National College of Art & Design; the National Irish Visual Arts Library; the National Library of Ireland; the Royal Irish Academy; the Royal Dublin Society Library and the Chester Beatty Library. The staffs of the following collections have been most helpful: the Victoria and Albert Museum; the National Portrait Gallery; the Fitzwilliam Museum, Cambridge, and the Royal Collections, London.

Dr Paul Caffrey, *National College of Art & Design*
Dublin, October 2000

Catalogue text:

The miniatures have been arranged in chronological order of artist as far as knowledge of the dates permit. All measurements are in centimetres, height by width, (or diameter in the case of circular miniatures). For ease of reading, signatures and inscriptions are given without raised letters, where used. References in the text are abbreviated, and are cited in full in the bibliography.

*denotes an abbreviated inscription

/ denotes a change of line or break in an inscription

Illustrations:

Miniatures in the main catalogue are generally illustrated actual size.

Abbreviations:

ARA
Associate of the Royal Academy

DNB
Dictionary of National Biography

GEC
G.E.Cockayne *The Complete Peerage* (1910–59, 13 vols.)

NGI
National Gallery of Ireland, Dublin

NGL
National Gallery, London

NLI
National Library of Ireland, Dublin

NMI
National Museum of Ireland, Dublin

NPGL
National Portrait Gallery, London

RA
Royal Academy of Arts, London; Royal Academician

RDS
The Dublin Society (founded 1731), Royal Dublin Society (after 1820)

RHA
Royal Hibernian Academy; Royal Hibernian Academician

SNPGE
Scottish National Portrait Gallery, Edinburgh

UM
Ulster Museum, Belfast

V&A
Victoria and Albert Museum, London

WCL
Wallace Collection, London

YCBA
Yale Center for British Art, New Haven

Glossary of Materials, Terms and Techniques

Anneal, toughen by gradually diminishing heat in the kiln when firing an enamel miniature. This process is used to adhere the layers of metallic oxide paint to the enamel surface.

Brushstrokes or Brushwork, the style of manipulation of the brush with the resulting effects on the application of paint on the support. In miniature painting, it becomes the individual handwriting of the miniaturist and is a vital clue to identification.

Enamel Technique, painting with pigments made from metallic oxides that are applied in overglazes to a vitreous enamel surface on a metal base.

Flux, the substance mixed with metallic oxide pigments that make it flow so that it may be applied like paint. In enamelling oil is used.

Gouache, opaque colours, usually mixed with white pigment ground in water and thickened with gum and honey. This was a common characteristic of miniature painting on ivory , especially the painting of clothing details.

Hatch, Hatching, Hatched Lines, paint in thin lines, usually parallel. Cross-hatching is when the lines of paint overlap.

Linear, brushstrokes of long, narrow lines of uniform breadth.

Luminosity, full of light, allowing the ivory support to show through and reflect the light thrown on the miniature, which was the desired effect and appeal of ivory painting.

Metallic Oxide, compound of oxygen with another element, or with organic radical, used as a pigment in enamel miniature painting.

Paste, the white enamel covering of the metal support.

Plumbago, from *plumbum*, the Latin for lead ore, denoting black lead, which is in fact graphite. Sharpened pieces were used for drawing portraits on vellum.

Scraper, miniaturists working on ivory used a scraper of penknife to scratch highlights in the dry paint.

Stipple or Stippling, painted or drawn in dots.

Watercolour, pigment mixed with gum made from fish lime and water had been used by medieval manuscript illuminators. From the sixteenth century, miniaturists mixed pigment with gum arabic and water when painting on vellum. When dissolved in water, the indissoluble grains of pigment are dispersed and the luminosity of the colours increases. The transparency of watercolour allows light to pass through the colour and reflect off the surface beneath. Vellum or ivory was the perfect colour on which to work.

Miniature Painting in Ireland and England 1650–1850: Works on Vellum, Ivory and Enamel

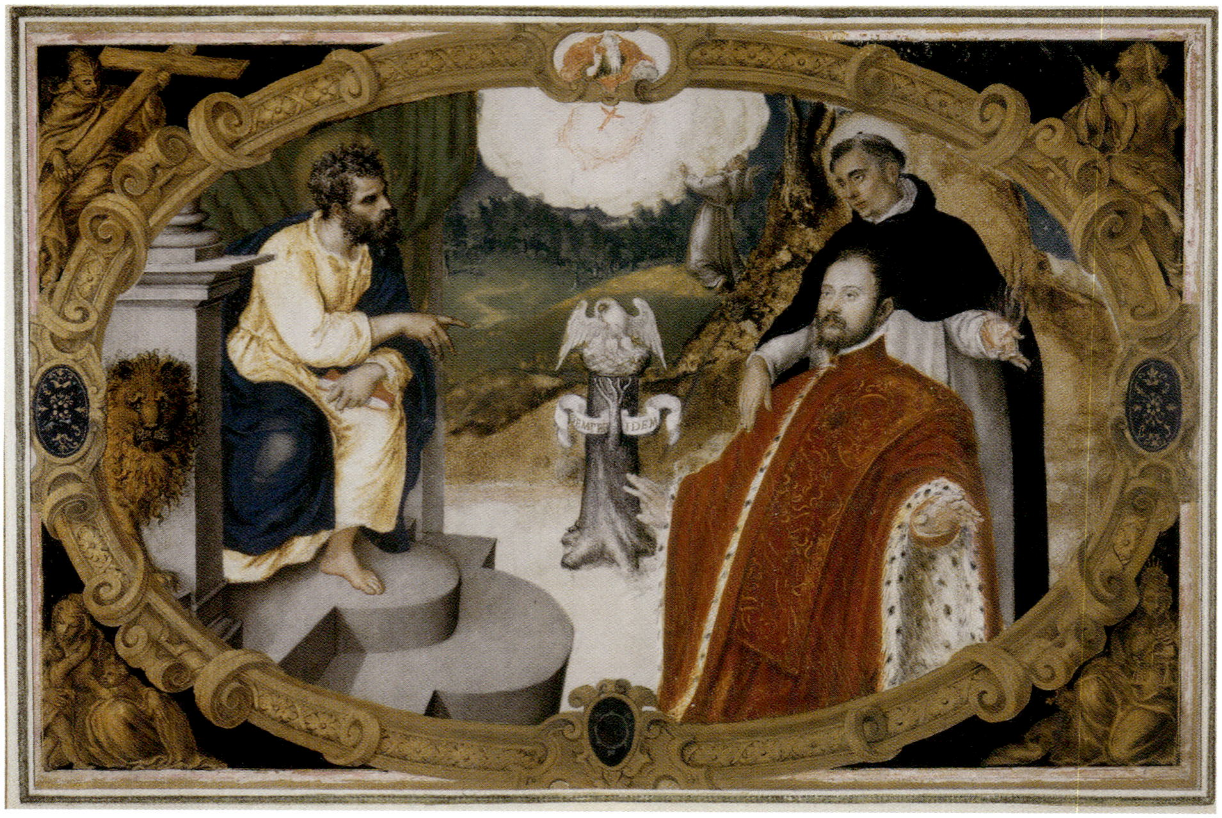

1. A Procurator of the Molin family presented to St Mark by St Vincent Ferrer, 21.5 x 33, gold paint and tempera with varnish on vellum
VENETIAN SCHOOL (c.1550/1600)
Purchased at Christie's, London, Duke of Somerset Sale, 1890 (NGI 2328)

The Origins of Miniature Painting

The techniques of miniature painting originated in gouache and watercolour painting on vellum. The first such miniatures were decorated initial capitals in manuscripts. With time, these became increasingly elaborate and ornamented. Their design later expanded, and the illuminator ultimately provided not merely decorated capital letters, but illustrations to the text, known in the medieval period as *historiae*. These were referred to as illuminations or limnings, deriving from Latin *illuminare* to light up, enlighten or embellish. The outline of the capital letter was drawn on the sheet of vellum with a piece of sharpened red lead. The Latin for red lead or vermilion is *minium. Miniare* is to colour red (with red lead)[1] and the illuminator was termed a *miniator*.

Since the seventeenth century, the term miniature has been applied by extension to all types of illustration in manuscripts. The English word carries a connotation of small or minute, and often the etymology is mistaken.[2] The decorated capitals in a Gospel or Book of Hours could illustrate any aspect of the text but often took the form of a picture of a devotional image, or a symbolic representation of an evangelist. During the late middle ages, it became increasingly popular for patrons to be portrayed in texts commissioned for a private chapel or given to a religious institution. These donor portraits were the first miniature portraits. A mid-sixteenth century example on vellum by an anonymous Venetian artist is *A Procurator of the Molin family presented to St Mark by St Vincent Ferrer* (Illus. 1). The portrait of the procurator (an agent or magistrate in Italy), in contemporary sixteenth century dress, is prominent in the composition. The mystical significance is underlined by the background details of a dying pelican, an emblem of Christ's sacrifice on the cross, and St Francis receiving the stigmata. A border with God the Father and personifications of Justice, Faith, Hope and Charity frame the image.[3]

In secular texts such as the charter, grant of arms, letters patent or other form of legal document, the ruling monarch was usually represented in the capital letter. Waterford City Corporation has Royal Charters spanning from King John (1215) to George IV (1815), including the illuminated Charter Roll of the 1370s, with a portrait of the reigning monarch, Edward III (exhibited at the Museum of Waterford Treasures).[4] Herald-painters, who were responsible for devising coats of arms and creating genealogies, used the same materials as miniaturists. They sometimes painted portraits inset into family trees. The testimonial to the character of William III by Daniel Mahony (active c.1738) exemplifies this practice (Illus. 2). There, the vellum is inscribed with text. It includes an added portrait of William III, copied from an engraving after Kneller. The ornamentation in the margins is derived from Celtic interlace patterns, and is reminiscent of the Irish manuscript illumination tradition.

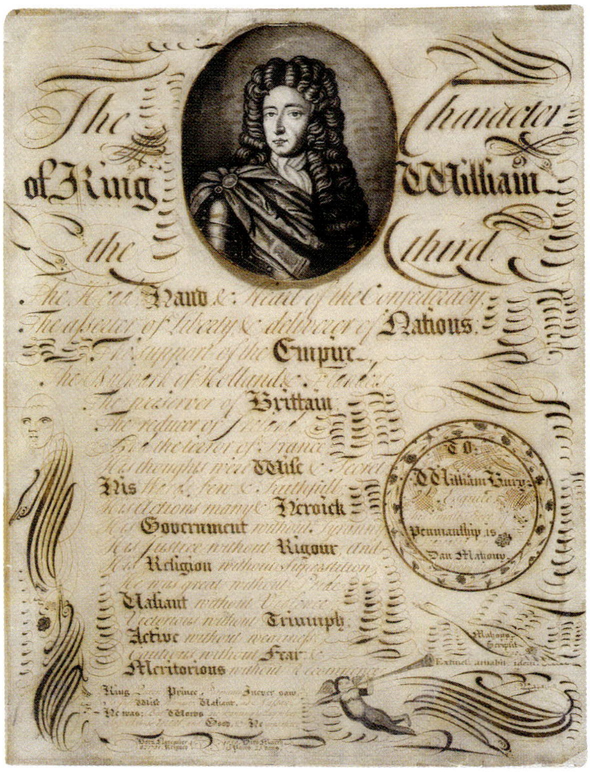

2. *A Testimonial to King William III's character*, 1738, ink and wash on vellum
DANIEL MAHONY (active c.1738)
Presented by Mr V. Newman, 1981
(NGI 7927)

From Manuscript to Miniature

With the rapid growth of printing, the hand-illuminated manuscript became less important. Illuminators transferred their activities to other commissions. Among these were small devotional images on vellum. Some were designed to be framed and displayed on the wall of a domestic interior. Others became a feature of lockets, which were worn as jewellery. Thus pictures previously confined to manuscript decoration became liberated from the page to become the first independent miniature portraits. The miniaturist continued to paint on vellum and used the same materials and techniques of painting as the manuscript illuminator. From the earliest times, the miniature and the miniaturist have been associated with specific materials and techniques that define their craft.

By the sixteenth century, the freestanding portraits were usually called *limnings* or *pictures in little*. They were generally painted in watercolour on vellum, and were quite small in size. The idea of a small portrait was not new. There is an established tradition of renaissance portrait medals, a tradition based on the revival of the antique classical tradition of casting images of the emperor or monarch's head on a medal, or striking it on a coin, carving a head in a gem or stone as an intaglio or carving in a cameo. At this stage of the development of the miniature portrait, two historical influences may be seen as predominant; manuscript illumination, and medallion portraiture.

The First Miniature Portraits

The earliest detached miniature portraits appear in France at the end of the fifteenth century. However, the development of the miniature is associated initially with the Netherlands. In England, the tradition first appears in the work of a family of Flemish miniaturists, the Horenbouts, or Horneboltes as they became known.[5] They were settled in London by the time the German artist Hans Holbein the Younger (1497/98–1543) paid his first eighteen-month visit to England in 1526.[6] Indeed, Holbein is said to have received instruction in miniature painting from one of them. The portrait of Henry VIII (1526), in its jewelled surround, by Lucas Hornebolte (d.1544) is one of the earliest independent portrait miniatures (Fitzwilliam Museum, Cambridge).[7] Holbein paid a second visit to England from 1532–36. Henry VIII commissioned him to paint miniature portraits, including that of his fourth bride *Anne of Cleves* (Victoria and Albert Museum, London). Holbein's miniatures appear to have been executed from drawings done from life. They consequently exemplify both Holbein's skill as a realist portrait painter and his mastery of the miniature technique. This confluence resulted in the finest miniature portraits ever painted.

By the time Holbein's work showed this characteristic mastery of the miniature, it had been long recognized as a portrait painted on a small scale in watercolour on vellum. Holbein's work shows yet another feature, which was to remain a characteristic of these portraits. Miniature portraits were personal and private likenesses, quite unlike larger oil portraits which were public images for general presentation and public display. During the late sixteenth century it became fashionable to wear miniature portraits as an ornament of dress. They were adorned with expensive jewels and worn in gold lockets and jewelled cases that could be elaborately decorated. The usual shape of miniatures changed from circular to oval so that they would fit more easily into lockets. Many of the early miniaturists did not come from a background in oil portraiture but in goldsmithing and its allied crafts which further emphasises the close relationship between the portrait as jewellery and ornament.

The Elizabethan Portrait

At the end of the sixteenth century, the miniature acquired a unique aesthetic which was not derived from full scale oil portraiture. The miniature image was not a naturalistic portrait. This separate form of jewelled portrait had an intimacy of its own, delicately painted, imbued with a charm, symbolism, enigmatic mottoes and often highly charged erotic meaning unknown in sixteenth century oil portraits. In the rarefied court of Elizabeth I, miniaturists led the way, and oil painters tried to imitate the effects of the miniature portrait. The very best of visual Elizabethan art and culture was expressed in the imaginative miniature portraiture of Nicholas Hilliard (c.1547–1619) and in the work of his pupil Isaac Oliver (1558/68–1617).[8] Hilliard's *Treatise concerning the Arte of Limning* (MS. in Edinburgh University Library) gives both technical information and an insight into the creation of miniatures.[9]

Seventeenth Century Miniatures

The political and social changes of the seventeenth century brought about a new interest in a more naturalistic portrait. This was reflected in the miniatures of the period.[10] However, the most important factor for miniaturists was the domination of portraiture by oil painters. Sir Anthony Van Dyck (1599–1641) had a profound effect on English portraiture during the seventeenth century. He established a model of portraiture that was adapted by portrait painters and miniaturists alike. Van Dyck introduced the spirit of the baroque, luxurious drapery, silvery texture of cloth and invented the Cavalier portrait (see catalogue entry 109).

The techniques of miniature painting were preserved within families of miniaturists who passed on the craft to the next generation.[11] Miniature painting survived as a distinct form of portrait in the work of John Hoskins (c.1595–1664/5) and his nephew, Samuel Cooper (1608/09–1672). Cooper was an exceptional miniaturist, a society portraitist with an international reputation. He managed to remain aloof from, or overcome, the political consequences of the Civil War, to paint the leaders of both the Commonwealth and the Restoration. His success lay not in revolutionary composition but in technical virtuosity and subtle observation of character and personality. The influence of Van Dyck may be detected in Cooper's bold brushstrokes and the liveliness of his portraits. Indeed Cooper was known as 'the Van Dyck in little'.[12]

Miniature Painting as a Social Accomplishment

Thomas Flatman (1635–1688) was the other great miniaturist of the second half of the seventeenth century. Flatman continued the tradition of brilliant naturalistic miniature portraits. Although often criticised for his dry technique, his portrait of Captain Bransby (catalogue entry 2) is technically accomplished and delicately painted after the manner of Cooper and Hoskins.[13] Flatman was an academic, a lawyer and poet and did not depend on miniature painting for a living. A development of the second half of the seventeenth century was that miniature painting became a pastime for gentlemen and formed part of polite and scholarly accomplishment.[14] It was no longer the sole province of artisans. A nobleman or gentleman would not only collect miniature portraits, but take lessons in painting. Thus, the noble ideal comprehended skill in poetry, music and miniature painting. Simon Digby, Bishop of Elphin (active 1668–1720) is the first known miniaturist of Irish birth, and was a gifted amateur. For him, miniature painting was a social accomplishment. His portraits of his colleagues and their wives assisted his preferment in the church (catalogue entry 3).

The Plumbago Portrait

Towards the end of the seventeenth century, a new technique of miniature painting was introduced to England and Ireland. The plumbago miniature, drawn in black lead or graphite, became popular from the 1660s. Plumbago originated in the allied book, illustration and engraving trades, probably in the Netherlands. Originally plumbagos were preparatory drawings for engravings. These were drawn on paper or card, material a great deal cheaper than vellum. Thomas Forster (c.1677–after 1712) was a leading plumbago miniaturist (catalogue entries 6–7).[15]

The Enamel Miniature and visiting Enamellists

Miniaturists, who made short visits, often brought a significant change to miniature painting in England and Ireland, affecting both stylistic and technical development of the miniature portrait (Illus. 3). The first miniaturist to paint on enamel in England was Jean Petitot (1607–1691) from Geneva. He came to England in the 1630s and was employed as an enamellist at the court of Charles I. The Swedish-born goldsmith and enamellist, Charles Boit (1662–1727), made lengthy stays from 1687 and 1703 and is viewed as part of the English School. Of his pupils, the most important was Christian Friedrich Zincke (1683/85–1767), who came from Dresden and remained in London. These were the artists who popularised enamel portrait painting in England. After Zincke, the most successful enamellist was Jean André Rouquet (1701– 1758) who left Switzerland and settled in London about 1723.

The enamel portrait was essentially a northern European type of portrait. It was already well known to William of Orange and, when he took the throne in 1688, he created the position of Enameller at the court. This set the seal on the fashion for enamel portraits, which spread in England and Ireland among his supporters. During this period, it became the custom among diplomatists to exchange enamel portraits, a custom already established in French courtly and diplomatic circles. The demand for enamel portraits in England was initially met by foreign enamellists who settled. This pattern is familiar to students of decorative stuccowork, where foreign craftsmen imported continental skills into Irish and English country houses. The Swede, Christian Richter (1678–1732), worked in London from 1702. Martin van der Meytens (1695–1770), born in Stockholm of Dutch extraction, came to London in 1714, staying until 1717, then went to Paris to study enamelling with Charles Boit (who had fled abroad to escape debts). Thereafter, van der Meytens went to work in Dresden, Venice and Rome before settling in Vienna. Jacques-Antoine Arlaud (1668–1746) was of French extraction, born in Geneva. He came to London in 1721 and stayed until 1729. Jean-Antoine Mussard (1707– after 1768) came from Geneva and worked in London, where he

Opposite:
3. Continental Enamellists who visited London
Presented by Sir Alfred Chester Beatty, 1951

MARTIN van der MEYTENS (1695–1770)
(?) John III, King of Poland, (1629–1696)
5.6 x 4.4, enamel on copper
(NGI 3600)

JEAN-ANTOINE MUSSARD (1707–after 1768)
Girl with a fruit basket, 1727
6.2 x 4.3, enamel on copper
(NGI 3602)

JEAN PETITOT (1607–1691)
Louis XIV, King of France, (1638–1715), c.1660
2.5 x 2, enamel on gold
(NGI 3252)

FRIEDRICH CHRISTOPH WEISBROD (1739–1803)
Portrait of a lady with a jewelled choker, 1755
2.6 x 3.9, enamel on copper
(NGI 3694)

GOTTFRIED HENDRIK RODE (1752–c.1793)
Portrait of a man in a pink coat, 1790
3.5 x 3, enamel on copper
(NGI 3711)

GOTTFRIED HENDRIK RODE (1752–c.1793)
Portrait of a lady with a pink bow, 1784
3.7 x 3.2, enamel on copper
(NGI 3712)

exhibited at the Society of Artists from 1763–68. Gottfried Hendrik Rode (1752–c.1793) was born in The Hague. He had been a pupil of the Swiss enamellist Johann Heinrich [von] Hurter (1734–1799), who had settled in London about 1777. Rode may have been working for Hurter, when he was in London during the early 1780s. Friedrich Christoph Weisbrod (1739–1803) from Stuttgart was also in London in the 1780s.

The Enamel Technique

Enamel miniatures are more closely connected with oil portraits, since enamelling is capable of reproducing the shiny quality of oil painting. The most common form of enamel miniature was a copy of an oil portrait. The technique was difficult and laborious. It necessitated drawing either from life or the oil portrait. The image was painted in metallic oxide paints, which were applied to a smooth vitreous enamel surface made from ground glass. The white enamel paste was applied to a metal base, usually copper or gold as these did not expand and contract in the firing unlike other metals. The metal base was dome shaped, and the convex side enamel (Thomas Moore, p. 128, is an exceptionally large example). This meant that any cracking, or pitting, that took place in the firing was confined to the reverse, so that on the other side there was a smooth white surface to which paint could be easily applied. The metallic oxide colours fused with the enamel in the firing. Colours so applied were not subject to fading, nor were they affected by dampness. The resulting picture had an attractive jewel-like quality. Miniature portraits of this type became the fashion from c.1700–40. It is clear that these miniatures are not painted *in* enamel so much as *on* enamel.[16] It will be appreciated that the eighteenth century enamelling technique described here is quite different from earlier techniques, such as *champlevé* or *cloisonné*, where enamels are poured into grooves or compartments on the metal support.

The Enamellists

After the departure of Charles Boit (1662–1727) from London in 1714, Christian Friedrich Zincke (1683/85–1767) became the foremost enamellist in

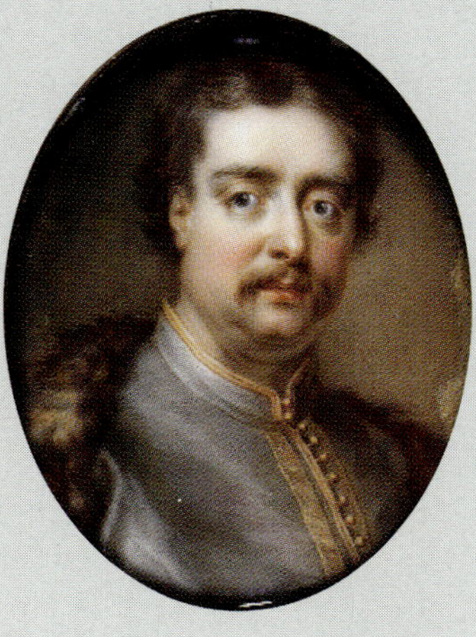

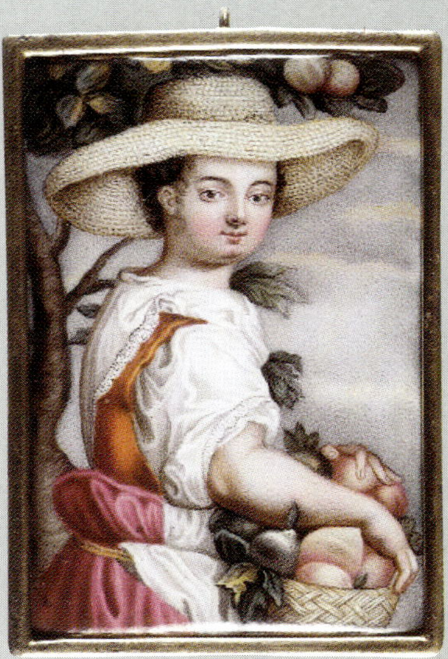

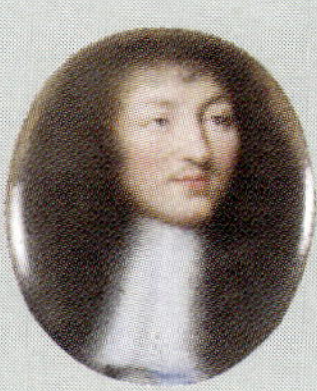

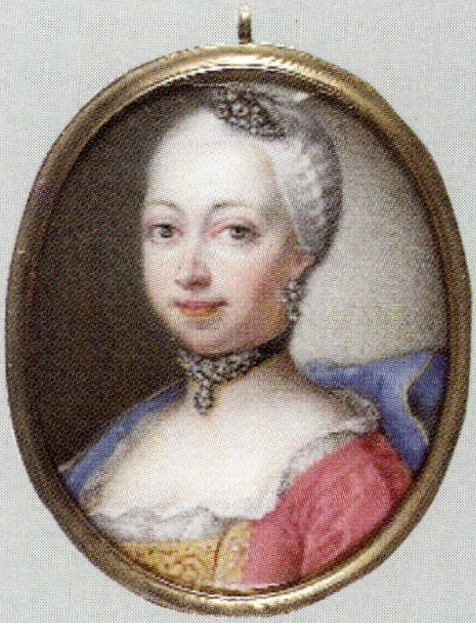

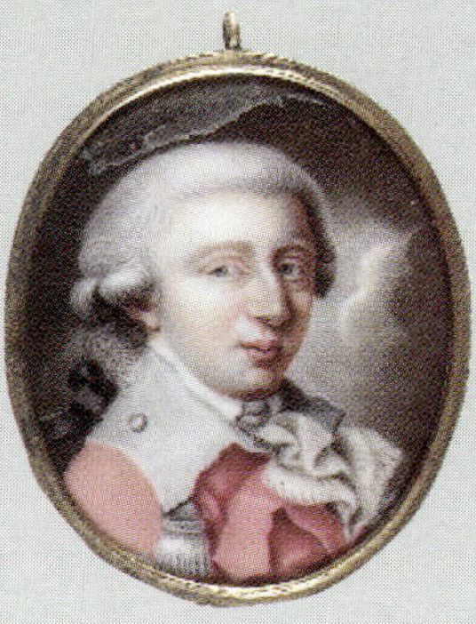

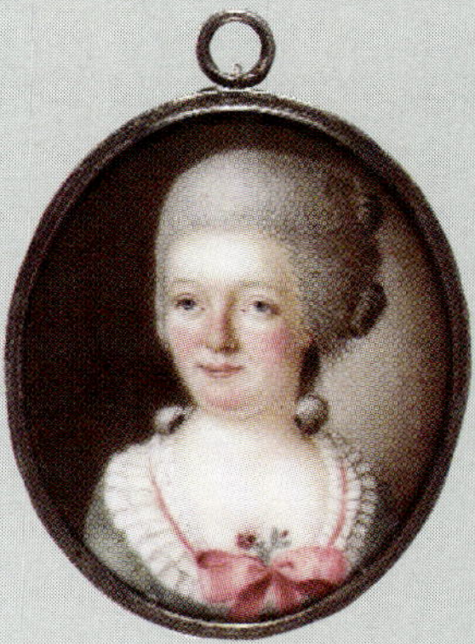

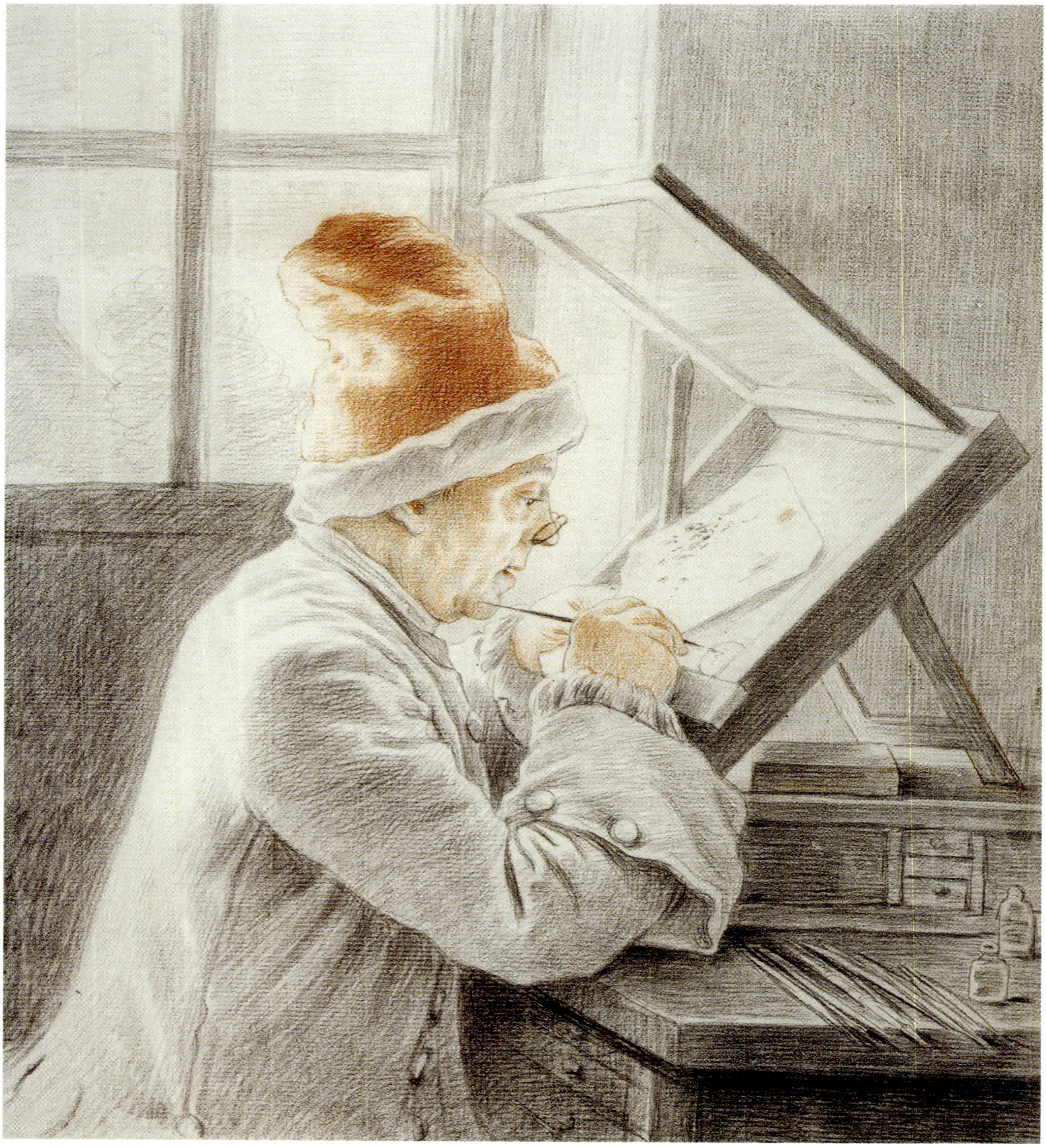

4. *Christian Friedrich Zincke, (1683/85–1767), painting a miniature of his daughter,* 1752
black and red chalk drawing
WILLIAM HOARE (1707–1792)
(British Museum, London P&D 1860-7-28-169)

England. The portrait of him (Illus. 4) by William Hoare (1707–1792) shows Zincke in 1752 working at his portable easel box. The glazed top reflects light down and keeps out dust. The miniature is securely held in the corner of the box, leaving his hands free for a palette and brush. There are drawers for the brushes and colours. A sense of order is underlined. Zincke was then in retirement and is shown keeping up his skill. He had been greatly helped by the patronage of George II. He created a format for the enamel portrait, which consisted of an almost full-face head and shoulders, or half-length composition, sometimes with drapery, so imitating lifesize oil portraiture. Many enamels were, in any case, copies or adaptations of full scale portraits, particularly those by Sir Godfrey Kneller (1646–1723). A practice was begun of frequently inscribing details of the sitter and date, in enamel, on reverse (Illus. 5). This was to culminate in the absurdly long inscriptions by the Bone family. Jean André Rouquet (1701–1758) was the best of Zincke's imitators, whose formula and technique were adopted by many enamellists. The German-born miniaturist Jeremiah Meyer (1735–1789) was apprenticed to Zincke and took on his technique (catalogue entry 47). Noah Seaman (active 1724–1741) and Irish-born enamellist, Nathaniel Hone (1718–1784) were close followers of Zincke. Hone's background was as a goldsmith and he spent most of his career in England, succeeding to much of the patronage formerly enjoyed by Zincke. Frequent self-portraits document Hone's wish to establish his status in the crowded London art world (Illus. 6–7). Only William Prewett (active 1733–1755), an English-born enamellist, managed to evolve what is clearly a unique and distinctive style (catalogue entry 17).

Subject, or cabinet enamels, form a distinct specialisation. Practitioners in this field included the Swiss-born miniaturist, George Michael Moser (1706–1783). Several enamellists and miniaturists worked as decorators of ceramics, and shared a common technique. William Craft (c.1730–1811) was employed by Wedgwood to decorate ceramics and later specialised in painting subject enamels (catalogue entry 43). William Russell Birch (1755–1834) painted large classical and mythological subjects (catalogue entry 66).

The Enamel Portrait as Jewellery

Of all the miniature techniques, these enamel miniatures were best suited to be worn as personal adornment. Most enamels of this type were set in gold pendants. Less commonly, they are found in lockets, brooches, rings, chatelaines, earrings or bracelets. In this period, even buttons, fans and buckles were decorated with enamel portraits. Though it was common for gold settings to be

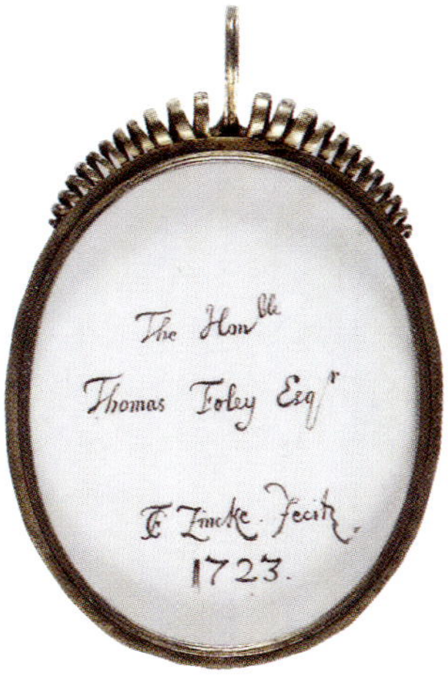

5. *Inscription and signature on reverse of The Hon. Thomas Foley* (catalogue entry 10)
CHRISTIAN FRIEDRICH ZINCKE
(1683/85–1767). (NGI 3594)

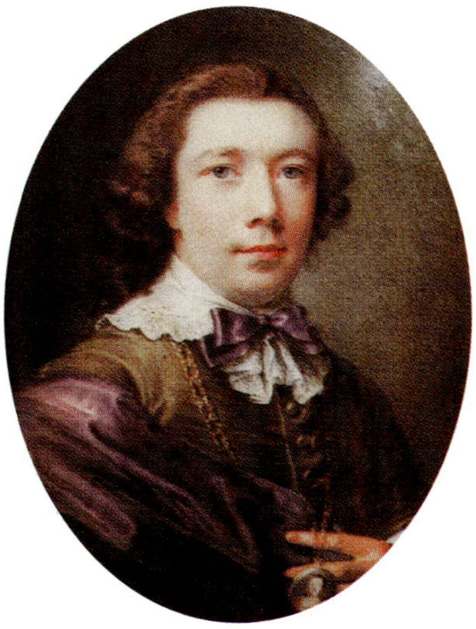

6. *Self-Portrait holding a miniature of his wife*, 1749
enamel miniature, 11 high
NATHANIEL HONE (1718–1784), (Untraced)
Hone's emulation of the celebrated Van Dyck *Self-Portrait*

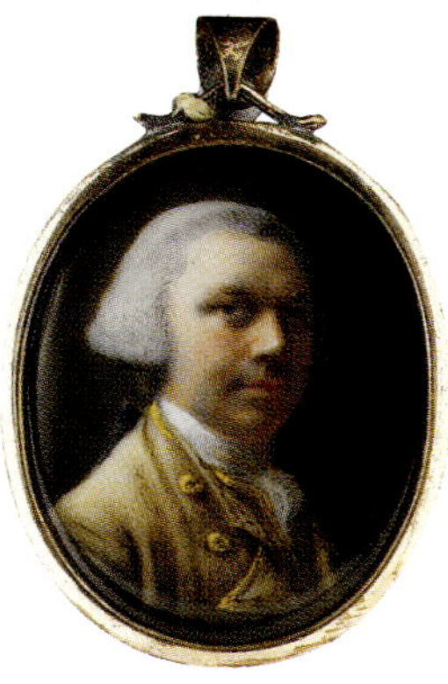

7. *Self-Portrait*, late 1750s
enamel miniature, 3.2 x 2.8
NATHANIEL HONE (1718–1784)
(Courtesy of the National Portrait Gallery, London cat. 1878)

8. Miniatures as Jewellery

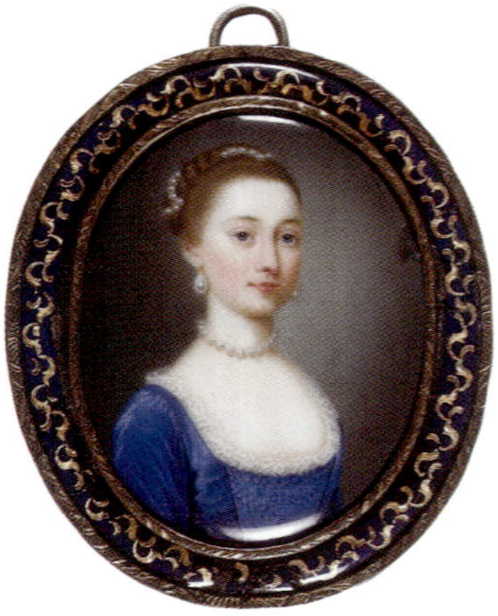

Portrait of a lady in a blue dress, with decorative surround
NATHANIEL HONE (1718–1784)
(NGI 7082)

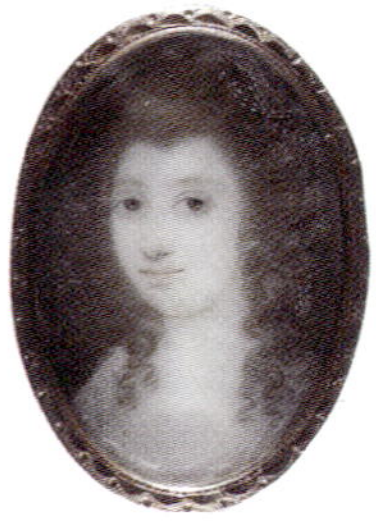

Portrait of a lady in a pink dress, set in a gold ring
ENGLISH SCHOOL (c.1770)
(NGI 7115)

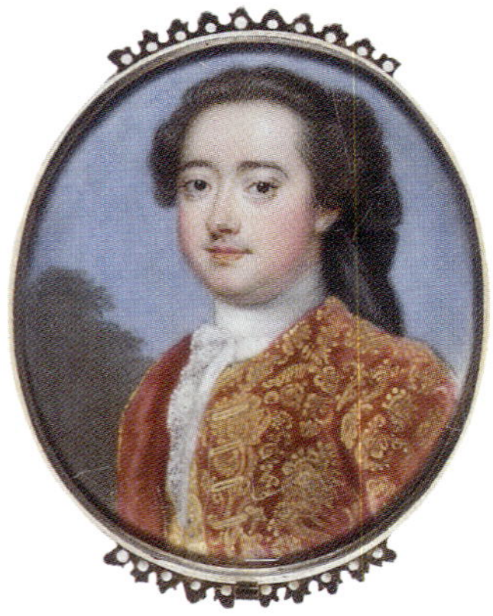

So-called portrait of 2nd Duke of Portland, with gold bracelet setting
CHRISTIAN FRIEDRICH ZINCKE
(1683/85–1767) (NGI 3765)

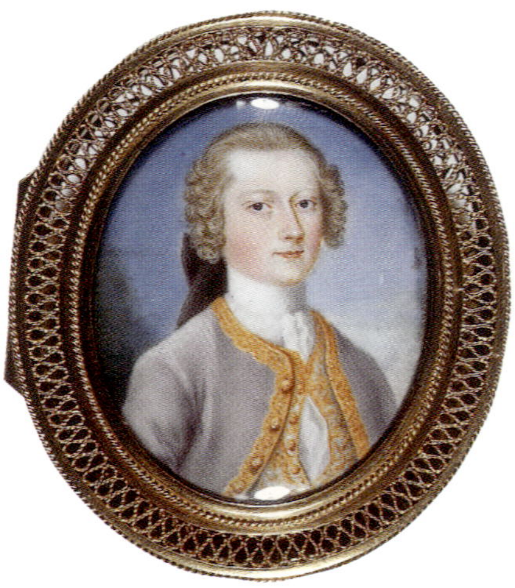

Portrait of a young man in a pale violet coat, set on a patch-box
CIRCLE OF GERVASE SPENCER
(c.1715–1763)
(NGI 7103)

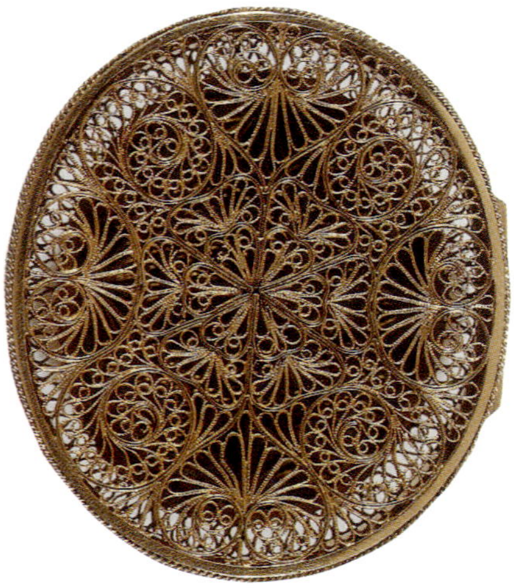

Reverse of NGI 7103

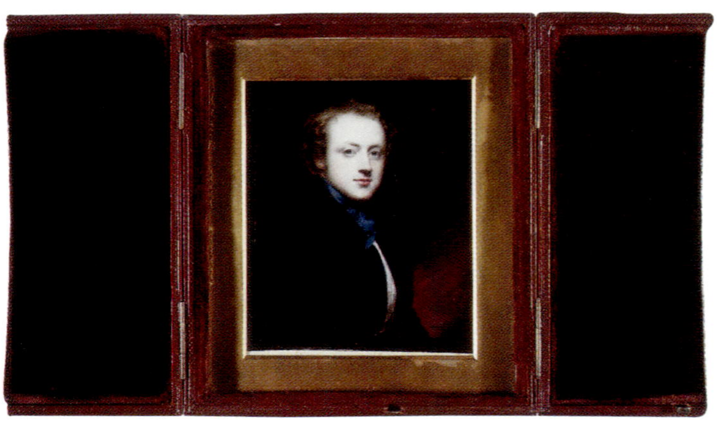

Self-Portrait, set in a leather display case, 1831
EDWARD ROBERTSON (1809–after 1840)
(NGI 7710)

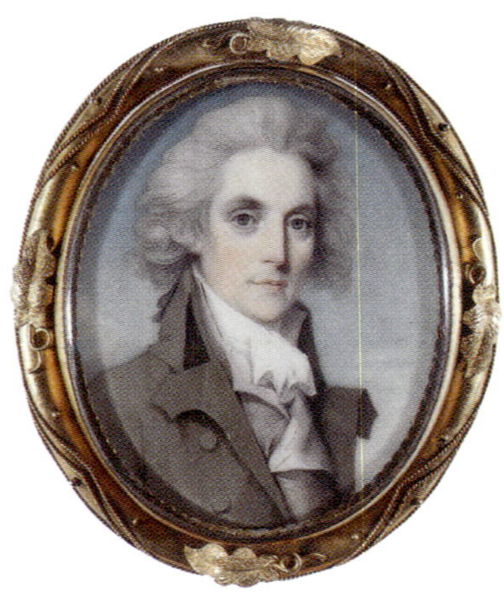

Colonel William Lane, set in a two-sided brooch, c.1870
IRISH SCHOOL (LATE 18TH CENTURY)
(NGI 7594)

elaborately embellished with jewels, the most common type of setting which survives is the plain oval pendant with a clasp of decorative scroll work. These would have been worn around the neck on a gold chain, ribbon or cord. This explains why the miniature was commonly worn as an object of adornment, a fashionable accessory and piece of jewellery (Illus. 8).

The Decoration of Boxes

As enamels are durable, and provided a covering for the image, it was common for miniature portraits to be found in decorative panels, and as ornaments to the lids of patch, powder or snuff boxes (Illus. 9). Sometimes miniatures were painted on watchcases and vinaigrettes. Objects such as these were used by both men and women. Taking snuff or powdered tobacco was popular at the end of the seventeenth century. Elaborate snuff-boxes and patch-boxes are a particularly eighteenth century phenomenon. The snuff-box formed an integral part of the ritual and etiquette, the vogue for snuff perhaps contributing to the popularity of enamel, as so many boxes were made with enamel portraits and scenes of everyday life. Black taffeta or silk patches were kept in special boxes called patch-boxes. Patches were fashion accessories but originally they may have served a defined cosmetic purpose, to hide disfiguring smallpox scars, or other spots and blemishes. The precious materials used by the enamellist, the jeweller and goldsmith in the manufacture of lockets and snuff-boxes demonstrate how the different crafts overlapped. Many of the enamellists came from a background in goldsmithing, rather than limning or oil painting.

The Enamel Miniature in Ireland

The first Irish miniature portraits painted by known professionals were those done by the enamellists. Before the enamellists, there were collections of miniature portraits in Ireland, but these do not survive. Also, before the enamellists, miniaturists were known to have worked in Ireland but no signed or authenticated works have survived from this era. The technique of enamelling was probably brought to Ireland by visiting or immigrant French goldsmiths.

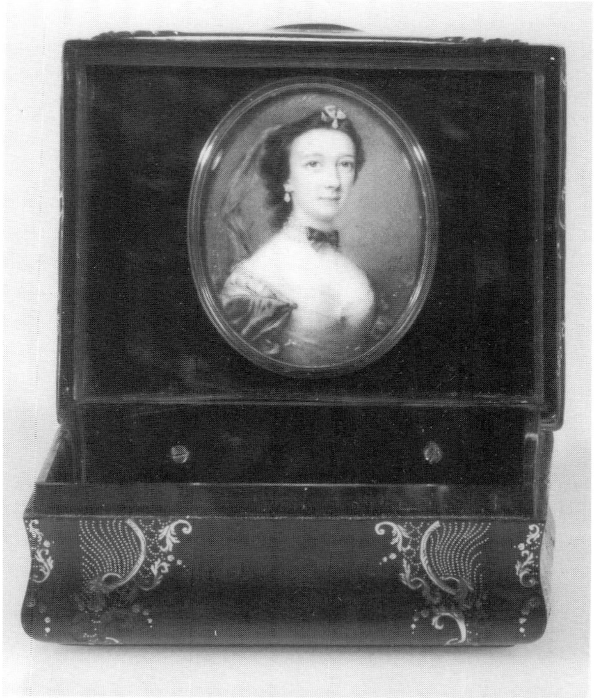

9. *Portrait of a lady*, 1750, enamel miniature 4.8 x 3.8 by NATHANIEL HONE (1718–1784), mounted inside a tortoiseshell snuff-box with gold rococo scroll work (Yale Center for British Art, Paul Mellon Collection B1974.2.56)

Nathaniel Hone would have become proficient before leaving for England. The technique of painting in metal oxides on enamel was practised by James Gwim (active 1720–1769), who worked as an engraver and maker of snuff boxes. This eccentric character went to manage the Battersea Enamel Works with a fellow Dubliner, John Brooks (active 1730–1756), who invented a method of painting in enamel on china. Peter Wingfield (1718–1777) was a watch engraver and goldsmith, who did enamel portraits and later worked in watercolour on ivory. George Mullins (active c.1755–1775) was painting lids of snuff-boxes for Thomas Wyse in Waterford during the 1750s, in between his career as a landscape painter. John Stordy (d.1799), a portrait enamellist, trained as a watchmaker making enamel plates for watches. His brother Charles Stordy (active c.1757) was an enamellist and member of the Guild of Cutlers, Painter Stainers and Stationers in Dublin. Rupert Barber (1719–1772) was one of the most underestimated of the enamellists who spent their career in Ireland. Like so many, Barber paid occasional visits to London and Bath. This virtuoso was apprenticed in London and Barber was a

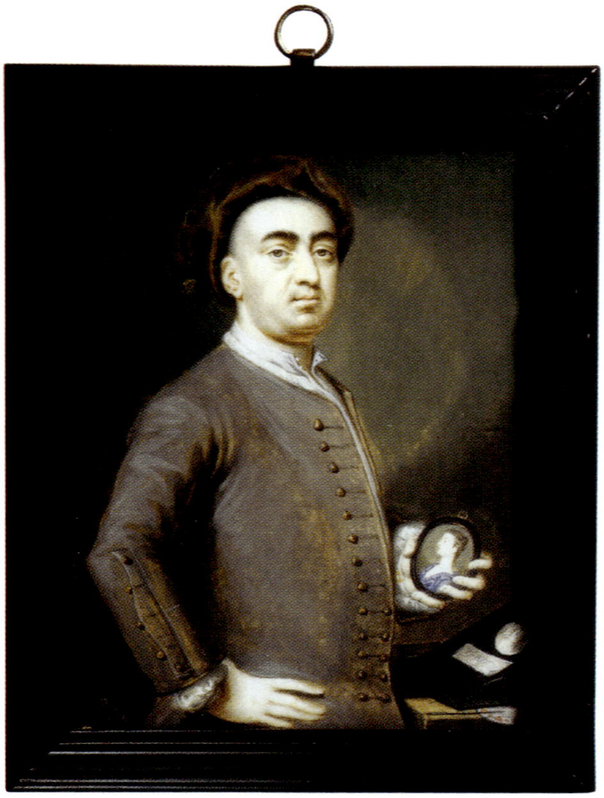

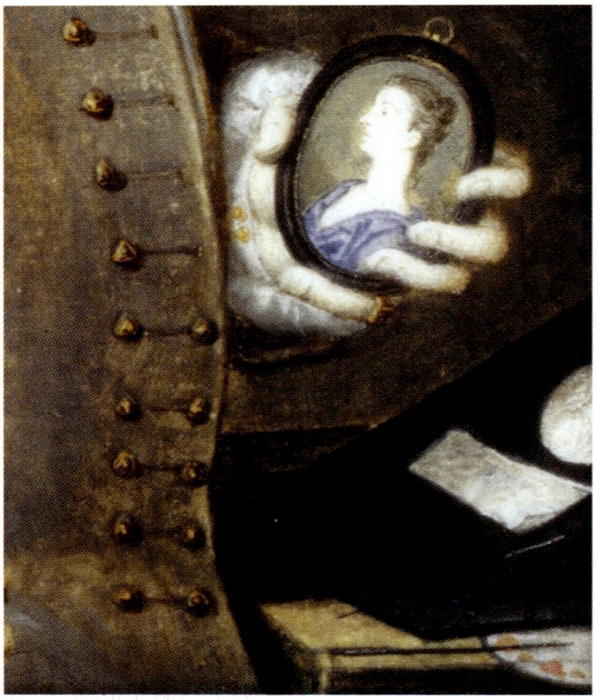

10. Self-Portrait holding a miniature, 1724
gouache on vellum miniature, 12.9 x 9.8
BERNARD LENS III (1682–1740)
(Ashmolean Museum, Oxford 1897. 58)

skilled draughtsman (catalogue entry 28), who painted more naturalistic portraits than Zincke or Nathaniel Hone. He worked on a larger scale and his miniatures are full of expression and individuality. Barber appears to have been particularly interested in capturing the sitter's personality and character.

The Introduction of Watercolour on Ivory Painting

The end of the seventeenth century saw the demise of the watercolour on vellum tradition and the popularity of enamelling and plumbago miniatures. Thereafter, came the introduction of ivory as a surface on which to paint portraits. The most important miniature painter in England at the beginning of the eighteenth century to make use of this new technique was Bernard Lens III (1682–1740). Lens (Illus. 10) is known to have painted his first portrait on ivory in 1707. The Venetian, Rosalba Carriera (1675–1757), is generally credited with inventing the watercolour on ivory technique.[17] She was an accomplished pastellist (NGI 3844–3849) but originally worked as a decorator of ivory snuff-boxes with watercolour *fondelli*. Her watercolour on ivory portraits, such as *Mrs Summers* (V&A), were popular with Grand Tourists. It was probably from examples brought back from Italy that Lens studied the technique.

The Ivory Technique

Although Lens is known to have painted on ivory in 1707, it took at least another thirty years before the watercolour on ivory miniature became the popular form of miniature painting. The reasons for the shift to ivory as a support for miniature portraits can be viewed as a change in fashion. It took many years before the possibilities of the translucent ivory surface were generally exploited and the taste for more informal portraits of the 1730s may also explain the reasons for the adoption of ivory. The formal stiff pose of enamel portraits became unfashionable. This quickly gave way to a new type of miniature painting, in which the sitter was dressed as he or she would be in their daily life.

Bernard Lens III painted in dotted stipple on to bare ivory, in a cautious attempt to prevent the watercolour paints from running. His work shows a heavy reliance on gouache (watercolour mixed with white), to cover the ivory surface, and create a matt effect. The technical problems encountered in dealing with the oily and difficult ivory surface posed a challenge to the first generation of ivory miniaturists. During the 1750s, these technical problems were overcome by degreasing the ivory surface, cutting the ivory thinner, and adding gum arabic to the watercolour.[18]

The Ivory Portrait

Once the technical difficulties were overcome and the quality of ivory portraits improved in the 1750s, public interest in the miniature portrait revived. Accuracy of portraiture was in demand. The informal, intimate, elegant image of the miniature portrait suited the taste of the age. The miniature, with its associations with courtship, marriage, and commemoration, required a likeness or accurate image. One interesting pair are the elderly lady and her grandson sealed back to back (Illus. 11). The quest for verisimilitude was an important theme in eighteenth century culture. As with enamel miniatures, ivory portraits formed an integral part of jewellery. They were worn in gold pendants, lockets, bracelets or rings. These miniatures were susceptible to damp, and to changes in temperature. Hence they were commonly encased in glass. Cyphers of the sitter's initials (catalogue entry 24), mottoes, a blazon of arms, personal inscription (Illus. 12), or monogram, were included. These portraits were given as presents to close friends, family members, exchanged during courtship, engagement or during a long separation during wartime or a period abroad. Miniature portraits became the traditional way of marking an event such as a marriage. They could be encased in a jewelled locket, or otherwise adorned with jewels and precious stones. Often these possessed some symbolic meaning, so that romantic ideas could be made permanent. Thus, rubies signified passionate love, diamonds, constancy in marriage, and pearls were sacred to Venus, the goddess of love. As part of the whole, the sitter's initials were often arranged in seed pearls. These settings became increasingly decorative and complex. It became usual to incorporate locks of the sitter's

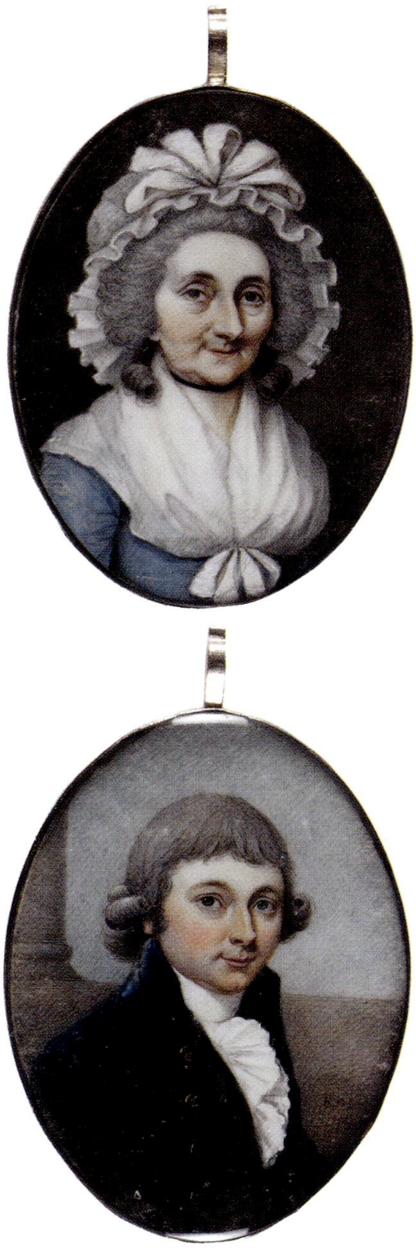

11. Portrait of a lady and her grandson, 1789 (in same frame) watercolour on ivory miniatures
SAMPSON TOWGOOD ROCH (1757–1847)
(NGI 19284)

12. Inscription on backing paper of Sarah Sophia Banks, 1768 (catalogue entry 37)
(NGI 2717)

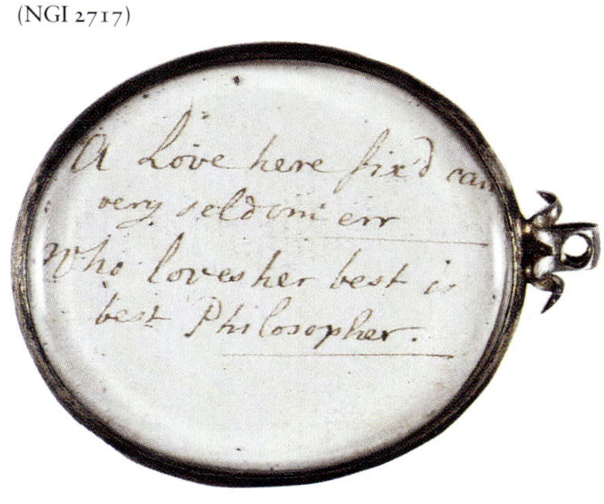

13. Hair patterns on reverses of miniatures

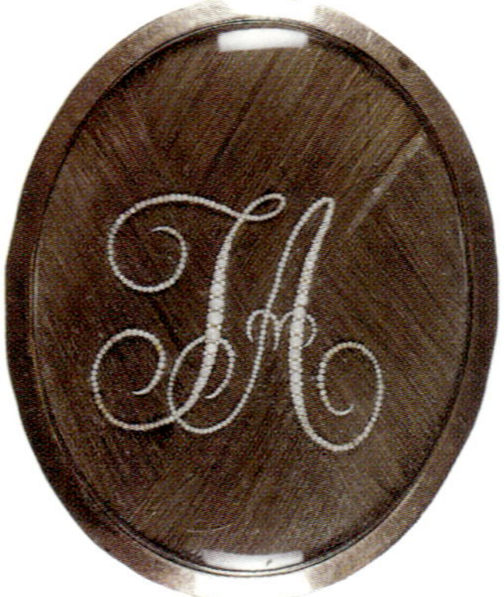

Interwoven hair with seed pearl initials TA
ENGLISH OR IRISH SCHOOL
(LATE 18TH CENTURY)
(NGI 7936)

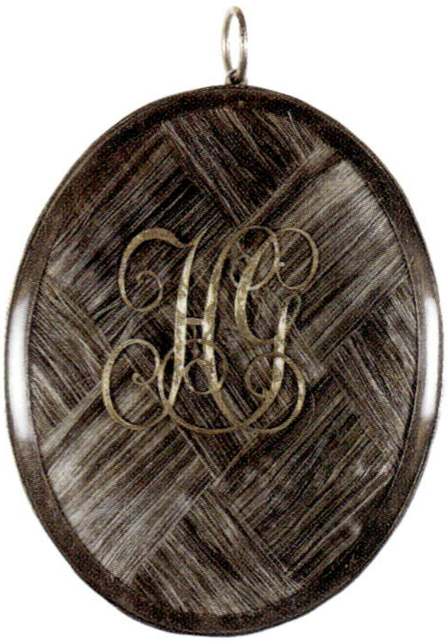

Interwoven hair with gilt initials HG, c. 1800
GEORGE LAWRENCE (c.1758–1802)
(NGI 7149)

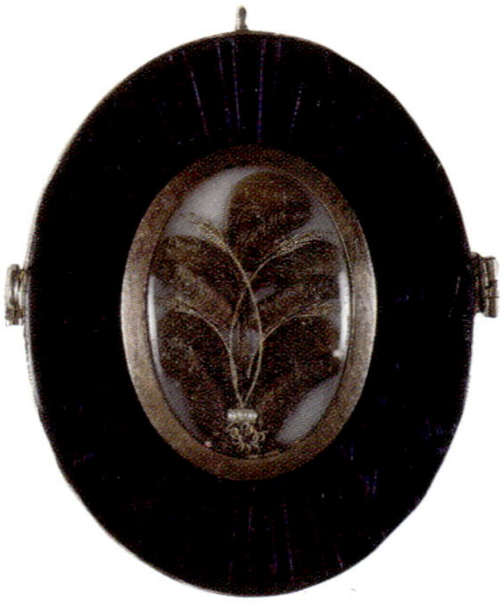

Locks of hair in feathered designs interspersed with gold filigree, 1793
GEORGE LAWRENCE (c.1758–1802)
(NGI 7078, cat. 85)

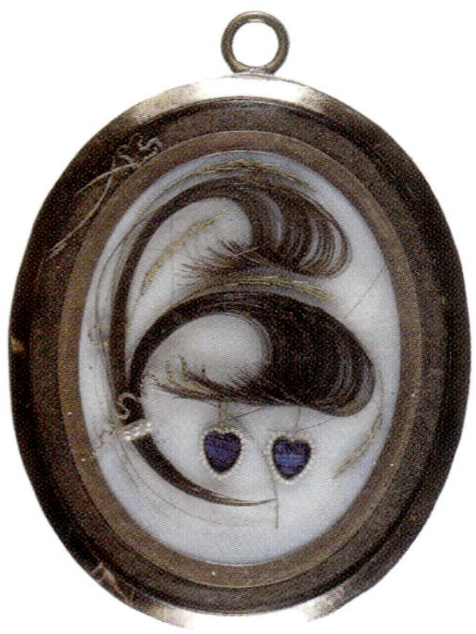

A pair of pearl edged hearts suspended from locks of hair and gold filigree, c.1810
GEORGE JACKSON (active c.1810)
(NGI 2376, cat. 117)

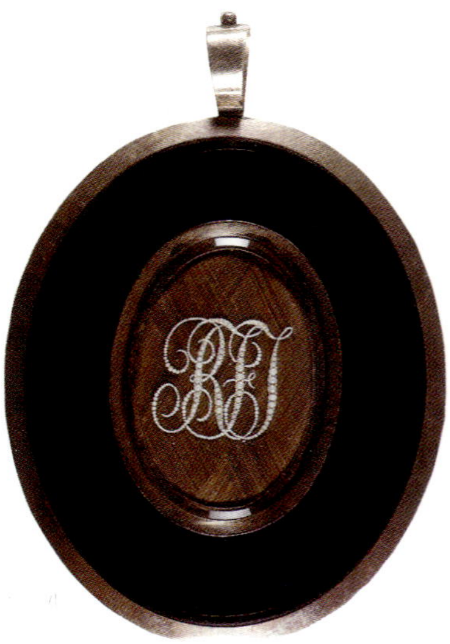

Interwoven hair with seed pearl initials RJT, 1800
SAMPSON TOWGOOD ROCH (1757–1847)
(NGI 7087, cat. 83)

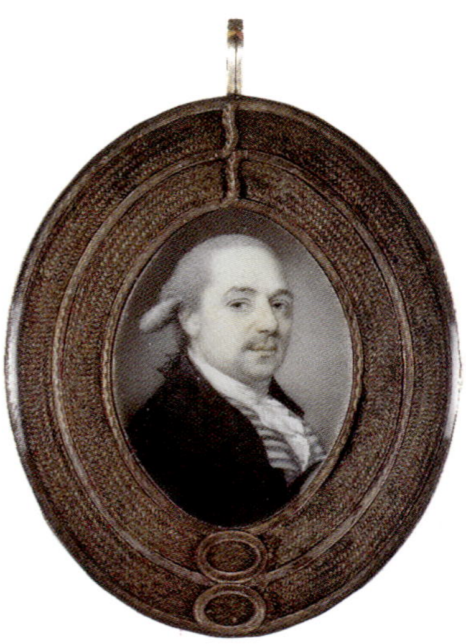

Gaspar Erck, with rope patterning on front and interwoven hair on reverse
SAMPSON TOWGOOD ROCH (1757–1847)
(NGI 19381)

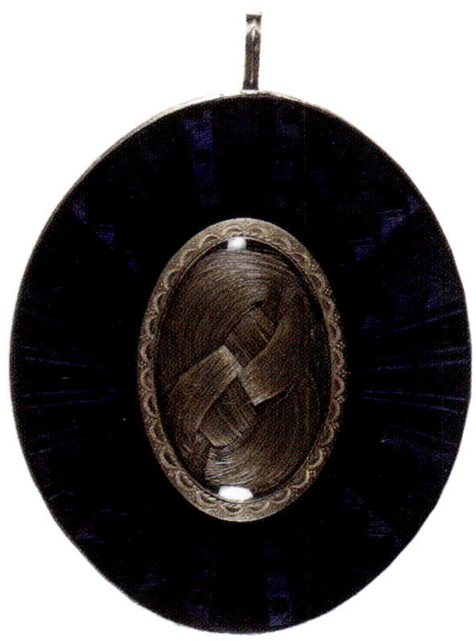

Reverse of NGI 19381

hair which was plaited or interwoven on the reverse (Illus. 13).

The commemorative or memorial miniature also became common. As forms of mourning became increasingly elaborate, and the cult of widowhood arose, the miniature became part of mourning dress. The miniature took on the role of reliquary. The widow would wear the image of the deceased, and the locket would contain a lock of his braided hair. The oil portrait of *Mrs Frances J. Hadden* (NGI 1728), by the obscure nineteenth century Irish artist Ambrose Fortune, shows her in the black mourning dress of widowhood, wearing a veil, and with a miniature portrait of her husband in a brooch pinned centrally below the white collar of her dress (Illus. 14). Some miniature portraits were worn on a chain. This formed part of the dress of either men or women. Women often wore miniatures pinned to the breast, either consciously, or unconsciously, signifying that the sitter was close to their heart. Men often wore miniatures on chains, at the waist or on a watch chain with or without a seal. Ivory miniatures encased in glass decorated snuff, powder and patch boxes in the same way as the enamel portraits.

The 'Modest School'

With the revival of interest in the miniature in about 1750, their quality and quantity improved. Reynolds has characterised the portraits of this era as those of the 'Modest School'.[19] This epithet refers to both the small scale of the miniatures and the modest presentation of the sitter. At this time, practitioners experimented with the technique and developed their own individual styles of painting which was partly the result of changes in taste, and also a response to the technical difficulties of manipulating watercolour on ivory. The first to achieve success with this new technique was again Nathaniel Hone (1718–1784). Hone contributed to the improvement of the technique by using linear brush strokes of watercolour mixed with gum arabic, which helped the watercolour to adhere to the ivory surface.

A remarkable number of this group of miniaturists were of Irish birth. Luke Sullivan (1705–1771) was trained as an engraver. Sullivan painted miniatures in delicate, short linear, brushstrokes, building up

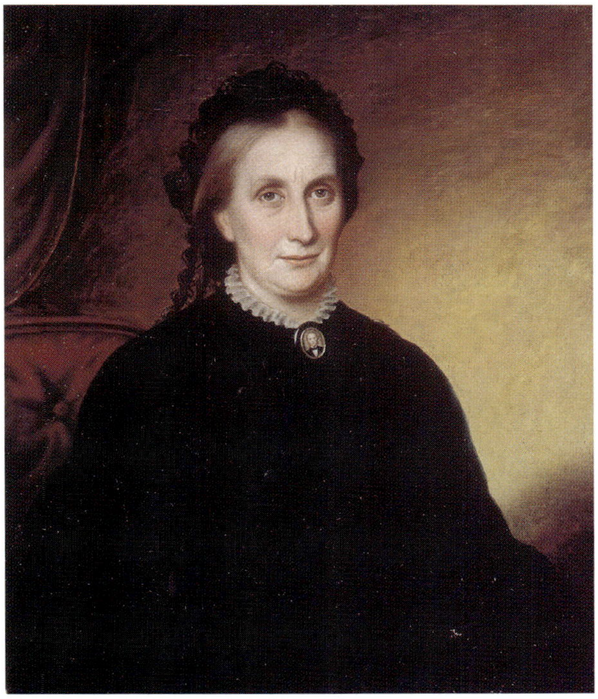

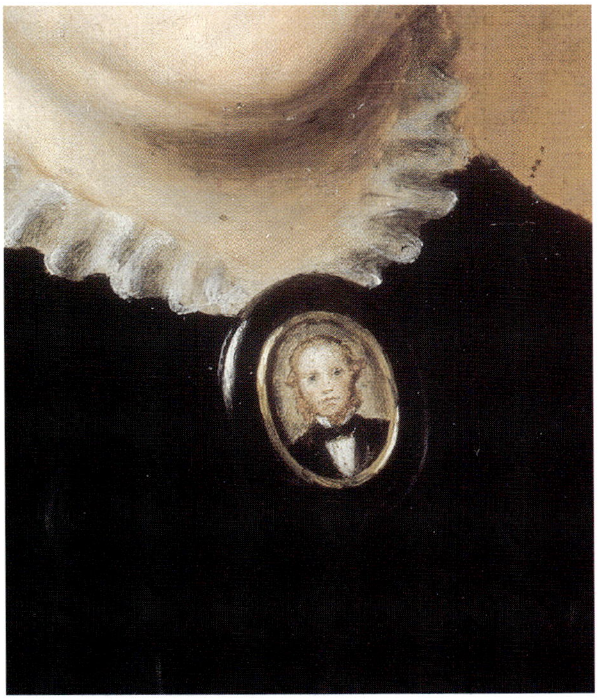

14. Mrs Frances J. Hadden, oil painting and detail of miniature
AMBROSE FORTUNE (19TH CENTURY)
(NGI 1728)

the lines of watercolour like the lines in an engraving. Sullivan was greatly influenced by French rococo engraving and his miniature portraits have the prettiness associated with this period of French painting. He achieved his effects by the use of powdery colour harmonies of greys and blues, indefinite outlines and the distant gaze of the sitter. Thomas Frye (c.1710–1762), also of Irish birth, trained both as an engraver and oil painter. He captured the textures of cloth and gave his miniatures a silvery look by applying short linear brushstrokes, which have the quality of engraving.

Ireland in the Mid-century: Hamilton, Reily and O'Keeffe

During the 1750s, Dublin became a centre of 'Modest School' miniature painting. The most important event that influenced the work of miniaturists was the taking over of Robert West's (active 1740s–1770) private drawing school by the Dublin Society in 1746. This was to become the Drawing Schools of the Dublin Society (those of Landscape and Ornament, and Architecture, opened later). Students were taught drawing and, on graduation, often apprenticed to a miniaturist. In all, at least forty-one miniaturists who worked in Ireland are known to have been trained at the Dublin Society. Gustavus Hamilton (c.1739–1775), James Reily (active 1745–1780/88) and Daniel O'Keeffe (1740–1787) attended the Schools and established Dublin as a centre of miniature painting.

The New Era of the Watercolour on Ivory Portrait

Samuel Collins (1735–1768), firstly at Bath and then in Ireland, worked in watercolour on ivory in quite a different way. He was one of the first miniaturists to fully exploit the ivory surface of the miniature, not covering the ivory completely with paint, but allowing the surface to show through, producing a characteristic effect. Jeremiah Meyer (1735–1789), in his watercolour on ivory portraits, introduced a linear style of painting in fine long brushstrokes that did away with stippling and hatching techniques. This style consisted of brushstrokes that criss-crossed in the areas of shadow but allowed much of the ivory surface to shine through. Meyer's linear brushstrokes were imitated and adapted by the miniaturists for the rest of the eighteenth century.

The work of John Smart (1741/43–1811), Richard Crosse (1742–1810), Ozias Humphry (1742–1810) and Richard Cosway (1742–1821) marked a new era in miniature painting. Their background and education was quite different to those of the previous generation of miniaturists. All were formally taught drawing at William Shipley's Academy in London. This had a profound impact on the quality of miniature painting in England although artists' tools were little changed (Illus. 15).

Exhibitions became important public events to promote a miniaturist's work. In 1760, the Society of Artists was formed. This society held annual exhibitions of the work of miniaturists. The first exhibition included the work of Nathaniel Hone, Meyer, Crosse and Cosway. From 1765–80, the Society of Artists in Ireland held exhibitions which included miniatures by James Ballard (active 1753–1792), Charles Forrest (active 1765–1787), Charles Robertson (1760–1821), Robert Wade (active c.1765–1785) and Gustavus Hamilton, James Reily, and Daniel O'Keeffe, already mentioned.

The Royal Academy, London, was inaugurated in 1768. Among its founder members were the miniaturists Nathaniel Hone and Jeremiah Meyer. At the Royal Academy, miniatures were displayed in a group around the chimneypiece in the Great Room (Illus. 16). Miniaturists vied with one another to paint larger pictures which might more easily gain public attention. They came under pressure to present their sitters in classical poses and themes. This is evident in the work of James Scouler (c.1740–1812) and Richard Crosse. There was a renewed influence of oil portraiture on the miniature. Nathaniel Hone however was more ambitious than his fellow practitioners. He longed for the challenge of history painting so much, that he abandoned the miniature portrait altogether. His elder son, Horace Hone (1754/56–1825/27), was to be one of the most accomplished late eighteenth century watercolour on ivory miniaturists, and is still underrated. He began painting in the 'Modest School' style taught to him by his father. Despite these early influences, Horace Hone developed his own style loosely based on the Meyer-Cosway mode. The size of his ivories

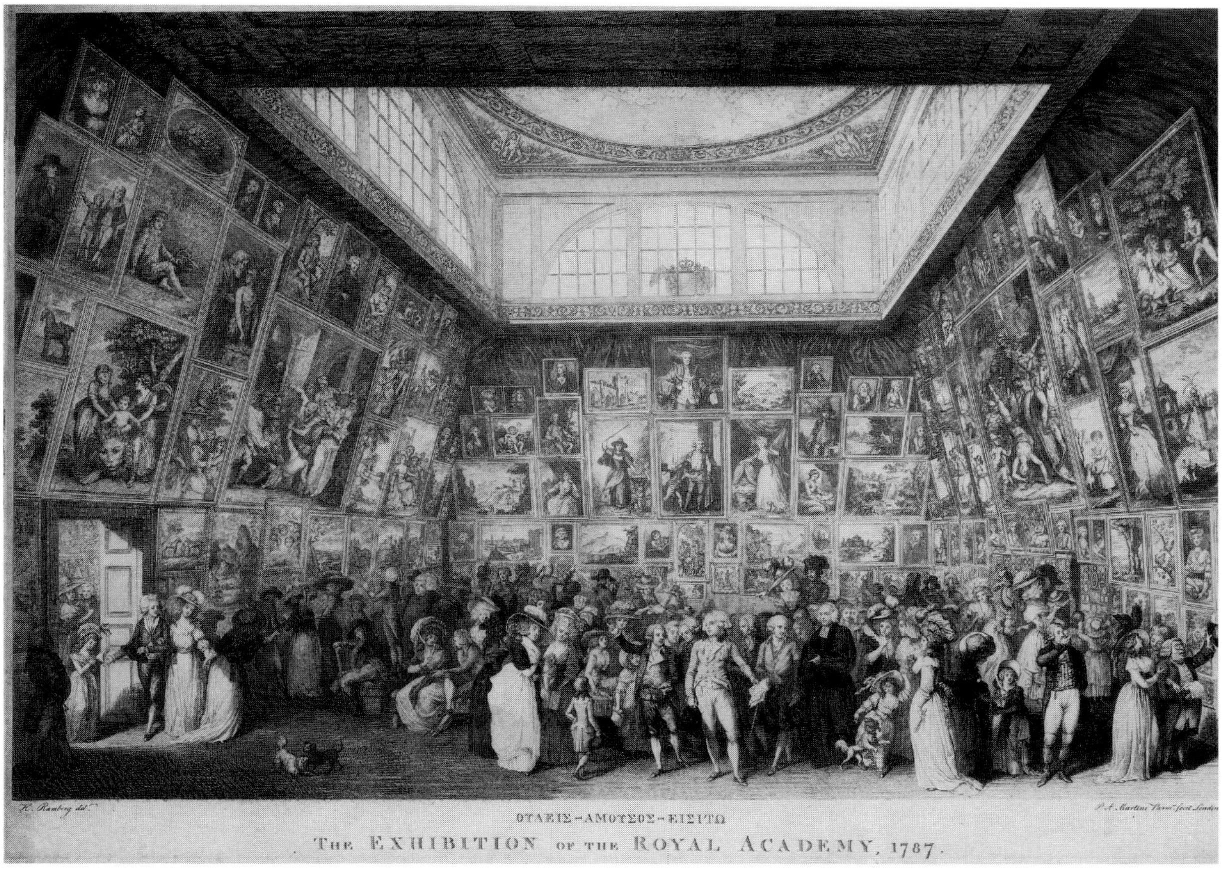

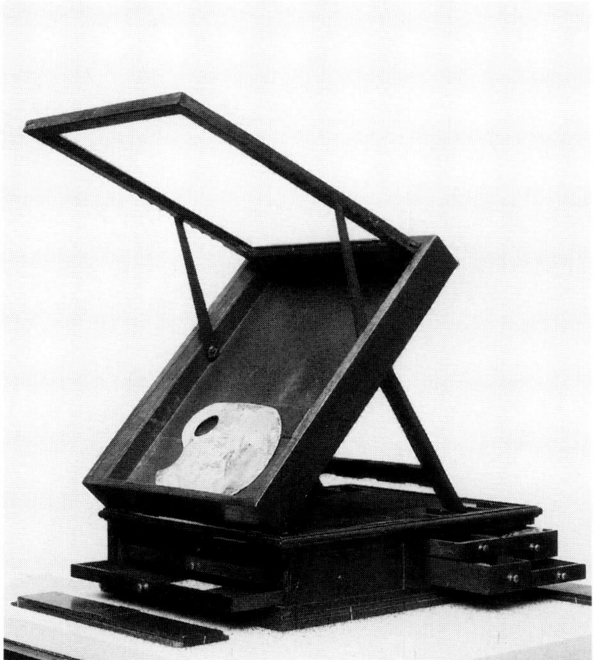

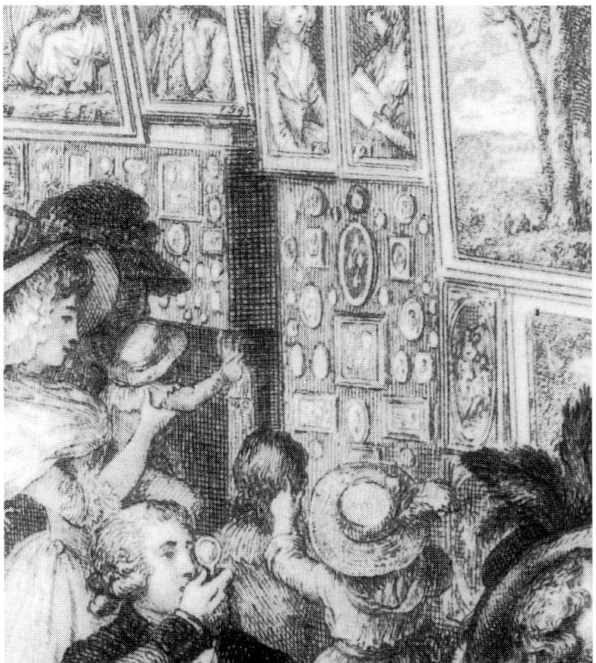

15. The portable miniature painter's desk of Richard Crosse (1742–1810)
(Victoria and Albert Museum, London p10–1925)
The glazed top lifts to diffuse the light on the ivory laid on the slanting ledge.

16. The Exhibition of the Royal Academy at Somerset House, 1787 line engraving, with detail of miniatures (lower right)
PIETRO ANTONIO MARTINI (1739–1797)
after JOHANN HEINRICH RAMBERG
(1763–1840). (Royal Academy, London)

increased, and he adopted linear brush strokes of curving parallel lines. Horace Hone was a close friend of the Irish miniaturist Sampson Roch (1757–1847, catalogue entries 81–83). Hone's influence may be seen on Roch's later, larger miniature portraits. Roch combined his own innate neatness of technique with an elegance and freeness of painting he derived from Hone's style.

Richard Cosway popularised the use of cloudy sky backgrounds and painted the face in short linear grey brushstrokes and the hair in soft masses. This produced the most imitated miniature style of the 1770s and 1780s. At this time, it became fashionable to paint miniatures, not of a head of the sitter, but of the sitter's eye (examples in the V&A). Adam Buck (1759–1833, Illus. 17) was exceptional

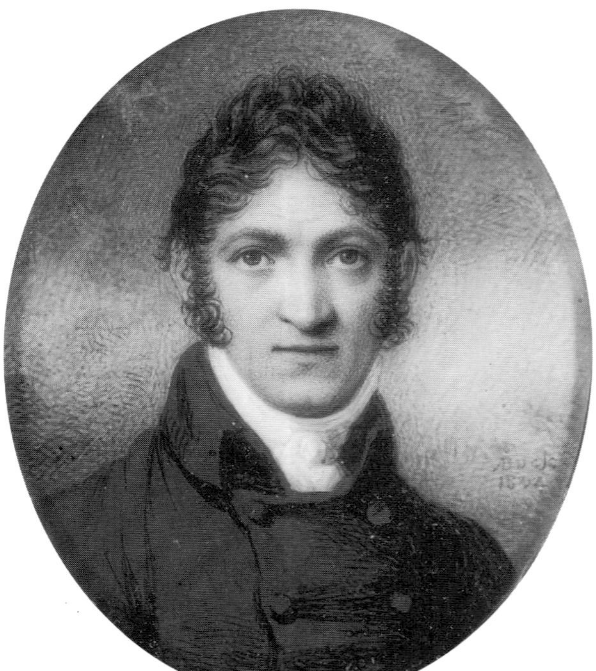

17. *Self-Portrait*, 1804, watercolour on ivory miniature, 6.4 x 5.7
ADAM BUCK (1759–1833)
(Victoria and Albert Museum, London 801–1892)

Opposite:
18. Portrait of a lady with an artist's folio, 1803
watercolour over black chalk, 39 x 29
ADAM BUCK (1759–1833)
(NGI 7738)

by virtue of his admiration for classical Greek and Roman art, an interest that pervades his portraits. Miniature painting on ivory was particularly appropriate for exposition of neo-classical taste, since the whiteness of the ivory could replicate the effect of marble. He was able to achieve the desired effect by the use of muted colours, linear brushstrokes and classical drapery, allowing much of the unpainted or thinly painted ivory to show through. A change may be observed in miniatures painted during the 1790s. Adam Buck and John Comerford (c.1770–1832) began to paint small whole-length portraits in watercolour on card or paper. These portraits, with details of an interior, or in outdoor settings, were effectively contractions of full-scale oil portraiture, and constitute a new development (Illus. 18). At this time, George Chinnery (1774–1852) exercised particular influence on the miniature portrait. Again, Chinnery's works were larger than those of his immediate predecessors. His works aspire towards his oil portraits in composition, and in the use of freer brushwork than characteristically employed by the previous generation of miniaturists.[20] There was to be a converse effect on his later career in China, where the small-scale oil portraits (NGI 785) have the glowing colours of miniatures.

The Cabinet Miniature

Cabinet miniatures were popular throughout the eighteenth century. These were miniatures, hung on walls, or painted to be part of interior decoration. These were usually larger in size than the general run of portrait miniatures, and were rectangular in shape. They were usually framed in wooden frames and often arranged in decorative groups on a wall or in a cabinet. In the eighteenth century these arrangements were confined to the most private, informal rooms of a house such as a boudoir or cabinet-room, rooms used for informal entertainment by family and close friends. Often, the sitters were painted in undress, or informal pose.

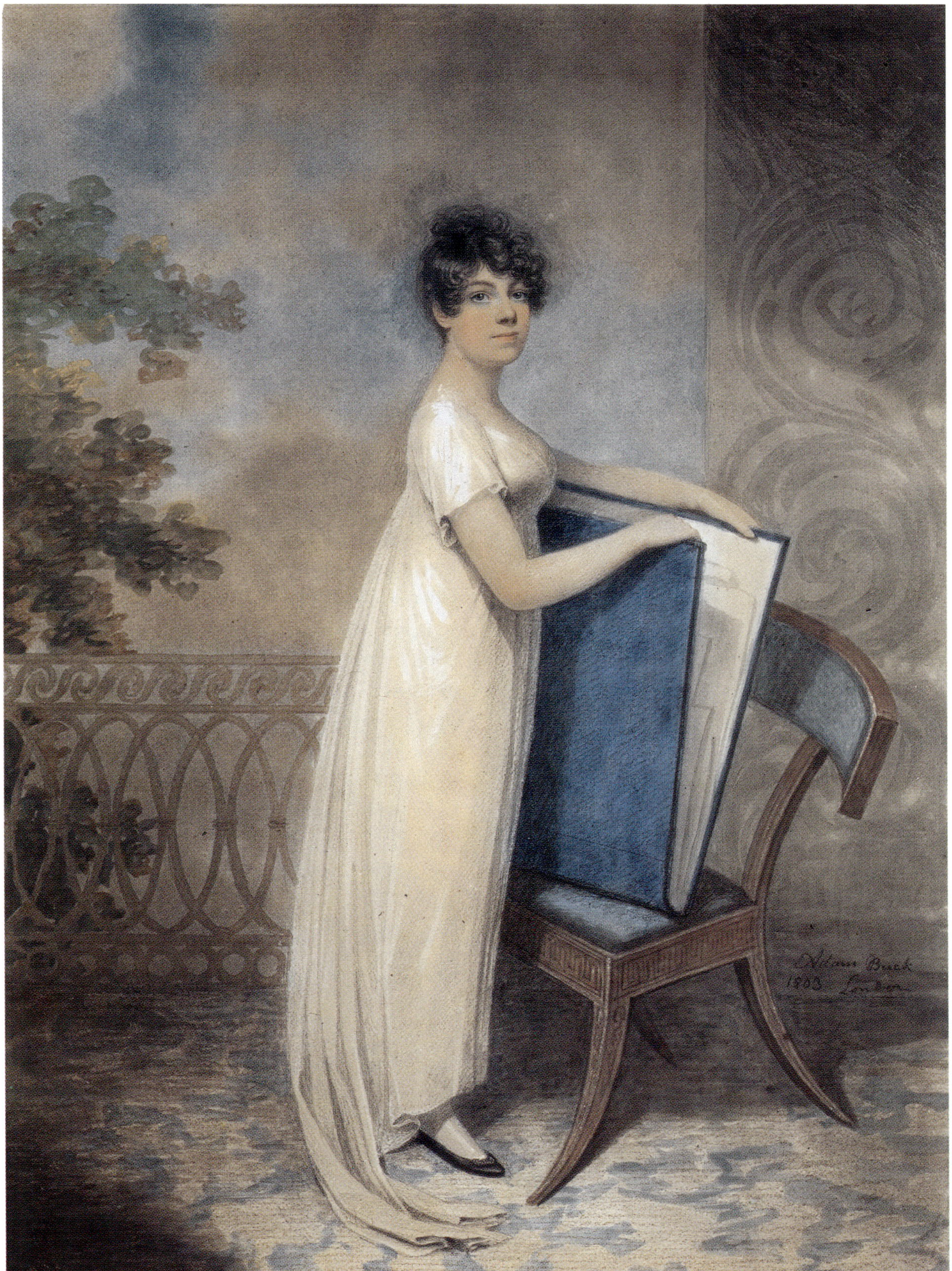
Adam Buck
1803 London

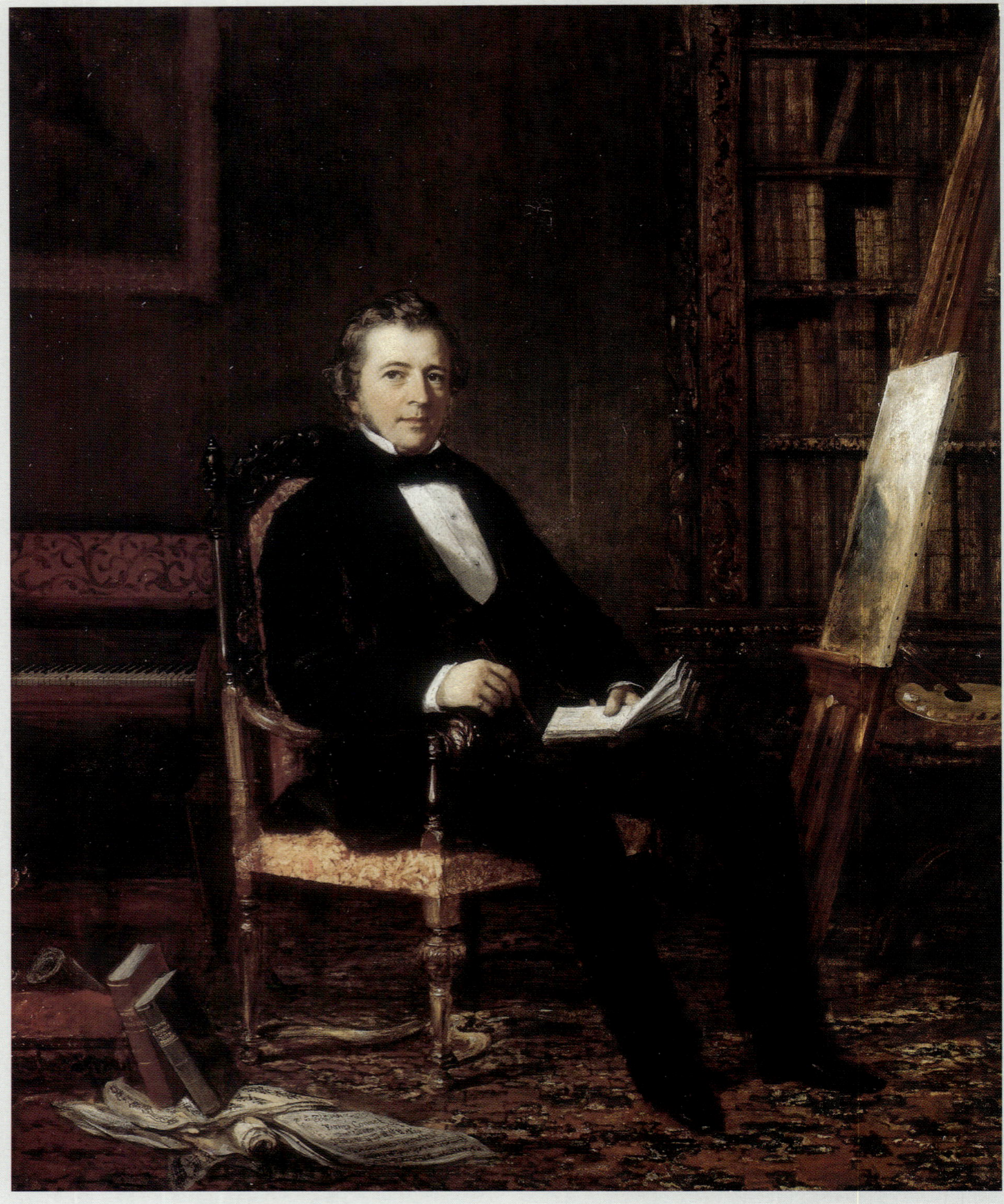

22. *Samuel Lover, (1797–1868), Miniaturist, Composer and Novelist, seated by his easel,* 1856 oil painting
JAMES HARDWOOD (1816–1872),
purchased in 1872 for the portrait collection.
(NGI 142)

of £2,000 to purchase some of the portraits in the exhibition.[23] Although the application was refused, the second Director of the Gallery, Henry Doyle (1827–1892), a miniaturist and portrait painter, set about purchasing portraits (Illus. 22), and these formed the nucleus of a National Portrait Gallery. A room was set aside in 1884 for the display of Irish portraits and was called the National, Historical and Portrait Gallery. There were over 160 exhibits (oils, drawings, Illus. 23, watercolours and prints), as yet no miniatures, and a catalogue published for a penny. The first full catalogue of the collection appeared in the 1898 Gallery guide by Sir Walter Armstrong and the last in 1928. The artistic merit of these portraits was a secondary consideration. Miniatures were soon acquired as they were often the only extant portraits of historical personalities. Many of the engraved images of revolutionary leaders, such as those of Robert Emmet, were taken from miniatures too. Miniatures were displayed with other media in a cluttered arrangement. The locket miniatures were displayed in vitrines. This arrangement, typical of the late nineteenth century, remained the same until the 1970s, when the separate identity of a National Portrait Collection was temporarily put in abeyance.

In 1876, the first miniature was purchased for the National Gallery of Ireland's collection. This was the portrait of Richard Burke by Henry Bone (catalogue entry 68). It was bought from Mrs Catterson Smith for fifteen guineas and was an inauspicious start to the miniature collection as it was stolen in 1880 (recovered in 1905). The collection of miniatures evolved in the early years through purchases. In 1886, miniatures by John Comerford were bought from Viscount Powerscourt for the sum of £40. Many of them were unfinished, including portraits of Sir Thomas Esmonde, Judge Kelly and Richard Power, the comic actor. In 1889, the self-portrait of Charles Byrne (catalogue entry 84) was purchased for £10 from Miss F. Byrne, a member of his family, and the self-portrait of G. Jackson was bought at Christie's (the price not recorded). Two early portraits by Thomas Gainsborough, bought for £5 5s in 1894 fall within the miniature canon. In 1906, the large enamel of Thomas Moore (catalogue entry 113)

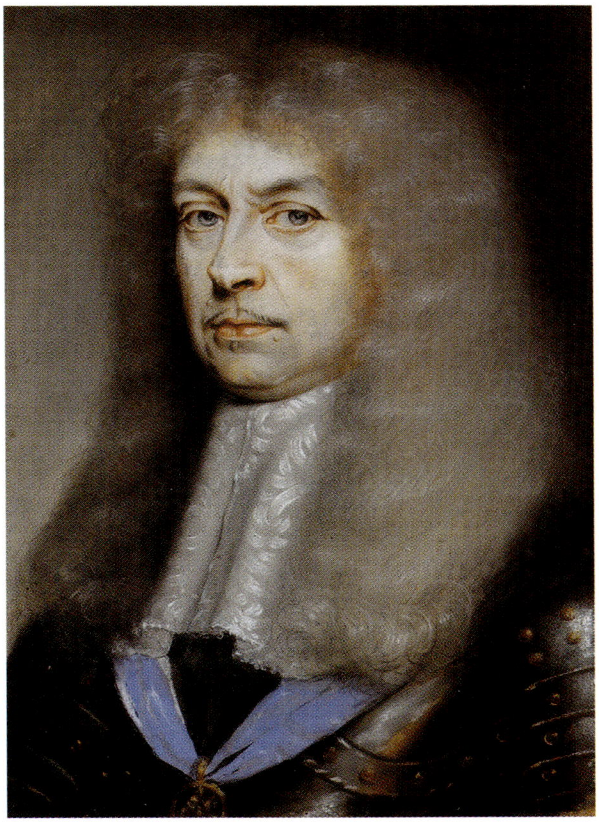

23. *James Butler, 1st Duke of Ormonde, (1610–1688),* 1670s pastel
EDMUND ASHFIELD (active 1669–c.1700)
This was another of Henry Doyle's purchases for the portrait collection. Ashfield is recorded as also having been a miniature painter, but no examples have been identified.
(NGI 6292)

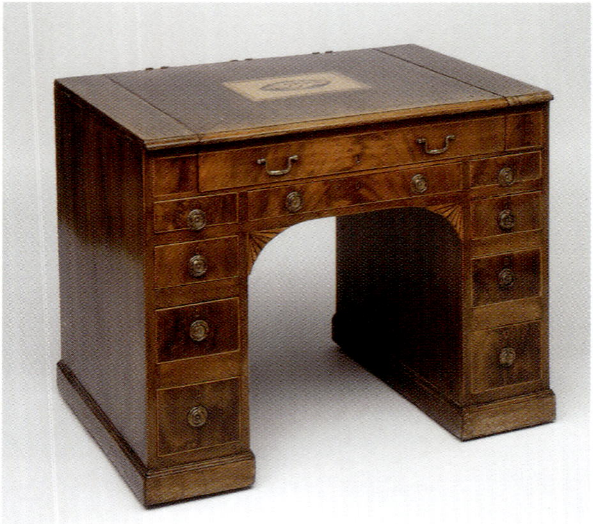

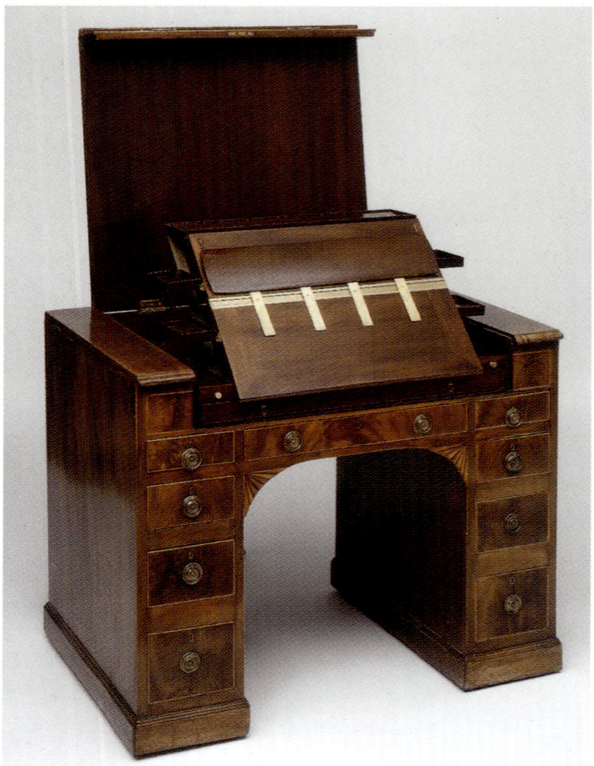

24. *Charles Robertson's miniature painter's desk* (NGI 12000)

Opposite:
25. *Charles Robertson (1760–1821), at his miniature painter's desk,* c.1820 watercolour
HENRY KIRCHHOFFER (1781–1860)
(NGI 2523)

was purchased for £36. In 1907, the self-portrait of Horace Hone (catalogue entry 75) was purchased for £25 from Horace Buttery, a London dealer who also sold oil paintings to the Gallery and carried out conservation.

Miniatures were purchased throughout the early years of the last century. John Bogle's portrait of Sir George Pickering (catalogue entry 61) was bought in Dublin for £4 from Mr R.A. Jones. In 1920, Nathaniel Hone's portrait of Sarah Sophia Banks (catalogue entry 37) was purchased for £35 and the intriguing portrait of Thomas Murphy (NGI 2719, p.180) for £5 12s 3d, at the Francis Wellesley Sale, held by Sotheby's, when some Old Master drawings and Mrs Mary Delany's 'Sketchbook' of mounted drawings, were also acquired.

The miniature collection owes much to gifts, such as those between 1901 and 1905 from Mr E. Stanley Robertson, the great-grandson of the miniaturist, Charles Robertson (1760–1821) and his brother Walter Robertson (c.1750–1801). These included the portrait of Walter Robertson by Charles Robertson (catalogue entry 90), Charles Robertson's mahogany and satinwood miniature painting desk (Illus. 24), and the watercolour portrait of him at this desk in 7, Holles Street, Dublin, by Henry Kirchhoffer (1781–1860, Illus. 25), a unique record of an Irish miniaturist in his studio. Robertson is dressed in a black frock coat and knee breeches, the clothes of an established professional. This is echoed in his surroundings, with marble busts, a classical column and drapery. The quality of the desk and the well-appointed studio are indicative of the social standing of a successful Dublin miniaturist. When closed, it appears an ordinary piece of domestic furniture, with scallop inlay in satinwood. When opened up, it contains an adjustable easel with brass slats and a wooden tray on a string pulley. There are drawers for storing ivory, paints, palettes and brushes, and trays for them and water. Despite having both desk and watercolour, precisely how the easel functioned is unclear. In 1904, the fine pair of portraits of Vice-Admiral Plampin and his wife by Adam Buck were bought from Mrs Wallis of Co. Dublin. The same year, a Buck watercolour was presented by Hugh Lane, whose generosity in gifts and eventual bequest

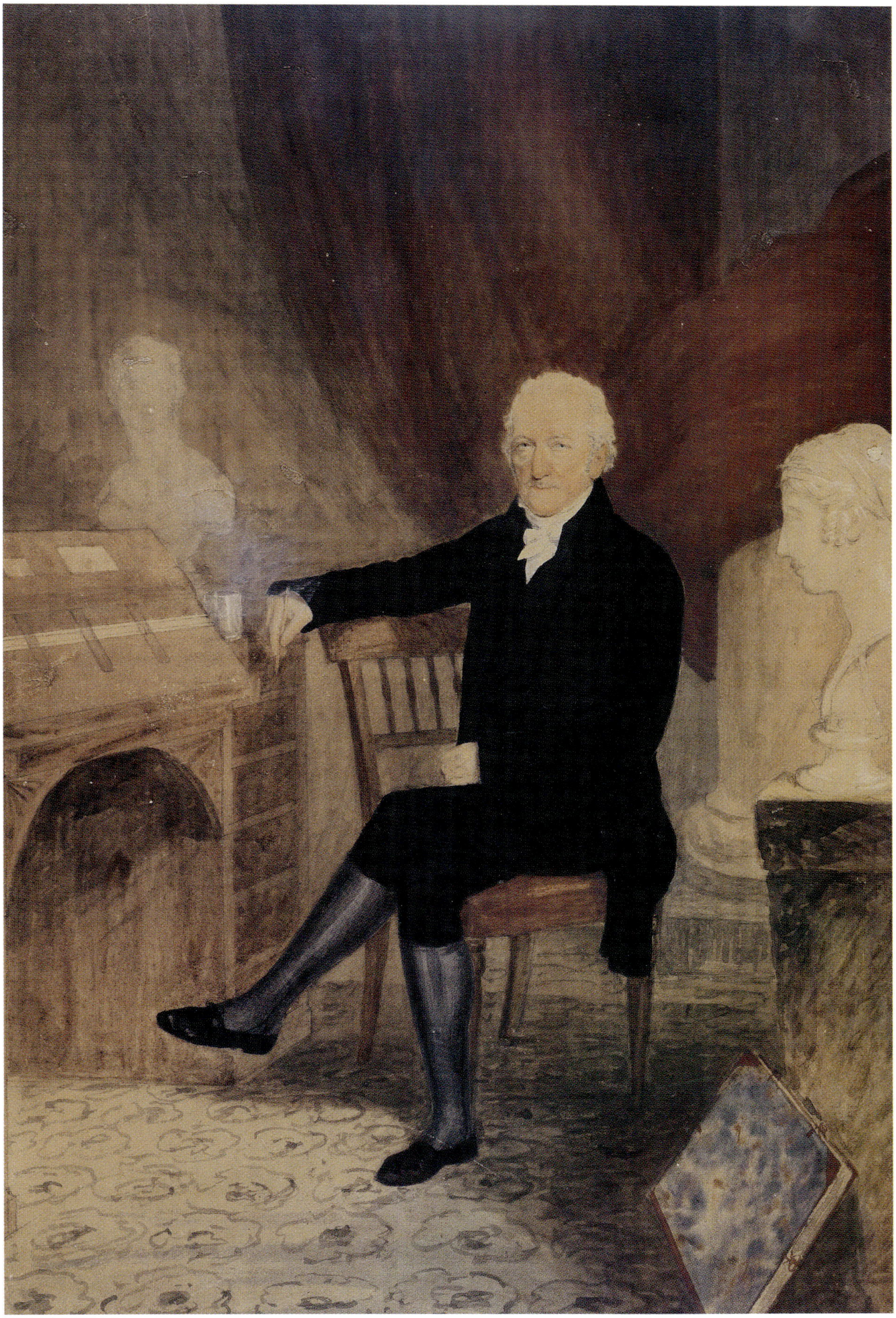

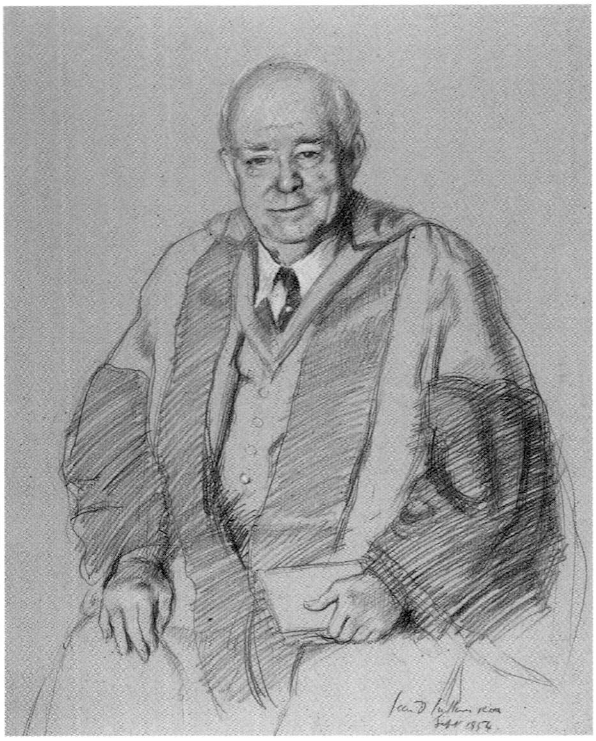

26. Sir Alfred Chester Beatty, (1875–1968),
1954 drawing
SEÁN O'SULLIVAN (1906–1964)
(NGI 3567)

of paintings and monies was to contribute substantially to the collection.

The Friends of the National Collections of Ireland was founded in 1924 and their first presentation was a miniature portrait on ivory of Mrs Coote by John Comerford (NGI 2739, p. 161). It was donated by Lucius O'Callaghan, then Director of the National Gallery of Ireland no doubt, setting a good example.[24] In 1924, Edward Martyn bequeathed an anonymous miniature portrait of an ancestor (NGI 2745, p. 179), together with an oil by Claude Monet (NGI 852) and two pastels by Edgard Degas (NGI 2740–2741). In 1925, Horace Hone's portrait of Sarah Siddons (catalogue entry 76) and four portraits of other members of the Hone family by Horace Hone were presented by Mrs C. H. Hone. As with the purchasing of paintings, the war years did not preclude buying a Samuel Lover self-portrait miniature (catalogue entry 123) from a London firm in 1942, to add to a chalk drawing bought in 1901. A significant bequest was the outstanding Richard Cosway self-portrait (catalogue entry 58) bequeathed by Miss Meta Grace in 1949, with another Cosway portrait.

The Gallery's collection of miniatures was greatly enhanced by the donation of 209 miniatures given in 1951 by [Sir] Alfred Chester Beatty (1875–1968, Illus. 26).[25] The Minute Book only singled out 'important examples of the work of Jean Petitot and Henry Bone'[26]. This was Chester Beatty's first donation to an Irish collection and principally a collection of English and French miniatures. It came with two cabinets, which still house nearly all the miniatures in the Gallery. There are superb examples of the principal European enamellists (many outside the scope of this publication). The majority came from the Jacob Nachemsohn Collection of enamels. This was a key collection of authenticated works, formed in the 1920s (though some signatures were misinterpreted).[27] Their eventual home in Dublin has gone unnoticed until now. Nothing has been learnt about Nachemsohn, despite extensive enquiries. Chester Beatty's background in minerals and earlier interests in oriental objects in precious materials might explain their attraction for him, together with his wish to collect objects of the highest quality in whatever field. Miniatures in this collection include examples by Lucius Barber (catalogue entry 30), attributed to Rupert Barber (catalogue entry 29), William Bate (catalogue entry 105), William Charles Bell (catalogue entries 130–31), William Russell Birch (catalogue entries 66–67), Charles Boit (catalogue entries 4–5), Henry Bone (catalogue entries 69, 71–73), Henry Pierce Bone (catalogue entries 109–10), Peter Joseph Bone (catalogue entries 115), William Bone (catalogue entries 118–20), Samuel Collins (catalogue entries 46), William Craft (catalogue entries 42–44), Sarah, Countess of Essex (catalogue entry 93), William Essex (catalogue entry 114), Marcus Gunter (catalogue entry 16), Nathaniel Hone (catalogue entries 33, 35–36), Johann Heinrich [von] Hurter (catalogue entry 45), Giuseppe Macpherson (catalogue entry 38), Jeremiah Meyer (catalogue entry 47), George Michael Moser (catalogue entries 19–20), William Prewett (catalogue entry 17), Godfried Hendrik Rode (Illus. 4), Jean André Rouquet (catalogue entries 13–14), James Scouler (catalogue entries 55), Noah Seaman (catalogue entry 15), John Simpson (catalogue entries 127–28), Gervase Spencer (catalogue entries 24–27) and Christian Friedrich Zincke (catalogue entries 10–12).

In 1967, Mrs Christina Edgeworth Colvin presented a rare, signed and dated, miniature by Andrew Dunn of an ambitious Irish Bishop (catalogue entry 107) with other portraits. The collection was further expanded in 1969 by the transfer of the National Museum of Ireland's collection of 235 miniatures (135 Irish and English, Illus. 27)[28]. The National Museum of Ireland had been purchasing miniatures since the 1890s and always exhibited miniatures as part of their collection of decorative art. Details of their acquisition by the National Museum are published in this catalogue for the first time.[29] In 1917, Dr George Sigerson's Collection of miniatures (mainly French, but with three Cosway portraits and a Horace Hone) had been loaned to the museum, where it was catalogued and exhibited,[30] but not subsequently acquired. The collection transferred from the National Museum included several donations and bequests: Thomas L. Longfield gifts (1897 and 1908), Miss Frazer gift (1900), Miss C. Henry gift (1900), Martelli Williams bequest (1904), W.E. Gumbleton gift (1911), Miss A. E. Bagge-Hearn gift (1913), Miss R. F. Sharff gift (1919), the Todd Mercer bequest (1924), Miss Gardiner bequest (1929), an anonymous donation of Ellis family portraits (1939), Miss Amy Colston gift (1942), Mrs E. B. Day gift (1946), Miss Alison Kinchela bequest (1948), Mrs Maev Sullivan gift (1949), which included Samuel Cooper's *Sir Thomas Anthony* (catalogue entry 1) and Adam Buck's *Portrait of a young lady seated on a sea wall* (catalogue entry 88), Mr J. W. Jellet gift (1949), Miss Lettice Digby Cooke gift (1950) and Mrs Gladys Gorges gift (1958). In 1982, two miniatures by Andrew Rymsdyck (1754–1786), were transferred also.

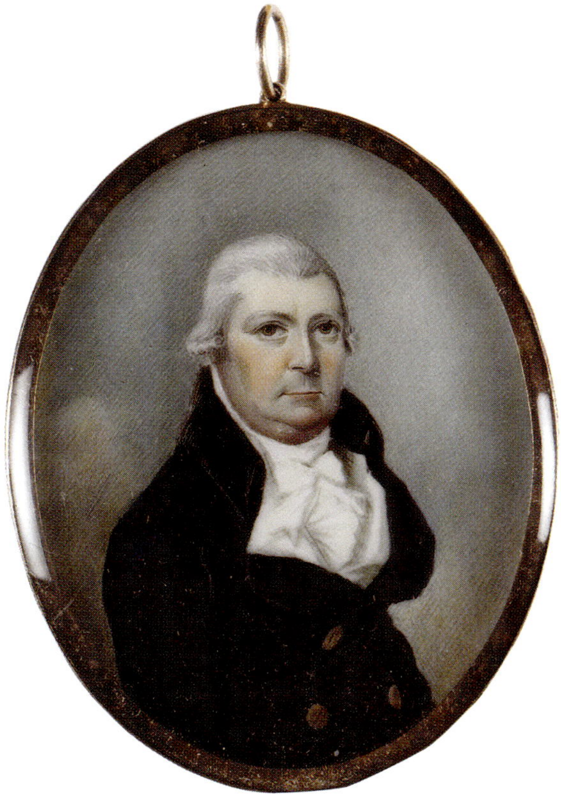

27.*Hamilton Gorges of Kilbran, Co. Meath, (c.1739–1822)*, c.1800 watercolour on ivory miniature.
GEORGE LAWRENCE (c.1758–1802)
One of the miniatures transferred from the NMI, 1969.
(NGI 7149)

In 1974, important material by Samuel Lover (1797–1868) was bequeathed by Mrs Ella Herbert Bartlett, the artist's great granddaughter (including catalogue entry 124). The Sir Andrew Armstrong

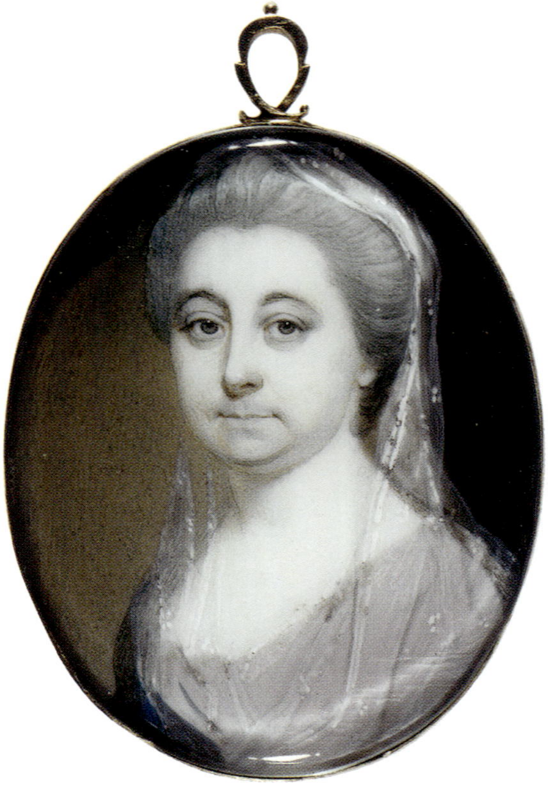

28. Mrs Henry Barnard,
watercolour on ivory miniature
RICHARD CROSSE (1742–1810)
(NGI 19269)

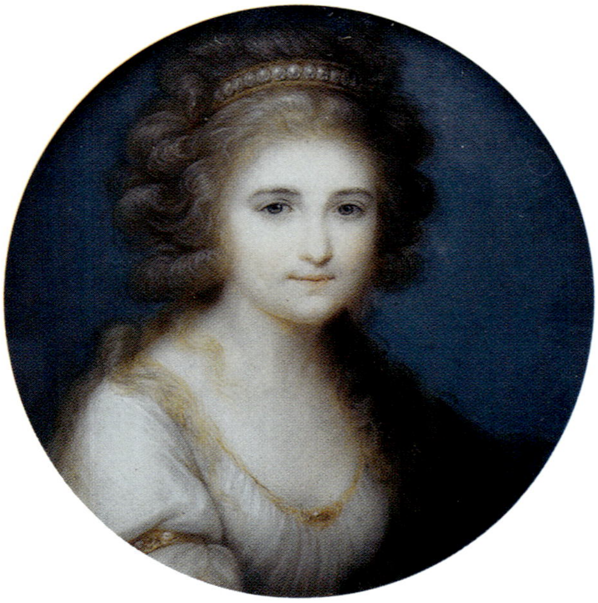

29. Mrs Daniel Mussenden, (born Fridiswide Bruce, d.1785), c.1780 watercolour on ivory miniature
FRENCH SCHOOL (c.1780)
(NGI 19281)

bequest in 1981 included six miniatures of his ancestors. The Miss Mary A. McNeill Bequest of fifty Irish and English miniatures in 1985 (Illus. 28) came from a Belfast historian and miniatures collector, who had specialised in miniatures by Irish artists and or of Irish sitters.[31] The silhouettes and continental artists are not covered here, but the portrait of the beautiful *Mrs Daniel Mussenden* (Illus. 29), in whose memory the Earl-Bishop of Derry named the Mussenden Temple at Downhill, Co. Antrim, illuminates the later development of watercolour on ivory miniatures in France. The Irish and English miniatures included fifteen artists not represented before (some only identified after acquisition). There are significant portraits by John Barry (catalogue entry 104), Henry Bone (catalogue entry 70), Penelope Carwardine (catalogue entry 41), John Comerford, Richard Crosse (catalogue entry 56), George Engleheart (catalogue entry 62), Thomas Flatman (catalogue entry 2), Thomas Forster (catalogue entries 6–7), Nathaniel Freese, William Grimaldi (catalogue entry 63), Jean-Francois-Marie Hüet-Villiers (catalogue entry 103), Ozias Humphry (catalogue entry 57), Bernard Lens III (catalogue entry 9), Jeremy Meyer, Edward Miles (catalogue entry 64), George Place (catalogue entry 94), Charles Robertson (catalogue entries 91–91), Sampson Towgood Roch, John Smart (catalogue entries 53–54) and Luke Sullivan (catalogue entry 18).

In 1989, the Gallery's collection was further augmented by five Erck family portraits bequeathed by Dr Silver Deane Oliver. The artists were identified as Frederick Buck, Gustavus Hamilton and Sampson Towgood Roch (Illus. 13) and provide a rare instance where a group of high quality miniatures has stayed together. Purchases are now generally reserved for rarities, such as the unknown man by Charles Forrest for £225 in 1983 (catalogue entry 65), the portrait of William Ashford by John Comerford for £4,850 in 1995 (catalogue entry 100), or the pair of late miniatures by Thomas Frye for £7,169 also in 1995 (catalogue entries 22–23). An additional work by the Liverpool miniaturist, Thomas Hazlehurst, which shared its catalogue number with another, is an added bonus (Illus. 30). This attractive portrait of an

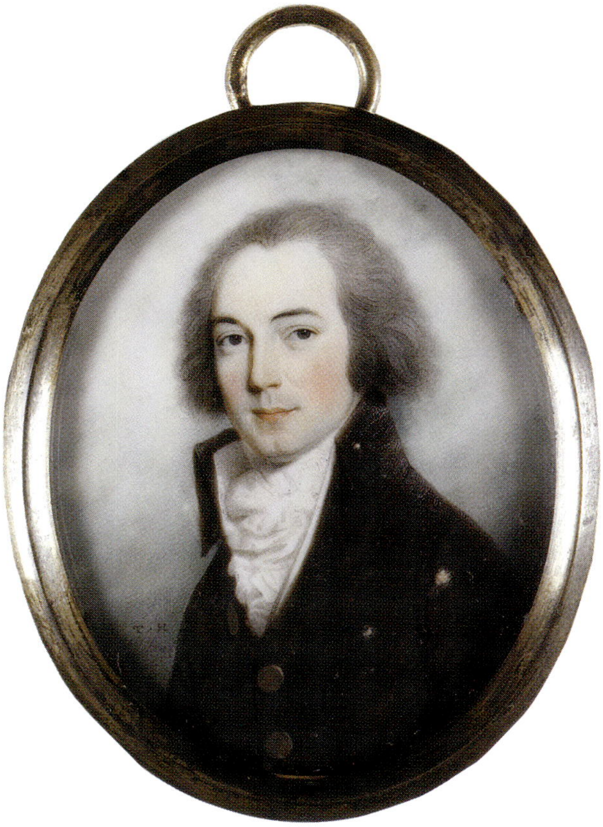

30. Portrait of a man in a brown coat, 1790s
watercolour on ivory miniature
THOMAS HAZLEHURST (c.1740–1821)
(NGI 19588)

unknown man is painted with the bright luminosity of the Regency period. It had been conflated with a portrait of the Duke of Wellington.

No collection can be all-encompassing, but the Gallery's represents two hundred years of the finest exponents of miniature painting on both sides of the Irish Sea.

Footnotes:

1. In Latin, *minianus* (red leaded) and *miniatulus* (painted red) are derived from *minium*.
2. A full etymology of the word miniature and a history of the origins of the portrait miniature are given in Colding 1953, pp. 9–19.
3. London 1974, no. 19. NGI 1983, p. 712.
4. Walton 1992, *passim*, especially pp. 4–10.
5. Strong 1983, pp. 12–44. Coombs 1998, pp. 15–16.
6. Piper 1957, pp. 36–55. Strong 1983, pp. 45–53.
7. Bayne-Powell 1985, pp. 129–301.
8. Strong 1983, *passim*.
9. Thornton and Cain 1981, *passim*. Hilliard's Treatise was unpublished in his lifetime.
10. Murdoch *et al.* 1981, pp. 85–87.
11. Murrell in Murdoch *et al.*, 1981, pp. 1–16. Murrell in Bardo 1978, pp. 29–39.
12. Piper 1957, pp. 115–25. Murdoch *et al.*, 1981, pp. 104–20. Murdoch 1997, pp. 115–17.
13. Murdoch *et al.* 1981, pp. 148–53. Murdoch 1997, pp. 205–06.
14. Murdoch *et al.* 1981, pp. 149–50. Coombs 1998, pp. 54–57.
15. Sumner 1988, pp. 115–17.
16. Speel 1998, pp. 101–03.
17. Walker 1992, catalogue no. 126.
18. Colding 1953, pp. 122–42. Murrell in Murdoch *et al.*, 1981, pp. 16–24. Coombs 1998, pp. 84–86.
19. Reynolds 1988, pp. 105–14.
20. Caffrey 1999, pp. 11–12, 49–50.
21. Walker 1999, pp. 305–07.
22. Noon in Murdoch *et al.*, 1981, pp. 207–09.
23. NGI 1981, p. xx
24. Exhibition, Dublin 1999, p. 112.
25. NGI 1983, Appendix 8, pp. 817–18. He was knighted in 1954 a few months before his portrait was drawn by Seán O'Sullivan (Illus. 26).
26. NGI Archive.
27. Williamson 1926, pp. 1–26.
28. NGI 1983, Appendix 8, pp. 824–26.
29. Annotated typescript list of miniatures transferred from the NMI to the NGI, 17 April 1969 (NGI Archive).
30. NMI 1917, *List of French Portrait Miniatures Etc. Lent by George Sigerson Esq MD to the National Museum Dublin.*
31. Wynne 1986, pp. 36–41, gives a full biography. Collection catalogued in Le Harivel and Wynne 1986, pp. 104–35.

Chronological Catalogue of Irish and English Miniatures 1650–1850

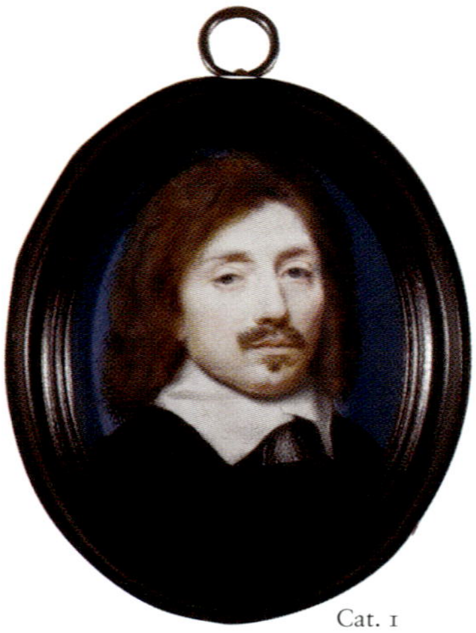

Cat. 1

1. *Sir Anthony Thomas*, 1647

SIGNED AND DATED: *S.C. 1647*
LATER INSCRIPTION ON REVERSE OF FRAME: *Sr Anthony Thomas Knt*
4.6 x 3.3, watercolour on card
Set in a turned wood cabinet frame.
PROVENANCE: presented to the NMI by Mrs Maev Sullivan, Dublin, 1949; transferred from the NMI, 1969.
NGI 7045
LITERATURE: NGI 1983, p. 76.

SAMUEL COOPER

London 1608/09~1672 London

Cooper, possibly of Dutch descent, was the son of Richard Cooper and Barbara Hoskins. He was taught miniature painting by his uncle, John Hoskins the elder (c.1595–1664/65). Cooper's brother Alexander (d.1660) was also a miniaturist. Samuel Cooper may have worked in France, Holland and Germany. He was well established in London with his own studio in Henrietta Street, Covent Garden, by 1642, where he was highly successful. Cooper was the leading miniaturist of his day. There is a probable self-portrait in the Victoria and Albert Museum. He enjoyed both Royalist and Commonwealth patronage and in 1663 was appointed miniature painter to Charles II. Cooper had wide intellectual interests, was an accomplished linguist and musician and counted among his circle John Aubrey, Samuel Butler, John Evelyn, Thomas Hobbes and John Milton. Cooper's wife, Christina Turner of York, was the aunt of the poet Alexander Pope.

LITERATURE: Vertue 1929–52, Notebook II, p. 129. Foster 1914, *passim.* Long 1929, pp. 81–91. Foskett 1974, *passim.* Murdoch *et al.* 1981, pp. 104–20. Reynolds 1988, pp. 47–60. Murdoch 1997, pp. 115–17.

Cooper's portrait of Sir Anthony Thomas is a fine example of his early style of miniature portrait painting, which was executed during the Civil War. Cooper was influenced by oil portraiture and the work of Van Dyck, with the result that his miniatures are broadly painted. The illumination of the face shows the influence of his teacher John Hoskins. Cooper paints the details of the face with long lines of red-brown hatching.

Sir Anthony Thomas is presented as a fashionably dressed young man against a brilliant blue background. The sitter has modish long hair, worn down to his shoulders, a moustache and tuft of beard under his lower lip. He wears a white lawn falling collar which is tied with two draw strings, and the tassel of the draw string is shown. A cloak is draped asymmetrically over his right shoulder.

THOMAS FLATMAN

London 1635~1688 London

Flatman was educated at Winchester and New College, Oxford, where he was elected to a Fellowship in 1656. He was called to the Bar in 1662, and was a poet and writer as well as miniaturist. From c.1660–83 he had a busy practice as a miniaturist in London, where his clients were drawn from professional and intellectual circles. Flatman was influenced by Samuel Cooper's technique, which

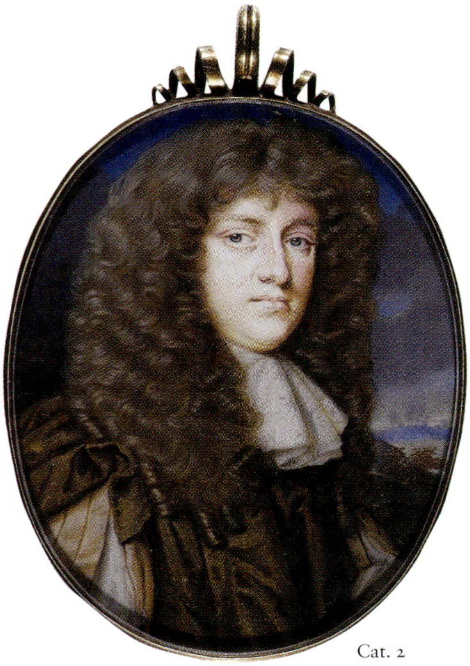

Cat. 2

was based on building up the sitter's face in reddish-brown hatching. He was a friend of Henry Purcell, Charles Cotton, Isaak Walton and members of the Royal Society, of which he became a member in 1668. He was part of a distinguished group of miniaturists, which included Matthew Snelling (1621–1678), Charles Beale (1631–1705), and Mary Beale (1633–1691). A self-portrait from 1673 is in the Victoria and Albert Museum, London.

LITERATURE: Long 1929, pp. 154–55. Murdoch *et al.* 1981, pp. 148–53. Reynolds 1988, pp. 68–71. Murdoch 1989, pp. 254–57. Lloyd and Remington 1996, p. 128. Murdoch 1997, pp. 205–06.

2. *Captain Robert Bransby RN*, c.1670

SIGNED: *TF* (in monogram)
7.4 x 5.9, watercolour on vellum
Set in a gold oval pendant frame.
PROVENANCE: collection of the Rt. Hon. Lord Hastings; collection of Mrs Robinson; purchased by Miss Mary A. McNeill at Christie's, London, 10 June 1963, lot 164; Miss Mary A. McNeill Bequest, 1985.
NGI 19241
LITERATURE: Le Harivel and Wynne 1986, p. 107.

Flatman's portrait of Captain Bransby is highly characteristic of his miniature painting style and technique. This portrait is part of a group of portraits of unknown sitters he painted during the 1670s. It is remarkably similar in style and execution to a *Portrait of a Man*, c.1670 (Royal Collection)[1], and *Unknown Man*, dated 1675 (Ashmolean Museum, Oxford). The sitter is brought forward in the miniature and dominates a distant landscape. The portrait is neatly drawn in a clear graphic style. The red-brown flesh tones used in the painting of the sitter's face and blue sky in the background are characteristic of Flatman's work.

Captain Bransby wears a large full bottomed wig made from real hair. He is elaborately dressed in a dull gold coloured cloak over a salmon coloured coat. It was fashionable in the seventeenth century to slash the sleeves of the coat as a display of luxury and to reveal the cloth beneath. In this example the slashing reveals Bransby's white linen shirt. He has a white linen neck cloth. The costume suggests that the portrait was painted c.1670.

REFERENCE: 1. Lloyd and Remington 1996, p.128.

SIMON DIGBY

b. (?) Co. Down, active Cos. Meath/ Limerick/ Roscommon 1668~1720 Lacken, Co. Roscommon)

Simon Digby was Bishop of Limerick from 1678 and later of Elphin (1691–1720). He was educated at Trinity College, Dublin and was then made Rector of Dunshaughlin, Co. Meath, and chaplain to the Earl of Ossory, Lord Deputy. He married Elizabeth Westenra, the daughter of Warner Westenra, and they had eight sons and eight daughters. His skill as a miniaturist was noted during his lifetime, and was viewed as an important social accomplishment. Digby's portrait miniatures are the earliest extant miniatures painted by a miniaturist of Irish birth. A self-portrait with his family is illustrated in Strickland (plate XX).

LITERATURE: Strickland 1913, vol. 1, pp. 277–78; Burke's 1889, p.1193.

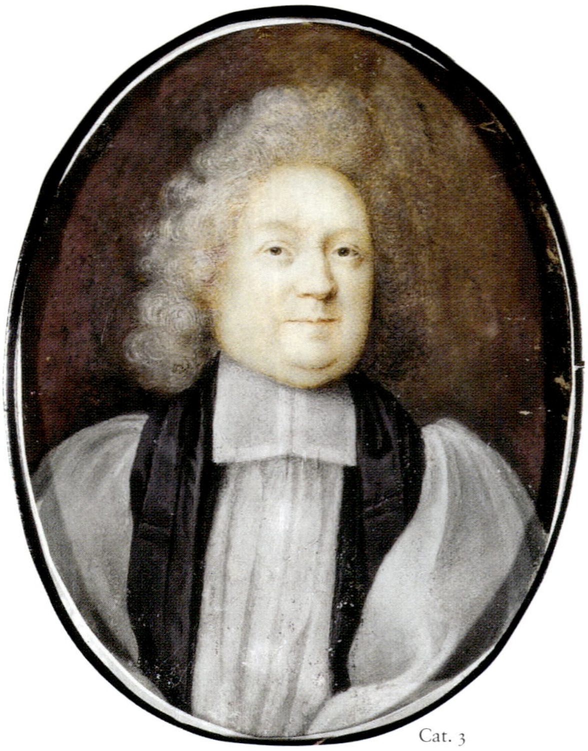

Cat. 3

3. *John Tillotson, (1630–1694), Archbishop of Canterbury*, c.1692

INSCRIBED ON BACKING PAPER: *Archbp. Tillotson.*
9.3 x 7.2, gouache and watercolour on vellum, pasted on card
Set in a black rectangular wooden cabinet frame with an oval inset.
PROVENANCE: by descent in the Digby Family at Landenstown, Co. Kildare; purchased by the landscape painter George Petrie (1790–1866) at auction in Dublin; presented by Petrie to Henry R. Dawson, Dean of St Patrick's, Dublin; purchased by the NMI, 1895; transferred from the NMI, 1969.
NGI 7221
EXHIBITED: Dublin 1970, no. 32.
LITERATURE: NGI 1983, p. 104.

John Tillotson studied at Clare Hall, Cambridge, where he was appointed a Fellow in 1651. He was a well-known preacher in London in the 1660s. In 1664 he married Miss French, a niece of Oliver Cromwell. In 1670 he was made Prebendary of Canterbury Cathedral, then Dean in 1670, and from 1689 until his death in 1694 was Archbishop of Canterbury.[1] This miniature would probably have been painted during that time. Tillotson was famous for his published sermons and a great favourite of William and Mary.

Digby was an accomplished miniaturist working in watercolour on vellum. In this portrait, the vellum support shows through in the painting of the sitter's face, which is built up in dotted stipple brushstrokes. The dark maroon background is painted in blotchy brushstrokes and the paint forms dark rivulets. Tillotson's ecclesiastical dress is painted in long flat brushstrokes in gouache, watercolour mixed with white pigment. A comparable portrait by Digby, in watercolour on vellum, of *John Hough, (1651–1743), Bishop of Worcester,* is in the NPGL.

REFERENCE: 1. DNB vol. XIX, pp. 872–78.

CHARLES BOIT

Stockholm 1662~1727 Paris

Boit, though born in Sweden, was of French extraction. He probably learned the technique of painting on enamel from Pierre Signac (c.1624–?1684) at the Swedish Court. He went to live in England in 1687, where he was helped to establish himself as a miniaturist by his fellow Swede, Michael Dahl (1656–1743). Boit was appointed enamellist to William III in 1696. He was employed by Queen Anne, but because of financial difficulties, fled to Paris about 1714. In 1717, he was made an *Agrée* of the Académie Royale. Tsar Peter the Great and Philippe, Duc d'Orleans, Regent of France, were among his patrons. Christian Friedrich Zincke was his most important pupil (see catalogue entries 10–12).

LITERATURE: Clouzot 1924, p. 26; Nisser 1927, *passim*; Long 1929, pp. 35–36; Reynolds 1988, pp. 87–91.

4. *Portrait of a man in a blue coat*, c.1710

SIGNED: *Cboit* (CB in monogram)
4.1 x 3.5, enamel on copper
Set in an oval gilt metal frame.
PROVENANCE: Jacob Nachemsohn Collection, 1926; presented by Sir Alfred Chester Beatty, 1951.
NGI 3651
LITERATURE: Williamson 1926, p. 18. NGI 1983, p. 13.

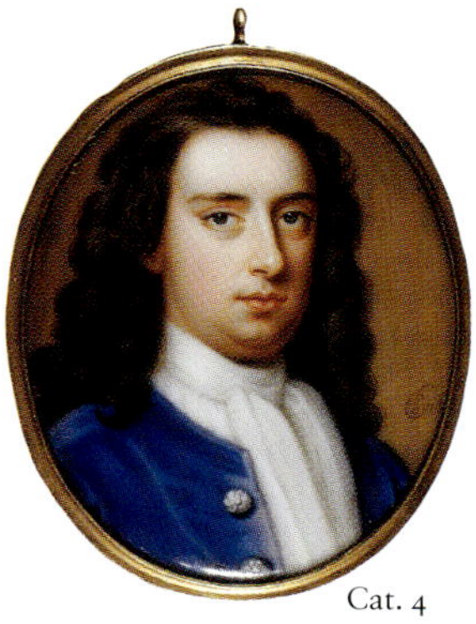

Cat. 4

Boit's technical proficiency is apparent from this portrait which is a representative example of his work. The portrait is smoothly painted against a plain brownish background and it shows Boit's typical use of rich blues and pinks. His stylistic and technical influence may be seen in the work of his pupil Zincke (see catalogue entries 10–12). The sitter is not wearing a wig but his natural hair has been enriched with hair extensions of long curls at the back. He wears a blue coat with silver buttons and a plain white linen neck cloth.

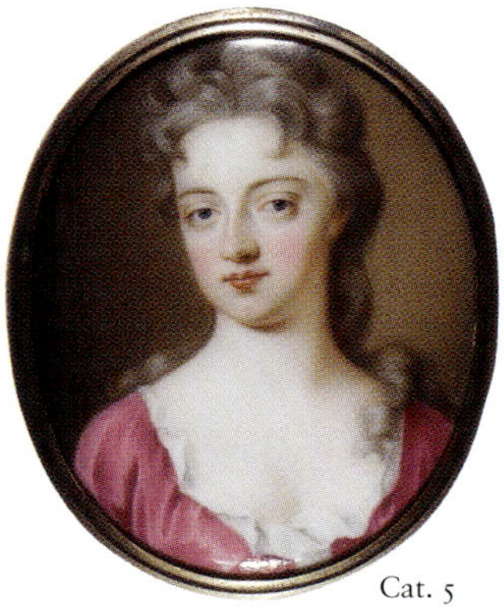

Cat. 5

5. *Portrait of a lady in a pink dress,* c.1710

SIGNED: *C.boit pinx:*
4.5 x 3.6, enamel on copper
Set in an oval gilt metal frame.
PROVENANCE: Jacob Nachemsohn Collection, 1926; presented by Sir Alfred Chester Beatty, 1951.
NGI 3752
LITERATURE: Williamson 1926, p. 18. NGI 1983, p. 13.

This miniature exemplifies Boit's intimate and informal portraits of female sitters. The subject wears her own hair arranged in loose locks. She is in a state of undress, in a pink wrapping gown, with a white chemise showing. The costume suggests that the portrait was painted c.1710.

THOMAS FORSTER

(?) Northumberland c.1677~
after 1712 London

Very little is known for certain about the life and *oeuvre* of Thomas Forster. He was possibly born in Northumberland. Forster had a very distinguished clientele and he probably worked in Ireland. In the 1690s he was part of the entourage of James Butler, 2nd Duke of Ormonde (1655–1745), and was well patronised by Ormonde and his supporters. He may have been related to the plumbago draughtsman Charles Forster (active 1709–1717).

LITERATURE: Goulding 1916, pp. 122–23. Bell and Poole 1925–26, pp. 73–79. Sumner 1988 pp. 115–21. Reynolds 1996, catalogue nos. 34–37.

6. *Portrait of a man,* 1702

SIGNED AND DATED: *T Forster Delin 1702*
10.9 x 8.4, plumbago on card
Set in a turned wood oval cabinet frame.
PROVENANCE: purchased by Miss Mary A. McNeill at Christie's, London, 31 March 1981, lot 13; Miss Mary A. McNeill Bequest, 1985.
NGI 19242
LITERATURE: Le Harivel and Wynne 1986, p. 107.

Forster did portraits in plumbago on card which was a popular medium for miniature portraits during the period 1660–1720. Plumbago was the predecessor of the lead pencil, its name deriving from the Latin *plumbum* meaning black lead or graphite, the crystalline form of carbon. These portraits were drawn like line engravings with finely pointed pieces of graphite, or plumbago pencil, on vellum or card.

The unidentified sitter in this portrait wears a lavish full bottomed wig which is arranged asymmetrically over one shoulder, which usually indicates a military officer. He is dressed in a fashionably tight fitting coat with a steinkirk cravat made of white linen which is loosely twisted and threaded through a button hole. Forster's plumbagos capture the texture of cloth, his portraits exemplify his adroitness at drawing the details of dress.

Similar plumbago portraits by Forster are in the Metropolitan Museum of Art, New York and

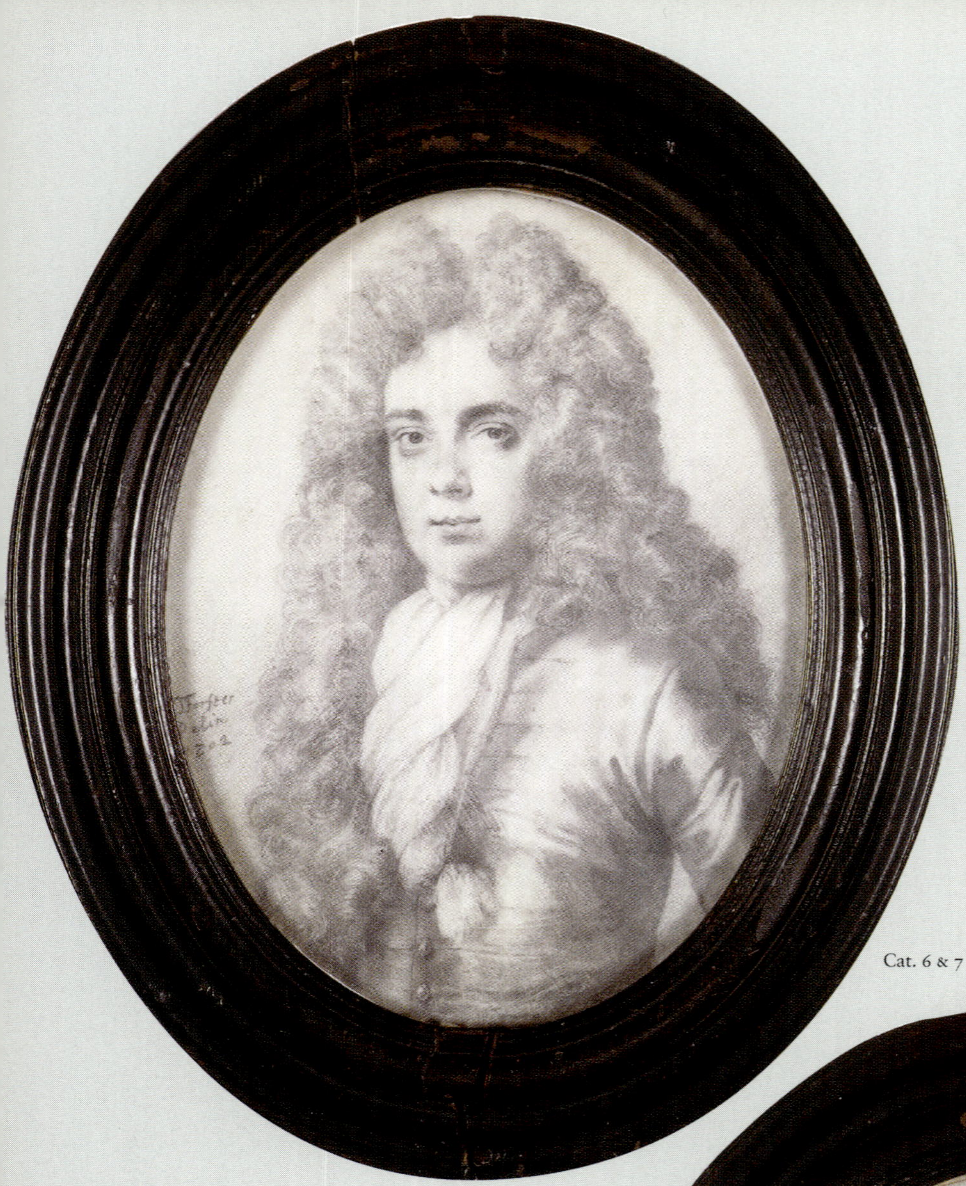

Cat. 6 & 7

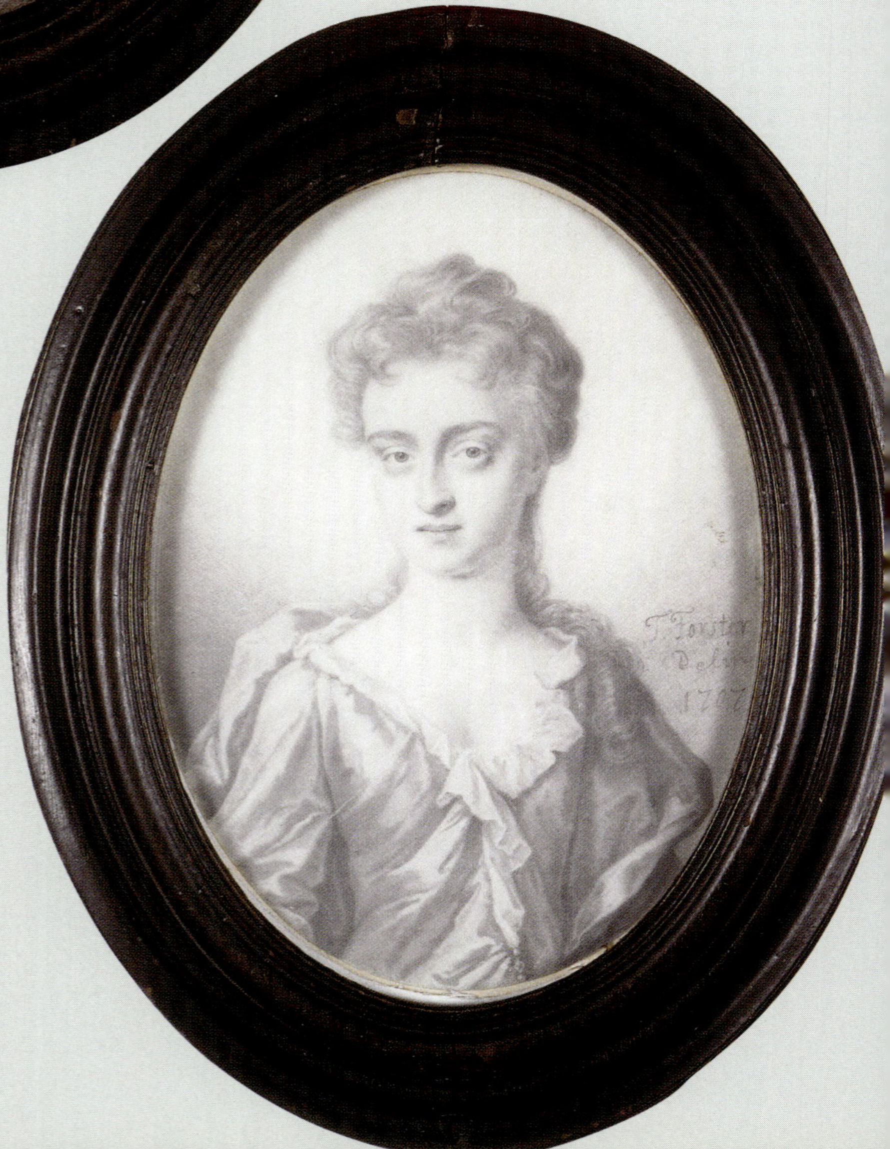

Holburne Museum of Art, Bath. The twelve Bath portraits are of all of sitters with Irish connections.[1]

REFERENCE: 1. Sumner 1988, pp. 115–21.

7. *Portrait of a lady*, 1707

SIGNED AND DATED: *T Forster Delin 1707*
10.7 x 8.1, plumbago on card
Set in a turned wood oval cabinet frame.
PROVENANCE: purchased by Miss Mary A. McNeill at Christie's, London, 31 March 1981, lot 12; Miss Mary A. McNeill Bequest, 1985.
NGI 19243
LITERATURE: Le Harivel and Wynne 1986, p. 108.

The sitter wears a wrapping gown, with a low white linen chemise underneath and a jewelled clasp attached to the front of the gown. Her own hair falls in loose locks behind her shoulders. A cloak falls nonchalantly over one shoulder. This adds to the air of informality typical of miniature portraiture.

ENGLISH SCHOOL
EARLY 18TH CENTURY

8. *Charles I, King of England, (1600–1649)*

1.8 x 1.7, watercolour on card
Set in an oval enamel bracelet setting, the case has a floral pattern on the reverse and is edged with paste diamonds.
PROVENANCE: purchased by the NMI, 1910; transferred from the NMI, 1969.
NGI 7112
LITERATURE: NGI 1983, p. 131.

Charles I was the younger son of James I and crowned King in 1625. With refined taste and sensibility, he was to be a major patron and collector, employing talents such as Rubens, Van Dyck and Inigo Jones and buying, in particular, works from the Gonzaga Collection. It was his autocratic behaviour, a French Catholic wife and reliance on favourites like the Duke of Buckingham, which alienated him from Parliament and much of the populace. The ensuing Civil War (1642–49) led to his defeat and capture by Oliver Cromwell and the Parliamentary forces. He was tried and executed in 1649. Considered by many a victim, the Church of King Charles the Martyr (c.1676) in Tunbridge Wells was built in his memory.

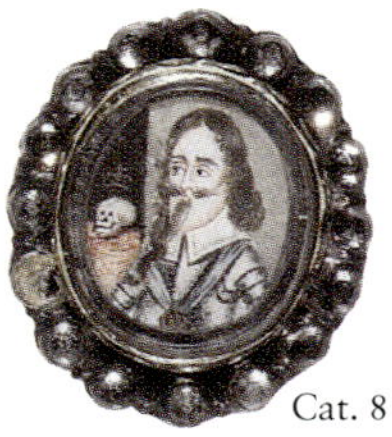

Cat. 8

Charles I is shown full face with long dark hair worn asymmetrically over his shoulder in military style, moustache, and pointed beard. He wears a broad white linen collar over armour and the ribbon and badge of the Order of the Garter. The crowned skull alludes to the triumph of the Stuart succession over death (the execution of Charles I in 1649). This miniature belongs to a large group of commemorative miniatures of Charles I that were painted in the late seventeenth and early eighteenth century and which would have been worn by the royalist supporters of the Stuarts as a badge of allegiance. This jewelled portrait demonstrates the fact that miniatures were important signifiers of political identity as well as objects of adornment and part of dress.

BERNARD LENS III

London 1682~1740 London

Lens was the son of Bernard Lens II (1659–1725), a mezzotint engraver and drawing master, and grandson of Bernard Lens I (c.1631–1708), an engraver. He was probably taught miniature painting by his father. He attended Kneller's Academy in Great Queen Street, Westminster. He is recorded as a member of the artists' Rose and Crown Club. Bernard Lens III was appointed Painter in Enamel and Cabinet Painter to George I in 1726 and continued under George II. He worked as a drawing master and taught members of the royal family as well as Horace Walpole. Two of his sons, Andrew Benjamin (c.1713–after 1779), and Peter Paul (c.1714–c.1750), were miniaturists.

LITERATURE: Vertue 1929–52, Notebook III, p. 50. Long 1929, pp. 266–69. Reynolds 1988, pp. 94–97. Bignamini 1991, pp. 54, 75.

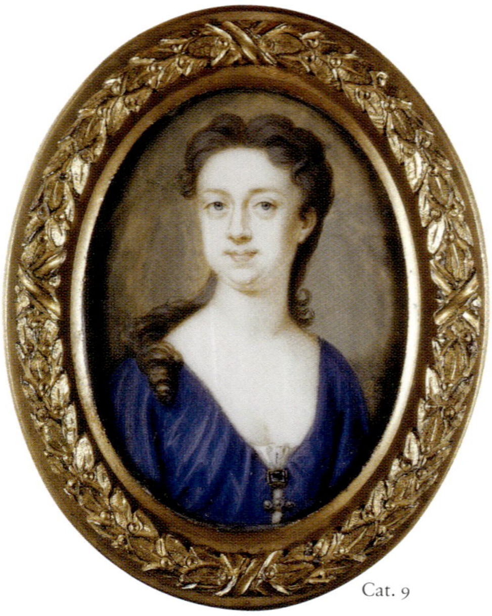

Cat. 9

9. *Portrait of a lady in a blue dress,* c.1715
SIGNED: *BL* (in monogram)
6.1 x 4.1, watercolour on ivory
Set in a nineteenth century oval ormolu frame.
PROVENANCE: purchased as a portrait of Ann Austin by Miss Mary A. McNeill at Christie's, London, 12 May 1964, lot 46; Miss Mary A. McNeill Bequest, 1985.
NGI 19246.
LITERATURE: Le Harivel and Wynne 1986, p. 110.

Lens' miniature is the earliest portrait painted on ivory in the NGI collection. Bernard Lens' early work was painted on vellum, but from 1708 he used ivory and was one of the first miniaturists in England to do so. The Venetian, Rosalba Carriera (1675–1757), is credited with the invention of the technique and it is not known how Lens learnt it. He was probably familiar with her work from examples brought back to England from Venice by grandees, such as the 4th Earl of Manchester, returning from their Grand Tour.

Technically Lens's miniatures are similar to those by Carriera, as in the use of watercolour, gouache and a greenish-brown shading in this work. In characterisation and presentation of his sitter's, Lens was influenced by Kneller's full-scale oil portraits. He would have been very familiar with his work and even attended Kneller's Academy. In this miniature portrait the sitter is quite mechanically posed. Lens presents his sitter with her hair loosely falling over her shoulder. She is in a state of undress with a white chemise showing underneath her wrapping gown which is held together by a pearl and table cut jewelled clasp.

CHRISTIAN FRIEDRICH ZINCKE

Dresden 1683/85~1767 London

Zincke was the son of a Dresden goldsmith. He came to England in 1706 where he was apprenticed to the enamellist Charles Boit (1662–1727). Zincke dominated the market for enamel portraits in the early part of the eighteenth century and was greatly favoured by George II, Frederick, Prince of Wales and Princess Amelia. He had many pupils and is known to have taught William Prewett (active 1735–1750, see catalogue entry 17) and Jeremiah Meyer (1735–1789, see catalogue entry 47).

LITERATURE: Vertue 1929–52, Notebook III, p. 64. Murdoch *et al.* 1981, pp. 164–70. Crookshank and Glin 1969, p. 76. Caffrey 1999, p. 19.

10. *The Hon. Thomas Foley, (d.1766), later 2nd Baron Foley of Kidderminster,* 1723
INSCRIBED, SIGNED AND DATED ON REVERSE (Illus. 6): *The Honble. / Thomas Foley Esqr / CF Zincke fecit / 1723* (CF in monogram)
4.5 x 3.7, enamel on gold
Set in a gold oval pendant frame.
PROVENANCE: Jacob Nachemsohn Collection, 1926; presented by Sir Alfred Chester Beatty, 1951.
NGI 3594
EXHIBITED: 1969–70 Dublin, London and Belfast, no. 116.
LITERATURE: Williamson 1926, p. 18. NGI 1983, p. 736.

The Hon. Thomas Foley is fashionably dressed in a wig. He wears a very expensive fine lace fronted shirt and white linen neck cloth. Foley succeeded his father as Lord Foley of Kidderminster in 1732 and died unmarried in 1766.[1] This miniature portrait exemplifies Zincke's established formula of the 1720s and 1730s. Attention is given to posing the sitter's head. The face no longer fills the enamel, as it did in

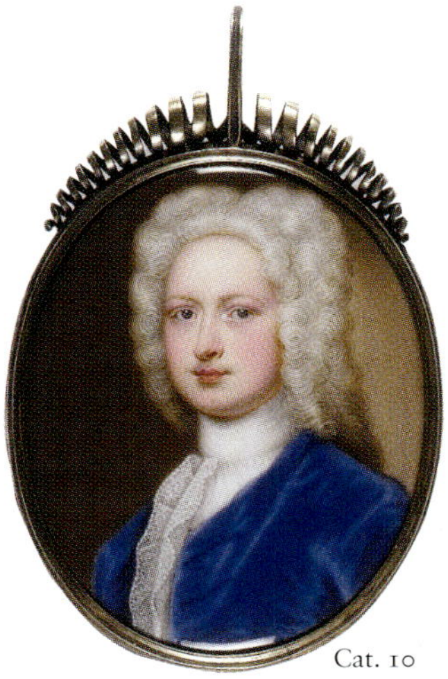
Cat. 10

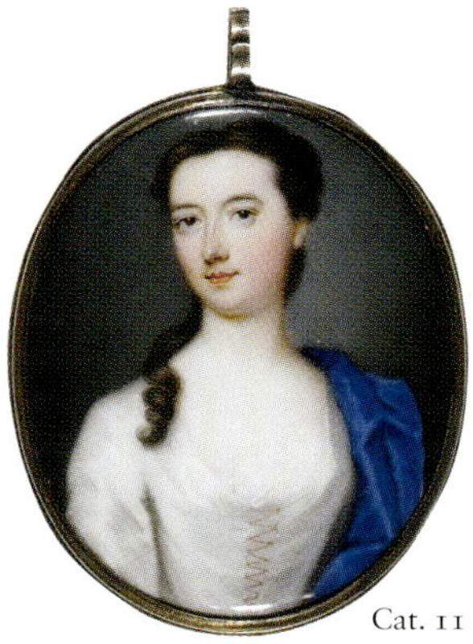
Cat. 11

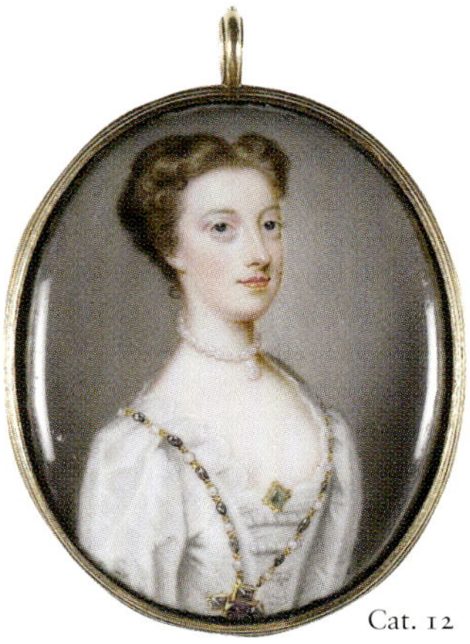
Cat. 12

earlier work, and greater attention is paid to painting the details of the coat and wig. Zincke's characteristic red stippling may be seen in the modelling of the face with each red dot blended together to form pinkish red cheeks. The plain drab background is typical of his work.

REFERENCE: 1. GEC vol. V, p. 535.

11. *Lady Dorothy Boyle (1724–1742) daughter of the 4th Earl of Cork and 3rd Earl of Burlington,* 1739

INSCRIBED, SIGNED AND DATED ON REVERSE:
Lady / Dorothy Boyle / Born May 14th / 1724 / CF Zincke Fecit / 1739 (CF in monogram)
4.4 x 3.6, enamel on copper
Set in a gold oval pendant.
PROVENANCE: Jacob Nachemsohn Collection, 1926; presented by Sir Alfred Chester Beatty, 1951.
NGI 3597
EXHIBITED: 1969–70 Dublin, London and Belfast, no. 117.
LITERATURE: Williamson 1926, p. 18. NGI 1983, p. 736.

Lady Dorothy Boyle was one of three daughters of Richard Boyle, 3rd Earl of Burlington, (1694–1753), the great patron of the arts, architect and supporter of Palladianism. She was fifteen when this portrait was painted and died three years later.[1]

Zincke's miniature is typical of his standard portraits of female sitters and follows his established formula. The sitter wears a low cut fashionable dress with zig-zag lacing and a contrasting piece of deep blue silk draped over her shoulder against a blue-grey background. The sitter's face is turned to the right and hair falls over her right shoulder. Zincke used red stippling and plenty of deep blue cobalt in his enamels. The lips are painted in contrasting shades of red.

REFERENCE: 1. GEC vol. II, pp. 432–33. Burke's 1889, p. 556.

12. *Margaret Cavendish, Duchess of Portland, (born Harley 1715–1785), wife of the 2nd Duke,* 1735

INSCRIBED, SIGNED AND DATED ON REVERSE:
Margaret Cavendishe / Duchess of Portland / CF Zincke fect. / 1735 (CF in monogram)
4.5 x 3.7, enamel on copper
Set in a gold oval locket engraved with a cipher of the sitter's initials surmounted by a ducal coronet.
PROVENANCE: presented by Sir Alfred Chester Beatty, 1951.
NGI 3744
LITERATURE: NGI 1983, p. 737.

This finely executed enamel is an example of Zincke's most accomplished work. The flatness associated with many of his portraits of women has been avoided here by meticulous attention to details of the sitter's jewellery, hair and dress. The Duchess of Portland is dressed in fanciful costume, with a scallop edged dress and elaborate jewellery. The face is painted in characteristic pinkish-red dot stippling.

The Duchess was the only daughter and heir of Edward Harley, 2nd Earl of Oxford and Mortimer, and her portrait was painted shortly after her marriage to the Duke of Portland in 1734. She was celebrated by Prior as *My Noble, Lovely little Peggy.*[1]

The Oxford and Portland families were significant patrons of the enamel miniaturists and some of the finest work of the 1720s and 1730s was executed for them. An earlier portrait of this sitter with her father was painted by Zincke in 1727 and was recorded in an account of the collection of the Duke of Portland, which contained 25 miniatures by Zincke.[2] The Duchess of Portland was a close friend of Mrs Delany. Mrs Delany records on 9 January 1784 that, after having her hair done, she visited the Duchess where they spent the afternoon looking at miniatures, gems and intaglios.[3] The Duchess was a great collector. She purchased the Portland Vase and was an accomplished wood turner.[4]

REFERENCES: 1. GEC vol. X, pp 592–93. Burke's 1889, p. 1126. 2. Goulding 1916, pp. 1–224. Adams and Lewis 1968–70, pp. 1–34. 3. Llanover 1861–62, vol. VI, p. 201; 4. *ibid.*, vol. VIII, pp. 472, 485.

JEAN ANDRÉ ROUQUET

Geneva 1701~1758 Charenton, near Paris

Rouquet was the son of French Protestants who fled to Switzerland. He settled in London about 1723, where he worked for the next thirty years. He was highly successful and according to Vertue, charged ten guineas per miniature portrait. Rouquet was a friend of William Hogarth and David Garrick. In 1753, he went to live in Paris where he joined the Académie Royale and published an account of English art entitled *L'État des Arts en Angleterre* (1755) which was well regarded. He exhibited at the Paris Salon 1753–57 but died insane.

LITERATURE: Vertue 1929–52, Notebook III, p. 96. Long 1929, p. 378. Reynolds 1988, pp. 102–03.

13. *Portrait of a man in a blue coat*, c.1750

SIGNED: *R*

4.2 x 3.5, enamel on copper

Set in a gold oval pendant frame.

PROVENANCE: Jacob Nachemsohn Collection, 1926; presented by Sir Alfred Chester Beatty, 1951.

NGI 3656

LITERATURE: Williamson 1926, p. 19. NGI 1983, p. 669.

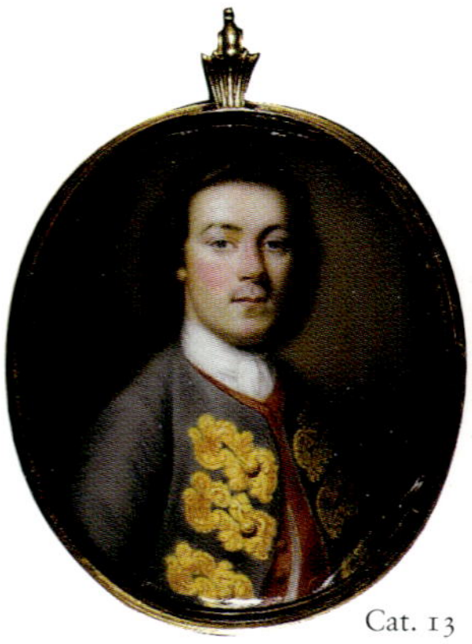

Cat. 13

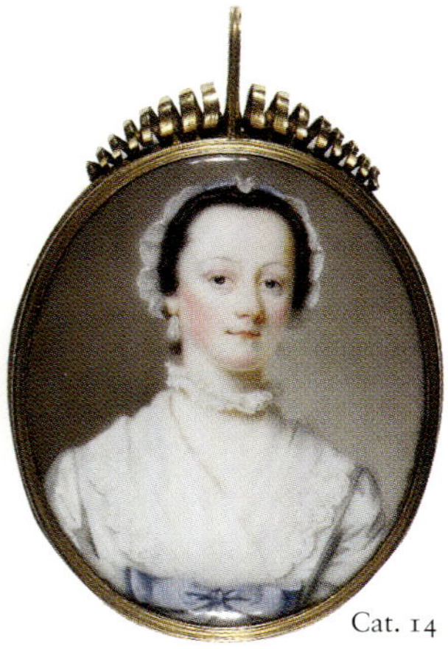

Cat. 14

This is a good example of Rouquet's work. Signed enamels by him are rare. There is an overall elegance and prettiness that is quite unlike Zincke or Richter's work. The eyes are slightly protruding, and the lower lips are painted as slightly moist. The sitter's costume is particularly carefully painted, as is evident in the details of the blue coat, with decorative gold frogging, and the pink waistcoat. As Rouquet worked somewhat in the manner of Zincke, his unsigned work is often given to Zincke, or an anonymous artist working in his style.

14. *Portrait of a lady with a blue bow*, c.1750

SIGNED: *R*

4.2 x 3.5, enamel on copper

Set in a gold oval pendant frame.

PROVENANCE: Jacob Nachemsohn Collection, 1926; presented by Sir Alfred Chester Beatty, 1951.

NGI 3649

LITERATURE: Williamson 1926, p. 20. NGI 1983, p. 669.

Rouquet was adept at painting the details of dress and jewellery. This elegantly dressed young lady wears lace around her neck, which was the height of fashion for 1750. She has a handkerchief shawl around her shoulders with a blue bow at her waist. She wears large pear-shaped drop pearl earrings. Rouquet's enamels are painted in minute stipple that blends together to produce a smooth surface. The plain background is typical of his work.

NOAH SEAMAN

active England 1724~1741

Little is known for certain about this miniaturist. He may have been brother of oil portraitist Enoch Seeman (c.1694–1744), and miniaturist Isaac Seaman (d.1751), brought to London by their father, a portraitist from Danzig, or may be related to the miniaturist Abraham Seaman (active 1724–1731).

LITERATURE: Foskett 1987, p. 641.

15. *Portrait of a lady in a blue dress,* 1728

SIGNED AND DATED ON REVERSE: *Noah Seaman pinx. / 1728*

4.9 x 3.9, enamel on copper

Set in a metal pendant frame, later adapted as a brooch.

PROVENANCE: transferred from the NMI, 1969.

NGI 7330

LITERATURE: NGI 1983, p. 675.

Signed and dated enamel portraits by Noah Seaman are rare. He worked closely to Zincke's style and technique. Seaman was a skilful enamellist and particularly adept at painting the textures of costume and textiles. He caught the subtle variation of colour as light falls on the cloth of a sitter's dress. This unknown lady wears a wrapping gown with white chemise underneath, which has folded linen at the front like a stomacher. The scarcity of his work after 1730 suggests that he could not compete with Zincke who dominated the market for enamels. There are some deep scratches and damage to the enamel surface. *Portrait of a man in a blue coat* (NGI 3612) has stylistic differences and is less securely attributed to Seaman.

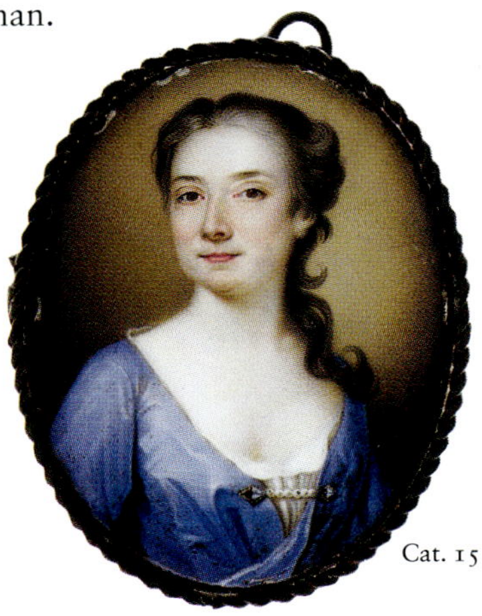

Cat. 15

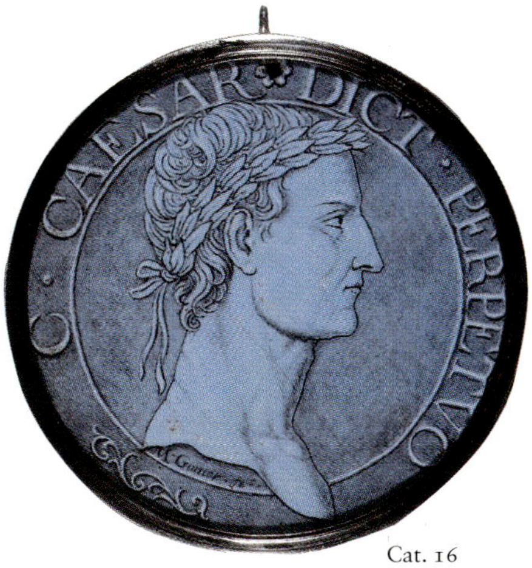

Cat. 16

MARCUS GUNTER

active London 1725~1736

Gunter was working as an enamellist and goldsmith in London in 1725. Very little is known of his life or work and he is principally remembered for his enamels of Roman Emperors done in the same year as a copy after David Teniers II (1610–1690).

LITERATURE: Long 1929, p. 183. Charleston 1956, pp. 61–68. Foskett 1987, p. 553.

16. *Gaius Julius Caesar (c.100–44 B.C.), General and Dictator,* 1725

SIGNED: *M. Gunter. fet*

5 diam., enamel on copper

Unframed.

PROVENANCE: Jacob Nachemsohn Collection, 1926; presented by Sir Alfred Chester Beatty, 1951.

NGI 3700

LITERATURE: Williamson 1926, pp. 23–24. Charleston 1956, pp. 61–68. NGI 1983, p. 190.

Caesar's profile in enamel is part of a group of twelve enamels executed by Gunter in 1725. There are seven enamels in the NGI collection, which comprise profile portraits of Julius Caesar, Otho, Germanicus, Domitian, Vespasian, Nero and Tiberius. Five enamels of Augustus, Claudius, Vespasian, Galba and Vitellius are in the Victoria and Albert Museum, London. All twelve were in the Jacob Nachemsohn Collection in 1926 and one of Vespasian is dated.[1] They would have been executed for a collector and probably housed in a cabinet. They are identified from inscriptions on the portraits, and from

Suetonius' history of the lives of the first twelve Caesars (with the exception of Caligula and Titus who are not included in the extant group of enamels). The iconography of the Roman Emperors and generals is taken from Hubert Goltzius' (1526–1583) *Icones Imperatorem Romanorum* (1557).[2]

REFERENCES: 1. Williamson 1926, pp. 23–24. 2. Anjou 1956, pp. 43–50. Charleston 1956, pp. 61–68.

WILLIAM PREWETT

active London 1733~1755

Said to have been born in Suffolk, little is known about Prewett's life, except that he was a pupil of Zincke. He is one of the best of the English-born enamellists, evolving his own distinctive, and different, style. As signed enamel portraits by him are extremely rare, very often second-rate enamels, in the manner of Zincke, are attributed to him. He is not mentioned by contemporary chroniclers, George Vertue or Horace Walpole.

LITERATURE: Long 1929, p. 351. Murdoch *et al.* 1981, pp. 168–69.

17. *Portrait of a man in a brown coat,* c.1740

SIGNED: *W. Prewett pinx*

4.6 x 3.7, enamel on copper

Set in a nineteenth century ormolu frame.

PROVENANCE: Jacob Nachemsohn Collection, 1926; presented by Sir Alfred Chester Beatty, 1951.

NGI 3610

LITERATURE: Williamson 1926, p. 20. Foskett 1972, vol. 1, p. 457. NGI 1983, p. 647.

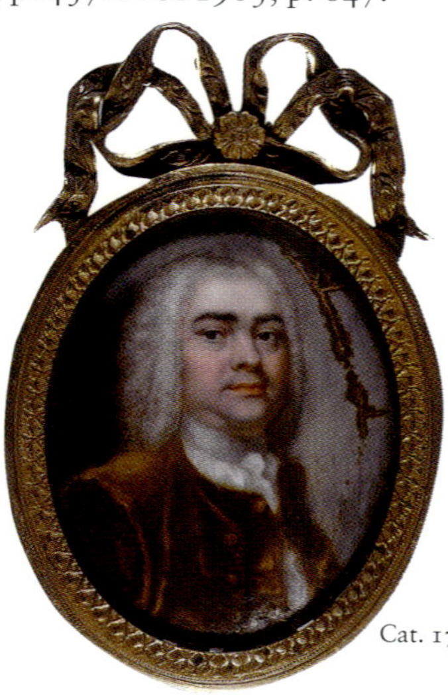

Cat. 17

This is an important work by Prewett, as it is a rare signed example. It exemplifies his original and distinctive style. Prewett's work is wholly unlike the work of enamellists C.F. Zincke (1683/85–1767, catalogue entries 10–12) or Noah Seaman (active 1724–1741, catalogue entry 15). His portraits are distinguishable by being more naturalistic and lively. The effect is produced by the use of more flesh-like tones in the painting of the sitter's face. He has managed to break away from the pinkish stipple associated with Zincke and Nathaniel Hone. This enamel portrait has many of the qualities of work in watercolour on ivory. The sitter wears a wig and a cinnamon-brown coat and matching waistcoat, which was a popular colour throughout the 1740s. He has a plain white linen neck cloth and shirt.

LUKE SULLIVAN

Co. Louth 1705~1771 London

Sullivan was born in Ireland, but spent his entire career as a miniaturist in England. He worked as an assistant to William Hogarth (1697–1764) and to the engraver Jacques-Philippe Le Bas (1707–1783). As a result of Le Bas' influence, Sullivan worked in a fully-fledged French rococo style. Sullivan, a colourful character, who resided at taverns and brothels, was described by J.T. Smith (1828) as: *a handsome lively fellow; but, being too much attached to what are denominated the good things of this world,...died in a miserable state of disease and poverty.*

LITERATURE: Pasquin 1796, pp. 16–17. Smith 1828, vol. II, pp. 211–12. Smith 1845, pp. 25–26. Long 1929, p. 426. Caffrey 1999, p. 21.

18. *Portrait of a man in mushroom coloured coat,* c.1765

SIGNED: *LS* (in monogram)

3.8 x 3.3, watercolour on ivory

Set in a rococo gold pin brooch decorated with a border of flowers.

PROVENANCE: purchased by Miss Mary A. McNeill at Christie's, London, 19 December 1972, lot 67; Miss Mary A. McNeill Bequest, 1985.

NGI 19248

LITERATURE: Le Harivel and Wynne 1986, p. 111.

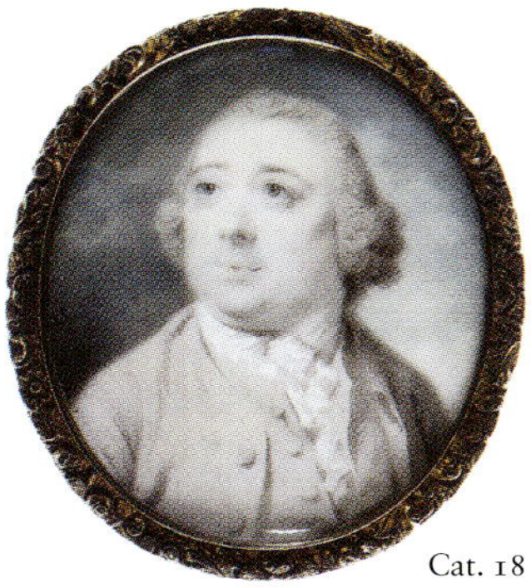

Cat. 18

Sullivan's date of birth would place him early in the chronological sequence of miniature painters, but he did not take up miniature painting until the late 1750s. He worked almost exclusively in watercolour on ivory and created a highly individual style that consisted of building up the portrait in minute curved lines. Sullivan often painted his sitters as if looking away from the viewer into the distance. The pose, range of grey powdery tones and frame give the portrait a French rococo feel.

GEORGE MICHAEL MOSER RA

Schaffhausen, Switzerland 1706~
1783 London

Moser was the son of a metal worker. He studied in Geneva and then settled in London in 1726 where he was employed to chase brass work for furniture, also as a medallist and enamellist. Moser was principally a decorator of boxes, watch cases, bracelets and seals. He worked for George II and taught George III drawing before his accession. He was a member of the artists' Rose and Crown Club, and a friend of Oliver Goldsmith and Dr Johnson. Moser established his own private Academy, which later merged with the St Martin's Lane Academy. He was Director of the St Martin's Lane Academy in 1746–47 and was an original member of the Society of Artists with which he exhibited from 1760–67. He was a founder member of the Royal Academy, the first Keeper, and an exhibitor from 1769–70. His daughter, Mary Moser RA (1744–1819), was a renowned flower painter, and he taught his nephew Joseph Moser (1748– 1819). He died at Somerset House and is buried at St Paul's, Covent Garden.

LITERATURE: Long 1929, pp. 303–04. Bignamini 1991, pp. 50, 116, 121–22.

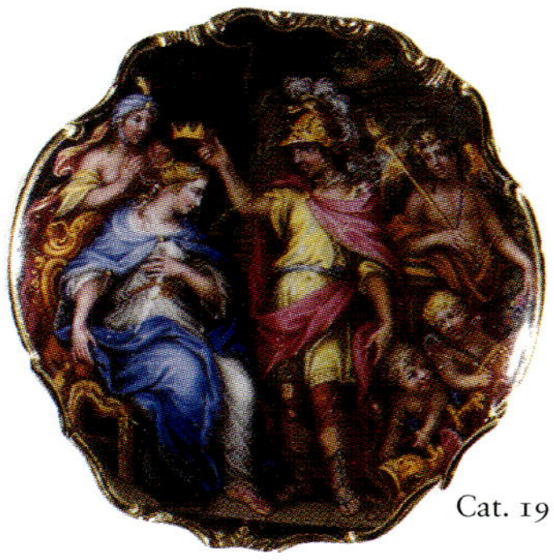

Cat. 19

19. *The Wedding of Alexander and Roxana*, c.1730

SIGNED: *G M Moser fecit*
4.2 diam., enamel on gold, edged with gold border
Originally set in the lid of a box.
PROVENANCE: presented by Sir Alfred Chester Beatty, 1951.
NGI 3736
LITERATURE: NGI 1983, p. 555.

This enamel shows Alexander the Great (356–323 BC), King of Macedonia, at the moment of his marriage to Roxana, a former Persian captive. Alexander, the military genius, dressed in a cloak and helmet, crowns Roxana, who is seated. His companion Hephaestion, and two amoretti, are present. The subject of Alexander and Roxana was a very popular theme for decorative work, such as this enamel. Its romantic subject and theme of marriage was appropriate for miniatures, which were often commemorative pieces that were exchanged during an engagement, or at the time of a marriage. Signed work by Moser is extremely rare and this is an excellent example of his decorative work executed for the lid of a snuff, patch or powder-box. It dates from early in his career.

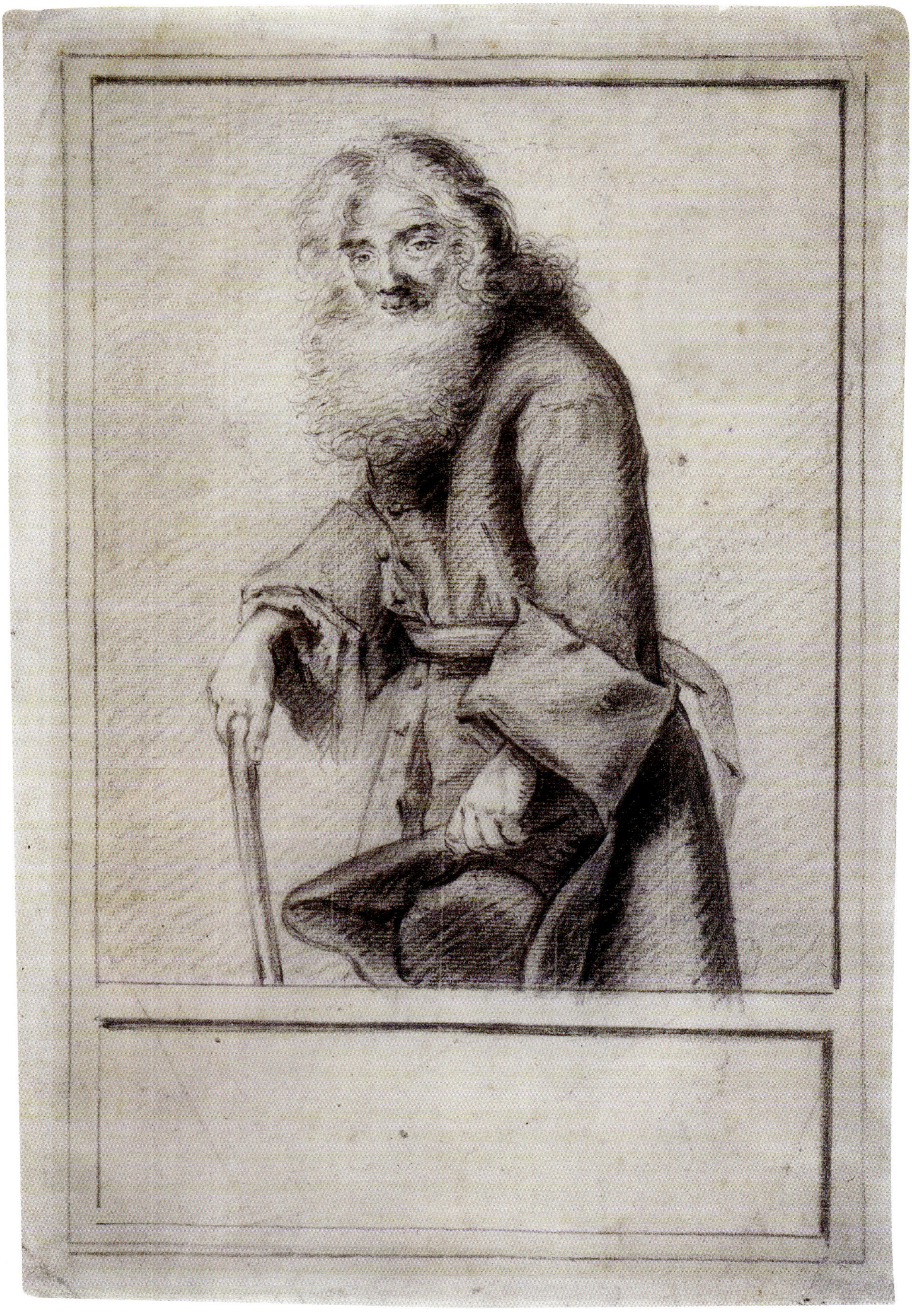

Cat. 28, see previous page

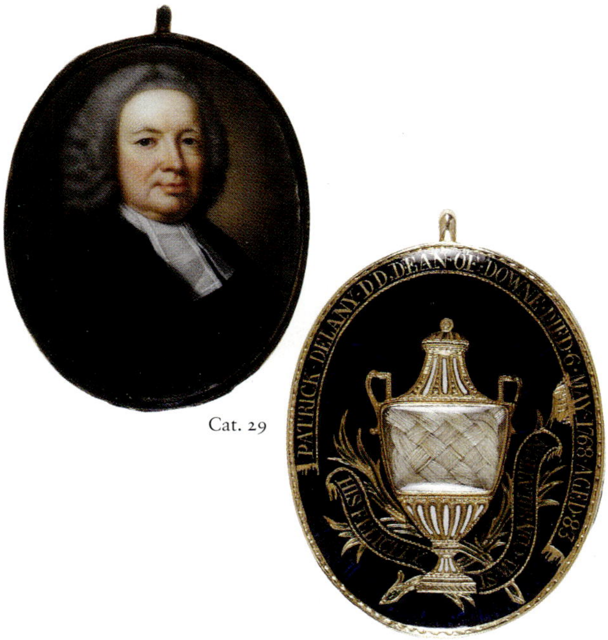

Cat. 29

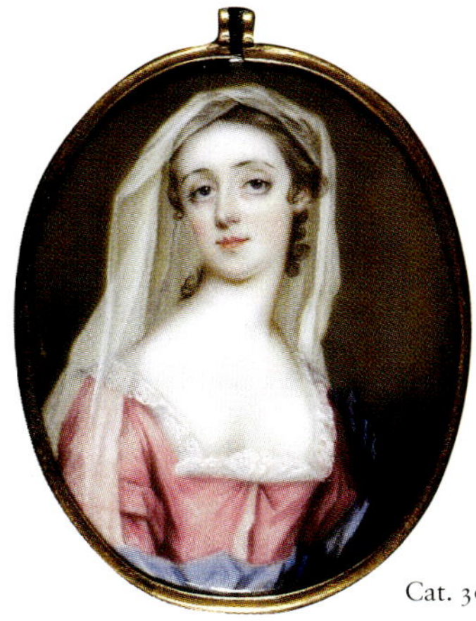

Cat. 30

Attributed to RUPERT BARBER

29. Dr Patrick Delany, (1684/85–1768), Dean of Down, c.1740

INSCRIBED ON REVERSE: *PATRICK DELANY D.D. DEAN OF DOWNE DIED 6 MAY 1768 AGED 83 HIS FELICITY IS MY CONSOLATION*

4.8 x 3.8, enamel on copper

Set in a gold and blue glass pendant locket, the reverse is decorated with an urn painted in white enamel with gold fluting. A lock of the sitter's hair is set into the urn beneath a cut crystal.

PROVENANCE: presented by Sir Alfred Chester Beatty, 1951.

NGI 3728

EXHIBITED: 1970 Dublin, no. 48 (incorrect illustration).

LITERATURE: NGI 1983, p. 394.

Dr Delany was educated at Trinity College, Dublin where he was elected Fellow. He married twice, both times to rich widows. He entertained generously at his house, Delville. Through his wife, Mary Delany, the celebrated diarist, letter writer and artist, he was appointed Dean of Down.[1]

The attribution of this enamel portrait to Rupert Barber is based on a comparison with the signed and dated enamel of William Thompson (New Orleans Museum of Art), also executed in the 1740s. From 1743–60s, Barber was living with his wife, a niece of Dean Delany at Delville.

REFERENCE: 1. DNB vol. V, pp. 760–61.

LUCIUS BARBER

Dublin 1720~1767 London

Lucius Barber has been traditionally recorded as a Swedish miniaturist who worked in England, but he was the brother of enamellist Rubert Barber, hence son of Rupert Barber and the poetess Mary Barber. Barber exhibited at the Society of Artists exhibitions in London from 1763 to 1766 and lived in Haymarket.

LITERATURE: Long 1929, p. 13; Foskett 1987, p. 484.

30. Portrait of a lady, known as Peg Woffington (1714/18–1760)

SIGNED: *B*

5.2 x 4, enamel on gold

Set in a gold pendant frame.

PROVENANCE: presented by Sir Alfred Chester Beatty, 1951.

NGI 3705

LITERATURE: NGI 1983, p. 6.

Traditionally this miniature portrait has been described as a portrait of Peg Woffington, the popular comic actress who was born in Dublin, the daughter of a bricklayer.[1] At the age of eight, she played the part of Captain Macheath in Madame Violant's Lilliputian company. She was engaged by Rich in 1740 to appear at Covent Garden as Sylvia in Farquhar's *Recruiting Officer*. She was loved for her charm and vivacity. Her instant success led to her playing many leading roles. While acting the part of Roxana to Mrs Bellamy's Statira, she drove her off the stage and stabbed her. She had many lovers and for a time she lived with David Garrick. Amongst accepted portraits are Andrew Miller's 1745 mezzotint after John Giles Eccardt (NGI 10367) and John Lewis' 1753 oil (NGI 579 AND NPGL), which share an oval face and theatrical air with this sitter, whose costume might date her about 1730.

REFERENCE: 1. DNB vol. XXI, pp. 752–55.

Attributed to LUCIUS BARBER

31. *Mr Redington of Co. Galway,* c.1760

LABEL ON REVERSE INSCRIBED: *Portrait / of / Mr Redington / Galway / enamelled / on / gold / valuabl.* [sic]

3.2 x 2.7, enamel on gold (damaged)

Set in a gold pendant frame in a leather case.

Formerly catalogued as Henry Bone (1755–1834).

PROVENANCE: presented to the NMI by Mrs Maev Sullivan, Dublin, 1949; transferred from the NMI, 1969.

NGI 7044

LITERATURE: NGI 1983, p. 16.

The attribution of this enamel to Lucius Barber is on stylistic grounds. The sitter's slightly hooded eyes are characteristic. He also painted drapery in an angular fashion. Mr Redington is dressed in a coat, elaborately embroidered with a gold decorative edging and waistcoat, a white linen shirt, and has a black solitaire or ribbon around his neck. The enamel is cracked down the centre and across the sitter's face.

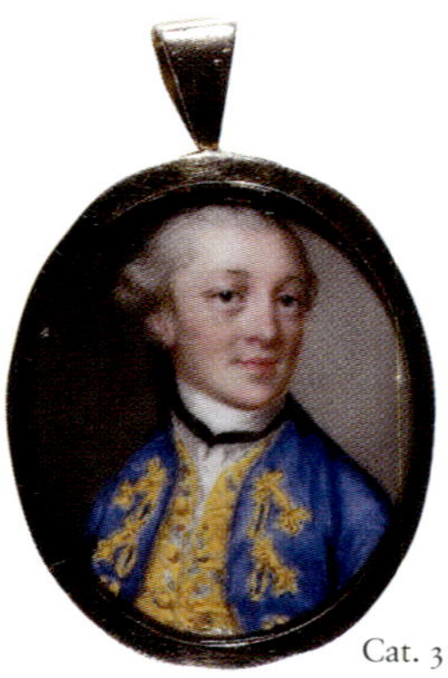

Cat. 31

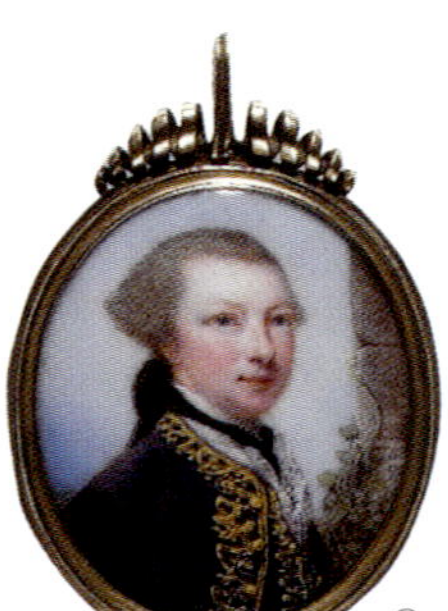

Cat. 33

NATHANIEL HONE RA (THE ELDER)

Dublin 1718~1784 London

Son of a Dublin merchant, he was descended from Dutch goldsmiths and married an heiress at York in 1742. Hone was working as an enamellist and miniaturist in watercolour on ivory from c.1740. He was in London by 1748 and living at Henrietta Street from 1752. Nathaniel Hone occupies an important place in the history of Irish and English miniature portrait painting. After Zincke's decline, from 1746 onwards, Hone succeeded him as the foremost enamel miniaturist of his day. Hone's talent was recognised by his contemporaries. However his contribution to the technical development of miniature painting on enamel, and in watercolour on ivory, and virtuosity as a miniaturist, have not been given any attention in accounts of his life. Hone is known as an oil painter and founder member of the Royal Academy in 1768. His naturalistic approach to painting miniature portraits owed much to William Hogarth (1697–1764), and Thomas Hudson (1701–1779), and anticipates his later development as an oil painter and portraitist.

LITERATURE: Pasquin 1796, pp. 9–10. Edwards 1808, pp. 99–103. Strickland 1913, vol. I, pp. 515–23. Long 1929, pp. 219–20. Crookshank and Glin 1969, pp. 47–49 and 78. Crookshank and Glin 1978, pp. 86–69. Le Harivel 1992, *passim.*

32. *William Capell, 3rd Earl of Essex (1697–1743),* 1747

SIGNED AND DATED: *NHone / 1747* (NH in monogram)

3.8 x 3.4, enamel on copper

Framed in an elaborate nineteenth-century filagree pendant setting.

PROVENANCE: transferred from the NMI, 1969.

NGI 7331

LITERATURE: NGI 1983, p. 296.

Hone's enamel technique is exemplified by this portrait. He uses minute dotted stipple in painting the shaded areas of the face and pinkish stipple in the shading of the sitter's cheeks. Hone painted costume details in strong colours. The gold brocade on the Earl of Essex's blue coat is meticulously overpainted

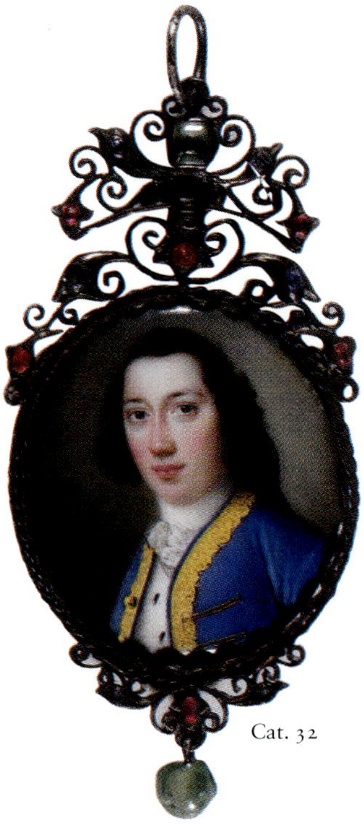

Cat. 32

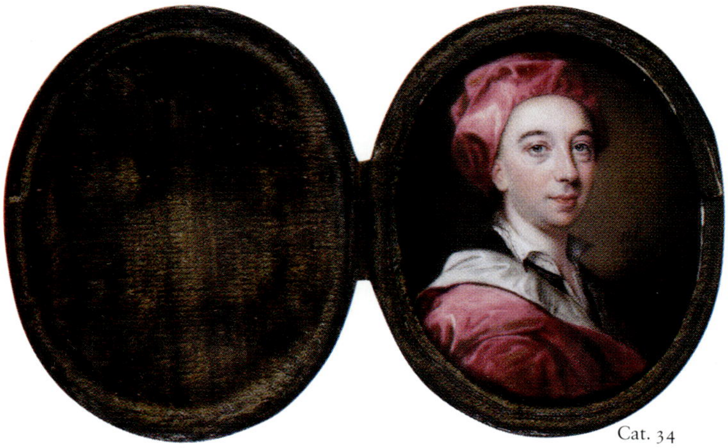

Cat. 34

in opaque yellow. Unusually he wears an ermine decorated waistcoat. Although this enamel is of interest technically, it is a rather lifeless portrait. This lack of characterisation in the sitter's expression may be explained by the fact that it is a copy of an earlier portrait painted in the 1720s or 1730s. This enamel was executed four or five years after the sitter's death. It would have been commissioned by his widow, or one of his six daughters, as a commemorative portrait, and worn as a memorial.

33. *Portrait of a young man in a purple coat,* 1750

SIGNED AND DATED: *NH / 1750* (NH in monogram)
2.8 x 2.5, enamel on copper
Framed in an oval gold pendant.
PROVENANCE: Jacob Nachemsohn Collection, 1926; presented by Sir Alfred Chester Beatty, 1951.
NGI 3666
LITERATURE: Williamson 1926, p. 18. NGI 1983, p. 295.

In contrast with Hone's enamel of the Earl of Essex, this portrait is more freely painted in stipple and parallel hatched lines. The sitter's cheeks are in characteristic pink stipple. The shading of the face is built up in short hatched lines which create an indefinite outline around the mouth and nose. Hone carefully paints the details of the brocade and button's on the coat and waistcoat; the lace edged shirt is overpainted in opaque white. The sitter wears a tie back wig and untied solitaire. The sky blue background and ivy-clad rustication are unusual elements in a miniature of this date. The ivy is emblematic and has traditionally been a symbol of friendship, fidelity and marriage.

34. *Portrait of a man in a pink turban,* 1751

SIGNED AND DATED: *NH /1751* (NH in monogram)
4.6 x 3.8, enamel on copper
Framed in a contemporary eighteenth-century leather case.
PROVENANCE: Miss M. J. Alexander; presented by Charles Dickinson, her executor, after 1924.
NGI 7471
LITERATURE: NGI 1983, p. 296.

The sitter is portrayed informally in this intimate portrait. He is shown in his own home wearing a house cap or turban instead of a wig and a banyan or dressing gown with a white open neck linen shirt. The fashionable informality and less rigid pose are in keeping with the taste for unpretentious portraits in the mid-eighteenth century.

This miniature would not have been worn, but was kept in its leather case, or placed open on a table where it could be viewed. The slight increase in size of this enamel has allowed for the introduction of drapery in the background. The use of pink, particularly in the painting of the sitter's face, is again typical of Hone's enamels.

35. *Sir Henry St John Bt.*, 1763

SIGNED AND DATED: *NH / 1763* (NH in monogram)
INSCRIBED AND DATED ON REVERSE: *Sr. Henry St. John Bart. / AEt 26, 1763.*
3.4 x 2.8, enamel on gold
Framed in a gold oval pendant.
PROVENANCE: Jacob Nachemsohn Collection, 1926; presented by Sir Alfred Chester Beatty, 1951.
NGI 3663
EXHIBITED: 1969–70 Dublin, London and Belfast, no. 126.
LITERATURE: Williamson 1926, p. 18. NGI 1983, p. 295. Le Harivel 1992, p. 14.

Hone's mature enamel painting technique and style of portraiture may be seen in this miniature. The portrait is crisply drawn and there is an overall neatness of modelling which is built up in minute hatched lines and stipple. Hone used strong colours, such as the deep blue and contrasting yellow in the painting of the sitter's military style and brocade. Sir Henry St John wears his own hair, which is dressed, and a lace edged white linen shirt. The same deep blue is used in painting the eyes and there is a hint of blue in the shading.

36. *Portrait of a man in a purple coat*, 1764

SIGNED AND DATED: *NH / 1764* (NH in monogram)
2.7 x 2.3, enamel on gold
Framed in a gold oval pendant.
PROVENANCE: Jacob Nachemsohn Collection, 1926; presented by Sir Alfred Chester Beatty, 1951.
NGI 3635
LITERATURE: Williamson 1926, p. 20. NGI 1983, p. 295.

Hone's enamel is well drawn and there is an attempt at characterisation. He uses subtle gradations of purple in the painting of the coat and the sitter's face. The use of pink and purple stipple is characteristic of Hone work on enamel. The sitter's coat is edged with fur and he wears a fashionable, lace edged, white linen shirt.

37. *Sarah Sophia Banks (1744–1818)*, 1768

SIGNED AND DATED: *NH / 1768* (NH in monogram)
INSCRIBED ON BACKING PAPER: *A Love here fix'd can / very seldom err / Who loves her best is / best Philosopher.*(Illus. 12).
4.5 x 3.8, watercolour with gouache highlights on ivory
Framed in an oval metal pendant with the inscription under glass on the reverse (Illus. 12).
PROVENANCE: purchased at Sotheby's, London, Mr Francis Wellesley Sale, 1920.
NGI 2717
EXHIBITED: 1969–70 Dublin, London and Belfast, no. 127.
LITERATURE: NGI 1983, p. 295. Butler 1990, p. 15.

Sarah Sophia Banks of Revesby Abbey, Lincolnshire, was the only sister of Sir Joseph Banks, Bt., (1743–1820), the great explorer, naturalist, botanist and President of the Royal Society. She never married and was a collector of objects of natural history, books and coins. Sir Joseph Banks presented her coins and engravings to the British Museum after her death.[1]

Sarah Sophia Banks is elegantly dressed in the fashions of the 1760s and informally posed. She wears a pink wrapping gown over a white lace edged

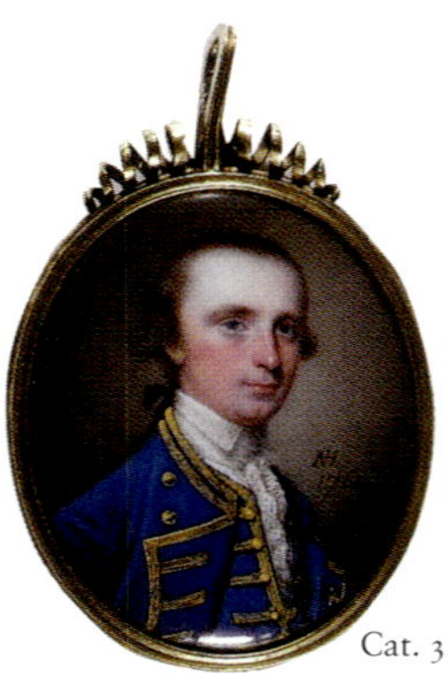

Cat. 35

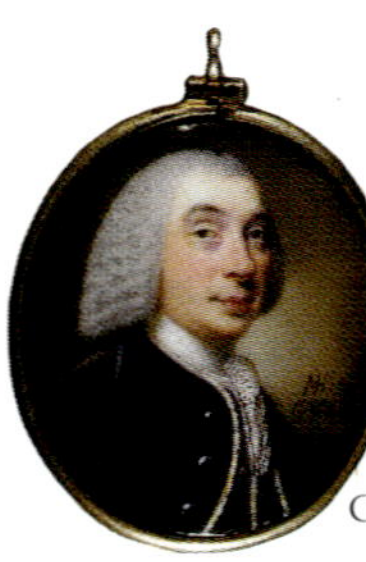

Cat. 36

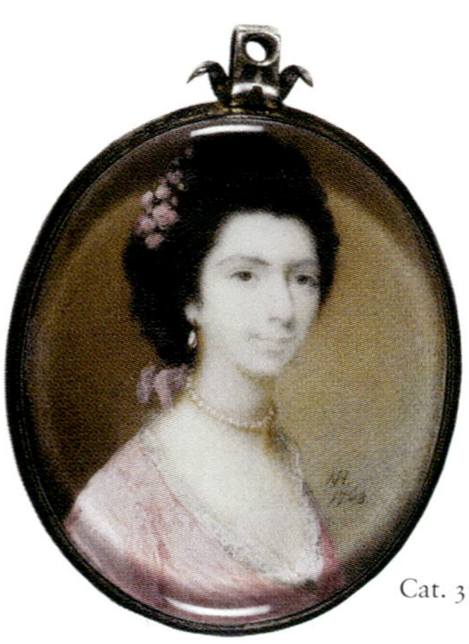

Cat. 37

chemise. Little pink roses are in her hair and a string of pearls loosely tied behind her neck with a ribbon. The pearl drop earrings are overpainted in opaque white highlights. This portrait was painted when she was 24 and must have been kept as a token of affection by an admirer.

Hone overcame the technical difficulties of painting in watercolour on ivory during the 1750s. This miniature shows his mastery of the technique. Working on a larger scale than his enamels, Hone allows the luminous white ivory support to show through in the painting of pale white powdered flesh. By the 1770s, soon after this portrait was painted, Hone stopped painting miniatures and devoted his attention to full-scale oil painting.

REFERENCE: 1. DNB vol. I, p. 1053.

GIUSEPPE (JAMES OR JOSEPH) MACPHERSON

Florence 1726~after 1778 (?) Florence

He was the son of Donald Macpherson, a footman in the service of Alexander, 2nd Duke of Gordon and reputed to have been a pupil of Pompeo Batoni (1708–1787), in Rome. Macpherson painted miniatures in watercolour and enamel. In 1742, he was elected *novizio* of the Florentine Academy. He is known to have worked in Florence, Milan, Germany, Paris (1754) and London (1754) and specialised in making enamel copies of paintings for the Grand Tour market. He was commissioned by Lord Cowper to paint miniature copies on ivory of sixty-four self-portraits of artists, including his own, in the collection of Grand Duke Cosimo at the Uffizi, Florence. In 1767 Cowper exhibited the enamels at SS. Annunziata in an exhibition organised by the Florentine Academy. Lord Cowper gave the collection to George III.[1]

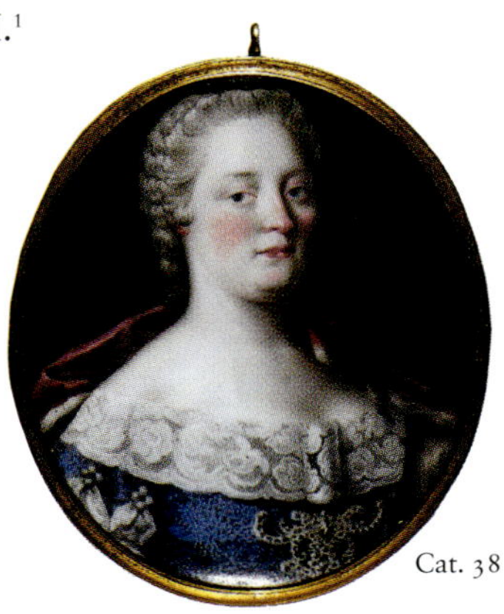

Cat. 38

LITERATURE: Long 1929, p. 285. Fleming 1959, pp. 166–67. Webster 1972, pp. 1145–46; Ingamells 1997, p. 627.

REFERENCE: 1. Walker 1992, pp. 232–48.

38. *Empress Maria Theresa, (1717–1780), Archduchess of Austria, Queen of Bohemia and Hungary,* late 1740s

SIGNED AND DATED ON REVERSE: *Macpherson fecit* 174... (last digit missing)

4.2 x 3.8, enamel on copper

PROVENANCE: Jacob Nachemsohn Collection, 1926; presented by Sir Alfred Chester Beatty, 1951.

NGI 3624

LITERATURE: Williamson 1926, p. 24. NGI 1983, p. 494.

An early enamel by Macpherson, this miniature is painted in a fairly free style with fine linear modelling and strong shadows. It depicts Maria Theresa, the elder daughter of the Emperor Charles VI, (1685–1740), whom she succeeded in 1740. Maria Theresa was Archduchess of Austria, Queen of Hungary and Bohemia, and Holy Roman Empress. This portrait shows her wearing a blue dress with gold embroidery and edged with a white lace border. Over her shoulders is placed an ermine edged coronation robe. She has blue eyes and wears a white powdered wig.

Macpherson's enamel miniature is based on a portrait by Jean Étienne Liotard (1702–1789). Liotard was in Vienna in 1743 and did several portraits of Maria Theresa and her family. He made a state pastel portrait of Maria Theresa at the time of her coronation in 1745.[1] He then did other copies in pastel and miniature versions on enamel and on ivory. An engraving by Johann Christoph von Reinsperger (1747), a pupil of Liotard, is also thought to derive from it. An enamel version by Liotard, painted at Lyon in 1747, is in the Rijksmuseum, Amsterdam. Macpherson's enamel is similar to two watercolour on ivory portraits after Liotard in the Royal Collection[2], especially catalogue number 735 in pose and characterisation.

REFERENCES: 1. Loche and Rothlisberger 1978, no. 64.
2. Walker 1992, pp. 262–63, catalogue numbers 733 and 735.

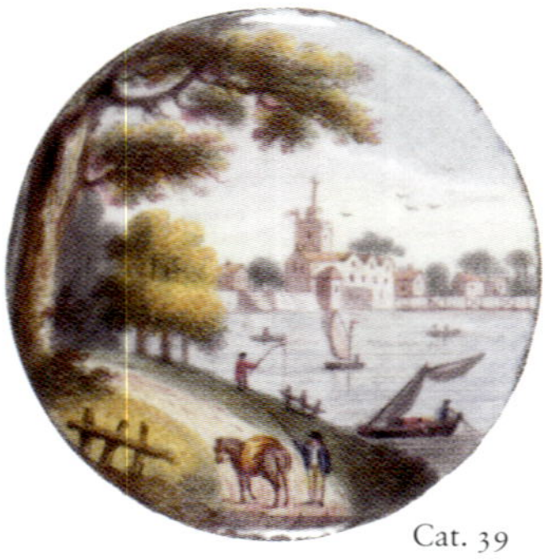
Cat. 39

ENGLISH SCHOOL (c.1750)

39. *All Saints, Fulham, London*, c.1750

4.1 diam., enamel on copper
Unframed.
PROVENANCE: presented by Sir Alfred Chester Beatty, 1951.
NGI 3679
LITERATURE: NGI 1983, p. 129.

In the eighth century Bishop Waldhere of London obtained the lands of Fulham, thus establishing a long association between Fulham and the Bishops of London. In the churchyard, to the left of the Church of All Saints, Fulham, there are ten tombs of former Bishops of London. The interior of the church is filled with seventeenth century monuments. The church was rebuilt in 1880–81 and the medieval tower, refaced in 1845, when the wooden spire was removed, is all that remains of the earlier structure.[1]

Originally this decorative enamel would have been set into the lid of a snuff or patch box. It shows a scene from everyday life on the river Thames. The background is dominated by the Church and old Putney Bridge, which was built in 1729. Part of the fifteen span wooden bridge may be seen to the right of the church.

REFERENCE: 1. Weinrib and Hibbert 1983, pp. 18, 298.

AFTER JOSIAH WEDGWOOD

Burslem, Staffordshire 1730–
1795 Etruria, Staffordshire

Born into a family of potters, Wedgwood entered into partnership with Thomas Whieldon in 1754 and in 1759 set up his own business which still flourishes. His ability as a master potter, and business acumen in developing wider markets were largely responsible for the expansion of the Staffordshire pottery industry. He opened a larger factory, called Etruria in 1769. He is known for his cream-coloured earthenware, jasper ware and basalt ware and established the taste for neo-classical design in English ceramics (particularly employing John Flaxman, 1755–1826).

LITERATURE: Reilly 1992, *passim.*

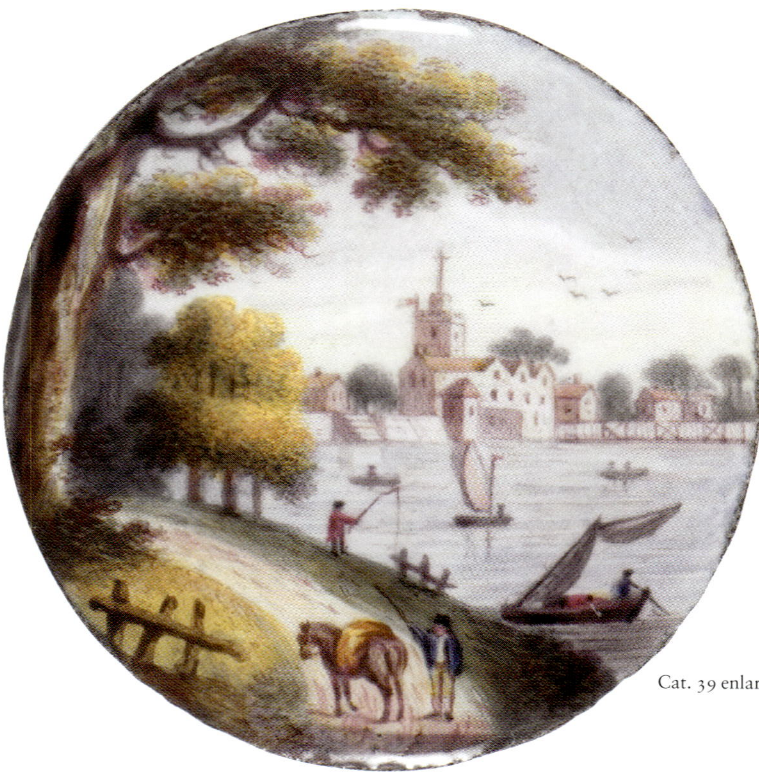
Cat. 39 enlarged

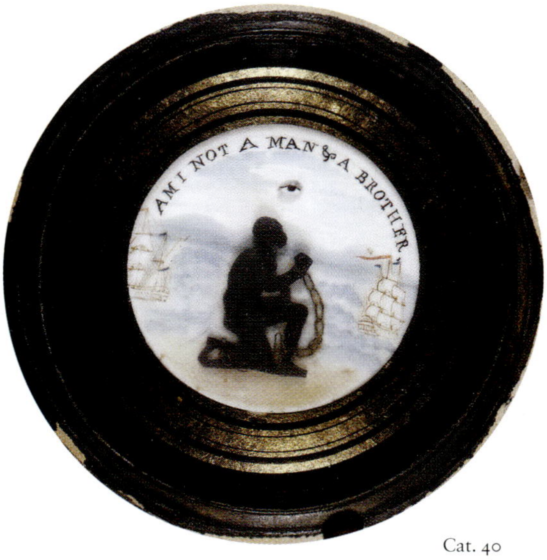

Cat. 40

40. *Am I not a Man and a Brother*, c.1790

3.8 diam., ivory, metal and watercolour on ivory
Set in a circular wooden cabinet frame.
PROVENANCE: presented by Sir Alfred Chester Beatty, 1951.
NGI 3722

In 1787 Josiah Wedgwood designed and produced a ceramic cameo depicting a black male in chains with the words AM I NOT A MAN AND A BROTHER for the Society for the Abolition of the Slave Trade. These anti-slavery medallions were intended to be worn by abolitionists and their supporters. They were set into metal mounts, snuff-boxes, hairpins or bracelets. A contemporary account described them:

> *At length the taste for wearing them became general, and thus a fashion, which usually confines itself to worthless things, was seen for once in the honourable office of promoting the cause of justice, humanity and freedom.*[1]

This ivory miniature version is based on the Wedgwood medallion and was probably copied from the retail medallion, which was plagiarised and manufactured by the Staffordshire pottery T. & J. Hollins, or a brass medal that was struck c.1790.[2]

Although the known medallions are quite similar, the NGI miniature contains some differences. It has a seascape with two slave-ships and a distant shore with hills in the background. In the blue sky, a stylised eye is centrally placed which is symbolic of God the Father.

REFERENCES: 1. Guyatt 2000, p. 93. 2. *ibid*, p. 97.

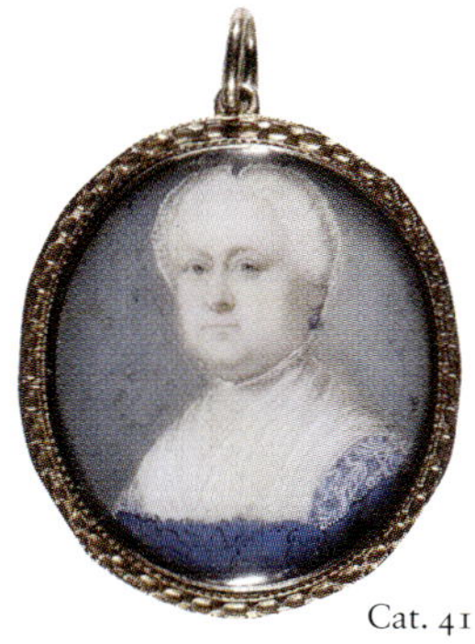

Cat. 41

PENELOPE CARWARDINE

Withington, Herefordshire c.1730–1801 London

Penelope Carwardine was the elder of six daughters of John and Anne Carwardine of Thinghills Court, Herefordshire. Her reckless father ruined the family's finances and Penelope turned to portrait painting as a means of earning a living. By 1754 she was an established miniaturist but did not paint after her marriage to Mr Butler, a London church organist, in c.1772. Her work of the 1750s shows some influence from Bernard Lens III (1682–1740, catalogue entry 9). Ozias Humphry (1742–1810, catalogue entry 57) painted her portrait in 1767.[1]

LITERATURE: Long 1929, p. 64; Foskett 1987, p. 507.
REFERENCE: 1. Williamson 1918, opp. p. 78.

41. *Portrait of a lady in a blue dress*, c.1760

SIGNED: *PC*
3 x 2.6, watercolour on ivory
Framed in a gold pendant setting with bright-cut engraving around the edge. A lock of the sitter's hair in encased on reverse.
PROVENANCE: purchased by Miss Mary A. McNeill at Christie's, London, 18 February 1969, lot 154; Miss Mary A. McNeill Bequest, 1985.
NGI 19255
LITERATURE: Le Harivel and Wynne 1986, p. 114.

Carwardine's miniature is neatly painted with attention paid to the details of dress and jewellery. The sitter wears a blue dress with a white fichu, or lace shawl, over her shoulders, and blue clasp earrings.

WILLIAM CRAFT

(?) Tottenham, Middlesex c.1730–1811 London

Craft was an enamellist who painted portraits, landscapes and subject pictures. He is known to have decorated clock-faces and watch-cases. Williamson believed that Craft was the brother of Thomas Craft, a decorator at the Bow porcelain factory. An artist named William Craft entered the Royal Academy Schools in 1774 but there is considerable disagreement on the actual identity of Craft. Foskett suggests that there may be two different miniaturists, William Craft (or Croft) and William Hopkins Craft, but the problem of identity remains unsolved. There are signed portrait and subject miniatures by both W. and W. H. Craft, but they are in similar style. Craft worked as a ceramics decorator for Josiah Wedgwood (who found him troublesome) at his Chelsea studio from 1769–71. He was known as Croft, as in the record of his death when a pensioner of the Charter House, London.

LITERATURE: Williamson 1926, p. 12. Long 1929, pp. 105–06. Foskett 1987, pp. 518–19.

42. *Self-Portrait,* 1780

SIGNED AND DATED: *W Craft / 1780*

INSCRIBED, SIGNED AND DATED ON REVERSE: *Portrait / of / W: CRAFT / Enamel Painter / 1780*

3.1 x 2.7, enamel on copper

Set in a gold pendant frame.

PROVENANCE: Jacob Nachemsohn Collection, 1926; presented by Sir Alfred Chester Beatty, 1951.

NGI 3668

LITERATURE: Williamson 1926, p. 18. NGI 1983, p. 81.

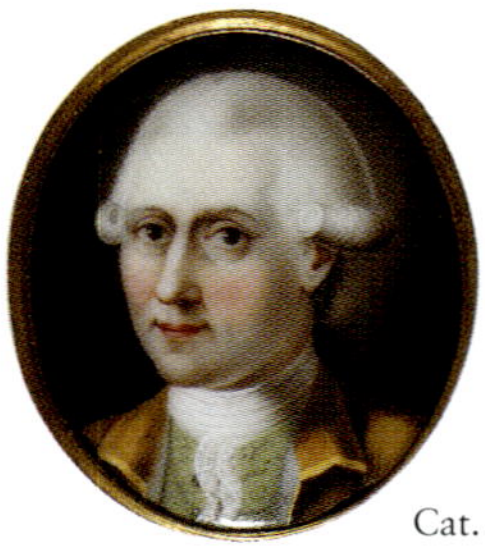

Cat. 42

Craft presents himself as a successful professional man in a powdered wig with a tie bag. He wears a white linen neck cloth and shirt which is edged with lace and a light-green waistcoat. Although Craft would appear to be quite young in this portrait, it is not a sophisticated work and could be the same artist as *The Judgement of Paris*.

43. *The Judgement of Paris,* 1782

SIGNED AND DATED: *W:Craft. / 1782*

10.2 x 14.2, enamel on copper

Unframed.

PROVENANCE: Jacob Nachemsohn Collection, 1926; presented by Sir Alfred Chester Beatty, 1951.

NGI 3582

LITERATURE: NGI 1983, p. 81.

Craft's large decorative oval plaque depicts the Judgement of Paris, the most popular mythological theme in art. Paris, the Trojan Prince, was abandoned as a child to avoid the prophecy that he would destroy his homeland, and brought up as a shepherd. Unknowingly, the three goddesses, Juno, Venus and Minerva, turned to him to judge who should be awarded the apple inscribed 'For the Fairest' which had been thrown by the goddess of discord amongst the gods at the marriage of Peleus and Thetis. Paris is attended by Cupid, as he awards the golden apple to Venus, who had promised him the hand of the most beautiful woman in marriage. This was to be Helen, whose abduction led to the Trojan War. The enamel may originally have decorated the lid of a box, as the subject frequently appears on decorative miniatures and snuff or patch boxes.

Although he did some portraits from life, Craft's colouring was very harsh and his technique more suited to decorative enamels. He specialised in subjects, usually with a patriotic theme, which were used as decorative panels on a box, or piece of furniture. *The Judgement of Paris* is a good example. The colouring is quite strong and there is an overuse of purple tones in the shading. The weak figures, and liking for patterns, point to this being his own composition.

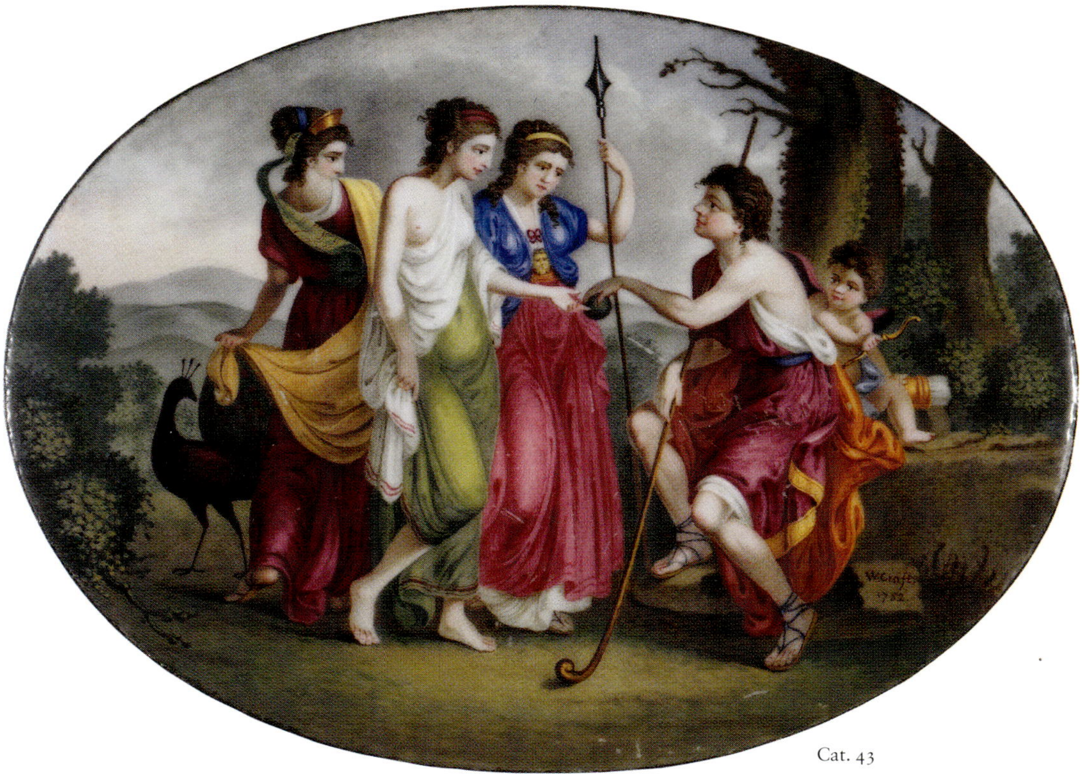

Cat. 43

44. *Francis Bacon, 1st Baron Verulam and Viscount St Alban, (1561–1626), Lord Chancellor,* 1793
(Illustrated overleaf)

INSCRIBED, SIGNED AND DATED ON REVERSE: *Natural / History in Ten Centuries / by Lord Bacon / Royal Society / founded / 1660 / W:H: Craft fect. / 1793 / from a portrait in the Royal Society / Sir Joseph Banks / President*

17 x 14, enamel on copper

Oval gilt metal frame.

PROVENANCE: Jacob Nachemsohn Collection, 1926; presented by Sir Alfred Chester Beatty, 1951.

NGI 3585

LITERATURE: Williamson 1926, p. 19. NGI 1983, p. 81.

Francis Bacon was educated at the University of Cambridge. He was called to the Bar and appointed King's Counsel. With the accession of James I, he was knighted and in 1613 he was constituted Attorney General and member of the Privy Council. In 1617 he was made Lord Keeper of the Great Seal and the following year Lord High Chancellor of England. He became Baron Verulam in 1618 and Viscount St Alban three years later.[1] In 1620 Bacon was convicted of corruption, admitted his offence, was fined £40,000, and imprisoned. On his release, he devoted his time to writing, and was the first important writer of essays in English.[2]

Craft's large oval enamel of Lord Bacon is after a contemporary portrait by Abraham Van Blyenberch (active 1617–1622) at the Royal Society, London. Van Blyenberch, in the circle of Paul Van Somer and Daniel Mytens, is thought to have visited England around 1618, but there are few portraits known by him.[3] Bacon, dressed in black and russet, with gold oversleeves, wears a deep white frill collar and white cuffs and a high black felt hat. He is leaning on a table upon which a red cloth seal bag with the royal coat of arms is placed. In his left hand is a scroll with the inscription: *To the Right Honble. Francis, Lord Verulam, Lord Chancellor of England 1619*. The intended recipient of Craft's enamel is not known.

REFERENCES: 1. Burke's 1889, pp. 77–78. 2. DNB vol. II, pp. 800–32. 3. Waterhouse 1978, p. 53.

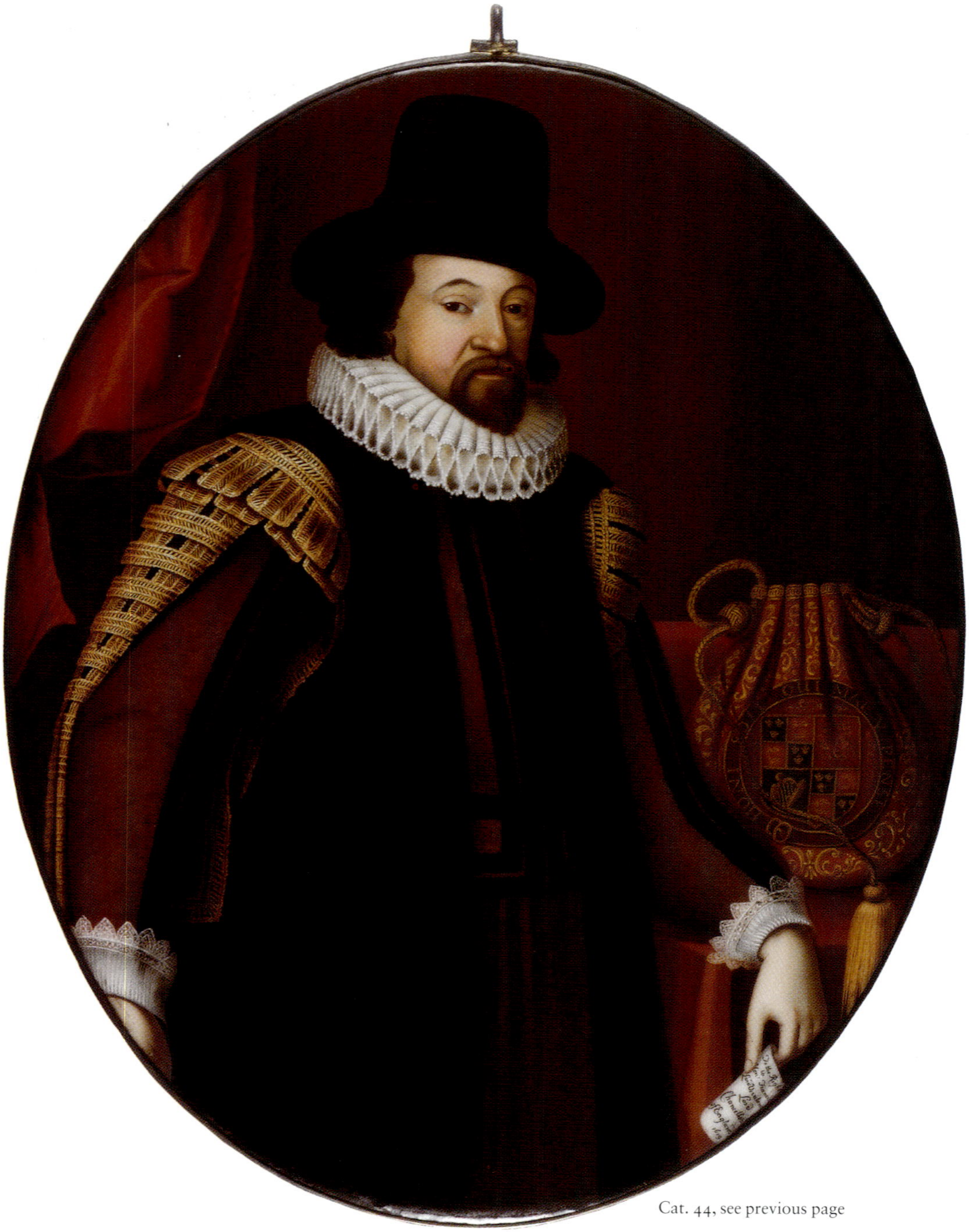

Cat. 44, see previous page

JOHANN HEINRICH [VON] HURTER

Schaffhausen, Switzerland 1734–
1799 Düsseldorf

Hurter was working in Berne, The Hague, and at Versailles, before he settled in London about 1777, supposedly on the advice of Lord Dartrey. He exhibited at the Royal Academy from 1779–81. Hurter worked mainly as a copyist. From 1785–87 he was working at Schaffhausen, Karlsruhe, The Hague and Paris before returning to London. In London he established a factory that manufactured mathematical

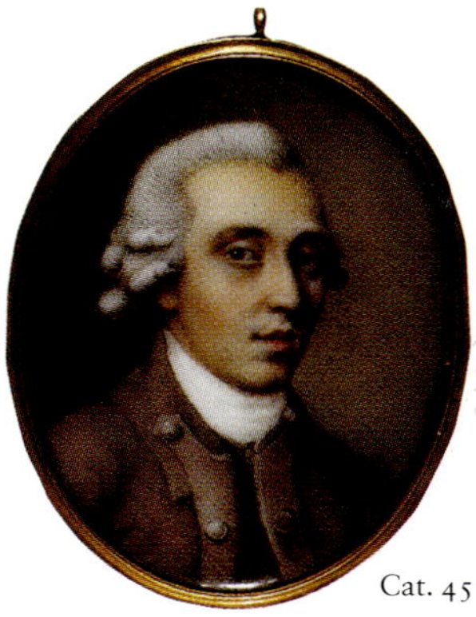

Cat. 45

and scientific instruments. Latterly he divided his time between London and Germany. His son Charles (or Carl) Ralph Hurter (active 1780–91), was also a miniaturist.

LITERATURE: Long 1929 pp. 232–33. Foskett 1987, pp. 573–74.

45. *Tiberius Cavallo, (1749–1809), Natural Philosopher,* 1783

INSCRIBED, SIGNED AND DATED ON REVERSE: *Tiberius Cavallo / F.R.S. / born in Naples / March the 30th / 1749 / Hurter pint. Londini / 1783*
4.5 x 3.6, enamel on copper
Set in an oval gilt metal pendant frame.
PROVENANCE: Jacob Nachemsohn Collection, 1926; presented by Sir Alfred Chester Beatty, 1951.
NGI 3611
LITERATURE: Williamson 1926, p. 21. NGI 1983, p. 713.

Tiberius Cavallo was born in Naples and went to live in England at an early age. He carried out experiments on electricity and magnetism. He was a distinguished scientist, inventor, and was admitted a fellow of the Royal Society in 1779.[1] Hurter generally specialised in painting enamel copies of historical portraits and this is one of his rare portraits of a contemporary in London. The strong linear modelling, deep shadows and plain stippled background are indicative of Hurter's work.

REFERENCE: 1. DNB vol. III, pp. 1246–47.

SAMUEL COLLINS

Bristol 1735~1768 Dublin

Collins practised miniature painting at Bath where, included amongst his pupils, was the miniaturist Ozias Humphry (1742–1810, see catalogue entry 57). In about 1762, Collins left Bath because of financial difficulties, and moved to Ireland, where he painted miniatures until his death in 1768. Collins signed his work with his initials, and, as a result, his miniatures are often confused with those by Samuel Cotes (1734–1818).

LITERATURE: Pasquin 1796, p.28. Smith 1828, vol. II, p. 357. Strickland 1913, vol. I, p. 190. Caffrey 1999, p. 23.

46. *Portrait of a lady with a white collar,* 1761

SIGNED AND DATED: *S.C. 1761*
3.6 x 3.1, enamel on copper
Set in an oval gilt metal frame.
Formerly catalogued as Samuel Cotes (1734–1818)
PROVENANCE: Jacob Nachemsohn Collection, 1926, catalogued as Samuel Cotes; presented by Sir Alfred Chester Beatty, 1951.
NGI 3731
LITERATURE: Williamson 1926, p. 20. NGI 1983, p. 78.

Collins worked in watercolour and enamel. This is an example of his work on enamel which is characteristically softly painted with indefinite outlines. The distant gaze of the sitter gives the portrait a rococo feel. Collins's initials are painted in smooth strokes of the brush unlike Cotes, who signed his work in initials made up of several strokes.

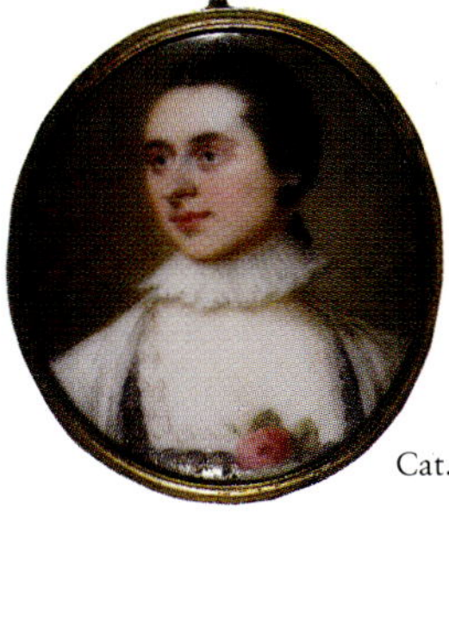

Cat. 46

JEREMIAH MEYER RA

Tübingen, Germany 1735~1789 Kew, Surrey

Meyer was the son of a portrait painter who brought him to England at the age of fourteen. He studied at the St Martin's Lane Academy where he was known as Jeremy Meyer. On leaving the Academy, he was apprenticed to Zincke from 1757–58, at a cost of £200, (with an additional £200 for materials), where he learned the craft of the enamellist (see catalogue entries 10–12). Meyer was responsible for the portrait of George III which was used in the design of the coinage. In 1764, he was appointed Miniature Painter to the Queen and Painter in Enamel to the King. Meyer exhibited miniatures at the Society of Arts in 1760 and at the Society of Artists in 1761–63, 1765 and 1767. He was a Director of the Incorporated Society of Artists. In 1768 he signed the *Memorial of the Royal Academy* and was a founder member of the Royal Academy, where he exhibited from 1769–83.

In 1763 Meyer married the painter Barbara Marsden (b.1743). George Romney (1734–1802) painted a group portrait of the Meyer family (private collection). Their daughter Mary was painted as *Hebe* (Ascott, Buckinghamshire National Trust) by Joshua Reynolds, who was a friend of the family. Meyer's pupils included Richard Collins (1755–1831) and Diana Hill (active 1775–1844). He was one of the most influential miniaturists of the eighteenth century. Meyer worked both in enamel and watercolour and developed two very distinct styles of painting to suit the different media. Meyer's ivories are painted in a very linear style, which was emulated by many miniaturists after 1770 and was influential on the development of the miniature in the last quarter of the eighteenth century.

LITERATURE: Papendiek 1887, vol. II, pp. 52–53. Graves 1907, p. 164. Long 1929, pp. 293–96. Foskett 1987, pp. 599–600. Bignamini 1991, pp. 116, 121.

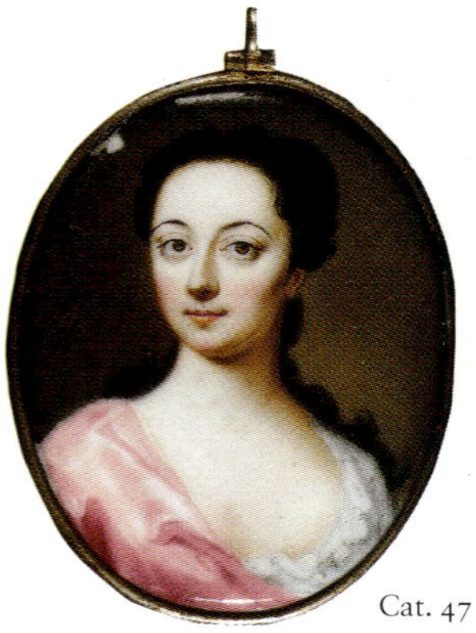

Cat. 47

47. *Portrait of a young lady in a pink dress*, c.1760

SIGNED: *JM* (in monogram)
4.3 x 3.5, enamel on copper
Set in an oval gilt metal frame.
PROVENANCE: Jacob Nachemsohn Collection, 1926; presented by Sir Alfred Chester Beatty, 1951.
NGI 3636
LITERATURE: Williamson 1926, p. 20. NGI 1983, p. 506.

This enamel portrait is an example of Meyer's very early work painted before he evolved his own individual style. It was painted during, or shortly after, his apprenticeship with Zincke in 1757–58 and is painted with Zincke's technique, having the rather stiff pose associated with his work. It has the feel of an apprentice piece. The sitter's facial appearance tallies with a date of mid–1750s for this miniature, though the presentation of the sitter's costume, the pink drape and white chemise, could suggest a much earlier date. The enamel is technically accomplished, the colours are well blended and the sitter is placed against a plain grey background.

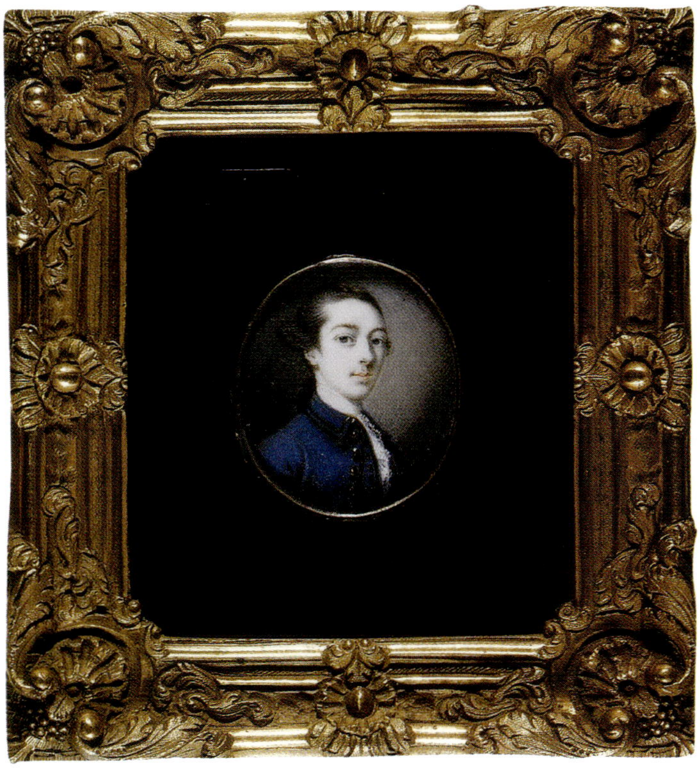

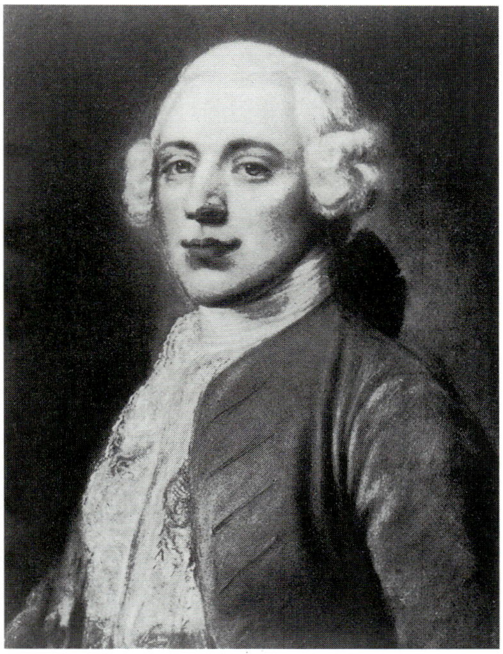

32. *Self-Portrait*, c.1760 pastel
GUSTAVUS HAMILTON
(Untraced)

Cat. 48

GUSTAVUS HAMILTON

(?) Co. Meath c.1739~1775 Dublin

Hamilton was one of the first miniaturists to study at the Dublin Society's Drawing Schools. He was taught there by Robert West (active c.1740–1770). Hamilton was awarded prizes for drawing in 1755 and 1756.[1] He worked for Samuel Dixon (active 1748–1769) colouring his *basso-relievo* prints and tried his hand at his own botanical watercolours (NGI 7932). Hamilton spent his entire career working in Ireland and exhibited his work at the Society of Artists in Ireland from 1765–73. He is buried at St Werburgh's, Dublin, where a plaque was erected in his memory.

LITERATURE: O'Keefe [*sic*] 1826, vol. I, pp. 18–19. Strickland 1913, vol. I, pp. 426–27; Breeze 1985, p. 13. Caffrey 1999, p. 23.

REFERENCES: 1. RDS Minute Book 1750–56, vol. III: 3 April 1755, 2 December 1756. RDS Proceedings, 1769–70, vol. VI, p. 230.

48. *Self-Portrait*, 1759

SIGNED AND DATED: *GHP / 1759*

3.1 x 2.8, watercolour with gouache on ivory

Set in a gold oval pendant with a lock of the sitter's hair under glass on the reverse, mounted in a nineteenth century rococo-revival ormolu frame.

PROVENANCE: purchased by the NMI, 1909; transferred from the NMI, 1969.

NGI 7117

LITERATURE: NGI 1983, p. 230.

Formerly catalogued as *Portrait of a Gentleman*, it can be compared with a pastel self-portrait of Hamilton illustrated in Strickland.[1] (Illus. 32). The facial similarities, also the painting of the eyes and angle of the head, all suggest that this is a self-portrait.

Hamilton's idiosyncratic style of miniature painting is apparent in this work. The eyes and eyebrows are exaggerated in size and painted in dark browns and black. The details of the blue coat with black trim, and lace edged shirt, are picked out in overpainted gum laden gouache. The slight stiffness associated with Hamilton's work may be seen too.

REFERENCE: 1. Strickland 1913, vol. I, plate XXIX.

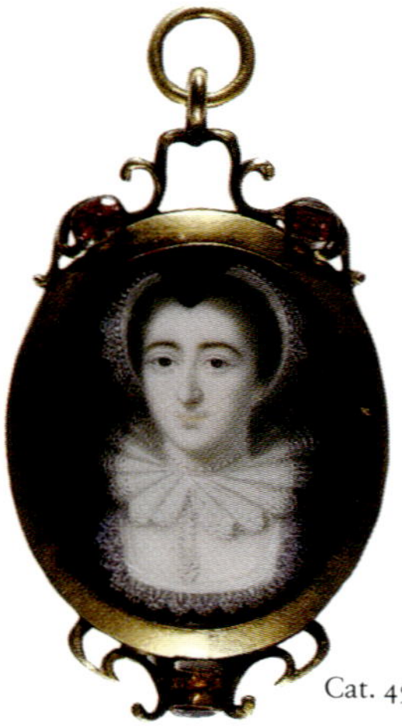

Cat. 49

49. *Portrait of a lady in Elizabethan costume,* 1764

SIGNED AND DATED: *Hamn. / 1764*
3.4 x 2.8, watercolour with gouache on ivory
Set in an oval metal pendant frame.
PROVENANCE: purchased from Mr M. D'Alton, Dublin, 1910.
NGI 7322
LITERATURE: NGI 1983, p. 231.

It was fashionable in the eighteenth century to wear, and be painted in, what was considered to be Elizabethan or old English dress, confused in the popular imagination with Shakespearean costume, and, in fact, an amalgam of earlier periods with Van Dyck of the 1630s. The sitter in this portrait is not strictly wearing Van Dyck, or masquerade costume and it more specifically recalls the earlier miniatures of Nicholas Hilliard (1547–1619), and Isaac Oliver (1558/68–1617). Hamilton paints the minute details of the lace head-dress, with its widow's peak, ruff and collar, in white opaque gouache. This makes the detail stand out against the dark background and is characteristic of Hamilton's work on a very small scale.

JAMES REILY

active Dublin 1745~1780/88 Dublin

Reily was educated at the Blue-Coat School, Dublin (1745–48) and was sent as a pupil to Robert West (1748). In 1753, he was awarded a prize for drawing by the Dublin Society.[1] He was apprenticed to Samuel Dixon (active 1748–1769), where he was employed hand colouring *basso-relievo* subjects of birds and flowers. Reily then set up his own practice as a miniaturist in Capel Street and later in Grafton Street, Dublin. He exhibited at the Society of Artists in Ireland in 1765–70, 1772, 1773 and 1779.

LITERATURE: Pasquin 1796, p. 17. O'Keefe [*sic*] 1826, vol. I, p. 19. Vicars Griffith 1852, p. 36. Strickland 1913, vol. II, p. 274. Breeze 1985, p. 23.
REFERENCE: 1. RDS Minute Book 1750–56, vol. III: 15 February 1753.

50. *Portrait of a lady in a pink dress,* 1764

SIGNED AND DATED: *I Reily / 1764*
3.8 x 3.2, watercolour on ivory
Set in a gold locket with a lock of the sitter's hair on reverse.
PROVENANCE: purchased by the NMI, 1908; transferred from the NMI, 1969.
NGI 7086
LITERATURE: NGI 1983, p. 657.

The sitter wears a pink dress, with a lace stomacher, and a trim of cloth tied in a bow around her neck. In her hair is a lace edged pompon. Reily developed his own individual style made up of criss-crossing lines. His work does not have clear outlines and precision. The blue-grey tinge in the flesh tones of the face is the result of discolouring due to the lead oxide in the paint.

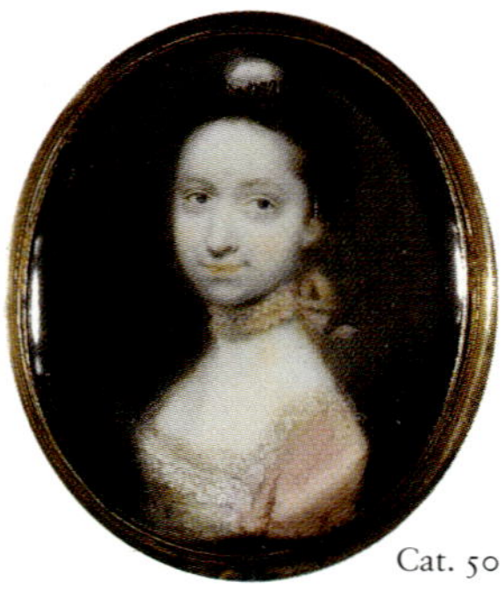

Cat. 50

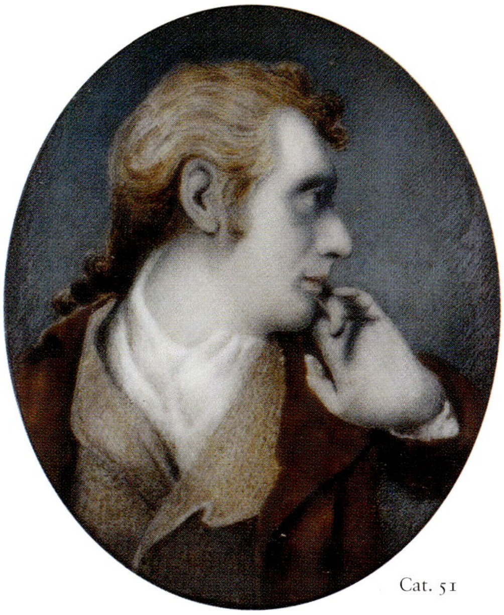

Cat. 51

DANIEL O'KEEFFE

Dublin 1740~1787 London

O'Keeffe was educated at the Dublin Society Drawing Schools. He is recorded as a pupil in 1754[1] and was awarded prizes for drawing in 1755, 1756 and 1757. He was apprenticed to Samuel Dixon (active 1748–1769) and like Gustavus Hamilton and James Reily coloured *basso-relievo* subjects of birds and fruit. By 1762 he was established as a miniaturist in Temple Bar, Dublin. He worked in London, where he exhibited at the Free Society of Artists in 1769 and 1783, and at the Royal Academy between 1771 and 1786. O'Keeffe worked in Bath about 1776 and had to leave Salisbury in 1777 as a result of debt. He died from consumption in London.

LITERATURE: Pasquin 1796, p. 27. O'Keefe [*sic*] 1826 vol. I, p. 2, pp. 19–20.

REFERENCE: 1. RDS Minute Book 1750–56, vol. III: 16 June 1754, pp. 304, 337, 339, 389.

51. *John O'Keeffe, (1747–1833), Actor, Playwright and the artist's brother,* 1776

INSCRIBED, SIGNED AND DATED ON REVERSE OF FRAME: *John O'Keeffe / the Celebrated Actor / Author & Landscape Painter / Daniel O'Keeffe pinxt. / Dublin 1776*

7.7 x 6.5, watercolour on ivory

Set in a nineteenth century black *passe-partout* frame with a brass acorn clasp.

PROVENANCE: presented by Mrs Frank Vickerman, 1977.

NGI 7795

LITERATURE: NGI 1983, p. 598.

John O'Keeffe was born in Abbey Street, Dublin, and educated at the school in Cook Street founded in 1750 by Father John Austin, S.J.[1] At the age of six, he was attending West's Academy and was recorded as a pupil by the Dublin Society in 1754.[2] John O'Keeffe started his career as a miniaturist but, according to Pasquin, *he left the polite arts for the stage, and performed, what is termed low comedy with success in Dublin and London.*[3] He published his autobiography *Recollections of the Life of John O'Keefe written by himself*, in 1826.[4] This portrait was painted in Dublin before O'Keeffe went to London in 1779. It is an extremely rare miniature by his brother, Daniel O'Keeffe. The profile pose and gesture give a suitably theatrical air to this portrayal of a professional actor. The excessive blues in the shadows may be due to the discolouring of skin tones.

REFERENCES: 1. DNB vol. XIV, pp. 966–68. 2. RDS Minute Book 1750–56, vol. III: 16 June 1754. 3. Pasquin 1796, p. 27. 4. O'Keefe [*sic*] 1826, *passim*.

ROBERT WADE

active Dublin c.1765~1785 Dublin

Very little is known about Wade and his work is rare. He practised as a miniaturist in Dublin, initially in Exchequer Street. Strickland records an advertisement that he moved to 61, [south] Great George's Street in 1780 (after exhibiting for the only time at the Society of Artists in Ireland). He charged one guinea for painting a miniature portrait on ivory. From 1782–85, he worked in Parliament Street and thereafter at 7, Essex Bridge.

LITERATURE: Strickland 1913, vol. II, p. 492. Breeze 1985, p. 28. Caffrey 1999, p. 25.

52. *Richard Ellis, (1744–1814)*, c.1780

INSCRIBED ON REVERSE: *Richard Ellis / 1744 / 1814*
3 x 2.1, watercolour on ivory
Cabinet frame.
Formerly catalogued as Irish School (early 19th century)
PROVENANCE: purchased by the NMI, 1939; transferred from the NMI, 1969.
NGI 7186
LITERATURE: NGI 1983, p. 397.

Wade's miniature of Richard Ellis would originally have been framed in a gold locket. The identification of this miniature, as painted by him, rests on the comparable technique of a signed miniature portrait of Joseph Leeson after Pompeo Batoni (private collection).[1]

REFERENCE: 1. Caffrey 1999, p. 25.

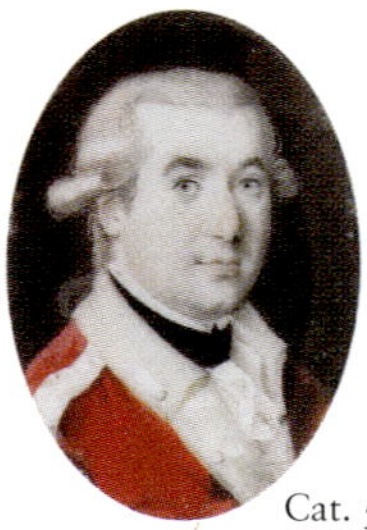

Cat. 52

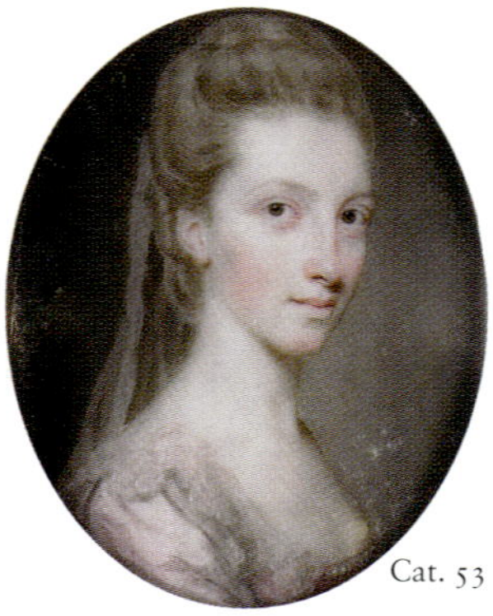

Cat. 53

JOHN SMART

near Norwich, Norfolk 1741/43~ 1811 London

His exact date and place of birth are not known. Smart studied at William Shipley's Academy in St Martin's Lane in 1755. In that year, he submitted a drawing to the Society of Arts competition and came second to Richard Cosway (see catalogue entries 58–59). In the next three competitions, Smart took first prize. He exhibited at the Society of Artists from 1762–83, and between 1772 and 1778 held the Society's offices of Director, Vice-President and President. His first wife eloped with the watercolourist William Pars (1742–1782), and he subsequently lived with, or married, three other women. In 1785, he moved to Madras, returning to London in 1795. Amongst various self-portraits are examples dated 1797 (V&A) and 1802 (Cleveland Museum of Art).

LITERATURE: Foskett 1964, *passim*.

53. *Mary Cholmondeley*, (d.1806), 1775

SIGNED AND DATED: *J.S. 1775.*
4 x 3.3, watercolour on ivory
Set in an oval pendant frame.
PROVENANCE: purchased by Miss Mary A. McNeill at Christie's, London, 27 October 1959, lot 75; Miss Mary A. McNeill Bequest, 1985.
NGI 19260
LITERATURE: Le Harivel and Wynne 1986, p. 117 (date given as 1774).

Mary Cholmondeley was the sister of the future Lady Bellingham (p. 80).[1] She remained a spinster and was killed in a carriage accident while accompanying Caroline, Princess of Wales.[2] Smart portrays her in a pink masquerade dress with a Van Dyck lace edged collar and a veil falling from her hair. He usually painted his sitters with very dark brown eyes which may be seen in this miniature. Smart used flat matt, colours applying microscopic stippling to model the face and shadows.

REFERENCES: 1. Burke's 1889, p. 282. 2. Information from J. Bellingham.

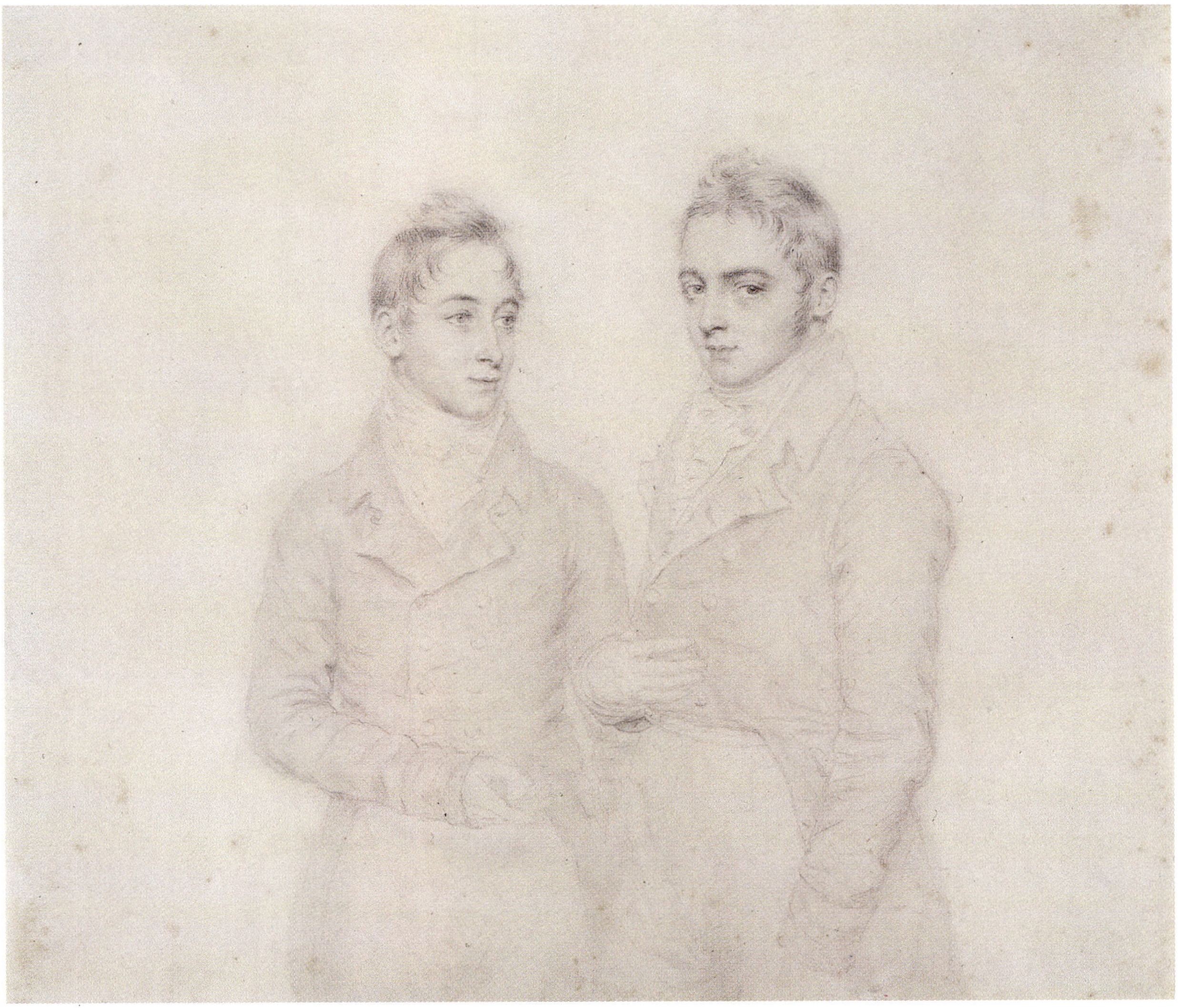

Cat. 54

54. *(?) Henry Wigram, (1791–1866), and a brother, sons of Sir Robert Wigram, Bt., of Wexford,* 1805
17.2 x 19.9, pencil on paper
PROVENANCE: by descent in the Wigram/Fitzwygram family to the Revd. Sir Clifford Wigram, Bt.; purchased by Miss Mary A. McNeill at Christie's, London, 27 October 1959, London, lot 92; Miss Mary A. McNeill Bequest, 1985.
NGI 19265
LITERATURE: Le Harivel and Wynne 1986, p. 120.

The two sitters are sons of Sir Robert Wigram (1743–1830), a Wexford merchant. The drawing was probably done in 1805 when Sir Robert Wigram was created a baronet and sat to Smart.[1] Traditionally they have been called Henry (1791–1866), and Thomas Wigram (dates unknown) but Wynne has suggested that they are Money (1790–1873), and James Wigram (1793–1866).[2] Sir Thomas Wigram had at least 15 sons (and five daughters) which makes exact identification difficult. The sitters were young men when this drawing was done and could be any of his elder sons.[3] This is a fine specimen of Smart's preliminary sketches, which were drawings (sometimes with wash or watercolour), done on paper.

REFERENCES: 1. Foskett 1964, pl. XXIV, fig. 86. 2. Le Harivel and Wynne 1986, p. 120. 3. Burke's 1889, pp. 552–53; 1928, pp. 2412–15.

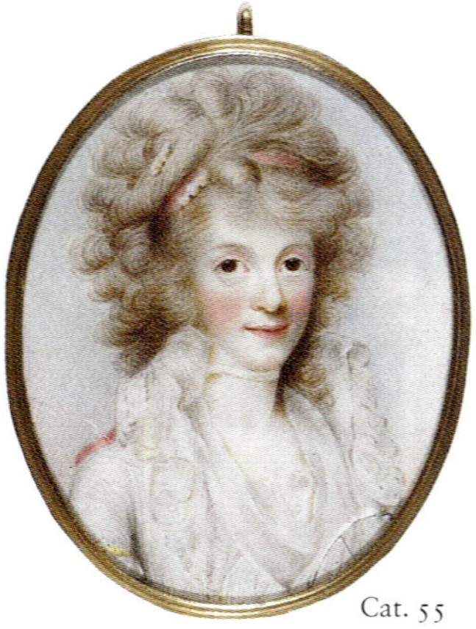

Cat. 55

JAMES SCOULER

Edinburgh c.1740~1812 London

Scouler studied at the Academy attached to the Duke of Richmond's Gallery of Casts at Richmond House in Whitehall, and at the St Martin's Lane Academy. The Society of Arts awarded him a prize for drawing in 1755. He exhibited at the Society of Artists from 1761–68, at the Free Society of Artists in 1767, and at the Royal Academy from 1780–87. Scouler spent most of his career in London, but may have visited India.

LITERATURE: Long 1929, pp. 391–92. Foskett 1987, pp. 640–41.

55. *Miss J. Spicer, (active 1801–02), Enamellist,* 1801

SIGNED AND DATED ON REVERSE: *J.S. 1801*
4.6 x 3.8, enamel on copper
Set in a gilt metal pendant frame.
PROVENANCE: Jacob Nachemsohn Collection, 1926; presented by Sir Alfred Chester Beatty, 1951.
NGI 3653
LITERATURE: Williamson 1926, p. 19. NGI 1983, p. 675.

Miss J. Spicer, the daughter of the miniaturist Henry Spicer (1743–1804), specialised in painting enamel portraits. She exhibited twice at the Royal Academy 1801–02. Her sister, M.A. Spicer, (active 1799–1803), was also a miniaturist.[1] Enamels by Scouler are rare. The influence of John Smart's stipple shading on Scouler is evident in this portrait. Smart almost certainly did not paint enamels (enamel copies of his work were done by others), but as Smart and Scouler shared the same initials there is a certain amount of confusion as to the exact attribution of miniatures. There is a crack on the enamel surface in the lower right corner.

REFERENCE: 1. Foskett 1987, p. 654.

RICHARD CROSSE

Knowle, Devon 1742~1810 Knowle, Devon

Crosse was born deaf and dumb. Having shown a talent for drawing, he was sent to London to study at William Shipley's drawing school and at the Academy attached to the Duke of Richmond's Gallery of Casts at Richmond House in Whitehall, which was first opened to students in 1758. He won a prize for drawing in the Society of Arts competition in 1758, exhibited at the Society of Artists from 1760–91, at the Free Society of Artists from 1761–66, and at the Royal Academy from 1770–96. Crosse was appointed Painter in Enamel to George III in 1788. He was an outstanding miniaturist and his distinguished clientele included the Prince of Wales, the Dukes of Cumberland and Gloucester. His miniature painter's desk is in the Victoria and Albert Museum, London (Illus. 15).

LITERATURE: Long 1929, pp. 109–10; 1929a, pp. 61–94. Foskett 1987, p. 520.

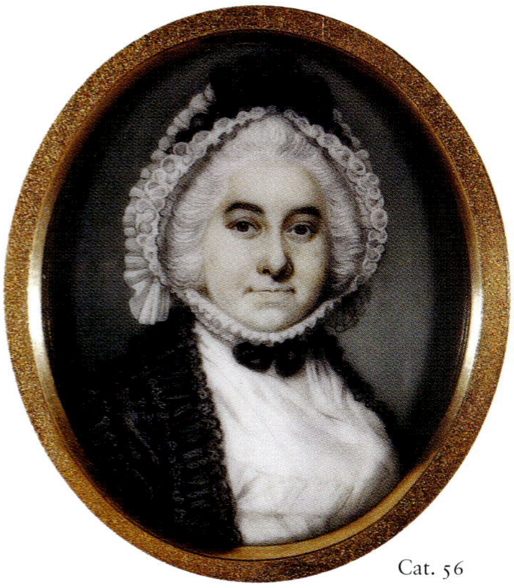

Cat. 56

56. *Mrs John Harrison*, 1792

INSCRIBED LATER ON REVERSE OF FRAME: *Painted by Richard Crosse 1792. Bill... Harrison / dated 17th Feb. £10.10.*
5.7 x 4.9, watercolour on ivory
Set in a 19th century *passe-partout* frame.
PROVENANCE: purchased by Miss Mary A. McNeill at Christie's, London, 13 November 1962, lot 22; Miss Mary A. McNeill Bequest, 1985.
NGI 19266
LITERATURE: Le Harivel and Wynne 1986, p. 120.

Mrs Harrison is presented dressed as a widow. She wears a variant of mourning dress, a black shawl, and an elaborate closed cap with black ribbon. The greenish-blue tint in the shading and the plain dark background are indicative of Crosse's work.

OZIAS HUMPHRY RA

Honiton, Devon 1742~1810 London

Humphry's father was a wigmaker and dealer in textiles, his mother a lacemaker. In 1757 he was apprenticed to William Shipley in London to improve his drawing of lace design. He studied at the St Martin's Lane Academy and at the Duke of Richmond's Gallery of Casts at Richmond House in Whitehall. In 1760, he went to Bath, where he was apprenticed to the miniaturist Samuel Collins (1735–1768, see catalogue entry 46). When Collins left for Dublin, Humphry took over his practice. At Joshua Reynolds' suggestion, he moved to London in 1764. He exhibited at the Society of Artists from 1765–71. In 1773 he went to Italy with George Romney (1734–1802), having the aspiration of becoming a history painter. Humphry returned to London in 1777 and exhibited with the Royal Academy. He was elected ARA in 1779 and RA in 1791. His oil paintings were not a success and he continued to work as a miniaturist. From 1784–87 he was in India. His eyesight began to fail and he turned to crayon portraiture (for example *Elizabeth Farren*, NGI 3869). He was appointed Painter in Crayon to the King in 1792. By 1797–98 he was blind and could no longer paint.

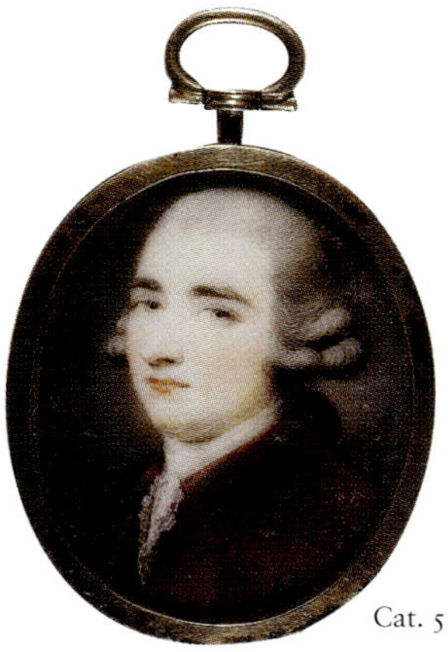

Cat. 57

LITERATURE: Graves 1907, p. 125. Williamson 1918, *passim*. Long 1929, pp. 229–31. Foskett 1987 pp. 572–73. Reynolds 1988, pp. 134–48.

57. *Major-General Webb, (1703–1773)*, c.1760

3.6 x 3.2, watercolour on ivory
PROVENANCE: collection of The Hon. Lady Shelley-Rolls; purchased by Miss Mary A. McNeill at Christie's, London, 13 February 1962, lot 7; Miss Mary A. McNeill Bequest, 1985.
NGI 19270
LITERATURE: Le Harivel and Wynne 1986, p. 123.

Webb was an officer in the Eighth Dragoon Guards. He rose to the rank of Major, fought at Dettingen (1743) and Fontenoy (1745). He was promoted to the rank of Lieutenant-Colonel, commanding officer of the Eighth. In 1755 he was made Colonel of the 48th Foot, being promoted to the rank of Major-General in 1759. In 1761 he was made a Lieutenant-General. Having been transferred to the Eighth Foot in 1766, he was given command of the 14th Dragoons in 1772.[1] He is depicted here out of uniform.

Although unsigned, this miniature displays all of the characteristics of a miniature portrait by Humphry. It is neatly drawn and the features of the sitter's face are suggested by stipple shading, notably around the nostrils. Humphry had an idiosyncratic method of painting eyes and eyebrows. The eyes have a dreamy or sleepy quality and the eyebrows are drawn in long parallel lines. In this portrait, both aspects are apparent.

REFERENCE: 1. Letter from Miss E. Talbot Rice, National Army Museum, London (NGI dossier 19270).

RICHARD COSWAY RA

Okeford, Devon 1742~1821 London

Cosway was the son of the headmaster of Blundell's School, Tiverton. In about 1754 he was apprenticed to Thomas Hudson (1701–1779) in London. He later studied and taught at William Shipley's drawing school. He attended life-drawing classes in St Martin's Lane and the Academy attached to the Duke of Richmond's Gallery of Casts at Richmond House in Whitehall. From 1755–60 his drawings won prizes at the Society of Arts annual competitions. He exhibited work at the Society of Arts in 1760, the Free Society of Artists, 1761–64 and 1766, and at the Society of Artists from 1767–69. In 1766 he was a member of the Incorporated Society of Artists. He entered the Royal Academy Schools in 1769. Cosway exhibited at the RA from 1770–1806, becoming ARA in 1770 and RA in 1771 (included in *The Academicians of the Royal Academy*, 1772, by Johann Zoffany, Royal Collection). An oil painter of variable quality, Cosway excelled as a miniaturist. It was his connection with the Prince of Wales (later Prince Regent and George IV) and his circle that gave his life and work great glamour. He became Principal Miniature Painter to the Prince of Wales in 1786. Cosway was a connoisseur and virtuoso who amassed an Old Master collection, which included paintings by Rubens and Rembrandt, drawings by Holbein, Giulio Romano, Rubens and Watteau, as well as decorative *objets d'art*, rococo furniture and sculpture. This formed a backdrop for the lavish entertainments the Cosways gave at Schomberg House in Pall Mall. Cosway was artistic advisor to the Prince of Wales and was influential in forming the collections at Carlton House.

. In 1781, Cosway married the artist Maria Hadfield (1759/60–1838), who was born and brought up in Italy. She the daughter of Charles Hadfield, owner of a chain of inns in Italy which were frequented by Grand Tourists. Hadfield was from Manchester of Irish descent. Together, the Cosways were one of the most glamorous couples in London and Paris. Maria Cosway had a scandalous affair with Thomas Jefferson when he was American ambassador in Paris. After her husband's death, she established at Lodi the Collegio delle Grazie, a school for young ladies, and the Fondazione Cosway (Instituto Maria SS. Bambina, Lodi), which houses a collection of Richard Cosway's drawings.

LITERATURE: Williamson 1897 and 1905, *passim.* Graves 1907, pp. 64–65. Long 1929, pp. 94–103. Allan 1968, pp. 211, 213–17. Foskett 1987, pp. 355–64, 517. Reynolds 1988, pp. 124–32. Bignamini 1991, pp. 115, 118. Lloyd 1995, *passim.*

58. *Self-Portrait in Elizabethan Costume,* c.1790

7.1 x 5.7, watercolour on ivory

FRAMED IN A GOLD LOCKET SET WITH PEARLS AND ENGRAVED ON REVERSE: *R. Cosway, R.A. 1740–1821 by R. Cosway.* A lock of the artist's interwoven hair is set into the reverse of the miniature.

PROVENANCE: bequeathed by Miss Meta Grace, 1949. NGI 3024

EXHIBITED: 1972–73 Bucharest and Budapest, no. 13. 1995–96 Edinburgh and London, no. 71.

LITERATURE: NGI 1983, p. 78. Foskett 1987, p. 517. Lloyd 1995, p. 119.

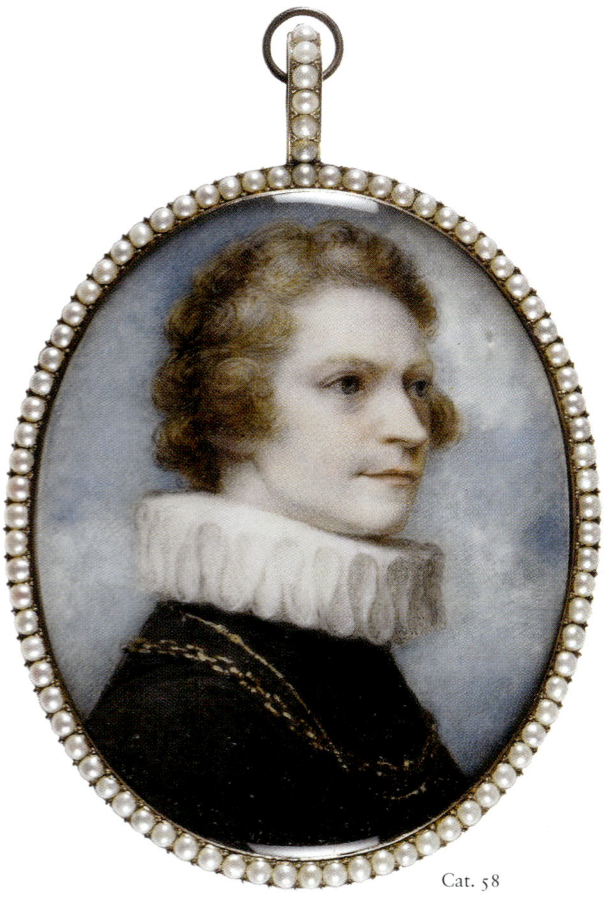

Cat. 58

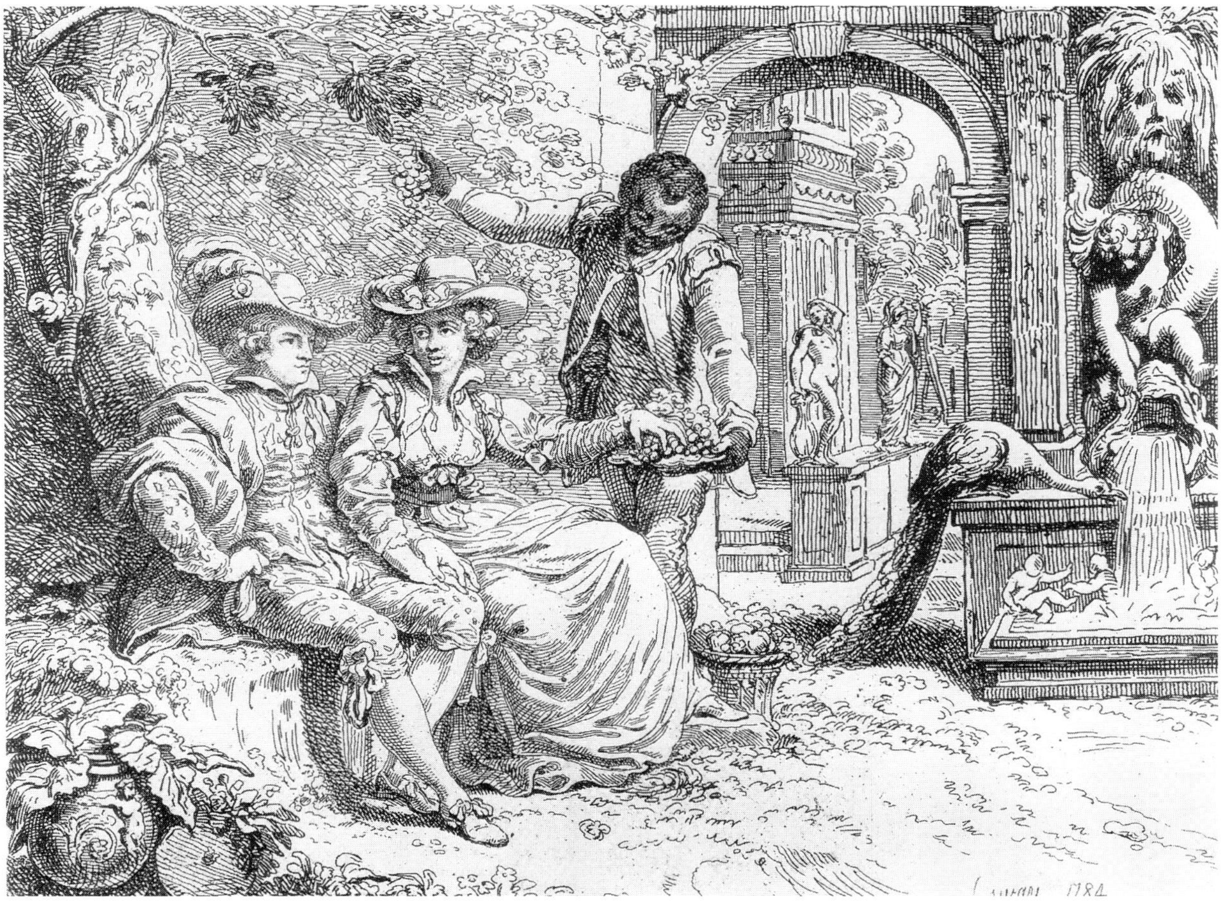

33. Self-Portrait with his wife Maria,
1784 etching, 20.9 x 24.8
RICHARD COSWAY
(Whitworth Art Gallery, University of Manchester
p. 20239)

Cosway was a small, foppish and flamboyant man. His love of fashion and self-advertisement set him apart and he was often satirized in caricature, such as *The Macaroni Painter* mezzotint after George Dawe (1828). Cosway painted a large number of self-portraits in different guises. In some other examples he is dressed in Van Dyck dress for a masked ball (oil in, Attingham Park, Shropshire, National Trust), paying homage to busts of Michelangelo and Rubens (drawing in Fondazione Cosway, Lodi), with his wife in an exotic garden, like Rubens and Hélène Fourment, (black and red chalk drawing in Fondazione Cosway, Lodi and related etching, Illus. 33), as a dandy or macaroni (miniature in Metropolitan Museum of Art, New York), as a Spanish grandee (pencil and watercolour in Huntington Library and Art Gallery, San Marino, California), as Esau (pencil and watercolour in Uffizi, Florence) and as a mystical figure (pencil and watercolour in Worcester Art Museum, Worcester, Mass.). In contrast, there is a self-portrait when an old man (miniature in Fitzwilliam Museum, Cambridge).

Cosway was in his late 40s when he painted this self-portrait, loosely painted against a sky-blue and cloudy background, which are typical features of his miniatures. He is dressed in Elizabethan masquerade costume with a ruff and gold chains. His natural hair is a fashion of the 1780s popularised by the Prince of Wales (Illus. 19). The image is of a rather idealised, younger and slimmer, man than contemporary portraits would suggest. There is a comparable watercolour self-portrait in the National Portrait Gallery, London, also painted c.1790, with similar frizzled hair, but in contemporary dress. In choosing Elizabethan costume for NGI 3024, Cosway is both highly fashionable and placing himself within the miniature portrait tradition by making reference back to the golden age of the English Renaissance miniature.

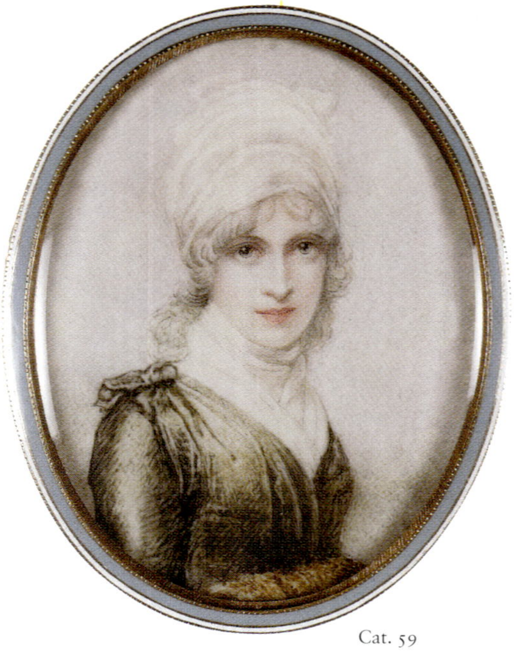

Cat. 59

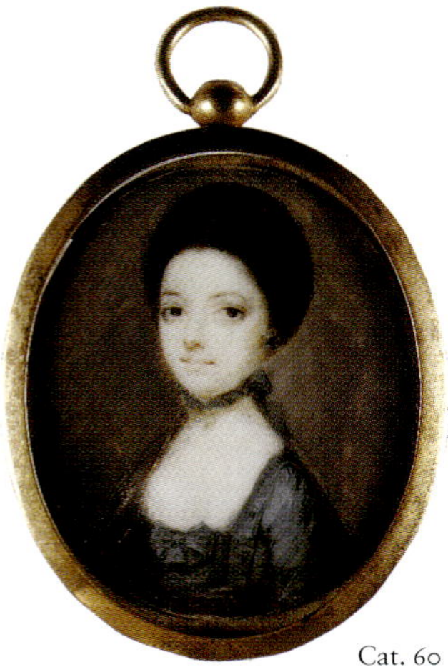

Cat. 60

59. *Mrs Moffat,* 1797

INSCRIBED, SIGNED AND DATED ON BACKING PAPER:
Rdus Cosway R.A. Primarius Pictor Serenissimi Walliae Principis Pinxit 1797
7.5 x 5.8, watercolour on ivory
Gold pendant frame.
PROVENANCE: Massey Mainwaring Collection (recorded by old label on reverse); bequeathed by Miss Meta Grace, 1949.
NGI 3023
LITERATURE: NGI 1983, p. 78.

During the 1790s, Cosway was painting some of his best work, using tones of grey and blue and minimal detail, but the costume in this miniature has more the feel of a sketch and the background is pale and unfinished. The sitter is rather dull and lifeless. Cosway's Latin inscription alludes to his royal appointment in 1786.

JAMES BALLARD

active Dublin 1753~1792 Dublin

Ballard studied at the Dublin Society Drawing Schools and was awarded prizes for drawing in 1753, 1754 and 1756.[1] He exhibited 50 miniatures at the Society of Artists in Ireland during the years 1766 to 1777. Ballard worked as a drawing teacher in Dublin. His portrait of Dean Swift was engraved in 1775.

LITERATURE: Strickland 1913, vol. 1, pp. 19–20. Breeze 1985, pp. 1–2. Caffrey 1999, p. 23.
REFERENCE: 1. RDS Minute Book 1750–56, vol. III: 15 February 1753, 16 June 1754, 3 April 1755 and 2 December 1756.

60. *Portrait of a lady in a blue dress,* 1768

SIGNED AND DATED: *J. Ballard / 1768*
4.6 x 3.5, watercolour with gouache on ivory
Set in a gilt metal pendant frame.
PROVENANCE: purchased by the NMI, 1887; transferred from the NMI, 1969.
NGI 7073
LITERATURE: NGI 1983, p. 5.

Ballard's watercolour on ivory miniature is typical of much of the work which was produced in Dublin during the 1760s, which Reynolds (1988) has called the 'Modest School'. The sitter wears a blue dress, with grey cloak, and a matching blue ribbon at her neck. Her hair is fashionably high for the 1760s. Ballard uses a lot of gouache which has a dull effect. The eyes and hair are painted in black gouache. The translucent long lines of grey gouache in the background allow some of the ivory to show through.

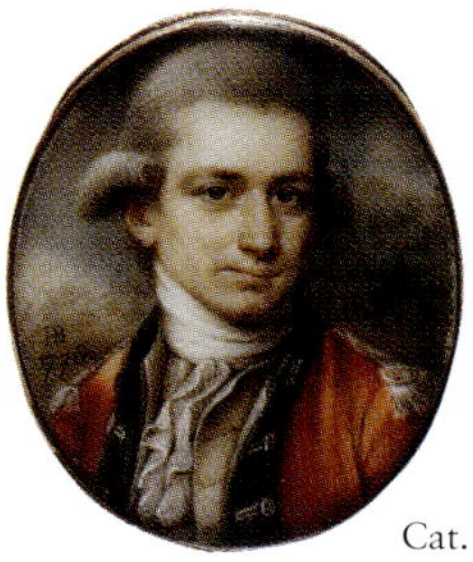

Cat. 61

JOHN BOGLE

Scotland c.1746~1803 Edinburgh

Bogle was a kinsman of the Earls of Menteith through his mother Mary Graham. He was educated at the drawing school in Glasgow and in 1769 married Marion Wilson in Edinburgh. He practised as a miniaturist in Edinburgh, and in London after 1770 for most of the period to 1790. Bogle exhibited at the Society of Artists in 1769–70, and at the Royal Academy from 1772–94 (except 1774). He was an acquaintance of Fanny Burney whom he accompanied to the trial of Warren Hastings at Westminster Hall. In 1800 he returned to Edinburgh.

LITERATURE: D'Arblay 1891, vol. II, p. 361. GEC vol. VIII, p. 677. Long 1929, pp. 33–34. Foskett 1987, p. 494. Reynolds 1988, pp. 143–44.

61. *Sir George Pickering*, 1776

SIGNED AND DATED: *JB 1776*
3.4 x 2.9, enamel on copper
Set in a gold bracelet setting, later adapted to a brooch.
PROVENANCE: purchased from Mr R.A. Jones, Dublin, 1903.
NGI 2552
LITERATURE: NGI 1983, p. 13.

Bogle was adept at capturing the character of his sitters and this portrait is a good example of his understated, but perceptive characterisation. Sir George Pickering is well posed against an indefinite background. He wears a military style jacket with upturned collar. His powdered hair is swept back and curled over his ears. Bogle used minute stippling to build up his portraits and the shading is done in grey stippling. This dense use of stippling in the painting of hair produces a woolly effect.

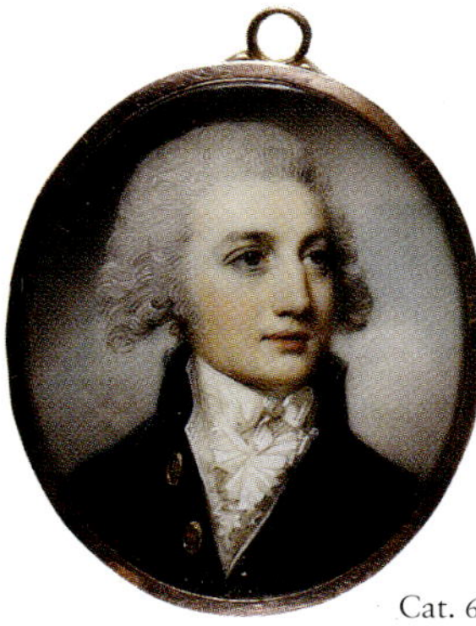

Cat. 62

GEORGE ENGLEHEART

Kew, Surrey 1750/53~1839
Blackheath, London

Engleheart was the son of a German plaster modeller and entered the Royal Academy Schools in 1769 (the same year as Richard Cosway), when he is recorded as being 16 years old. He later studied under Joshua Reynolds, copying oil portraits in miniature, and with the Irish landscape painter George Barret (1728/32–1784). Engleheart worked principally in London where he had a studio in Hertford Street, Mayfair. He exhibited at the Royal Academy from 1773–1822. In 1789 he was appointed Miniature Painter to George III in succession to his friend, the miniaturist Jeremiah Meyer (see catalogue entry 44). Engleheart was a friend of George Romney (1734–1802), William Blake (1757–1827), and the poet William Cowper (1731–1800). About 1813 he retired to his country house near Hounslow. His fee book has survived and provides a complete account of his sitters from 1775 to 1813. A profile self-portrait (c.1803) is in the NPGL. His nephew John Cox Dillman Engleheart (1782/84–1862), and Thomas Richmond (1771–1837), were pupils.

LITERATURE: Williamson and Engleheart 1902, *passim*. Long 1929, pp. 141–43. Foskett 1987, pp. 535–56.

62. *Portrait of a man in a blue coat*, late 1780s

3.9 x 3.3, watercolour on ivory
PROVENANCE: purchased by Miss Mary A. McNeill from A.G. Tite, London, June 1962. Miss Mary A. McNeill Bequest, 1985.
NGI 19272
LITERATURE: Le Harivel and Wynne, 1986, p. 124.

Engleheart's elegant style of miniature painting was similar to Cosway. He was a prolific miniaturist and could be formulaic. This portrait is beautifully drawn but has a slightly rushed feel to it and there is little individuality or characterisation of the fashionable sitter. The forward positioning of the sitter in the picture plane and the use of a cloudy sky background are typical of Engleheart's work, as are the relatively small scale, absence of a signature, emphasis on the eyes, and the wiry painting of the powdered hair. These are characteristics of Engleheart prior to c.1795, after which there is a marked increase in the size of the ivory. His subdued palette, blue-grey hatching and angular brushstrokes in the painting of the costume give the portrait a crispness. The upturned collar of his coat and hairstyle suggest that this miniature was painted in the late 1780s.

WILLIAM GRIMALDI
(MARCHESE GRIMALDI)
London 1751~1830 London

Grimaldi was born in Shoreditch, the fourth and eldest surviving son of Alexander, 7th Marchese Grimaldi, a descendant of a branch of the noble Genoese family. From 1764–66 he studied miniature painting with his uncle Thomas Worlidge (1700–1766). Grimaldi painted in watercolour and enamel and was practising as a miniaturist at Chester in 1774. He exhibited at the Free Society of Artists 1768–70, the Society of Artists 1772, and at the Royal Academy 1786–1830. He was working in Paris from 1777–83 but settled in London in 1785. Grimaldi was appointed Miniature Painter to the Duke and Duchess of York (1791) and Enamel Painter to the Prince of Wales, afterwards George IV, from 1804 to c.1824 and is well represented in the Royal Collection. There is a drawing of him at his painting desk by Mary Grimaldi (after Louisa Edmeads, 1785–1873, his daughter) in the NPGL.

LITERATURE: Grimaldi 1873, *passim.* Long 1929, pp. 180–81. Foskett 1987, p. 552.

63. *Hester Frances, Lady Bellingham, (born Cholmondeley, 1763–1844), wife of 1st Bt.,* c.1795

LABEL ON FRAME INSCRIBED: *Lady Frances Bellingham / Sale of Bellingham Property. /*
9.3 x 7.7, watercolour on ivory
Set in a cabinet frame.
Formerly catalogued as English School (c.1785).
PROVENANCE: by descent in the Bellingham Family, Castle Bellingham, Co. Louth; sold at the Castle Bellingham Sale, 1956; Louis Wine and Co., Dublin, where purchased by Miss Mary A. McNeill, September 1957; Miss Mary A. McNeill Bequest, 1985.
NGI 19283
LITERATURE: Le Harivel and Wynne 1986, p. 130.

Hester Frances Bellingham was the extremely rich younger daughter of the Hon. and Revd. Robert Cholmondeley and Mary Woffington (sister of the actress Peg Woffington) and granddaughter of the 3rd Earl of Cholmondeley. In 1783 she married William Bellingham (d.1826) of Castle Bellingham, Co. Louth, who had been secretary to William Pitt.[1] He was made a Baronet in 1796 (third creation) as recognition of his service. After her husband's death, Augustus Foster of Glyde Court, Co. Louth wrote to his brother Frederick Foster, on 7 January 1829:

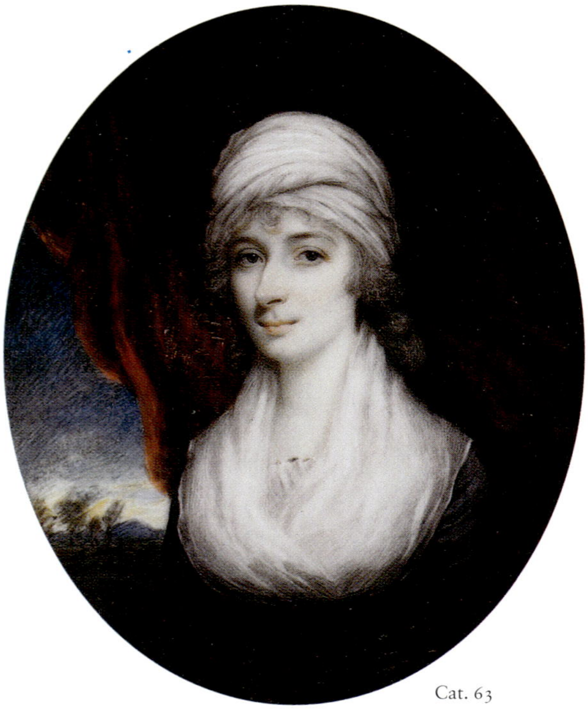

Cat. 63

Sir Wm. Bellingham's widow lives at present at / Castle Bellingham and I believe occasionally at / Dunany... She is an English woman and to be / lauded for her love of Ireland that takes her to Louth tho' she / might of course stay over in England without incurring censure.[2]

The identification of Grimaldi as the painter of this elegant portrait[3] is based on stylistic and technical evidence. Grimaldi was an accomplished miniaturist who specialised in painting relatively large miniatures. A favourite device of his was the use of drapery in the background and a distant landscape. In this portrait, deep red drapery contrasts against a dark blue sky. The distinctive shading on the face, particularly in the dark blue shading of the nostrils and the lower lip in hatched lines are additionally characteristic. This miniature exemplifies his technique of painting in watercolour mixed with gum arabic which gives the portrait a glossy finish.

In Grimaldi's portrait, her costume is very much of the later 1790s, with a white fichu over her shoulders and wrapped headdress in the Greek style. An oil portrait of her about the same date, by an unknown artist, is still in the Bellingham family.

REFERENCES: 1. Burke's 1889, pp. 124, 282. 2. Inscribed on a card attached to the reverse of the frame, probably in the hand of Miss Mary A. McNeill. 3. First made verbally by Foskett.

EDWARD MILES

Great Yarmouth 1752~1828 Philadelphia

Miles was encouraged to study drawing by a surgeon, for whom he worked as an errand-boy. He moved to London in 1771 and attended the Royal Academy Schools in 1772. Miles exhibited miniatures at the RA from 1775–97, amongst them copies in miniature of portraits by Reynolds. From 1779–82 he was living in Norwich. In 1792 he was appointed Miniature Painter to Frederica, Duchess of York and in 1794 to Queen Charlotte. From 1797 to 1806 he worked in St Petersburg and was appointed Court Painter to the Tsars Paul I and Alexander I. Long has suggested that Miles was influenced by the Russian miniaturist Augustin Ritt (1765–1799) and must have known the French miniaturist Jean-Laurent Mosnier (1743/44–1808), who was a court painter in St Petersburg. Miles emigrated to the United States of America where he was based in Philadelphia from 1807 until his death in 1828. In 1810 he was a founder member of an Academy, the Society of Artists (later the Columbian Society of Artists), where he taught drawing. His miniatures are unsigned.

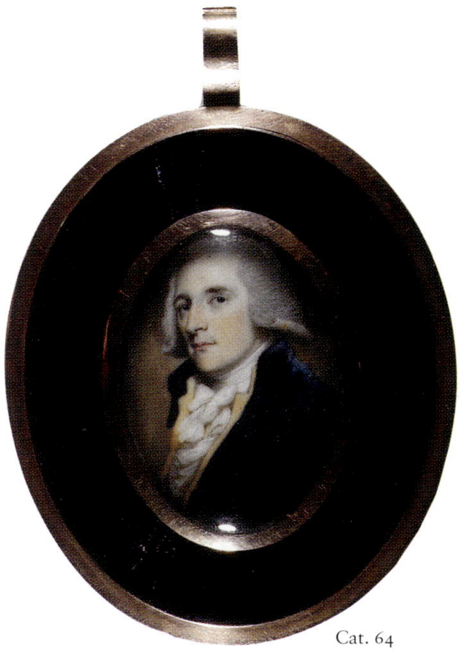
Cat. 64

LITERATURE: Long 1929, p. 297. Foskett 1987, p. 600. Reynolds 1988, pp. 149–50. Johnson 1991, p. 20.

64. *George Augustus Chichester, 2nd Marquess of Donegall (1769–1844),* c.1795

4 x 2.8, watercolour on ivory

Set in a gold and blue glass oval pendant frame. Locks of the sitter's hair are plaited and displayed against opalescent glass on the reverse.

PROVENANCE: purchased by Miss Mary A. McNeill at Christie's, London, 21 February 1961, lot 25; Miss Mary A. McNeill Bequest, 1985.

NGI 19273

The 2nd Marquess of Donegall was MP for Carrickfergus, Co. Antrim, from 1798–99 when he succeeded to the marquessate. He became a Privy Councillor in Ireland and was made a Knight of St Patrick in 1821. He was Lord Lieutenant of Co. Donegal from 1831 until his death in 1844. In 1795 he married Anna May (d.1849), an illegitimate daughter of Sir Edward May, Bt.[1] This miniature may have been painted as a token of affection during his engagement, or to commemorate their marriage.

Miles' handling of the details of the sitter's face is typical of his work. The eyes, nose and mouth are well drawn and the lips clearly defined. He uses slightly pale tones of watercolour that have a yellowish tinge. In contrast, the costume and hair are softly painted. The Marquess of Donegall wears a blue coat and buff coloured waistcoat, with a white linen shirt and neck cloth.

REFERENCE: 1. Burke's 1889, p. 431.

CHARLES FORREST

active Dublin 1765~1787 Dublin

Forrest entered the Dublin Society's School of Figure Drawing on 17 October 1765. He was awarded a prize of £6 for drawings in chalk on 25 June 1772.[1] He worked in chalk and pastel (NGI 7351–7355) as well as watercolour on ivory. Forrest exhibited miniatures at the breakaway Academy of Artists exhibition in Dublin in 1774 and at the Society of Artists in Ireland exhibition in 1780.

LITERATURE: Strickland 1913, vol. 1, p. 375. Breeze 1785, p. 11.

REFERENCE: 1. RDS *Proceedings* 1765–66, vol. II, p. 230; 1771–72 vol. VIII, p. 455.

65. *Portrait of a man in a maroon coat,* 1775

SIGNED AND DATED: *Forrest 1775*

3.7 x 3.2, watercolour on ivory

Set in a gold oval frame.

PROVENANCE: purchased, from Miss Elaine Fitzpatrick, Dublin, 1983.

NGI 19180

LITERATURE: Le Harivel and Wynne 1984, p. 58.

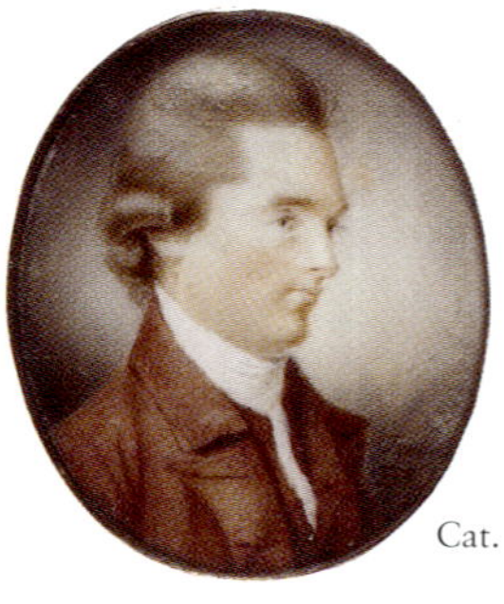

Cat. 65

The cool grey-blue shading and powdery tones of Forrest's watercolour miniatures are similar to the colours he uses in his pastel portraits. The distant gaze of the sitter and pale colouring are reminiscent of work by Luke Sullivan (1705–1771), see catalogue entry 18). Few miniatures by Forrest are known, but a comparable portrait, dated 1777, of an unknown lady, is in a private collection.[1]

REFERENCE: 1. Caffrey 1999, p. 26.

WILLIAM RUSSELL BIRCH

Warwick 1755~1834 Philadelphia

Birch was a pupil of miniaturist Henry Spicer (1743–1804), from whose house he exhibited two enamel mythological subject miniatures at the Society of Artists exhibition in 1775. In 1784 he was awarded a silver palette by the Society of Arts. He exhibited work at the Royal Academy from 1781–94. Birch invented a new colour, a shade of brownish red that could be used by enamellists and was called Birch's red (a compound of cinnabar and copper). In 1791 he published a book of engravings *Délices de la Grande Bretagne*. About 1794 he went to the United States of America, with a recommendation from Benjamin West (1738–1820). Birch settled in Philadelphia, where he worked as an enamellist and published views of Philadelphia and of American country houses. Birch's autobiography, a fifty-one page manuscript, is in the archive of the Historical Society of Pennsylvania, Philadelphia (Birch Papers). His son Thomas Birch (1779 or 1787–1851) assisted him in America.

LITERATURE: Long 1929, p. 31. Brockway 1933, pp. 94–96. Ross 1940, pp. 5, 20. Foskett 1987, p. 493.

66. *Romeo and Juliet,* 1783

SIGNED AND DATED: *W.Birch. 1783*

10.4 x 12, enamel on copper

Gilt metal frame.

PROVENANCE: Jacob Nachemsohn Collection, 1926; presented by Sir Alfred Chester Beatty, 1951.

NGI 3584

LITERATURE: Williamson 1926, p. 23. NGI 1983, p. 12.

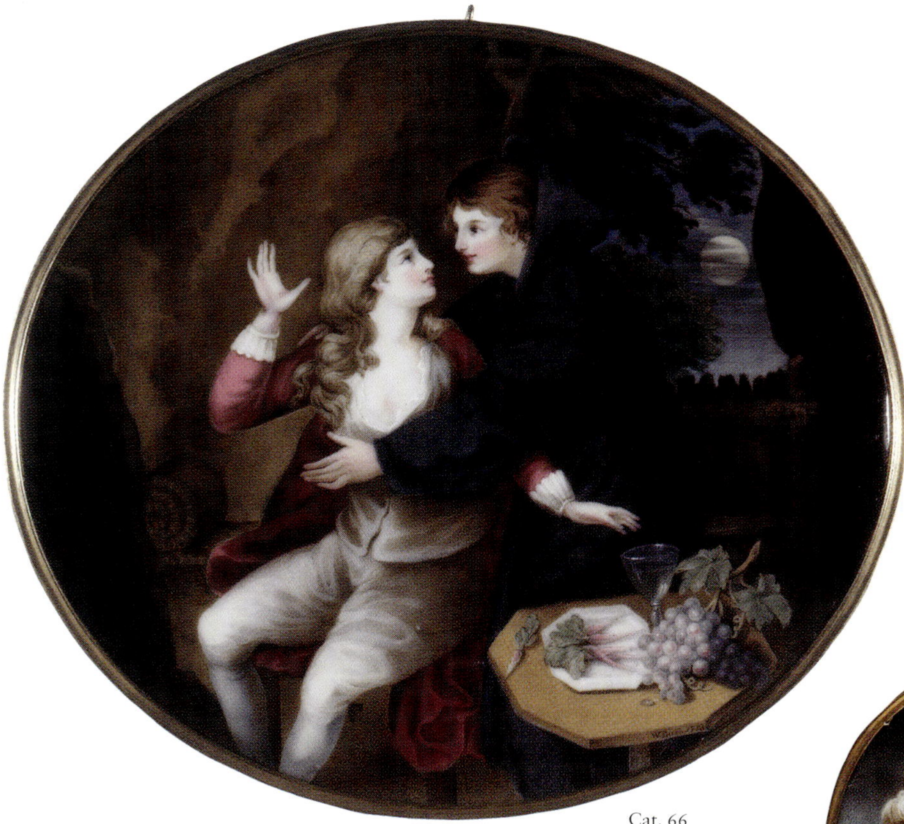

Cat. 66

The subject was previously identified as *Vertumnus and Pomona*. Ovid's *Metamorphoses* (14) relates how Vertumnus tried to woo the goddess Pomona in various disguises, but without success. Disguised as an old woman, he was allowed into her garden, and when he revealed his true self she was overcome. Here both figures are young and the setting is a cave by moonlight, rather than a garden. Given the man's hooded disguise, woman's undressed hair, sepulchral couch in the background, and prominent glass, this is more likely to be the last scene from Shakespeare's tragedy *Romeo and Juliet*. In David Garrick's popular revised text (1749), where he added seventy-five lines, the two doomed lovers are briefly reunited at the Capulet tomb, to which Juliet has been taken after seeming to die. They then take poison together. Birch's female figure wears fanciful dress associated with the 18th century theatre and reacts with stylised gestures. These, with the cloudy night, recall the 1753 print of Mrs Bellamy and Garrick in the roles.[1] The foreground display of still-life is a visual balance, with bunch of grapes, wine glass, and unexpectedly, a dish of radishes. In contrast to William Craft (catalogue entry 43), the colouring is more successful, with subtle gradations of tone and Birch was also an accomplished draughtsman.

REFERENCE: 1. Lennox-Boyd *et al.* 1984, pp. 50–51.

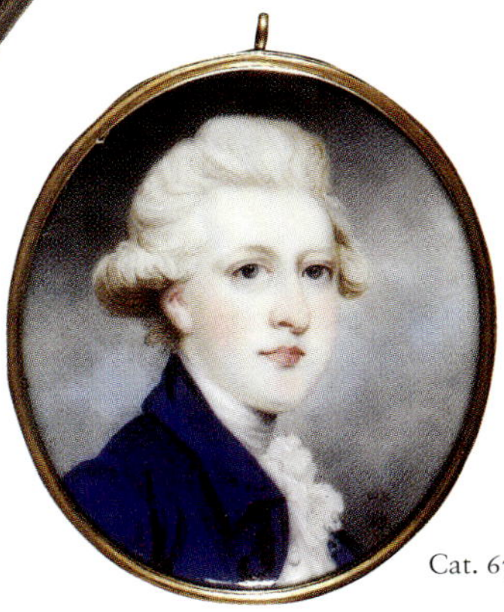

Cat. 67

67. *Portrait of a young man in a blue coat*, 1783

SIGNED AND DATED: *W.B. / 83*
4.5 x 3.9, enamel on copper
Set in an oval gilt metal pendant frame.
PROVENANCE: Jacob Nachemsohn Collection, 1926; presented by Sir Alfred Chester Beatty, 1951.
NGI 3654
LITERATURE: Williamson 1926, p. 26. NGI 1983, p. 12.

Birch was technically brilliant and an excellent draughtsman. The sitter has dark eyes which are usually slightly exaggerated in Birch's enamels. Posed against a grey-blue cloudy sky, he wears a dark blue coat, and white linen neck cloth and shirt, with a frill down the front.

HENRY BONE RA

Truro, Cornwall 1755~1834
Somers Town, near London

Bone was the son of a woodcarver and cabinet-maker. He began his working life, in 1771, as a decorator of hard-paste china at William Cookworthy's factory in Plymouth. Bone was then apprenticed to Richard Champion of Bristol in 1772. He went to London c.1778 where he was employed decorating lockets, fans, watches and jewellery. Bone painted watercolour on ivory miniatures from life, but was a prolific enamellist, who specialised in painting copies of oil portraits by a wide range of portrait painters, including Joshua Reynolds, John Hoppner, fellow Cornishman John Opie, and Thomas Lawrence. He was helped in his career by Dr John Wolcot (see catalogue entry 115). Between 1781 and 1832 he exhibited over 240 enamels at the Royal Academy and he also exhibited at the Free Society of Artists, British Institution and Society of British Artists.

In 1801 he was appointed Enamel Painter to George, Prince of Wales and thereafter to George III, George IV, and William IV. George, Prince of Wales, commissioned him to make large-scale enamel copies of work of mythological and religious subject pictures by Reynolds and others. Some of these were elaborately framed and hung in the Prince of Wales's private bedroom at Carlton House. In 1822, Bone exhibited *Portraits of Illustrious Characters from the Reign of Elizabeth I* in his house at 15, Berners Street. Many of these are now at Kingston Lacy, Dorset (National Trust). His portrait was painted with a backdrop of some, in 1828, by his son, William Bone (NPGL). By 1832, Bone's eyesight had failed. An extensive historical set of enamels, *Portraits of Illustrious Englishmen* was begun by Bone and finished after his death by his eldest son Henry Pierce Bone (1779–1855, see catalogue entries 109–10).

Bone was frequently mentioned in Joseph Farington's diary. Bone's enamelling technique and method of firing is recorded in Benjamin Haydon's diary and by Susan Sibbald. Three volumes of preparatory drawings by Bone are in the NPGL and have been fully catalogued (Walker 1999). From these contemporary accounts of his working methods, and from the drawings in the National Portrait Gallery London, Bone's technique of enamelling is known. He first made a preliminary drawing in pencil, which was transferred to transparent tracing paper in ink, and then to a primed copper or brass plate to be painted and fired into the finished enamel. The drawings were carefully stored for future use. These were annotated, possibly by himself, or one of his sons. Bone taught several of his children to paint and five of his children and two grandchildren became miniaturists.

LITERATURE: DNB vol. II, p. 805. Hett 1926, pp. 141–43. Long 1929, pp. 37–39. Garlick *et al.* 1978–84. pp. 1280, 2269, 2274, 2614, 4295. Foskett 1987, p. 495. Reynolds 1980, pp. 311–17, 343–44; 1988, p. 151. Walker 1992, pp. 269–315; 1999, pp. 305–67.

68. *Richard Burke, (1758–1794), Politician and son of Edmund Burke,* 1790

INSCRIBED, SIGNED AND DATED ON BACKING PAPER: *Richard Burke / son of Edmund Burke / obit. Aug 2 1794 at 38 / Heny. Bone / Pinxt 1790 / Russell Street / Bloomsbury*

8.5 x 6.5, watercolour on ivory

Set in a black *passe-partout* frame with a gilt metal inset and acorn clasp.

PROVENANCE: purchased from Mrs A. Catterson Smith, Dublin, 1876. This miniature was stolen from the NGI in 1880 and recovered in 1905.

NGI 7323

LITERATURE: NGI 1914, p. 305. NGI 1983, p. 16.

Richard Burke was the only son of the statesman, orator, and writer, Edmund Burke (1729–1797). In January 1792, on the invitation of the Catholic General Committee, he came to Dublin for four months, where he was appointed Parliamentary Agent for the Committee who sought to end the Penal Laws. In 1794 he was appointed Chief Secretary for Ireland but died before taking up the post. His father was deeply affected by his death, after which he withdrew from public life.[1]

This portrait of Burke is a rare watercolour on

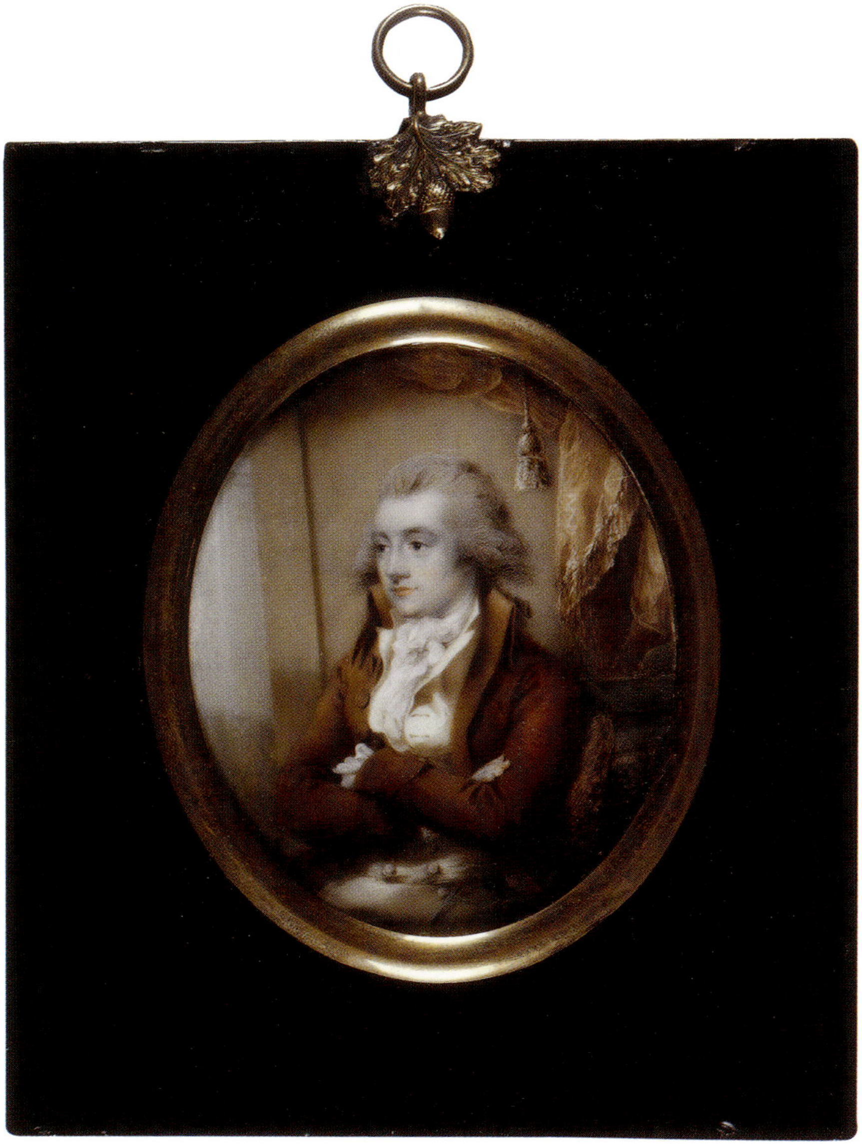

Cat. 68

ivory miniature by Bone. It could have been painted from life. Richard Burke is posed against drapery in the background wearing a brown coat, buff coloured waistcoat and white linen shirt and neck cloth. His hair is fashionably powdered for 1790. There is a strong blue tinge to the shading of the sitter's face which may be the result of lead discolouring in the paint. The sitter has a slightly orange complexion, which is probably discolouring.

REFERENCE: 1. DNB vol. II, pp. 345–65.

69. *Benjamin West, (1738–1820), Artist,* 1801 (Illustrated overleaf)

SIGNED AND DATED: *H. Bone 1801*

INSCRIBED, SIGNED AND DATED ON REVERSE: *Benjamin West P.R.A. / Historical Painter to His Majesty / London / Novr. 1801 / Painted by Henry Bone A.R.A. / Enamel Painter to His Royal Highness / The Prince of Wales after a picture / by B. West Painted 1800.*

16 x 12.8, enamel on copper

Gilt metal frame.

PROVENANCE: Bone Sale, London, June 1836, lot 6; Jacob Nachemsohn Collection, 1926; presented by Sir Alfred Chester Beatty, 1951.

NGI 3571

EXHIBITED: 1804 Royal Academy, no. 355.

LITERATURE: Williamson 1926, p. 19. NGI 1983, p. 15. Erffa and Staley 1986, p. 453. Walker 1999, p. 349.

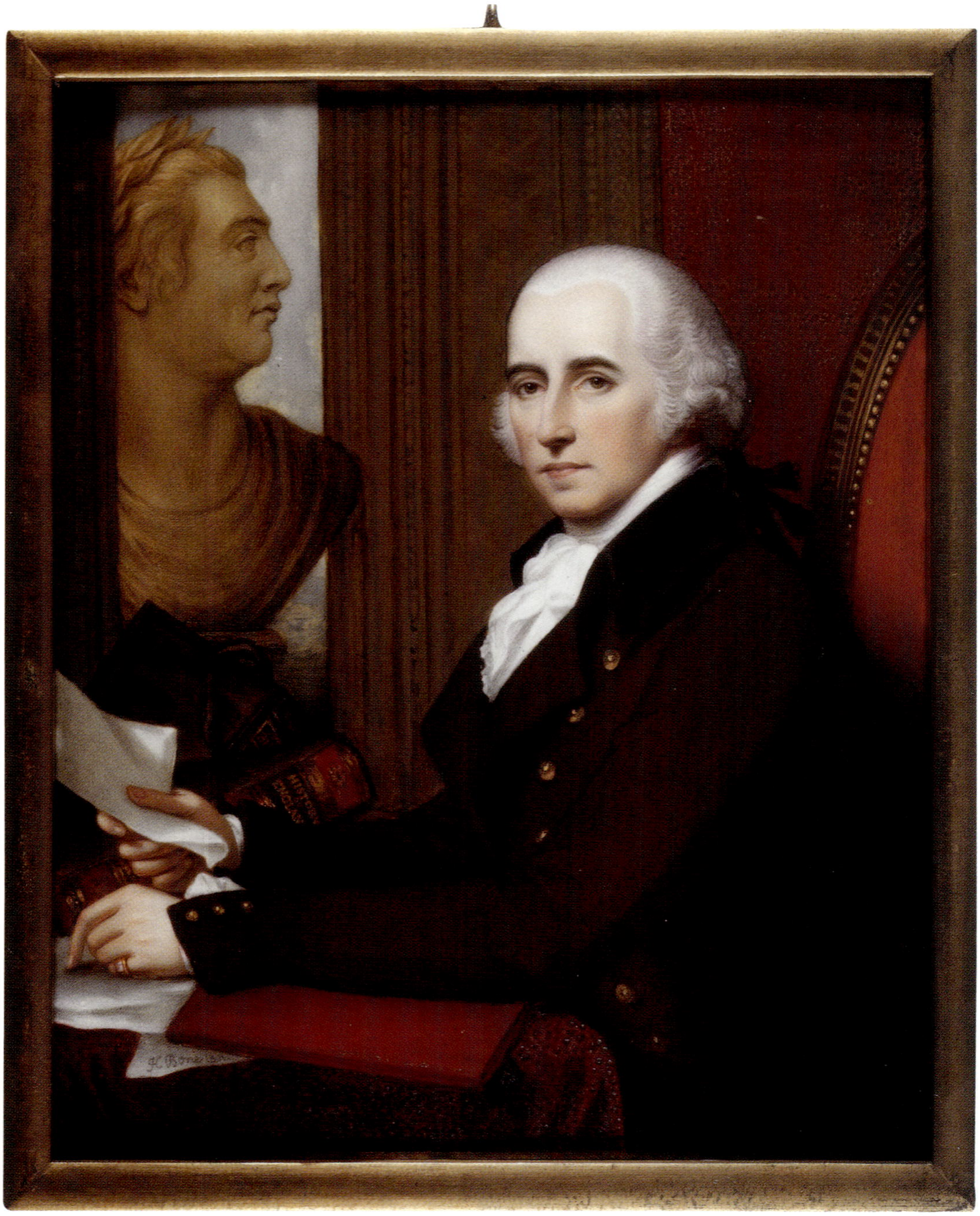

Cat. 69

Benjamin West, the American painter, spent three years in Italy. He set up as a portrait painter in London in 1763 and became a founder member of the Royal Academy. He succeeded Reynolds as President of the RA in 1792. This enamel was copied from a self-portrait by West which was painted in 1793. In the original portrait, the paper under West's left hand is painted with the inscription: *Benjamin West, Esq / Painted this picture in 1793*. West was elected a member of the Society of Dilettanti in 1792, and in 1818 he presented his self–portrait to the Society. It is in the collection of the Society of Dilettanti, at Brooks's, St James's, London.[1]

West, in a brown coat with black collar and white cravat is shown as the President of the Royal Academy. He is seated in the President's chair holding the charter of the RA in his right hand. On the table in front of him are two books that represent the twin sources of his inspiration, one is a *History of England* and the other a Bible. In the background, there is a bust of his principal patron, George III, which is probably his own invention.[3]

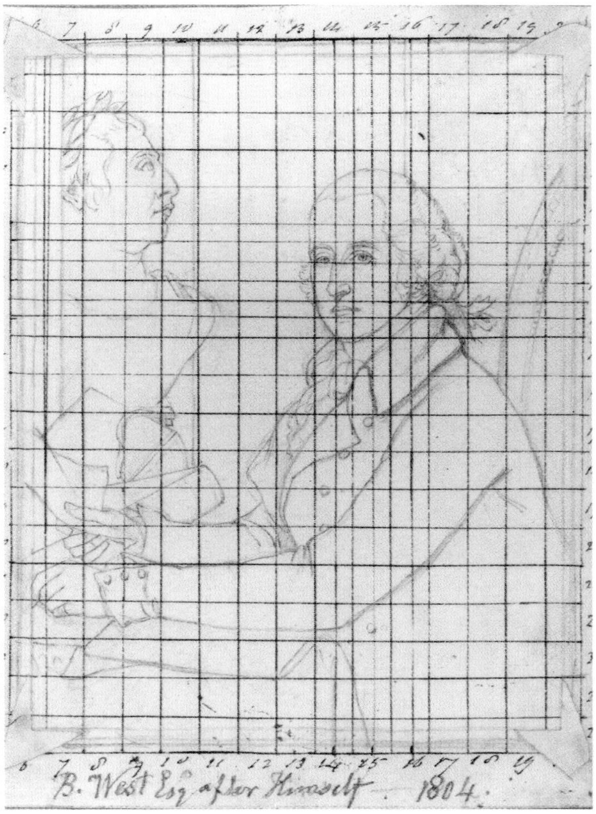

34. Drawing of Benjamin West portrait, 1804, HENRY BONE (NPGL)

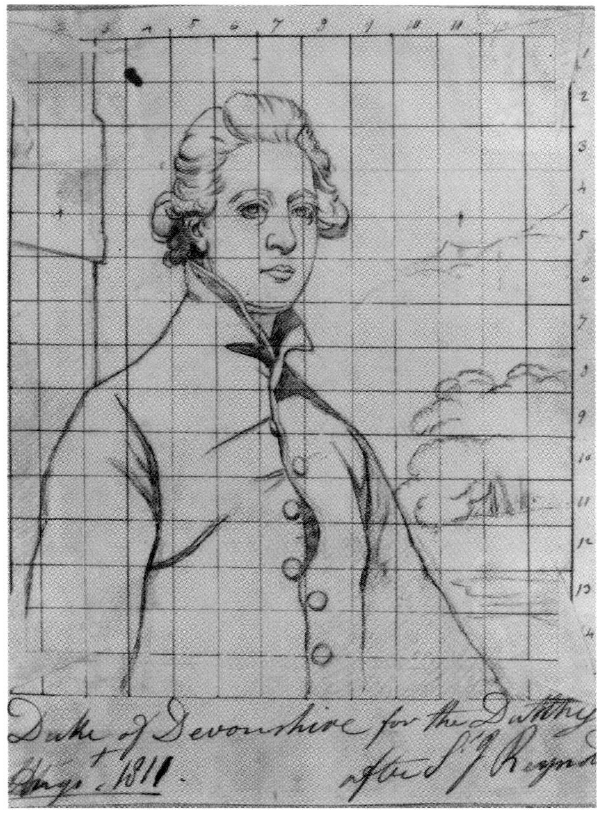

35. Drawing of 5th Duke of Devonshire portrait, 1811, HENRY BONE (NPGL)

A preparatory drawing by Bone, dated 1804 (Illus. 34), for an enamel, taken to be NGI 3571, is in the National Portrait Gallery, London (vol. I, p. 88, drawing c).[2] The date appears to be an error.[3]

REFERENCES: 1. Ford 1991, p. 141. 2. Walker 1999, p. 349, no. 542. 3. Erffa and Staley 1986, p. 453.

70. *William Cavendish, 5th Duke of Devonshire, (1748–1811),* 1811 (Illustrated overleaf)

INSCRIBED AND SIGNED ON REVERSE: *Bone / William 5th Duke of / Devonshire*

15.5 x 12.7, enamel on copper

Black wooden cabinet frame with gilded inset.

PROVENANCE: purchased by Miss Mary A. McNeill at Christie's, 20 June 1967, lot 5; Miss Mary A. McNeill Bequest, 1985. NGI 19274

EXHIBITED: 1811 Royal Academy, no. 321.

LITERATURE: Le Harivel and Wynne 1986, p. 125. Foskett 1987, p. 302.

William Cavendish, 5th Duke of Devonshire, succeeded to the dukedom on the death of his father in 1764. He was Lord High Treasurer of Ireland and Governor of Co. Cork from 1766 until 1793.[1] His first wife was the great beauty and leader of fashion, Georgiana, daughter of the first Earl Spencer. He was a Whig. Both he and his wife were intensely interested in politics. After her death at the age of 48, William Cavendish married Lady Elizabeth Foster, daughter of Frederick Augustus, Earl-Bishop of Derry, and widow of John Thomas Foster of Co. Louth, who had been living with the Duke and Duchess in a *ménage-à-trois* for some time.[2]

Bone's preparatory drawing for this enamel (Illus. 35) is in the National Portrait Gallery, London (vol. III, p. 21, drawing b). It is inscribed: *Duke of Devonshire for the Dutchy after Sr J. Reynolds Augst 1811*. Reynolds' original portrait was exhibited at the RA in 1776 and is at Althorp Park, Northamptonshire. An unfinished version of Bone's enamel was sold at the Bone sale in 1836.[3] Bone captures the quality of the oil portrait, Reynolds' brushstrokes and the subtle green colouring.

REFERENCES: 1. GEC vol. IV, pp. 346–48. 2. Burke's 1889, pp. 178, 422. 3. Walker 1999, p. 322.

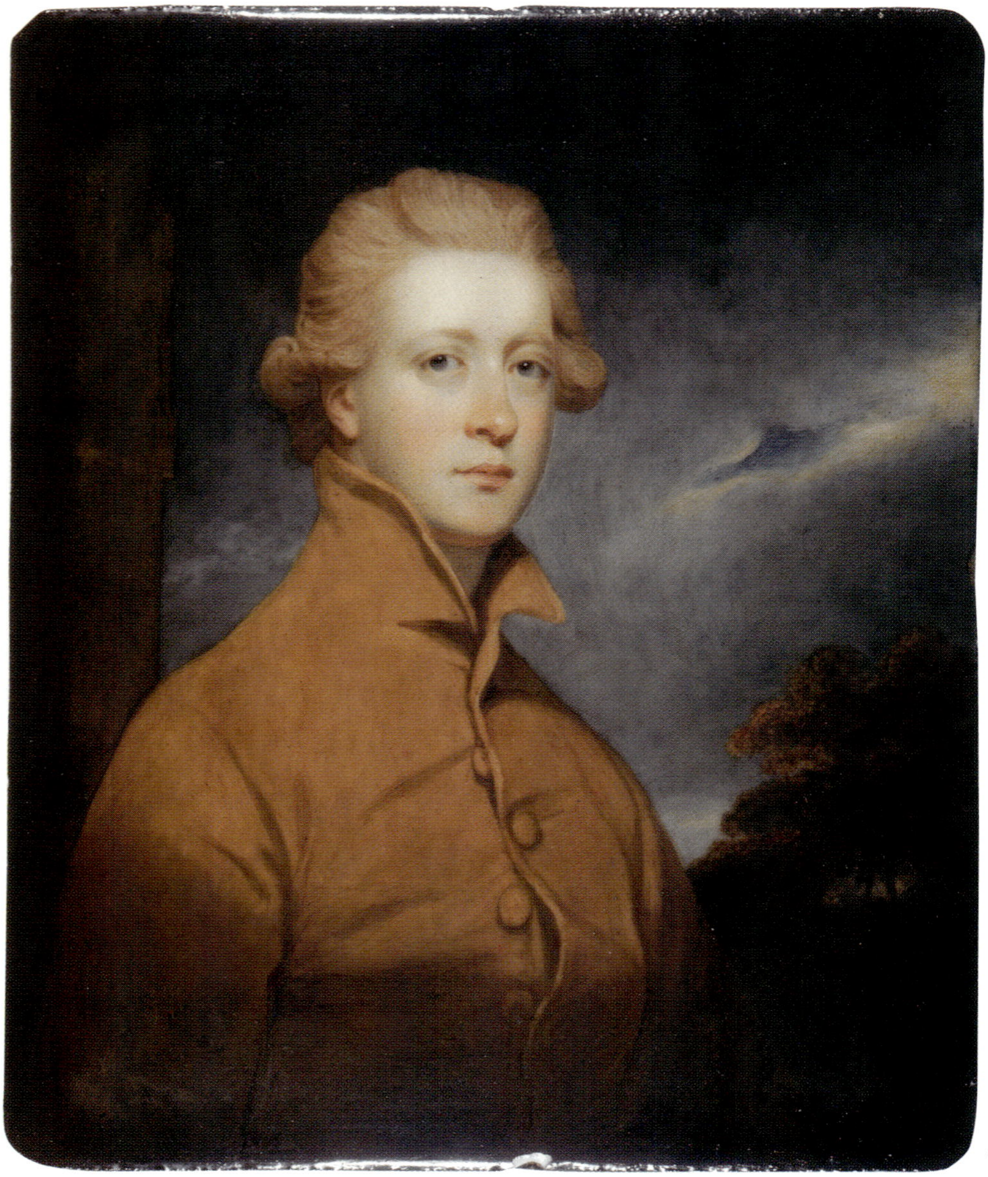

Cat. 70

71. *The Good Shepherd,* 1818

SIGNED: *HBone* (HB in monogram)

INSCRIBED, SIGNED AND DATED ON REVERSE: *The Good Shepherd / London / Aug. 1818 / Painted by Henry Bone R.A. / Enamel Painter in Ordinary / to His Majesty & Enamel Painter / to His R. H. the Prince Regent / after the Original by / Murillo in the collection / of (and painted for) Sir Simon / H. Clarke Bart. / Oak Hall, / Middlesex*

20.3 x 15.4, enamel on copper

Gilt metal frame.

PROVENANCE: Jacob Nachemsohn Collection, 1926; presented by Sir Alfred Chester Beatty, 1951. NGI 3569

LITERATURE: Williamson 1926, p. 19. NGI 1983, p. 14.

This is a reduced copy of a painting by Bartolomé Esteban Murillo (1617–1682). It is faithful with slight alteration to the face, and shows the very young, beardless, figure of Christ, holding a staff, and surrounded by sheep in a landscape. The subject is found in early Christian art and was revived during

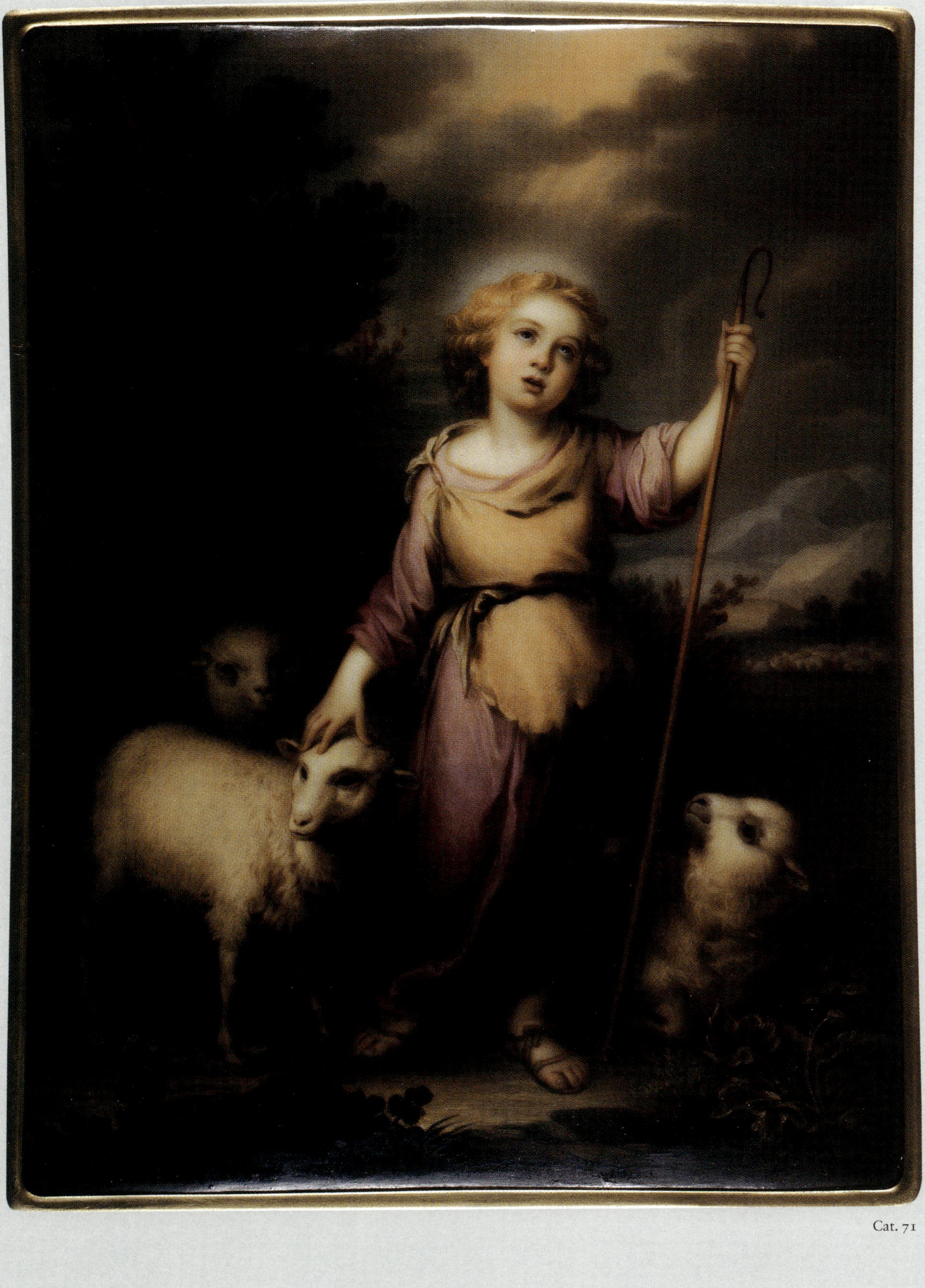

Cat. 71

the baroque period. Henry Bone specialised in painting enamel copies of Old Master pictures, the vogue for them established by the Prince of Wales. The enamels did not fade and so were ideal for display and interior decoration. The second volume of drawings by Bone in the National Portrait Gallery, London, is full of religious and mythological pictures. There are three after Murillo, whose work was highly sought after in England and Ireland from the 18th century onwards. *The Holy Family*, NGI 1719, for example, was brought from Spain by John Blackwood of Soho Square, in 1760. No great country house gallery was complete without a Murillo.

Bone's preparatory drawing for this enamel is in the NPGL (vol. II, p. 55, drawing b). It is inscribed: *Good Shepherd. Original by Murillo, collection of Sir S. Clarke–for Sr Simon H. Clarke Bart. Augst 1814* [deleted] *1818*[1] (Illus. 36). Murillo's canvas was then in the collection of Sir Simon Houghton Clarke, grandson of the Jamaican planter Philip Houghton.[2] It is now in a private collection and on loan to Birmingham Museum and Art Gallery[3] (Illus. 37). The pendant, and closely related, *Infant St John with the lamb*, is in the National Gallery, London. They were painted for the inaugural festivities of S. Maria la Blanca, Seville, in 1665 and displayed on an altar in the Plaza.

REFERENCES: 1. Burke's 1889, p. 294; 2. Walker 1999, p. 356, fig. 174. 3. Walker incorrectly states that the picture was in the collection of Sir Hugh Lane and is now in the NGI. The confusion may have come from the present owner having the same surname. See Iñiguez 1980, catalogue number 204. There are only two other treatments of the subject, in the Prado, Madrid and a German collection.

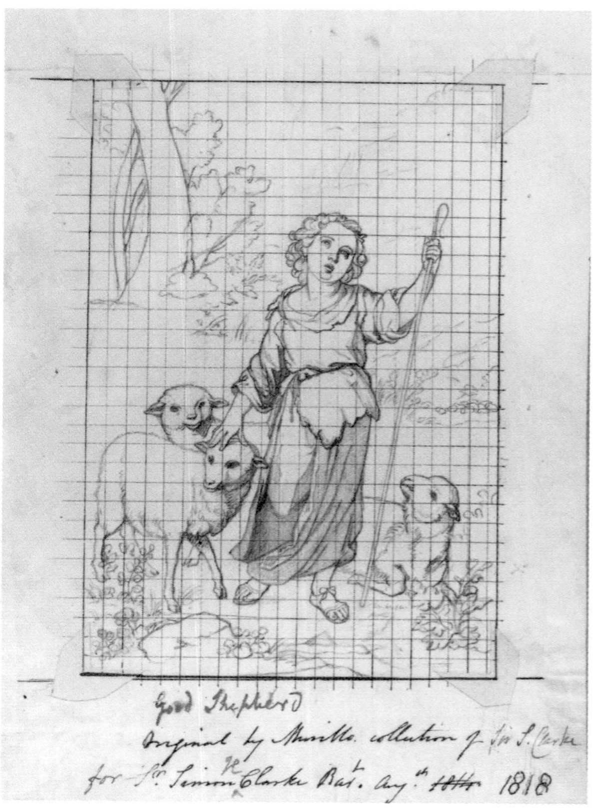

36. Drawing of The Good Shepherd, 1818
HENRY BONE
(NPGL)

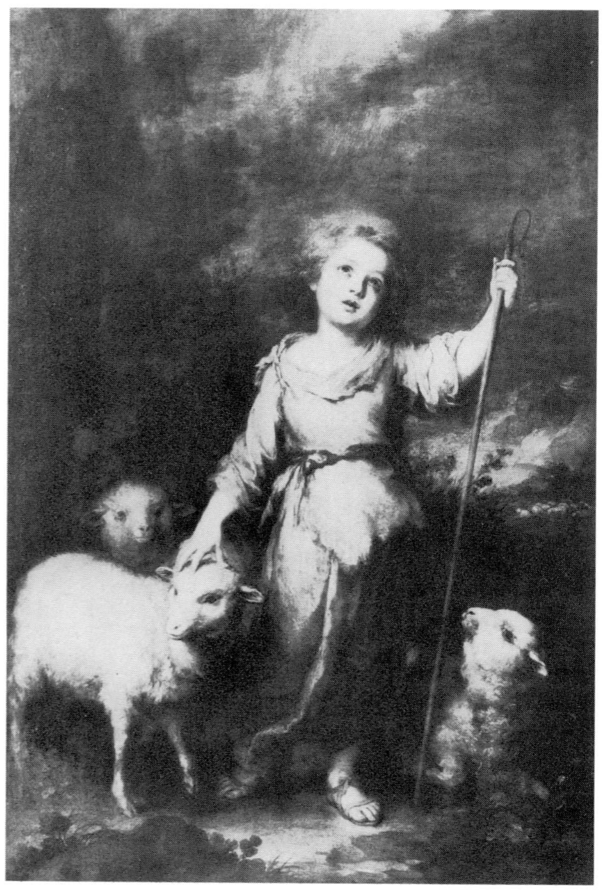

37. The Good Shepherd, c.1665
BARTOLOMÉ ESTEBAN MURILLO
(Private Collection)

72. *Henry VII, King of England , (1457–1509)*, 1824

INSCRIBED, SIGNED AND DATED ON REVERSE: *Henry VII / London / Aug. 1824 / Painted by Henry Bone R.A. / Enamel Painter to His Majesty / etc Enl. Painter to His R. H. / The Duke of York etc etc / after the Original at / Hatfield Herts*

9.4 diam, enamel on copper

Gilt metal frame

PROVENANCE: an enamel of Henry VII was sold in the Bone Sale, June 1836 which may have been this one; Jacob Nachemsohn Collection, 1926; presented by Sir Alfred Chester Beatty, 1951.

NGI 3575

LITERATURE: Williamson 1926, p. 24. NGI 1983, p. 15

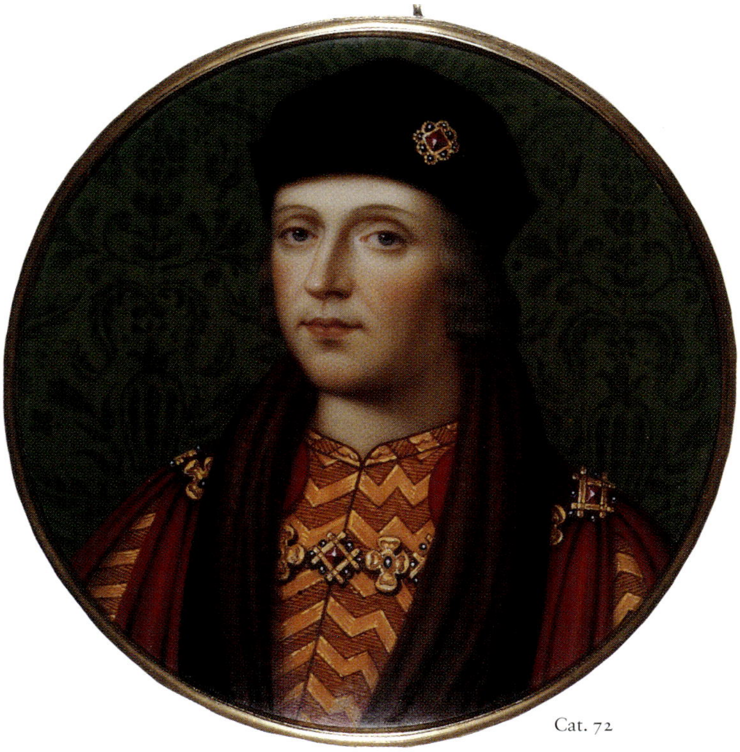

Cat. 72

Henry VII ruled from 1485–1509, after the defeat of Richard III at the Battle of Bosworth Field. He married Elizabeth of York and established the Tudor Dynasty. The finest portraits of him are those by Michael Sittow (NPGL), and probably from a death mask, by Florentine sculptor, Pietro Torrigiano (V&A and the tomb in Henry VII's Chapel, Westminster Abbey). The original for this enamel is at Hatfield House, Hertfordshire and now given to an anonymous painter c.1500.[1] Bone makes the King seem much younger in his version. His preparatory drawing (Illus. 38) is in the NPGL (vol. I, p. 46, drawing b) and inscribed: *Henry VII – Mabuse in the Collection of the Marquis of Salisbury Hatfield House.*[2] Another version of this portrait by Bone is in the Royal Collection (BP 422352). This is an example of Bone's historical enamel portraits, which he popularised.

REFERENCES: 1. Auerbach and Kingsley Amis 1971, p. 34, illus. 8. 2. Walker 1999, p. 330.

38. Drawing of Henry VII portrait
HENRY BONE
(NPGL)

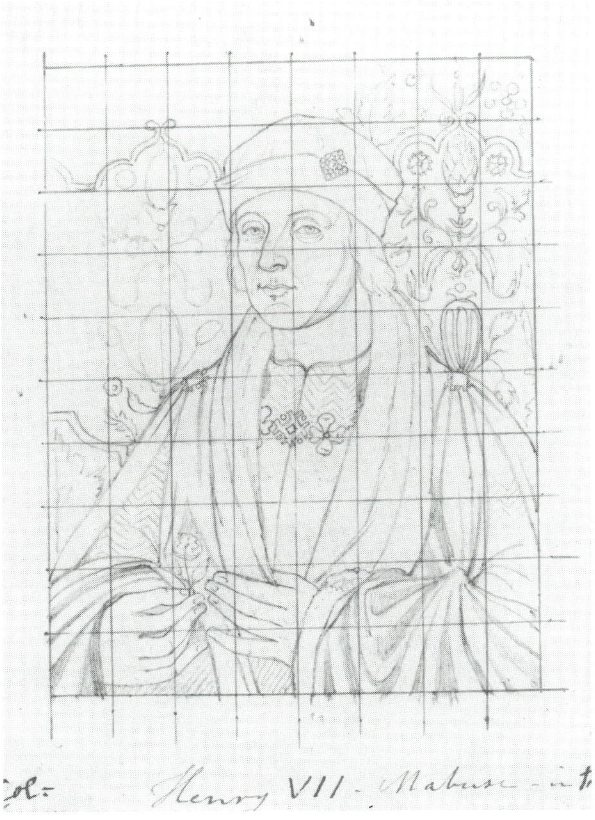

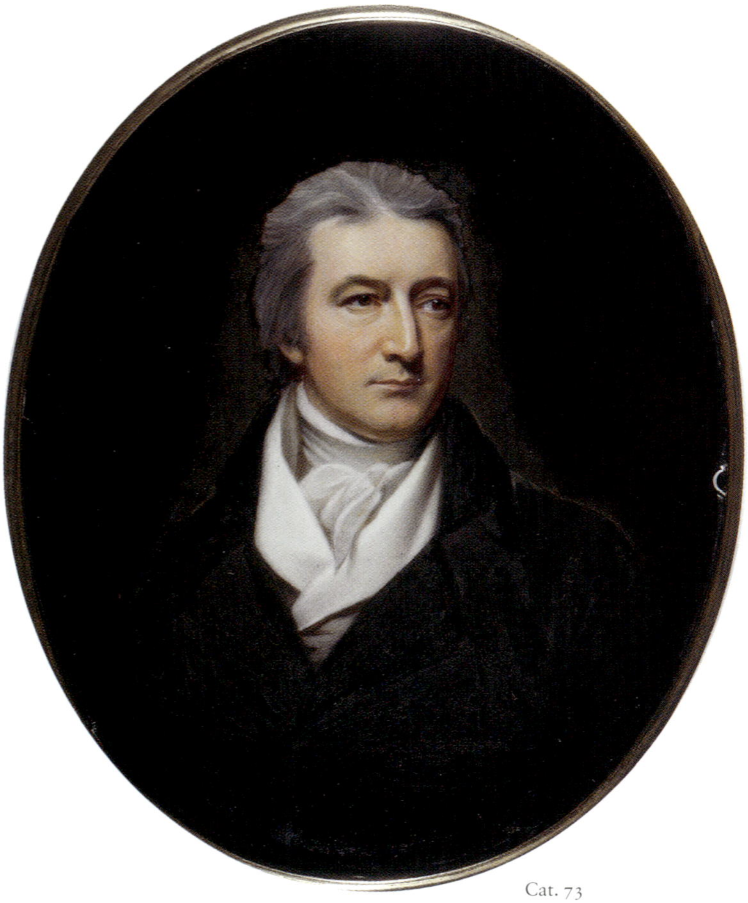

Cat. 73

73. *Henry Bone, (1755–1834), Enamellist,* 1830

INSCRIBED, SIGNED AND DATED ON REVERSE:
Henry Bone R.A. etc etc etc / London / 1830 / Painted by Hy Bone RA / Enamel Painter to His / Majesty the King after / the Original by J. Opie / RA etc
11.8 x 9.8, enamel on copper
Gilt metal frame.
PROVENANCE: Jacob Nachemsohn Collection, 1926; presented by Sir Alfred Chester Beatty, 1951.
NGI 3574
LITERATURE: Williamson 1926, p. 23. NGI 1983, p. 15.

Bone's enamel self-portrait derives from an oil portrait painted by his friend and fellow Cornishman, John Opie, in 1799. Opie presented the portrait to Bone and it was in the Bone family until 1891, when purchased by the National Portrait Gallery, London. Bone carried out several enamel copies of the portrait. One, dated 1802, is illustrated by Foskett[1] and another version, dated 1809, is listed by Walker.[2]

Bone wears a black coat with a dark green velvet collar, white waistcoat and white neckcloth and tie. He is posed against a plain dark brown background. Bone and Opie were both greatly helped in their careers by Dr John Wolcot (see catalogue entry 115). Bone copied numerous oil portraits by Opie.[3]

REFERENCES: 1. Foskett 1972, plate 21. 2. Walker 1985, vol. I, p. 56. 3. Walker 1999, p. 362.

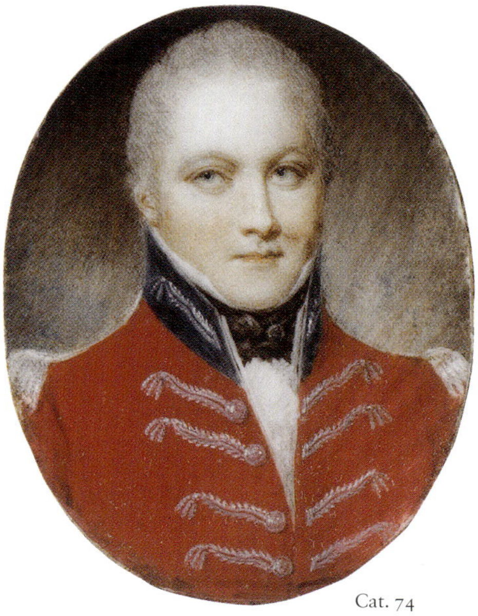

Cat. 74

SAMUEL SHELLEY

London 1756~1808 London

Shelley was born in Whitechapel and was a successful London miniaturist. He was admitted to the Royal Academy Schools in 1774 aged 17. In 1770 he was awarded a prize by the Society of Arts. He exhibited at the Society of Artists in 1773 and 1775 and at the Royal Academy from 1774 to 1804. Edward Nash (1778–1821) and Alexander Robertson (1772–1841) were his pupils.

LITERATURE: Long 1929, pp. 396–98. Foskett 1987, p. 643.

74. *General Duffield, Hanover Guards,* c.1800

7.4 x 6, watercolour on ivory

Oval pendant frame, now placed in a gilt cabinet frame.

Former catalogued as English School (late 18th century)

PROVENANCE: Bequeathed by Todd Mercer to the NMI, 1924; transferred from the NMI, 1969.

NGI 7014

LITERATURE: NGI 1983, p. 128.

Shelley was an excellent draughtsman and his work is characterised by the use of greenish-yellow flesh colour, found in the background also. He used watercolour mixed with a lot of gum arabic, which gives the miniature the appearance of oil paint.

HORACE HONE RA

London 1754/56~1825/27 London

Horace Hone was the second son Nathaniel Hone RA (1718–1784, see catalogue entries 32–37). He was taught miniature painting in watercolour on ivory and on enamel by his father, who used him for the model of a boy sketching from a cast (NGI 1297). In 1770, Horace Hone attended the Royal Academy Schools in London and exhibited at the RA from 1772 to 1822, being appointed ARA in 1779. Horace Hone settled in Dublin in 1782, brought over by Lady Temple, when her husband was Lord Lieutenant. Lady Temple was Baroness Nugent of Carlanstown in her own right in the peerage of Ireland. Through her social connections in Ireland, and with the backing of the Viceregal court, she ensured that Hone received ample patronage. Hone was so renowned that he was appointed Miniature Painter to the Prince of Wales in 1795. He had an extensive practice which was badly affected by the Act of Union, when many of his fashionable patrons moved to London. Hone worked almost exclusively in Ireland until 1804, when he returned to London. He spent part of 1804 in Bath. For some time afterwards he lived in London in the house of his patron, Richard, 7th Viscount Fitzwilliam of Merrion (founder of the Fitzwilliam Museum, Cambridge), where he re-established himself as a miniaturist. Hone had long suffered from mental illness and his decline, from 1805, is recorded in *The Diary of Joseph Farington.* He died in London and is buried in the grounds of St George's Chapel, Bayswater Road.

LITERATURE: Pasquin 1796, p. 31. Mulvany and Gandon 1846, pp. 138–41. Strickland 1913, vol. I, pp. 508–13. Long 1929, pp. 217–18. Garlick *et al.* 1978–84, vol. VIII, p. 3068; vol. X, p. 3706; vol. XV, p. 5374. Caffrey 1999, p. 29.

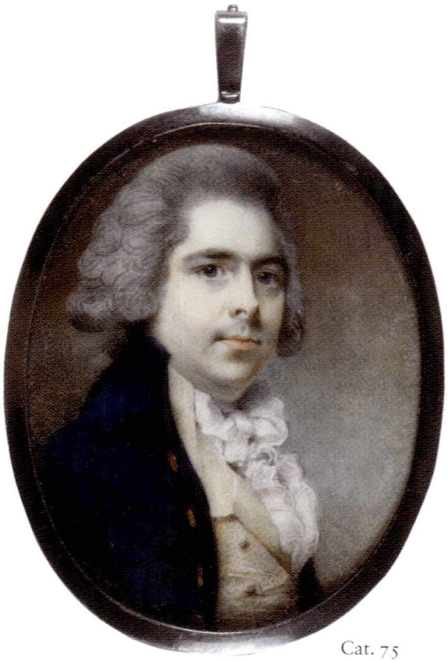

Cat. 75

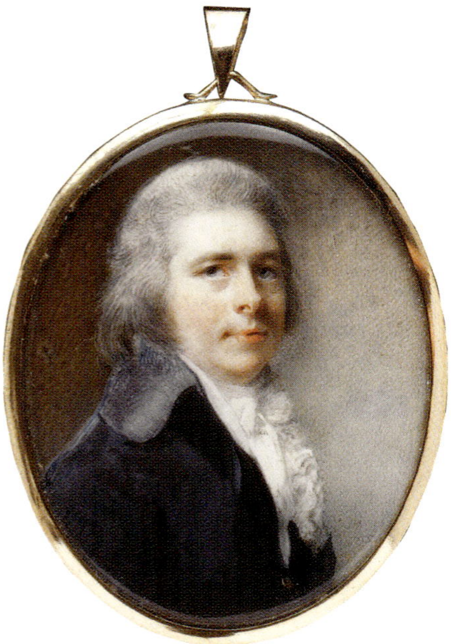

39. *Self-Portrait*, 1795 watercolour on ivory miniature, 6.7 x 5.1
HORACE HONE
(Courtesy of the National Portrait Gallery, London - cat. 1879)

75. *Self-Portrait*, c.1785

SIGNED ON BACKING PAPER: *Mr H Hone / ARA*
6.5 x 5, watercolour with gouache on ivory
Set in a silver-gilt oval pendant.
PROVENANCE: purchased, from Mr Horace Buttery, London, 1907.
NGI 2612
EXHIBITED: 1969–70 Dublin, London and Belfast, no. 134.
LITERATURE: NGI 1983, p. 293.

Hone's self-portrait would have been painted in Dublin during the 1780s, when he was starting out as a fashionable miniaturist and painting some of his finest work. It was painted before he began to suffer from illness, depression and financial difficulties. Hone presents himself as a successful, well-dressed young man, posed against a russet and blue background. His powdered hair is frizzled in the style popularised by the Prince of Wales. The hair is painted in broad curving lines of watercolour. He wears a white linen neck cloth and shirt with a frill down the front. His dark blue coat is fashionably cut with a high collar and he wears a buff coloured, double-breasted, waistcoat. The highlights of the shirt, and shading of the coat, are painted in flat brushstrokes of matt gouache. A slightly more melancholic, but comparable, watercolour on ivory self-portrait, painted in 1795, is in the National Portrait Gallery, London (Illus 39). An enamel, painted in 1804, is in the Art Institute of Chicago.

During the 1770s, the size of the ivory support gradually increased allowing for larger portraits to be painted. Horace Hone's self-portrait exemplifies his mature watercolour style, which is painted with characteristic curving parallel linear brush strokes. The shading of the face is done using minute blue parallel lines. Washes of colour are applied thinly in the areas of the face and background. The washes of colour and lightly brushed strokes allow more ivory to show through, which gives the surface luminosity and fully exploits the watercolour on ivory technique.

76. *Mrs Sarah Siddons, (born Kemble, 1755–1831), Actress,* 1784

SIGNED AND DATED: *HH 1784* (HH in monogram)
INSCRIBED, SIGNED AND DATED ON REVERSE:
Mrs Siddons / Painted in Dublin / by Horace Hone ARA / 1784
9.2 x 7.6, watercolour on ivory
Set in a 19th century black *passe-partout* frame with a floral clasp.
PROVENANCE: thought to have been in the collection of the Hon. Mrs O'Neill in 1785; presented by Mrs C.H. Hone, 1925.
NGI 7318
LITERATURE: NGI 1983, p. 293. Asleson 1999, p. 20.

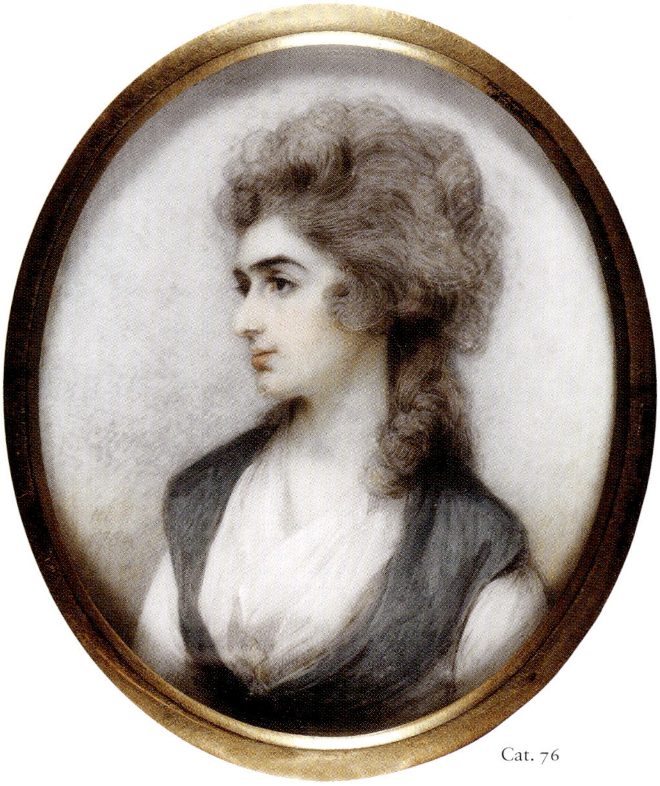

Cat. 76

Mrs Siddons, the English tragic actress, came to Dublin, encouraged by the success of her brother John Philip Kemble who had been in Dublin since 1781. Mrs Siddons made her triumphant debut in *Isabella* on 21 June 1783 at the Smock Alley Theatre in Dublin.[1] Hone's miniature portrait was painted during her second visit to the city in the summer of 1784. Although she did not enjoy her stay, nor like the inhabitants, her performances were a great success.

The theatre provided an important source of commissions for miniaturists who were anxious to supply the demand for images of famous actors and actresses of the day. Although Sarah Siddons was a well established actress by 1782, this is one of her earliest known portraits. Richard Crosse also painted a miniature of her (V&A). The leading portraitists of the day depicted her, including Thomas Gainsborough in semi-profile c.1783–85 (NGL), Joshua Reynolds as *The Tragic Muse* in 1784 (Huntington Art Gallery, San Marino), Gilbert Stuart c.1785 and John Downman in 1787 (both in NPGL). Hone's miniature was, however, engraved and became the popular and easily recognisable image of the actress.

Cat. 76 detail

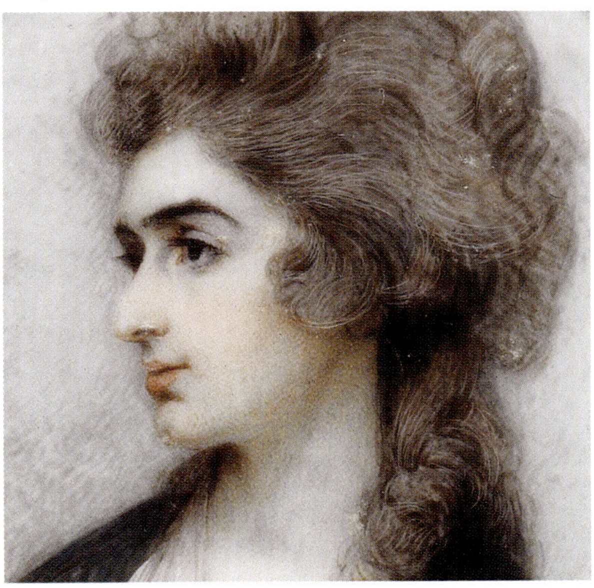

Siddons was as much admired for her classical beauty as her acting ability. Hone captures her magnificence in this head and shoulders, three-quarter profile portrait. Siddons is posed looking away from the viewer in a thoughtful gaze that shows off her features. Hone uses the elaborate *à la conseilleur* hairstyle, and cross-over mantle, to form a composition that is well suited to the oval shape. The hair, loosely swept up, is painted in long curving parallel brushstrokes. The dark areas have been scored with a scraper to reveal the ivory support beneath. The shading of the face and blue shadows are painted in stipple. This miniature exemplifies Hone's mature style of painting. It is a relatively large miniature, perfectly drawn. Hone fully exploits the

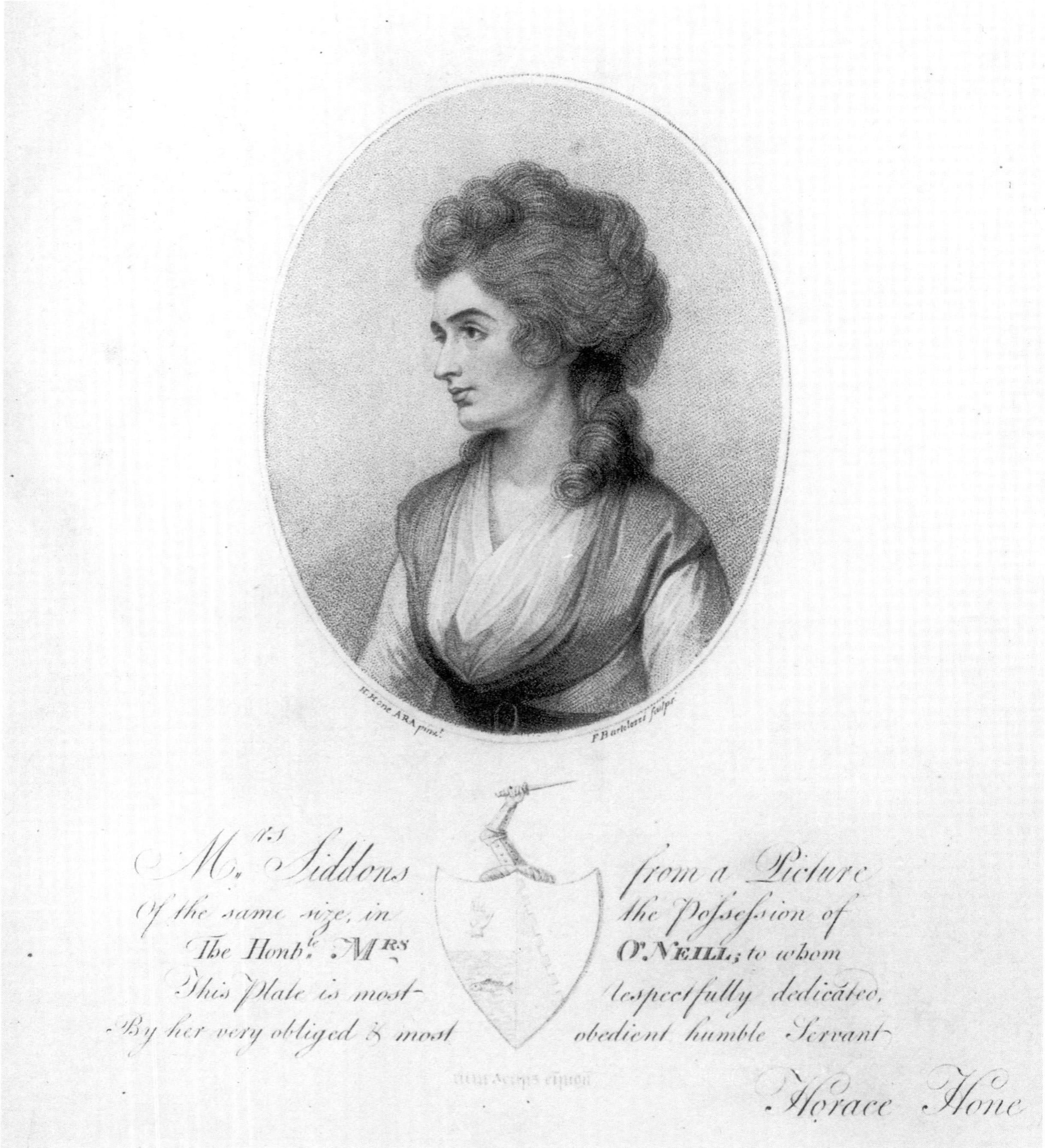

40. Print after Sarah Siddons watercolour miniature, 1785
FRANCESCO BARTOLOZZI after HORACE HONE
(NGI 10310)

ivory by leaving much of the surface unpainted and exposed, to allow the luminosity of the support come through.

Hone did several versions of his portrait of Mrs Siddons in watercolour and enamel and had them engraved. Today, two other watercolour on ivory versions of Hone's portrait of Mrs Siddons are known and they are both dated 1784. One is in the collection of the Royal Shakespeare Theatre, Stratford-upon-Avon. The other, of her facing in the opposite direction, was last recorded in a private collection in 1934.[2] The NGI portrait may have been the one in the collection of the Hon. Mrs O'Neill, which was engraved by Francesco Bartolozzi (1727–1815) and published in London, 1785 (NGI 10310, Illus. 40). The following advertisement appeared in *Freeman's Journal* in December 1784 and January 1785.

Engraved by Bartolozzi and published by H. Hone at 108 Capel Street, Dublin, in 1785; price to subscribers, plain, black or red, five shillings; non subscribers three half crowns; proof, or coloured, impressions, half a guinea.

Strickland describes the print[3] as being dedicated to Mrs Siddons, in whose possession the original miniature was, and that this was the miniature sold at Christie's in 1885 for £42. A miniature of her by Hone was exhibited in 1904 at the Guildhall Exhibition, as part of the Earl of Mayo's collection of theatrical portraits.

An enamel version of the NGI portrait of Mrs Siddons, signed by Hone and dated 1786, was executed with her wearing a hat and different clothes. This version is in a private collection.[4] Hone executed a later enamel portrait, based on NGI 7318, which was exhibited at the Royal Academy in 1822. This enamel portrait was engraved in stipple by G.F. Phillips (active 1815–1832) and published in London in 1825 (NGI 10308, Illus. 41).

REFERENCES: 1. Mrs Siddons also appeared in Cork, DNB, vol. XVIII, p. 197. 2. Exhibition London 1975, entry 104, as belonging to Miss Catherine Evans Gordon in 1934. 3. Strickland 1913, vol. 1, p. 513. 4. sold Sotheby's, Geneva, 25–27 May, 1993 and illustrated in Asleson 1999, p. 20.

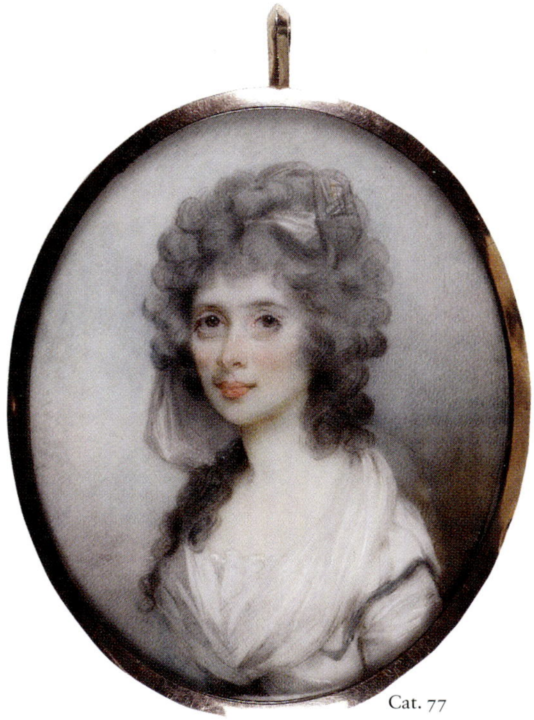

Cat. 77

77. *Portrait of a lady in a white dress,* 1791

SIGNED AND DATED: *HH / 1791* (HH in monogram)
6.5 x 5.2, watercolour on ivory
Set in a gold oval pendant with a blue glass border on the reverse. A lock of the sitter's hair is interwoven under a raised central panel of clear glass.
PROVENANCE: presented by Mrs C. H. Hone, 1925.
NGI 7321
EXHIBITED: 1969–70 Dublin, London and Belfast, no. 138
LITERATURE: NGI 1983, p. 294.

This is another fine example of Hone's skill in watercolour on ivory. By 1791, hairstyles, especially for ladies, became more elaborate and the larger miniatures made it possible to incorporate the fashionable large curled type depicted here. The unknown sitter is fashionably dressed and has a handkerchief shawl popular around 1790.

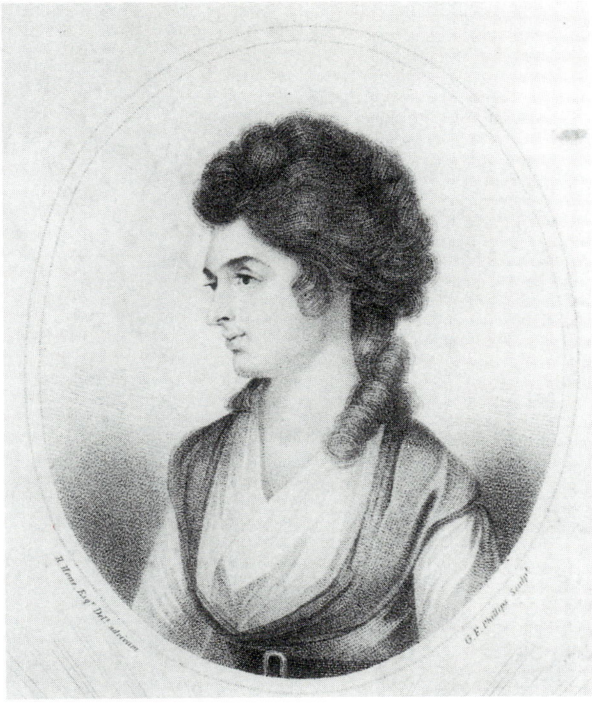

41. *Print after Sarah Siddons enamel miniature,* 1825
G.F. PHILLIPS after HORACE HONE
(NGI 10308)

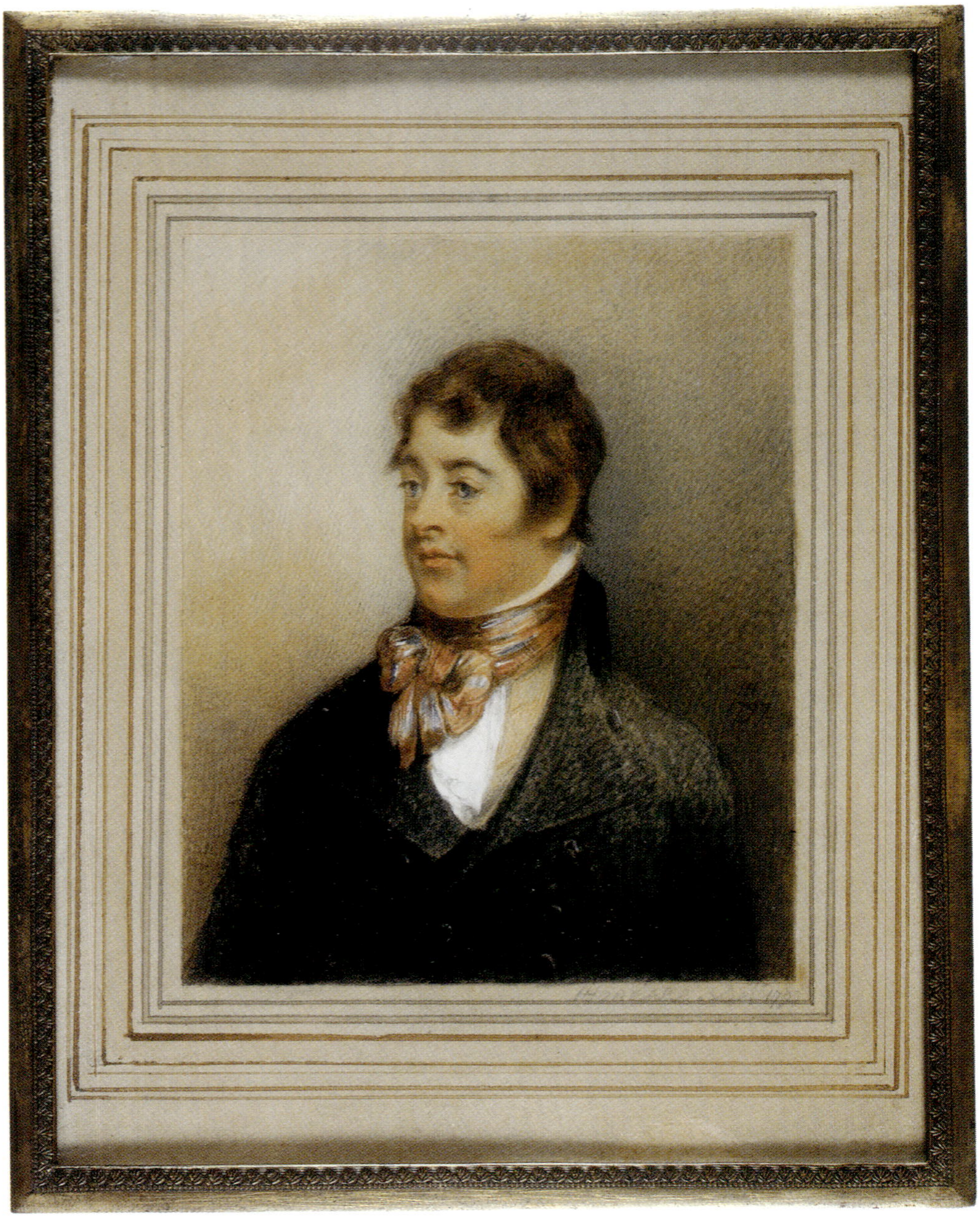

Cat. 78

78. *Lord Edward Fitzgerald (1763–98)*, 1797

SIGNED AND DATED: *HH / 1797* (HH in monogram)
10.8 x 8.8, watercolour on paper
Framed in a black leather case with a velvet and brass border.
NGI 2156
ENGRAVED: in mezzotint by T.W. Huffam (active 1825–c.1855) and published in Madden's *United Irishmen* (1843, vol. II, 2nd series, opposite p. 97, see NGI 11138, Illus. 43).
PROVENANCE: presented by Lt.-Col. W. Fitzgerald, 1884.
LITERATURE: NGI 1983, p. 292.

Lord Edward Fitzgerald was a son of the 1st Duke and Duchess of Leinster. After military service in America and Canada, he became MP for Kildare and, inspired by the French Revolution, pursued radical politics. He joined the United Irishmen and was on the committee organising the 1798 Uprising. After the leaders were arrested, he was on the run until betrayed and mortally wounded during his arrest. He died in Newgate Gaol, Dublin. With his honest nature and courage, he was already a popular hero[1]. Hone portrays him against a cloudy sky background. He has fashionably cropped short hair, echoing the style of the French Republic, and is wearing a predominantly red and blue patterned neckcloth and light-blue coat. The portrait is painted in Hone's characteristic parallel and hatched brushstrokes.

Hone's portrait of Lord Edward, dated 1797, is based on a watercolour on ivory miniature which he painted in 1795 (Private Collection, exhibited at the Gorry Gallery, Dublin, 1991, Illus. 42).[2] It is usually stated that Hone's portrait is derived from an oil portrait by Hugh Douglas Hamilton (1740– 1808)[3]. Hamilton however, first painted Lord Edward during the winter of 1796[4] and may have been influenced by Hone's composition. In Hamilton's portrait, Lord Edward wears a red neck cloth, buff coloured waistcoat and dark blue coat. In later versions, painted after Lord Edward's death, the neck cloth was painted plain white.

Hone would have kept the watercolour on paper portrait as a stock portrait from which to paint miniatures and images for engravings. After Lord Edward's death in 1798 there was a great public demand for images of him. Hone's portrait was engraved and Lord Edward is shown wearing the patterned neck cloth (Illus. 43). Horace Hone had a thriving business copying miniatures and adapting full scale oil portraits for the miniature portrait and engraving market. There was a popular demand for images of heroes and famous public figures such as Lord Edward Fitzgerald and Lord Charlemont, whom Hone painted several times. These portraits were in turn engraved providing an additional source of income for miniaturists.

REFERENCES: 1. DNB vol. VII, pp. 110–11. 2. The watercolour on ivory miniature is signed *HH* (in monogram) and dated 1795, Caffrey 1991, p. 10. 3. NGI 1983, p. 292 and NGI 1988, p. 235. 4. Tillyard 1997, p. 218.

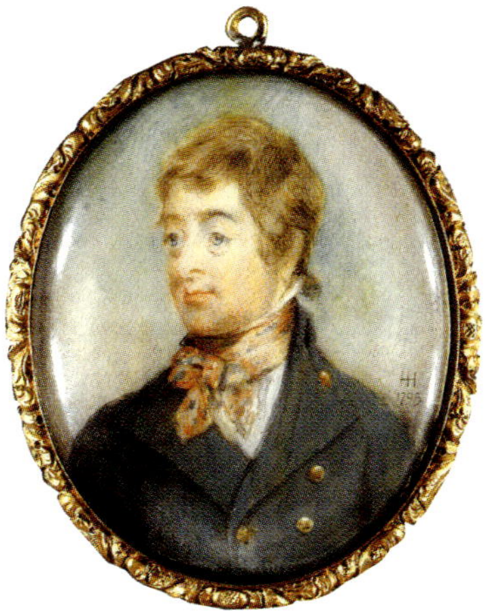

42. *Lord Edward Fitzgerald*, 1795
watercolour on ivory miniature, 5 x 4
HORACE HONE
(Private Collection, courtesy of the Gorry Gallery).

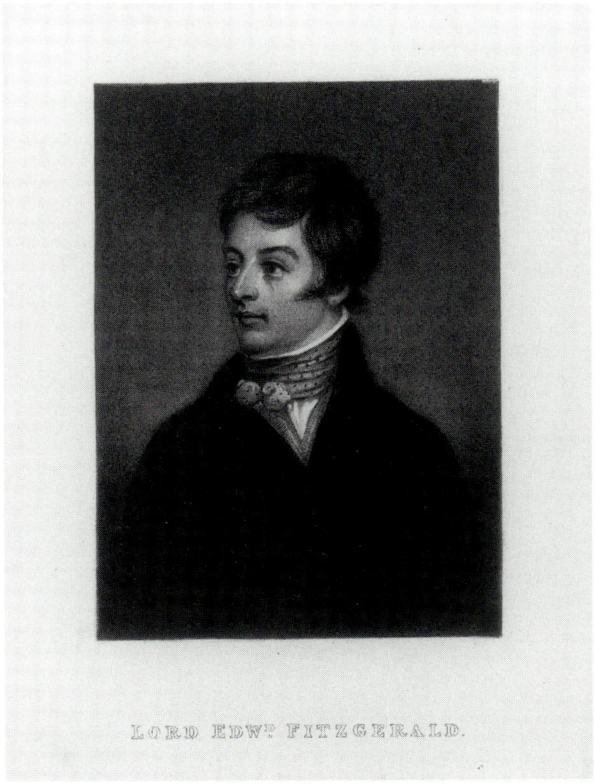

43. *Print after Lord Edward Fitzgerald watercolour miniature*, 1843
T.W. HUFFAM after HORACE HONE
(NGI 11138)

79. *James Gandon, (1743–1832), with the Custom House, Dublin in the background*, 1799

12.7 x 10.5, watercolour, gouache and pencil on card
Cabinet frame with ebonised and gilt wood.
PROVENANCE: presented by Nathaniel Hone (the Younger) RHA, 1884.
NGI 2157
LITERATURE: Wynne 1967, p. 532. NGI 1983, p. 292.

James Gandon was a pupil of Sir William Chambers, exhibiting and publishing architectural designs from 1767. He was brought over to Dublin in 1781 to build a new Custom House. Despite his many critics, he was to grace the city with a series of neo-classical structures, mostly ornamented with sculpture by Edward Smyth. These comprise the Custom House (1781–91), Four Courts (1786–1802), House of Lords Portico (1784–c.89), Military Infirmary (1786), the original Carlisle (now O'Connell) Bridge and King's Inns (from 1795). He also designed villas around Dublin, but had less success in country houses with the exterior only completed at Emo Court, Co. Laois (c.1790–98) and the dramatic stable yards at Carrigglas Manor, Co. Longford (c.1795). Gandon retired to Lucan, Co. Dublin, in 1808.

Gandon is presented pointing over his shoulder to a view of his recently completed masterpiece, the Custom House, Dublin. He wears a reddish-brown coat with a fur collar, double-breasted white waistcoat, white linen shirt with a white neck cloth, frill and black cravat. He was a close friend of Horace Hone. A biography of Hone is included in Mulvany and Gandon's *Life of James Gandon*.[1] Hone's watercolour on card portrait would have been painted as a preliminary portrait for a watercolour on ivory, enamel, or engraved portrait of Gandon. Hone kept the portrait as a stock image of the architect from which to paint miniatures. Hone did several finished miniatures of Gandon based on this portrait

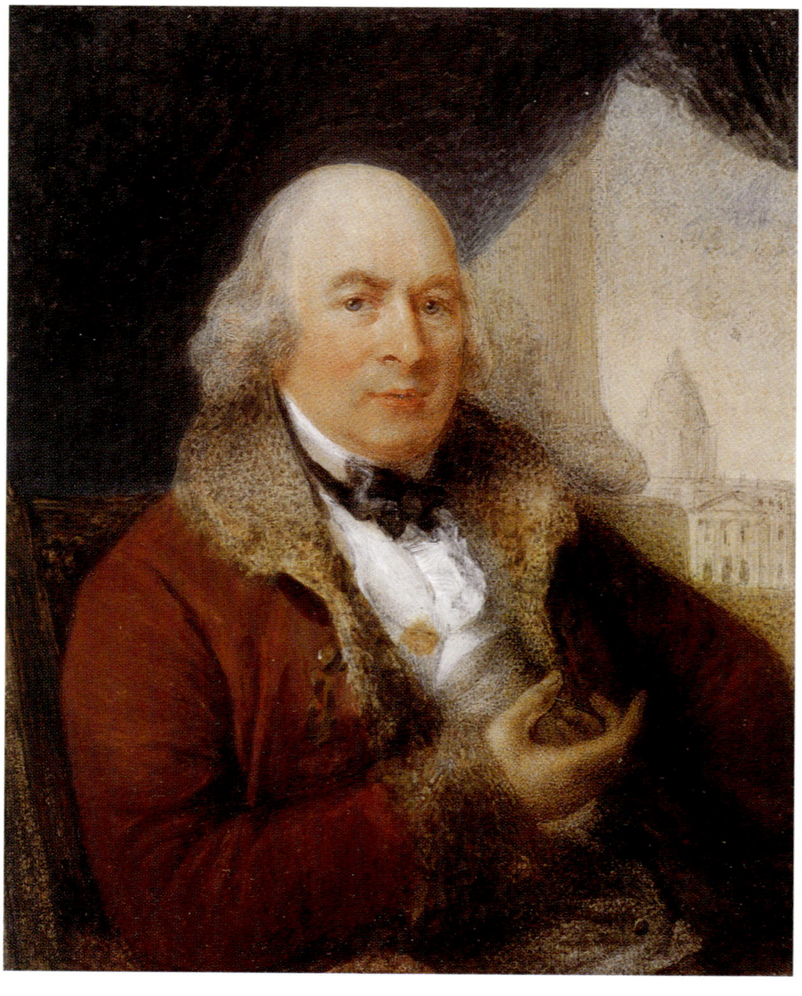

Cat. 79

44. *James Gandon*, 1806 enamel miniature, 8.8 high
HORACE HONE
(By courtesy of the Syndics of the Fitzwilliam Museum, Cambridge)

45. *Print after James Gandon watercolour miniature*, 1846
HENRY MEYER after HORACE HONE
(NGI 10833)

and his enamel portrait executed in 1806 (Fitzwilliam Museum, Cambridge, Illus. 44), which omits the Custom House, was clearly based on the NGI portrait. The Fitzwilliam enamel is signed and dated 1799, when the original portrait from life was done. It is inscribed on the reverse as executed in 1806.[2]

A version of Horace Hone's portrait of Gandon, which may have been NGI 2157, was engraved in mezzotint by Henry Meyer (c.1782–1847) as the frontispiece to Mulvany and Gandon's *Life of James Gandon* (1846), see NGI 10833, Illus. 45.

REFERENCES: 1. Mulvany and Gandon 1846, pp. 138–41. McParland 1985, p. 189. 2. Bayne-Powell 1985, p. 125.

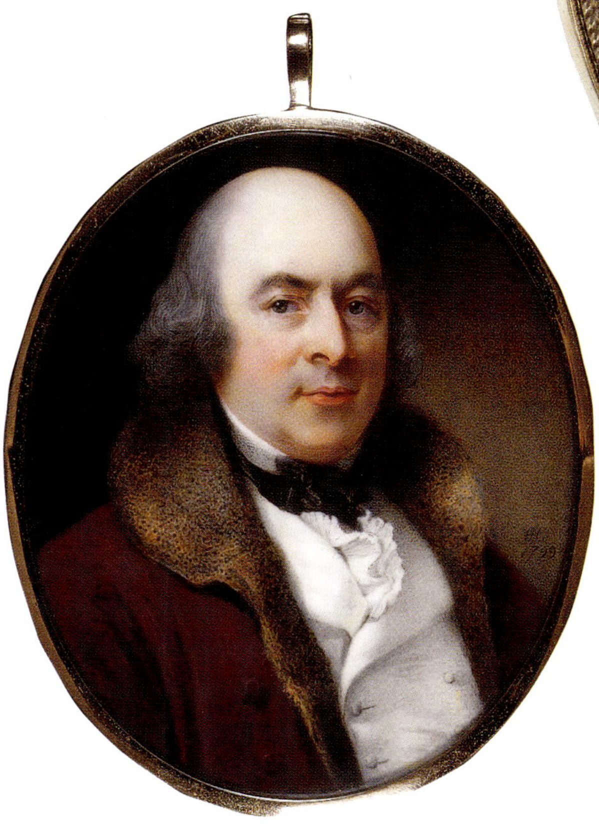

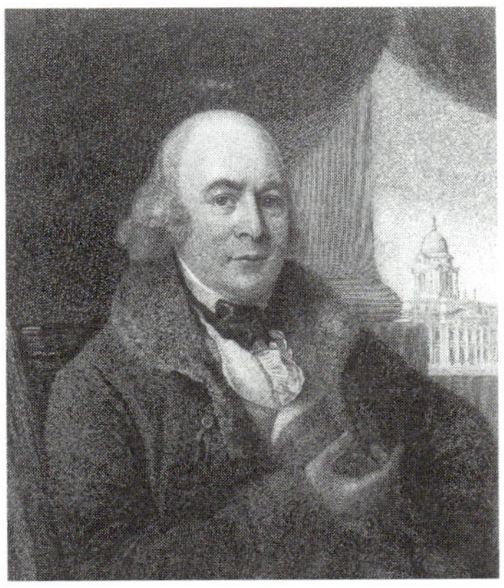

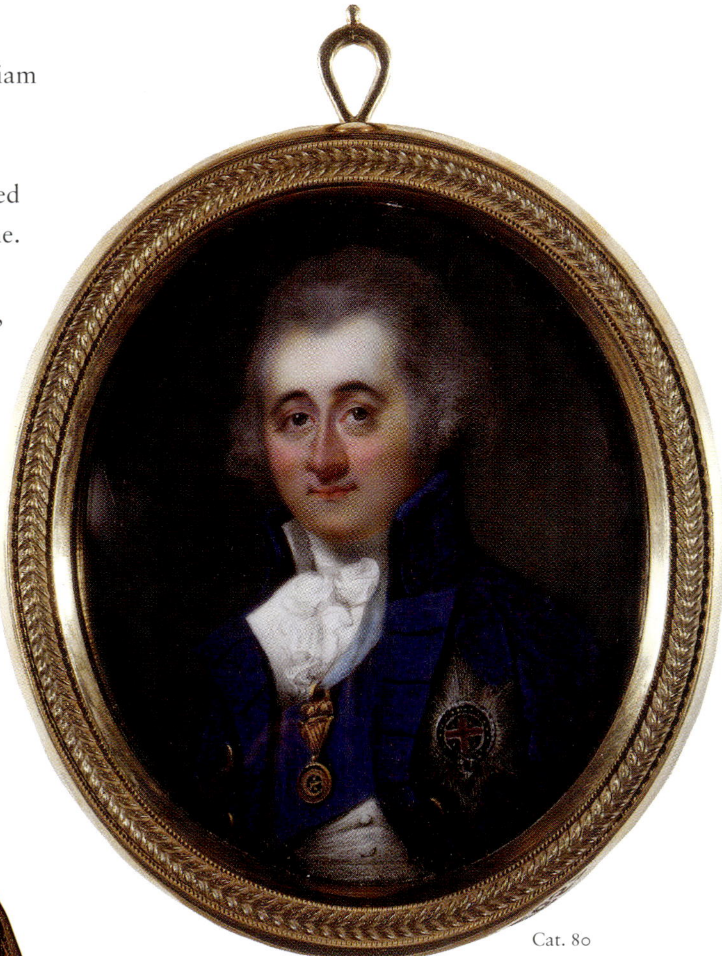

Cat. 80

80. *Charles Manners, 4th Duke of Rutland, (1754–1787), Lord Lieutenant of Ireland,* 1805

SIGNED AND POSTDATED: *HH. / 1787*
(HH in monogram)
INSCRIBED, SIGNED AND DATED ON REVERSE: *London 1805 / Charles, Duke of Rutland, / Lord Lieutt. of Ireland / Feby 1784 / Died there Octr. 24th.1787 / This Enamel, Painted by Horace / Hones A.R.A. 1805 from the/ Original Water Colour picture / painted in Dublin / and was the last picture / the Duke sat for, / London 1805*
9 x 7.5, enamel on copper
Oval gilt metal frame.
PROVENANCE: by family descent; bequeathed by Miss Eleanor Hone, 1912.
NGI 2657
EXHIBITED: 1969–70 Dublin, London and Belfast no. 139. 1971 Cork, no. 196.

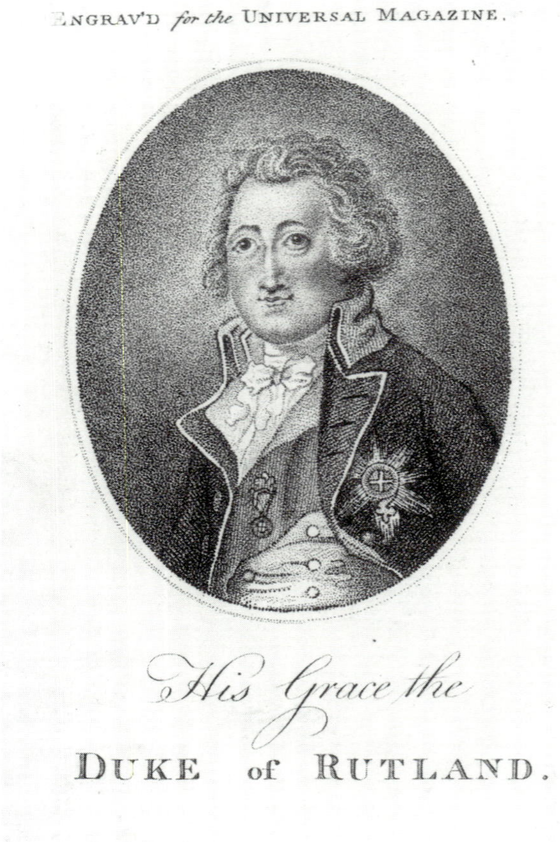

46. *Print after watercolour version of 4th Duke of Rutland miniature,* 1790
ENGLISH SCHOOL (1790) after HORACE HONE
(NGI 11322)

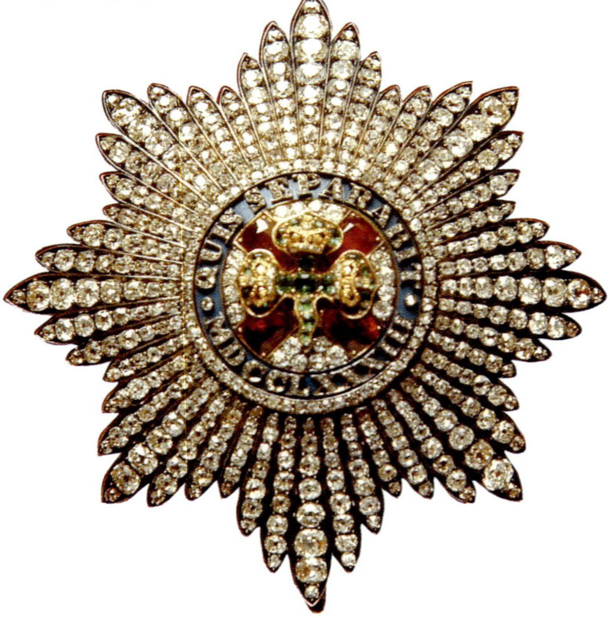

47. *Reduced replica of the Star of the Grand Master of the Knights of St Patrick,* c.1890 silver and gold, with diamonds, rubies and emeralds, 8.5 x 8.5
R.& S. GARRARD and CO.
(NGI 12068)

The Duke of Rutland had been Lord Steward of the Bedchamber and Lord Privy Seal when he was appointed Lord Lieutenant in 1784. He was extremely popular in Ireland because of the lavish entertainments that he provided[1] and Barrington noted he *was an amiable and extravagant peer without any particular talent, except for conviviality.*[2] He died in office. The fountain designed by Francis Sandys on Merrion Square (1791) was erected in memory of the Duke by his grieving widow and has a relief portrait of him in Coade stone. He was a noted patron of the arts and architecture and supported the foundation of a public picture gallery, with Peter de Gree (1751–1789) as Keeper. The Duke was a friend of Reynolds and an advocate of Gandon's work.

This is a formal miniature portrait. The sitter is portrayed as Lord Lieutenant of Ireland wearing the eight-pointed star of the cross of St George and the dark blue ribbon of the Most Noble Order of the Garter, as well as the sky-blue ribbon and badge of the Most Illustrious Order of St Patrick. The Order of St Patrick was founded in 1783 for Irish Peers and the Lord Lieutenant was *ex officio* Grand Master. A replica of the Grand Master's Diamond Star (stolen in 1907), belonging to the 6th Earl of Milltown, is in the NGI (Illus. 47).

Horace Hone's enamel miniature is based on a watercolour portrait (untraced) which he painted from life in 1787, the year of the Duke's death. This was engraved anonymously in stipple for the *Universal Magazine and Review* London, February 1790 (NGI 11322, Illus. 46). Although Horace Hone did enamels throughout his career, he produced more enamels based on watercolour portraits, and copies of oil portraits, during the period 1804–10 and Farington records[3], that in 1805 Hone had 'returned mainly to *enamel* painting'.

REFERENCES: 1. GEC vol. XI, pp. 269–70. 2. Barrington 1833, vol. 2, p. 225. 3. Garlick *et al.* 1978–84, vol. VIII, p. 3068.

SAMPSON TOWGOOD ROCH

Youghal, Co. Cork 1757~1847
Ardmore, Co. Waterford

Roch was the elder son of William and Mary Roch of Youghal, Co. Cork. He was deaf and dumb from birth. At an early age he showed a great talent for drawing, and was encouraged to paint. Roch was probably taught privately as there is no record of him studying at the Dublin Society's Drawing School. By 1779 he was established as a miniaturist in Dublin and was making frequent trips to England. Roch employed an assistant, Charles Byrne (1757–c.1810), who acted as his interpreter and was also a miniaturist (see catalogue entry 84). In 1792 he went to live permanently in Bath where he had a large practice attracting many distinguished clients and Royal patronage. Bath became a fashionable resort, after the discovery of the Roman baths in 1755. It was customary for visitors to have a miniature portrait painted. Roch returned to live at his family house at Woodbine Hill, Co. Waterford, after the death of his wife in 1822. There he continued to paint and he did numerous sketches of everyday country life which are a unique record of pre-Famine Ireland (Ulster Folk Museum, Cultra). He is buried at Ardmore, Co. Waterford. Roch's portrait was painted in watercolour on ivory by his friend, Horace Hone, in 1795, which with a self-portrait, late in life, still belong to a collateral branch of the Roch family (Caffrey 1986a, front cover and p. 14).

LITERATURE: Caffrey 1986a, pp. 14–20.

81. *Mrs Mangan, (born Hoey)*, 1788

SIGNED AND DATED: *S Roch / 1788*
6.7 x 5.1, watercolour on ivory
Framed in a gold oval pendant. The reverse is engraved with bright-cut decoration, surrounding locks of the sitter's interwoven hair, with her initials JM in gold, set in the centre.
PROVENANCE: purchased, from Miss Langan, Termonfeckin, Co. Louth, 1903.
NGI 2532
EXHIBITED: 1969–70 Dublin, London and Belfast, no. 145. 1976 Dallas, no. 91.
LITERATURE: NGI 1983, p. 664.

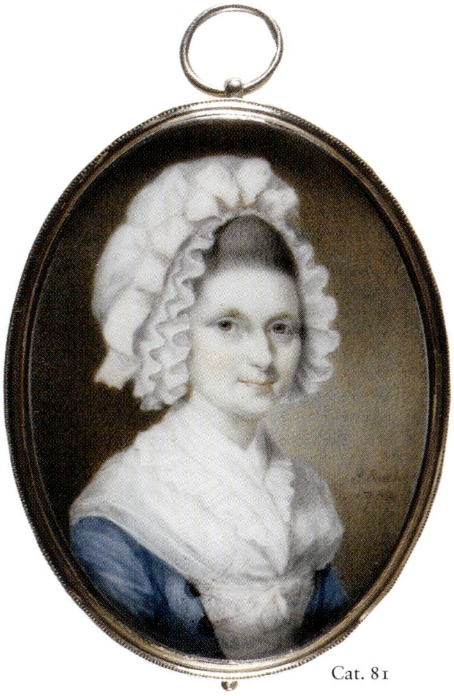

Cat. 81

This miniature dates from Roch's Dublin period before he moved to Bath. Mrs Mangan (formerly catalogued as Mrs Morgan), is modestly attired in a dress with lacing in the front, which would have been old-fashioned for that time. Her head is covered with a round cap and she wears a handkerchief shawl around her shoulders. The round cap was an important item of informal headdress throughout the eighteenth century. As hairstyles became larger in the 1780s and early 1790s, so did the round cap. In this miniature it forms an important decorative device.

Roch's miniature portraits are characterised by his distinctive minute linear brushstrokes. His work is extremely neat and carefully painted. Details of the sitter's face and clothes are painted in short parallel linear brushstrokes, which are closely spaced, creating a smooth surface. An idiosyncratic feature of his work is that he paints portraits with an incipient smile. This is the result of the use of stipple shading in the painting of the corners of the lips and cheeks.

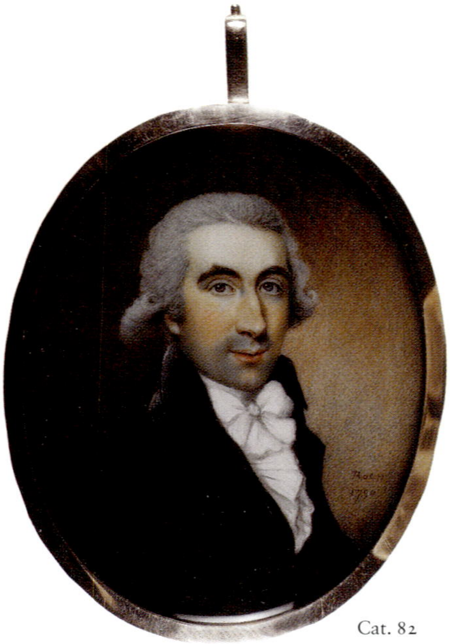

Cat. 82

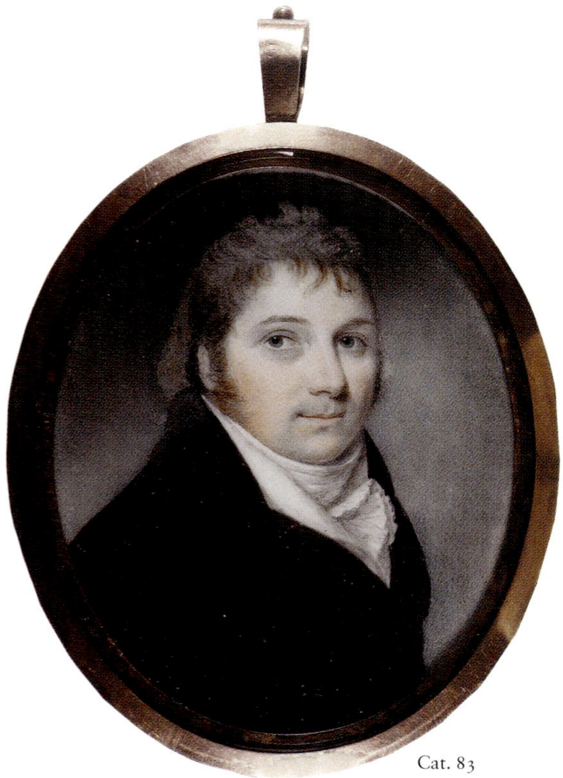

Cat. 83

82. *Portrait of a man in a grey-blue coat*, 1790
SIGNED AND DATED: *ROCH / 1790*
6.5 x 5, watercolour on ivory
Framed in an oval gold pendant with a lock of the sitter's interwoven hair in the reverse.
PROVENANCE: purchased, from Hibernian Antiques, Dublin, 1971.
NGI 7356
EXHIBITED: 1976 Dallas, no. 92.
LITERATURE: NGI 1983, p. 664.

Roch's careful style of painting hardly varied throughout his career and he remained uninfluenced by the larger and more freely painted work of his contemporaries, such as that of his close friend Horace Hone (see catalogue entries 75–80). Roch's trademark neatness and the sitter's incipient smile mark this miniature as typical of his work.

83. *Mr R. James Tisdall of Rathcoole, Dunleer, Co. Louth*, c.1800
7.5 x 6.1, watercolour on ivory
Set in an oval gold and blue glass pendant frame. A lock of the sitter's hair is interwoven with his initials in seed pearls on the reverse (Illus. 13).
PROVENANCE: purchased by the NMI, 1914; transferred from the NMI, 1969.
NGI 7087
LITERATURE: NGI 1983, p. 664.

This miniature was probably painted on one of Roch's frequent visits to Ireland during the period he was living in Bath. The subtle variation of the sitter's face are meticulously painted. The attribution to Roch is based on comparable portraits, which are carefully painted with minute stippling, and the sitter's depiction with Roch's characteristic incipient smile.

CHARLES BYRNE

Dublin 1757~c.1810 Dublin

Byrne was a pupil of Sampson Towgood Roch (1757–1847, see preceding entries), and acted as Roch's interpreter and assistant. In about 1791, he was employed as a miniaturist by Hutchinson's, a firm of jewellers in Dame Street, Dublin. Byrne must have gone to live in England when Roch left in 1792. He practised in London, where he exhibited at the Royal Academy in 1800 and the Society of Artists of Ireland in 1802. Pasquin describes him as eccentric, but by the time of his death, he had become insane.

LITERATURE: Pasquin 1796, p.33. Ryan 1821, vol. I, pp. 296–97. Graves 1905–06, vol. II, p. 73. Caffrey 1986a, pp. 17–18. Stewart 1990, p. 98.

84. *Self-Portrait,* late 1790s

7.6 x 5.9, watercolour on ivory

Set in a black *passe-partout* frame.

PROVENANCE: by descent through a collateral branch of the artist's family; purchased from Miss F. Byrne, 1889.

NGI 2304

EXHIBITED: 1969–70 Dublin, London and Belfast, no. 140.

LITERATURE: NGI 1983, p. 44.

Although Byrne was taught by Roch, their work has little in common. There is none of Roch's finesse of detail, nor his neatness (see catalogue entries 81–83). Byrne uses blotchy brushstrokes and dark stippling to create a brooding self-portrait of an artist, now known to have been on the verge of insanity.

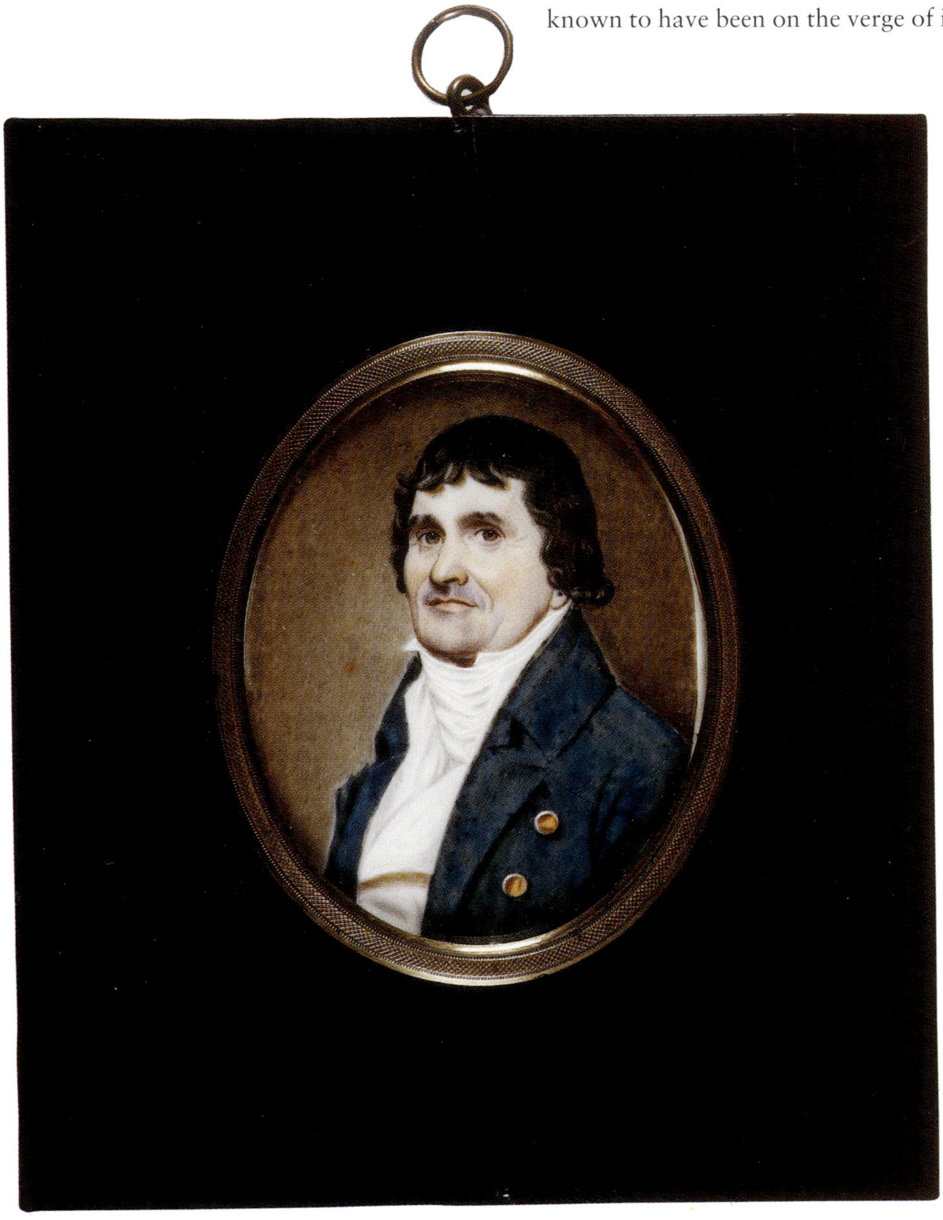

Cat. 84

GEORGE LAWRENCE

Dublin c.1758~1802 Dublin

Lawrence was part of a distinguished Dublin family of miniaturists. His brothers John Lawrence (active 1771–1793) and Robert Lawrence (active 1794–1820) were also practitioners. George Lawrence entered the Dublin Society's Drawing Schools in 1771. On 26 May 1774, Lawrence was awarded a prize for a drawing of a head and figure.[1] After leaving the school, he worked as a miniaturist and pastellist. His studio was at 35, Grafton Street and in the 1780s he moved to 35, South Frederick Street. Printed labels give his prices as a guinea for either a miniature or pastel portrait, which later increased to two guineas.

LITERATURE: Strickland 1913, vol. II, p. 12. McGuire 1936, pp. 206–9; Caffrey 1999, p. 31.

REFERENCE: 1. RDS Proceedings 1773–74, vol. X, p. 434.

85. *Portrait of a man in a blue coat*, 1793

SIGNED AND DATED: *G. Lawrence / Dubln / 1793*

6.6 x 5.1, watercolour with gouache on ivory

Framed in an oval gold pendant, later adapted as a brooch. The reverse has locks of the sitter's hair arranged in feathered designs, interspersed with gold filigree against a blue glass background. These form strands of wheat which stem from three seed pearls (Illus. 13).

PROVENANCE: purchased by the NMI, 1915; transferred from the NMI, 1969.

NGI 7078

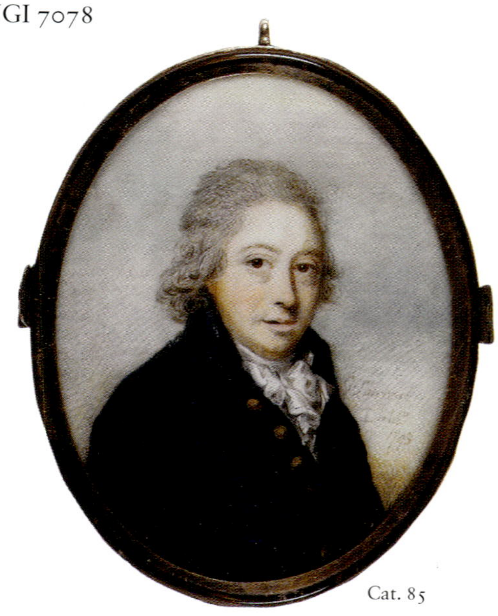

Cat. 85

Lawrence's fine linear brushwork is similar to Horace Hone's, especially the curving parallel lines used to paint the sitter's hair in this portrait. Lawrence's technique is characterised by painting in broadly spaced parallel lines of watercolour, which may clearly be seen in the background. The sitter's blue coat is painted in gouache, as are the white highlights of the white linen shirt and neck cloth.

This miniature is framed and presented as a commemorative portrait. It may have been painted from life, but would have been reframed after the sitter's death. The reverse is decorated with emblems of mortality and mourning. Single strands of gold filigree in the shape of ears of wheat sprout from seed pearls. This is a symbolic representation of the Last Judgement (harvest). The pearls are associated with earthly love and were traditionally worn by widows during mourning.

ADAM BUCK

Cork 1759~1833 London

Buck was the elder son of Jonathan Buck, a silversmith of Castle Street, Cork. Unlike his brother Frederick (1771–1840, see catalogue entries 101–02), he did not attend the Dublin Society Drawing Schools, and his artistic training is unknown. He worked as a miniaturist and painter of small whole-length portraits in Cork where he evolved his own decorative neo-classical style. Pasquin states that he was self-taught and worked in Dublin for several years. In 1795, Buck moved permanently to London. He lived in Piccadilly and then Soho, and exhibited at the Royal Academy from 1796–1833. He was keenly interested in Antique Greek and Roman vase painting and published a prospectus for a book on Greek vase painting in 1811. It was intended to be a continuation of Sir William Hamilton's *Collection of Engravings from Ancient Vases* (1791–97). Only one instalment of ten etched outlines was issued in 1812. His neo-classical taste is shown by the 1813 watercolour self-portrait with his family (YCBA) and self-portrait miniature (Illus. 17, V&A). Buck made a speciality of small full-length watercolour portraits (Illus. 18) and many portraits and fancy subjects by him were engraved, generally in colour stipple and aquatint (V&A and BM).

LITERATURE: Pasquin 1796, p. 41. Jenkins 1988, pp. 448–57. Crookshank and Glin 1994, pp. 125–56.

86. *Vice-Admiral Robert Plampin, (1762–1834)*, 1803

SIGNED AND DATED: *ABuck / 1803* (AB in monogram)
7 x 5.6, watercolour on ivory
PROVENANCE: purchased from Mrs Wallis, Swords, Co. Dublin, 1904.
NGI 2553
EXHIBITED: 1969–70 Dublin, London and Belfast, no. 142. 1976 Dallas, no. 89.
LITERATURE: NGI 1983, p. 25.

Plampin joined the navy in 1775 and distinguished himself in the Napoleonic Wars. He was promoted to the rank of Vice-Admiral in 1825. From 1825–28 he was Commander-in-Chief in Ireland.

Adam Buck's unique style of miniature painting was imbued with neo-classical spirit. Restraint in the use of colour, leaving areas of the ivory base exposed, and skilful drawing are characteristics of his work. Buck builds up his portraits in minute linear brushstrokes with clearly defined outlines. He paid great attention to painting details of dress and hair, which by 1800, were in the neo-classical fashion. In this portrait, the sitter has fashionably dishevelled 'Brutus' cropped hair and long sideburns.

87. *Mrs Robert Plampin, (born Fanny Milchel, 1780–1864)*, 1803

SIGNED AND DATED: *ABuck 1803* (AB in monogram)
7 x 5.5, watercolour on ivory
Set in a later cabinet frame (Daniel Egan, Dublin)
PROVENANCE: purchased from Mrs Wallis, Swords, Co. Dublin, 1904.
NGI 2554
EXHIBITED: 1969–70 Dublin, London and Belfast, no. 143. 1976 Dallas, no. 90.
LITERATURE: NGI 1983, p. 25.

Painted with the same delicacy as the portrait of her husband, Mrs Plampin wears her hair with curls tied up at the back in the Grecian style, ultra fashionable in 1803. To complement her hairstyle, she wears a suitably classical, high waisted muslin dress, with a low cut décolletage in imitation of classical statuary.

Buck uses the established convention of posing pairs of portraits of husband and wife so that the sitter's face one another. Pairs of miniatures such as these were usually painted to commemorate an event such as an engagement, or, in this case, it was most likely to have been their marriage. There is another Buck portrait of her in antique profile, framed in its original gold pendant frame, in the Draper Gift at Kenwood House, London.[1]

REFERENCE: 1. Formerly in the collection of the late R.L. Bayne-Powell, sold at Sotheby's, London, October 1994, lot 75; see Edwards 1997, pp. 208–09, no. 93.

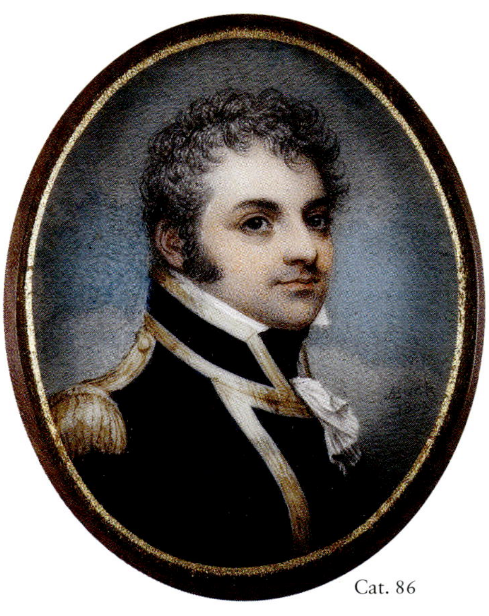

Cat. 86

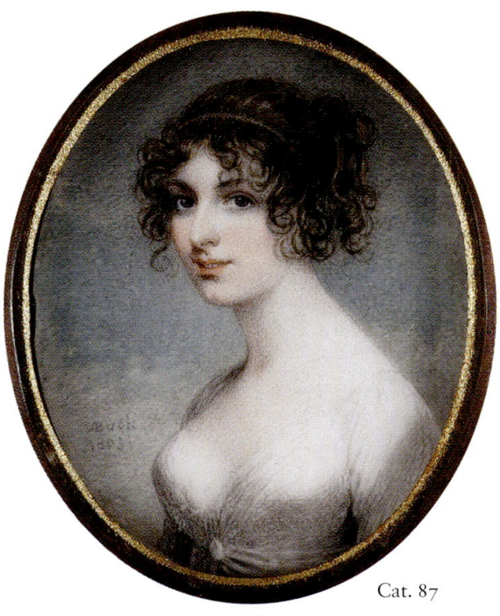

Cat. 87

88. *Young lady seated on a sea wall,* c.1800

8.5 diam., watercolour on ivory
Framed in a circular leather case (top lost), now set in a gilt frame.
PROVENANCE: presented to the NMI by Mrs Maev Sullivan, Dublin, 1949; transferred from the NMI, 1969.
NGI 7171
LITERATURE: NGI 1983, p. 27.

This cabinet miniature is an example of Buck's decorative work and the composition of this unusual circular miniature is skilfully devised. The girl's large be-ribboned cap, and the flowing folds of cotton in her high-waisted dress, form a pattern that echoes the circular shape of the ivory support. The face and shoes are painted in washes of carnation red and contrast with the blue of the ribbon in her cap. Typical of Buck's work is the painting of the sky background and the way the ivory support is left unpainted to form the whitest parts of the clouds.

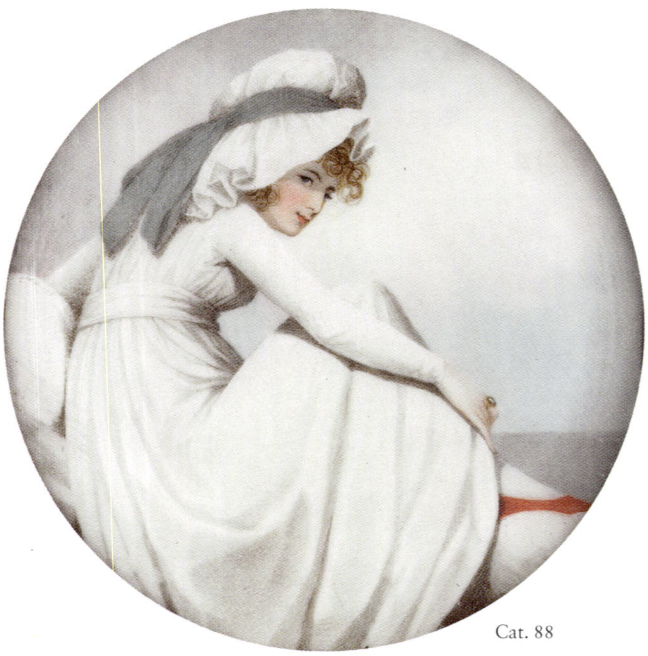

Cat. 88

JOHN CAMILLUS HONE

London 1759~1836 Dublin

John Camillus Hone was the younger son of Nathaniel Hone RA (1718–1784, see catalogue entries 32–37), and brother of Horace Hone ARA (1754–1825/27, see catalogue entries 75–80). In 1769, his portrait entitled *The Piping Boy* (NGI 440) was painted by his father. He was taught to paint miniatures in watercolour on ivory and on enamel by his father and exhibited at the Royal Academy from 1776–80. About 1790 he settled in Dublin and was appointed Engraver of Dies in the Stamp Office by the Lord Lieutenant. This appears to have been his main employment in later years. Few works by him are known.

LITERATURE: Strickland 1913, vol. I, pp. 514–15.

89. *Portrait of an elderly man in a brown coat,* 1773

SIGNED AND DATED: *I.H. / 1773*
3.4 x 2.8, watercolour on ivory
Framed in a gold bracelet setting, later adapted as a brooch.
Provenance unknown.
NGI 7334
LITERATURE: NGI 1983, p. 294.

J.C. Hone's portrait of a rather unprepossessing old man clearly shows the influence of Nathaniel Hone's style and technique of miniature painting. The small size is reminiscent of work of the 1750s. The crude dotted stippling in the background is unusual for a work dated 1773.

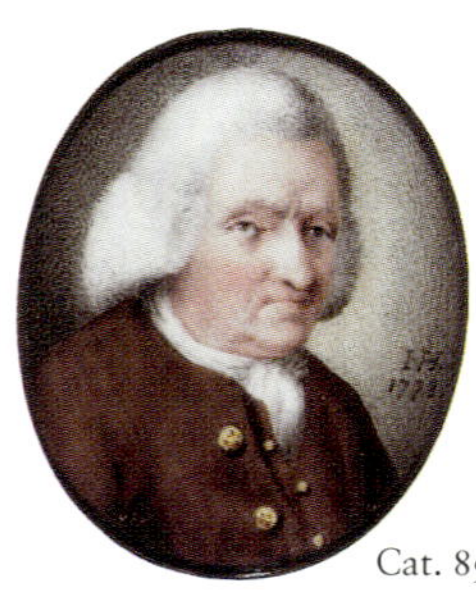

Cat. 89

CHARLES ROBERTSON

Dublin 1760~1821 Dublin

Robertson was born into a prominent Dublin family of jewellers and miniaturists. He spent most of his career in Dublin, apart from one prolonged period in London from 1785–92, and a shorter stay in 1806. During the last ten years of his life, he was active in seeking the establishment of an Irish painting academy, but died two years before the establishment of the Royal Hibernian Academy. He was in partnership with his elder brother, the miniaturist, Walter Robertson (c.1750–1802). Charles Robertson deployed a distinctive use of colour in his miniature portraits, using a particular slate grey-blue in the flesh tones. His portraits are neatly executed, with finely applied, minute, brushstrokes. As Robertson rarely signed his miniatures, they are difficult to identify. The National Gallery of Ireland has Robertson's miniature painting desk in its collection (Illus. 23) and a watercolour portrait of him working in his studio (Illus. 24) by Henry Brooke Kirchhoffer RHA (c.1781–1860).

LITERATURE: Pasquin 1796, p. 13. Graves 1905–06, vol. 4, p. 78. Strickland 1913, vol. II, pp. 284–86. Breeze 1985, p. 25.

Cat. 90, see next page

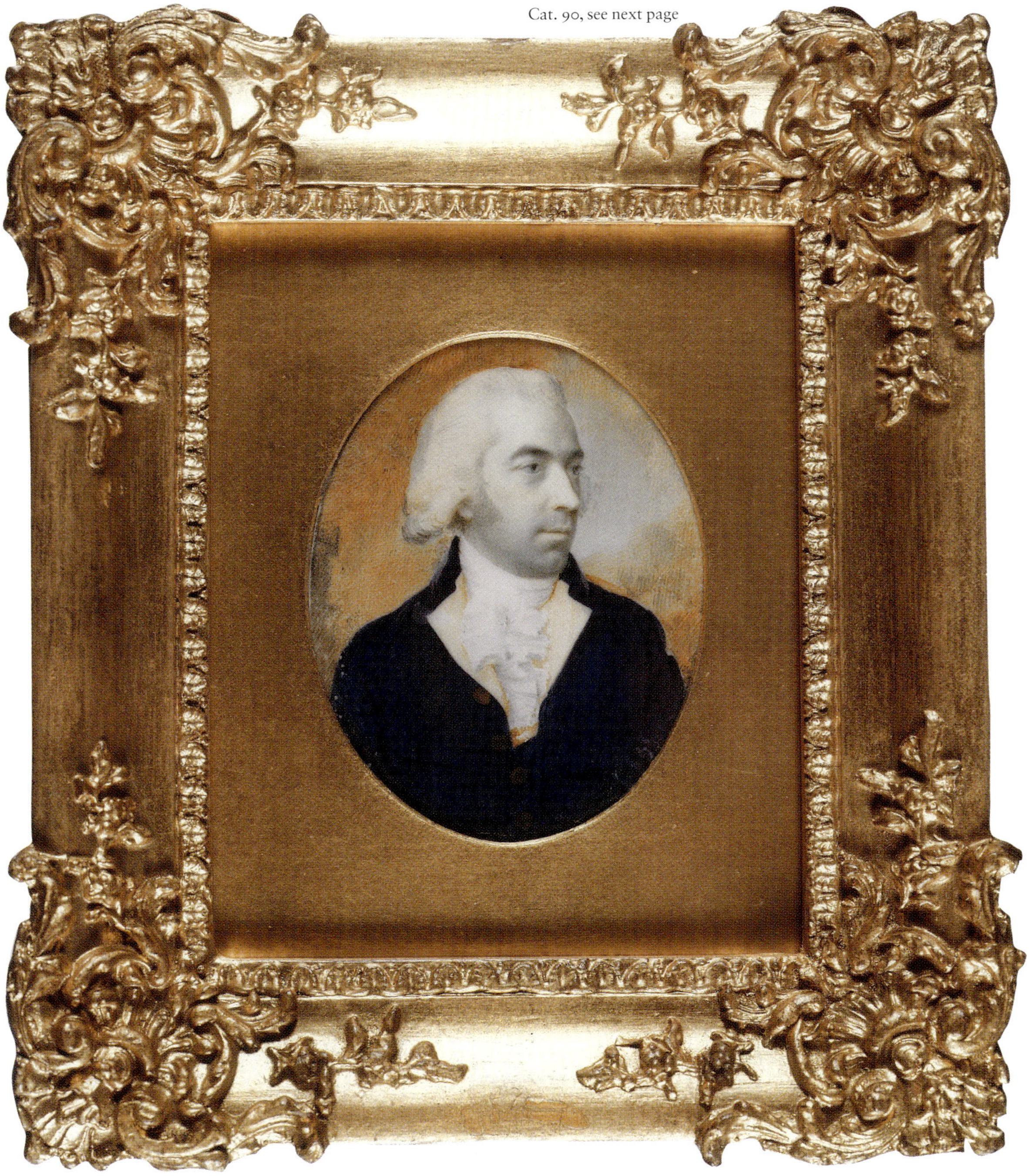

90. *Walter Robertson, (c.1750–1801), Miniaturist and the artist's elder brother,* c.1780

(Illustrated p. 109)

7.5 x 5.9, watercolour on ivory

Set in a nineteenth century, rococo revival, carved and gilded frame (Daniel Egan, Dublin).

PROVENANCE: by descent in the artist's family to his great-grandson Mr E. Stanley Robertson, and presented by him, 1903.

NGI 2524

LITERATURE: NGI 1983, p. 662.

Walter Robertson studied at the Dublin Society's School of Figure Drawing, which he entered on 17 October 1765. He was awarded a prize of £2 for drawings of human heads and figures in 1766.[1] He was an established miniaturist in Dublin during the years 1768–84 and in London from 1784–92. On his return to Dublin he was declared bankrupt and a considerable amount of his property was sold.[2] Robertson was a friend of the American painter Gilbert Stuart (1755–1828), and when Stuart returned to America in 1793, accompanied him. In America he was known as 'Irish Robertson', to distinguish him from the two Scottish miniaturists of the same name, Archibald and Alexander. In 1794, he was commissioned to paint a miniature of George Washington which was engraved several times.[3] In 1795, he went to India where he died in 1802.[4]

This characteristic portrait by Charles Robertson demonstrates his soft manner of painting and use of grey tones in the treatment of the sitter's face and the background. The composition and indirect gaze of his brother are typical of his work. There is a smaller miniature of Walter Robertson by Charles Robertson in a private collection.[5]

REFERENCES: 1. RDS Proceedings 1765–66, vol. II, p. 230; 1766–7, vol. III, p. 517. 2. Strickland 1913, vol. II, pp. 284–86. 3. Bolton-Smith 1984, pp. 4–5, 52. 4. Foster 1930–31, vol. XIX, pp. 1–18 and 1933, vol. XXI, pp. 108–9. 5. Caffrey 1999, p. 27, no. 38.

91. *Portrait of a lady in a white dress,* c.1800

5.9 x 4.9, watercolour on ivory

Gold pendant setting with interwoven locks of the sitter's hair framed on reverse.

PROVENANCE: purchased by Miss Mary A. McNeill, at Christie's, London, 21 February 1961, lot 39. Miss Mary A. McNeill Bequest, 1985.

NGI 19276

LITERATURE: Le Harivel and Wynne 1986, p. 126.

The sitter is fashionably dressed for around 1800. She wears a high-waisted white dress with a frill around the edge of the décolletage. Her white bonnet is tied with a scarf. The portrait is in Robertson's distinctive style, typically unsigned, and romantic in mood. This atmosphere is created by painting in lightly applied minute short linear brushstrokes. The background is painted in parallel lines of blue and grey. Subtle variations of colour and pale tones blend into each other and his outlines are slightly fuzzy. The blue-grey tones are also indicative of him.

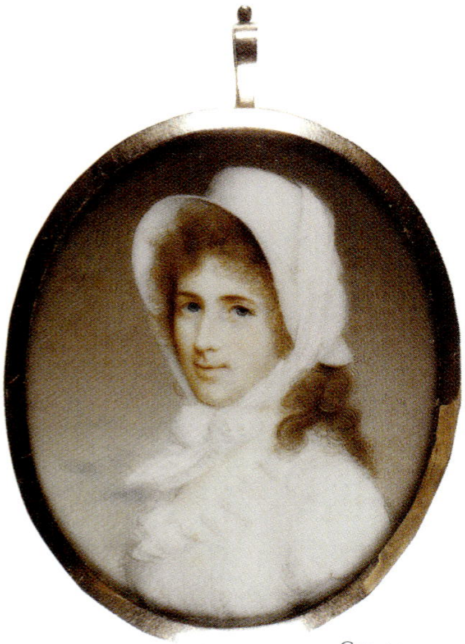

Cat. 91

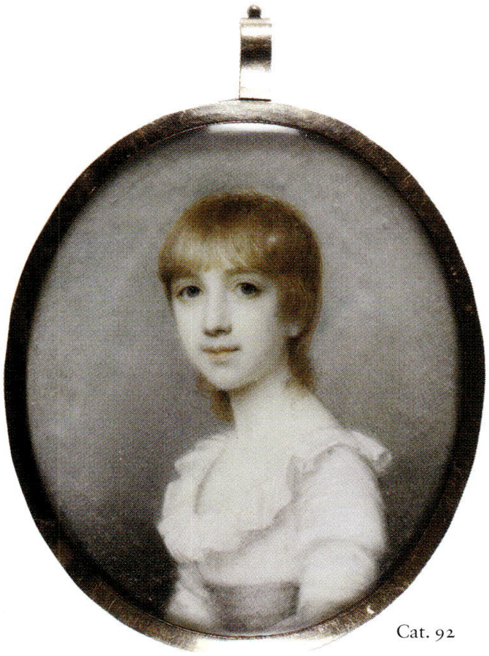

Cat. 92

92. *Portrait of a young girl*, c.1800

6.5 x 5.5, watercolour on ivory
Framed in a gold pendant setting with locks of the sitter's hair interwoven on the reverse
PROVENANCE: purchased by Miss Mary A. McNeill at Christie's, London, 7 November 1961; Miss Mary A. McNeill Bequest, 1985.
NGI 19277
LITERATURE: Le Harivel and Wynne 1986, p. 126.

The young girl is posed against a grey-blue sky background. She wears a white dress with a blue band around her waist. This miniature portrait exemplifies Robertson's style of painting, in the use of pale colours and parallel linear brushstrokes. His presentation has a romantic and often sentimental feel which is achieved in this portrait by slightly exaggerating the painting of her dark eyes.

SARAH, COUNTESS OF ESSEX (LADY MALDEN)

(?) St Helena c.1761~1838 London

Born Sarah Bazett, the daughter of Henry Bazett of St Helena, she married, firstly, Edward Stephenson and, secondly, in 1786, George Capell-Coningsby, Viscount Malden, who succeeded his father as 5th Earl of Essex in 1799. They later separated and she lived in London. She specialised in painting enamel copies of oil pictures.

LITERATURE: Burke's 1889, p. 518. Garlick *et al.* 1978–84, vol. X, p. 3506. Foskett 1987, p. 596.

93. *Sophonisba*, 1810 (Illustrated overleaf)

SIGNED AND DATED: *S Essex Pinx / 1810*
15.7 x 12.5, enamel on copper
PROVENANCE: Jacob Nachemsohn Collection, 1926; presented by Sir Alfred Chester Beatty, 1951.
NGI 3581
LITERATURE: Williamson 1926, p. 23. NGI 1983, p. 141.

Sophonisba is usually represented as a beautiful and lavishly dressed woman and was a popular subject for seventeenth century artists. She was the daughter of Hasdrubal, the Carthaginian general at the time of the second Punic War. She married Syphax, a prince of neighbouring Numidia, which was allied to Rome, and succeeded in turning him against the Romans. Her husband was defeated and captured by Masinissa, another Numidian leader, who fell in love with Sophonisba and also married her. Scipio demanded that she be sent to Rome, to prevent further unrest, but her husband begged her to commit honourable suicide, which she did, with composure and serenity, drinking a cup of poison sent by him.[1]

During the early part of the nineteenth century it was extremely fashionable to collect and display enamel copies of Old Master pictures. The theme, here, of virtuous self-sacrifice would have had additional appeal. This enamel was copied from a picture, known then as *Sofonisba Regina* by Titian (c.1480– 1576), which was in the collection of Lord Kinnaird. Until recently, NGI 3581 was thought to be after the celebrated *Portrait of a lady in a fur wrap* (c.1535) by Titian in the Kunsthistorisches Museum, Vienna (in Germany by the early 18th century). It is actually from Lord Kinnaird's version of the Titian, which had been earlier copied by Henry Bone (1755–1834). He made an enamel version in 1808, which was exhibited at the Royal Academy the same year.[2] Both copies include a modesty drape across Sophonisba's breast and flowers in the corner. The original oil picture was sold at Christie's, 28 June 1816, lot 96, and is untraced.

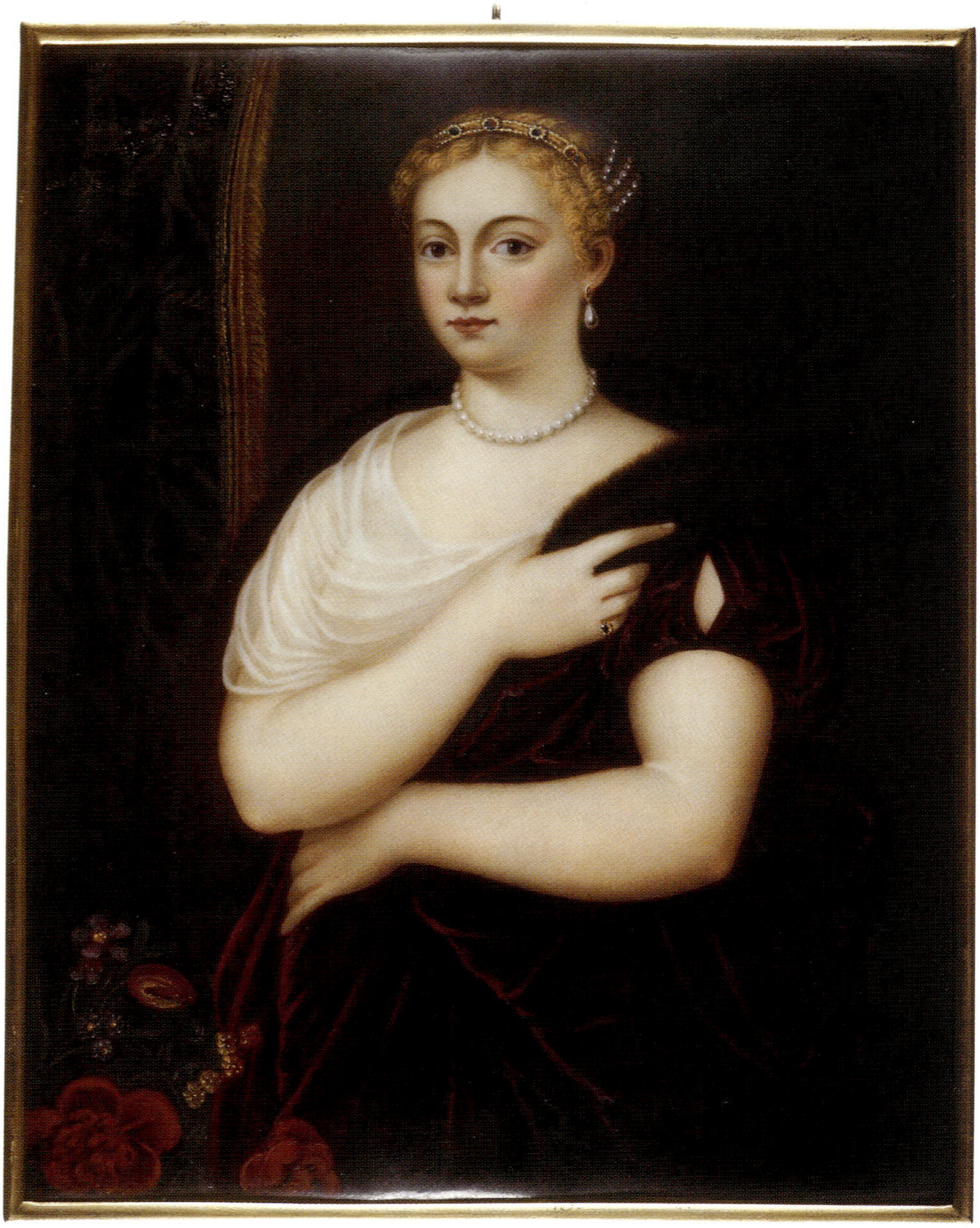

Cat. 93

Given the closeness in date of the Countess of Essex's miniature copy to Bone's, and their similar technique, it is surprising that there is no record of their meeting, or her perhaps taking instruction from him. She might, in fact, have had access to the same preliminary drawing, now in the NPGL. Equally, her technique is close to that of Bone. She was a proficient enamellist but, in this example, the copper has quite severely buckled in the firing, creating an undulating effect on the surface of the enamel.

REFERENCES: 1. Lemprière 1984, pp. 638–89. 2. Walker 1999, p. 359, no. 679, fig. 187.

GEORGE PLACE

Dublin c.1763~1805 Lucknow, India

Place was the son of a Dublin wholesale linen draper. He was trained at the Dublin Society Schools, which he entered on 7 December 1775.[1] Place practised in Dublin until 1791, when he went to London and York. Along with Sampson Towgood Roch (see catalogue entries 81–83) and Adam Buck (see catalogue entries 86–88), Place was one of the most accomplished Irish miniaturists to work in England during the 1790s. Like Samuel Andrews (?1767–1807) and George Chinnery (1774–1852), Place went to work in India, where he died.

LITERATURE: Pasquin 1796, p. 31. Strickland 1913, vol. II, p. 246. Caffrey 1999, p. 30.
REFERENCE: 1. RDS Proceedings 1775–76, vol. XII, p. 43.

94. *John F (possibly Hall)*, c.1790

INSCRIBED ON BACKING PAPER: John I.... [?Hall]
6.5 x 5, watercolour on ivory
Oval gold frame.
Formerly catalogued as English School (c.1780)
PROVENANCE: Miss Mary A. McNeill Bequest, 1985.
NGI 19280
LITERATURE: Le Harivel and Wynne, 1986, p. 128.

Place rarely signed his work and the attribution of this miniature to him rests entirely on his idiosyncratic style of painting and the technical details of the miniature. This miniature displays the two characteristic features of Place's style: a blue cloudy background and slightly exaggerated painting of the sitter's dark brown eyes. He tended to use a lot of blue in the shading of the face. In this example he paints the eyelids with long brushstrokes. There are portraits for comparison in the Victoria and Albert Museum, London.

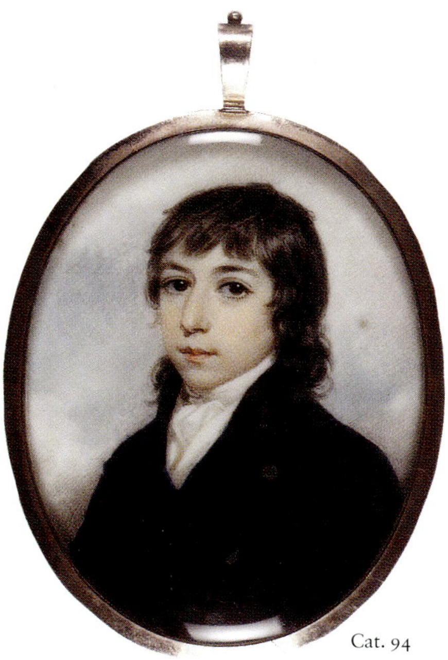

Cat. 94

JOHN COOKE

Dublin 1770~1805 Dublin

Cooke studied at the Dublin Society Schools. He was admitted to the Figure Drawing School on 2 November 1786.[1] He worked as a miniaturist in Dublin where he exhibited miniatures at the Society of Artists of Ireland exhibitions from 1800 to 1803.

LITERATURE: Strickland 1913, vol. I, p. 204. Stewart 1990, pp. 145–46. Caffrey 1999, p. 57.
REFERENCE: 1. RDS Proceedings 1786–87, vol. XXIII, pp. 5 and 25.

95. *Portrait of a young man in a brown coat*, 1800

SIGNED AND DATED: *J Cooke pinx 1800*
6.2 x 5, watercolour on ivory
Framed in a gold oval pendant.
PROVENANCE: purchased from Mr R. Harris, 1905.
NGI 2581
EXHIBITED: 1969–70 Dublin, London and Belfast, no. 153.
LITERATURE: NGI 1983, p. 75

The pose of the sitter and brushstrokes are reminiscent of work by Charles Robertson (1760–1821, see catalogue entries 90–92). The face is modelled in detail while the sky background and sitter's coat are painted in blotches of colour.

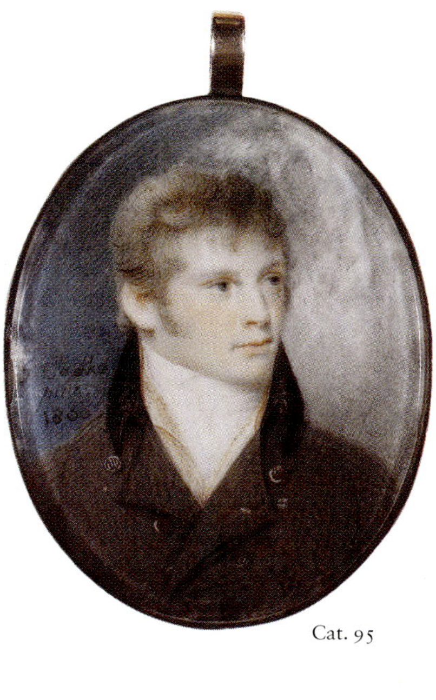

Cat. 95

JOHN COMERFORD

Kilkenny c.1770~1832 Dublin

John Comerford was the most prolific and successful miniaturist who spent his entire career in Ireland. He studied at the Dublin Society Schools in the late 1780s and received a drawing certificate in 1790 and a silver medal in 1791.[1] On leaving, Comerford divided his time between Kilkenny and Dublin. He was greatly influenced by the English artist George Chinnery (1774–1852), whom he met when Chinnery worked in Dublin 1795–1802. Chinnery's work was more freely painted in bold, broad, brushstrokes on relatively large pieces of ivory (examples in V&A). The larger cabinet miniature portraits allowed for more elaborate compositions, half-length portraits to be painted, and the inclusion of backgrounds or studio props such as a column or a piece of furniture. This new approach to miniature painting was quite different to the minutely detailed and highly finished technique perfected by Horace Hone (1754/56–1825/27, see catalogue entries 75–80), or Sampson Towgood Roch (1757–1847, see catalogue entries 81–83), that dominated miniature painting in Dublin during the 1790s.

Comerford adapted Chinnery's technique in formulating his own idiosyncratic style of miniature painting. Some of his work is both boldly painted, with finely finished details. The backgrounds are usually painted in broadly spaced parallel lines of varying dark blue and greyish tones with yellow cross-hatching. A characteristic, peculiar to Comerford's miniatures, is the reddish brown shading used in painting the sitter's face. The head is particularly well drawn and usually finely modelled in grey hatching giving a soft effect. In painting dress and details of costume, Comerford mixes his colours with gum arabic which produces flat areas of paint. He was particularly adept at painting the fashionable windswept men's hairstyles current in the early years of the nineteenth century. Comerford exhibited miniatures in Dublin in 1804, 1810, 1812 and 1813. In 1804, and again in 1809, he exhibited at the Royal Academy, London. Comerford was elected to the committee of the Society of Artists of Ireland and became its Vice-President.

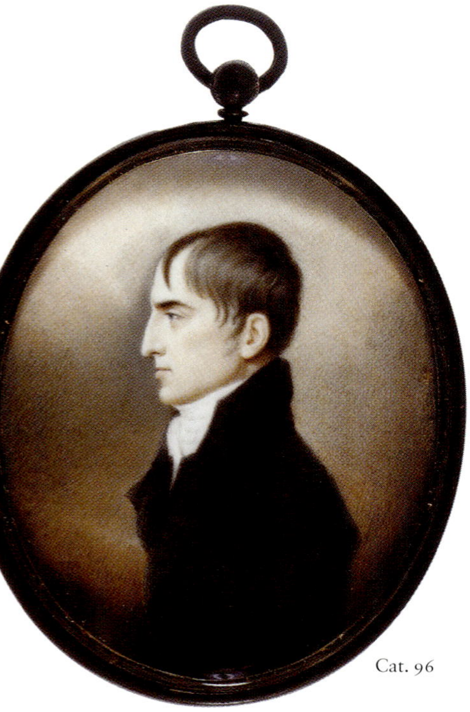

Cat. 96

From 1800 to 1823 (except for the years 1805–08), a variety of societies of artists held exhibitions in Dublin. Comerford was a popular figure in Irish artistic circles and he numbered among his friends Thomas James Mulvany RHA (1779–1845), who began his career as a miniaturist, Gaspar Gabrielli (active 1805–30), Vincent Waldré (c.1742–1814), James Gandon (1743–1823), Edward Smyth (1749–1812) and William Ashford (1746–1824). Thomas Sautell Roberts RHA (c.1760–1826) and Comerford collaborated in their work, Comerford often adding the figures or portraits to Roberts' landscapes.

Comerford taught Samuel Lover RHA (1797–1868, see catalogue entries 122–26) and John Doyle (1797–1868) to paint. His influence as a miniaturist may also be seen in the work of Thomas Clement Thompson RHA (1778/80–1857, see catalogue entry 108), who studied with Comerford.

LITERATURE: Mulvany and Gandon 1846, pp. 153–54. Strickland 1913, vol. I, pp. 194–202. Wynne in Crookshank and Glin 1969, p. 69. Stewart 1990, pp. 139–41. Conner 1993, pp. 31–46. Caffrey 1986, p. 52; 1987, pp. 42–47. Turpin 1995, pp. 96–97. Caffrey 1999, pp. 11–5 and 65–75 (List of known portraits painted by John Comerford).

REFERENCE: 1. RDS Proceedings 1789–90, vol. XXVI, p. 98; 1790–1, vol. XXVII, p. 81; 1820, vol. LVI, p. 35.

96. *Robert Emmet (1778–1803), Patriot,* c.1803

6.9 x 5.7, watercolour on ivory

ENGRAVED ON REVERSE OF THE CASE: *Robert Emmet / Born March 4th 1778 / Died Sep. 20th 1803* and inscribed on the reverse of Robert Temple Emmet's calling card: *Robert Emmet / Irish Patriot / My Great Grand Uncle / painted by Comerford / Dublin from a sketch made / at his trial*

Framed in a silver-gilt pendant, placed in a leather case.

PROVENANCE: by descent in the family of Emmet's brother Thomas Addis Emmet to Dr Thomas Addis Emmet of New York (grandnephew of Emmet); presented by Mr R. Emmet to the Government 1969 and transferred to the NGI, 1970.

NGI 7341

EXHIBITED: 1971 Cork, no. 21. 1976 Dallas, no. 97.

LITERATURE: NGI 1983, p. 65.

Son of a Dublin physician, Robert Emmet showed an early flair for oratory while at Trinity College. He was forced to leave University after joining the United Irishmen and he lived in France until 1802, lobbying support for an invasion to free Ireland. Back in Dublin from October 1802, he worked on assembling arms and recruits. An explosion in a depot precipitated an uprising on 23 July 1803, when Emmet and a handful of supporters marched on Dublin Castle, killing the Lord Chief Justice and his nephew. The rising failed and Emmet was arrested on 25 August. At his one-day trial at Green Street Court House on 19 September, he delivered a famous speech on liberty. He was hanged outside St Catherine's Church, Thomas Street.[1]

Miniatures of patriots and politicians were always popular in Ireland and were worn or displayed as expressions of political and national aspirations. In the period after the 1798 Uprising, and the abortive one of 1803, portraits of the leaders of the United Irishmen and the executed leaders such as Emmet were popular. Comerford and James Petrie (1750–1819) did sketches at Emmet's trial in 1803 (Petrie: NGI 7885–7886). Their work was later engraved (Illus. 48) and their profile portraits remain the seminal image of Emmet. Comerford's was based on a sketch done from life and owes much to the French republican tradition of portraiture. This is a sympathetic portrayal with delicate finish. A cruder version (NGI 2081) was painted by Henry Doyle (1827–1892).

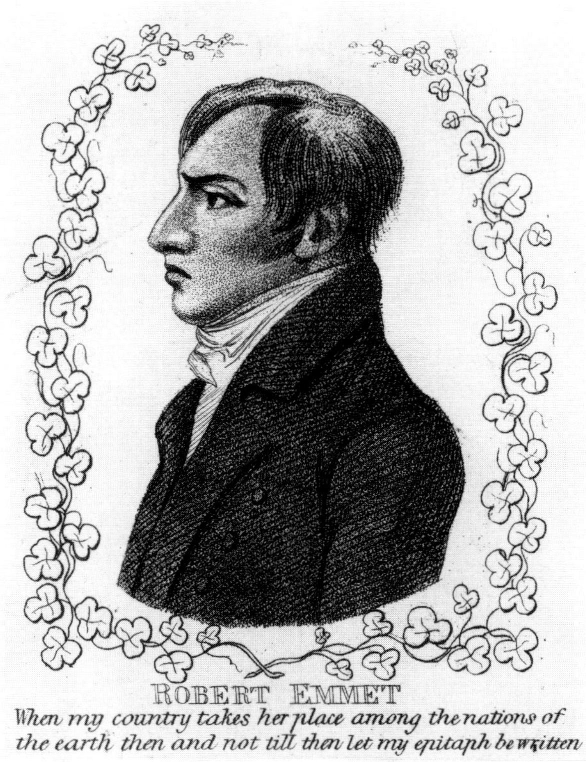

48. Anonymous commemorative print of Robert Emmet
after JAMES PETRIE
(NGI 11219)

REFERENCE: 1. DNB Vol. VI, pp. 180–81.

97. *Thomas Ellis, M.P., (1774–1832),* 1802 (Illustrated overleaf)

SIGNED AND DATED: *J. Comerford / 1802*

INSCRIBED ON REVERSE: *Thomas / Ellis of Abbotstown / sometime MP / for City of Dublin / Master in Chancery / B.1774. d.1832 / Castleknock / Buried in Castleknock / Ch Yard / Co. Dublin.*

7.2 x 5.8, watercolour on ivory

Framed in a gilt metal oval pendant.

PROVENANCE: presented to the NMI, 1939; transferred from the NMI, 1969.

NGI 7143

LITERATURE: Bence-Jones, 1978, p. 1. NGI 1983, p. 65.

President of the Royal Hibernian Academy in 1823, a year after this portrait was painted. William Cuming's oil portrait of Ashford was destroyed when the RHA building was burned in 1916.[2]

Comerford was a close friend of Ashford and he did several portraits of him.[3] He exhibited an earlier drawing of Ashford at the Society of Artists of Ireland exhibition in Dublin in 1802, which was engraved by Thomas Nugent in 1803.[4] This intimate miniature portrait shows a much older, bespectacled, painter, informally posed at work in his fur-lined dressing gown with a palate and brush in his hand. He was, in reality, painting little by this date. George Chinnery (1774–1852) encouraged Comerford to paint larger miniatures in imitation of oil portraits, of which this cabinet portrait is an example. It is relatively large and painted in broad brushstrokes of watercolour paint which are laden with gum arabic. The gum arabic gives the surface a glossy finish and the appearance of oil paint.

REFERENCES: 1. McParland 1985, p. 206. 2. Strickland 1913, vol. 1, plate II. 3. Mulvany and Gandon 1846, pp. 153–54. 4. Strickland 1913, vol. 1, plate II (second portrait).

FREDERICK BUCK

Cork 1771~1840 Cork

Frederick Buck was the younger son of Jonathan Buck, a silversmith of Castle Street, Cork. His brother was the miniaturist Adam Buck (1759–1833, see catalogue entries 86–88). On 5 December 1782 he was admitted to the Dublin Society Schools where he attended the Figure Drawing School and the Ornament School.[1] He does not appear to have excelled as a student, as his name does not appear in any of the list of prizes awarded by the Society. Buck returned to Cork, where he established himself as the leading miniaturist in the city. He had a large patronage and was particularly successful during the Napoleonic wars, when Cork was a significant military and naval centre. As it was a port of embarkation, Buck supplied the demand for keepsake miniatures of the young officers before they set off for war. He had a large output and twice as many examples as previously thought have now been identified in the NGI Collection.

LITERATURE: ffolliott 1984, pp. 46–50. Caffrey 1999, pp. 55–56.

REFERENCE: 1. RDS Proceedings 1782–83, vol. XIX, p. 42.

101. *Major Conyngham Ellis of the 40th Regiment, (1783–1815)*, c.1800

INSCRIBED ON BACKING PAPER: *Major / Conyngham / Ellis 40 Reg / b 1783– / d. 1815 from / wounds...* [indecipherable] */ at Waterloo / Buried in France.*
6.4 x 5.3, watercolour on ivory
Gilt metal oval pendant frame.
Formerly catalogued as Adam Buck (1759–1833)
PROVENANCE: presented to the NMI, 1939; transferred from the NMI, 1969.
NGI 7144
LITERATURE: NGI 1983, p. 27.

The inscription identifies this as an Irish Major who died from his wounds in 1815 after the defeat of Napoleon at the Battle of Waterloo. Buck's work is formulaic, particularly his military portraits. He may have had assistants who were employed to paint the blue sky backgrounds, bodies and uniforms. Buck would then add the heads in pink flesh tones and fill in the details on the sitter's regiment. As a result, much of his work appears stiffly posed.

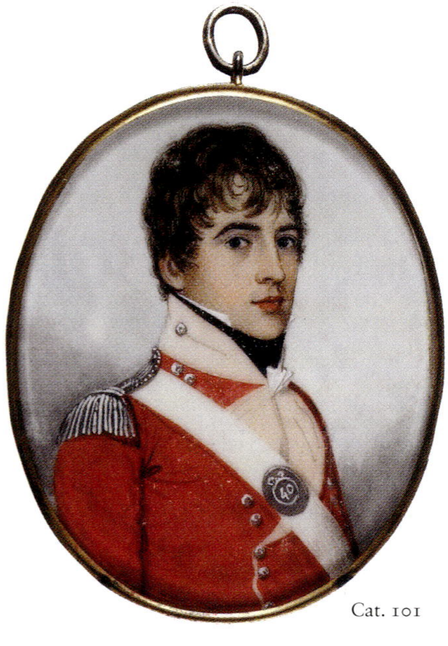

Cat. 101

102. *Mary O'Bryen*, 1807

INSCRIBED AND DATED ON BACKING PAPER: *My Dearest / Mother – / Mary O'Bryen / taken in / 1807 by Mr Buck / Cork*
6.3 x 5.3, watercolour on ivory
Set in a black *passe-partout* frame with a floral leaf clasp.
PROVENANCE: purchased by the NMI, 1915; transferred from the NMI, 1969.
NGI 7213
LITERATURE: NGI 1983, p. 28.

This is a good example of Buck's miniature portraits of a female sitter. She is posed against a pale blue sky and fashionably dressed in a white high-waisted dress, with her hair up in curls *à la grecque*. The rather elongated neck and shoulders are indicative of Frederick Buck's work.

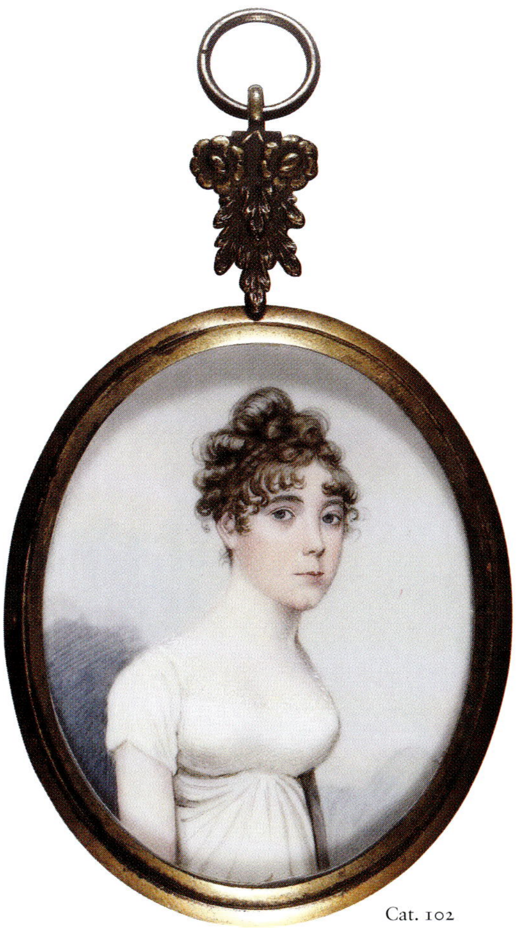

Cat. 102

JEAN-FRANÇOIS-MARIE HÜET-VILLIERS

Paris 1772–1813 London

Hüet was taught painting by his father. He adopted the name Hüet-Villiers after Villiers-sur-Orge where his father owned land. After serving in the army, he exhibited at the Salon from 1799 to 1812 and then went to England. He exhibited at the Royal Academy and the British Institution 1803–13. In 1805, he was appointed Miniature Painter to the Duke and Duchess of York and also painter to the exiled King of France. Hüet-Villiers worked in watercolour on ivory and marble, drew pastels, published some etchings and painted in oil. He painted portraits, mythological and fancy subjects.

LITERATURE: Long 1929, pp. 448–49. Foskett 1987, p. 572.

103. *George Macartney, 1st Earl Macartney, (1737–1806), Ambassador and Governor*, 1804
(Illustrated overleaf)

SIGNED AND DATED: *Villiers-Huet 1804*
INSCRIBED ON REVERSE OF FRAME: *Miniature by Villiers Huet 1804 / of / George, Earl Macartney, / b. 1737 d. 1806 / lot 224 in Sale of English Miniatures / 1750–1830 property of Lady Weardale /at Sotheby's, London, 14 May 1925 / R.S.L.*
8.9 x 7.1, watercolour on ivory
Oval pendant frame.
PROVENANCE: collection of Lady Weardale; sold at Sotheby's, London, 14 May 1925, lot 224; purchased by Anthony Thompson, January 1957; purchased by Miss Mary A. McNeill, date unknown; Miss Mary A. McNeill Bequest, 1985.
NGI 19289
LITERATURE: Le Harivel and Wynne 1986, p. 134.

George Macartney was born at Lissanoure, Co. Antrim. Macartney first visited Italy as a young man in 1761 and he was employed by Lord Holland as a tutor to young Stephen Fox in Geneva.[1] From 1764–68 he was Envoy and later Ambassador to Russia. He was Chief Secretary for Ireland from 1769–72. From 1775–79 he was Governor of

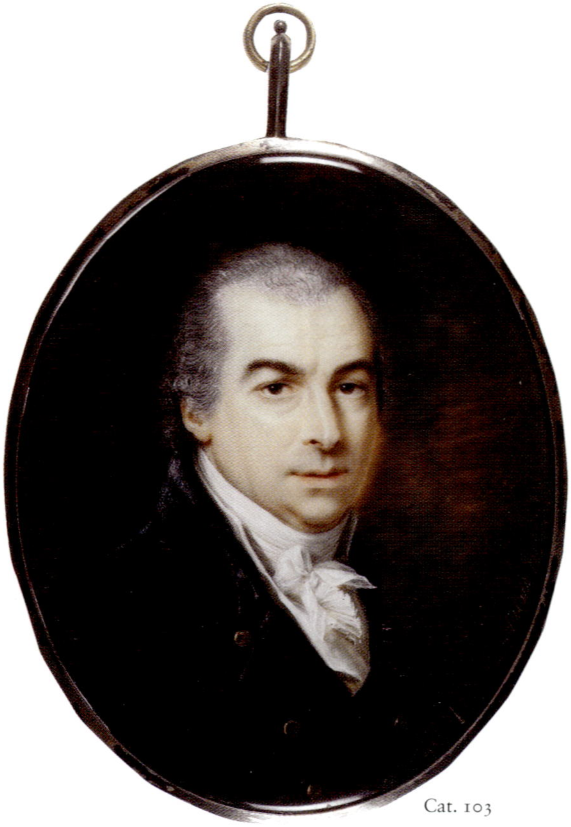

Cat. 103

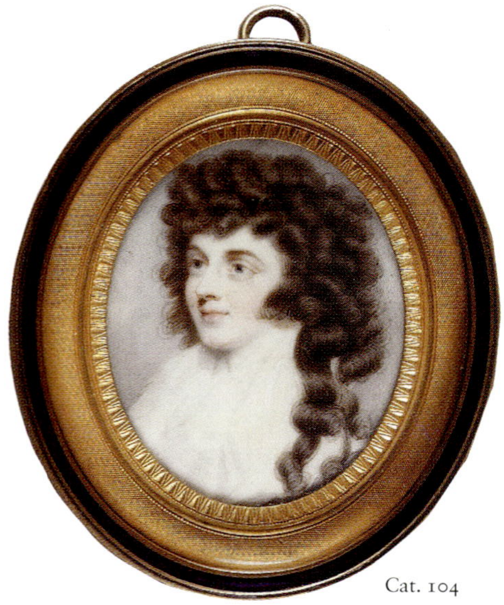

Cat. 104

Grenada, then Governor of Madras in 1781. In 1792 he was sent on a special Embassy to China, the first diplomatic contact between England and China. In 1795 he was sent on a confidential mission to Verona to the exiled Comte de Provence (later Louis XVIII of France).[2] While there, his portrait was drawn by an unknown artist (NPGL). From 1796–98 he was Governor of the Cape of Good Hope. He was created Baron Macartney in 1776 and Earl in 1794.[3] In his portrait, Hüet-Villier's uses watercolour mixed with gum arabic, which has an oily quality and gives the appearance of oil paint. The sitter is posed against a dark background. His hair is painted in grey wiry brush strokes.

REFERENCE: 1. Ingamells 1997, p. 621. 2. *ibid*, p. 621. 3. GEC vol. VIII, pp. 323–25.

JOHN BARRY

active London 1784~1827 (?) London

Very little is known about Barry's life and work. He exhibited at the Royal Academy from 1784 to 1827. He did not often sign his work, which may pass as by Thomas Hazlehurst (c.1740–1821).

LITERATURE: Long 1929, pp. 16–17.
Foskett 1987, p. 486.

104. *Portrait of a lady in a blue dress*, c.1790

4.4 x 3.5, watercolour on ivory
Gilt metal frame with a blue enamel border.
PROVENANCE: purchased by Miss Mary A. McNeill at Christie's, London, 20 October 1964, lot 36; Miss Mary A. McNeill Bequest, 1985.
NGI 19279
LITERATURE: Le Harivel and Wynne 1986, p. 128.

Very little is known about Barry's work, except that he had a distinctive style of painting which is exemplified by this miniature. Typical is the way the indeterminate contours of the sitter's white dress blend into the light-blue background. The detailed treatment of the curly locks of hair and curls is also characteristic.

WILLIAM BATE

active Dublin 1799~1845 (?) London

Bate was born into a family of Dublin jewellers and watchmakers. A William Bates (*sic*) is recorded as a pupil at the Dublin Society Schools in 1770,[1] but this could be a relation, as Bate's dated miniatures are much later. He was probably apprenticed to a member of his family, where he would have learned enamelling, which was used in the decoration of snuff-boxes, clock and watch faces, as well as in miniature portraiture. He worked as a watchmaker and miniaturist in Dublin. Later he had premises at

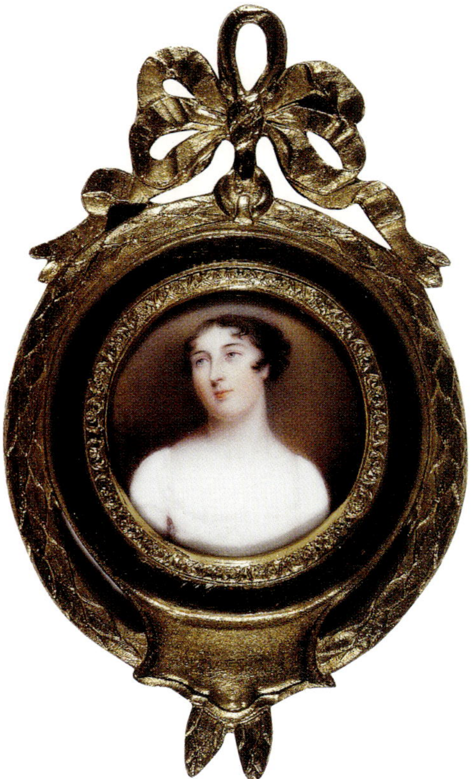

Cat. 105

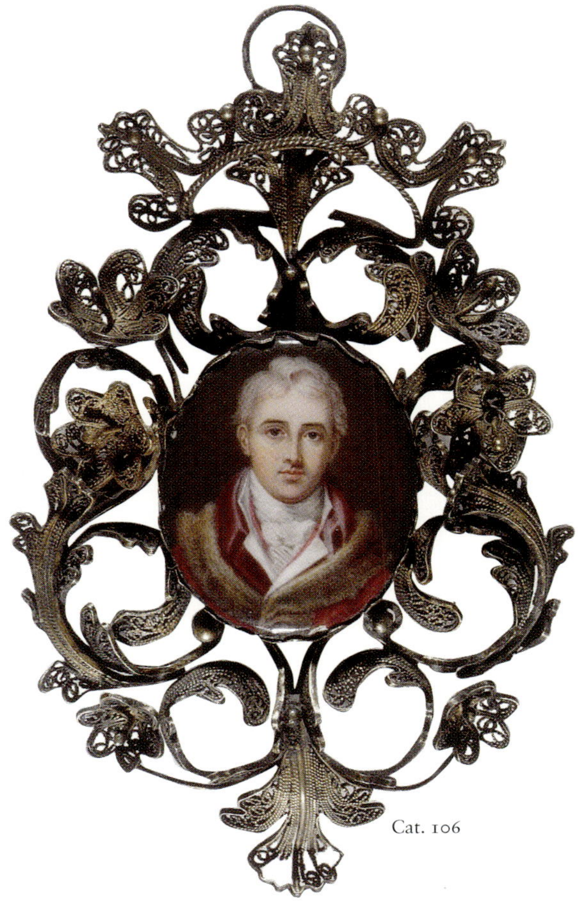

Cat. 106

Tivoli, Kingstown (Dun Laoghaire) and spent long periods in London. Bate exhibited miniatures at the Royal Academy from 1799 until 1827. About 1810, Bate was appointed Painter in Enamel to Princess Elizabeth, and Frederick, Duke of York (see NGI 3709). He had two sons, W.H. Bate (active 1808–27) and Thomas Bate (active 1809), both of whom were enamellists.

LITERATURE: Strickland 1913, vol. I, pp. 47–48.
REFERENCE: 1. RDS Proceedings, 1769–70, vol. VI, p. 107.

105. *Portrait of a lady in a white dress*, 1811

INSCRIBED, SIGNED AND DATED ON REVERSE:
Enamelled / by / Bate / Painter in Enamel / to H.R.H. / Princess Elizabeth / 1811
3.5 diam., enamel on copper
Set in an elaborate gilt metal frame.
PROVENANCE: Jacob Nachemsohn Collection, 1926; presented by Sir Alfred Chester Beatty, 1951.
NGI 3707
LITERATURE: Williamson 1926, p. 25. NGI 1983, p. 9.

Bate was primarily a copyist working from engravings, but this miniature of an unknown sitter was painted from life. It may be a posthumous portrait of Charlotte Edgeworth (1783–1807), being similar to the portraits by Elizabeth McCausland (active 1806–07, NGI 7549–7550, p. 183).

106. *Robert Stewart, Viscount Castlereagh, 2nd Marquess of Londonderry, (1769–1822)*, 1822

SIGNED: *WB* (in monogram)
INSCRIBED, SIGNED AND DATED ON REVERSE: *1822 Painted by Bate Painter to H.R.H. Princess Elizabeth*
3.9 x 3.2, enamel on copper
Set in an elaborate rococo-revival frame.
PROVENANCE: bequeathed by Lady Julia Fitzgerald, 1951.
NGI 2333
EXHIBITED: 1976 Dallas, no. 100.
LITERATURE: NGI 1983, p. 9.

Lord Castlereagh, the eminent statesman, was Secretary for Foreign Affairs. He was responsible for the Fourth Coalition of Great Britain, Russia, Prussia and Austria, which defeated Napoleon. He espoused Catholic Emancipation and the Union of Great Britain and Ireland. He was awarded the Order of the Garter. Castlereagh committed suicide in 1822.[1] Bate's enamel portrait is a commemorative miniature and was painted in the year of Castlereagh's death. Bate was an expert enamellist and he specialised in making copies of full-scale oil portraits, such as this version of Sir Thomas Lawrence's (1769–1830) portrait of Castlereagh. The original was exhibited at the Royal Academy in 1810, and is now in the National Portrait Gallery, London.

REFERENCE: 1. GEC vol. VIII, pp. 110–13.

ANDREW DUNN

active Ireland and London 1800~1820 London

Dunn may have been born in Dublin and attended the Dublin Society Schools under Francis Robert West (c.1749–1809). Dunn worked as a miniaturist in Waterford and Kilkenny before going to London. He returned briefly to Dublin in 1808 when he held an exhibition of his miniatures at the Dublin Society. Back in London, he exhibited at the Royal Academy from 1809–18 and sent works to various Dublin Societies of Artists from 1809 to 1819. Dunn was last recorded at 16, Norton Street, Fitzroy Square, in 1820.

LITERATURE: Herbert 1836, p. 55. Strickland 1913, vol. I, p. 309. Stewart 1990, pp. 204–05.

107. *Thomas Lewis O'Beirne, (c.1748– 1823), Bishop of Meath*, 1808

SIGNED AND DATED: *A. Dunn 1808.*

7.5 x 5.8, watercolour on ivory

PROVENANCE: presented by Mrs Christina Edgeworth Colvin, Oxford, 1967.

NGI 6314

EXHIBITED: 1809 Dublin, no. 200.

LITERATURE: NGI 1983, p. 121.

Thomas Lewis O'Beirne converted from Catholicism to Protestantism and rose to become Bishop of Meath. It was one of the wealthiest dioceses, with a recently completed neo-classical Bishop's Palace at

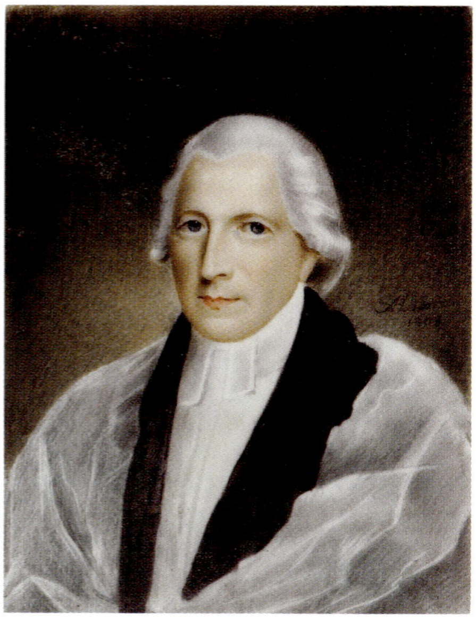

Cat. 107

Ardbraccan. Earlier in his career, he had been Rector of Templemichael, Longford, where his brother was an impoverished Catholic parish priest, known as 'The Dean'. O'Beirne was to ignore him later and gained a reputation as a notorious apostate.[1] His portrait suggests a more benign character. It is, significantly, a rare signed and dated miniature by Andrew Dunn. One trait of his is to slightly exaggerate the size of the pupil of the eye. The background and shading are painted in blotch stipple.

REFERENCE: 1. McNamee 1954, pp. 389, 555 and 652.

THOMAS CLEMENT THOMPSON RHA

Belfast c.1778~1857 Cheltenham

Thompson is thought to have been born in Belfast. He studied at the Dublin Society Schools where he was admitted to the Figure Drawing School on 7 July 1796.[1] Thompson was taught miniature painting by John Comerford (c. 1770–1832, see catalogue entries 96–100). He exhibited miniatures at the Society of Artists of Ireland 1801–02 and was working in Belfast during 1803. By 1809 he had taken up oil painting, which was to dominate his later career. He was exhibiting almost annually in Dublin from 1810–21, and then at the newly founded Royal Hibernian Academy from 1826–52. Thompson settled in London in 1817 and moved to Cheltenham in 1848. There is an oil self-portrait at his easel (NGI 575).

LITERATURE: Strickland 1913, vol. 2, pp. 438–49. Stewart 1995, pp. 707–08. Caffrey 1999, p. 49.
REFERENCE: 1. RDS Proceedings 1795–96, vol. II, p. 230. 1796–97, vol. III, p. 517.

108. *Mrs Reid, wife of Captain Reid of Co. Tipperary,* 1799

SIGNED AND DATED: *T Thompson / 1799*
6.8 x 5.6, watercolour on ivory
Gold oval pendant setting with a lock of the sitter's hair interwoven on the reverse.
PROVENANCE: purchased by the NMI, 1911; transferred from the NMI, 1969.
NGI 7084
LITERATURE: NGI 1983, p. 695.

The portrait is an early work which shows the influence of Comerford. His sitter's face is shaded in strong grey hatched lines. She is posed against a blue cloudy sky background which is broadly painted in parallel lines of colour. The dress is sketched in broad brushstrokes.

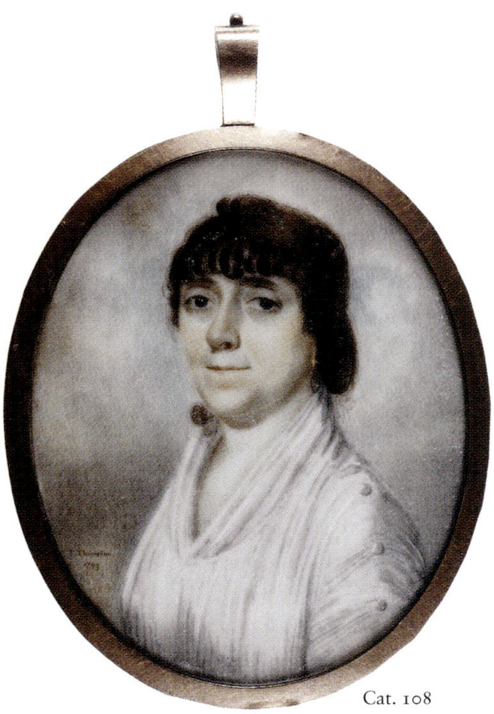

Cat. 108

HENRY PIERCE BONE

London (Islington) 1779~1855 London

Henry Pierce Bone was the eldest son of miniaturist Henry Bone (1755–1834, see catalogue entries 68–73). He assisted his father, so learning the craft of enamelling. He studied at the Royal Academy Schools from 1796 and exhibited work at the Royal Academy and British Institution from 1799 to 1855. Like his father he was prolific, and specialised in making enamel copies of oil paintings. He was appointed Enamel Painter to Queen Adelaide, the Duchess of Kent and her daughter, future Queen Victoria, in 1833, and to Prince Albert in 1841. In 1846 he published a catalogue of his enamels. Three of his children were enamellists: Charles Richard Bone (1809–c.1880), William Bone Junior (active 1827–1851) and Louisa Frances Bone (active c.1844).

LITERATURE: DNB vol. II, p. 806. Long 1929, pp. 40–41. Foskett 1987, pp. 495–96.

109. *William Villiers, Viscount Grandison, (1613–43),* 1838 (Illustrated overleaf)

INSCRIBED, SIGNED AND DATED ON REVERSE: *William Villiers Lord Grandison / London May 1838 Painted for / J.P. Ord Esq by Henry Pierce Bone / Enamel Painter to the Queen Dowager /& her R H the Duchess of Kent from the Original / by Van Dyck in the Collection of the Earl / of Clarendon The Grove. Herts.*
21 x 16.8, enamel on copper
Gilt metal frame.
PROVENANCE: Jacob Nachemsohn Collection, 1926; presented by Sir Alfred Chester Beatty, 1951.
NGI 3568
LITERATURE: Williamson 1926, p. 22. NGI 1983, p. 16.

Henry Pierce Bone's three-quarter length portrait is a copy of the full length portrait of Viscount Grandison by Van Dyck, which passed by descent in the Villiers family to the Earls of Clarendon (Illus. 49 overleaf). The enamel captures the stunning silk detail of the original. Grandison wears a red jacket with

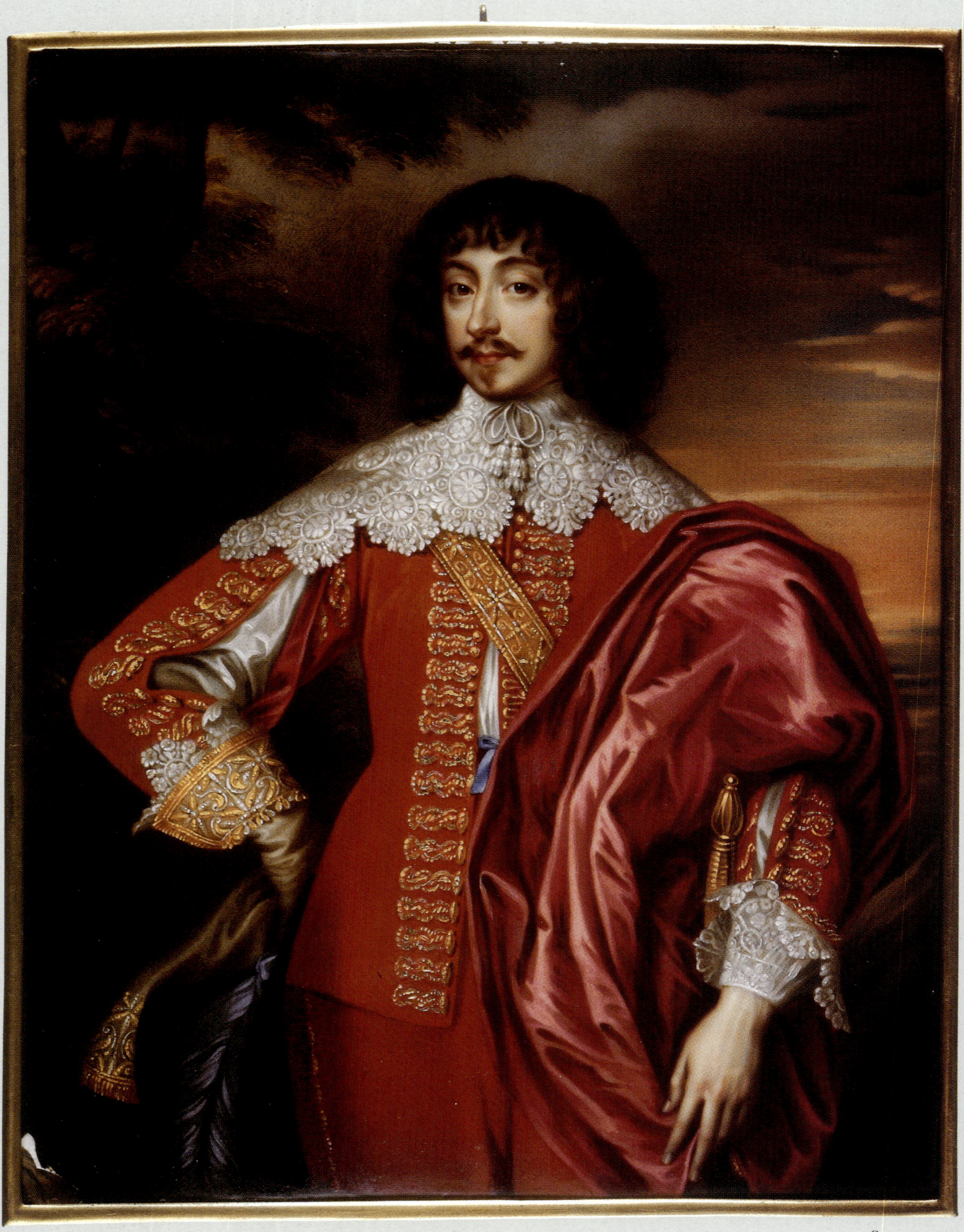

Cat. 109

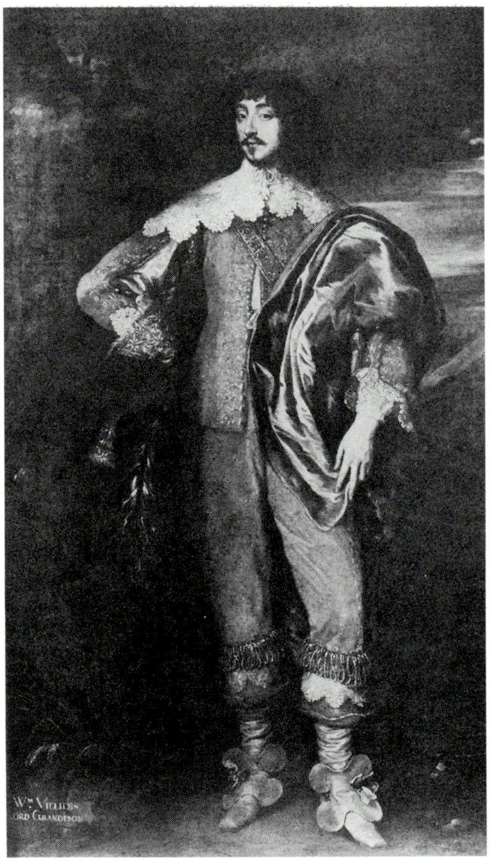

49. *William Villiers, Viscount Grandison*, c.1632
ANTHONY VAN DYCK
(Clarendon Park, Herts.)

gold embroidery and slashed sleeves which reveals his white shirt beneath. The shirt has a deep white lace collar and cuffs. Across his left shoulder is a red cloak and in his right hand he holds a black hat with a large blue feather. The enamel surface is chipped in the left corner. Van Dyck's portrait dates to his final years in England after 1632, when he was working for Charles I and his court, of which Grandison was a prominent member. He was a distinguished soldier and died from a wound he received at the siege of Bristol in 1643 during the Civil War.[1]

Bone's enamel was commissioned by J. Pickering Ord, of Edge Hill, Duffield, Derbyshire, who was a collector of enamel copies of Old Master paintings. Ord was a substantial patron of Henry Bone (Henry Pierce Bone's father), and other members of the family. He commissioned them to execute at least seventeen enamels.[2] At Clarendon Park, Henry Bone copied Van Dyck's *Countess of Newburgh*.

REFERENCES: 1. GEC vol. VI, p. 75. Burke's 1889, p. 764.
2. Walker 1999, pp. 306, 308, 365.

110. *Ninon de Lenclos, (1620–1705), Beauty and Courtesan*, 1845

INSCRIBED, SIGNED AND DATED ON REVERSE: *Ninon / de L'Enclos./ London Sepr. /1845. / Painted by Henry / Pierce Bone / Enamel / Painter to her Majesty & / H.R.H. Prince Albert / Etc From the original / by Mignard.*
5 x 4, enamel on copper
Set in an oval gilt metal pendant frame.
PROVENANCE: Jacob Nachemsohn Collection, 1926; presented by Sir Alfred Chester Beatty, 1951.
NGI 3618
LITERATURE: Williamson 1926, p. 25. NGI 1983, p. 17.

Ninon de Lenclos was a great beauty, salon hostess and wit. Her salon was frequented by St Evremond, Molière and the young Voltaire. Bone's enamel is a reduced copy of a portrait by Pierre Mignard (1612–1695), the principal court painter to Louis XIV. A portrait of her by Henry Bone (1755–1834) after miniaturist Jean Petitot, is in the Wallace Collection, London.[1]

REFERENCE: 1. Reynolds 1980, pp. 313–34.

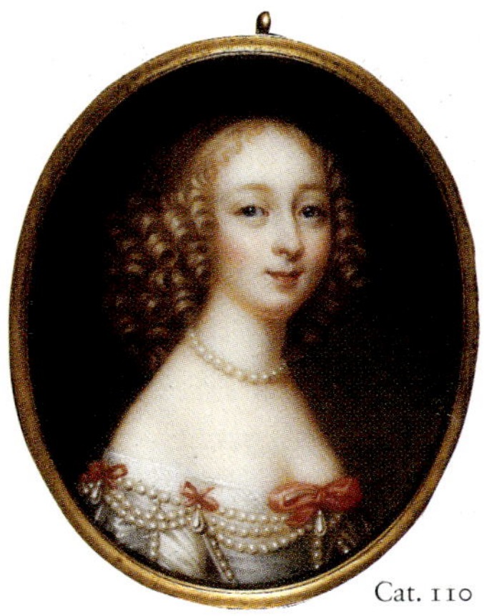

Cat. 110

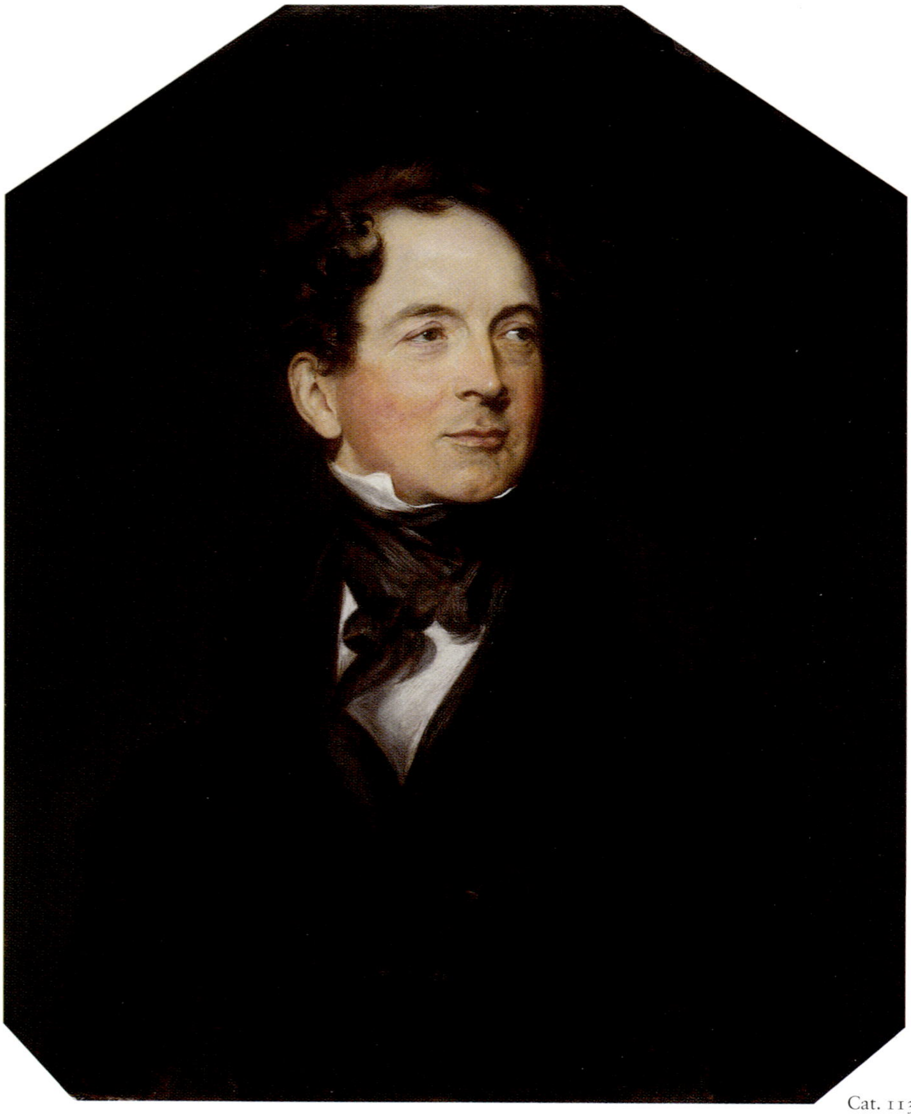

Cat. 113, as framed

WILLIAM ESSEX

(?) London 1784~1869 Brighton

Essex exhibited at the Royal Academy, British Institution, and the Society of British Artists from 1818 to 1864. He specialised in painting copies of portraits in enamel. In 1839, he was appointed enamel painter to Queen Victoria and in 1841, to Prince Albert. Essex taught the enamellists John Williams Bailey (1831–1914) and William Bishop Ford (1832–1922). His son William B. Essex (c.1823–1852) was also an enamellist.

LITERATURE: Foskett 1987, pp. 536–37.

113. *Thomas Moore, (1779–1852), Poet,* 1838

INSCRIBED, SIGNED AND DATED (under the frame): *Thomas Moore Esqr. / Painted after the Original Picture / by Sir Tho. Lawrence P.R.A. by / W. Essex. 1838. Enamel / Painter to Her Majesty*

Inscribed and signed on reverse of frame: *Thos. Moore Esqr / Author of the Irish Melodies etc etc / Painted from the Origl. picture / by Sir Thos. Lawrence P.R.A. / Wm. Essex Enamel painter / to Her Majesty & the Prince Consort. / 2 Osnaburgh Street / Regents Park*

33 diam., enamel on copper

Gilt cabinet frame (J.&W. Vokins, London).

PROVENANCE: purchased from Mr Horace Buttery, London, 1906.

NGI 4015

LITERATURE: NGI 1981, p. 47.

Thomas Moore was born in Dublin at 12, Aungier Street. On graduating from Trinity College, Dublin, in 1799, he went to London, where he established his literary reputation with his translation of the *Odes of Anacreon*, which was published in 1800. Moore's *Irish Melodies* (begun in 1807 and completed in 1834) was his greatest achievement. There are many portraits of him.

Essex's large portrait of Moore is copied from an incomplete head and shoulders portrait by Thomas Lawrence (1769–1830), sat for in 1829 and exhibited at the Royal Academy in 1830 (John Murray Collection).[1] The painterly qualities of the original oil and its brushwork are retained. The work is painted in enamel on a circular dish-shaped copper plate. The slightly domed shape of the copper helps to give strength to the base and prevented warping in the kiln when the enamel was being fired. The curved surface also adds depth to the portrait and allows the colours to fire with a smoother surface.

Essex would have made a preliminary drawing of Lawrence's portrait of Moore and then made a drawing on tracing paper. An outline was then transferred to the enamel surface. The details of the face and hair were painted first in metallic paints. When the image was painted, it was then fired in a kiln to fuse with the enamel surface. After this was achieved, the dark areas, costume and background, were painted in and fired.

REFERENCE: 1. Walker 1985, vol. 1, p. 345.

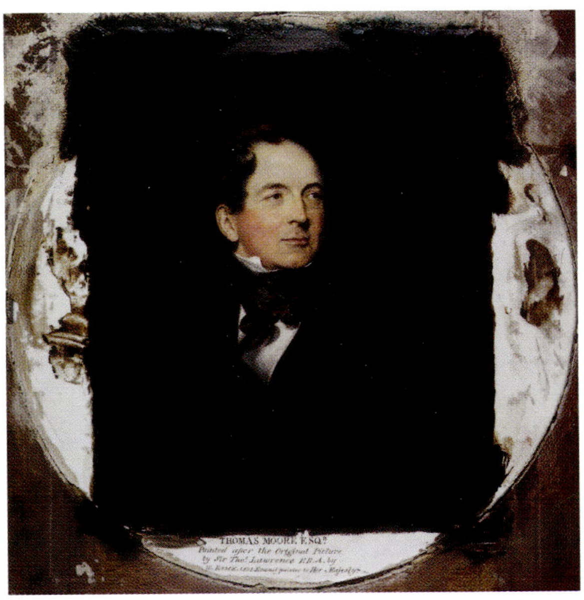

Cat. 113

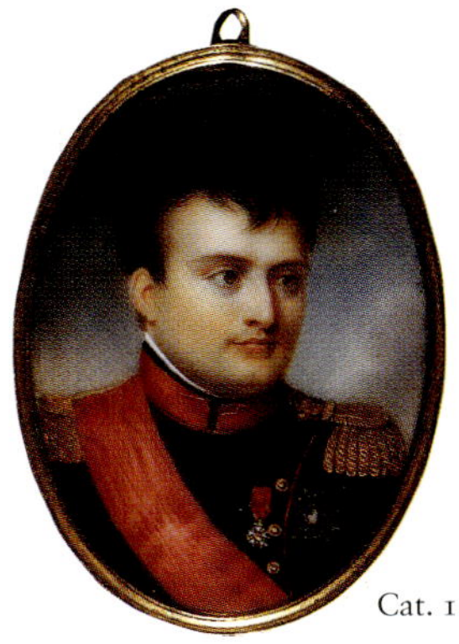

Cat. 114

114. *Napoleon I, Emperor of France (1769–1821)*, 1832

SIGNED: *W. Essex*

INSCRIBED, SIGNED AND DATED ON REVERSE: *W. Essex Pt. 1832 / Enamel Painter to H.R.H. the Princess Augusta*

4.2 x 3, enamel on copper

Oval gilt metal frame.

PROVENANCE: Jacob Nachemsohn Collection, 1926; presented by Sir Alfred Chester Beatty, 1951.

NGI 3617

LITERATURE: Williamson 1926, p. 25. NGI 1983, p. 142.

Napoleon I rose from the army to rule France as Emperor from 1804–14 and briefly returned from exile in 1815. Although often an enemy of England, he had his admirers even during periods of war and there was a great demand for portraits of him in his lifetime and afterwards. Napoleon is wearing the uniform of the *chasseurs-à-cheval*, dark green with a red collar and red piping, and the ribbon and cross of the Grand Eagle of the Legion of Honour with the Iron Crown of Lombardy. Essex painted this enamel after Jean-Baptiste-Jacques Augustin's (1759–1832) portrait of c.1810, the year in which Napoleon founded the Order of the Iron Crown of Lombardy. There are two such portraits by Augustin of Napoleon in the Wallace Collection, London.[1] Augustin was, with Jean-Baptiste Isabey (1767–1855), the leading French miniaturist of the early nineteenth century.

REFERENCE: 1. Reynolds 1980, pp. 197–98, nos. 169–70.

PETER JOSEPH BONE

London 1785~1814 near Toulouse

Peter Joseph Bone was taught enamelling by his father Henry Bone (1755–1834, see catalogue entries 68–73) whose preparatory drawings for enamels he reused in his own work. He was awarded a silver palette by the Society of Arts in 1800–01 for drawing. He later joined the army and died from wounds near Toulouse.

LITERATURE: Long 1929, p. 41. Foskett 1987, pp. 495–96.

115. *Dr John Wolcot, (1738–1819), Physician and Satirist 'Peter Pindar'*, 1801

INSCRIBED, SIGNED AND DATED ON REVERSE: *Doctor Walcot / Painted in Enamel after / a picture by John Opie Esqr / RA by Peter Joseph Bone / May 1801*
10.2 x 8.2, enamel on copper
Oval gilt metal pendant frame.
PROVENANCE: Jacob Nachemsohn Collection, 1926; presented by Sir Alfred Chester Beatty, 1951.
NGI 3580
LITERATURE: Williamson 1926, p. 22. NGI 1983, p. 17. Walker 1999, p. 350, no. 558.

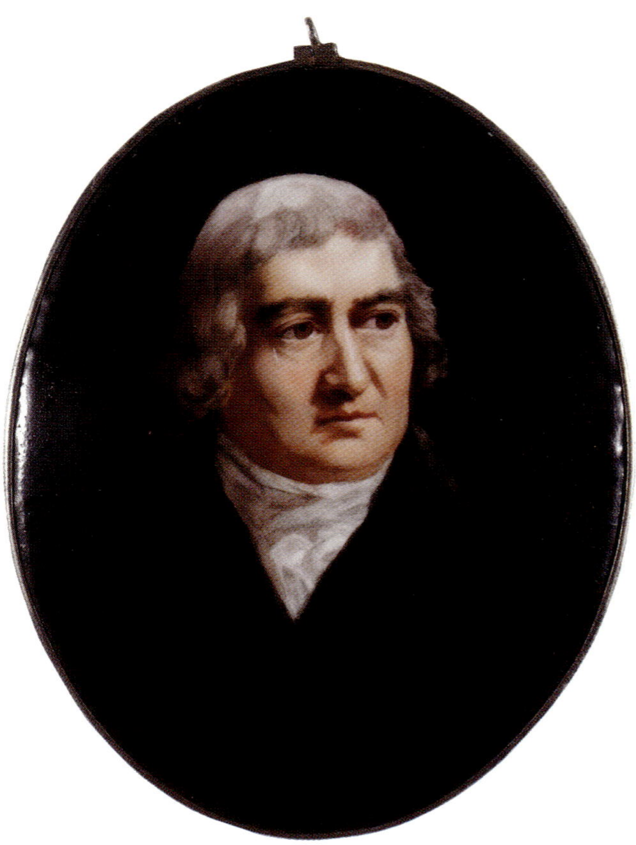

Dr John Wolcot was a physician and satirist who used the pseudonym 'Peter Pindar'. After studying medicine at Aberdeen he went to Jamaica, where he was physician to Sir George Trelawny, the governor, in 1767–69. He was ordained in 1769, but then forsook the church. He wrote more than seventy satirical works and, because of his knowledge of art, his best satires were on artists, such as Benjamin West (see catalogue entry 69). He became famous for his *Lyric Odes to the Royal Academicians* (1782–85).[1]

Walcot practised medicine in Cornwall, where he came into contact with the young painters, John Opie (1761–1807) and Henry Bone (1755–1834, see catalogue entries 68–73). He was responsible for promoting the young Opie as the 'Cornish Wonder' an untutored natural genius. Walcot gave up medicine and accompanied Opie to London. Peter Joseph Bone's father Henry Bone owed some his success as an enamellist to Wolcot, who was his patron. Wolcot wrote to Ozias Humphry recommending him for election to the Royal Academy.[2]

Henry Bone did preparatory sketches, probably from life, for enamel portraits of Wolcot, in 1793.[3] A version in watercolour on ivory, dated the same year, is in the Victoria and Albert Museum.

REFERENCES: 1. DNB vol. XXI, pp. 761–64. 2. Long 1929, p. 37. 3. Walker 1999, p. 350, no. 558.

WILLIAM JOHN NEWTON

London 1785~1869 London

He was the son of James Newton (1748–1804) the engraver. William Newton attended the Royal Academy Schools and exhibited at the Royal Academy and British Institution from 1808 to 1863. In 1833, he was appointed Miniature Painter to William IV and Queen Adelaide and in 1837 made Painter to Queen Victoria and knighted.

LITERATURE: Long 1929, pp. 311–12. Foskett 1987, p. 607.

Cat. 115

116. *Eliza O'Neill, (1791–1872), Actress, Mrs, later, Lady, Wrixon-Becher,* 1826

SIGNED AND DATED: *W.J. Newton. 1826*
18 x 13, watercolour on ivory
Cabinet frame (J.&W. Vokins, London).
PROVENANCE: purchased at Christie's, London, 1890.
NGI 2206
LITERATURE: Fleming-Williams 1971, p. 1784.
NGI 1983, p. 569.

Eliza O'Neill was born in Drogheda, the daughter of a stage-manager. She had a short but highly successful career as an actress, first in Belfast and then in Dublin and London. At Covent Garden in 1814 she played the role of Juliet to an ecstatic audience and was declared the successor to Sarah Siddons.[1] In 1819, she left the stage to marry William Wrixon-Becher, M.P. (1780–1850), of Ballygiblin, Mallow, Co. Cork, who was made a baronet in 1831.[2]

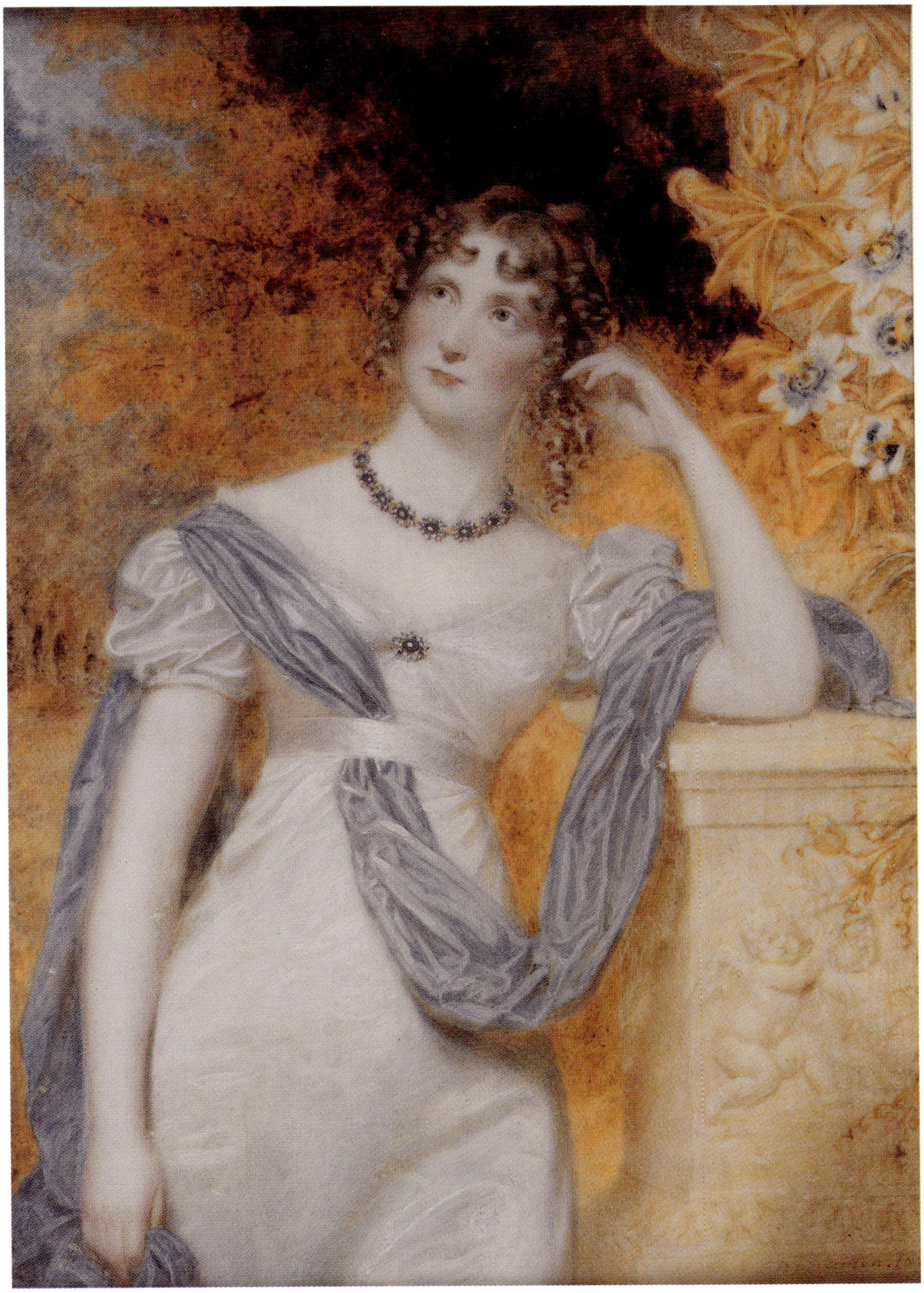

Cat. 116

Newton painted relatively large portraits on sheets of ivory, which allowed space for a background and props, such as the plinth in this cabinet portrait. By the 1820s, miniaturists were expected to aspire towards full-scale oil portraiture in composition and pose. O'Neill is shown in a romantic garden setting, posed gazing dreamily into the distance. A piece of drapery is artistically arranged across her shoulder, and she leans, in traditional reflective pose, on a plinth which has a classical relief carved on its side. She is framed with delicately painted passion flowers.

REFERENCES: 1. Fleming-Williams 1971, p. 1784.
2. Burke's 1889, p. 115.

G. JACKSON

active (?) Dublin c. 1810

Nothing is known of Jackson's life and work, who must have been presumed to be Irish when this miniature was acquired in the nineteenth century.

117. *Self-Portrait*, 1810

SIGNED AND DATED: *G Jackson 1810*
7.1 x 5.7, watercolour on ivory
Set in a gold oval pendant frame, which has an elaborate reverse containing two locks of the sitter's hair decorated with blue glass hearts and seed pearls (Illus. 13).
PROVENANCE: purchased at Christie's, London, 1889.
NGI 2376
LITERATURE: NGI 1983, p. 417.

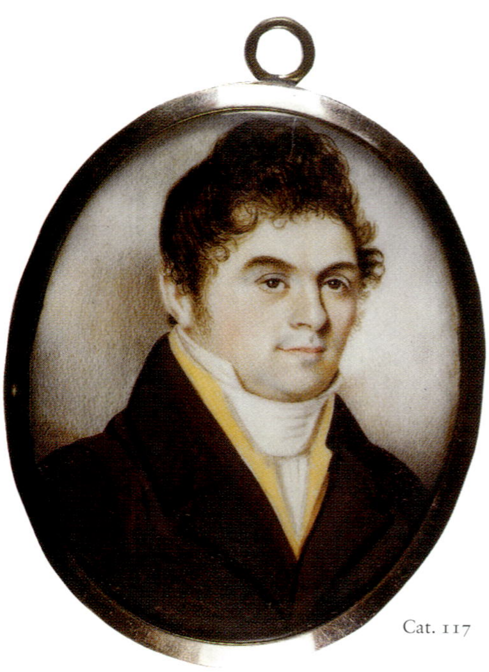
Cat. 117

Jackson's self-portrait is his only known work. It is well painted and shows Jackson as a fashionably dressed young man with short cropped hair.

WILLIAM BONE, SENIOR

active London 1815~1843 London

William Bone was the son of Henry Bone (1755–1834, see catalogue entries 68–73). He exhibited at the Royal Academy from 1815–43. In 1842 he was appointed Enamel Painter to the King of Hanover. He was taught enamelling by his father and he often reused preparatory drawings done by him.

LITERATURE: Long 1929, pp. 41–42. Foskett 1987, p. 496.

118. *Henry Bone, (1755–1834), Enamellist, the artist's father,* 1842

SIGNED: *WBone* (WB in monogram)
INSCRIBED, SIGNED AND DATED ON REVERSE: *Portrait of Henry Bone Esq RA born / at Truro in Cornwall Feby 6th 1755 died in / Somers Town near London Decr 17th 1834 / Painted in enamel by William Bone / one of his sons from an original picture / painted from life by the late Robert Trewick / Bone another of his sons. / The portrait in the background is that / of Elizabeth the wife of Mr Bone / London / May 1842*
16.1 x 13.4, enamel on copper
Gilt metal frame.
PROVENANCE: Jacob Nachemsohn Collection, 1926; presented by Sir Alfred Chester Beatty, 1951.
NGI 7338
LITERATURE: Williamson 1926, p. 22. NGI 1983, p. 18.

William Bone's enamel is a copy of an enamel portrait by Robert Trewick Bone of their father, exhibited at the Society of British Artists in 1831.[1] It shows Bone seated in the drawing room of his house, 15, Berners Street, Marylebone. It was a popular street for artists. John Opie, Henry Fuseli and the architect, William Chambers, had all lived there. On the wall behind Henry Bone, is a portrait of his wife, Elizabeth van der Meulen (1762–1826). William Bone's enamel, in this instance, was painted after Henry and Elizabeth

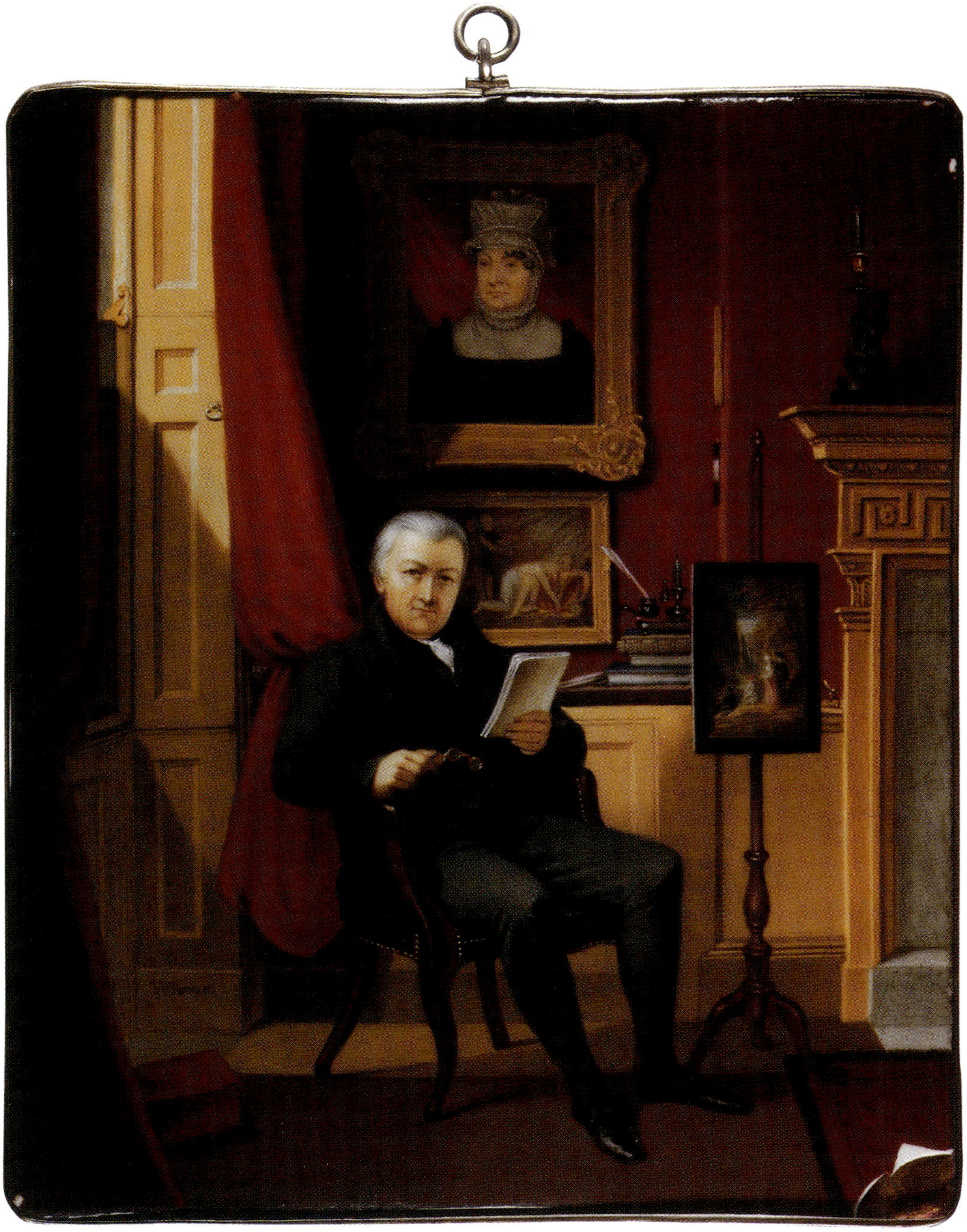

Cat. 118

Bone's death. The enamel surface is chipped in the right-hand corner. There is a watercolour on ivory portrait of Henry Bone by William Bone, painted during his father's lifetime, in 1828, in the NPGL. He is presented there more as a collector, than an artist. A portrait of Elizabeth van der Meulen by Henry Bone, dated 1779, the year before their marriage, is in the Victoria and Albert Museum.

REFERENCE: 1. Walker 1985, vol. I, p. 57.

119. *Charles James Fox, M.P., (1749–1806), Statesman,* c.1842 (Illustrated overleaf)

INSCRIBED SIGNED AND DATED ON REVERSE: *Rt Honble Charles James / Fox Born Jan 13 1749 / died Sept 1806 after the / original by Opie RA / Painted by WBone Enamel / painter to the King of / Hanover etc etc / London*

12 x 9.9, enamel on copper

Gilt metal frame.

PROVENANCE: Jacob Nachemsohn Collection, 1926; presented by Sir Alfred Chester Beatty, 1951.

NGI 3578

LITERATURE: Williamson 1926, p. 22. NGI 1983, p. 17.

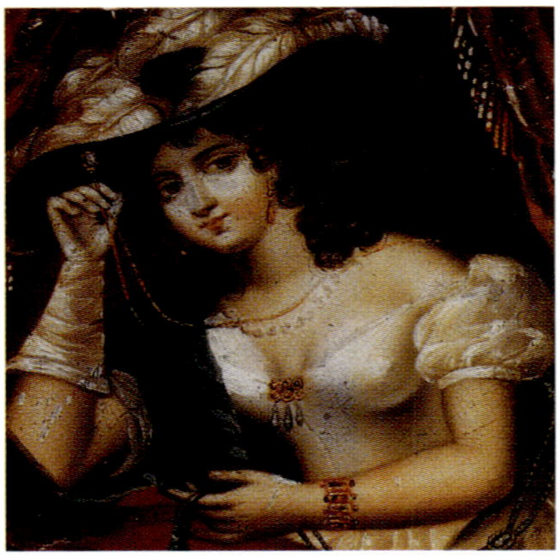

Cat. 122

122. *Imaginary portrait of Lady Morgan (born Sydney Owenson, 1776–1859), Author, at the Opera in the Theatre Royal,* late 1820s

SIGNED: *S.L.* 5.3 x 5.2, oil on metal
Cabinet frame.
PROVENANCE: presented to the NMI by Mrs Maev Sullivan, Dublin, 1949; transferred from the NMI, 1969.
NGI 7509
LITERATURE: NGI 1983, p. 476.

Lady Morgan, novelist, travel writer and art historian, was the daughter of an actor-manager, Robert Owenson (originally Mac Owen).[1] She was said to have been born on the mail boat on the Irish Sea on Christmas Day in 1776. When her father went bankrupt, she became a governess for the Fetherstonhaugh family at Bracklyn Castle, Killucan, Co. Westmeath, where she became well-known as a harpist. In 1805, she achieved national prominence with the publication of her collection of Irish music, one of the first to be compiled. The next year was marked by the publishing of her novel *The Wild Irish Girl*, which was based on events that took place in her father's family, and from reminiscences of time she spent in the West of Ireland. This book brought her a cult following and she became known as 'Glorvina' or 'The Wild Irish Girl'. In 1823 she published her biography of Salvator Rosa. She accepted the Marquess and Marchioness of Abercorn's invitation to stay with them at Barons Court, Co. Tyrone, and later married their physician, Thomas Charles Morgan, who was subsequently knighted.

In Dublin, the flamboyant Lady Morgan had her artistic salon at her house in Kildare Street, which Samuel Lover attended. She was the 'dictatress' of Irish artistic, theatrical, literary and musical society. Through her connections, Lover met important patrons and she encouraged him to paint and write musical comedy. Lover's portrait is an imaginary evocation of the young Lady Morgan and reflects his admiration for her. She is elaborately dressed in an evening gown and broad brimmed hat decorated with ostrich feathers. She is holding a pair of opera glasses and is seated in a box at the Theatre Royal, Dublin. She was, in reality, short, and not beautiful by the usual standards. Lady Morgan's favourite portrait was that as a Classical Sibyl by René Berthon (1776–1859), brought back from Paris (NGI 133). Lover painted several idealised portraits of her, and a version of this miniature is in the collection of the Royal Irish Academy. Another, less flattering, portrait, from a Lover drawing, was engraved by Robert Cooper (active 1795–1836) in 1825 (NGI 10959, Illus. 50). This miniature is a rare early example of Lover's work in oils.

REFERENCE: 1. DNB vol. XIII, pp. 924–26.

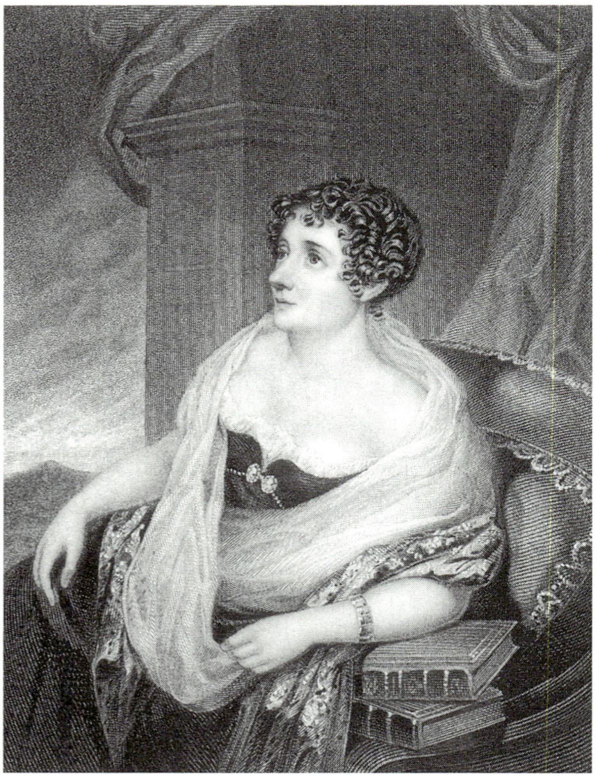

50. Print after drawing of Lady Morgan, 1825
ROBERT COOPER after SAMUEL LOVER
(NGI 20959)

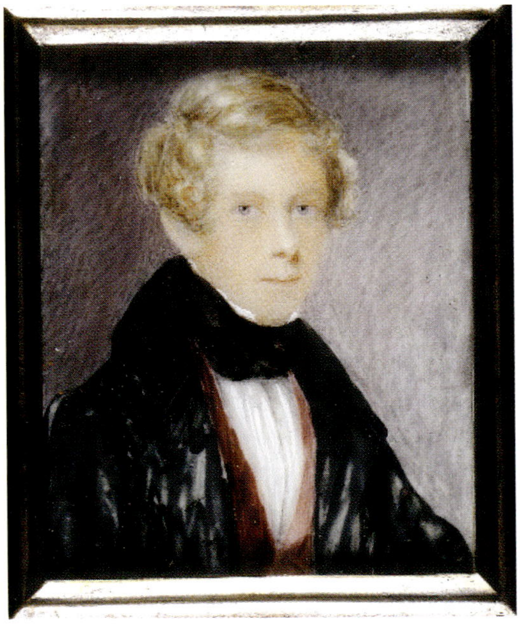

Cat. 123

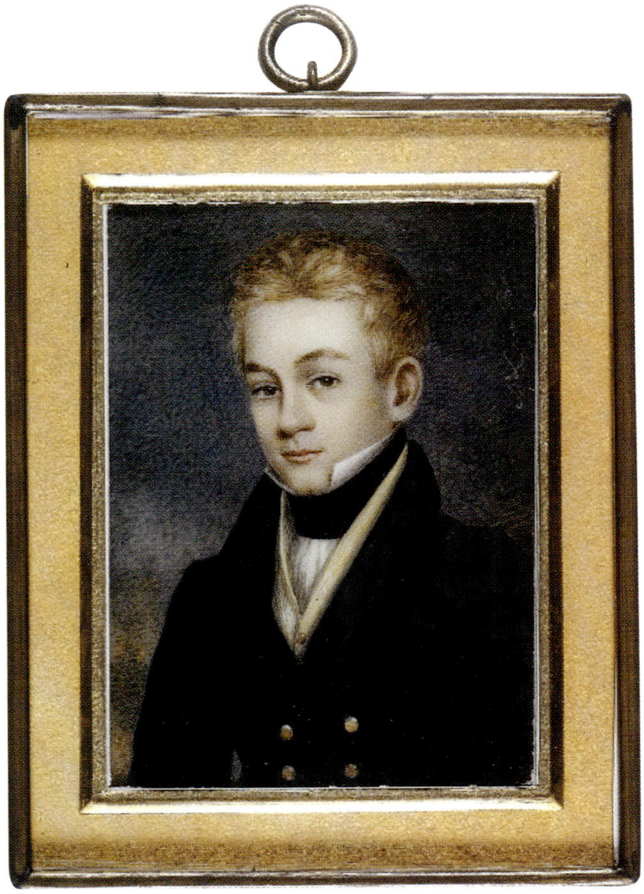

Cat. 124

123. *Self-Portrait*, c.1830
6.6 x 5.5, watercolour on ivory
Black *passe-partout* frame with an acorn clasp.
PROVENANCE: purchased at B.F. Stevens and Brown Ltd, London, 1942.
NGI 7340
EXHIBITED: 1976 Dallas, no. 98.
LITERATURE: NGI 1983, p. 476.

Lover's sketchy self-portrait is one of a series that he did during the 1820s and 1830s and tallies with the youthful appearance of an 1828 drawing (NGI 2432). The ivory support is relatively large, reflecting the taste for rectangular cabinet miniature portraits in the nineteenth century. Although this is an unfinished miniature, it illustrates the main characteristics of Lover's work: the loose painting of costume and, in the white areas, he ivory left unpainted, as in his treatment of the shirt and background.

124. *Portrait of a boy in a blue coat*, c.1830
SIGNED: *S. Lover pxt*
7.5 x 5.5, watercolour on ivory
Gilt metal cabinet frame with a velvet outer frame.
PROVENANCE: Bequeathed by Mrs Ella Herbert Bartlett, 1974.
NGI 7668
LITERATURE: NGI 1983, p. 478.

This portrait exemplifies Lover's finished miniature technique. The surface is smooth as a result of the application of minute brushstrokes loaded with gum arabic.

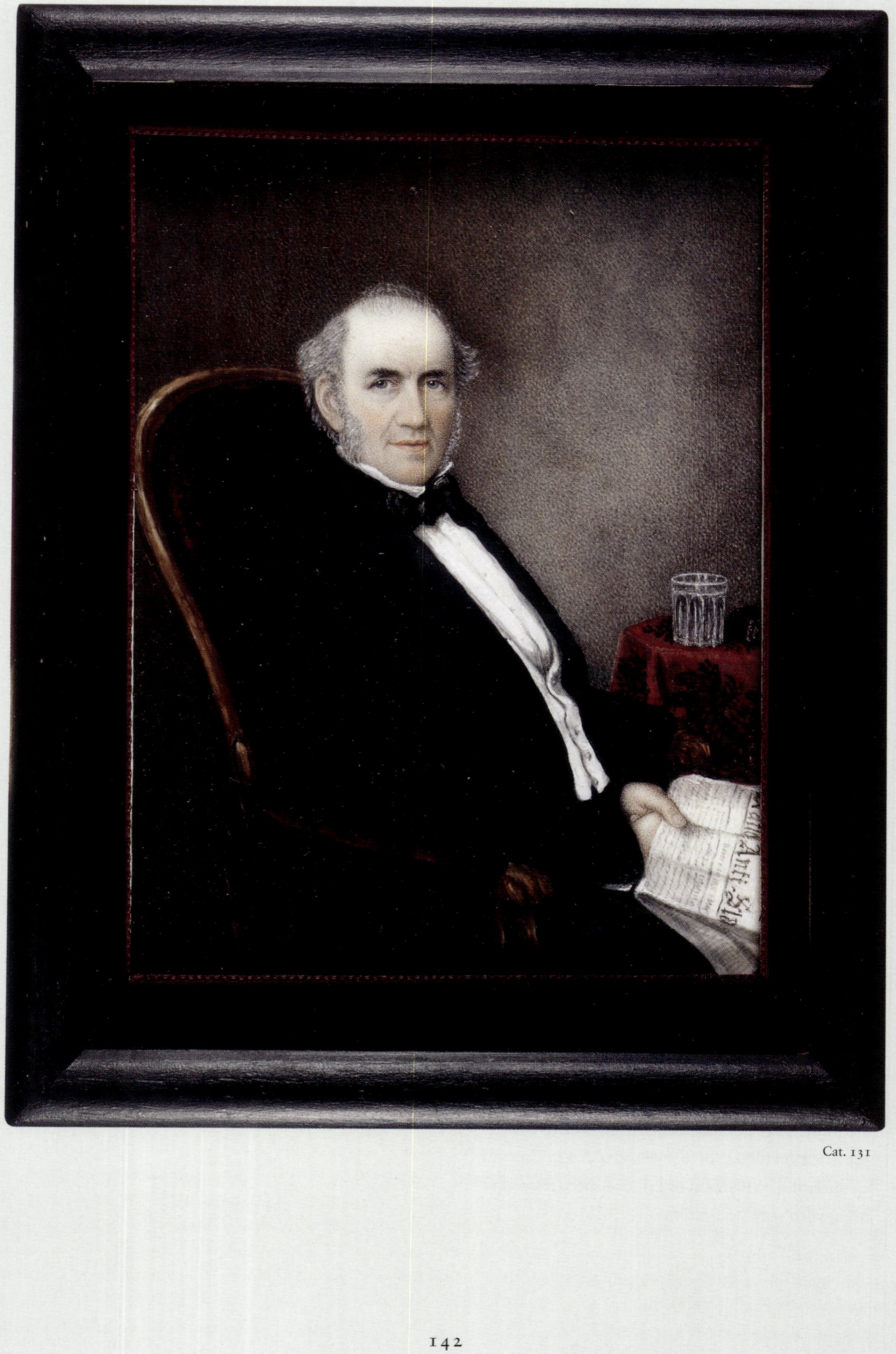

Cat. 131

B. BELL

active London 1849

This miniaturist remains obscure.

131. *James Haughton (1795–1873), Philanthropist*, 1849

INSCRIBED, SIGNED AND DATED ON BACKING CARD (now concealed): *James Haughton / painted by B. Bell / Moorfield / September / 1849*

16 x 12, watercolour on ivory

Wooden cabinet frame.

PROVENANCE: purchased from Miss Rose Black, Dublin, 1984.

NGI 19235

LITERATURE: Le Harivel and Wynne 1986, p. 44.

Haughton was born in Carlow and educated at Ballitore, Co. Kildare. He became a corn merchant in Dublin where he worked until his retirement in 1850. Haughton was brought up in the Society of Friends but became a Unitarian. He was a prolific writer of letters to the press where he aired his interests on social reform, the abolition of slavery, crime, capital punishment, land reform and the temperance movement. His main achievements were the establishment of the Dublin Mechanics Institute, the opening of Dublin Zoo and the National Botanic Gardens to the public on Sunday afternoons and the formation of the People's Garden in the Phoenix Park.[1]

Haughton is shown in a studio setting. With the Anti-Slavery tract in his hand, a book (probably the National Bible) and glass of water on the table beside him, Bell indicates his principal interests – Anti-Slavery, Unitarianism, and Temperance. During the 1840s and 1850s, the twin pressures of painting larger cabinet miniature portraits in imitation of oil portraits, and the impact of photography, affected miniature portraiture. Portraits had to be larger and more realistic, and there was a renewed interest in showing sitters as they were. The portrait of James Haughton shows the influence of photography on the miniature, as it tried to compete with the still, relatively expensive, daguerreotype and albumen print.

REFERENCE: 1. Webb 1878, p. 246.

Cat. 131, detail

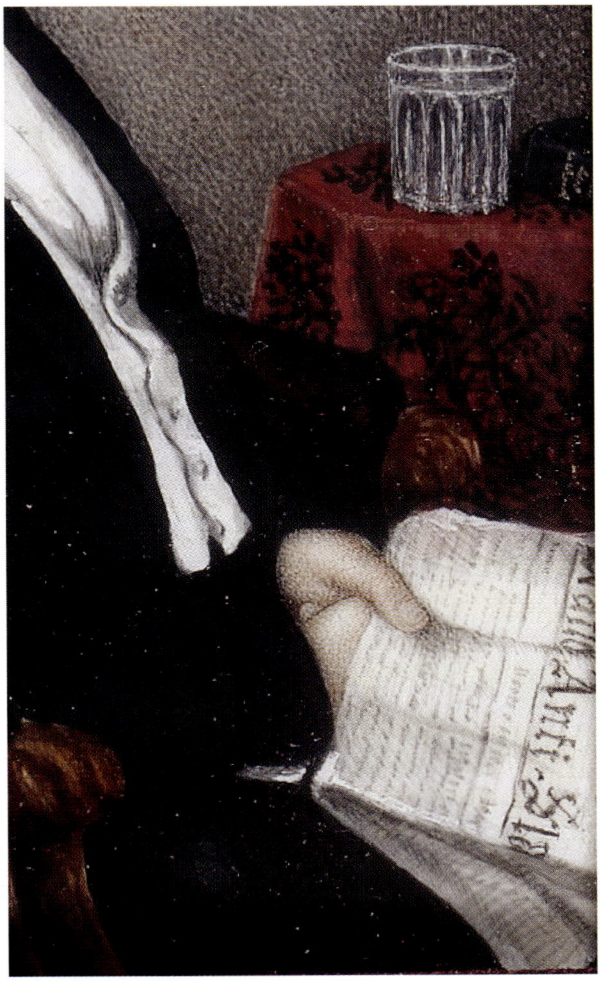

Bibliography

The bibliography includes both works cited in the catalogue and important publications on the subject of miniature painting in Ireland and England.

Allan 1968
David Allan, *William Shipley, Founder of the Royal Society of Arts*, London 1968.

Anjou 1956
Sten Anjou, 'Marcus Gunther's Designs for Jewellers 1684-1733', *Bulletin of Rohsska Konstslojdmuseet*, 1956, pp. 43-50.

Archer 1979
Mildred Archer, *India and British Portraiture 1770–1825*, London and New York 1979.

Asleson 1999
Robyn Asleson (ed.), *Sarah Siddons and her Portraitists*, Los Angeles 1999.

Auerbach and Kingsley Amis 1971
Erna Auerbach and C. Kingsley Amis, *Paintings and Sculpture at Hatfield House*, London 1971.

Bardo 1978
Pamela Pierrepont Bardo, *English and Continental Portrait Miniatures /The Latter-Schlesinger Collection, New Orleans Museum of Art*, New Orleans 1978.

Barrington 1833
Jonah Barrington, *Historic Anecdotes and Secret Memoirs*, London 1833.

Bayne-Powell 1985
Robert Bayne-Powell, *Catalogue of Portrait Miniatures in the Fitzwilliam Museum, Cambridge*, Cambridge 1985.

Bell and Poole 1925–26
C.F. Bell, and R.L. Poole, 'English Seventeenth-Century Portrait Drawings in Oxford Collections, II', *Journal of the Walpole Society*, 1925–26, vol. XIV, pp. 43–80.

Bence-Jones 1978
Mark Bence-Jones, *Burke's Guide to Country Houses, Volume I, Ireland*, London 1978.

Berg and Clifford 1999
Maxine Berg and Helen Clifford (eds.), *Consumers and Luxury*, Manchester and New York, 1999.

Bernard 1874
W. Bayle Bernard, *Life of Samuel Lover R.H.A. with selections from his papers*, London 1874.

Bignamini 1991
Ilaria Bignamini, 'George Vertue, Art Historian, and Art Institutions in London, 1689–1768', *Journal of the Walpole Society*, 1991, vol. LIV, pp. 1–148.

Birch c.1810
William Birch, *The Life of William Russell Birch, Enamel Painter, Written by Himself*, unpublished manuscript, 51 pp., Birch Papers, Historical Society of Pennsylvania, Philadelphia.

Blättel 1992
Harry Blättel, *International Dictionary Miniature Painters, Porcelain Painters, Silhouettists*, Munich 1992.

Bolton-Smith 1984
Robin Bolton-Smith, *Portrait Miniatures in the National Museum of American Art*, Chicago and London 1984.

Breeze 1985
George Breeze, *Society of Artists in Ireland Index of Exhibits 1765–80*, Dublin 1985.

Brockway 1933
Jean Lambert Brockway, 'William Birch: His American Enamel Portraits' *Antiques*, September 1933, no. 24, pp. 94–96.

Burke's 1889, 1891 and 1928
Burke's Illustrated Peerage and Baronetage, London 1889, 1891 and 1928.

Burke 1898
Bernard Burke, *A Genealogical and Heraldic History of the Landed Gentry of Great Britain and Ireland*, 2 vols., London 1898.

Butler 1990
Patricia Butler, *Three Hundred Years of Irish Watercolours and Drawings*, London 1990.

Caffrey 1986
Caffrey, Paul, 'Samuel Lover's Achievement as a Painter', *Irish Arts Review*, Spring 1986, vol. III, no. 1, pp. 51–54.

Caffrey 1986a
Paul Caffrey, 'Sampson Towgood Roch, Miniaturist', *Irish Arts Review*, Winter 1986, vol. III, no. 4, pp. 14–20.

Caffrey 1987
Paul Caffrey, 'John Comerford', *Irish Arts Review*, Autumn 1987, vol. IV, no. 3, pp. 42–47.

Caffrey 1991
Paul Caffrey, 'A Portrait of Lord Edward Fitzgerald' in *Catalogue of 18th, 19th and 20th Century Irish Paintings*, The Gorry Gallery, September 1991, p. 10.

Caffrey 1995
Paul Caffrey, 'Portrait of the Landscape Painter William Ashford' in *Catalogue of 18th, 19th and 20th Century Irish Paintings*, The Gorry Gallery, May 1995, p. 8.

Caffrey 1995a
Paul Caffrey, 'Irish Portrait Miniatures c.1700–1830', Unpublished Ph.D. Thesis, Southampton Institute 1995.

Caffrey 1999
Paul Caffrey, *John Comerford and the Portrait Miniature in Ireland c.1620–1850*, Kilkenny 1999 [catalogue of exhibition, Rothe House, Kilkenny and Hunt Museum, Limerick].

Cavalli-Björkman 1981
G. Cavalli-Björkman, *Svenskt Miniatyrmaleri*, Stockholm 1981.

Charleston 1956
Robert J. Charleston, 'Marcus Gunter a Note', *Bulletin of Rohsska Konstslojdmuseet*, 1956 pp. 61–68.

Clouzot 1924
Henri Clouzot, *Dictionnaire des Miniaturistes sur Email*, Paris 1924.

Colding 1953
Horben Holck Colding, *Aspects of Miniature Painting: Its Origins and Development*, Copenhagen, London and Edinburgh 1953.

Conner 1993
Patrick Conner, *George Chinnery 1774–1852 Artist of India and the China Coast*, Woodbridge, Suffolk 1993.

Coombs 1998
Katherine Coombs, *The Portrait Miniature in England*, London 1998.

Crookshank and Glin 1969
Anne Crookshank, and the Knight of Glin, *Irish Portraits 1660–1860*, catalogue of exhibition NGI, NPGL and UM 1969–70.

Crookshank and Glin 1978
Anne Crookshank, and the Knight of Glin, *The Painters of Ireland*, London 1978 (revised edition forthcoming 2001).

Crookshank and Glin 1994
Anne Crookshank, and the Knight of Glin, *The Watercolours of Ireland*, London 1994.

D'Arblay 1891
Madame D'Arblay (Fanny Burney), *The Diary and Letters of Madame D'Arblay*, 3 vols., London 1891.

DNB
Dictionary of National Biography, vols. 1-XXXI, London from 1909.

Edwards 1808
Edward Edwards, *Anecdotes of Painters*, London 1808. Facsimile reprint, London, 1970.

Edwards 1997
Sebastian Edwards, 'The Art and Business of Portrait Miniatures in England' in English Heritage, *Miniatures at Kenwood, The Draper Gift*, London 1997, pp. 11–15.

English Heritage 1997
Miniatures at Kenwood, The Draper Gift, London 1997.

Erffa and Staley 1986
Helmut von Erffa and Allen Staley, *The Paintings of Benjamin West*, New Haven and London 1986.

ffolliott 1984
Rosemary ffolliott, 'The Unmistakable Hand of Frederick Buck', *Irish Arts Review*, Summer 1984, vol. I, no. 2, pp. 46–50.

Fleming 1959
Fleming, John,, 'Giuseppe Macpherson: a Florentine Miniaturist' *Connoisseur*, November 1959, vol. 144, pp. 166–7.

Fleming-Williams 1971
Ian Fleming-Williams, 'Constable as a background painter', [Portrait of Eliza O'Neill], *Country Life*, 23 December 1971, p. 1784.

Folkenflik, forthcoming
Robert Folkenflik, 'Representations of Swift' in B. Connery (ed.), *Papers from the Tenth International Congress on the Enlightenment*, Delaware, forthcoming.

Ford 1991
Brinsley Ford, 'The Society of Dilettanti' in Philip Ziegler and Desmond Seward (eds), *Brooks A Social History*, London 1991.

Foskett 1963
Daphne Foskett, *British Portrait Miniatures*, London 1963.

Foskett 1964
Daphne Foskett, *John Smart the Man and His Miniatures*, London 1964.

Foskett 1972
Daphne Foskett, *A Dictionary of British Miniature Painters*, 2 vols., London 1972.

Foskett 1974
Daphne Foskett, *Samuel Cooper*, London 1974.

Foskett 1987
Daphne Foskett, *Miniatures: Dictionary and Guide*, Woodbridge, Suffolk 1987.

Foster 1898
Joshua Joseph Foster, *British Miniature Painters and their Works*, London 1898.

Foster 1914–16
Joshua Joseph Foster, *Samuel Cooper and the English Miniature Painters of the XVIIth Century*, London 1914–16.

Foster 1930–31
William Foster, 'British Artists in India 1760–1820', *Journal of the Walpole Society*, 1930–31, vol. XIX, pp. 1–88.

Foster 1933
William Foster, 'Additional Notes to British Artists in India, 1760–1820', *Journal of the Walpole Society*, 1933, vol. XXI, pp. 108–09.

GEC
G.E. Cockayne [revised by Vicary Gibbs and others] *The Complete Peerage*, 13 vols, London 1910–59.

Gabszewicz and Freeman 1982
Anton Gabszewicz and Geoffrey Freeman, *Bow Porcelain*, London 1982.

Garlick *et al.* 1978–84
Kenneth Garlick, Angus Macintyre and Kathryn Cave (eds.), *The Diary of Joseph Farington 1793–1821*, 15 vols., New Haven and London 1978–84.

Gorry 1989–2000
The Gorry Gallery *Catalogues of Exhibition of 18th, 19th and 20th Century Irish Paintings*, include miniatures (May 1989, September 1991, June 1995, September 1996, June 1997, December 1997, December 1998, June 2000, October 2000).

Goulding 1916
Richard W. Goulding, *The Welbeck Abbey Miniatures: A Catalogue Raisonné*, Oxford 1916.

Graves 1905–06
Algernon Graves, *The Royal Academy of Arts Exhibitors 1769–1804*, 8 vols., London 1905–06.

Grimaldi 1873
A.B. Grimaldi, *A Catalogue Chronological and Descriptive of Paintings, Drawings, & Engravings by and after William Grimaldi, RA*, London 1873.

Guyatt 2000
Mary Guyatt, 'The Wedgwood Slave Medallion: Values in Eighteenth-century Design', *Journal of Design History*, 2000, vol. 13, no. 2, pp. 93–105.

Gwynn 1930
Denis Gwynn, *Life of John Keogh*, Dublin 1930.

Harbison 1999
John Harbison, 'The Boy with the Squirrel Henry Pelham (1749–1806)', *Ireland of the Welcomes*, May-June 1999, vol. 48, no. 3, pp. 18–25.

Harbison 2000
John Harbison, 'Henry Pelham (1749–1806): Painter, Engraver, Engineer, Map-maker and Illustrator of Co. Clare's Antiquities' in Ciaran O Murchadha (ed.), *Co. Clare Studies Essays in Memory of Gerald O'Connell, Sean O Murchadha, Thomas Coffey and Pat Flynn*, Ennis 2000.

Herbert 1836
John Dowling Herbert, *Irish Varieties for the Last Fifty Years*, London 1836.

Hett 1926
F.P. Hett, *Memoirs of Susan Sibbald 1783–1812*, London 1926.

Hilliard 1981
Nicholas Hilliard, *A Treatise concerning the Arte of Limning*, critical edition by R.K.R. Thornton and T.G.S. Cain, Ashington and Manchester 1981.

Hughes 1952
G. Bernard Hughes, 'Old English Miniature Portraits', *Country Life Annual*, 1952, pp. 80–89.

Hutchinson 1968
Sidney C. Hutchinson, *The History of the Royal Academy, 1768–1968*, London 1968.

Iñiguez 1980
Diego Angulo Iñiguez, *Murillo*, 3 vols., Madrid 1980.

Ingamells 1997
John Ingamells (ed.), *A Dictionary of British and Irish Travellers in Italy 1701–1800*, New Haven and London 1997.

Jenkins 1988
Ian Jenkins, 'Adam Buck and the vogue for Greek vases', *The Burlington Magazine*, June 1988, vol. CXXX, no. 1023, pp. 448–57.

Johnson 1990
Dale T. Johnson, *American Portrait Miniatures in the Manney Collection*, New York 1990.

Le Harivel and Wynne 1984
Adrian Le Harivel and Michael Wynne, *National Gallery of Ireland Acquisitions 1982–83*, Dublin 1984.

Le Harivel and Wynne 1986
Adrian Le Harivel and Michael Wynne, *National Gallery of Ireland Acquisitions 1984–86*, Dublin 1986.

Le Harivel 1992
Adrian Le Harivel, *Nathaniel Hone,* Dublin 1992.

Lemprière 1984
John Lempriere, *Lempriere's Classical Dictionary*, London 1984 (first published 1788).

Lennox-Boyd *et al* 1974
Christopher Lennox-Boyd, Guy Shaw and Sarah Halliwell, *Theatre: the Age of Garrick*, London 1974.

Lister 1951
Raymond Lister, *The British Miniature*, London 1951.

Llanover 1861–62
Lady Llanover, *Autobiography and Correspondence of Mary Granville, Mrs Delany*, 6 vols, London 1861–62.

Lloyd and Remington 1996
Christopher Lloyd and Vanessa Remington, *Masterpieces in Little/Portrait Miniatures from the Collection of Her Majesty Queen Elizabeth II*, London 1996.

Lloyd 1995
Stephen Lloyd, *Richard and Maria Cosway Regency Artists of Taste and Fashion*, catalogue of exhibition, SNPGE and NPGL 1995–96.

Loche and Röthlisberger 1978
Renée Loche and M. Röthlisberger, *L'opera completa di Liotard*, Milan 1978.

Long 1929
Basil Somerset Long, *British Miniatures*, London 1929.

Long 1929a
Basil Somerset Long, 'Richard Crosse, Miniature and Portrait Painter', *Journal of the Walpole Society*, 1929, vol. XVII, pp. 61–94.

McGuire 1936
Edward A. McGuire, 'George Lawrence', *The Connoisseur*, 1936, vol. XCVII, pp. 206–09.

McNamee 1954
James J. McNamee, *History of the Diocese of Ardagh*, Dublin 1954.

McParland 1985
Edward McParland, *James Gandon/Vitruvius Hibernicus*, London 1985.

Mulvany and Gandon 1864
Thomas Joseph Mulvany and James Gandon, *The Life of James Gandon*, Dublin 1864. Facsimile edition edited by Maurice Craig, Dublin 1969.

Murdoch 1989
John Murdoch, 'Painting: From Astraea to Augustus' in B. Ford (ed.), *The Cambridge Cultural History of Britain, Vol. IV: The Seventeenth Century*, Cambridge 1989, pp. 235–65.

Murdoch 1997
John Murdoch, *Seventeenth-century English Miniatures in the Collection of the Victoria and Albert Museum*, London 1997.

Murdoch *et al.* 1981
John Murdoch, Jim Murrell, Patrick Noon and Roy Strong, *The English Miniature*, New Haven and London 1981.

NGI 1890
Catalogue of the Works of Art in the National Gallery of Ireland, Dublin 1890

NGI 1914
Catalogue of the Pictures and other works of art in the National Gallery of Ireland and the National Portrait Gallery, Dublin 1914.

NGI 1928
Catalogue of Pictures and other works of art in the National Gallery of Ireland and the National Portrait Gallery, Dublin 1928.

NGI 1981
National Gallery of Ireland Illustrated Summary Catalogue of Paintings, Dublin 1981.

NGI 1983
National Gallery of Ireland Illustrated Summary Catalogue of Drawings, Watercolours and Miniatures, (compiled by Adrian Le Harivel), Dublin 1983.

NGI 1988
Illustrated Summary Catalogue of Prints and Sculpture, (edited by Adrian Le Harivel), Dublin 1988.

NMI 1917
List of French Portrait Miniatures etc. Lent by George Siegerson, Esq., M.D. to the National Museum, Dublin, Dublin 1917.

Nisser 1927
W. Nisser, *Michael Dahl and the Contemporary Swedish School of Painting*, Uppsala 1927.

Noon 1979
Patrick Noon, *English Portrait Drawings and Miniatures/Yale Center for British Art*, New Haven 1979.

NPGL 1981
National Portrait Gallery Complete Illustrated Catalogue 1856–1979 (compiled by K.K. Yung), London 1981.

O'Brien 1951
Donough O'Brien, *Miniatures in the XVIII and XIX Centuries, An Historical and Descriptive Record*, London 1951.

O'Keefe 1826
John O'Keefe, *Recollections of the Life of John O'Keefe written by himself*, 2 vols, London 1826.

Papendiek 1887
Mrs Papendiek, *Court and Private Life in the Time of Queen Charlotte: being the journals of Mrs Papendiek*, (edited by Mrs Vernon Delves Broughton), 2 vols., London 1887.

Pasquin 1796
Anthony Pasquin [John Williams], *Memoirs of the Royal Academicians being an attempt to improve the national taste*, London 1796. Facsimile reprint (edited by R. W. Lightbown) London 1970.

Piper 1978
David Piper, *The English Face*, London 1978.

Pointon 1999
Marcia Pointon, 'Jewellery in eighteenth century England' in Maxine Berg and Helen Clifford (eds.) *Consumers and Luxury*, Manchester and New York 1999.

Pointon 1999a
Marcia Pointon, 'Wearing Memory: Mourning, Jewellery and the Body', in G. Ecker (ed.), *Trauer Tragen*, Munich 1999.

Reilly 1989
Robin Reilly, *Wedgwood*, 2 vols., London and New York 1989.

Reynolds 1980
Graham Reynolds, *Wallace Collection Catalogue of Miniatures*, London 1980.

Reynolds 1988
Graham Reynolds, *English Portrait Miniatures*, revised edition, Cambridge 1988.

Reynolds 1996
Graham Reynolds, *European Miniatures in the Metropolitan Museum of Art*, New York 1996.

Reynolds 1998
Graham Reynolds, *Fitzwilliam Museum handbooks/British Portrait Miniatures*, Cambridge 1998

Ribeiro 1995
Aileen Ribeiro, 'Portraying the Fashion, Romancing the Past: Dress and the Cosways' in Stephen Lloyd, *Richard and Maria Cosway Regency Artists of Taste and Fashion*, catalogue of exhibition, SNPGE and NPGL 1995–6.

Ribeiro 1997
Aileen Ribeiro, 'Fashion in Miniature', in English Heritage, *Miniatures at Kenwood The Draper Gift*, London 1997.

RDS 1733–62
Minute Book and Register of the Dublin Society, 1733–62, 4 vols, Library of the Royal Dublin Society.

RDS 1764–1800
Proceedings of the Royal Dublin Society, 1764–1800, vols. I–XXXVI, Dublin.

RIA 1801–03
Journal, 1801–03, Ms 24. K. 15. 2 vols., Royal Irish Academy, Dublin.

Ross 1940
Marvin Chauncey Ross, 'William Birch, Enamel Miniaturist', *American Collector*, 1940, vol. 9, pp. 5, 20.

Rouquet 1755
Jean André Rouquet, *The Present State of the Arts in England*, printed and translated by J. Nourse, London 1755. Facsimile reprint London 1970.

Rowell 1996
Christopher Rowell, 'A seventeenth-century Cabinet restored The Green Closet at Ham House', *Apollo*, April 1996, pp. 18–23.

Ryan 1821
Richard Ryan, *Biographica Hibernica A Biographical Dictionary of the Worthies of Ireland from the earliest to the present time*, London and Dublin, 1821.

Schidlof 1964
Leo R. Schidlof, *The Miniature in Europe*, 4 vols., Graz 1964.

Schneeberger 1958
P.F. Schneeberger, *Les Peintres sur Émail Genevois au XVIIe et XVIIIe siecles*, Geneva 1958.

Smith 1828
John Thomas Smith, *Nollekens and his Times*, 2 vols., London 1828. Edition annotated by Wilfred Whitten, 1920.

Smith 1845
John Thomas Smith, *A Book for a Rainy Day*, London 1845.

Speel 1987a
Erica Speel, 'Enamel Portrait Miniature – 17th Century, *Glass on Metal*, October 1987, vol. 6, no. 5, pp. 84–87.

Speel 1987b
Erica Speel, 'Enamel Portrait Miniatures – 18th Century' and 'Painting on Enamel – 18th Century', *Glass on Metal*, December 1987 vol. 6, no. 6, pp. 113–19.

Speel 1998
Erica Speel, *Dictionary of Enamelling History and Techniques*, Aldershot and Vermont 1998.

Stewart 1990
Ann Stewart, *Irish Art Loan Exhibitions 1765–1927*, vol. 1, A–L, Dublin 1990.

Stewart 1995
Ann Stewart, *Irish Art Loan Exhibitions 1765–1927*, vol. 2, M–Z and Vol. 3 Subject Index, Jersey and Dublin 1995.

Strickland 1913
Walter G. Strickland, *A Dictionary of Irish Artists*, 2 vols., Dublin and London 1913. Facsimile reprint Irish University Press, Shannon, 1968.

Strong 1983
Strong, Roy, *The English Renaissance Miniature*, London 1983.

Sumner 1988
Ann Sumner, 'Thomas Forster's Plumbagos', *The Antique Collector*, June 1988, pp. 115–21.

Sumner and Walker 1999
Ann Sumner and Richard Walker, *Secret Passion to Noble Fashion The World of the Miniature Portrait*, Bath 1999.

Sinebrychoffs 1983
Soumen Taideakatemia Miniatyyrit Miniatyrer, Sinebrychoffs Museum, Helsinki 1983.

Symington 1880
Andrew James Symington, *Life Sketch of Samuel Lover*, London 1880.

Tapp 1938
William H. Tapp, *Jefferyes Hamett O'Neale 1734–1801*, London 1938.

Taylor 1983
Lou Taylor, *Mourning Dress A Costume and Social History*, London 1983.

Tillyard 1997
Stella Tillyard, *Citizen Lord*, London 1997.

Turpin 1995
John Turpin, *A School of Art in Dublin since the Eighteenth Century*, Dublin 1995.

Verplanck 1997
Anne Verplanck, 'The Social meanings of Portrait Miniatures in Philadelphia, 1760–1820', in A.S. Martin and J.R. Garrison (eds.), *American Material Culture / The Shape of the Field*, Delaware and Tennessee, 1997.

Vertue 1929–52
George Vertue, *Vertue Notebooks I–VI* [transcribed and edited by A.J.K. Easdale], *Journal of the Walpole Society*, 1929–52
Notebook I, 1929–30, vol. XVIII: Notebook II, 1931–32, vol. XX: Notebook III, 1933–34, vol. XXII: Notebook IV, 1935–36 vol. XXIV: Notebook V, 1937–38, vol. XXVI: Index to Notebooks I–V, 1940–42, vol. XIX: Notebook VI, 1951–52, vol. XXX.

Vicars Griffith 1852
W. Vicars Griffith, 'Notices of the proceedings of the 'Dublin Society', in reference to their Drawing Schools from 1746–1750, and from 1761 to 1764, (the original records for these years having been lost) extracted from *Faulkner's Dublin Journal*, in *Royal Dublin Society Tenth Distribution Report of the Public Distribution of Premium awarded for 1851 to the Successful male and female students at the General Competition for Prizes in Drawing and Modelling being the second in connection with the Government School of Design*, Dublin 1852.

V&A 1981
Summary Catalogue of Miniatures in the Victoria and Albert Museum [not illustrated], London 1981.

Walker 1985
Richard Walker, *Regency Portraits/National Portrait Gallery*, 2 vols, London 1985.

Walker 1992
Richard Walker, *The Eighteenth and Early Nineteenth Century Miniatures in the Collection of Her Majesty the Queen*, Cambridge 1992.

Walker 1998
Richard Walker, *Miniatures/300 Years of the English Miniature Illustrated from the Collections of the National Portrait Gallery*, London 1998.

Walker 1999
Richard Walker, 'Henry Bone's Pencil Drawings in the National Portrait Gallery' *Journal of the Walpole Society*, 1999, vol. LXI, pp. 305–67 and figs. 97–188.

Walpole 1762–71
Horace Walpole, *Anecdotes of Painting in England*, 5 vols, London 1762–71.

Walton 1992
Julian C. Walton, *The Royal Charters of Waterford*, Waterford 1992.

Waterhouse 1978
Ellis Waterhouse, *Painting in Britain 1530–1790*, 4th edition, London 1978.

Webb 1878
Alfred Webb, *A Compendium of Irish Biography*, Dublin 1878.

Webster 1972
Mary Webster, 'A Scottish Miniaturist in Florence, *Country Life*, vol. CLI, 8 June 1972, pp. 1445–46.

Weinrib and Hibbert 1983
Ben Weinrib and Christopher Hibbert, *The London Encyclopedia*, London 1983.

Williamson 1905
George C. Williamson, *Richard Cosway, R.A. and his Wife and Pupils*, 2nd edition, London 1905.

Williamson 1918
George C. Williamson, *Life and Works of Ozias Humphry*, London 1918.

Williamson 1926
George C. Williamson, *Signed Enamel Miniatures of the XVIIth, XVIIIth & XIX Centuries*, [Jacob Nachemsohn Collection], privately published 1926.

Williamson and Engleheart 1902
George C. Williamson and Henry Engleheart, *George Engleheart 1750–1829: Miniature Painter to George III*, London 1902.

Winter 1948
Carl Winter, 'The British School of Miniature Portrait Painters', *Proceedings of the British Academy*, 1948, vol. XXXIV, pp. 1–19.

Wynne 1967
Michael Wynne, 'Tilly Kettle's Last Painting' [James Gandon], *The Burlington Magazine*, September 1967, vol. CIX, pp. 532–33.

Wynne 1970
Michael Wynne, 'A Note on Thomas Frye', *Quarterly Bulletin of the Irish Georgian Society*, 1970, vol. XIII, nos 2 and 3, pp. 38–44.

Wynne 1972
Michael Wynne, 'Thomas Frye (1710–1762)' [with outline catalogue], *The Burlington Magazine*, February 1972, vol. CXIV, pp. 76–84.

Wynne 1981
Michael Wynne, *National Gallery of Ireland Recent Acquisitions 1980–1981*, Dublin 1981.

Wynne 1982
Michael Wynne, 'Thomas Frye (1710–62) reviewed' [with supplement to catalogue], *The Burlington Magazine*, October 1982, vol. CXXIV, pp. 624–28.

Wynne 1986
Michael Wynne, 'The McNeill Bequest', *Irish Arts Review*, Winter 1986, vol. III, no. 4, pp. 36–41.

Exhibitions Cited

1809 Dublin
Society of Artists of Ireland, Dublin Society, Hawkins Street

1965 Edinburgh
British Portrait Miniatures, Edinburgh International Festival, 1965

1969–70 Dublin, London and Belfast
Irish Portraits 1660–1860, NGI, NPGL and UM

1970 Dublin
Church Disestablishment 1870–1970, NGI.

1971 Cork
Irish Art in the 19th century, Crawford Art Gallery, Cork.

1972–73 Bucharest and Budapest
British Portraits, British Council Exhibition, Museums of Fine Art, Bucharest and Budapest.

1974 London
Drawings from the National Gallery of Ireland, Wildenstein, London.

1975 London
The Georgian Playhouse, Hayward Gallery, London.

1976 Dallas
Irish Watercolours 1675–1925 from the National Gallery of Ireland, Dallas Museum of Fine Arts.

1995 Dublin
An Exhibition of 18th, 19th and 20th century Irish paintings, The Gorry Gallery, Dublin.

1995–96 Edinburgh and London
Richard and Maria Cosway, Regency Artists of Taste and Fashion, SNPGE and NPGL.

1999 Dublin
75 years of giving, The Friends of the National Collections of Ireland, Works of art donated by the Friends to the Public Collections of Ireland, RHA Gallagher Gallery, Dublin

Summary Catalogue of Irish and English Miniatures 1650–1850

PAUL CAFFREY AND ADRIAN LE HARIVEL

Updated from *NGI Illustrated Summary Catalogue of Drawings, Watercolours and Miniatures*, 1983; *Acquisitions 1984–1986*, with the Miss Mary A. McNeill Bequest of Miniatures and Silhouettes, and including subsequent accessions. Dates are given for the first entry by the artist.

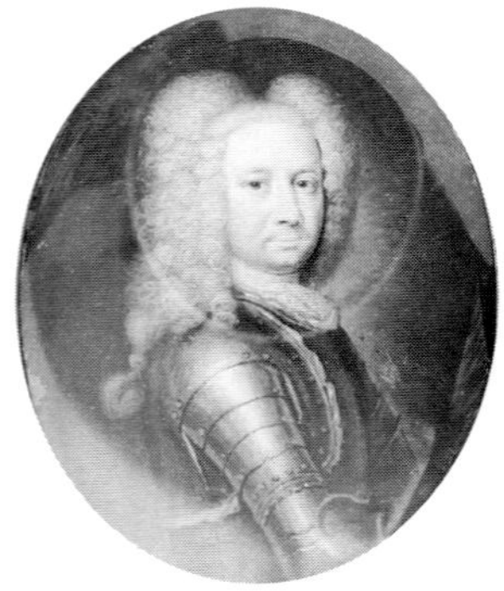

CIRCLE OF
JACQUES-ANTOINE ARLAUD
Geneva 1668 – 1746 Geneva
Portrait of a man in armour
6.5 x 5.1, watercolour on chicken skin. Transferred from the NMI, 1969 (where presented by Mrs M. Sullivan, 1949)
NGI 7023

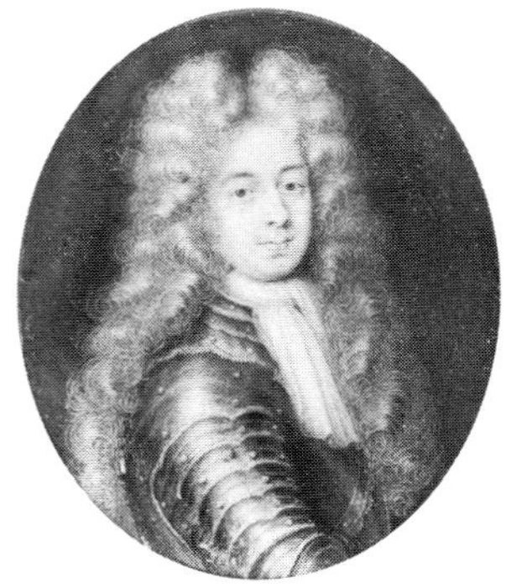

CIRCLE OF
JACQUES-ANTOINE ARLAUD
Arthur Chichester, 3rd Earl of Donegall, (1666–1706)
6.8 x 5.6, watercolour on card
Miss Mary A. McNeill Bequest, 1985
NGI 19244

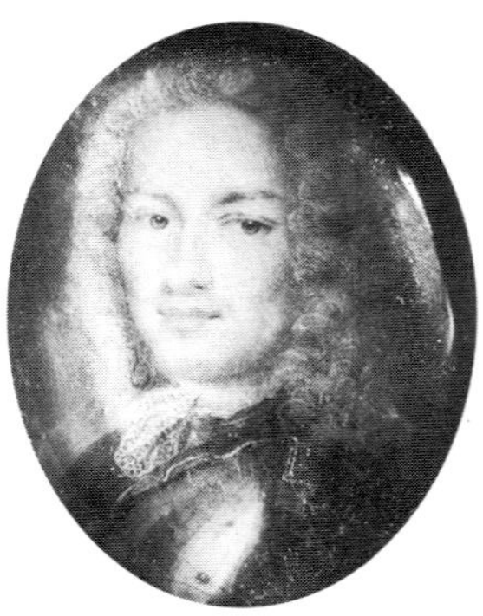

CIRCLE OF
JACQUES-ANTOINE ARLAUD
Portrait of a man in armour
3.7 x 2.9, watercolour on card
Miss Mary A. McNeill Bequest, 1985
NGI 19245

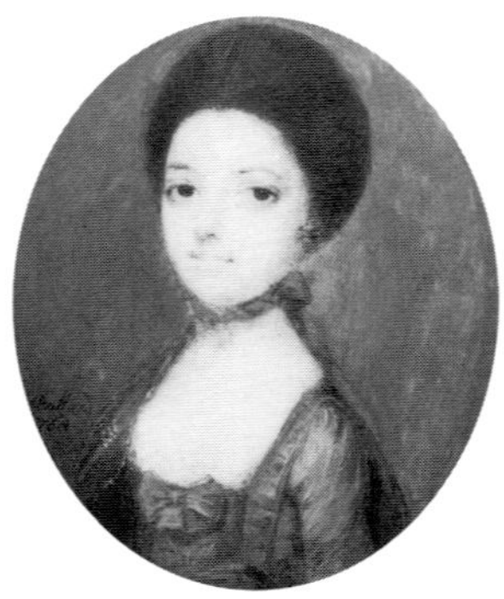

JAMES BALLARD
active Dublin 1753 – 1792 Dublin
Portrait of a lady in a blue dress, 1768
Signed and dated: *J. Ballard 1768*
4.6 x 3.5, watercolour with gouache on ivory. Transferred from the NMI, 1969 (where purchased 1887). NGI 7073. see p. 78.

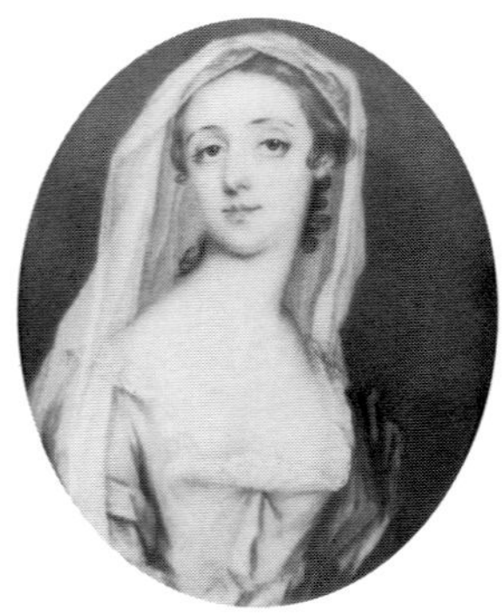

LUCIUS BARBER
Dublin. 1720 – 1767 London
Portrait of a lady, known as Margaret (Peg) Woffington, (1714/18–1760), Actress. Signed: *B*
5.2 x 4, enamel on gold
Presented by Sir Alfred Chester Beatty, 1951. NGI 3705.
see pp. 57–58.

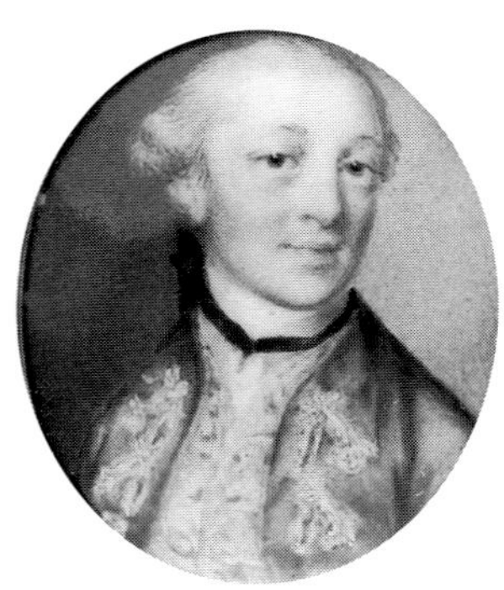

ATTRIBUTED TO LUCIUS BARBER
Mr Redington of Co. Galway, c.1760
3.2 x 2.7, enamel on gold
Transferred from the NMI, 1969 (where presented by Mrs M. Sullivan, 1949)
NGI 7044. see p. 58.

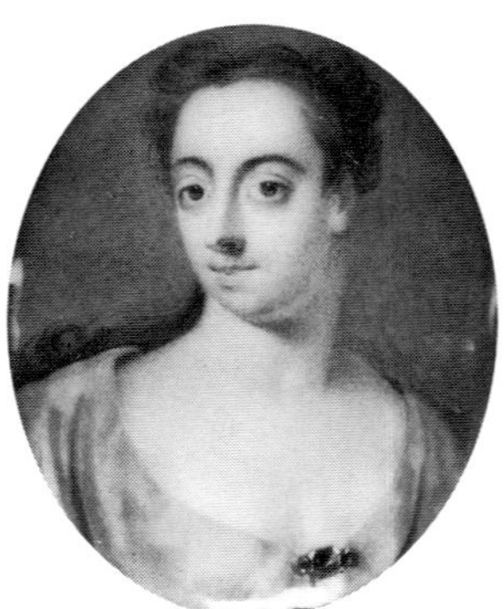

CIRCLE OF LUCIUS BARBER
Portrait of a lady in a pink dress
4.9 x 4, enamel on copper
Miss Mary A. McNeill Bequest, 1985
NGI 19271

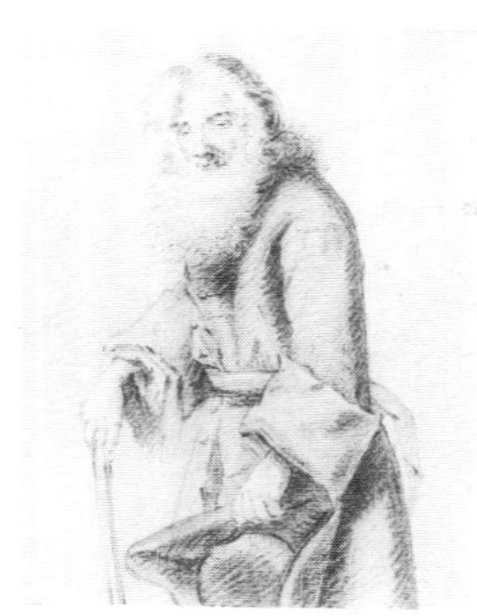

RUPERT BARBER
Dublin, 1719 – 1772 Dublin
William Thompson, a Dublin beggar, aged 114, (study for enamel miniature, 1744)
30.4 x 21.5, charcoal on paper
Presented by Mr H. Sinclair, 1921
NGI 2726. see pp. 55–56.

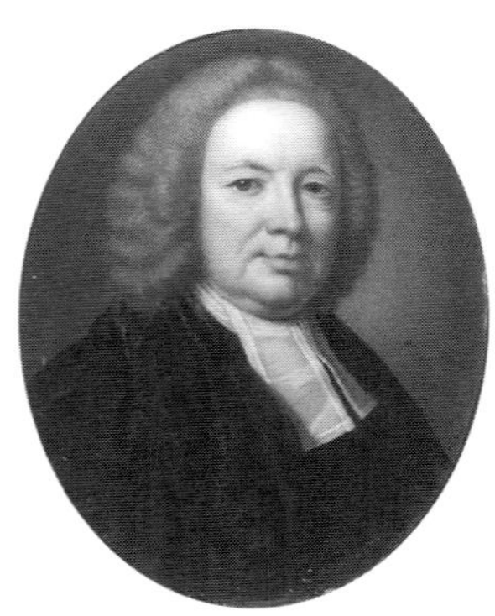

ATTRIBUTED TO RUPERT BARBER
Dr Patrick Delany, (1684/85–1786), Dean of Down, c.1740
4.8 x 3.8, enamel on copper
Presented by Sir Alfred Chester Beatty, 1951
NGI 3728. see p. 57.

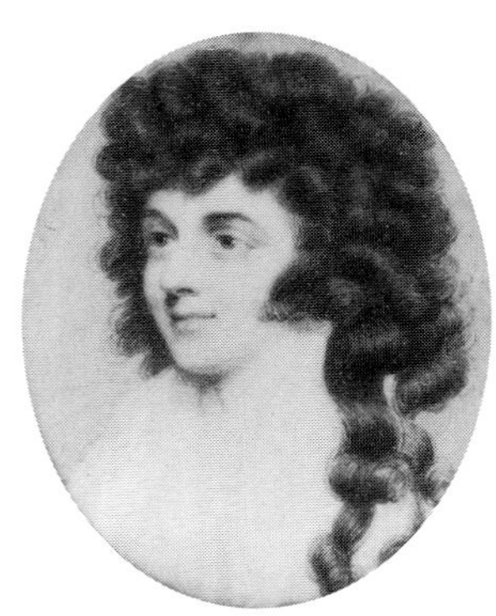

JOHN BARRY
active London 1784 – 1827 (?) London
Portrait of a lady in a blue dress, c.1790
4.4 x 3.5, watercolour on ivory
Miss Mary A. McNeill Bequest, 1985
NGI 19279. see p. 120.

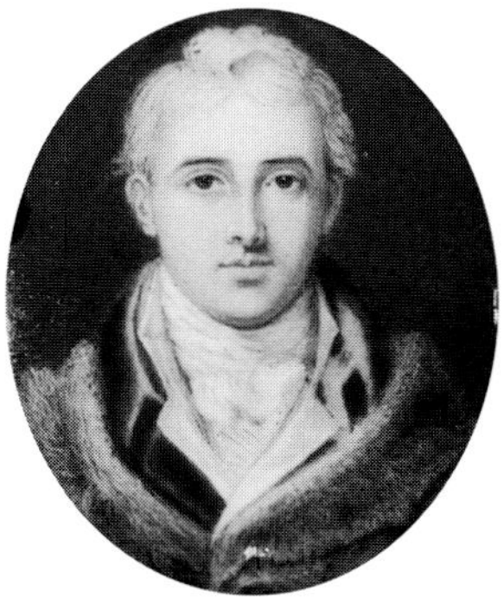

William Bate
active Dublin 1799 – 1845
(?) London. *Robert Stewart, Viscount Castlereagh, 2nd Marquess of Londonderry, (1769–1822),* 1822
(after T. Lawrence 1807–10 hl, NPGL). Inscribed, signed and dated on reverse: *1822 Painted by Bate**.
3.9 x 3.2, enamel on gold
Bequeathed by Lady Julia Fitzgerald, 1896. NGI 2333. see pp. 121–22.

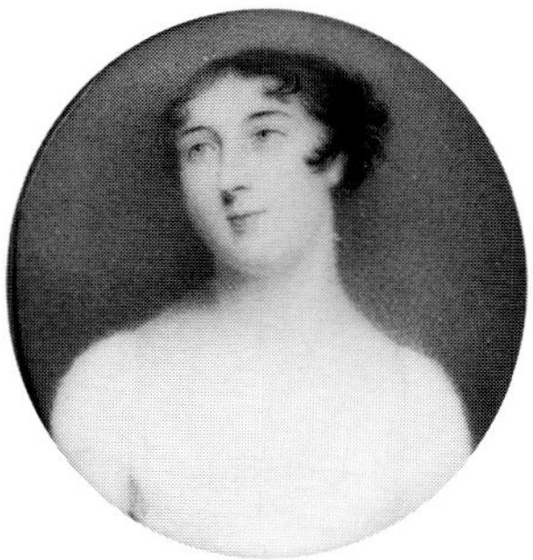

William Bate
Portrait of a lady in a white dress, 1811. Inscribed, signed and dated on reverse: *Enamelled by Bate*1811*. 3.5 diam, enamel on copper. Presented by Sir Alfred Chester Beatty, 1951
NGI 3707. see p. 121.

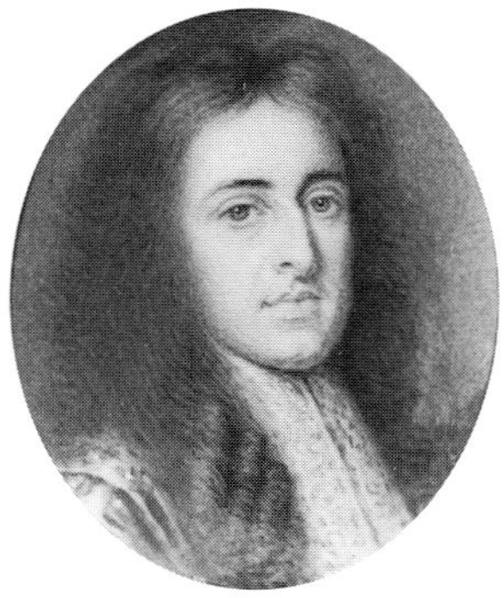

William Bate
Portrait of a man in armour, 1832
Signed and dated on reverse: *WB*(mono)*ate 1832*.
3.6 x 2.9, enamel on copper
Presented by Sir Alfred Chester Beatty, 1951
NGI 3708

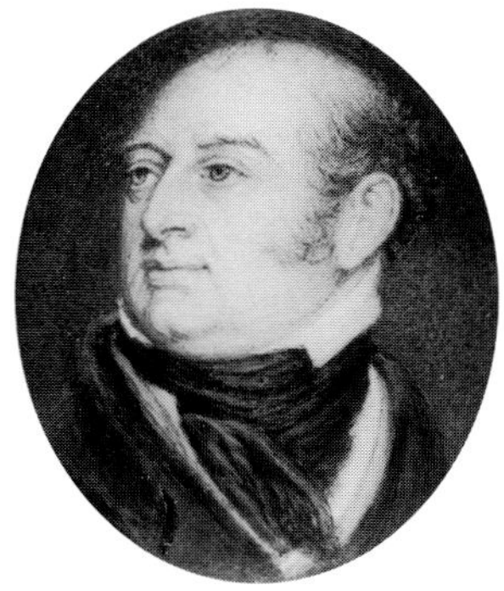

William Bate
Frederick, Duke of York, (1763–1827), son of George III,
1827 (after T. Lawrence exhibited 1822, untraced). Inscribed, signed and dated on reverse: *1827 by Ww. Bate**. 3.6 x 3, enamel on copper
Presented by Sir Alfred Chester Beatty, 1951. NGI 3709

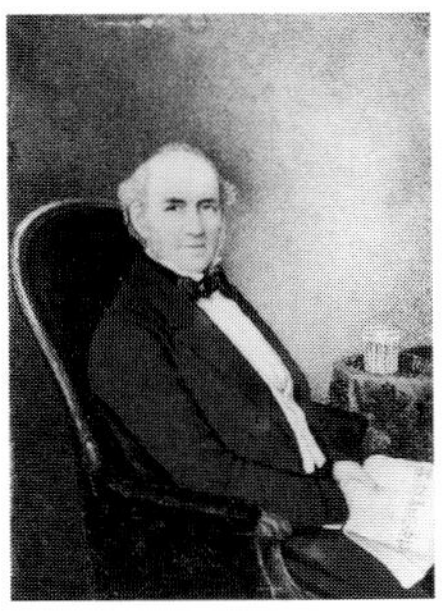

B. Bell
active London c.1849
James Haughton, (1795–1873), Social Reformer, 1849
Dated September 1849 on backing card. 16 x 12, watercolour on ivory. Purchased from Miss R. Black, 1984
NGI 19235. see pp. 142–43.

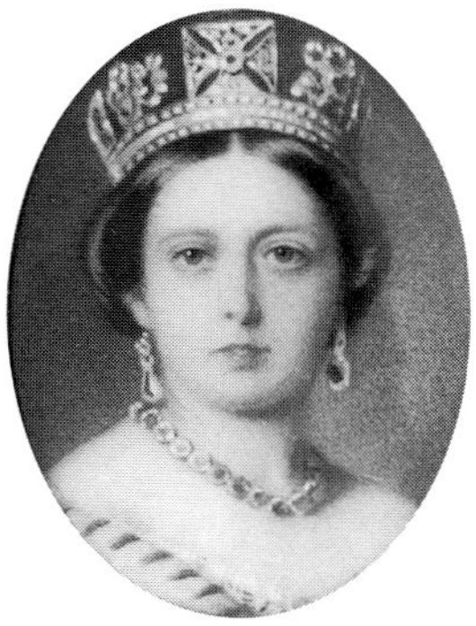

William Charles Bell
London c.1830 – 1904 London
Queen Victoria, (1819–1901), 1866. Inscribed, signed and dated on reverse: **by Bell 1866*
2.5 x 1.9, enamel on gold
Presented by Sir Alfred Chester Beatty, 1951
NGI 3627. see p. 141.

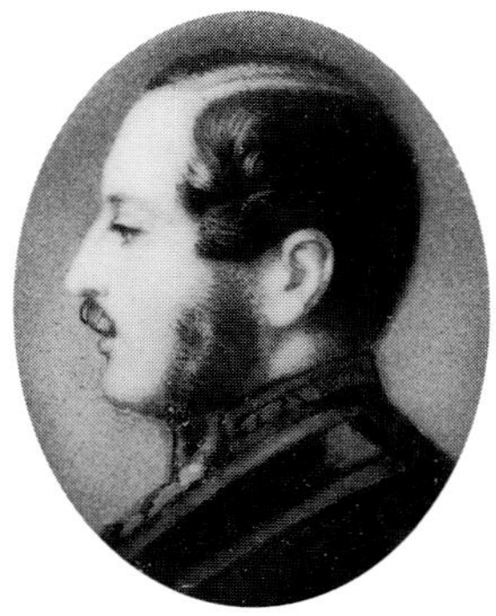

William Charles Bell
Prince Albert, (1819–1861), Consort of Queen Victoria, 1866
(after Winterhalter, Royal Collection)
Inscribed, signed and dated on reverse: **by Bell 1866*.
2.5 x 1.9, enamel on gold
Presented by Sir Alfred Chester Beatty, 1951. NGI 3628. see p. 141.

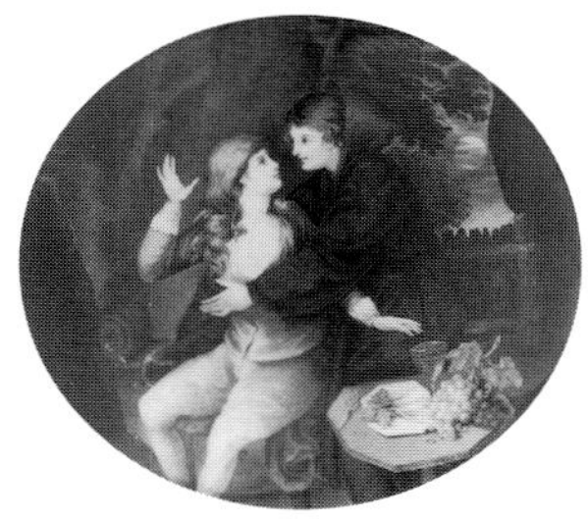

William Russell Birch
Warwick 1755 – 1834 Philadelphia
Romeo and Juliet, 1783
Signed and dated: *W.Birch. 1783*
10.4 x 12, enamel on copper
Presented by Sir Alfred Chester Beatty, 1951
NGI 3584. see pp. 82–83.

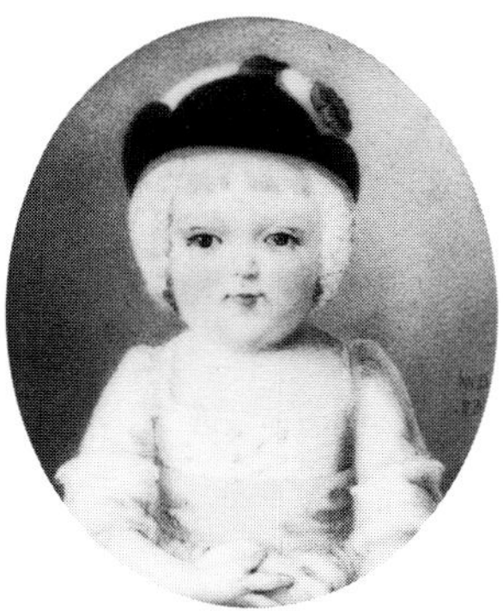

William Russell Birch
Portrait of a child with a black cap, 1783. Signed and dated: *W B 83*
4 x 3.5, enamel on copper
Presented by Sir Alfred Chester Beatty, 1951
NGI 3623

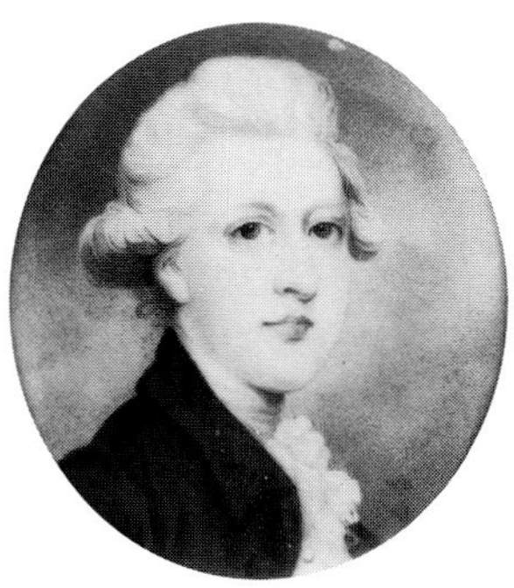

William Russell Birch
Portrait of a young man in a blue coat, 1783
Signed and dated: *W.B. 83*
4.5 x 3.9, enamel on copper
Presented by Sir Alfred Chester Beatty, 1951
NGI 3654. see p. 83

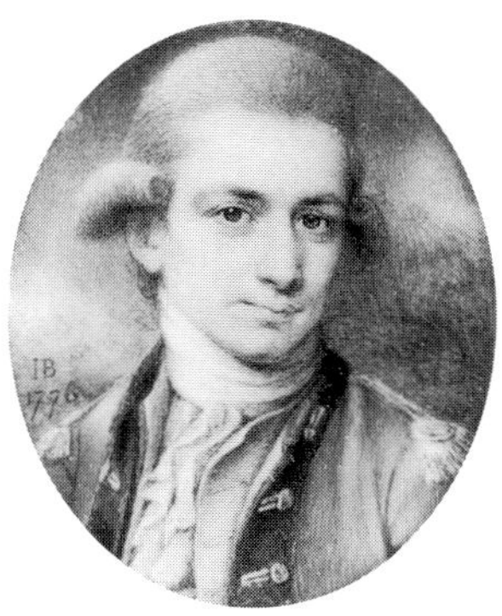

John Bogle
Scotland c.1746 – 1803 Edinburgh
Sir George Pickering, 1776
Signed and dated: *JB 1776*
3.4 x 2.9, enamel on copper, set in a brooch
Purchased from Mr R.A. Jones, 1903. NGI 2552. see p. 79.

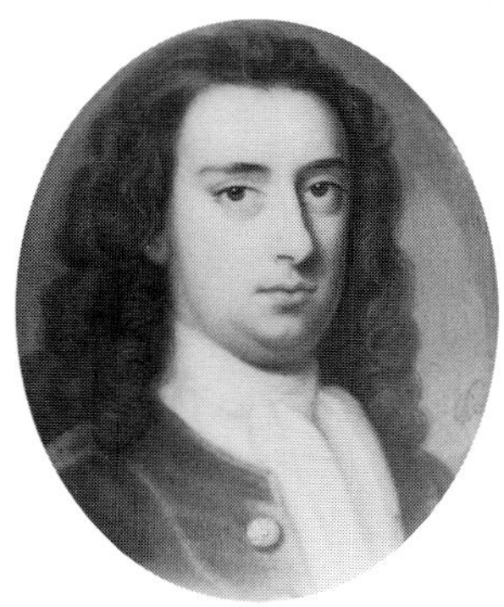

Charles Boit
Stockholm 1662 – 1727 Paris
Portrait of a man in a blue coat, c.1710
Signed: *CB*(in mono)*oit*
4.1 x 3.5, enamel on copper
Presented by Sir Alfred Chester Beatty, 1951
NGI 3651. see p. 42–43.

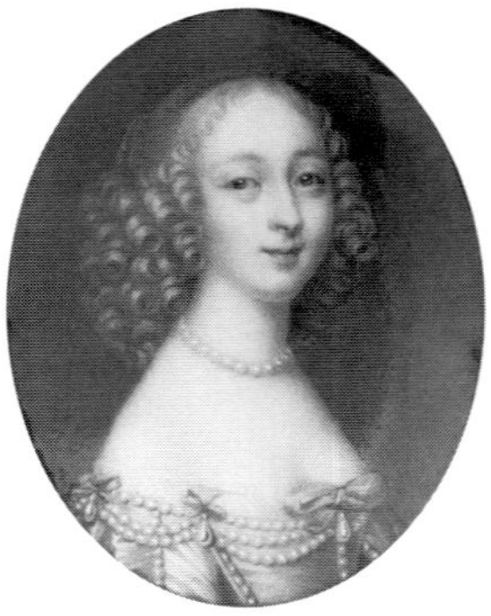

Henry Pierce Bone
Ninon de Lenclos, (1620–1705), Beauty and Courtesan, 1845
(after P. Mignard)
Inscribed, signed and dated on reverse: *London Sept. 1845. Painted by Henry Pierce Bone**
5 x 4, enamel on copper
Presented by Sir Alfred Chester Beatty, 1951
NGI 3618. see p. 125.

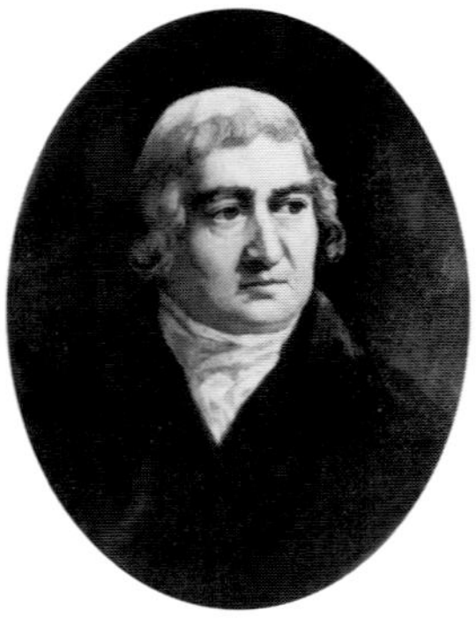

Peter Joseph Bone
London 1785 –
1814 near Toulouse
Dr John Wolcot, (1738–1819), Physician and Satirist 'Peter Pindar', 1801
(after J. Opie c.1793)
Inscribed, signed and dated on reverse: **by Peter Joseph Bone May 1801*
10.2 x 8.2, enamel on copper
Presented by Sir Alfred Chester Beatty, 1951
NGI 3580. see p. 130.

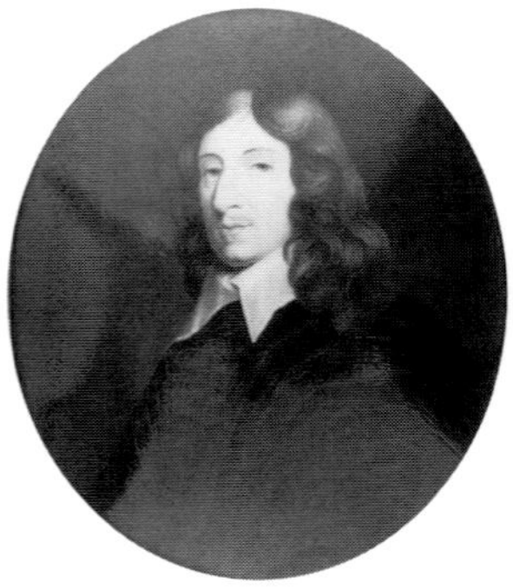

William Bone, Senior
active London 1815 –
1843 London
John Selden, (1584–1654), Writer and Politician
(after P. Lely c.1650)
Inscribed and signed on reverse: **Painted in Enamel by Wm. Bone**
11.9 x 9.9, enamel on copper
Presented by Sir Alfred Chester Beatty, 1951
NGI 3573

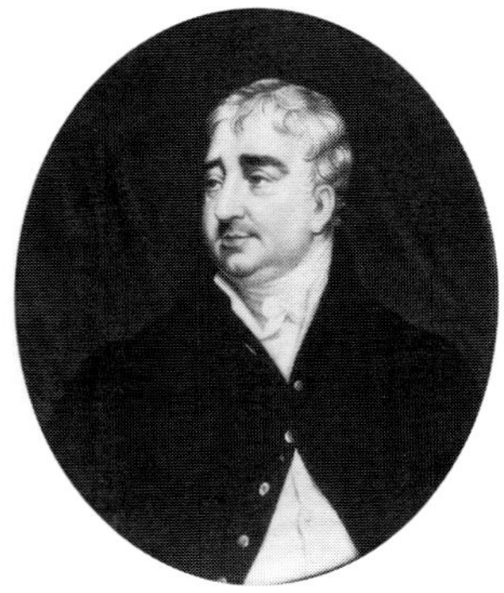

William Bone, Senior
Charles James Fox, M.P., (1749–1806), Statesman, c.1842
(after J. Opie 1804 wl, Holkham Hall, Norfolk)
Inscribed and signed on reverse: **Painted by WB*(in mono)*one**
12 x 9.9, enamel on copper
Presented by Sir Alfred Chester Beatty, 1951
NGI 3578. see pp. 133–34.

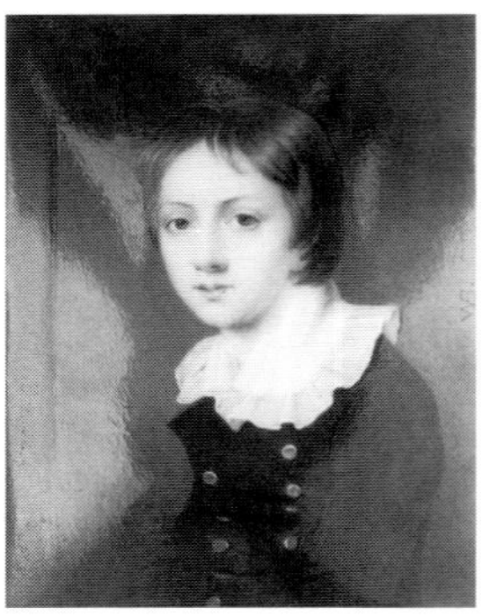

William Bone, Senior
Robert Trewick Bone, (1790–1840), Artist and brother, as a boy, 1834
(after H.P. Bone miniature)
Signed: *WB*(in mono)
Inscribed, signed and dated on reverse: **Painted in Enamel by William Bone*1834*
9.2 x 7.3, enamel on copper
Presented by Sir Alfred Chester Beatty, 1951
NGI 3579

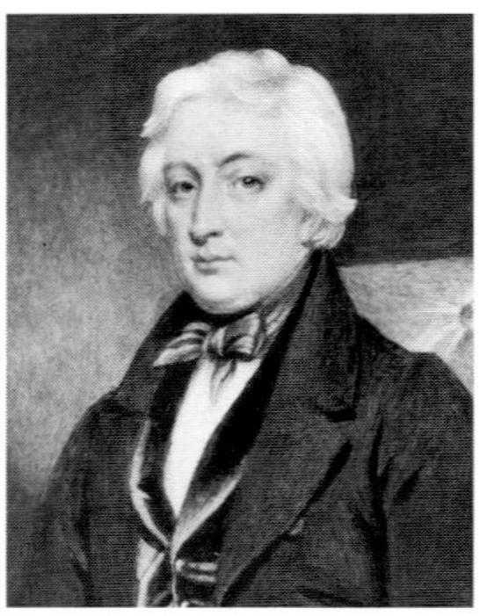

William Bone, Senior
(?) Portrait of a member of the Bone family
12.5 x 9.7, enamel on copper
Presented by Sir Alfred Chester Beatty, 1951
NGI 3588

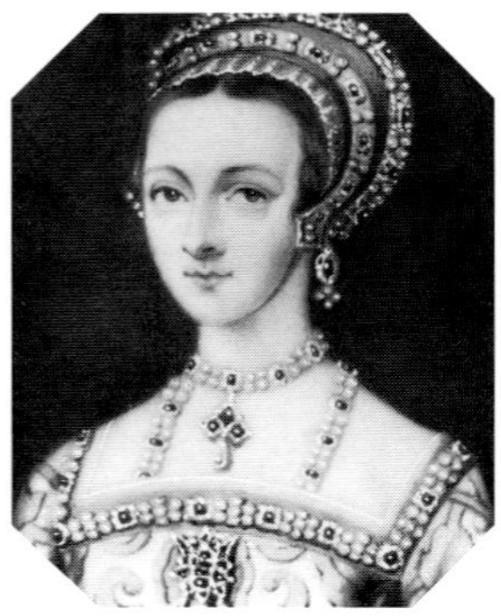

William Bone, Senior
Lady Jane Grey, (1537–1554), Pretender to the English Throne, 1831
(after English School 17th century wl, Seaton Delaval, Northumberland)
Signed: *WB*(in mono)
Inscribed, signed and dated on reverse: *London March 1831 Painted by William Bone**
3.9 x 3.2, enamel on copper
Presented by Sir Alfred Chester Beatty, 1951
NGI 3621

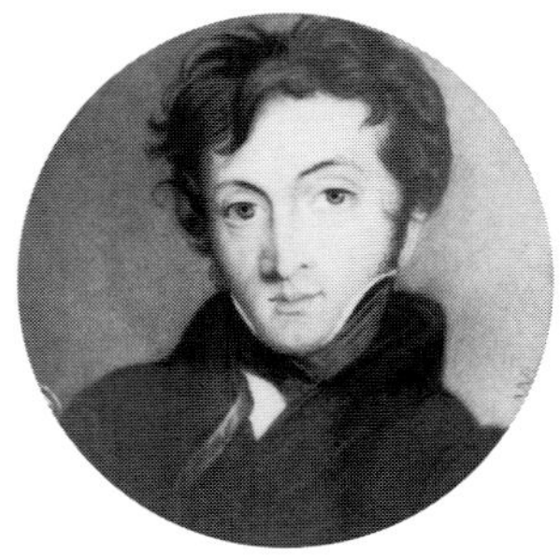

William Bone, Senior
Robert Trewick Bone, (1790–1840), Artist and brother, 1843. (after A. Chalon miniature)
Signed: *WB*(in mono). Inscribed, signed and dated on reverse: **Painted in enamel by Willm. Bone London 1843*. 4.7 diam., enamel on copper. Presented by Sir Alfred Chester Beatty, 1951.
NGI 3622. see p. 134.

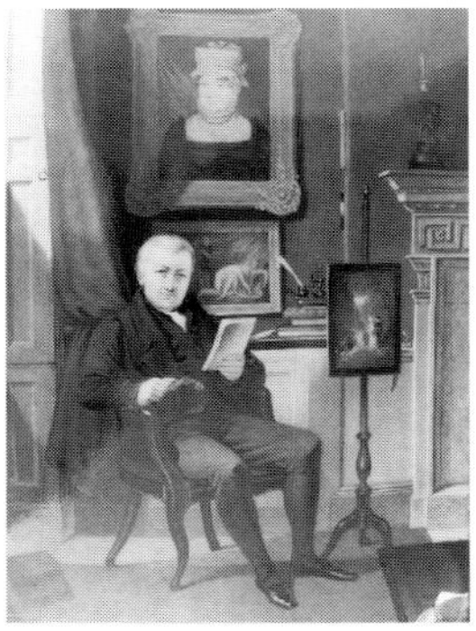

William Bone, Senior
Henry Bone, (1755–1834), Enamellist, the artist's father, 1842, (after R.T. Bone miniature exhibited 1831)
Inscribed, signed and dated on reverse: **painted in enamel by William Bone*London May 1842*
16.1 x 13.4, enamel on copper
Presented by Sir Alfred Chester Beatty, 1951.
NGI 7338. see p. 133.

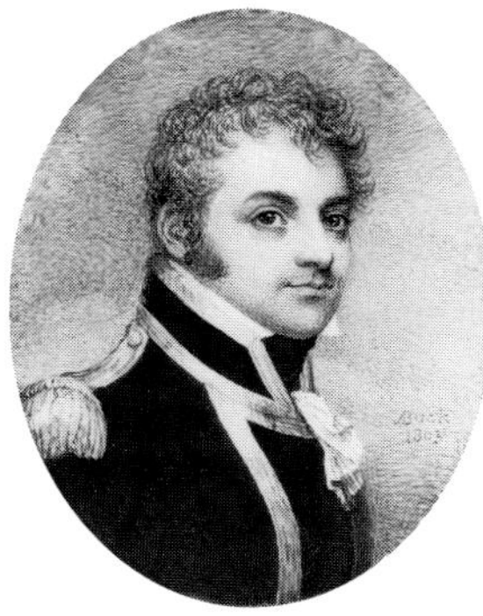

Adam Buck
Cork 1759 – 1833 London
Vice-Admiral Robert Plampin, (1762–1834), 1803
Signed and dated:
AB(in mono) *uck 1803*
7 x 5.6, watercolour on ivory.
Purchased from Mrs Wallis, 1904.
NGI 2553. see p. 107.

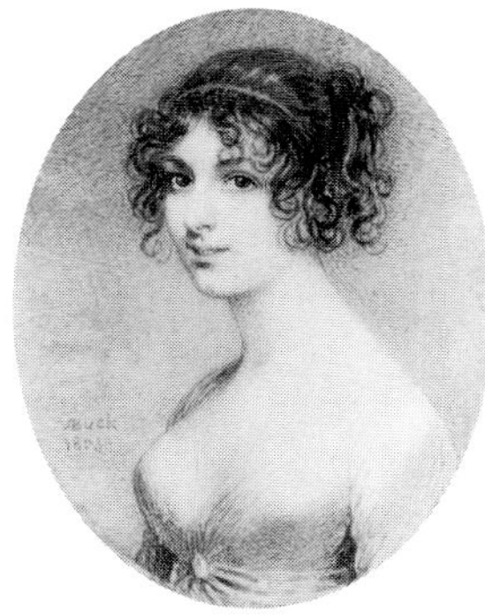

Adam Buck
Mrs Robert Plampin, (born Fanny Milchel), 1780–1864), 1803
Signed and dated:
AB(mono) *uck 1803*
7 x 5.5, watercolour on ivory
Purchased from Mrs Wallis, 1904
NGI 2554. see p. 107.

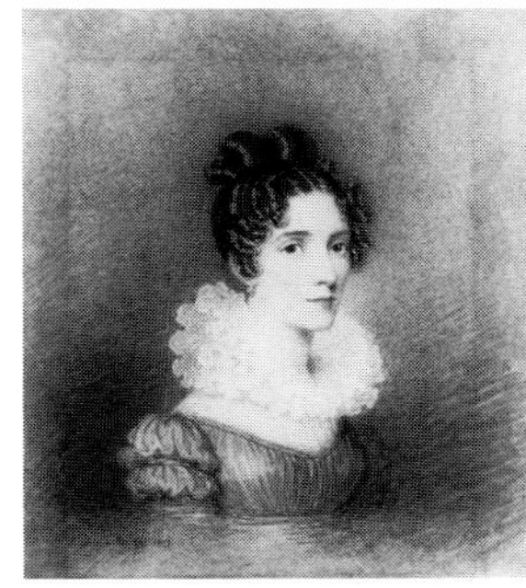

Adam Buck
Portrait of a young lady with a ruff, 1822
Signed and dated:
Adam Buck 1822
13.7 x 12.6, watercolour on card
Presented by Sir Hugh Lane, 1904
NGI 2555

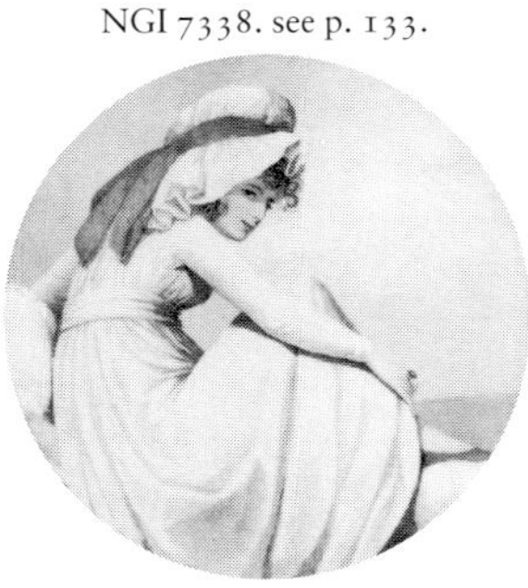

Adam Buck
Young lady seated on a sea-wall, c.1800
8.5 diam., watercolour on ivory
Transferred from the NMI, 1969 (where presented by Mrs M. Sullivan, 1949)
NGI 7171. see p. 108.

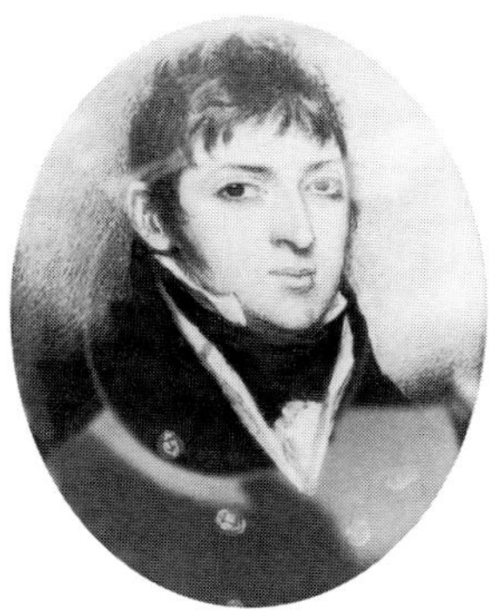

Attributed to Adam Buck
James L. Drummond
6.5 x 5, watercolour on ivory
Transferred from the NMI 1969 (where provenance unknown)
NGI 7093

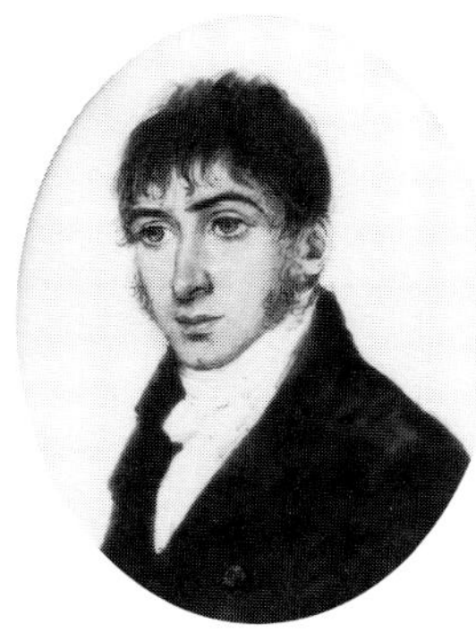

Frederick Buck
Cork 1771 – 1840 Cork
Sir Edward Stanley, (1769–1852), wine merchant and public official
6 x 5, watercolour on ivory
Presented by Mr E.S. Robertson, 1903
NGI 2530

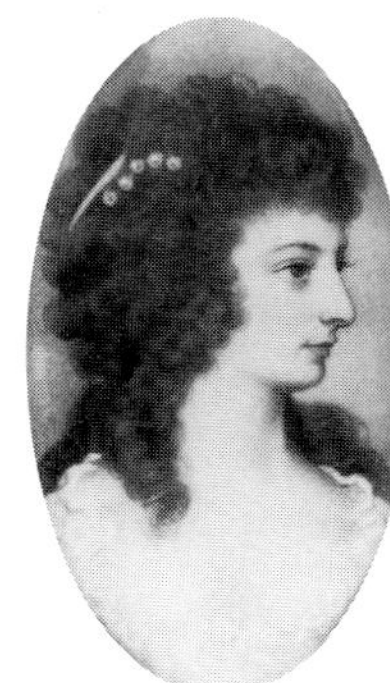

Frederick Buck
Miss Lombard
4.5 x 2.7, watercolour on ivory
Transferred from the NMI, 1969 (where purchased from sitter's granddaughter 1910)
NGI 7119

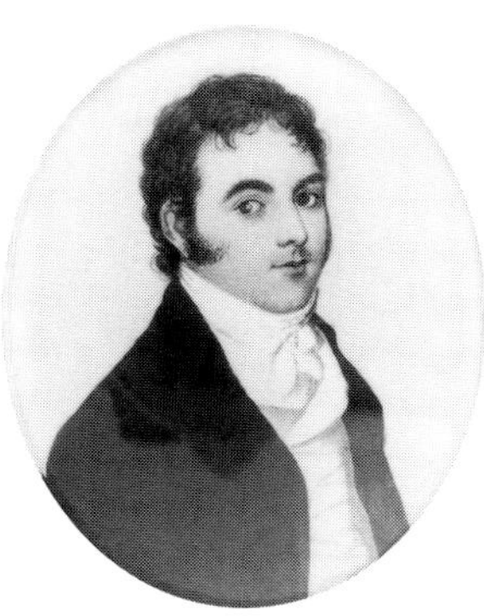

Frederick Buck
Thomas Ellis, (1774–1832)
7.3 x 5.2, watercolour on ivory
Transferred from the NMI, 1969 (where presented 1939)
NGI 7142

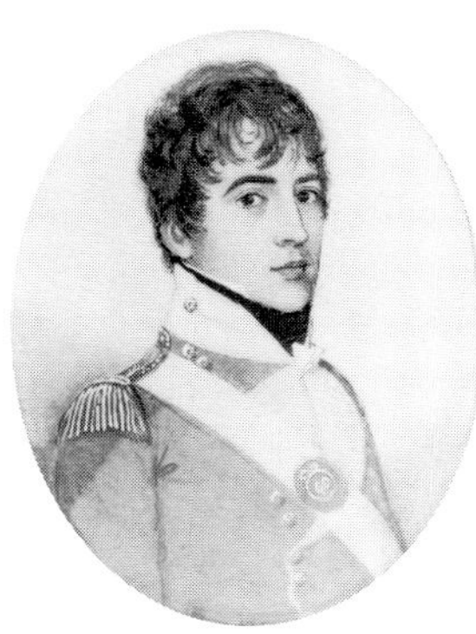

Frederick Buck
Major Conyngham Ellis of the 40th Regiment, (1783–1815), who died at the Battle of Waterloo,
c.1800. 6.4 x 5.3, watercolour on ivory. Transferred from the NMI, 1969 (where presented 1939)
NGI 7144. see p. 118.

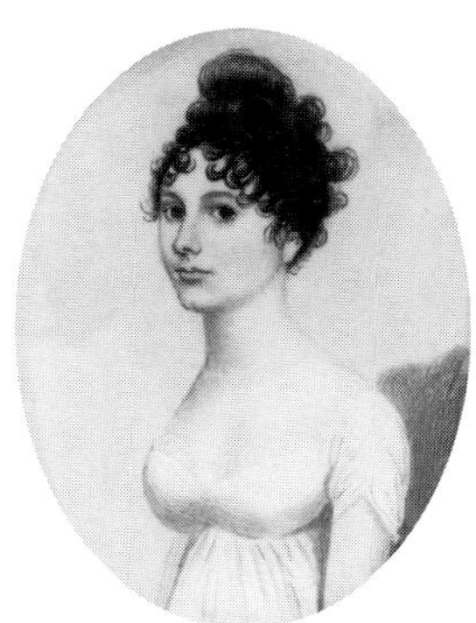

Frederick Buck
Barbara Elizabeth Turton, (born Ellis, 1772–1854)
6.8 x 5.1, watercolour on ivory
Transferred from the NMI, 1969 (where presented 1939)
NGI 7145

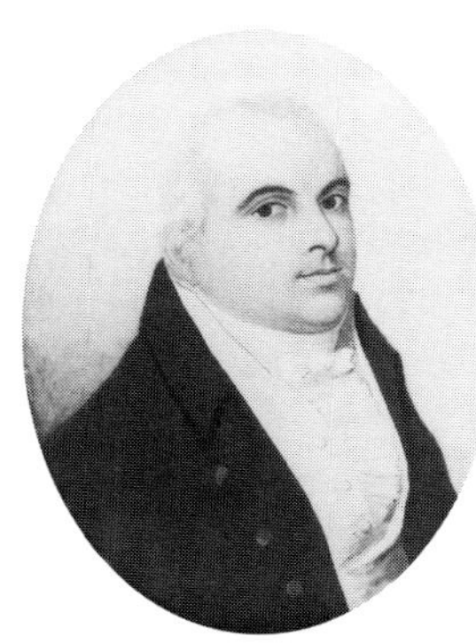

Frederick Buck
Lieutenant-Colonel T. Brownrigg of the 3rd Foot Regiment
7 x 5.7, watercolour on ivory
Transferred from the NMI, 1969 (where acquired 1946)
NGI 7146

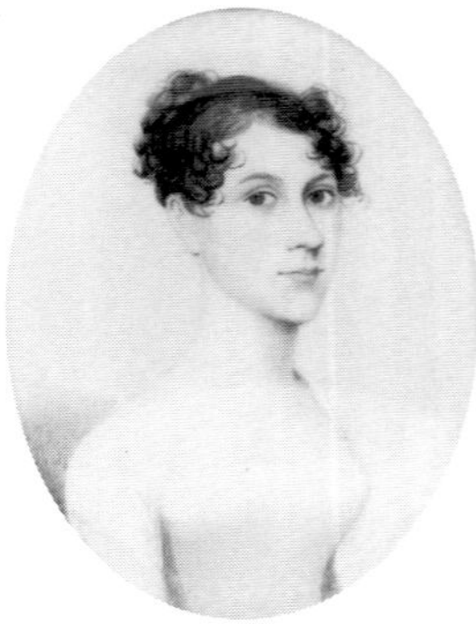

FREDERICK BUCK
Anne Ellis, (1787–1851)
6.6 x 5, watercolour on ivory
Transferred from the NMI, 1969
(where presented 1939)
NGI 7148

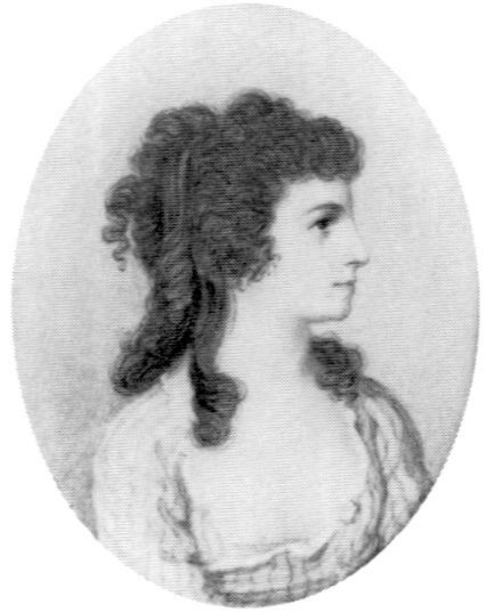

FREDERICK BUCK
Miss Buck, 1789
Dated 1789 on backing paper
4.4 x 3.5, watercolour on ivory
Transferred from the NMI, 1969
(where presented by
Mr J.W. Jellet, 1949)
NGI 7170

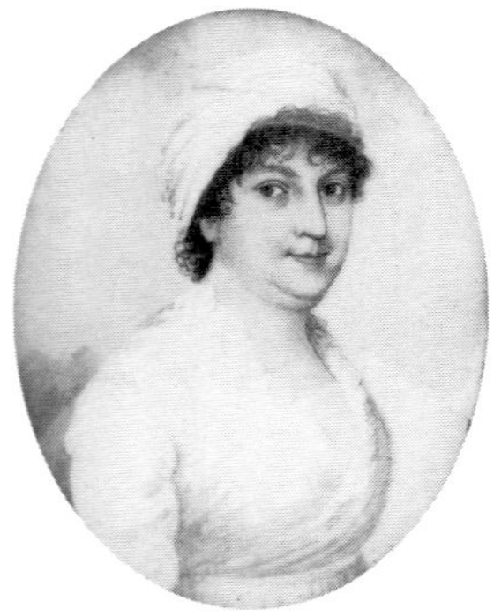

FREDERICK BUCK
Mrs Richard Ellis,
(born Mary Hilliard, d.1812)
6.3 x 4.8, watercolour on ivory
Transferred from the NMI, 1969
(where presented 1939)
NGI 7185

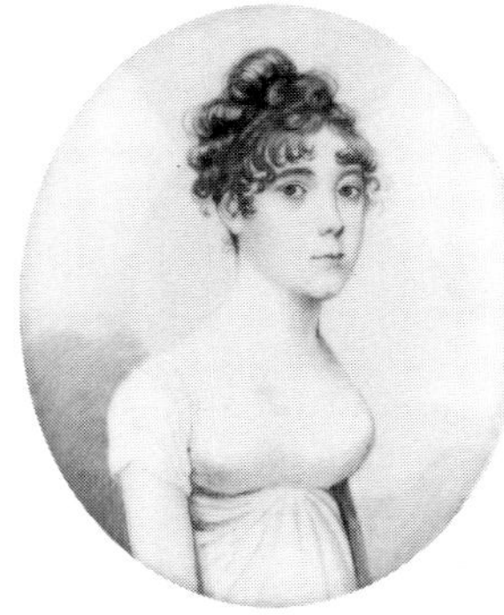

FREDERICK BUCK
Mary O'Bryen, 1807
Dated 1807 on backing paper
6.3 x 5.3, watercolour on ivory
Transferred from the NMI, 1969
(where acquired 1915)
NGI 7213. see p. 119.

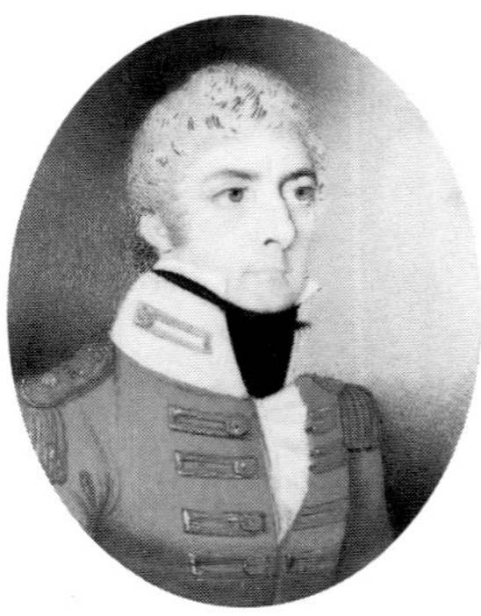

FREDERICK BUCK
Portrait of an Officer, c.1800
10.6 x 7.5, watercolour on ivory
Transferred from the NMI, 1969
(where purchased 1916)
NGI 7222

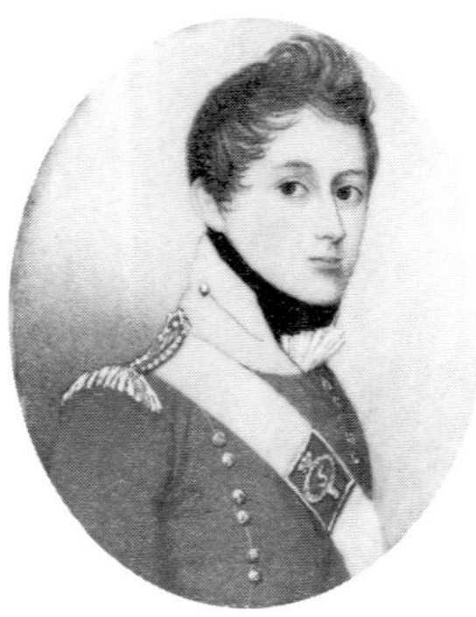

FREDERICK BUCK
Lieutenant John Trydell,
(1796–1831)
6.5 x 5.1, watercolour on ivory
Transferred from the NMI, 1969
(where provenance unknown)
NGI 7794

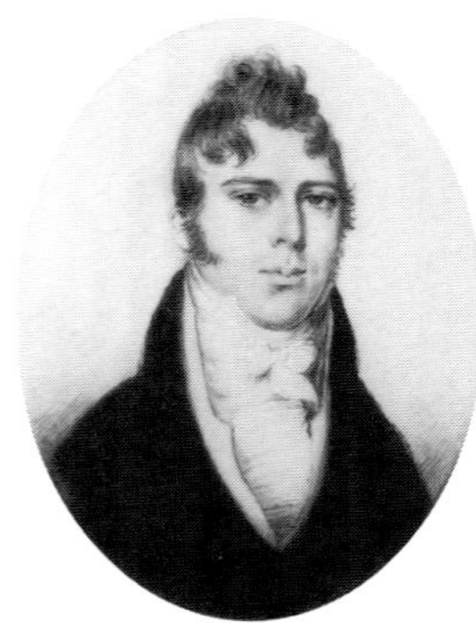

FREDERICK BUCK
A member of the Armstrong family
of Garry Castle, Co. Offaly
6.4 x 5, watercolour on ivory
Presented by Sir Andrew
Armstrong, Bt., 1981
NGI 7941

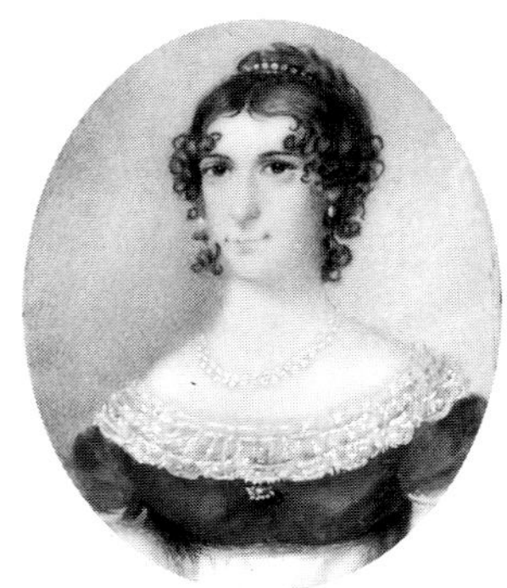

FREDERICK BUCK
Mrs Gaspar Erck,
(born Magdalen Lescure, d.1815),
(first wife of the following)
7.3 x 5.7, watercolour on ivory
Bequeathed by
Dr S.D. Oliver, 1989
NGI 19384

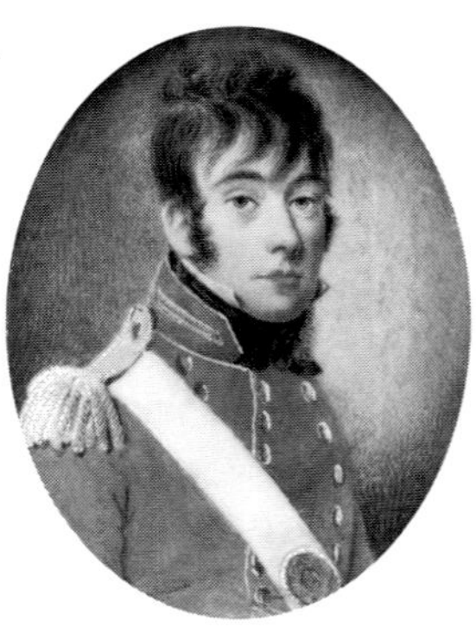

FREDERICK BUCK
Captain Gaspar Erck
6.9 x 5.2, watercolour on ivory
Bequeathed by
Dr S.D. Oliver, 1989
NGI 19385

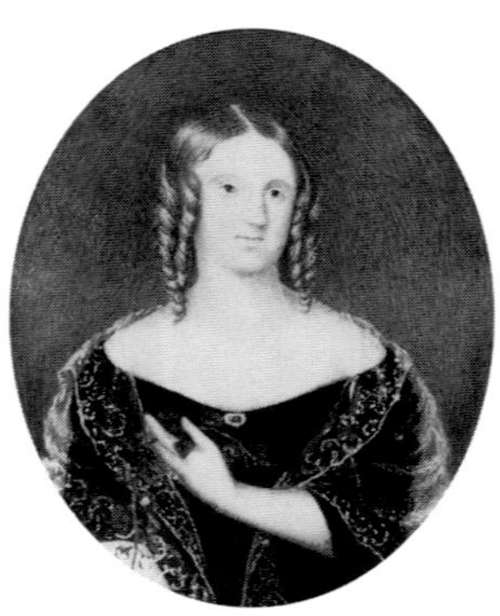

HARRIET BUNBURY
Ireland 1802 – 1888 Ireland
Selina Bunbury, (1802–1882),
Novelist and Traveller, c.1825
11.6 x 9.3, watercolour on card
Presented by Dr J.S. Crone, 1929
NGI 7314

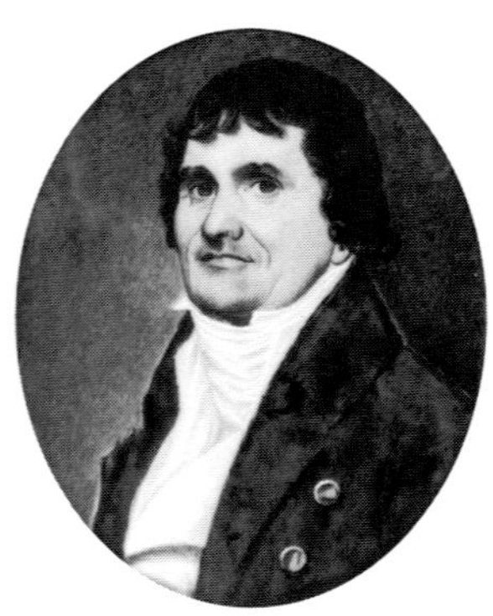

CHARLES BYRNE
Dublin 1757 – c.1810 Dublin
Self-Portrait, late 1790s
7.6 x 5.9, watercolour on ivory
Purchased from Miss F. Byrne,
1889
NGI 2034. see p. 105.

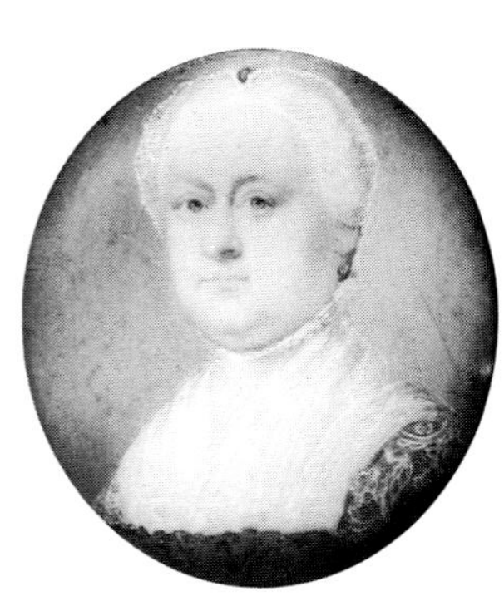

PENELOPE CARWARDINE
Withington, Herefordshire
c.1730 – 1801 London
Portrait of a lady in a blue dress,
c.1760. Signed: *PC*
3 x 2.6, watercolour on ivory
Miss Mary A. McNeill Bequest,
1985. NGI 19255. see p. 63.

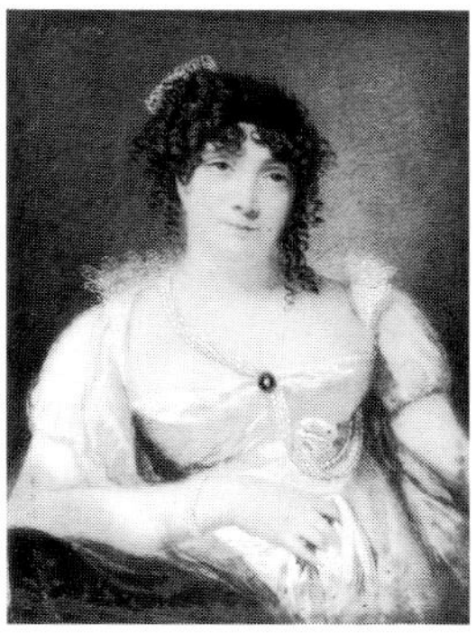

ALFRED EDWARD CHALON
Geneva 1780 – 1860 London
Maria (Mary Arabella), Marchioness of Lansdowne, (born Maddox, active 1805–1833), wife of the 2nd Marquess, c.1820.
Signed: *A. Chalon*
10.9 x 8.3, watercolour on ivory
Bequeathed by Professor J. Joly, great grandson of the sitter, 1934
NGI 2951. see p. 126.

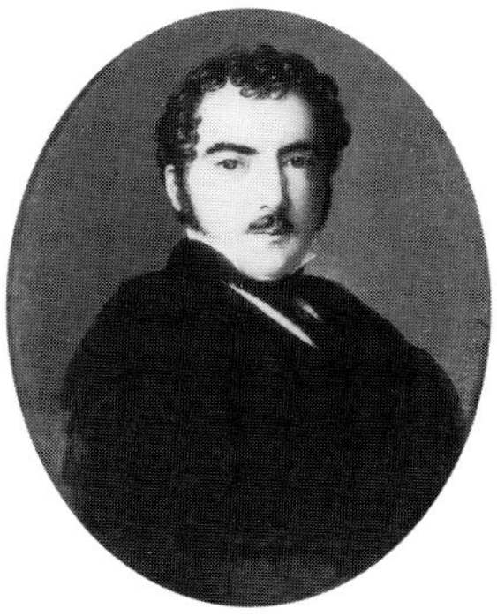

ALFRED EDWARD CHALON
Frederick Charles Spiridion, Count Lusi (m. 1818)
8 x 6.6, watercolour on ivory
Bequeathed by Professor J. Joly, grandson of the sitter, 1934
NGI 2952

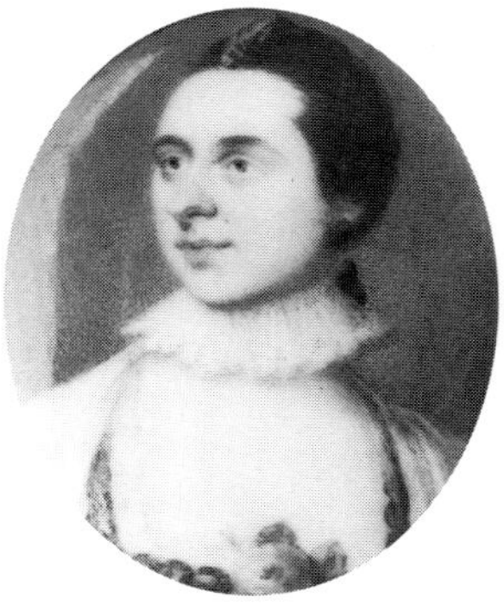

SAMUEL COLLINS
Bristol 1735 – 1768 Dublin
Portrait of a lady with a white collar, 1761
Signed and dated: *S.C. 1761*
3.6 x 3.1, enamel on copper
Presented by Sir Alfred Chester Beatty, 1951
NGI 3731. see p. 67.

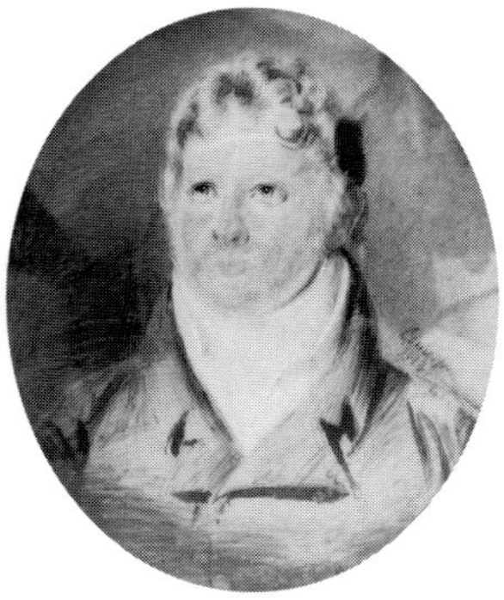

JOHN COMERFORD
Kilkenny c.1770 – 1832 Dublin
William Casey of Springfield, Co. Clare, 1813
Signed and dated: *Comerford 1813*
8.1 x 6.7, watercolour on ivory
Purchased from Sir Thomas Jones, 1891
NGI 2051

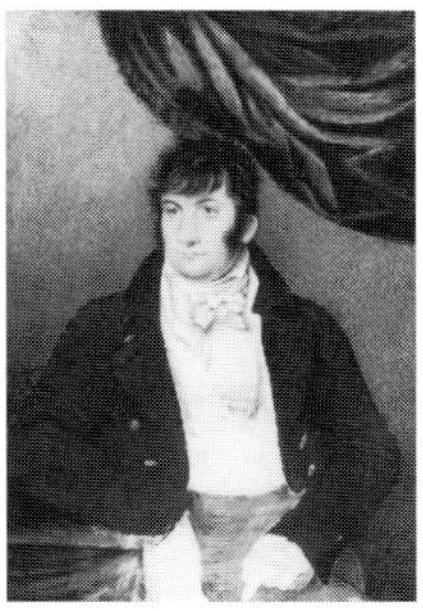

JOHN COMERFORD
Henry Sheares, (1753–1798), Barrister and brother of John Sheares
12.4 x 4.9, watercolour on ivory
Presented by the 7th Earl of Mayo, 1884
NGI 2052

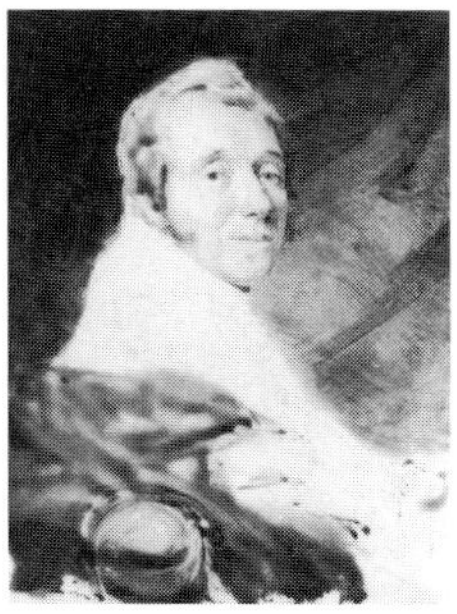

JOHN COMERFORD
Richard Power, Comedian and founder of the Kilkenny Theatre (unfinished), 1808/12
10.8 x 8.2, watercolour on ivory
Purchased from the 7th Viscount Powerscourt, 1886
NGI 2053

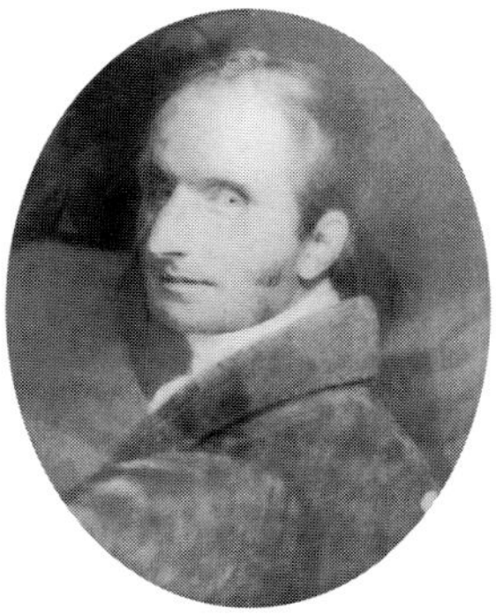

JOHN COMERFORD
Peter Atkinson, (1783/84–1817), 1817
Painted 1817 from a death mask and memory
7.1 x 5.7, watercolour on ivory
Presented by Dr G. Atkinson son of the sitter, 1888
NGI 2353

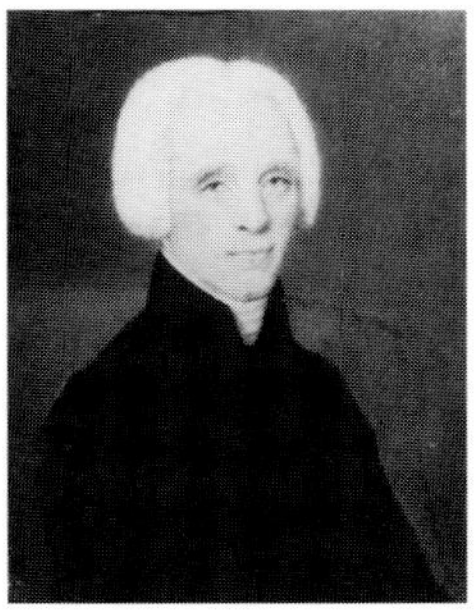

JOHN COMERFORD
The Hon. Charles Brodrick, (1761–1822), Archbishop of Cashel
8.4 x 6.6, watercolour on ivory
Purchased at Sotheby's, London, 16 May, 1923
NGI 2735

JOHN COMERFORD
Mrs Coote, 1804
Signed and dated on backing paper: *J. Comerford 1804*
6.9 x 5.8, watercolour on ivory
Presented by Mr L. O'Callaghan, through the Friends of the National Collections of Ireland, 1924. NGI 2739

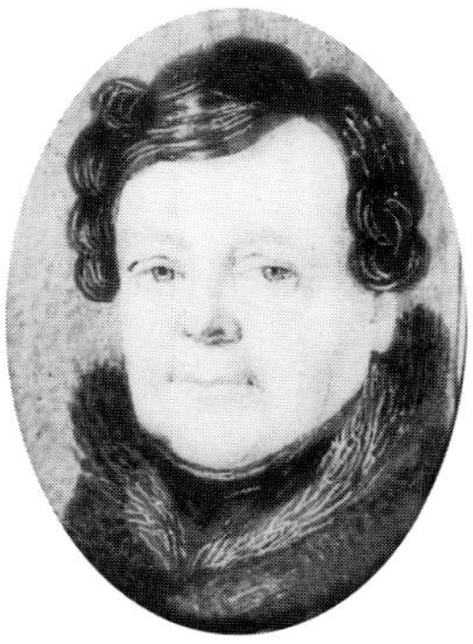

JOHN COMERFORD
Daniel O'Connell, M.P., (1775–1847), 'The Liberator', c.1820
2.2 x 1.6, watercolour on ivory
Presented by Mr D. Gwynn, 1930
NGI 2924. see p. 117.

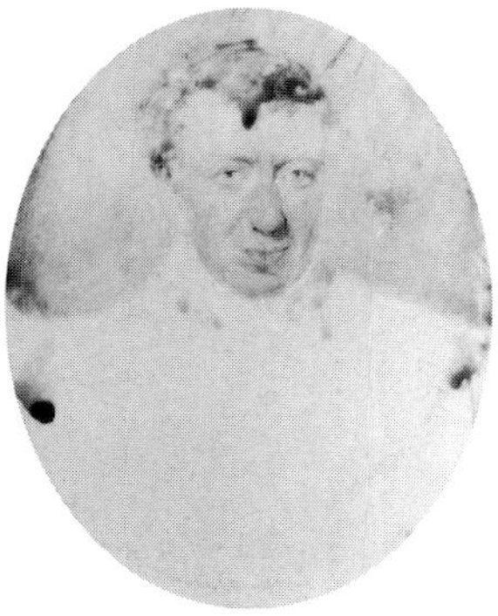

JOHN COMERFORD
Garret Trench (unfinished)
11 x 8.1, watercolour on ivory
Purchased from the 7th Viscount Powerscourt, 1886
NGI 3195

JOHN COMERFORD
Judge John Kelly (unfinished)
11.9 x 8.9, watercolour on ivory
Purchased from the 7th Viscount Powerscourt, 1886
NGI 3196

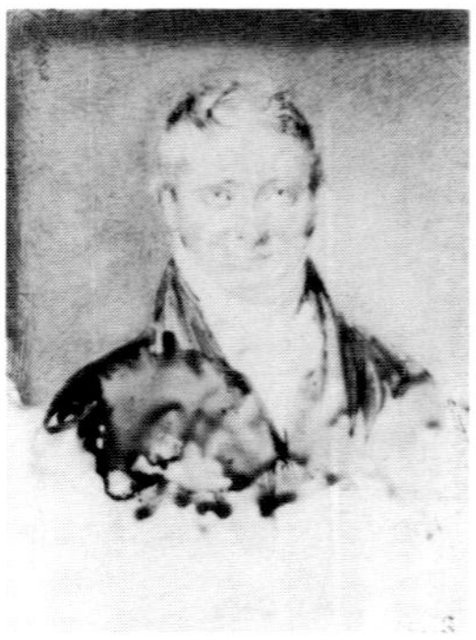

John Comerford
Sir Thomas Esmonde, Bt. (unfinished)
10.6 x 8.1, watercolour on ivory
Purchased from the 7th Viscount Powerscourt, 1886
NGI 3197

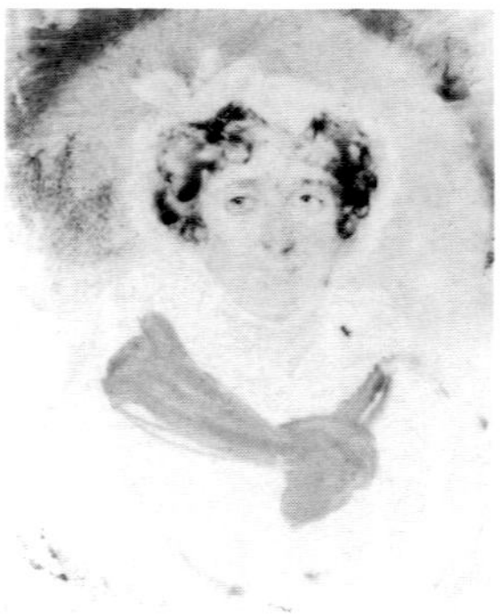

John Comerford
Portrait of a lady with a red shawl (unfinished)
10 x 8, watercolour on ivory
Purchased from the 7th Viscount Powerscourt, 1886
NGI 3198

John Comerford
Portrait of a man with white hair (unfinished)
10 x 7.5, watercolour on ivory
Purchased from the 7th Viscount Powerscourt, 1886
NGI 3199

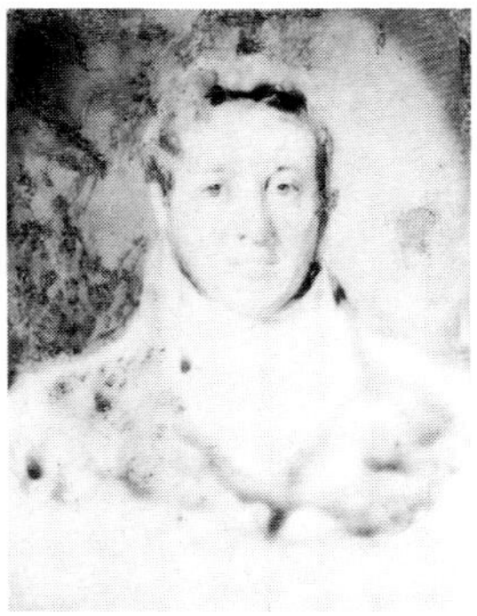

John Comerford
Portrait of a man in a brown coat (unfinished)
8.6 x 6.7, watercolour on ivory
Purchased from the 7th Viscount Powerscourt, 1886
NGI 3200

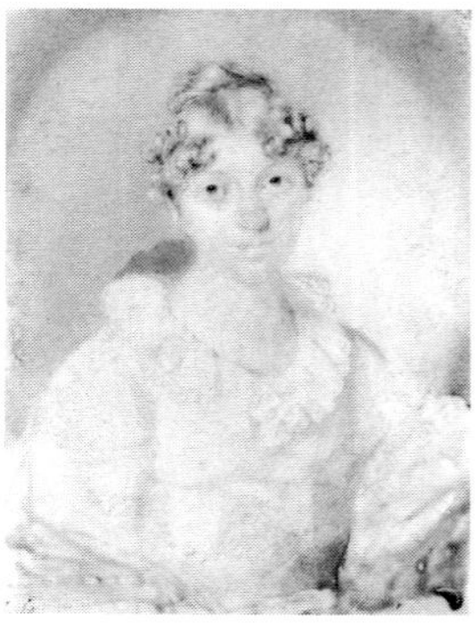

John Comerford
Portrait of a lady with a lace collar (unfinished)
10.7 x 8.2, watercolour on ivory
Purchased from the 7th Viscount Powerscourt, 1886
NGI 3201

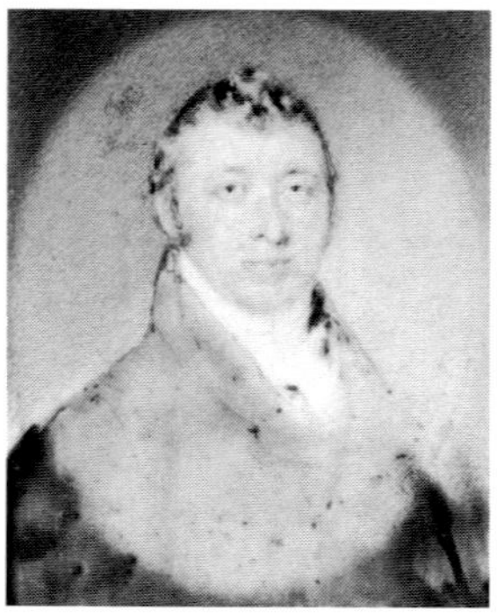

John Comerford
Portrait of a man in a blue coat (unfinished)
9.9 x 7.5, watercolour on ivory
Purchased from the 7th Viscount Powerscourt, 1886
NGI 3202

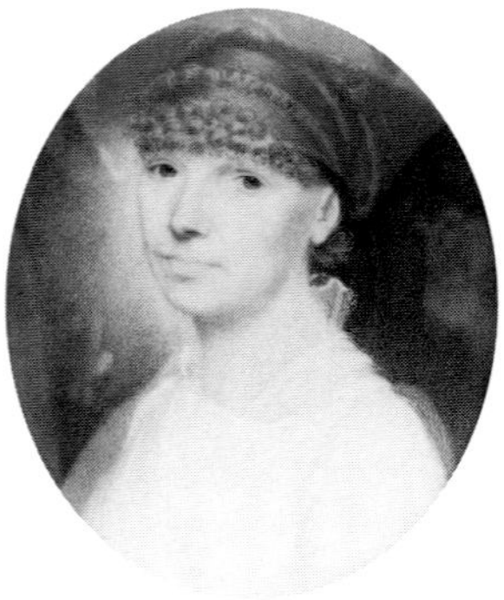

John Comerford
Elizabeth White
6.7 x 5.5, watercolour on ivory
Transferred from the NMI, 1969 (where presented by Miss C. Henry, 1900)
NGI 7070

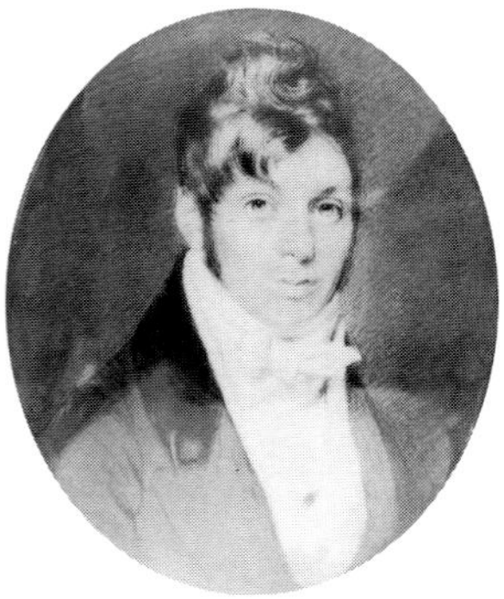

John Comerford
Portrait of a man in a grey-blue coat
7 x 5.8, watercolour on ivory, set in a brooch
Transferred from the NMI, 1969 (where purchased 1913)
NGI 7088

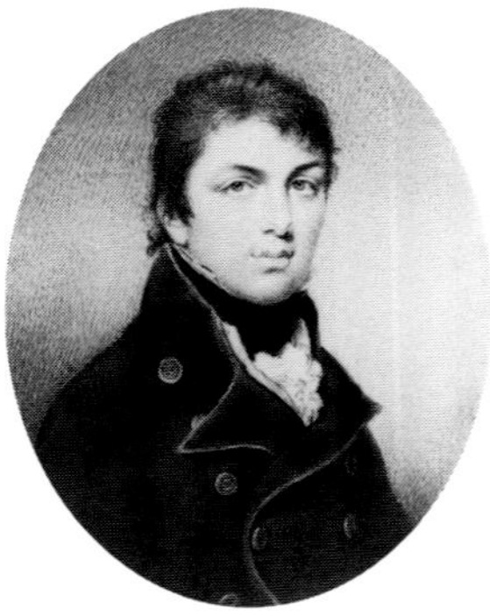

John Comerford
Portrait of a man in a blue coat with anchor buttons
8.3 x 6.7, watercolour on ivory
Transferred from the NMI, 1969 (where purchased 1914)
NGI 7089

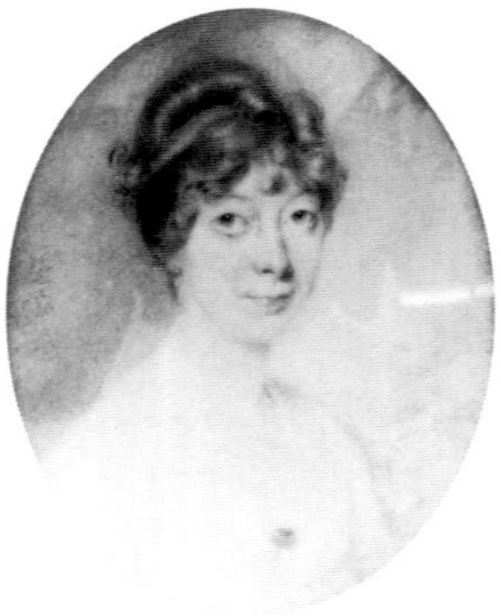

John Comerford
Mrs Thomas Ellis, (born Dymphna Monsell, 1780–1833), c.1802
6.8 x 5.2, watercolour on ivory
Transferred from the NMI, 1969 (where presented 1939)
NGI 7116

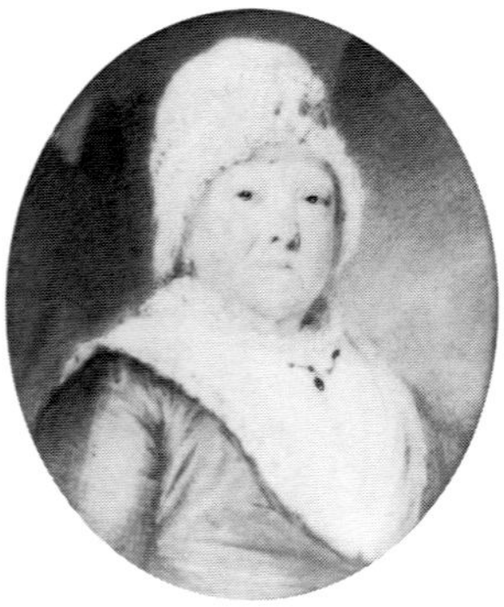

John Comerford
Miss or Mrs E.A.
7.6 x 6.2, watercolour on ivory
Transferred from the NMI, 1969 (where purchased 1915)
NGI 7141

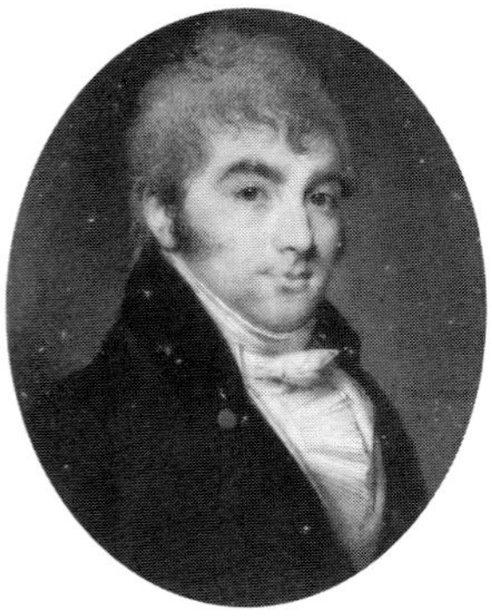

John Comerford
Thomas Ellis, M.P., (1774–1832), 1802
Signed and dated: *J. Comerford 1802*
7.2 x 5.8, watercolour on ivory
Transferred from the NMI, 1969 (where presented 1939)
NGI 7143. see pp. 115–16.

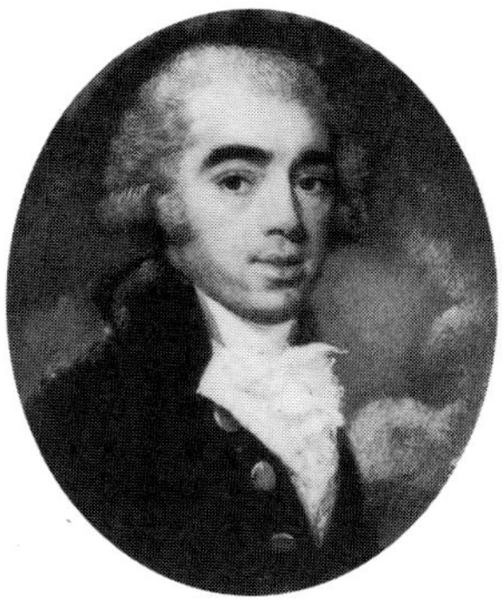

JOHN COMERFORD
J.R. Rogers, an Official of the Irish House of Commons
6.4 x 5.2, watercolour on ivory
Transferred from the NMI, 1969
(where presented by
Mrs M. Sullivan, 1949)
NGI 7150

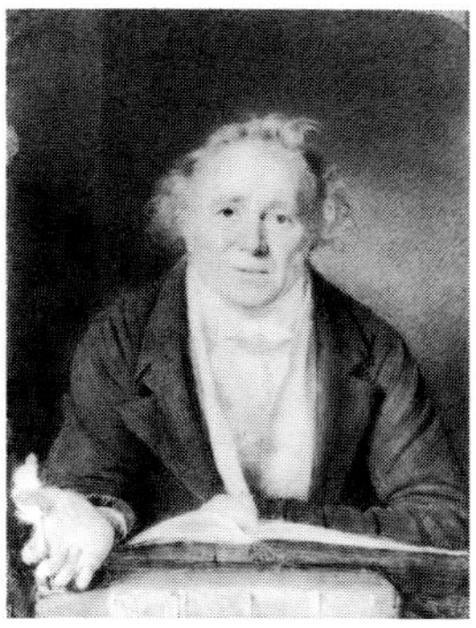

JOHN COMERFORD
John Keogh, (1740–1817), Catholic Leader, 1811
11.9 x 9.2, watercolour on ivory
Transferred from the NMI, 1969
(where presented by
Mrs M. Sullivan, 1949)
NGI 7200. see pp. 116–17.

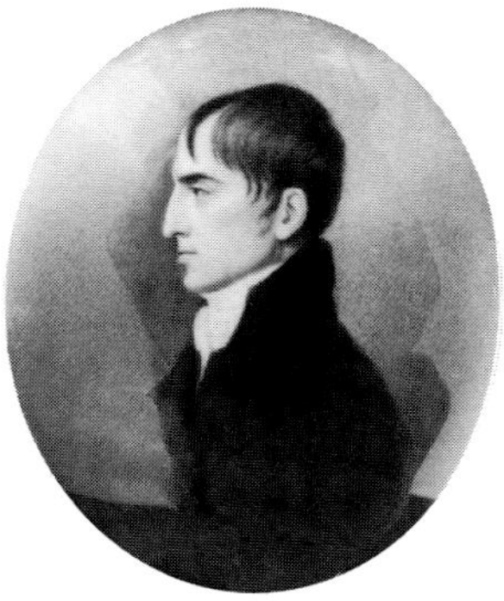

JOHN COMERFORD
Robert Emmet, (1778–1803), Patriot, c.1803
6.9 x 5.7, watercolour on ivory
Presented by Mr R. Emmet to the
Irish Government, 1969
and transferred
NGI 7341. see p. 115.

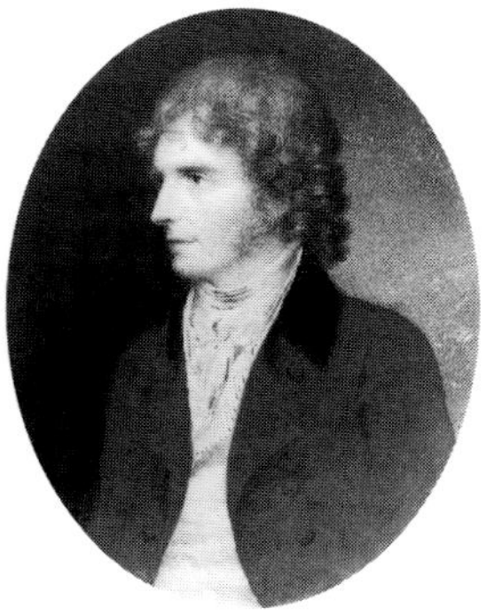

JOHN COMERFORD
Henry Joy McCracken, (1767–1798), United Irishman
7.8 x 6.2, watercolour on card
Purchased from
Mr G. Rooney, 1974
NGI 7711

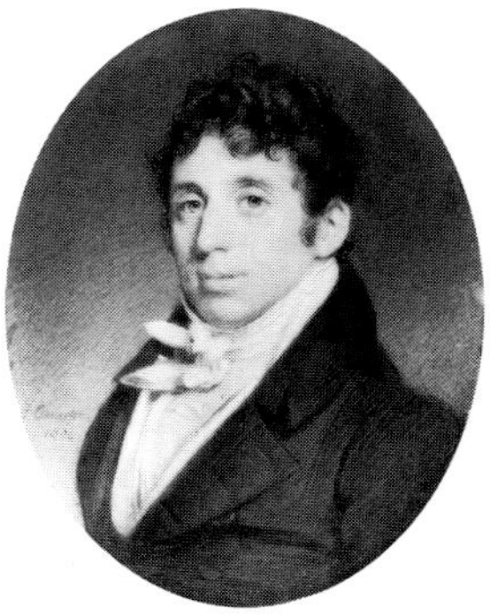

JOHN COMERFORD
Portrait of a man in a dark grey coat, 1804
Signed and dated:
J. Comerford 1804
7.3 x 5.8, watercolour on ivory
Miss Mary A. McNeill Bequest,
1985. NGI 19288

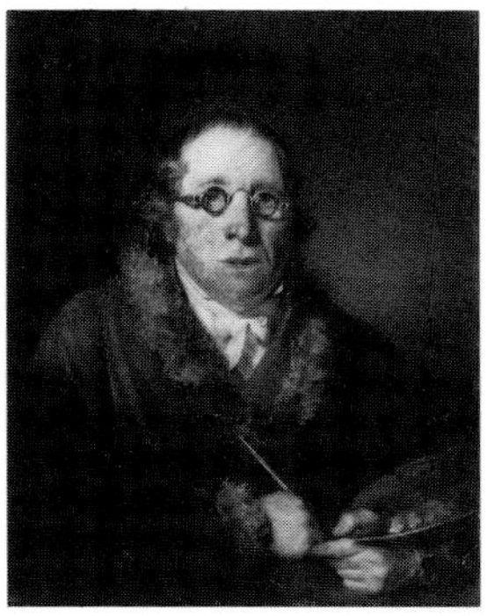

JOHN COMERFORD
William Ashford, (1746–1824), landscape painter and later first President of the Royal Hibernian Academy, 1822. Signed and dated: *J Comerford 1822.* 10.5 x 8.5, mixed media on ivory. Purchased from The Gorry Gallery, Dublin, 1995. NGI 19423. see pp. 117–18.

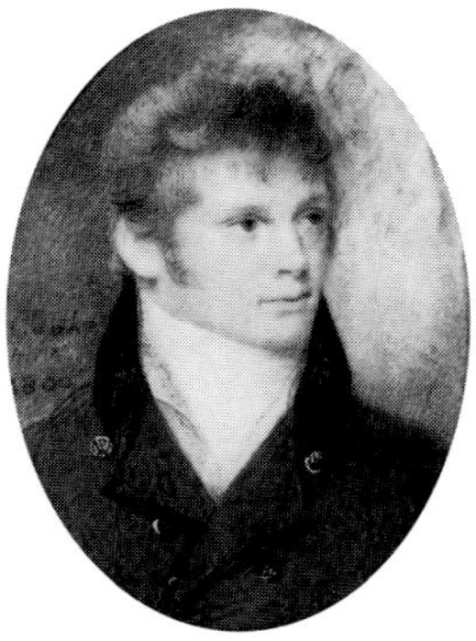

JOHN COOKE
Dublin 1770 – 1805 Dublin
Portrait of a young man in a brown coat, 1800
Signed and dated: *J Cooke pinx 1800.* 6.2 x 5, watercolour on ivory. Purchased from
Mr R. Harris, 1905
NGI 2581. see p. 113.

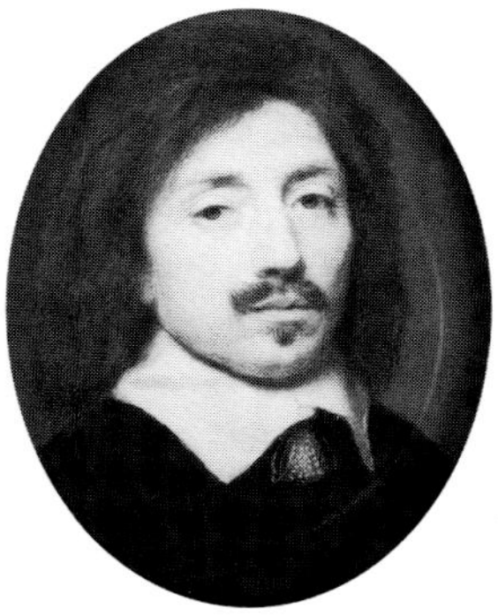

SAMUEL COOPER
London 1608/09 – 1672 London
Sir Anthony Thomas, 1647
Signed and dated: *S.C. 1647*
4.6 x 3.3, watercolour on card
Transferred from the NMI, 1969
(where presented by
Mrs M. Sullivan, 1949)
NGI 7045. see p. 40.

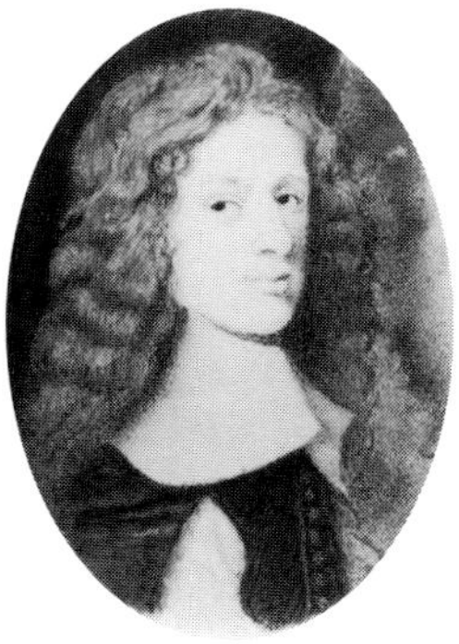

AFTER SAMUEL COOPER
Sir Samuel Morland, (1625–1695), Inventor (after undated miniature, V&A). 7.5 x 5.6, watercolour on ivory, 19th century
Transferred from the NMI, 1969
(where bequeathed by Miss
Gardiner, 1929). NGI 7138

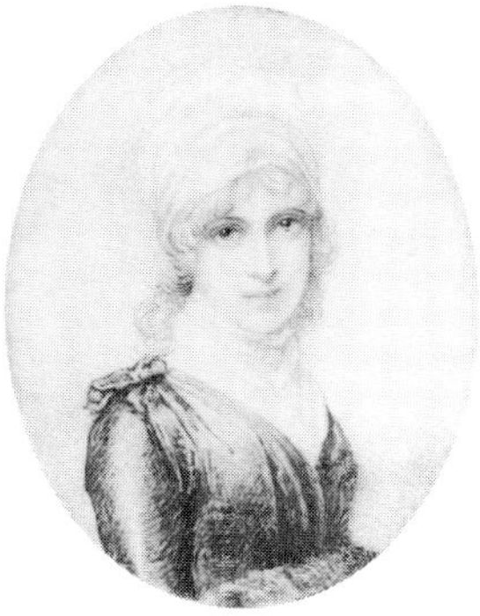

RICHARD COSWAY
Okeford, Devon 1742 – 1821
London. *Mrs Moffat,* 1797
Inscribed, signed and dated on backing paper: *Rdus Cosway R.A* Pinxit 1797*
7.5 x 5.8, watercolour on ivory
Bequeathed by Miss M. Grace,
1949. NGI 3023. see p. 78.

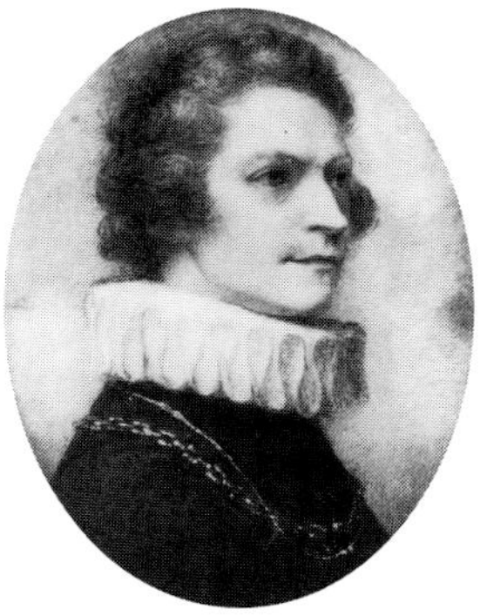

RICHARD COSWAY
Self-Portrait in Elizabethan costume, c.1790
7.1 x 5.7, watercolour on ivory
Bequeathed by Miss M. Grace,
1949
NGI 3024. see pp. 76–77.

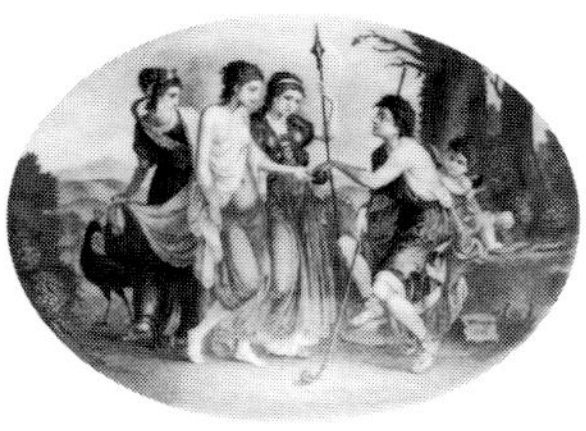

WILLIAM CRAFT
(?) Tottenham, Middx.
c.1730–1811 London
The Judgement of Paris, 1782
Signed and dated: *W:Craft. 1782.*
10.2 x 14.2, enamel on copper
Presented by Sir Alfred Chester
Beatty, 1951
NGI 3582. see pp. 64–65.

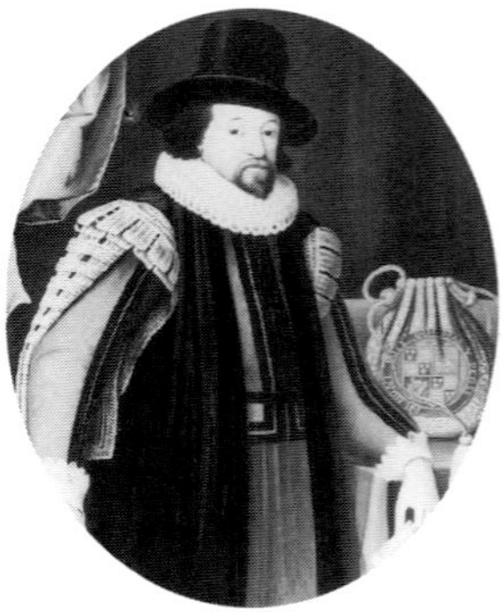

WILLIAM CRAFT
Francis Bacon, 1st Baron Verulam and Viscount St Alban, (1561–1626), Lord Chancellor, 1793, (after A. Blyenberch 1617/22, Royal Society, London). Inscribed, signed and dated 1793 on reverse. 17 x 14, enamel on copper. Presented by Sir Alfred Chester Beatty, 1951
NGI 3585. see p. 65–66.

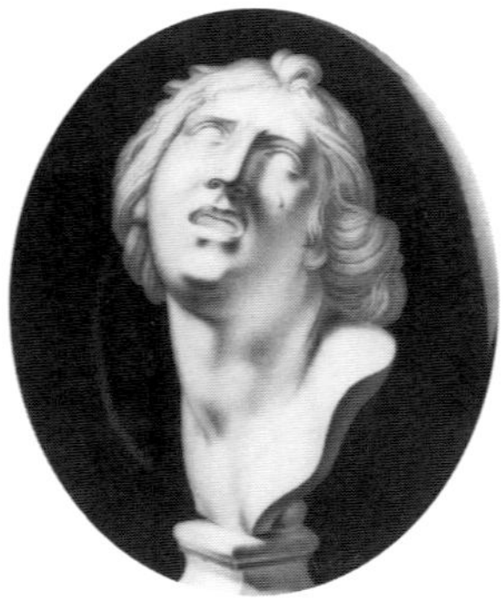

WILLIAM CRAFT
The Dying Alexander
(after the Antique sculpture, Uffizi, Florence)
Signed: *W: Craft*
6.8 x 5.8, enamel on copper
Presented by Sir Alfred Chester Beatty, 1951
NGI 3626

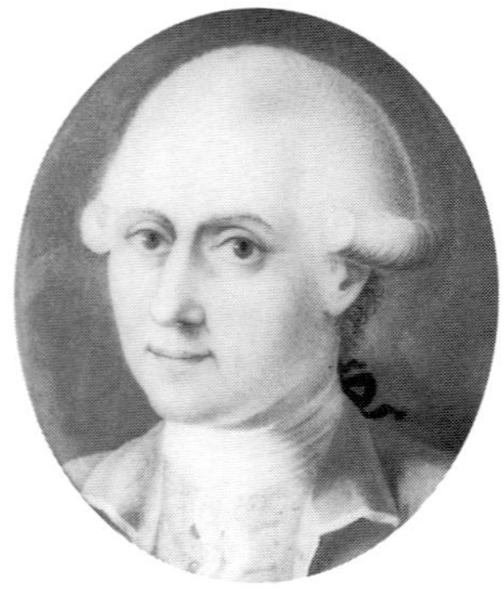

WILLIAM CRAFT
Self-Portrait, 1780
Signed and dated: *Craft 1780*
3.1 x 2.7, enamel on copper
Presented by Sir Alfred Chester Beatty, 1951
NGI 3668. see p. 64.

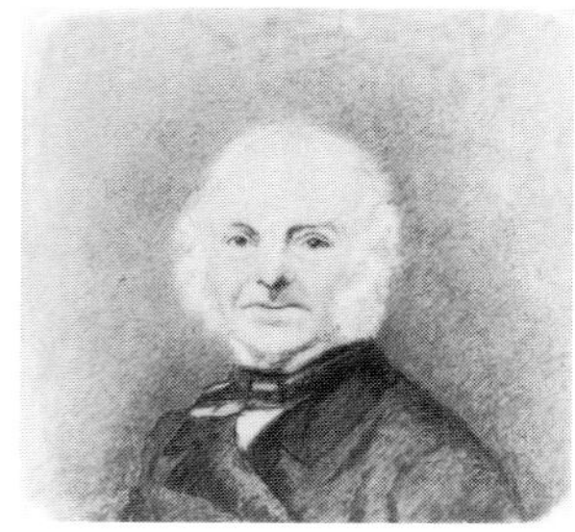

BESSIE CREGAN
active London 19th – 20th century
Martin Cregan (1788–1870), Artist, c.1850
4.5 x 4.8, watercolour on ivory
Bequeathed by the artist, great great granddaughter of the sitter, 1901
NGI 7482

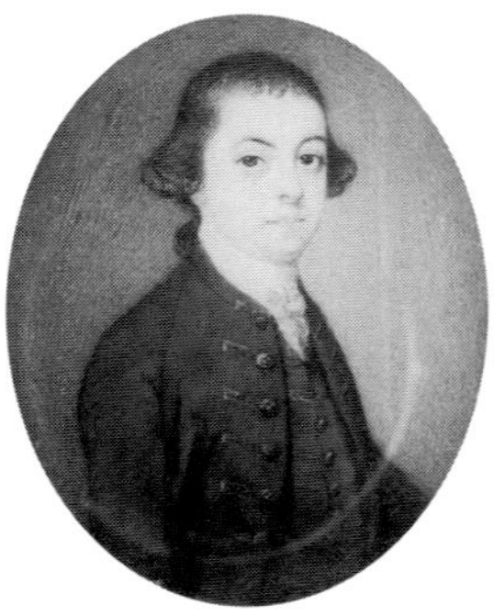

RICHARD CROSSE
Knowle, Devon 1742 – 1810 Knowle, Devon
William Courtenay, 2nd Viscount Courtenay and de jure *18th Earl of Devon, (1742–1788),* 1766
Dated 1766 on backing paper
5.8 x 4.8, watercolour on ivory
Transferred from the NMI, 1969 (where acquired 1906). NGI 7189

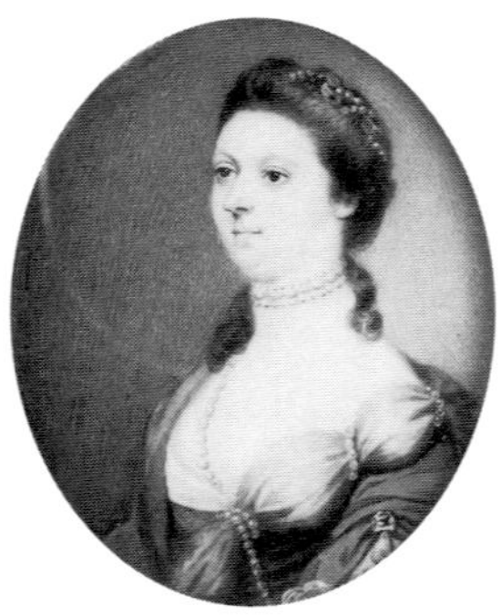

RICHARD CROSSE
Viscountess Frances Courtenay, (born Clack, active 1762–1782), wife of 2nd Viscount, c.1766
5.8 x 4.8, watercolour on ivory
Transferred from the NMI, 1969 (where acquired 1907)
NGI 7191

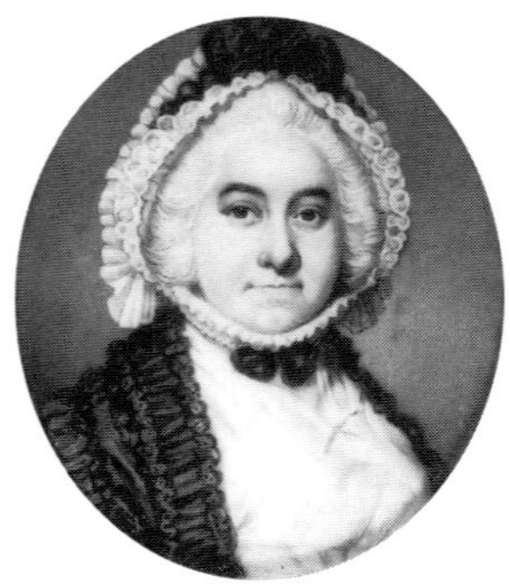

RICHARD CROSSE
Mrs John Harrison, (d.1803), 1792
Dated by later inscription on reverse of frame
5.7 x 4.9, watercolour on ivory
Miss Mary A. McNeill Bequest, 1985
NGI 19266. see pp. 74–75.

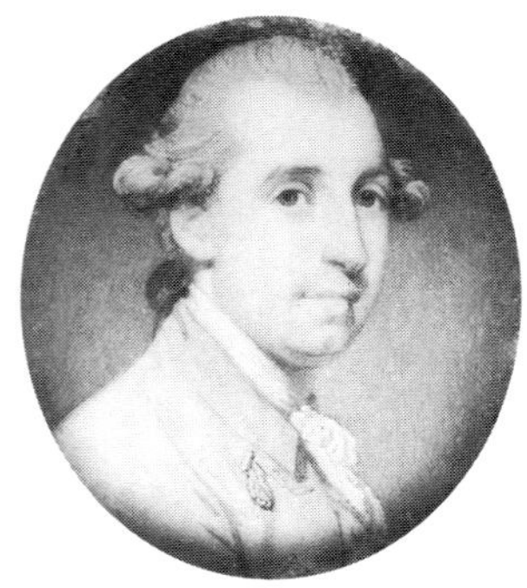

RICHARD CROSSE
John Beresford, M.P., (1738–1805), First Commissioner of Revenue in Ireland
3.4 x 3, watercolour on ivory
Miss Mary A. McNeill Bequest, 1985
NGI 19267

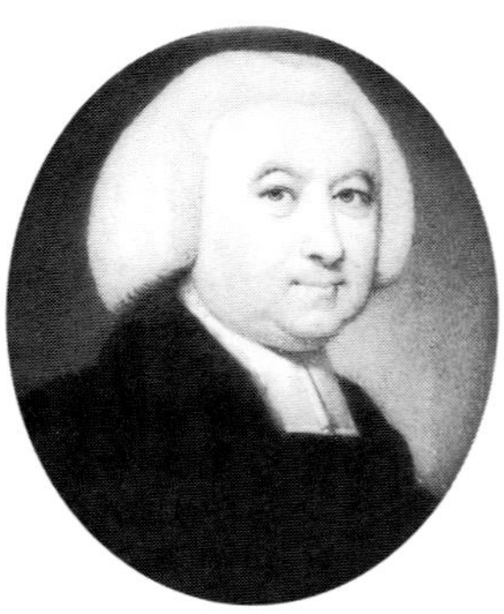

RICHARD CROSSE
Revd. Dr Henry Barnard
4.9 x 4, watercolour on ivory
Miss Mary A. McNeill Bequest, 1985
NGI 19268

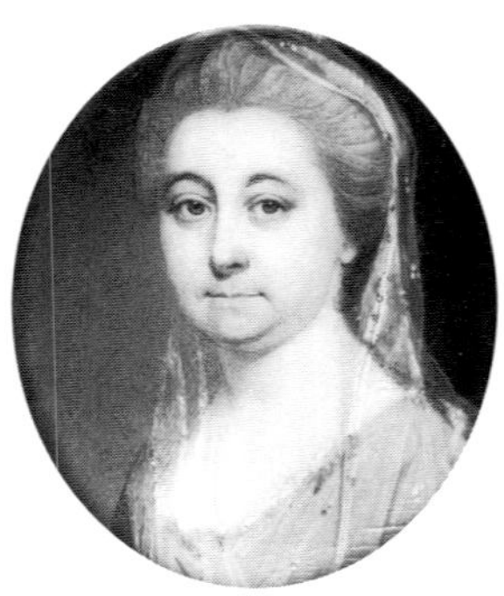

RICHARD CROSSE
Mrs Henry Barnard
4.9 x 4, watercolour on ivory
Miss Mary A. McNeill Bequest, 1985
NGI 19269. see Illus. 28.

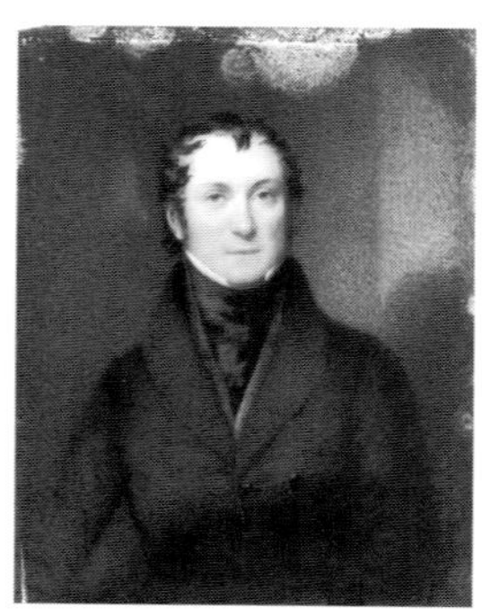

WILLIAM DENNING
active England c.1820
Portrait of a man
7.7 x 4, watercolour on card
Purchased from H. Graves & Co., London, 1886
NGI 2076

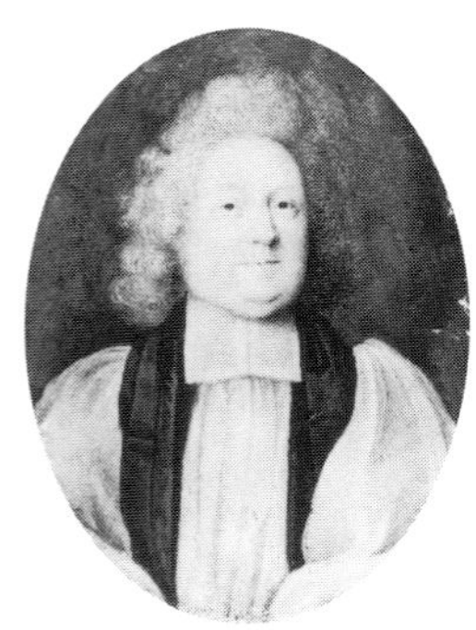

SIMON DIGBY (BISHOP OF ELPHIN)
active Ireland 1668 – 1720 Lacken, Co. Roscommon. *John Tillotson, (1630–1694), Archbishop of Canterbury,* c.1692. 9.3 x 7.2, gouache and watercolour on vellum, pasted on card. Transferred from the NMI, 1969 (where purchased 1895).
NGI 7221. see p. 42.

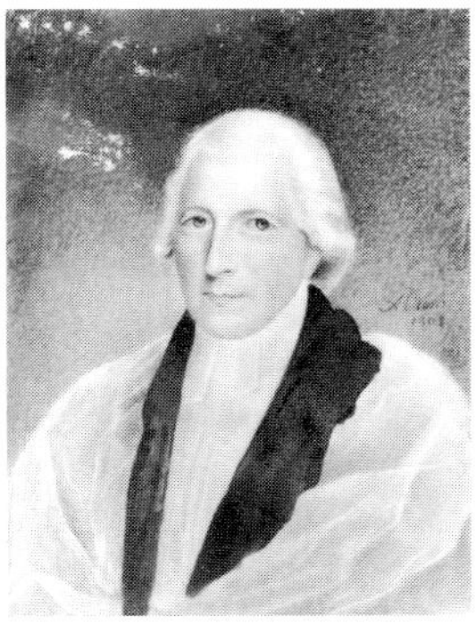

ANDREW DUNN
active Ireland and London
1800 – 1820 London
Thomas Lewis O'Beirne, (c.1748–1823), Bishop of Meath, 1808
Signed and dated: *A.Dunn 1808.*
7.5 x 5.8, watercolour on ivory
Presented by Mrs C.E. Colvin, 1967. NGI 6314. see p. 122.

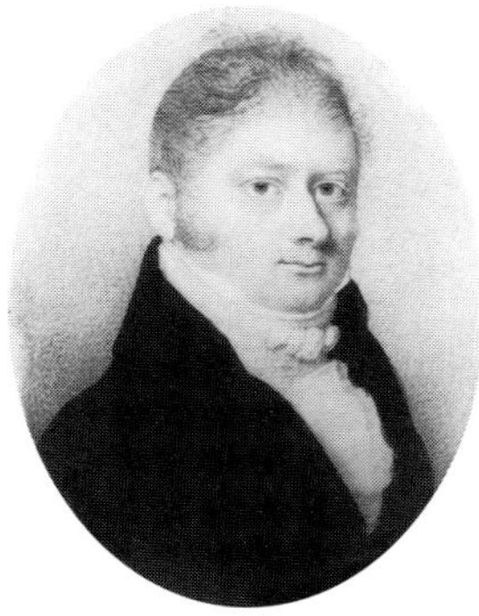

ANDREW DUNN
R.N. Bennett, Dublin Barrister
7 x 5, watercolour on ivory
Transferred from the NMI, 1969
(where acquired 1924)
NGI 7120

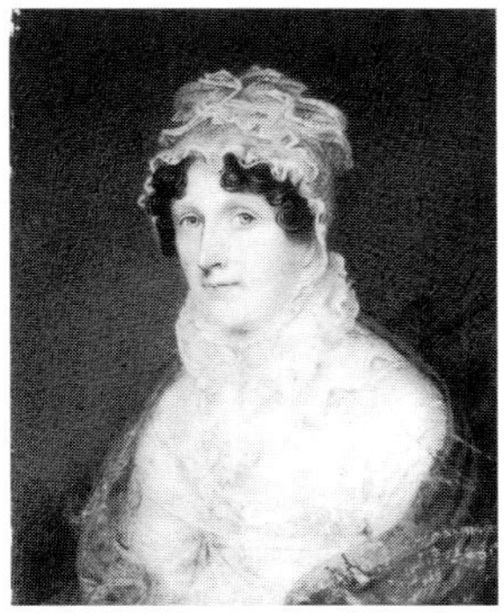

ANDREW DUNN
Viscountess Margaret Mountjoy, (born Wallis, active 1793–1839), 2nd wife of Luke Gardiner, Viscount Mountjoy
9.2 x 7.5, watercolour on ivory
Presented by Mr J.C. McFadden, in memory of his mother, 1981
NGI 7929

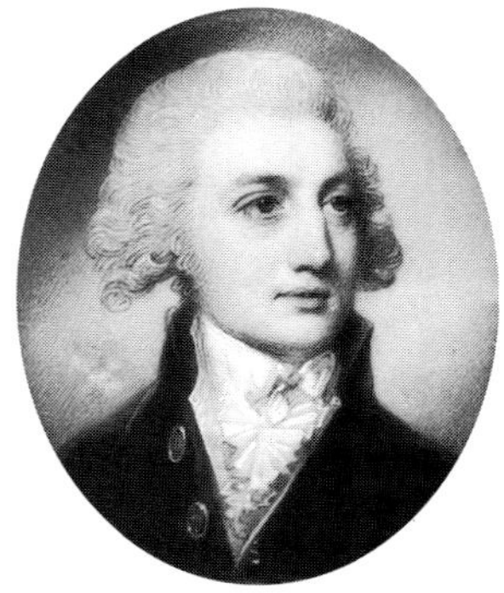

GEORGE ENGLEHEART
Kew, Surrey 1750/53 – 1839 Blackheath, London
Portrait of a man in a blue coat, late 1780s
3.9 x 3.3, watercolour on ivory
Miss Mary A. McNeill Bequest, 1985
NGI 19272. see pp. 79–80.

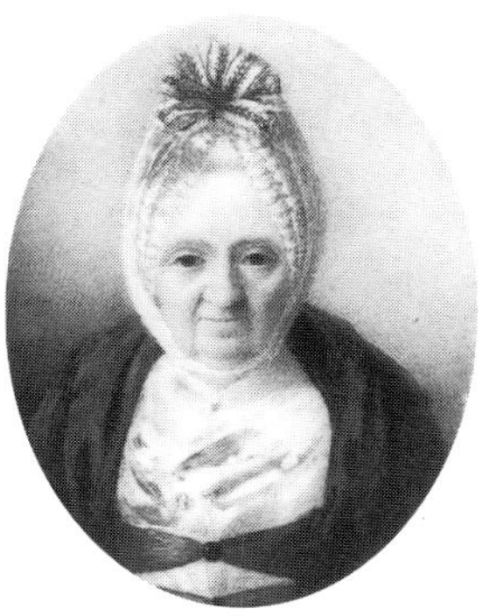

ATTRIBUTED TO GEORGE ENGLEHEART
Mrs Mary Harris of Salonica (born Bergoin)
5.9 x 4.7, watercolour on ivory
Transferred from the NMI, 1969
(where acquired 1891)
NGI 7181

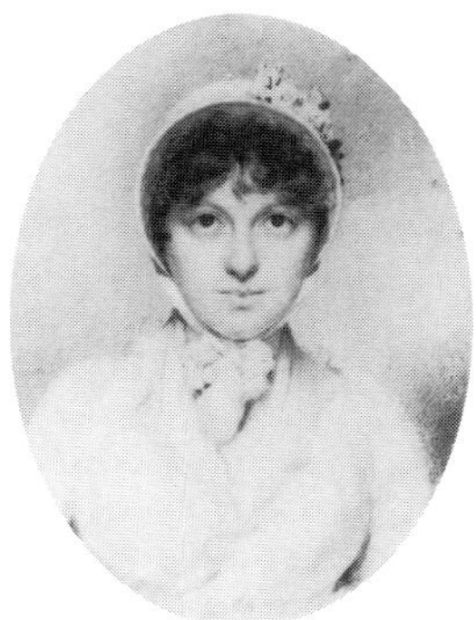

FOLLOWER OF GEORGE ENGLEHEART
Portrait of a lady with a white bonnet, 1821
Signed illegibly and dated 1821
7.8 x 6.2, watercolour on ivory
Transferred from the NMI, 1969
(where presented by Mrs M. Sullivan, 1949)
NGI 7024

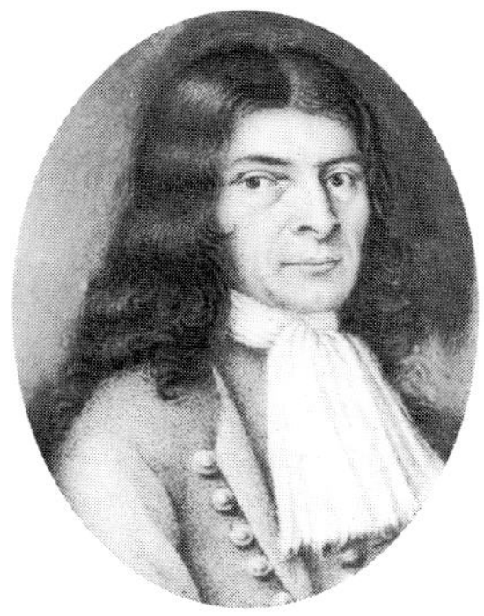

ENGLISH SCHOOL (17TH CENTURY)
Portrait of a man with long hair; heraldic device on reverse
4.5 x 3.5, enamel on copper
Presented by Sir Alfred Chester Beatty, 1951
NGI 3637

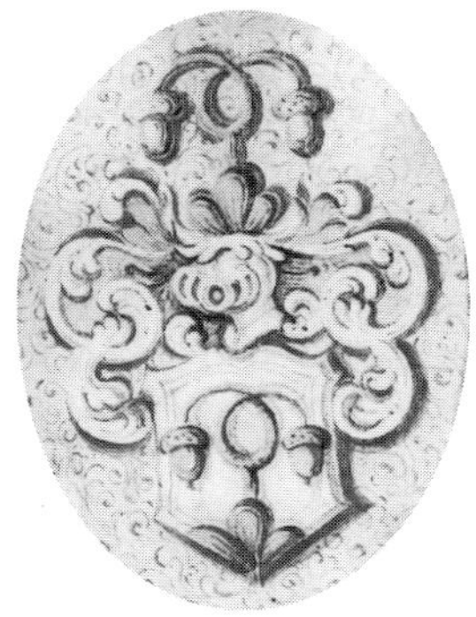

Reverse of NGI 3637

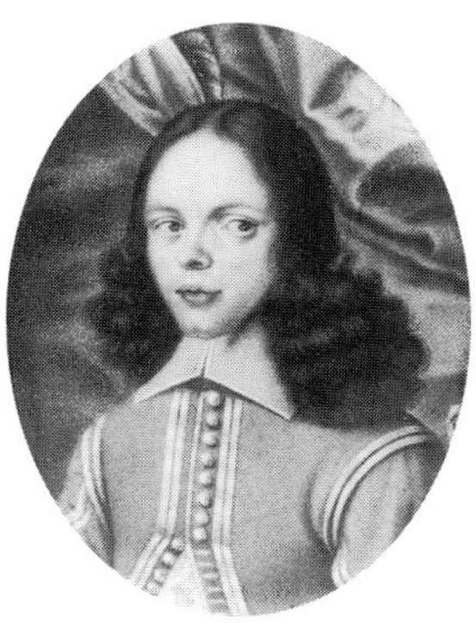

ENGLISH SCHOOL (17TH CENTURY)
Portrait of a man in a green coat
4 x 3.3, enamel on gold
Transferred from the NMI, 1969
(where purchased 1890)
NGI 7062

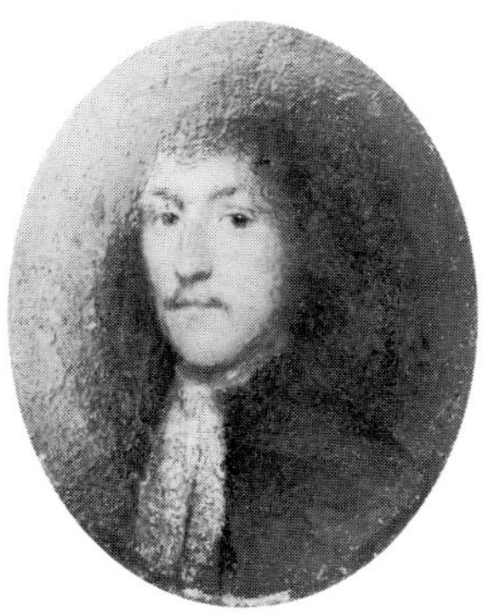

ENGLISH SCHOOL (17TH CENTURY)
Anthony Ashley Cooper, 1st Earl of Shaftsbury, (1621–1683), Statesman
4.8 x 3.9, oil on copper
Transferred from the NMI, 1969
(where presented by Mrs M. Sullivan, 1949)
NGI 7491

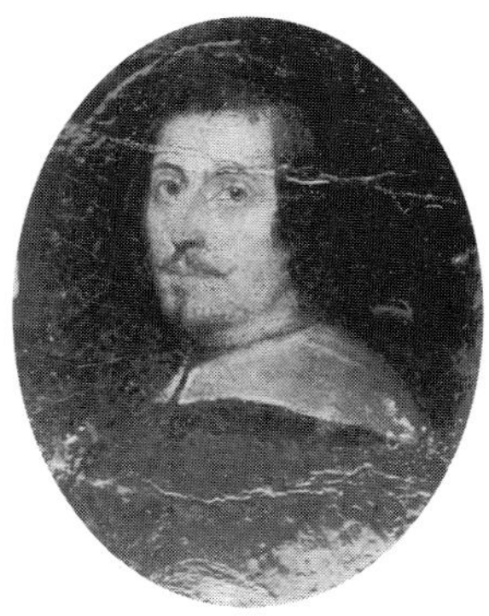

ENGLISH SCHOOL (17TH CENTURY)
Portrait of a man with a lace collar
4 x 3.2, oil on card
Transferred from the NMI, 1969
(where provenance unknown)
NGI 7492

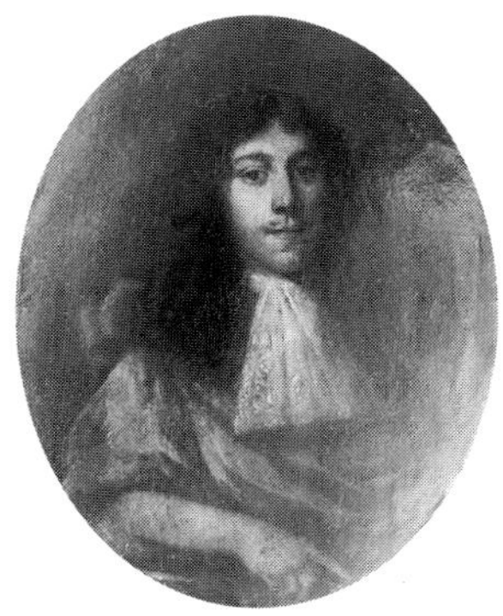

ENGLISH SCHOOL (17TH CENTURY)
Anthony Cowley, (1618–1667), Poet
12.2 x 9.7, oil on copper
Transferred from the NMI, 1969
(where provenance unknown)
NGI 7510

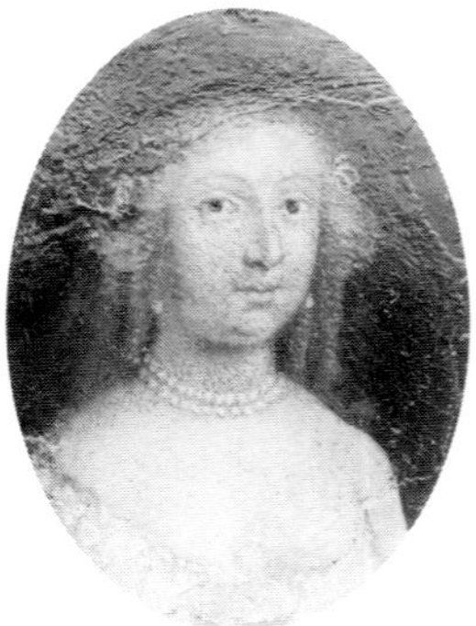

English School
(early 18th century)
Portrait of a lady in a white dress
7 x 5.2, oil on copper
Transferred from the NMI, 1969
(where provenance unknown)
NGI 7499

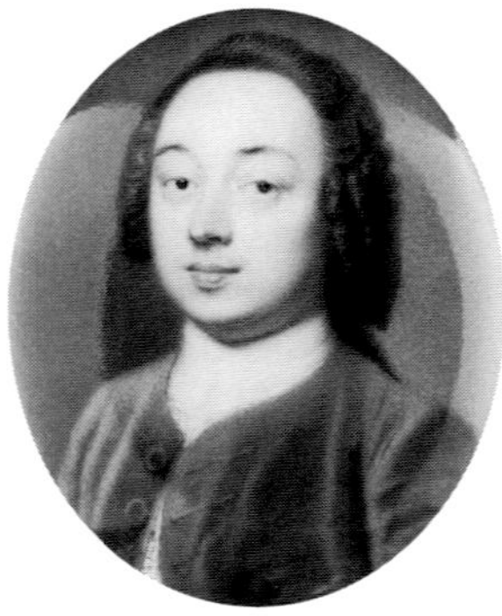

English School (c.1740)
Portrait of a young man in a mauve coat
3.7 x 4.1, enamel on copper
Presented by Sir Alfred Chester Beatty, 1951
NGI 3729

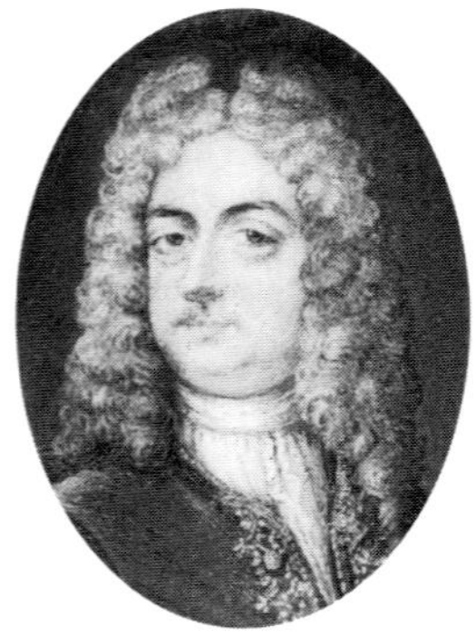

English School (c.1740)
*Arthur Chichester, 4th Earl of Donegall, (1695–1757), or Clotworthy Skeffington, 4th Viscount Massereene (active 1703–1738/39).*6.1 x 4.7, watercolour on ivory. Miss Mary A. McNeill Bequest, 1985
NGI 19275

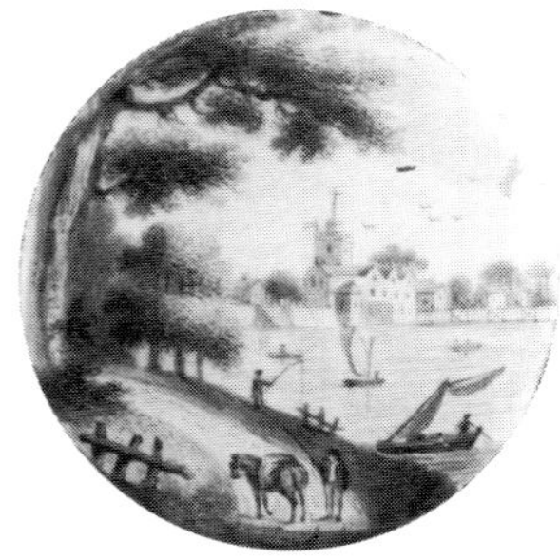

English School (c.1750)
All Saints, Fulham, London, c.1750
4.1 diam., enamel on copper
Presented by Sir Alfred Chester Beatty, 1951
NGI 3679. see p. 62.

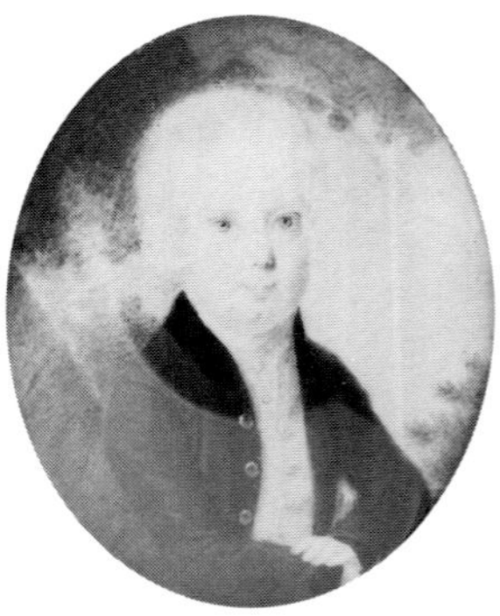

English School (c.1750)
Portrait of a boy in a blue coat
6.5 x 5.4, watercolour on ivory
Transferred from the NMI, 1969
(where bequeathed by Mr T. Mercer, 1924)
NGI 7053

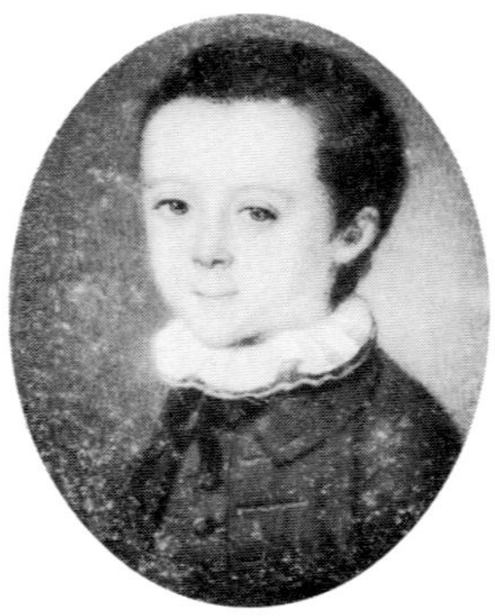

English School (c.1760)
Portrait of a young boy
3.3 x 2.7, watercolour on ivory
Miss Mary A. McNeill Bequest, 1985
NGI 19256

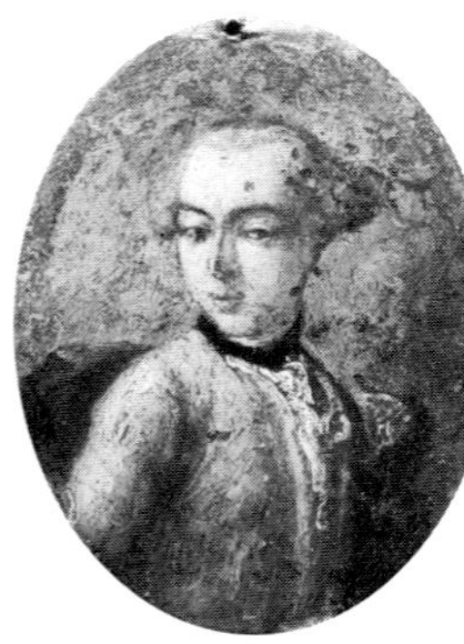

English School (c.1760)
Portrait of a man in a pink coat
11.6 x 9, oil on copper
Miss Mary A. McNeill Bequest, 1985
NGI 19257

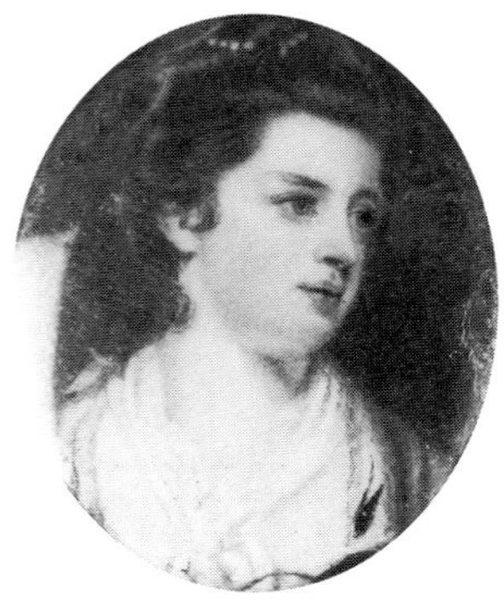

English School (c.1770)
Portrait of a young lady in a white dress
2.9 x 2.7, enamel on gold
Transferred from the NMI, 1969
(where presented by Mrs M. Sullivan, 1949)
NGI 7061

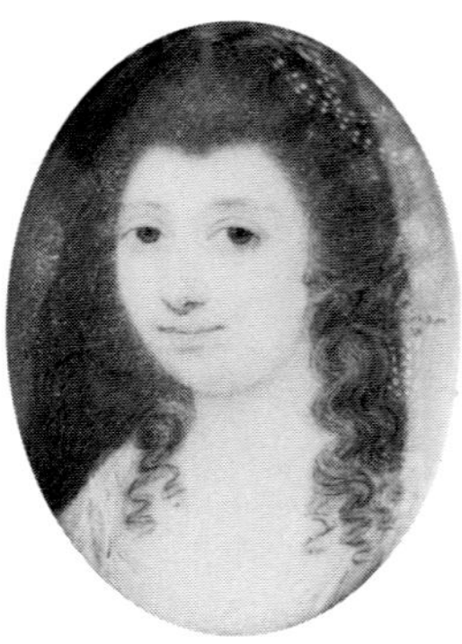

English School (c.1770)
Portrait of a lady in a pink dress
2.9 x 1.9, watercolour on ivory, mounted on a gold ring
Transferred from the NMI, 1969
(where purchased 1899)
NGI 7115. see Illus 8.

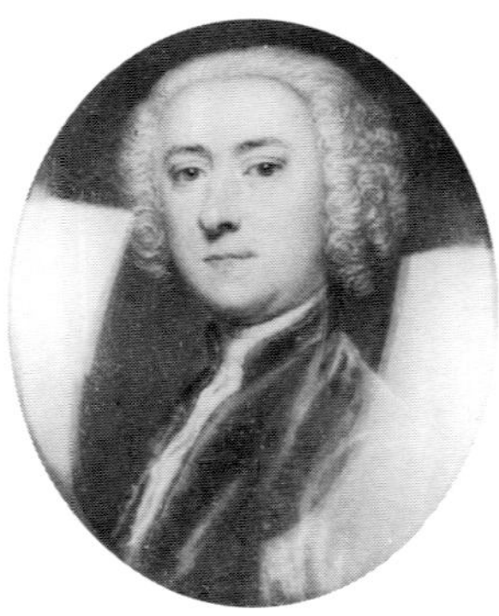

English School
(late 18th century)
Portrait of a man in a blue coat
4.7 x 3.9, enamel on copper
Presented by Sir Alfred Chester Beatty, 1951
NGI 3650

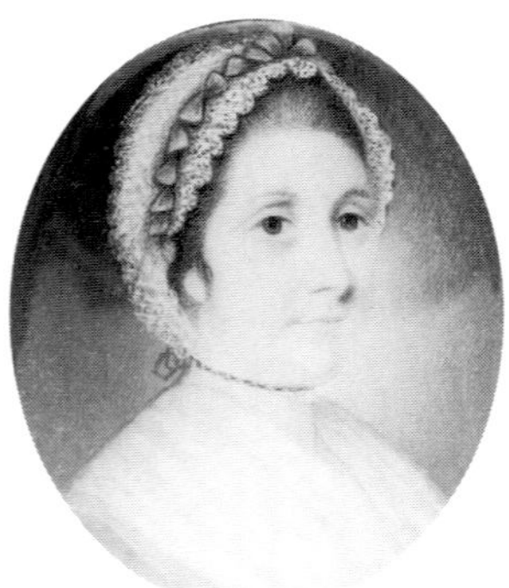

English School
(late 18th century)
Portrait of a lady with a lace cap
3.5 x 3, watercolour on ivory
Transferred from the NMI, 1969
(where acquired 1955)
NGI 7017

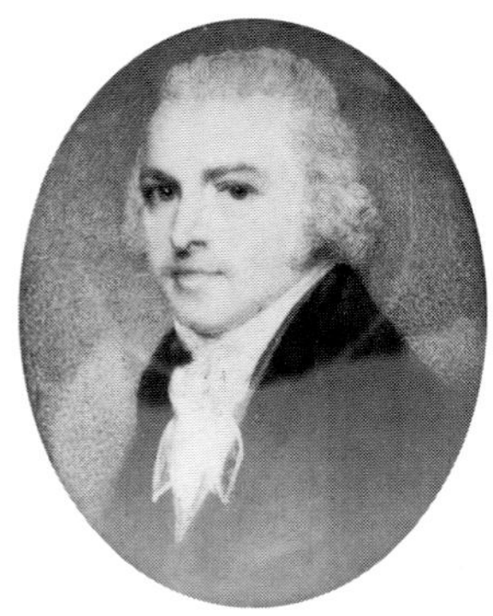

English School
(late 18th century)
Portrait of a man with a white cravat
7.2 x 5.6, watercolour on ivory
Transferred from the NMI, 1969
(where bequeathed by Mr T. Mercer, 1924)
NGI 7020

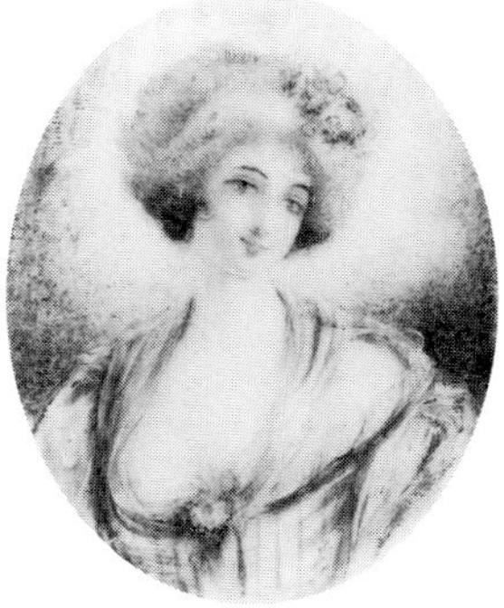

English School
(late 18th century)
Portrait of a lady with roses in her hair
5 x 4.1, watercolour on ivory
Transferred from the NMI, 1969
(where acquired 1954)
NGI 7043

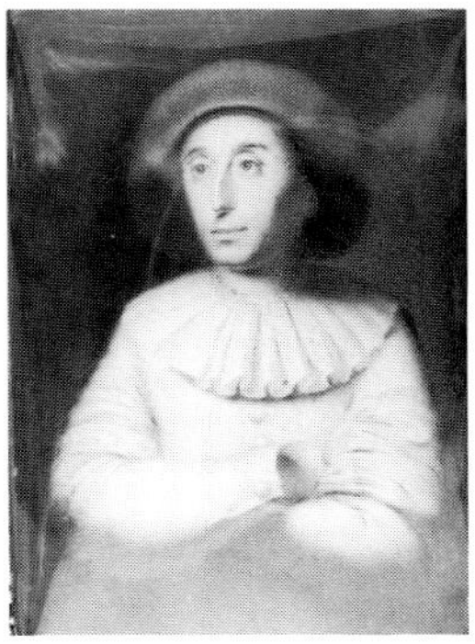

English School
(late 18th century)
Portrait of an actor, dressed as a Pierrot
6.2 x 4.4, enamel on copper
Transferred from the NMI, 1969
(where purchased 1891)
NGI 7055

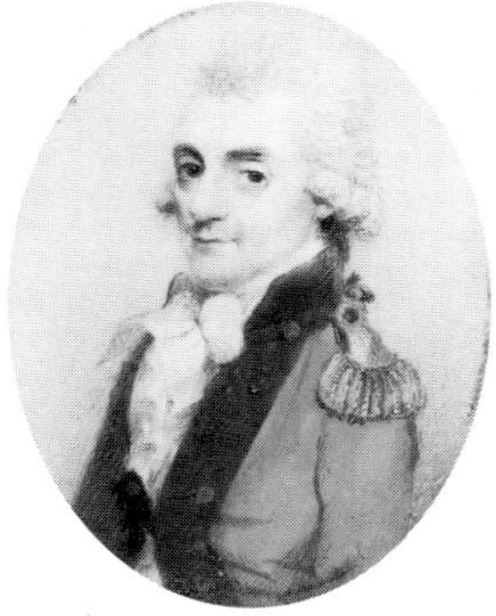

English School
(late 18th century)
Sir William Neville Hart, Bt., M.P.
6 x 4.8, watercolour on ivory
Transferred from the NMI, 1969
(where acquired 1891)
NGI 7179

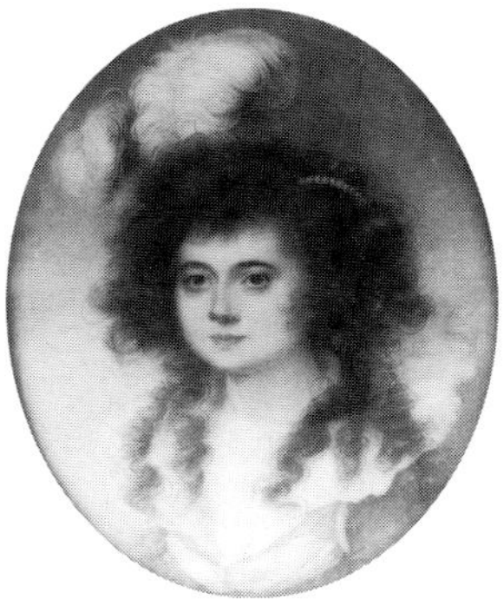

English School (c.1800)
Mrs Busby (born Camac)
5.3 x 4.4, watercolour on ivory
Purchased from Miss Huggard, 1973
NGI 7595

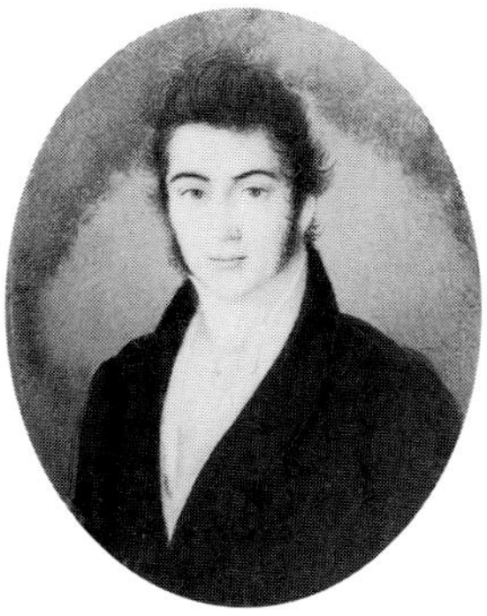

English School (c.1800)
Portrait of a man in a black coat
5.9 x 4.8, watercolour on ivory
Provenance unknown
NGI 18995

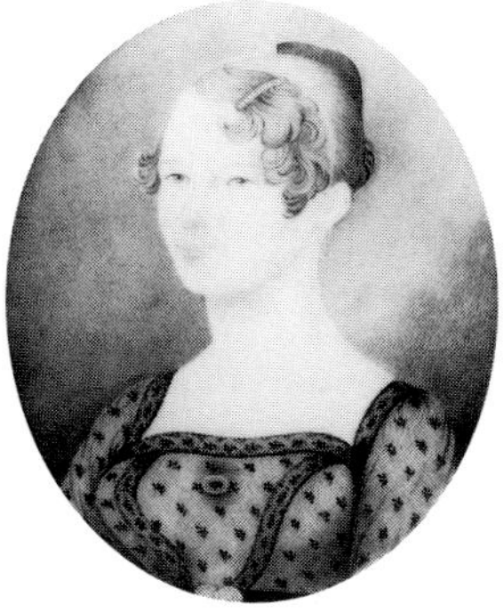

English School (19th century)
Portrait of a lady in a chiffon dress
6.4 x 5.1, watercolour on ivory
Transferred from the NMI, 1969
(where bequeathed by Mr T. Mercer, 1924)
NGI 7016

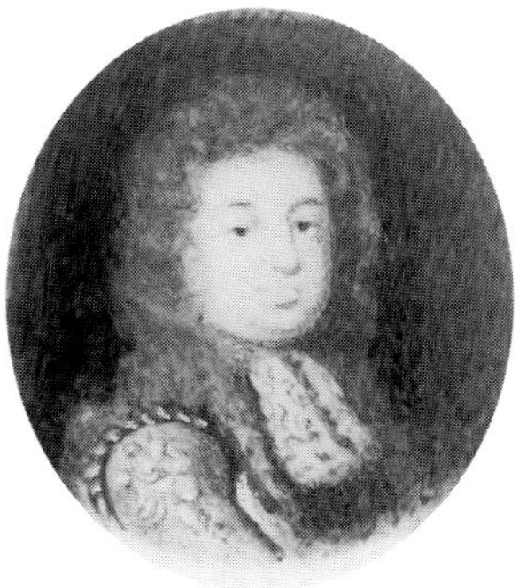

English School (19th century)
Portrait of a man with a wig
4.2 x 3.8, watercolour on ivory
Transferred from the NMI, 1969
(where bequeathed by Miss Gardiner, 1929)
NGI 7132

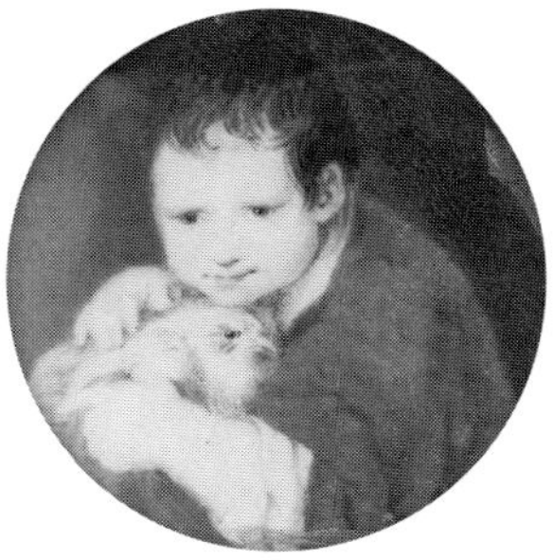

English School (19th century)
Portrait of a boy holding a bird
5 diam., watercolour on ivory, mounted on a tortoise shell patch-box
Transferred from the NMI, 1969
(where bequeathed by Mr T. Mercer, 1924)
NGI 7161

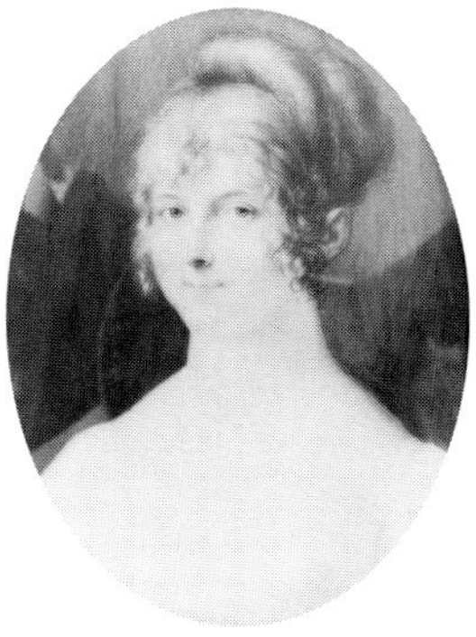

English School (19th century)
Portrait of a lady in a white dress
7.7 x 5.9, watercolour on ivory
Transferred from the NMI, 1969
(where bequeathed by Mr T. Mercer, 1924)
NGI 7162

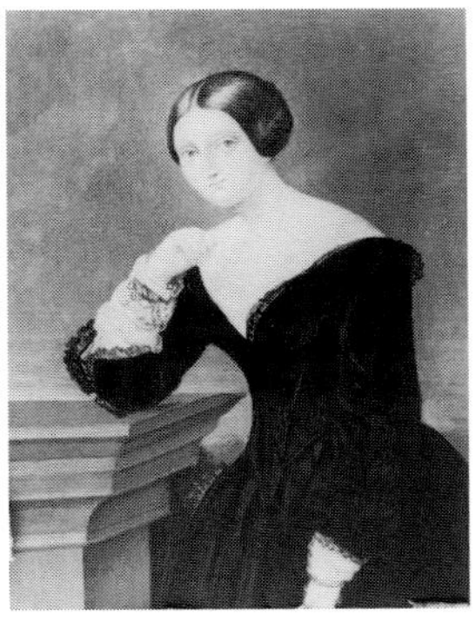

English School (19th century)
Portrait of a lady in a black dress
9.4 x 7.3, watercolour on ivory
Transferred from the NMI, 1969
(where bequeathed by Mr T. Mercer, 1924)
NGI 7163

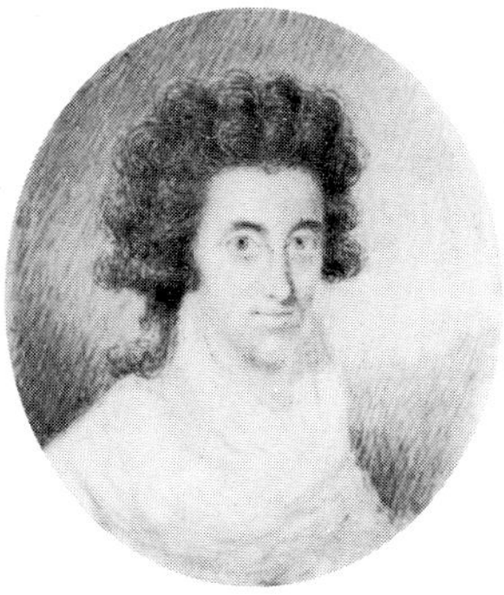

English School (19th century)
Portrait of a lady in a white dress
4.5 x 3.8, watercolour on ivory
Presented by the Friends of the National Collections of Ireland, 1974
NGI 7716

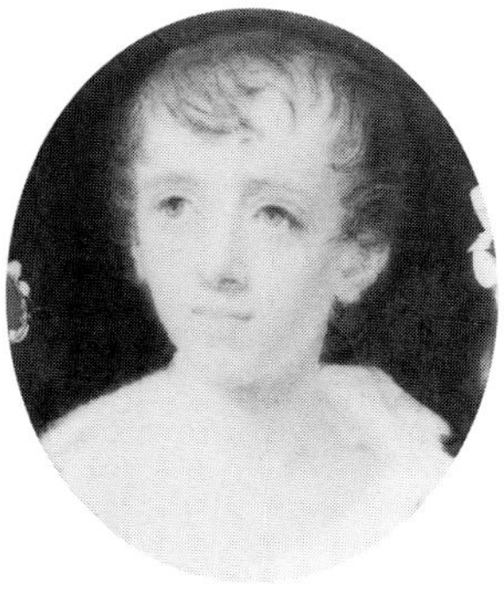

English School (19th century)
Portrait of a boy in a white shirt
5 x 4.5, enamel on copper (damaged)
Presented by the Friends of the National Collections of Ireland, 1974
NGI 7717

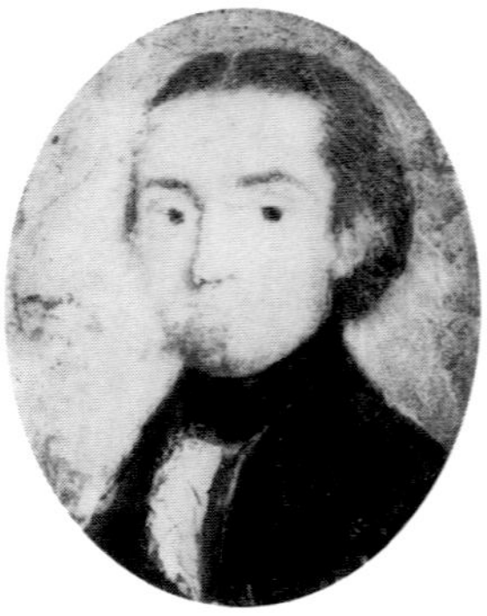

English School
(early 19th century)
Portrait of a man in a green coat
2.9 x 2.4, watercolour on ivory
Transferred from the NMI, 1969
(where bequeathed by
Mr T. Mercer, 1924)
NGI 7012

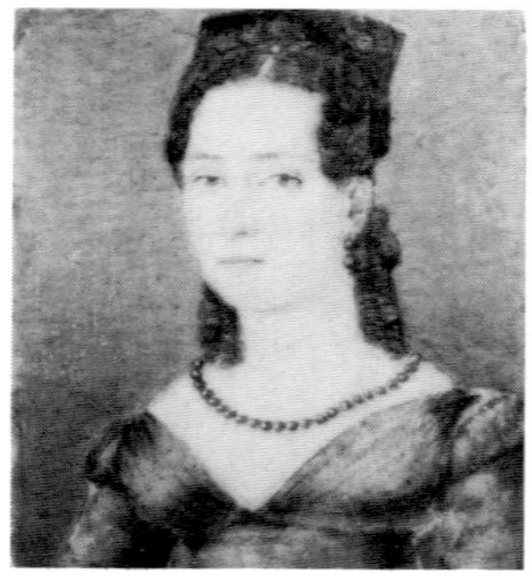

English School
(early 19th century)
Portrait of a lady in a pink dress
3.8 x 3.4, watercolour on ivory
Transferred from the NMI, 1969
(where bequeathed by
Mr T. Mercer, 1924)
NGI 7041

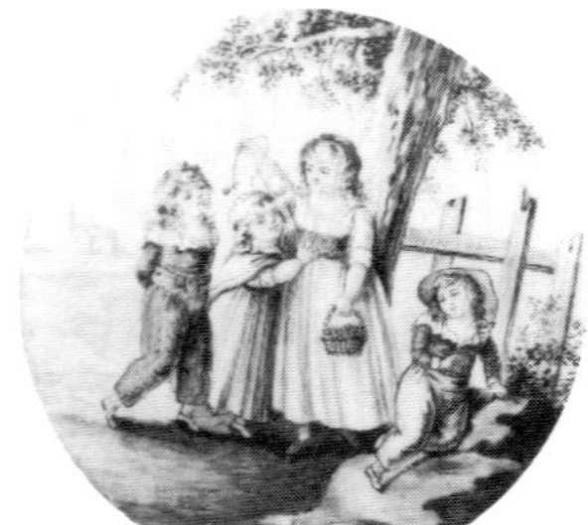

English School
(early 19th century)
Children playing beneath a tree
6.6 diam., watercolour on ivory
Transferred from the NMI, 1969
(where bequeathed by
Mr W.E. Gumbleton, 1911)
NGI 7208

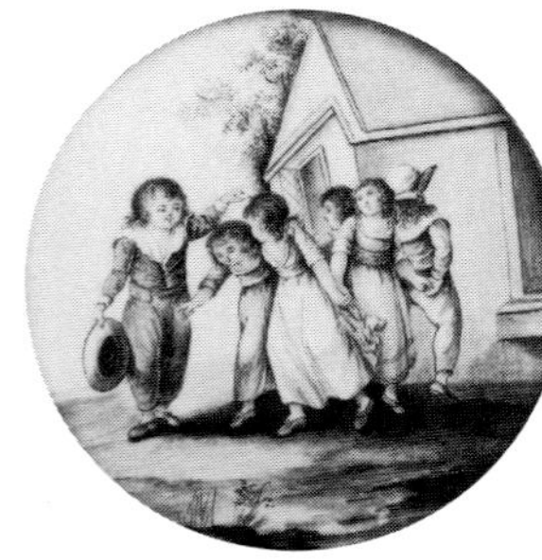

English School
(early 19th century)
Children playing in front of a cottage
6.8 diam., watercolour on ivory
Transferred from the NMI, 1969
(where bequeathed by
Mr W.E. Gumbleton, 1911)
NGI 7209

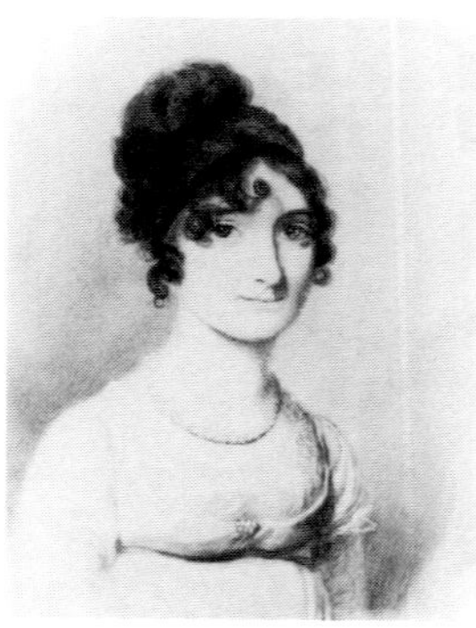

English School (c.1805)
Portrait of a lady in a white dress
9.4 x 6.9, watercolour on ivory
Transferred from the NMI, 1969
(where bequeathed by
Miss Gardiner, 1929)
NGI 7207

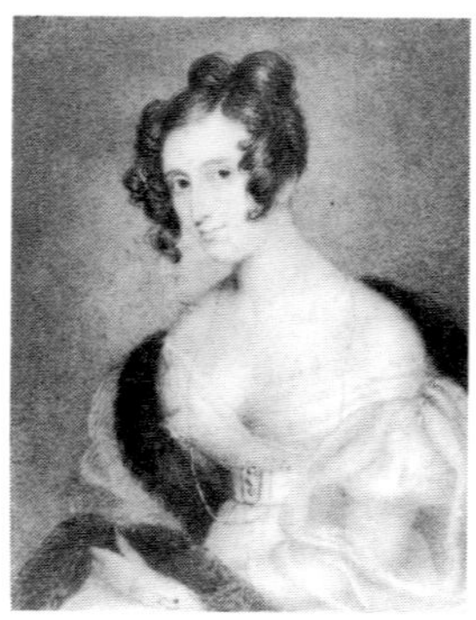

English School (c.1820)
Portrait of a lady with a fur wrap
11.4 x 9, watercolour on ivory
Transferred from the NMI, 1969
(where provenance unknown)
NGI 7545

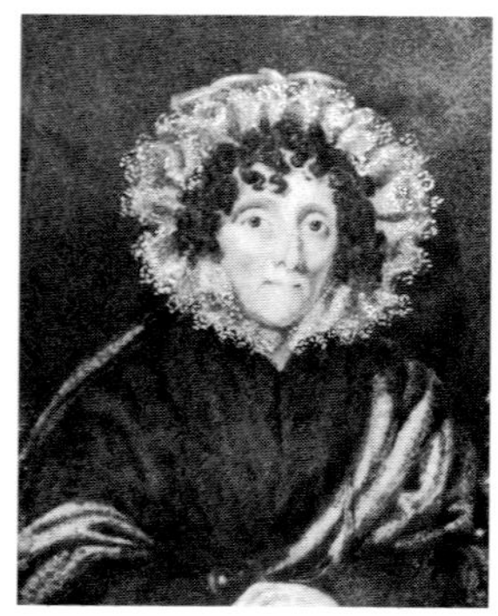

English School (c.1830)
Ann, Countess of Mornington, (born Hill, 1742–1831), Mother of the 1st Duke of Wellington
9.6 x 7.6, watercolour on paper
Purchased from Mr D. Egan, 1913
NGI 2685

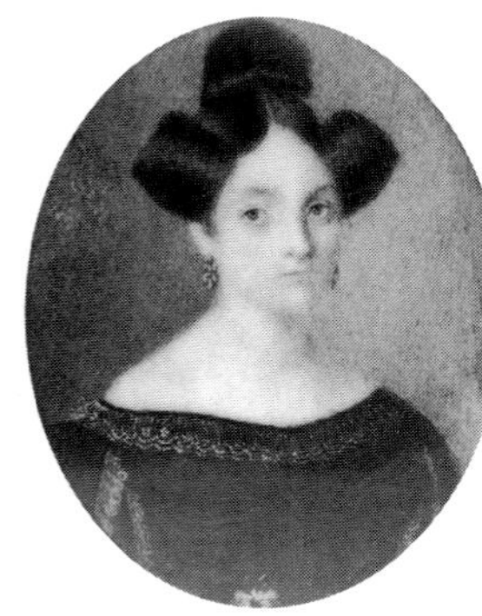

English School (c.1830)
Portrait of a lady in an indigo dress
5.7 x 4.6, watercolour on ivory
Transferred from the NMI, 1969
(where bequeathed by
Mr T. Mercer, 1924)
NGI 7174

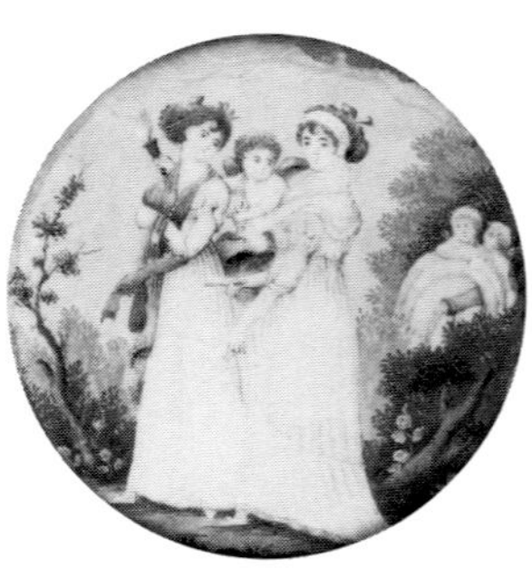

English School (c.1830)
Two ladies with a putto in a garden
6.6 diam., watercolour on ivory,
mounted on a patch-box
Transferred from the NMI, 1969
(where bequeathed by
Mr T. Mercer, 1924)
NGI 7176

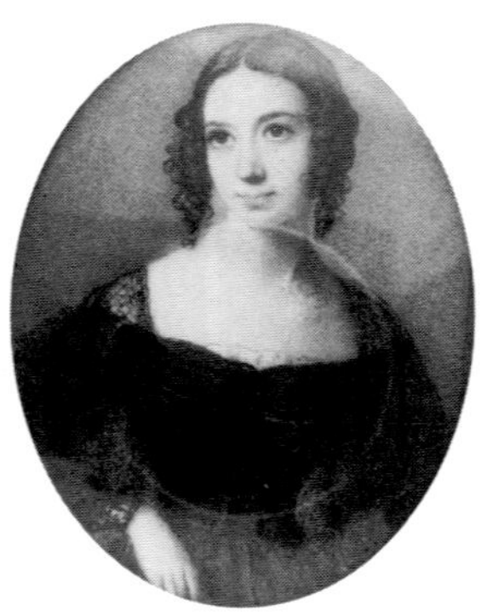

English School (c.1830)
Portrait of a lady in a black dress
9.5 x 4.5, watercolour on ivory
Transferred from the NMI, 1969
(where acquired 1891)
NGI 7183

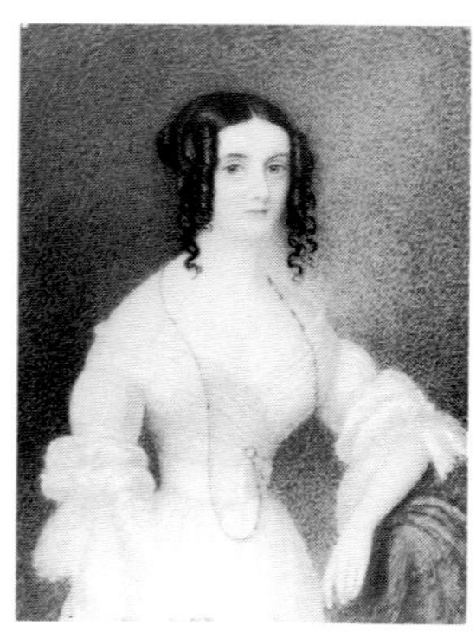

English School (c.1830)
Portrait of a lady in a white dress
10.5 x 8, watercolour on ivory
Transferred from the NMI, 1969
(where bequeathed by
Miss A. Kinchela, 1948)
NGI 7194

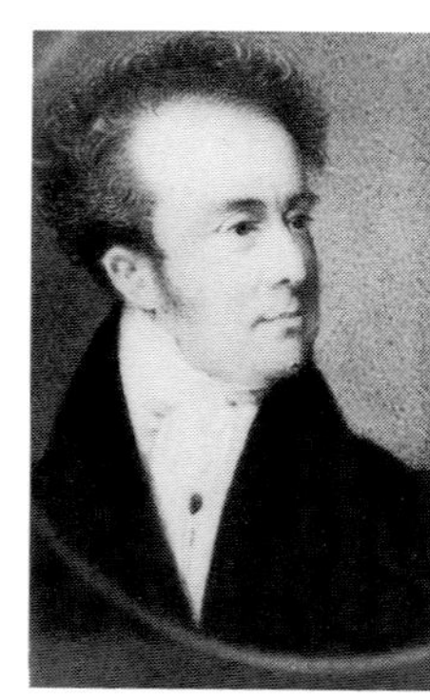

English School (c.1840)
Portrait of a man in a black coat
4.6 x 2.8, watercolour on ivory, set
in brass mount with doors
Provenance unknown
NGI 7540

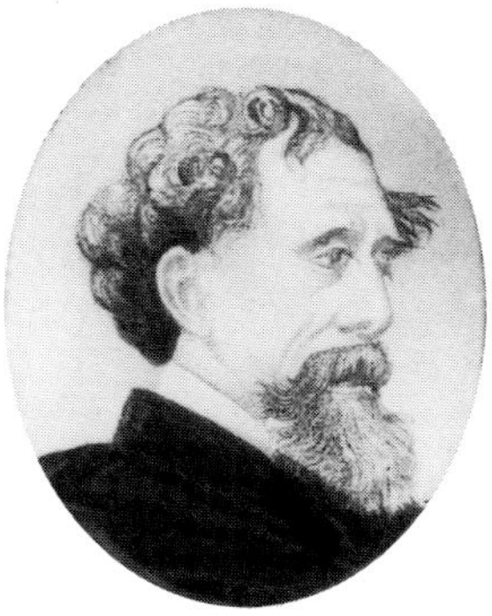

English School (c.1850)
Charles Dickens, (1812–1870), Author
2.7 x 2.2, enamel on copper
Presented by Sir Alfred Chester Beatty, 1951
NGI 3662

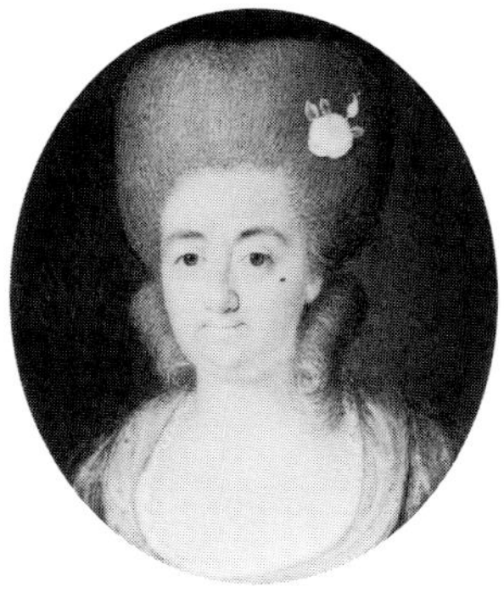

English or Irish School (18th century)
Portrait of an elderly lady with a rose in her hair
4.7 x 4, watercolour on ivory
Transferred from the NMI, 1969 (where bequeathed by Mr T. Mercer, 1924)
NGI 7038

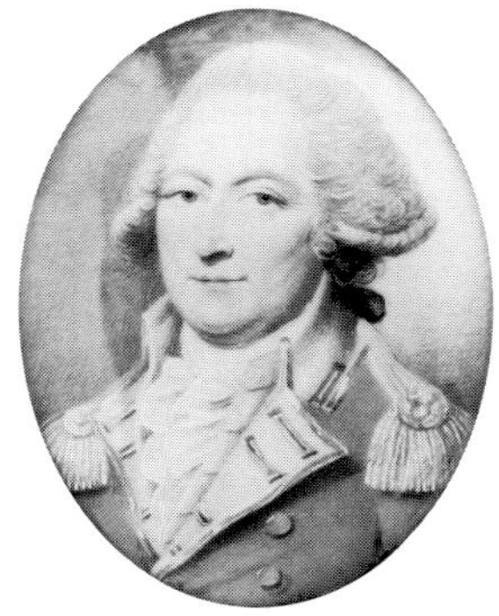

English or Irish School (c.1770)
Andrew Armstrong of the 14th Regiment (b.1732)
6.4 x 5.1, watercolour on ivory
Presented by Sir Andrew Armstrong, Bt., 1981
NGI 7935

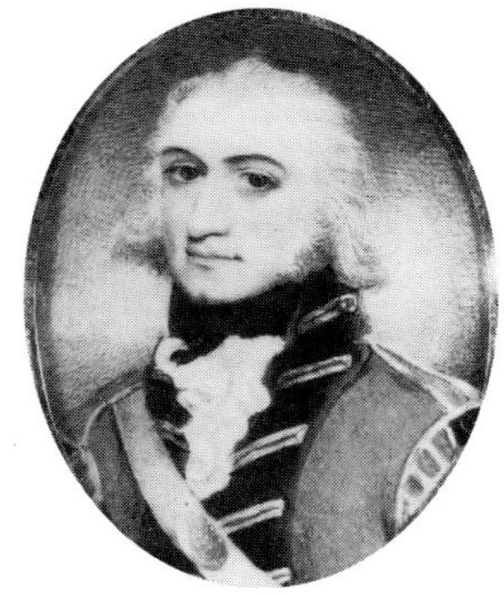

English or Irish School (late 18th century)
(?) Thomas St George Armstrong, 3rd son of Andrew Armstrong, (b.1765)
5.6 x 4.3, watercolour on ivory
Presented by Sir Andrew Armstrong, Bt., 1981
NGI 7936

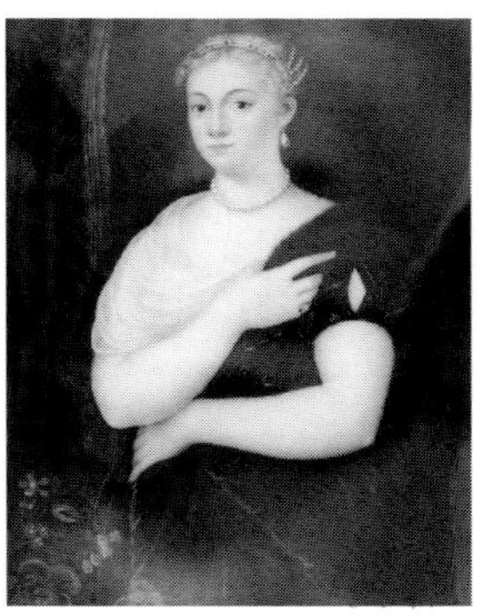

Sarah, Countess of Essex (Lady Malden)
(?) St Helena c.1761 – 1838 London.
Sophonisba, 1810 (after version of Titian). Signed and dated: *S Essex Pinx 1810.* 15.7 x 12.6, enamel on copper. Presented by Sir Alfred Chester Beatty, 1951
NGI 3581. see pp. 111–12.

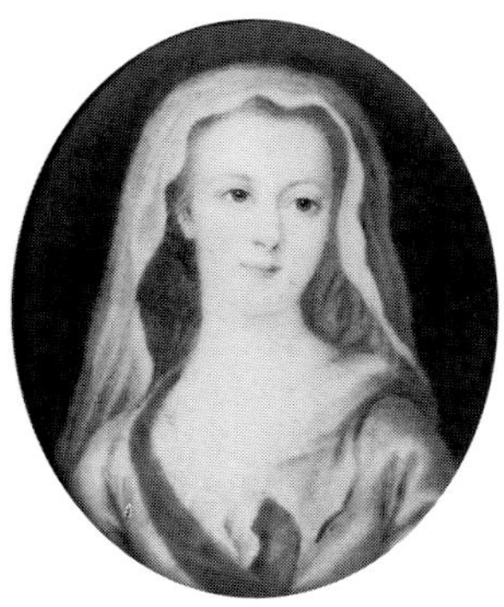

Sarah, Countess of Essex (Lady Malden)
Harriet Catharine, Duchess of Buccleuch, (born Townsend, 1773–1814), wife of 4th Duke, 1808. Inscribed, signed and dated on reverse: **SE Pinxt. 1808*
5.4 x 4.4, enamel on copper
Presented by Sir Alfred Chester Beatty, 1951. NGI 3629

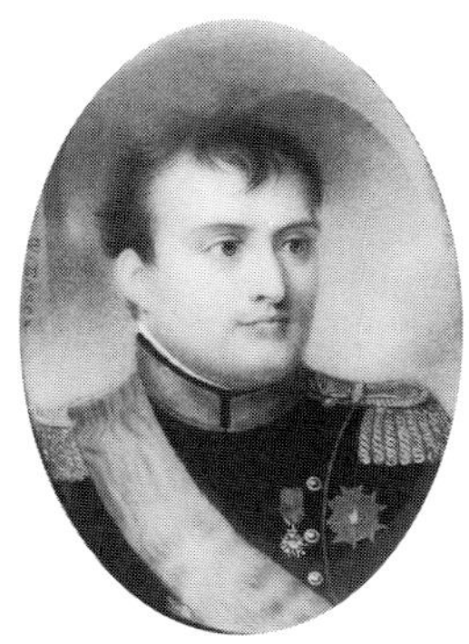

William Essex
(?) London 1784 – 1869 Brighton
Napoleon I, Emperor of France, (1769–1821), 1832 (after J.-B.-J. Augustin miniature c.1810)
Signed: *W. Essex.* Inscribed, signed and dated on reverse: ** W. Essex Pt. 1832*.* 4.2 x 3, enamel on copper
Presented by Sir Alfred Chester Beatty, 1951. NGI 3617. see p. 129.

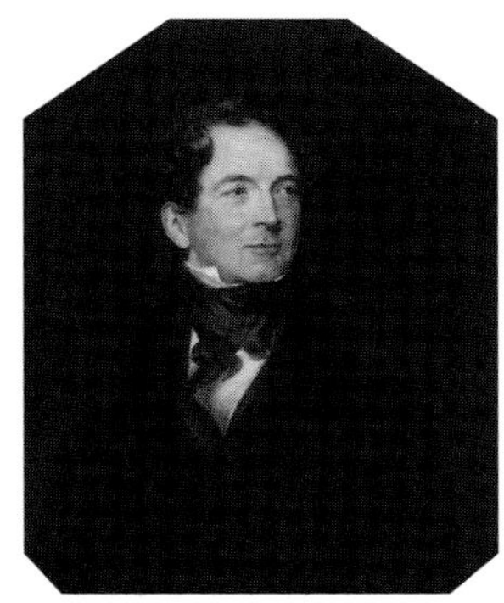

William Essex
Thomas Moore, (1779–1852), Poet, 1838 (after T. Lawrence 1829–30, private collection)
Inscribed, signed and dated: ** W. Essex. 1838.**
33 diam., enamel on copper
Purchased from Mr H.A. Buttery, London, 1906.
NGI 4015. see pp. 128–129.

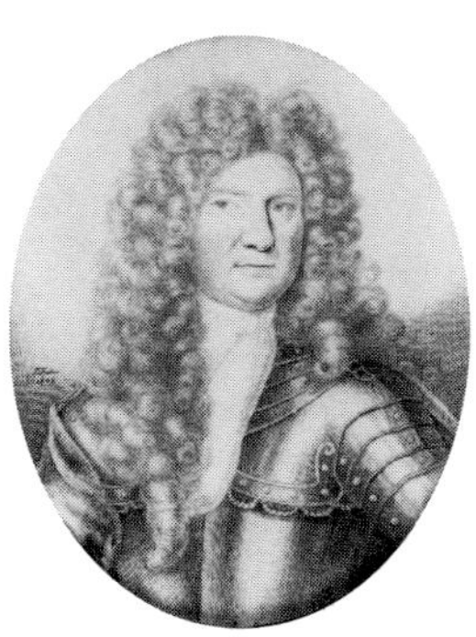

John Faber
The Hague 1650 – 1721 Bristol
Godert de Ginkel, 1st Earl of Athlone, (1644–1703), 1703
Signed and dated: *J: Faber 1703*
12.8 x 10.2, ink and silverpoint on paper. Purchased at Sotheby's, London, Mr F. Wellesley Sale, 1920. NGI 2718

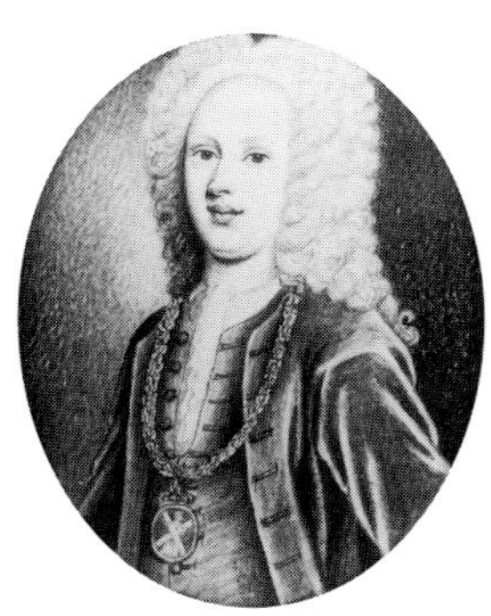

James Ferguson
Banffshire 1710 – 1776 London
Alexander Brodie of that Ilk, Lord Lyon King of Arms, (1697–1754), c.1727. 8 x 6.5, ink and wash on card. Transferred from the NMI, 1969 (where purchased 1910)
NGI 7204. see p. 52.

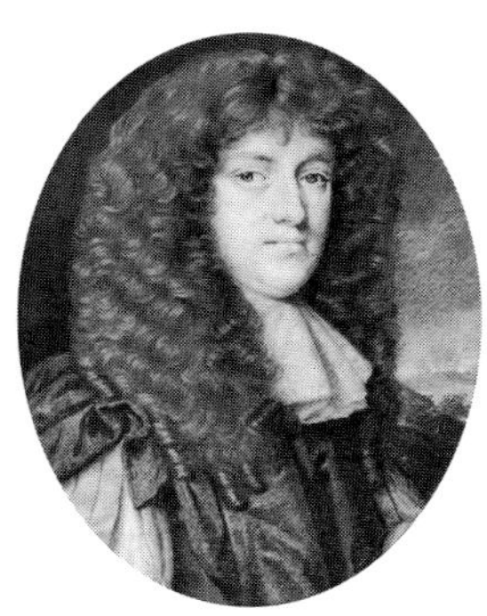

Thomas Flatman
London 1635 – 1688 London
Captain Robert Bransby, RN, c.1670. Signed: *TF*(in mono)
7.4 x 5.9, watercolour on vellum
Miss Mary A. McNeill Bequest, 1985
NGI 19241. see p. 41.

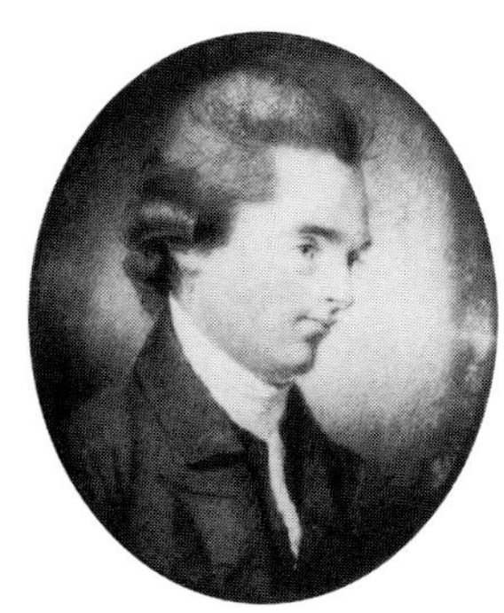

Charles Forrest
active Dublin 1765 – 1787 Dublin
Portrait of a man in a maroon coat, 1775
Signed and dated: *Forrest 1775*
3.7 x 3.2, watercolour on ivory
Purchased from Miss E. Fitzpatrick, 1983
NGI 19180. see p. 82.

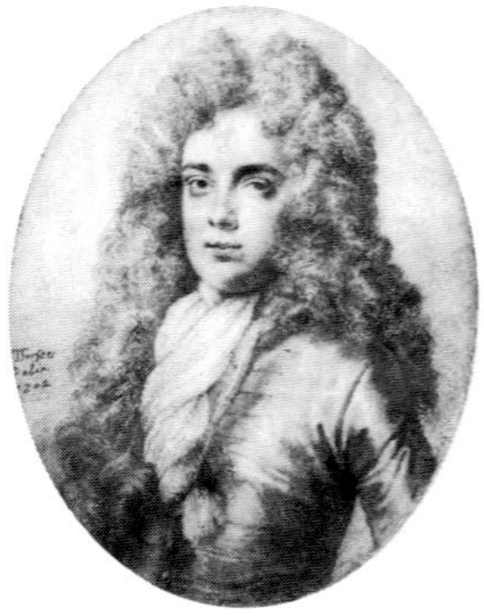

THOMAS FORSTER
(?) Northumberland c.1677 – after 1712 London
Portrait of a man, 1702
Signed and dated: *T Forster Delin 1702*
10.9 x 8.4, plumbago on card
Miss Mary A. McNeill Bequest, 1985. NGI 19242. see pp. 43–45.

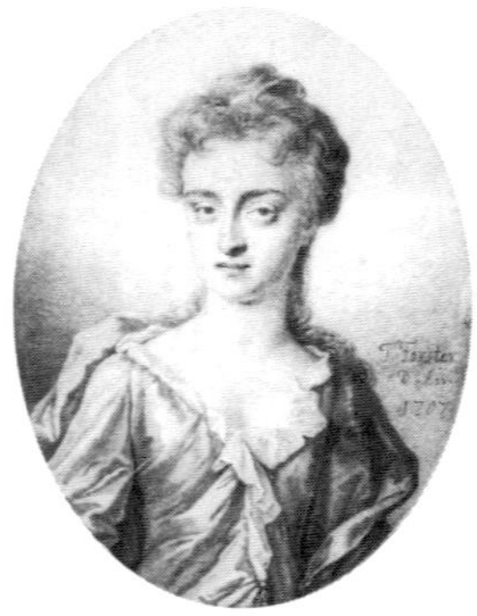

THOMAS FORSTER
Portrait of a lady, 1702
Signed and dated: *T Forster Delin 1707*
10.7 x 8.1, plumbago on card
Miss Mary A. McNeill Bequest, 1985
NGI 19243. see pp. 44–45.

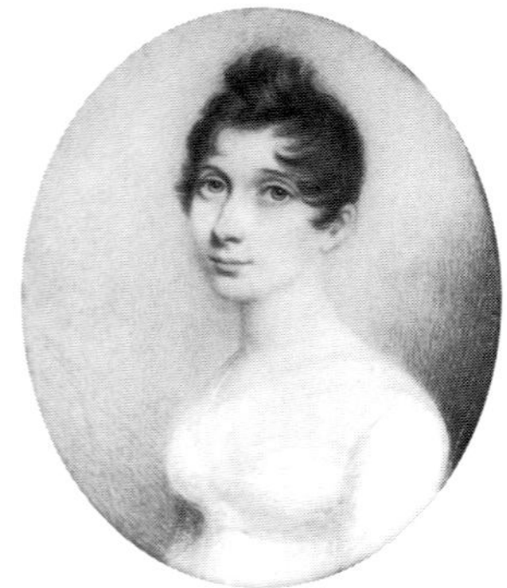

NATHANIEL FREESE
active London 1794 – 1814 London
Portrait of a lady in a white dress
7 x 5.7, watercolour on ivory
Miss Mary A. McNeill Bequest, 1985
NGI 19259

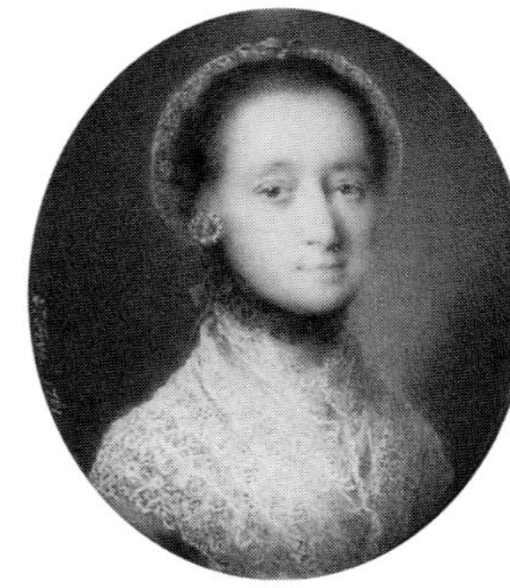

THOMAS FRYE
Dublin c.1710 – 1762 London
Portrait of a lady, (pendant to following), 1761
Signed and dated: *T. Frye 1761*
3.5 x 3, watercolour on ivory
Purchased with following at Phillips, London, 1995 (Lane Fund). NGI 19424. see p. 53.

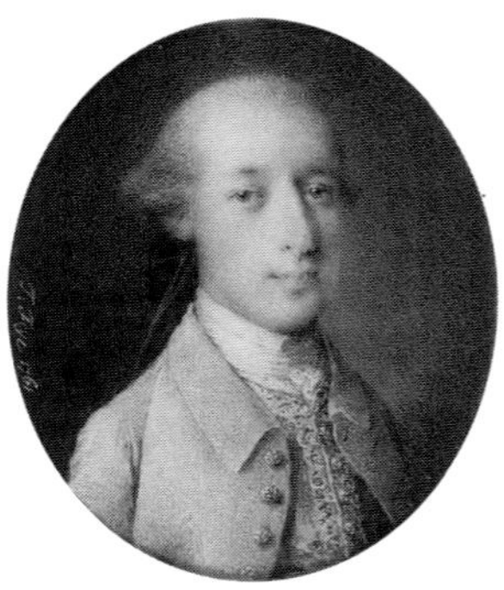

THOMAS FRYE
Portrait of a man, (pendant to above), 1761
Signed and dated: *T. Frye 1761*
3.5 x 3, watercolour on ivory
Purchased with preceding
NGI 19425. see p. 53.

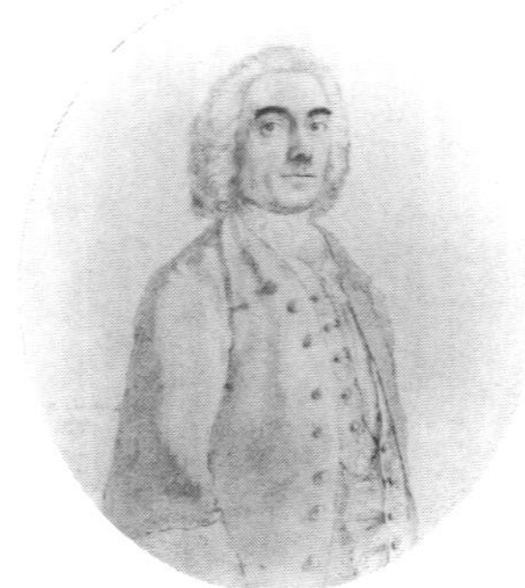

THOMAS GAINSBOROUGH
Sudbury, Suffolk 1727 – 1788 London
Portrait of a man, 1744
Signed and dated: *Tho: Gainsborough fecit 1743–4*
12.2 x 10.9, pencil on paper
Purchased from Mrs Snow, Waterford, 1894. NGI 2116

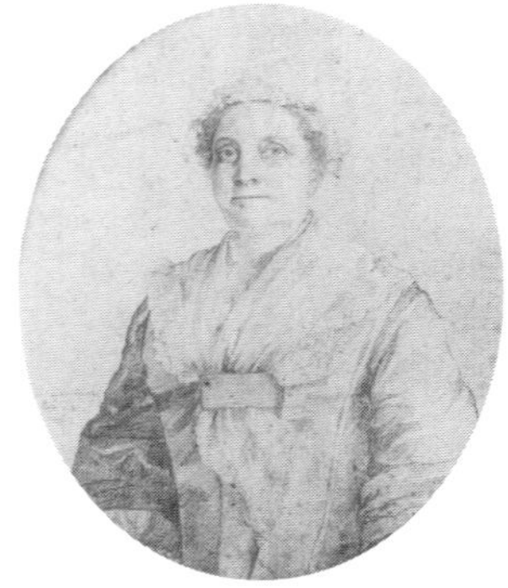

THOMAS GAINSBOROUGH
*Portrait of a lady,*1744
Signed and dated: *Tho Gainsborough fecit 1743–4*
12.2 x 10.9, pencil on paper
Purchased from Mrs Snow, Waterford, 1894. NGI 3211

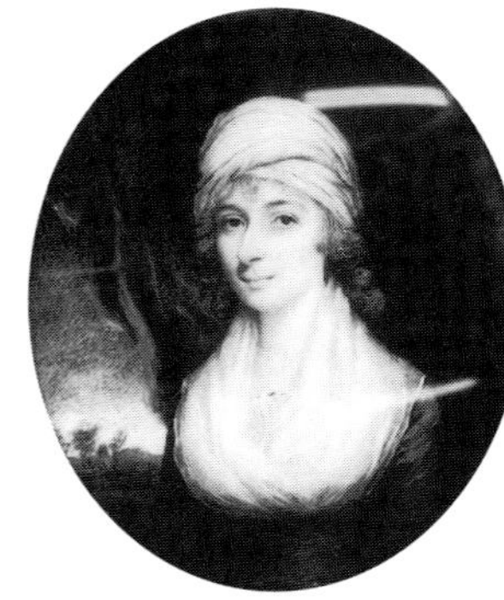

WILLIAM GRIMALDI (MARCHESE GRIMALDI)
London 1751 – 1830 London
Hester Frances, Lady Bellingham, (born Cholmondeley, 1763–1844), wife of 1st Bt., c.1795. 9.3 x 7.7, watercolour on ivory. Miss Mary A. McNeill Bequest, 1985.
NGI 19283. see pp. 80–81.

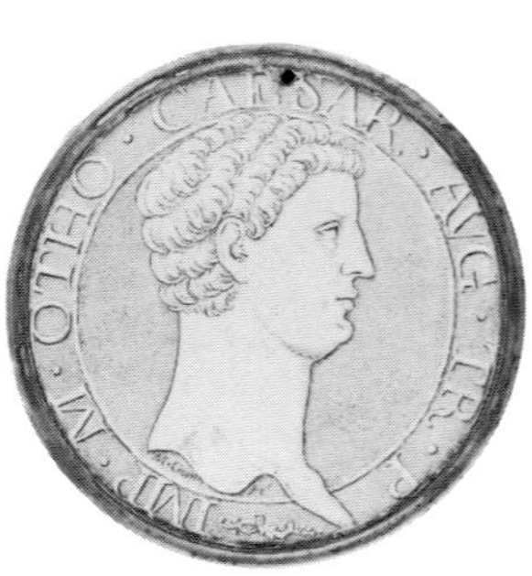

MARCUS GUNTER
active London 1725 – 1736
Heads of Caesars from Hubert Golzius' *Icones Imperatorum Romanorum* (1557). *Emperor Marcus Salvius Otho, (c.37–69AD)* , 1725. Signed: *M. Gunter. fet*
5 diam., enamel on copper
Presented by Sir Alfred Chester Beatty, 1951. NGI 3695

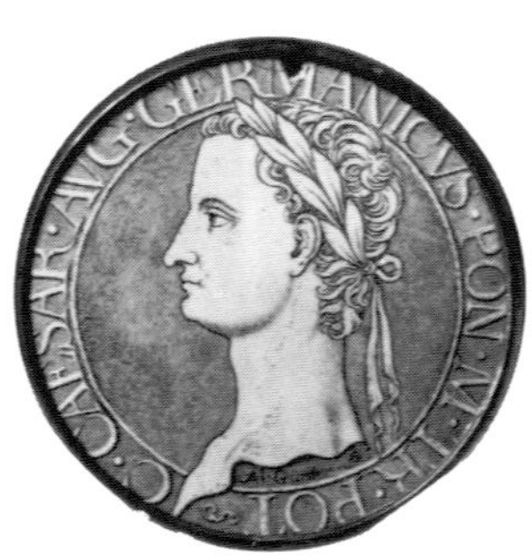

MARCUS GUNTER
Germanicus, (15BC–19AD), General, 1725
Signed: *M. Gunter. fet*
5 diam., enamel on copper
Presented by Sir Alfred Chester Beatty, 1951
NGI 3696

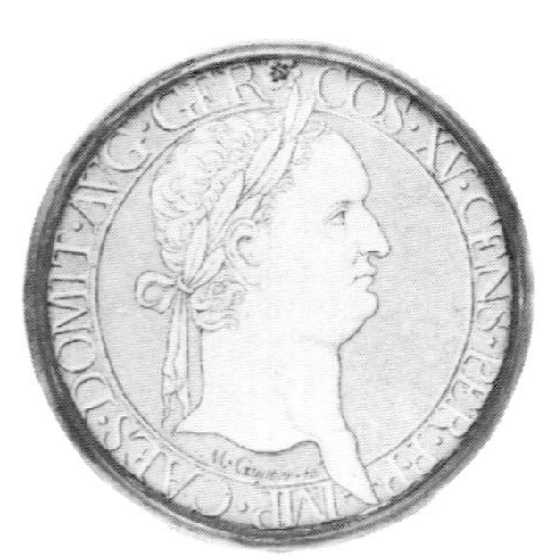

MARCUS GUNTER
Emperor Domitian, (51–96AD), 1725
Signed: *M. Gunter. fet*
5 diam., enamel on copper
Presented by Sir Alfred Chester Beatty, 1951
NGI 3697

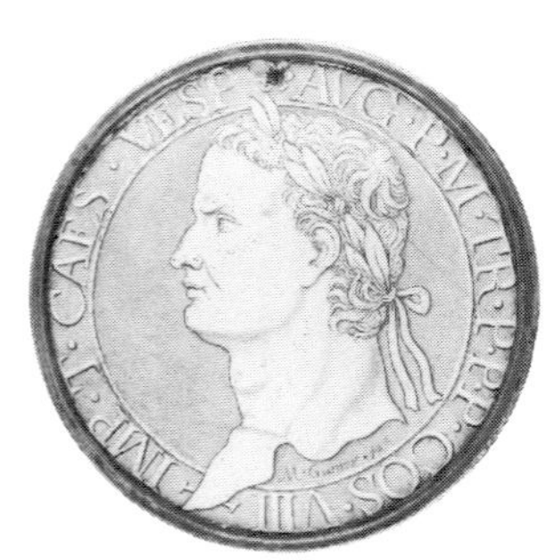

MARCUS GUNTER
Emperor Vespasian, (9–79AD), 1725
Signed: *M. Gunter. fet*
5 diam., enamel on copper
Presented by Sir Alfred Chester Beatty, 1951
NGI 3698

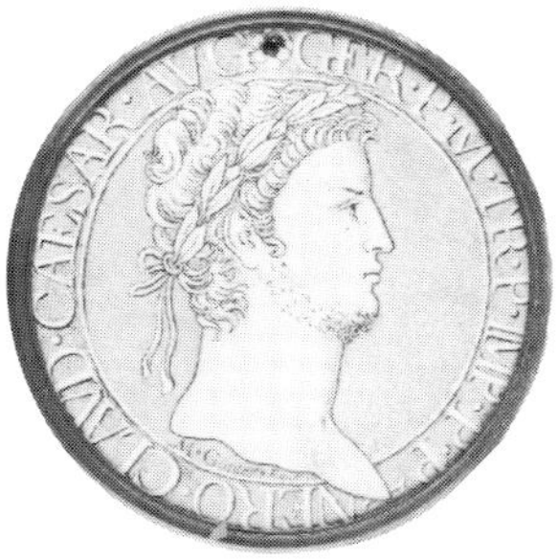

Marcus Gunter
Emperor Nero, (37–68AD), 1725
Signed: *M. Gunter. fet*
5 diam., enamel on copper
Presented by Sir Alfred Chester Beatty, 1951
NGI 3699

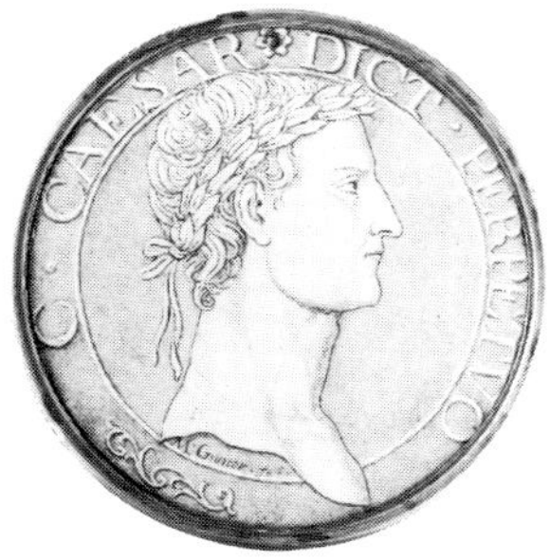

Marcus Gunter
Gaius Julius Caesar, (c.100–44BC), General and Dictator, 1725
Signed: *M. Gunter. fet*
5 diam., enamel on copper
Presented by Sir Alfred Chester Beatty, 1951
NGI 3700. see pp. 49–50.

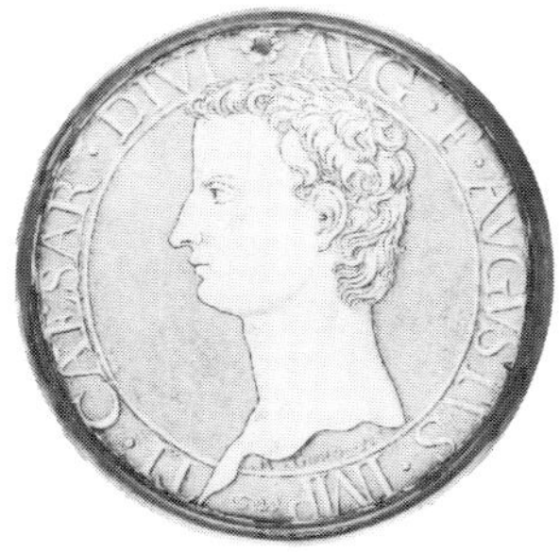

Marcus Gunter
Emperor Tiberius, (42BC–37AD), 1725
Signed: *M. Gunter. fet*
5 diam., enamel on copper
Presented by Sir Alfred Chester Beatty, 1951
NGI 3701

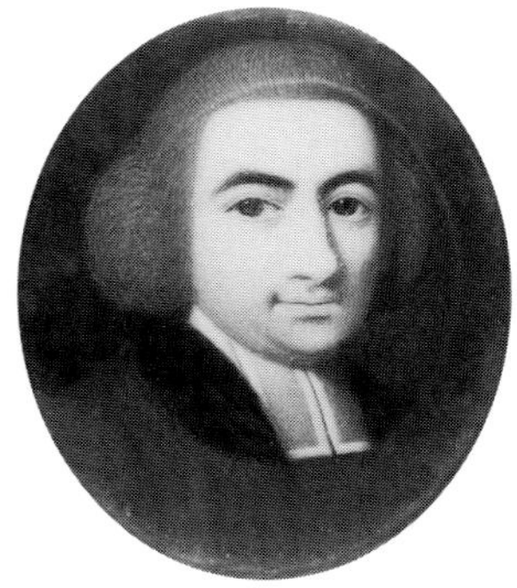

Gustavus Hamilton
(?) Co. Meath c.1739 – 1775 Dublin
Revd. Joshua Nunn, (1732–1802), Rector of Enniscorthy, Co. Wexford, 1767. Signed and dated: *Hamn.1767*. 3.5 x 3.1, watercolour on ivory. Transferred from the NMI, 1969 (where purchased 1927). NGI 7072

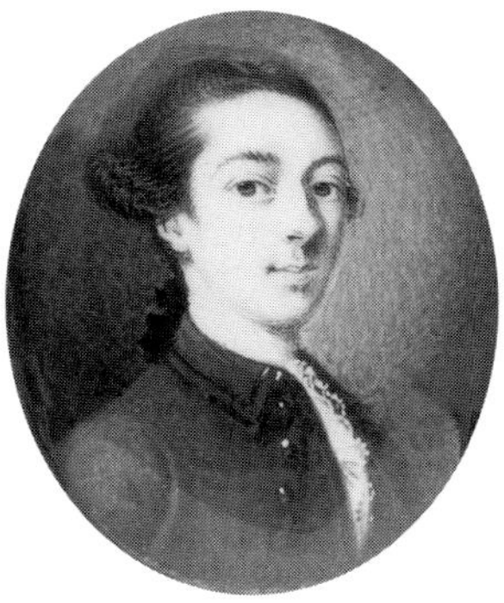

Gustavus Hamilton
Self-Portrait, 1759
Signed and dated: *GHP 1759*
3.1 x 2.8, watercolour with gouache on ivory
Transferred from the NMI, 1969 (where purchased 1909)
NGI 7117. see p. 69.

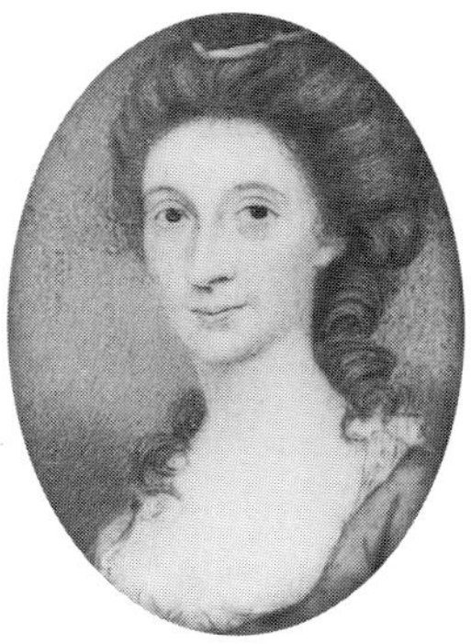

Gustavus Hamilton
Portrait of a lady in a blue dress
3.8 x 3, watercolour on ivory
Transferred from the NMI, 1969 (where acquired 1924)
NGI 7121

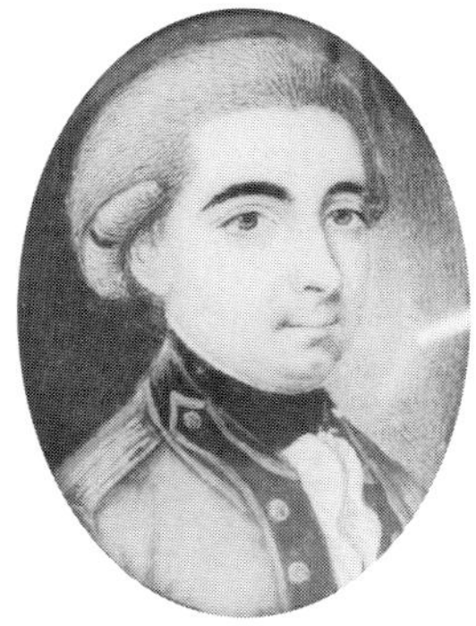

Gustavus Hamilton
Portrait of an Officer (initials E.S.)
3.8 x 3, watercolour on ivory
Transferred from the NMI, 1969 (where purchased 1891)
NGI 7147

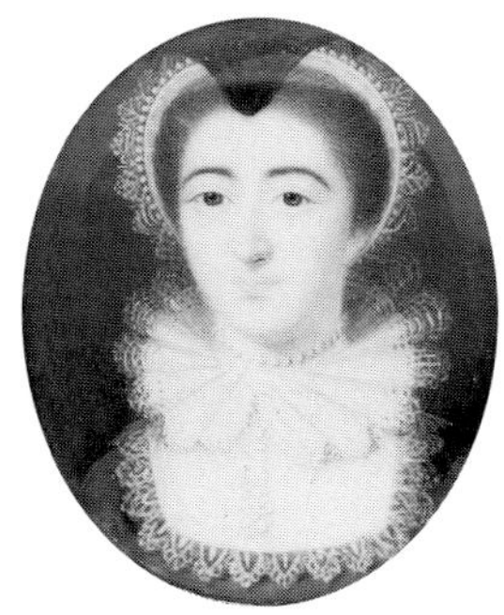

Gustavus Hamilton
Portrait of a lady in Elizabethan costume, 1764
Signed and dated: *Hamn. 1764*
3.4 x 2.8, watercolour with gouache on ivory
Purchased from Mr M. D'Alton, 1910. NGI 7322. see p. 70.

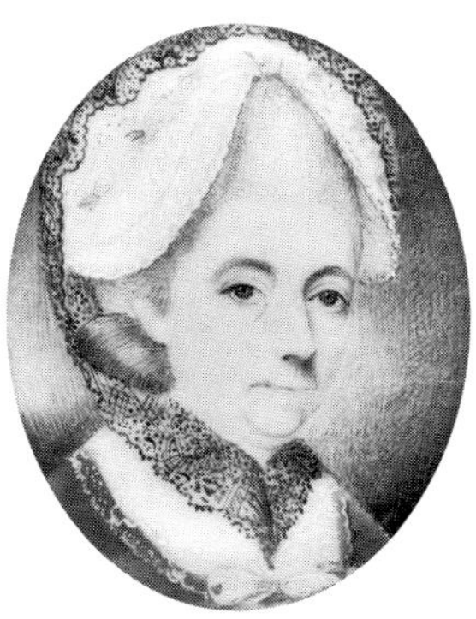

Gustavus Hamilton
Mary Gachet, c.1775
3.6 x 3.3, watercolour on ivory
Bequeathed by Dr S.D. Oliver, 1989
NGI 19383

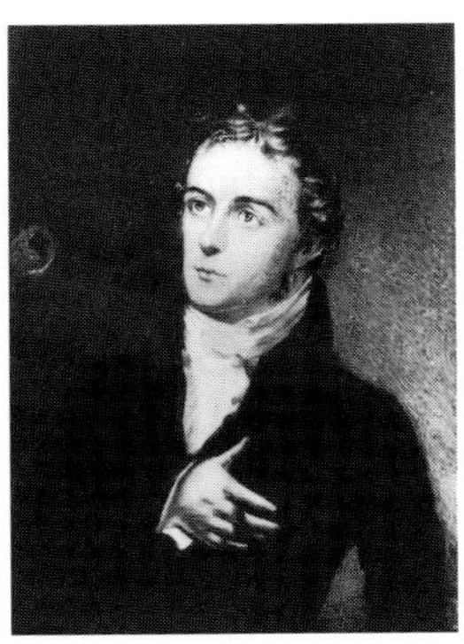

Joseph Patrick Haverty
Galway City 1794 – 1864 Dublin
Richard Lalor Sheil, M.P., (1791–1851), Playwright, c.1828
Dated c.1828 on reverse
11.6 x 8.7, oil and watercolour on ivory. Purchased from Miss M.A. Raye, 1893
NGI 2143

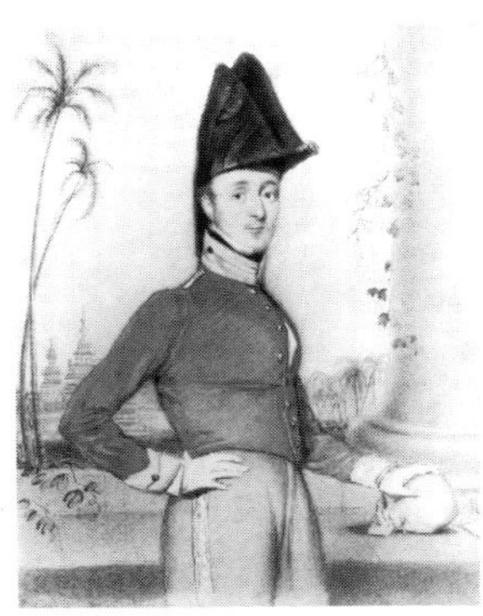

Thomas Hazlehurst
Liverpool c.1740 – 1821 (?)
Colonel Arthur Wellesley, (1769–1852), later 1st Duke of Wellington, when in India, c.1800
Signed: *T.H.*
6.4 x 5.4, watercolour on paper
Purchased from Mr D. Egan, 1913
NGI 2686

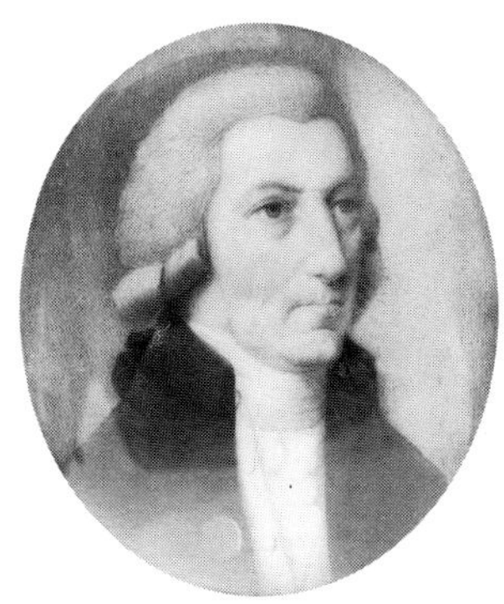

Thomas Hazlehurst
Captain John Hill
Signed: *T.H.*
3.5 x 3, watercolour on ivory
Transferred from the NMI, 1969 (where presented by Miss L.D. Cook, 1955)
NGI 7098

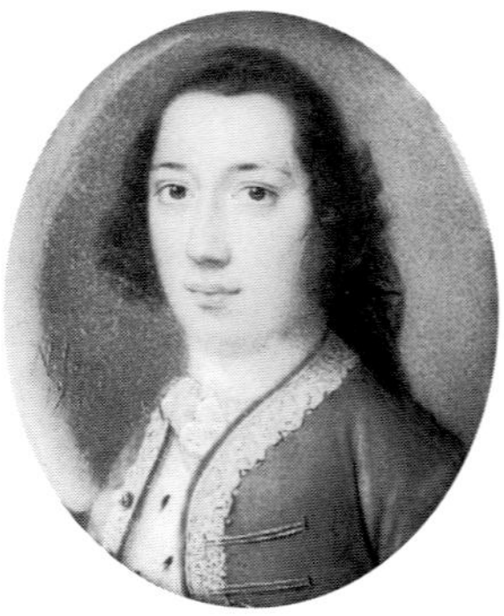

NATHANIEL HONE (THE ELDER)
William Capell, 3rd Earl of Essex, (1697–1742/43), 1747
Signed and dated:
NH(in mono) *one 1747*
3.8 x 3.4, enamel on copper
Transferred from the NMI, 1969
(where provenance unknown)
NGI 7331. see pp. 58–59.

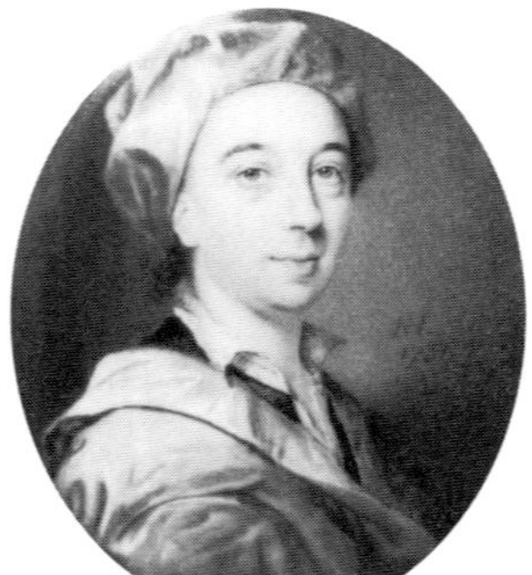

NATHANIEL HONE (THE ELDER)
Portrait of a man in a pink turban, 1751
Signed and dated:
NH(in mono) *1751.*
4.6 x 3.8, enamel on copper
Presented by Mr C. Dickinson, after 1924
NGI 7471. see p. 59.

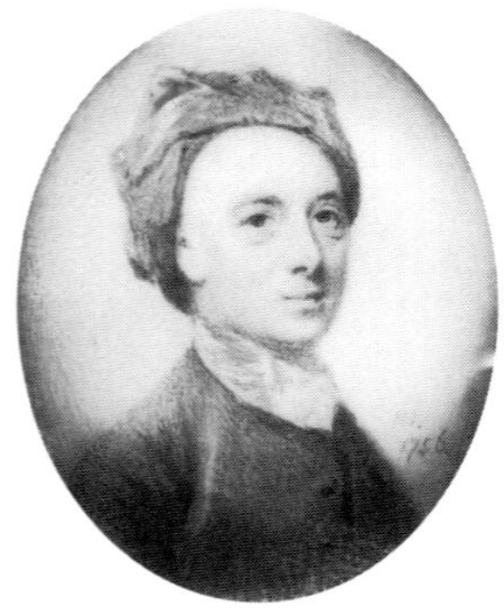

NATHANIEL HONE (THE ELDER)
Portrait of a man in a greenish-brown coat, 1756
Signed and dated:
NH(in mono) *1756*
3.4 x 2.9, watercolour on ivory
Miss Mary A. McNeill Bequest, 1985
NGI 19252

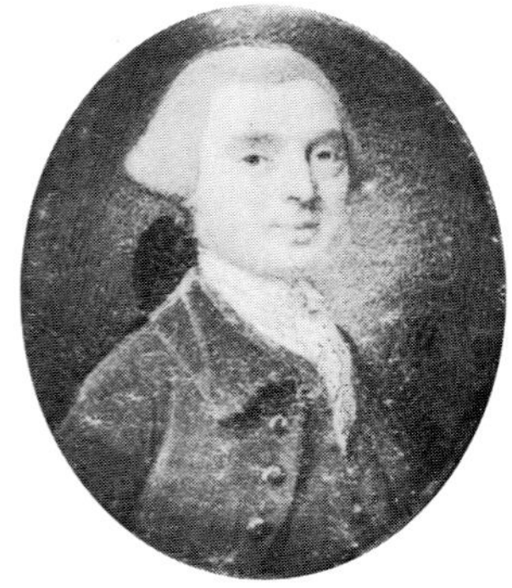

NATHANIEL HONE (THE ELDER)
Portrait of a man in a purple coat, 1763
Signed and dated:
NH(in mono) *1763*
3.2 x 2.7, watercolour on ivory
Miss Mary A. McNeill Bequest, 1985
NGI 19253

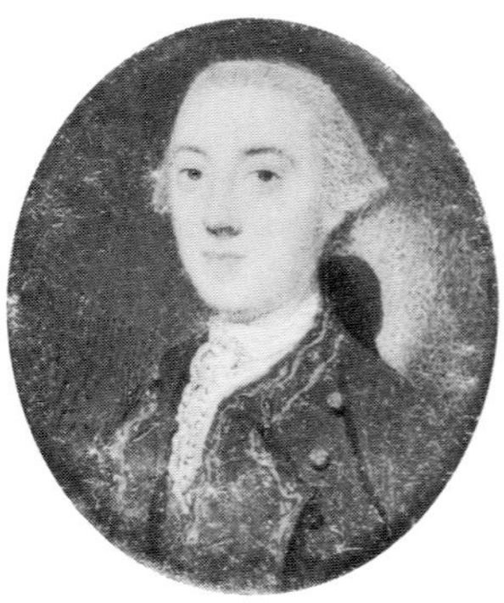

NATHANIEL HONE (THE ELDER)
Portrait of a man in a purple coat with gold braid, 1763
Signed and dated:
NH(in mono) *1763*
3.3 x 2.7, watercolour on ivory
Miss Mary A. McNeill Bequest, 1985. NGI 19254

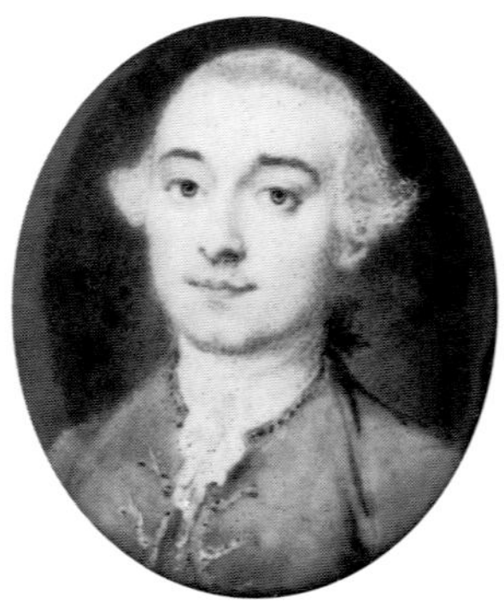

ATTRIBUTED TO
NATHANIEL HONE (THE ELDER)
Portrait of a man in a pink coat
3.1 x 2.7, enamel on copper
Transferred from the NMI, 1969
(where purchased 1899)
NGI 7071

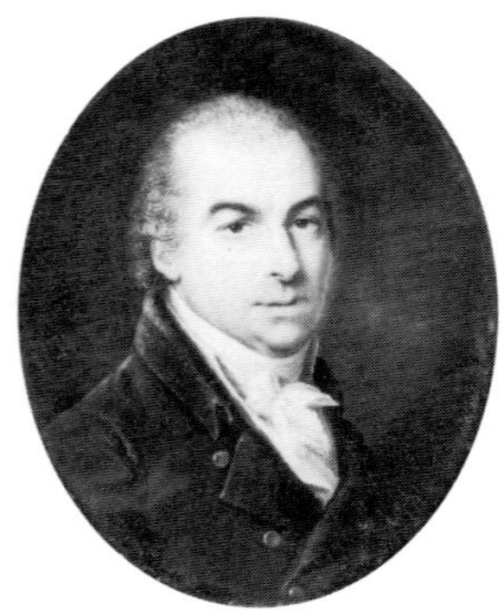

JEAN-FRANÇOIS-MARIE HÜET-VILLIERS
Paris 1772 – 1813 London
George Macartney, 1st Earl Macartney, (1737–1806), Ambassador and Governor, 1804
Signed and dated: *Villiers-Huet 1804.*
8.9 x 7.1, watercolour on ivory.
Miss Mary A. McNeill Bequest, 1985.
NGI 19289. see pp. 119–20.

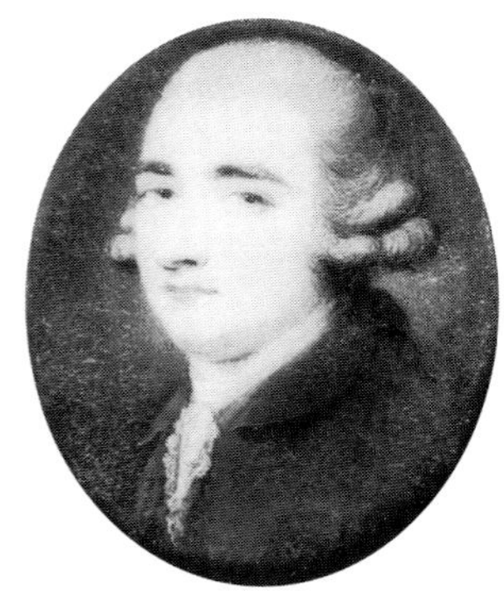

OZIAS HUMPHRY
Honiton, Devon 1742 – 1810 London
Major-General Webb, (1703–1773), c.1760
3.6 x 3.2, watercolour on ivory
Miss Mary A. McNeill Bequest, 1985. NGI 19270. see p. 75.

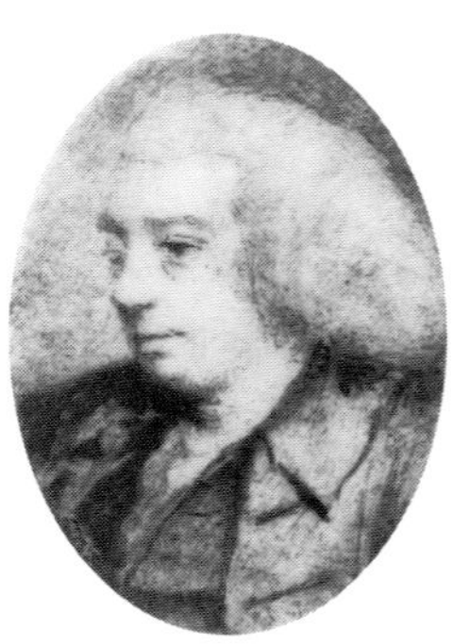

AFTER ROBERT HUNTER
Ulster c.1715/20 – c.1803 (?) Dublin
Dr Francis Hutcheson, (1728–1784), Composer (after NGI 905)
3.2 x 2.4, watercolour on ivory
Transferred from the NMI, 1969
(where presented by Mr T.H. Longfield, 1897). NGI 7081

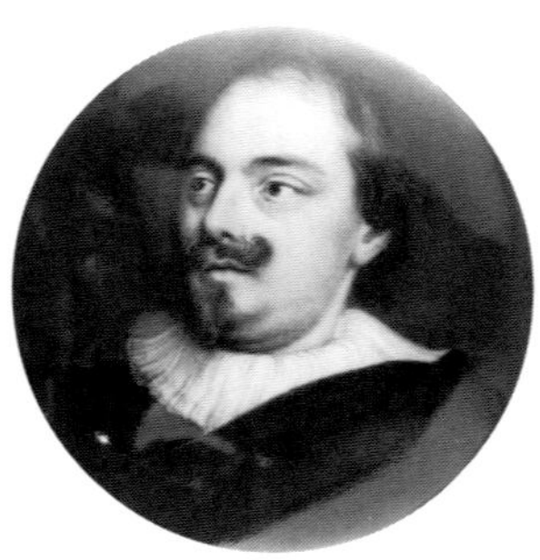

JOHANN HEINRICH [VON] HURTER
Schaffhausen, Switzerland
1734 – 1799 Düsseldorf
Portrait of a man in 17th century costume, 1777.
Signed and dated: *J Hurter. 1777.*
8 diam., enamel on copper
Presented by Sir Alfred Chester Beatty, 1951. NGI 3583

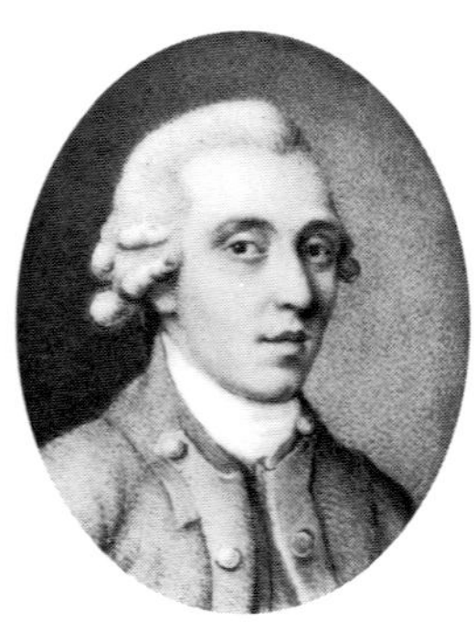

JOHANN HEINRICH [VON] HURTER
Tiberius Cavallo, (1749–1809), Natural Philosopher, 1783
Inscribed, signed and dated on reverse: **Hurter Pint. Londini 1783.* 4.5 x 3.6, enamel on copper
Presented by Sir Alfred Chester Beatty, 1951
NGI 3611. see p. 67.

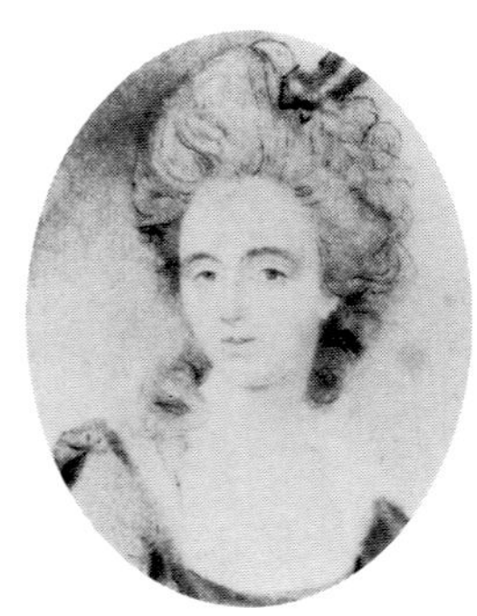

IRISH SCHOOL (18TH CENTURY)
Portrait of a lady in a blue dress
9 x 7, watercolour on paper
Purchased from
Mrs Catterson Smith, 1912
NGI 2673

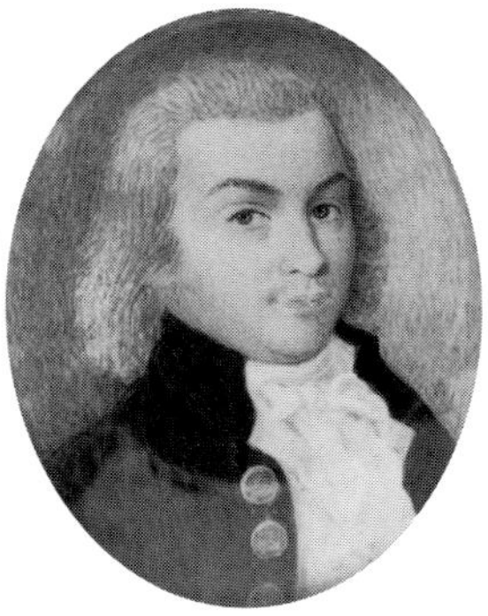

Irish School (18th century)
George Samuel Roderick
4.9 x 3.9, watercolour on ivory
Transferred from the NMI, 1969
(where presented by
Miss A.E. Bagge-Hearn,
granddaughter of sitter, 1924)
NGI 7076

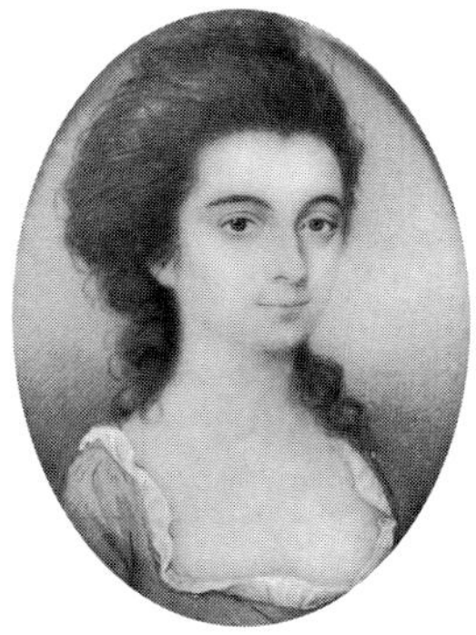

Irish School (c.1780)
Mrs John Erck,
(born Jane Marth Maignon)
4.2 x 3.1, watercolour on ivory
Bequeathed by
Dr S.D. Oliver, 1989
NGI 19382

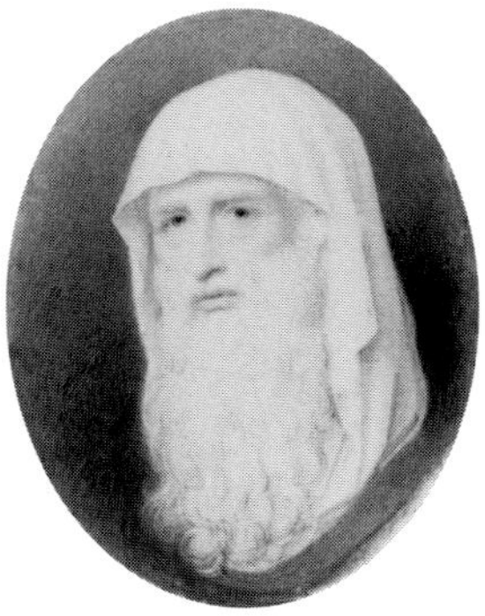

Irish School (c.1790)
The head of a Druid
8.1 x 6.7, watercolour on ivory
Transferred from the NMI, 1969
(where, presented by the friends
of the National Collections
of Ireland, 1926)
NGI 7167

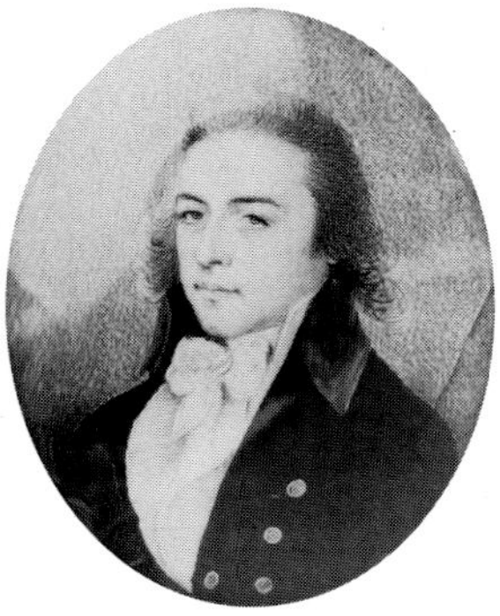

Irish School (c.1790)
(?) John Sheares, (1766–1798),
United Irishman
6.8 x 5.6, watercolour on ivory
Provenance unknown
NGI 7336

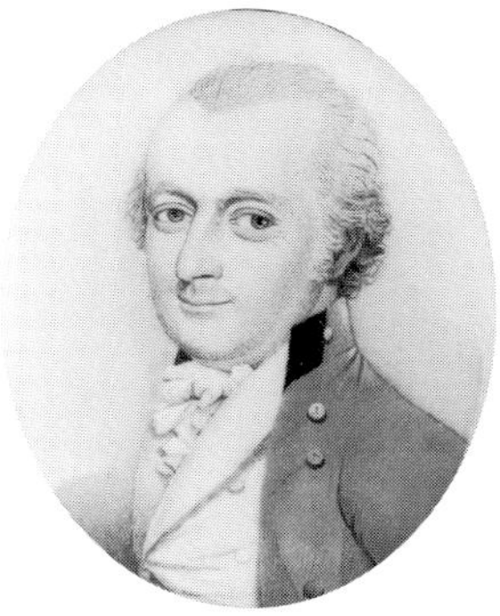

Irish School (c.1790)
Portrait of a member of the
Armstrong family
5.9 x 4.8, watercolour on ivory
Presented by Sir Andrew
Armstrong, Bt., 1981
NGI 7938

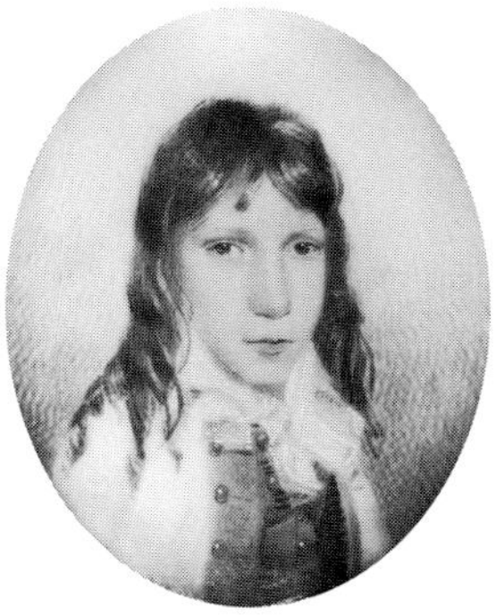

Irish School (c.1790)
Portrait of a boy
4.9 x 4.1, watercolour on ivory
Miss Mary A. McNeill Bequest,
1985
NGI 19285

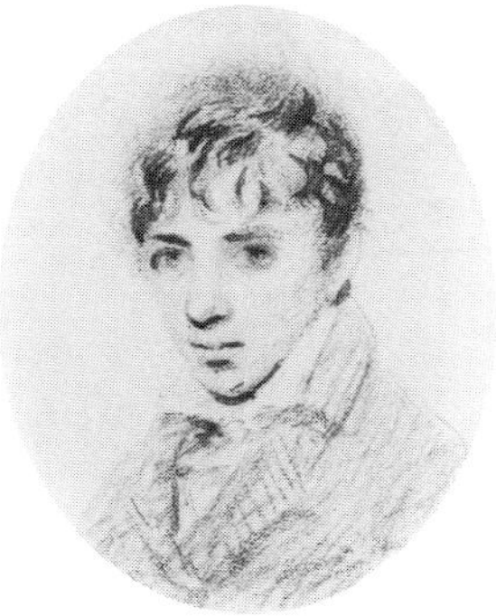

Irish School
(late 18th century)
George Petrie, (1790–1866),
Artist and Antiquary, as a boy
8.2 x 6.6, charcoal and
wash on paper
Purchased from
Mrs L. Rogers, 1950
NGI 3034

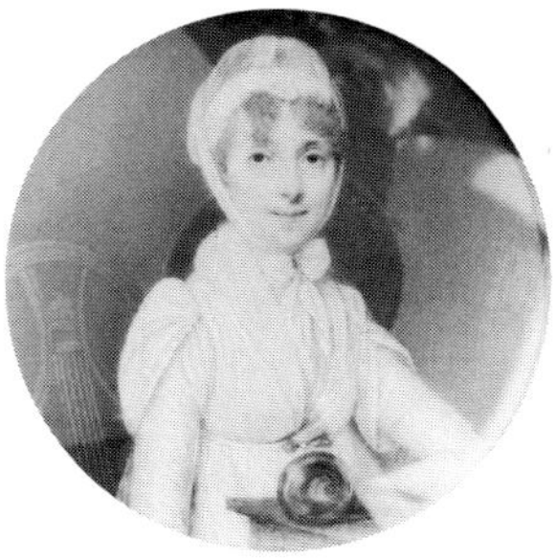

Irish School
(late 18th century)
Portrait of an elderly lady
with an ear trumpet
6.9 diam., watercolour on ivory
Transferred from the NMI, 1969
(where presented by
Miss A. Colston, 1942)
NGI 7057

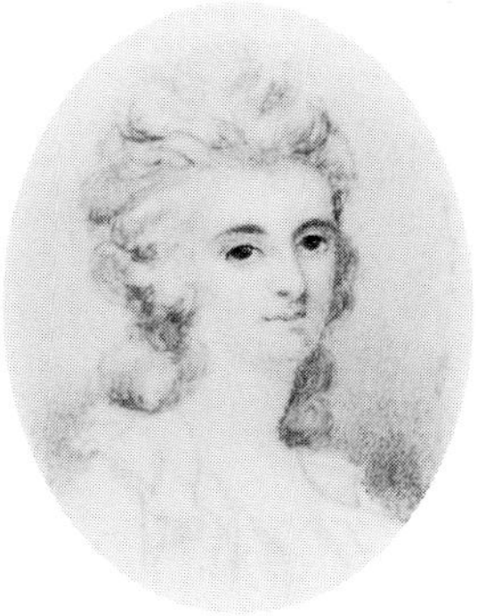

Irish School
(late 18th century)
Portrait of a lady in a white dress
(pendant to following)
6.1 x 4.7, watercolour on ivory
Transferred from the NMI, 1969
(where bequeathed by
Miss Gardiner, 1929)
NGI 7080

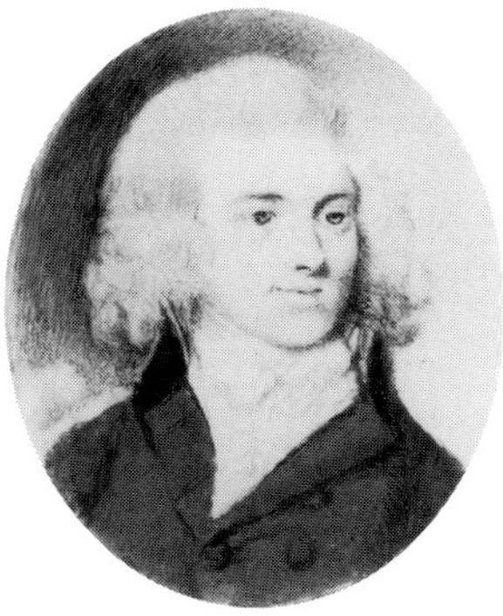

Irish School
(late 18th century)
Portrait of a man in an emerald
green coat (pendant to preceding)
5.9 x 4.5, watercolour on ivory
Transferred from the NMI, 1969
(where bequeathed by
Miss Gardiner, 1929)
NGI 7083

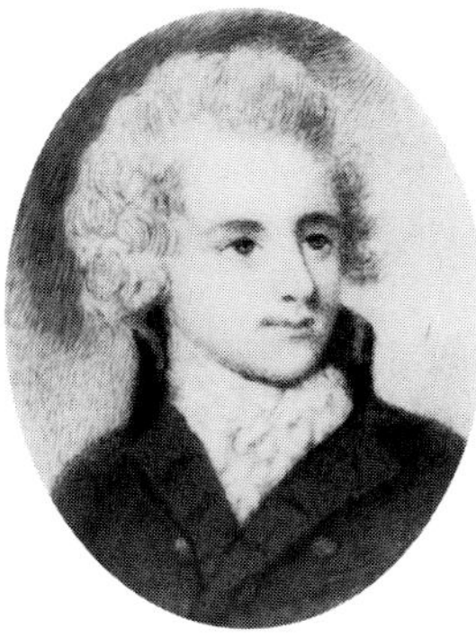

Irish School
(late 18th century)
Luke Gardiner, 1st Viscount
Mountjoy, (1745–1798)
6.5 x 5.2, watercolour on ivory
Transferred from the NMI, 1969
(where bequeathed by
Miss Gardiner, 1929)
NGI 7122

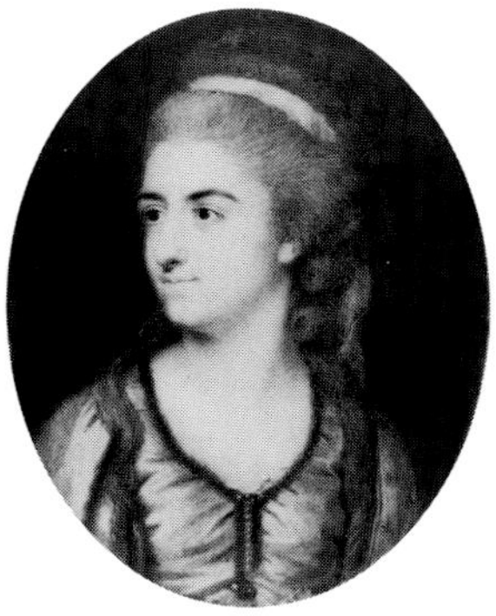

Irish School
(late 18th century)
Lady Elizabeth Hart,
(born Aspinal)
5.3 x 4.4, watercolour on ivory
Transferred from the NMI, 1969
(where acquired 1891)
NGI 7190

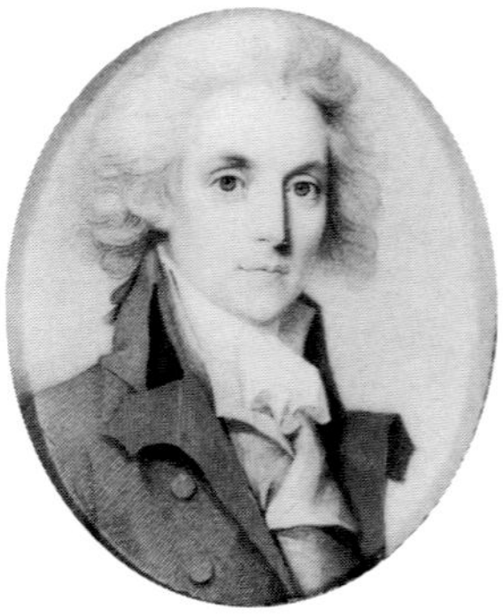

Irish School (late 18th century) and Irish School (c.1870), *Colonel William Lane, later Governor of St Helena; Frederick Willington, who served with the Royal Irish Regiment (?grandson of Colonel Lane) on reverse.*

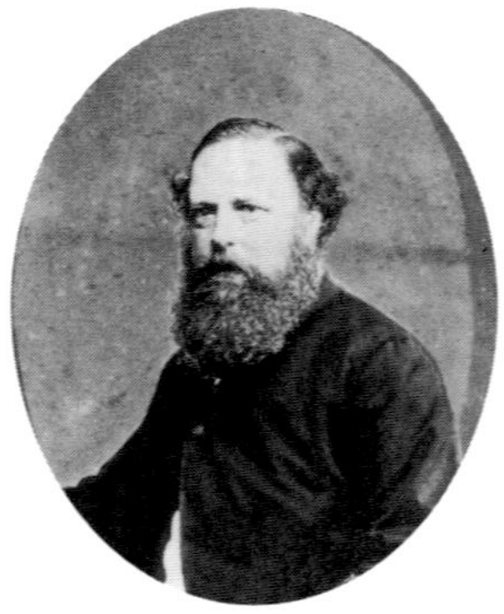

6.5 x 5, watercolour on ivory/ over photo on card, set in a gold brooch
Purchased from Miss Huggard, 1973. NGI 7594. see Illus. 8.

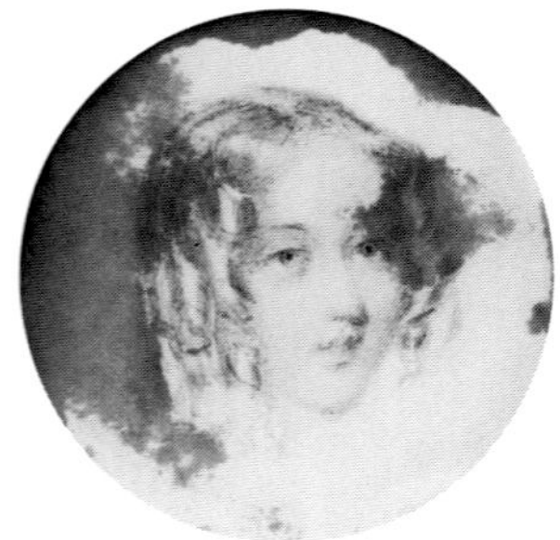

Irish School (19th century)
Portrait head of a young girl
6.2 diam., watercolour on vellum
Transferred from the NMI, 1969 (where bequeathed by Mr T. Mercer, 1924)
NGI 7155

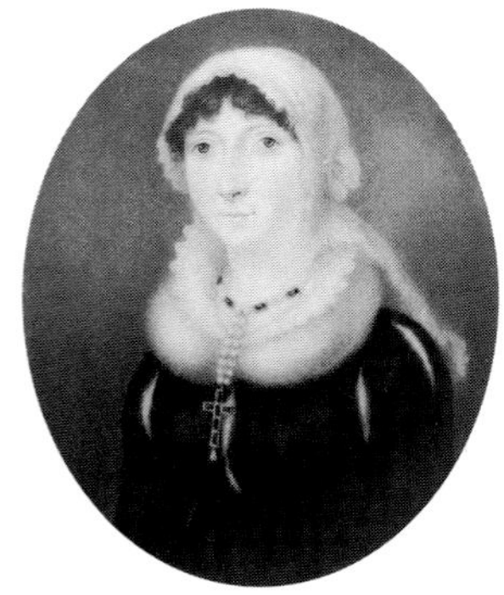

Irish School (19th century)
Portrait of a lady with a cross pendant
8.8 x 6.8, watercolour on ivory
Transferred from the NMI, 1969 (where bequeathed by Mr T. Mercer, 1924)
NGI 7175

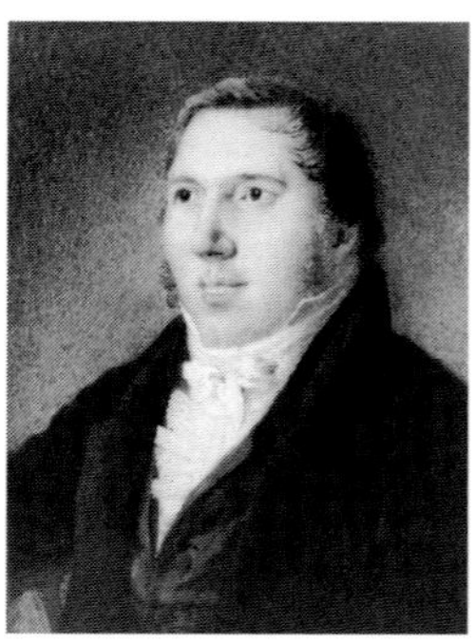

Irish School (c.1800)
Supposed portrait of Henry Sheares, (1753–1798), Barrister and brother of John Sheares
7.6 x 5.8, watercolour on ivory
Presented by the Misses Warren, 1930. NGI 2926

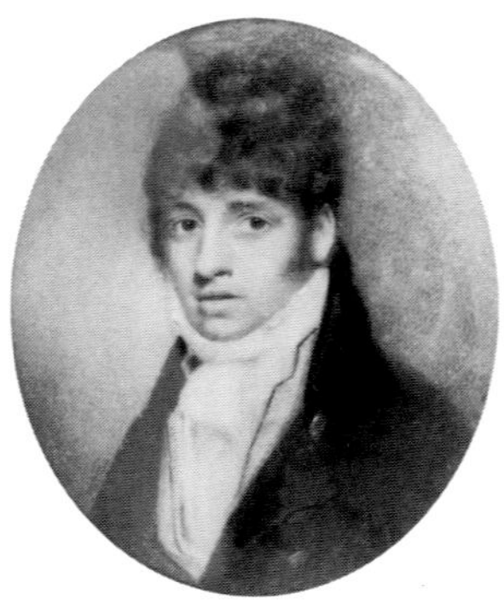

Irish School (c.1800)
John Howard Gorges of Kilbran, Co. Meath, (c.1780–1826)
6.7 x 5.8, watercolour on ivory
Transferred from the NMI, 1969 (where presented by Mrs G. Gorges, 1958)
NGI 7106

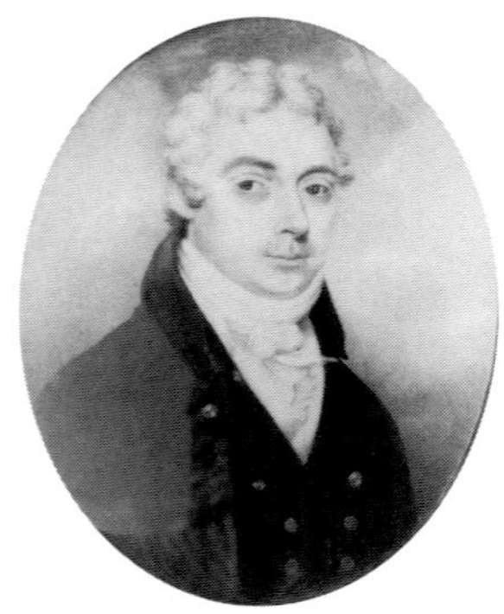

Irish School (c.1800)
Portrait of a member of the Armstrong family
7.1 x 5.7, watercolour on ivory
Presented by Sir Andrew Armstrong, Bt., 1981
NGI 7937

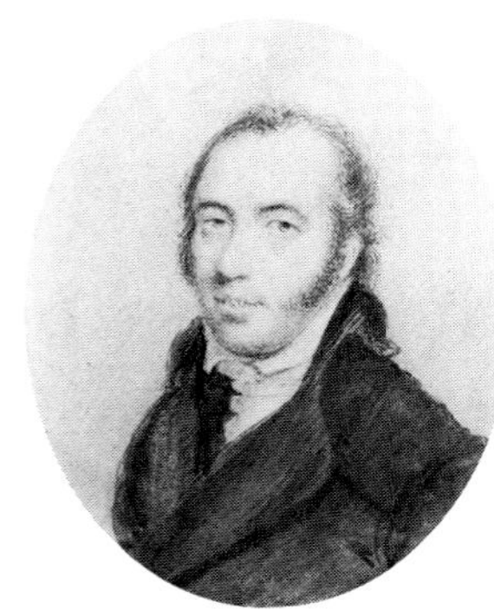

Irish School (c.1800)
Portrait of a man in a black coat
9.1 x 7.4, watercolour on card
Provenance unknown
NGI 19222

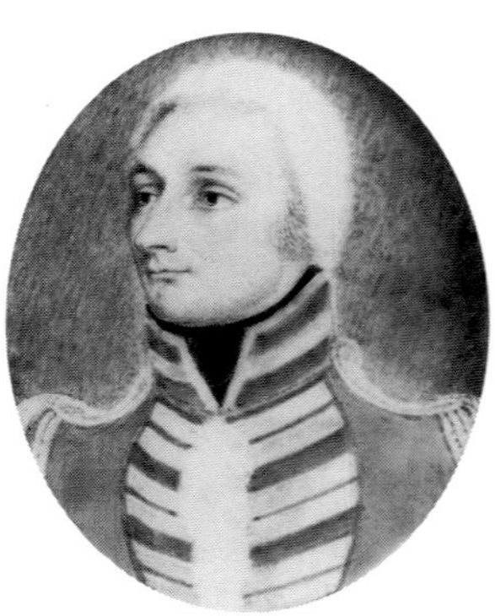

Irish School (early 19th century)
Portrait of an Officer
5.8 x 5, watercolour on ivory
Presented by Mr E.S. Robertson, 1903
NGI 2531

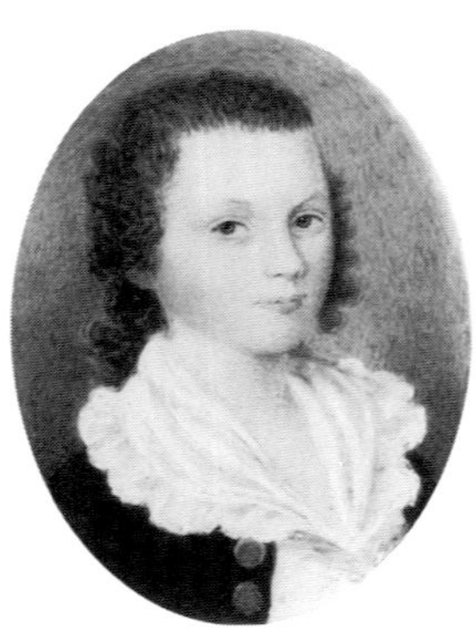

Irish School (early 19th century)
George Samuel Roderick, (?son of NGI 7076)
4.4 x 3.5, watercolour on ivory
Transferred from the NMI, 1969 (where presented by Miss A.E. Bagge-Hearn, 1913)
NGI 7074

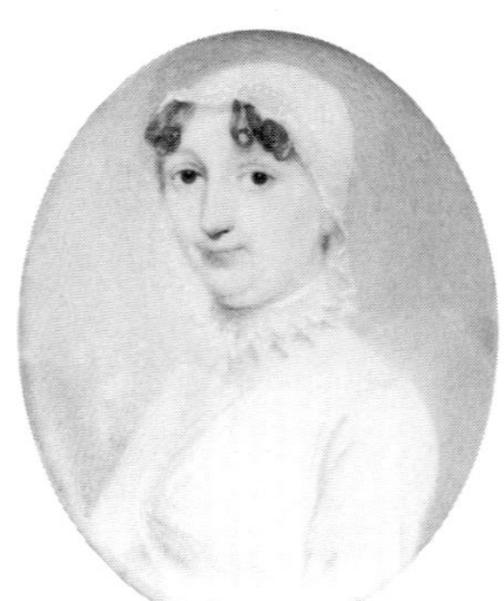

Irish School (early 19th century)
Catherine Coffey of Kilcumney, Co. Wicklow
6.9 x 5.5, watercolour on ivory, set in a brooch
Transferred from the NMI, 1969 (where purchased 1910)
NGI 7077

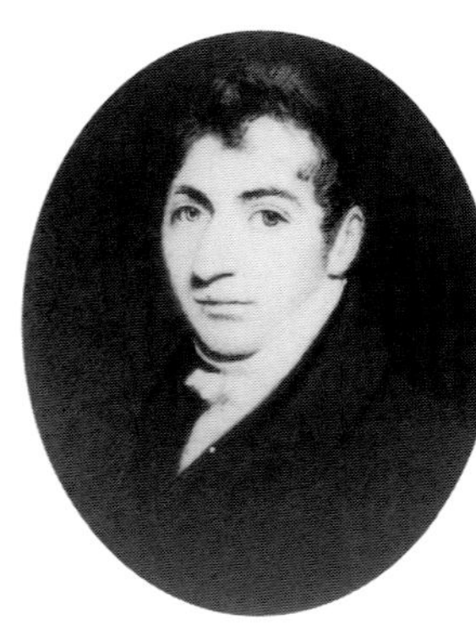

Irish School (early 19th century)
Mr G.
7.1 x 5.8, watercolour on ivory
Transferred from the NMI, 1969 (where presented 1911)
NGI 7085

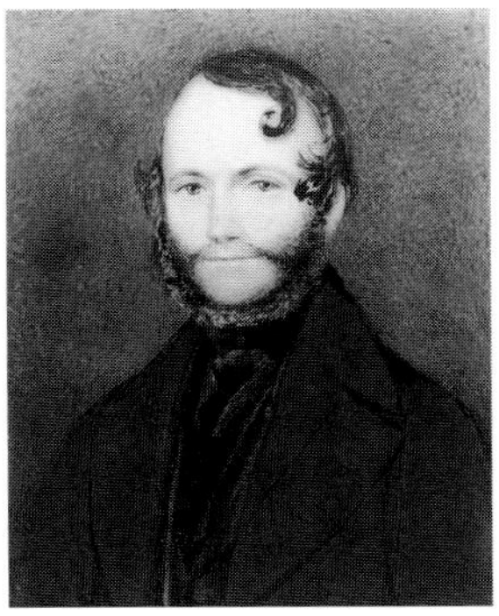

Irish School
(early 19th century)
Portrait of a man in a dark grey coat
6.5 x 5.2, watercolour on ivory
Transferred from the NMI, 1969
(where acquired 1947)
NGI 7105

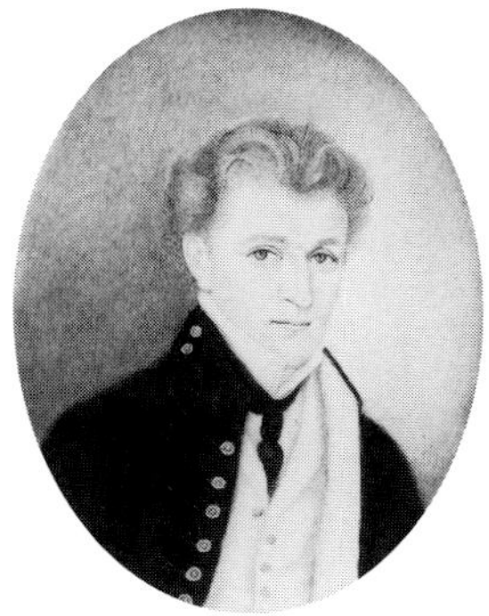

Irish School
(early 19th century)
Portrait of a young man in a blue coat
7.7 x 6.1, watercolour on ivory
Transferred from the NMI, 1969
(where presented by
Mrs G. Gorges, 1958)
NGI 7111

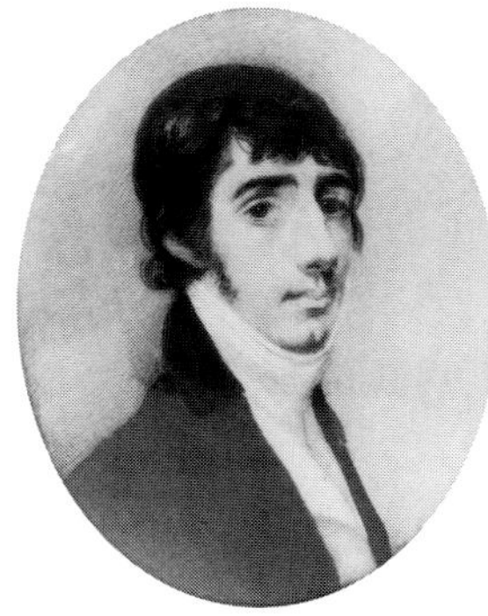

Irish School
(early 19th century)
Portrait of a young man in a blue coat
7.3 x 5.9, watercolour on ivory
Transferred from the NMI, 1969
(where purchased 1889)
NGI 7140

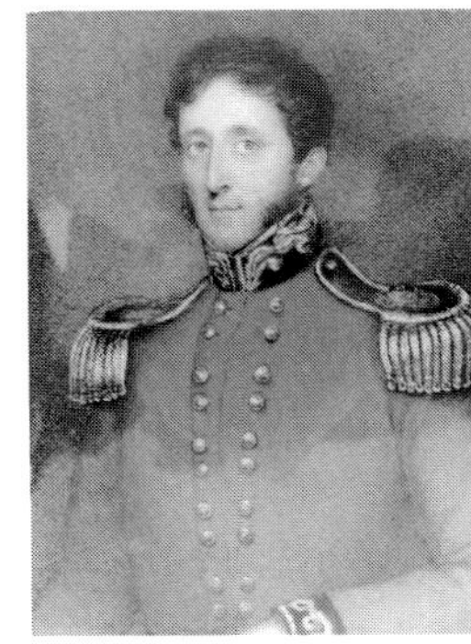

Irish School
(early 19th century)
William Daniel Kelly of Turrock, Co. Roscommon
11 x 8.1, watercolour on ivory
Transferred from the NMI, 1969
(where presented by
Mrs G. Gorges, 1958)
NGI 7164

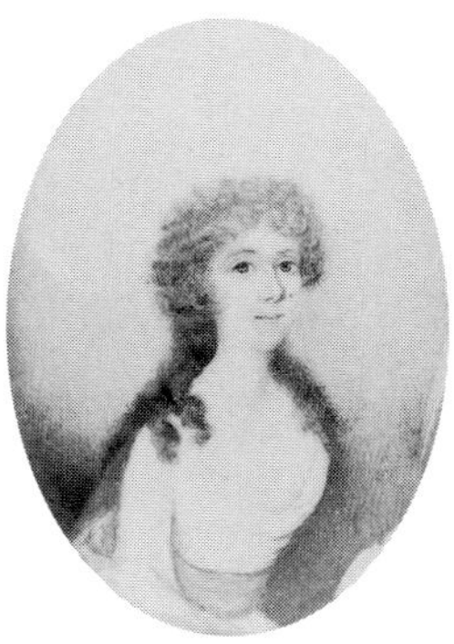

Irish School
(early 19th century)
Martha Richards of Solsboro, Co. Wexford
7.2 x 5.1, watercolour on ivory
Transferred from the NMI, 1969
(where presented by
Mrs G. Gorges, 1958)
NGI 7166

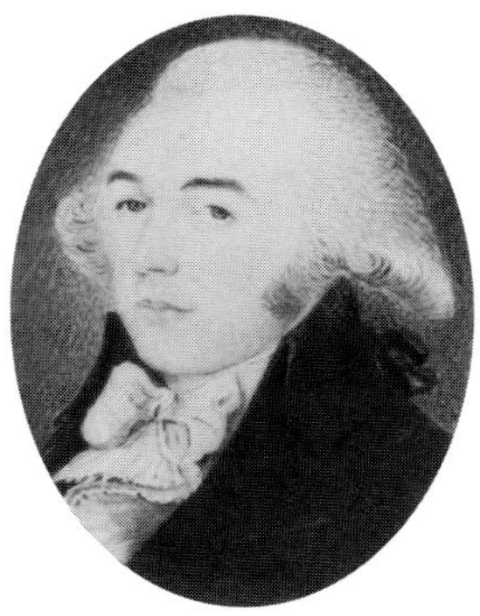

Irish School
(early 19th century)
John Sheares, (1766–1798), United Irishman
5.3 x 4.1, watercolour on ivory
Provenance unknown
NGI 7335

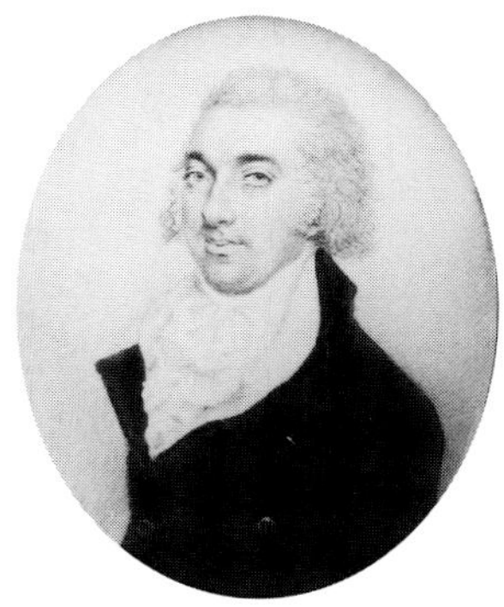

Irish School (c.1810)
Edward Martyn
7.5 x 5.8, watercolour on ivory
Bequeathed by Mr E. Martyn,
descendant of the sitter, 1924
NGI 2745

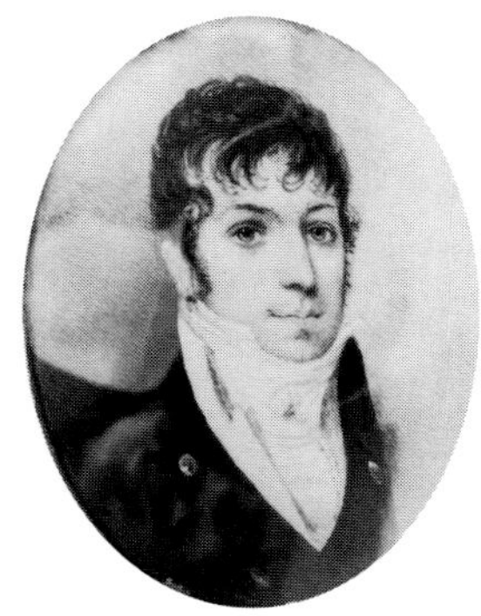

Irish School (c.1810)
Mr T.
6.7 x 5.3, watercolour on ivory
Transferred from the NMI, 1969
(where presented 1911)
NGI 7079

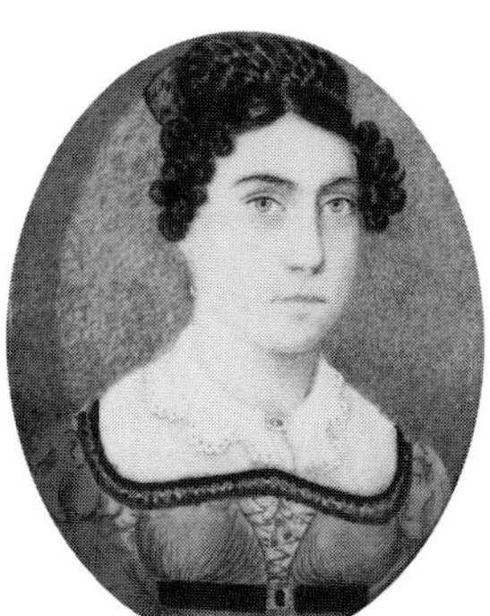

Irish School (c.1825)
Portrait of a lady in a brown dress
7.6 x 5.8, watercolour on ivory
Transferred from the NMI, 1969
(where presented by
Miss Frazer, 1900)
NGI 7225

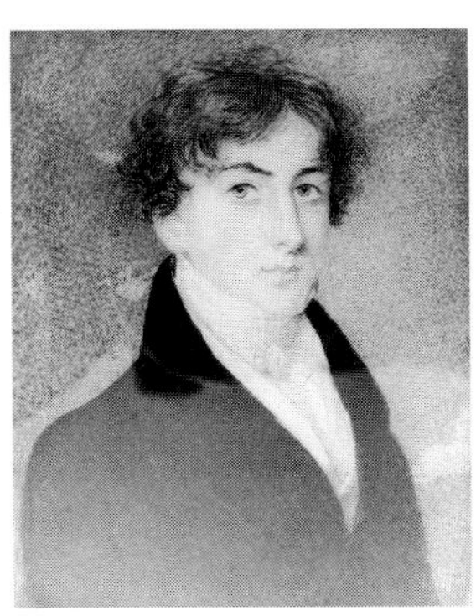

Irish School (c.1828)
Thomas Fortescue Ellis, (1808–1828)
8.8 x 7, watercolour on ivory
Transferred from the NMI, 1969
(where presented 1939)
NGI 7182

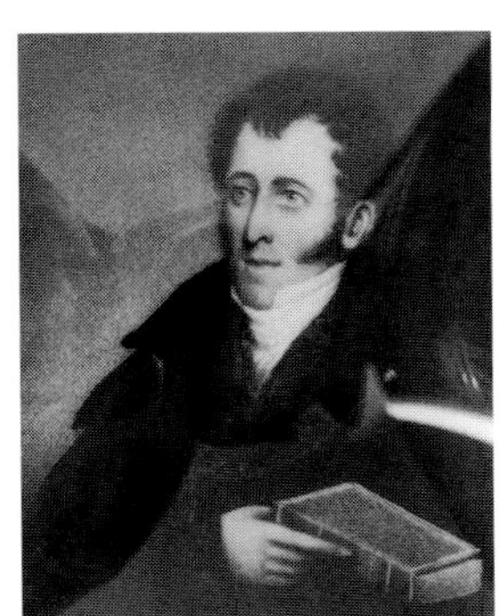

Irish School (c.1830)
William Daniel Kelly of Turrock, Co. Roscommon, holding a copy of Tasso
10 x 7.8, watercolour on ivory
Transferred from the NMI, 1969
(where presented by
Mrs G. Gorges, 1958)
NGI 7165

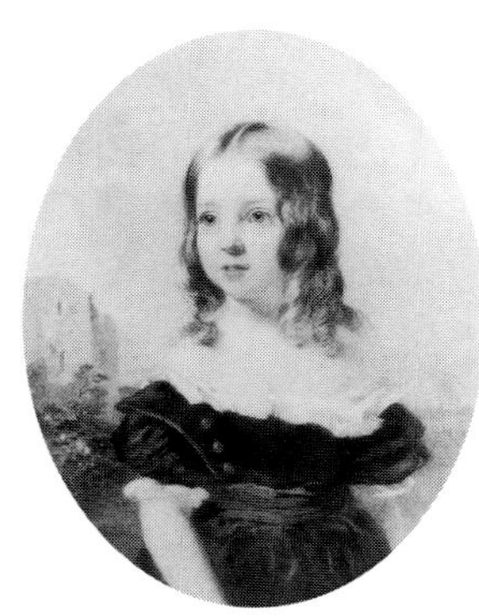

Irish School (c.1830)
Portrait of a girl against a landscape
12.5 x 12, watercolour on marble
Transferred from the NMI 1969
(where acquired 1924)
NGI 7199

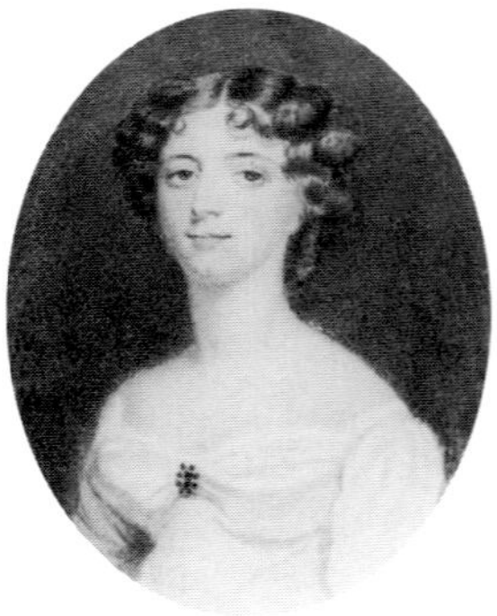

IRISH SCHOOL (c.1830)
Portrait of a young lady in a white dress
8.5 x 6.9, watercolour on ivory
Transferred from the NMI, 1969
(where bequeathed by
Miss Gardiner, 1929)
NGI 7215

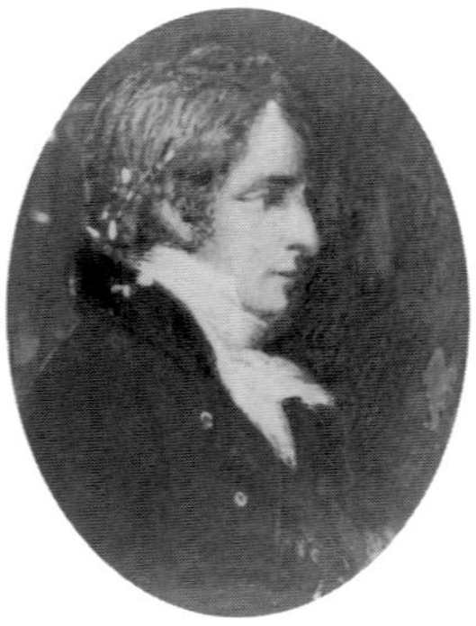

IRISH SCHOOL (c.1830)
Portrait of a man in a blue coat
7.5 x 5.8, watercolour on ivory
(damaged)
Provenance unknown
NGI 7541

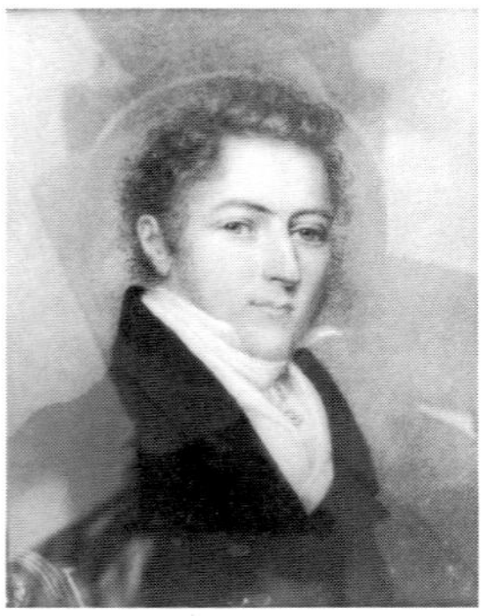

IRISH SCHOOL (c.1830)
Portrait of a member of the Armstrong family
7.9 x 6.3, watercolour on ivory
Presented by Sir Andrew
Armstrong, Bt., 1981
NGI 7939

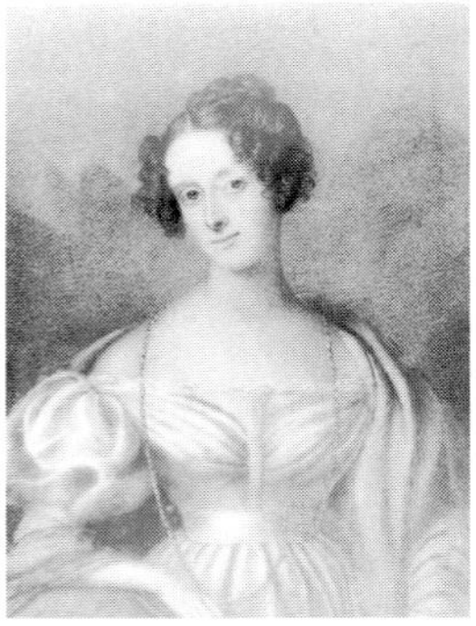

IRISH SCHOOL (c.1835)
Jane Kelly of Co. Roscommon, (1811–1884/85)
12.5 x 9.5, watercolour on ivory
Transferred from the NMI, 1969
(where presented by
Mrs G. Gorges, 1958)
NGI 7230

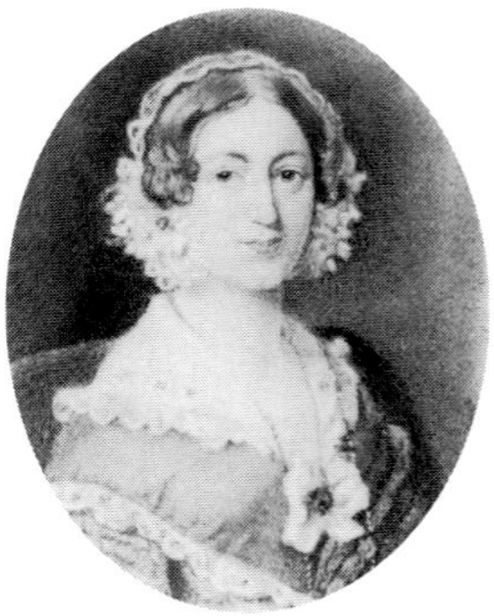

IRISH SCHOOL (c.1840)
Portrait of a lady in a blue dress
9.1 x 7.1, watercolour on ivory
Transferred from the NMI, 1969
(where bequeathed by
Miss Gardiner, 1929)
NGI 7217

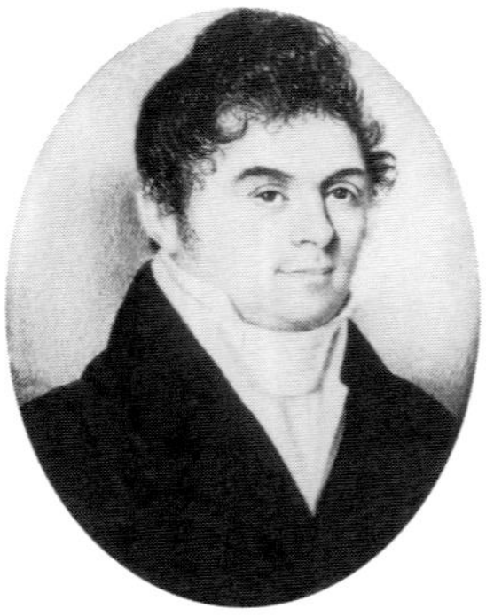

G. JACKSON
active (?) Dublin c.1810
Self-Portrait, 1810
Signed and dated: *G Jackson 1810*
7.1 x 5.7, watercolour on ivory
Purchased at Christie's,
London, 1889
NGI 2376. see p. 132.

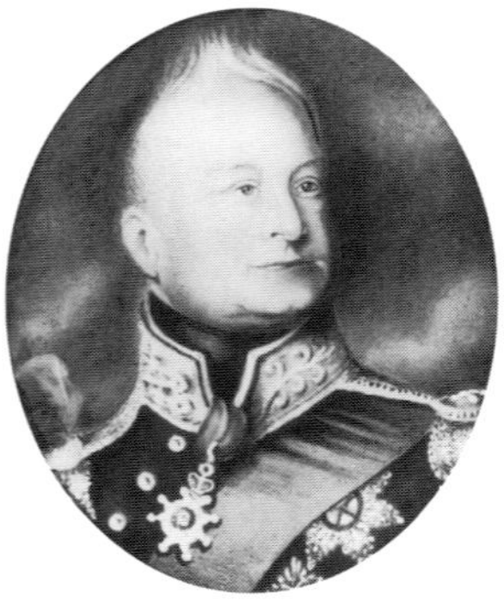

E. JAMES
active England c.1831
William IV, King of England, (1765–1837)
Signed and dated:
E James Jany 1831
3.6 x 3, enamel on copper
Presented by Sir Alfred Chester
Beatty, 1951. NGI 3771

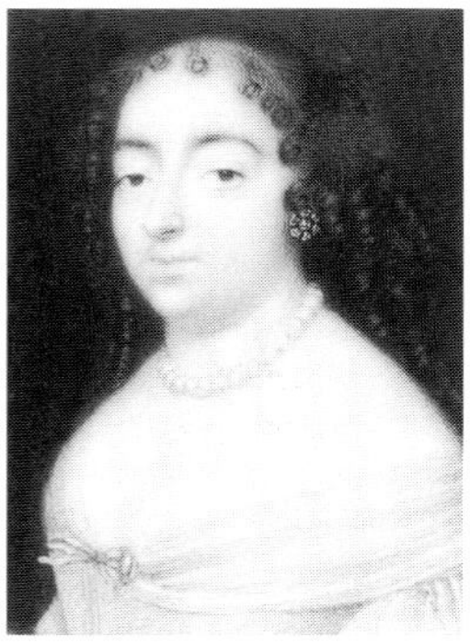

H. DE JANVRY
active England 1793 – 1800
Portrait of a lady with a pearl necklace
Signed on reverse: *HJ*
3.5 x 2.5, watercolour on ivory
Transferred from the NMI, 1969
(where acquired 1924)
NGI 7037

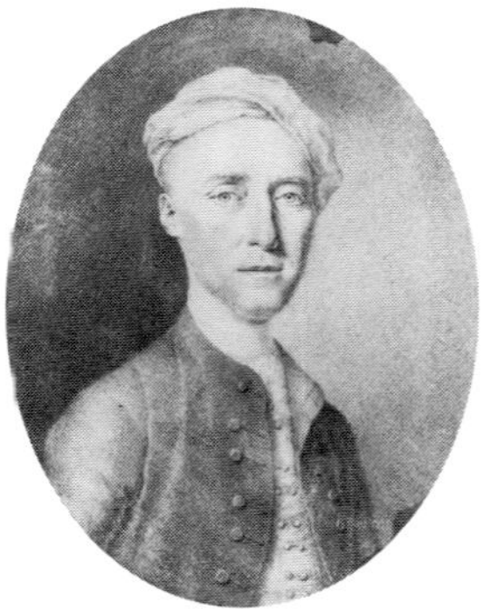

FOLLOWER OF CHARLES JERVAS
Shinrone, Co. Offaly c.1675 –
1739 London
Thomas Murphy, (b.1698), 1733
Inscribed on backing paper:
done in Jamaica 1733
12.4 x 9.8, pencil on paper
Purchased at Sotheby's, London,
Mr F. Wellesley Sale, 1920
NGI 2719

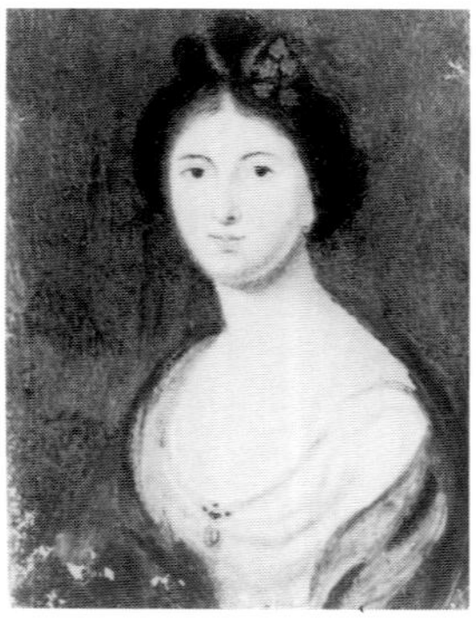

AFTER ANGELICA KAUFFMAN
Coire, Switzerland 1741 –
1807 Rome
Dorothea (Dolly) Monroe, (c.1750–1811), Celebrated Beauty
(19th century after NGI 405 hl,
1771). 9 x 6.9, watercolour on
ivory. Transferred from the NMI,
1969 (where provenance
unknown). NGI 7206

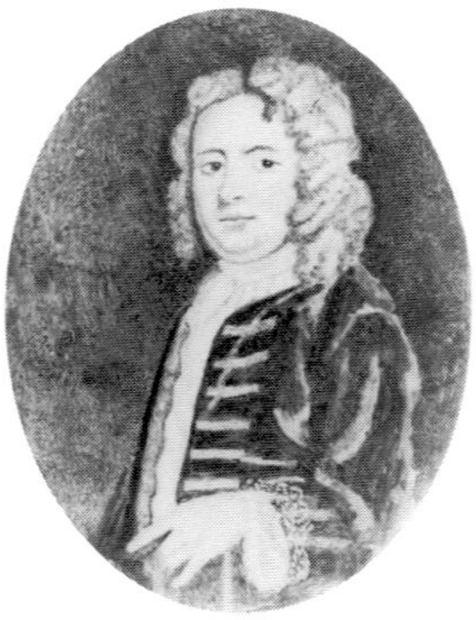

AFTER GODFREY KNELLER
Lübeck 1646 – 1723 London
Sir Richard Steele, (1672–1729), Essayist
(19th century after mezzotint of
Kneller of 1711, NPGL)
13 x 10, watercolour on ivory
Transferred from the NMI, 1969
(where provenance unknown)
NGI 7227

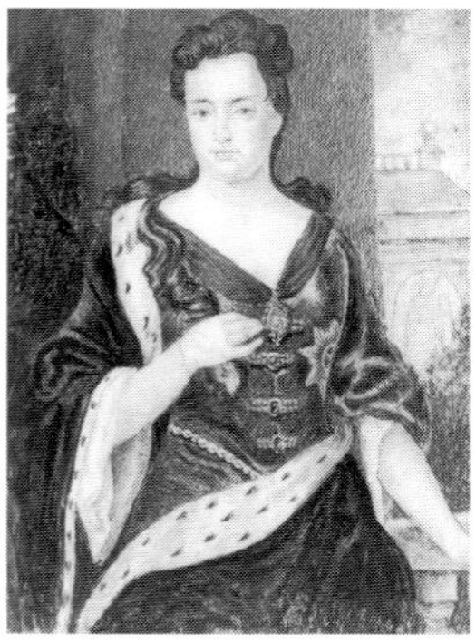

AFTER GODFREY KNELLER
Queen Anne, (1665–1714)
(19th century after Kneller c.1690)
11 x 8.2, watercolour on ivory
Provenance unknown
NGI 7685

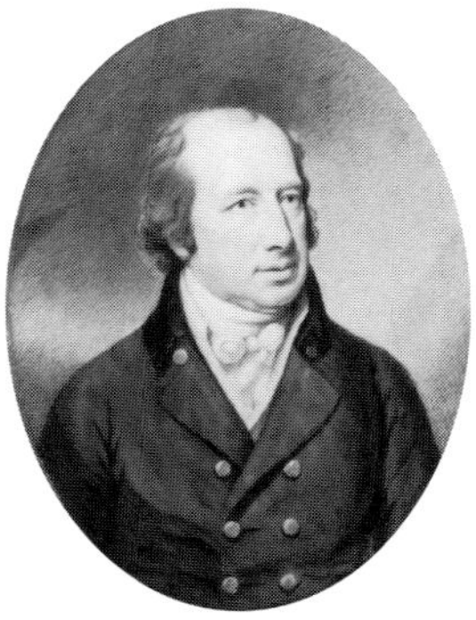

GEORGE LAWRENCE
Dublin c.1758 – 1802 Dublin
Sackville Hamilton, (1732–1818), Under-Secretary for Ireland
8.5 x 6.5, watercolour on ivory
Presented by Mrs T.H. Rice, 1900
NGI 2433

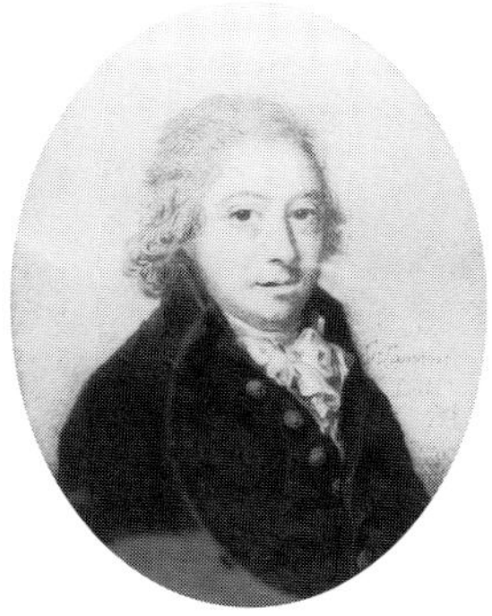

GEORGE LAWRENCE
Portrait of a man in a blue coat, 1793
Signed and dated: *G. Lawrence Dubln 1793*. 6.6 x 5.1, watercolour with gouache on ivory, set in a brooch. Transferred from the NMI, 1969 (where purchased 1915).
NGI 7078. see p. 106, Illus. 13.

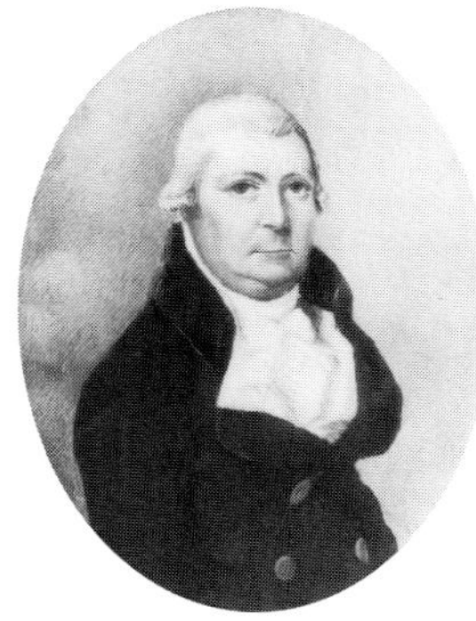

GEORGE LAWRENCE
Hamilton Gorges of Kilbran, Co. Meath, (1739–1802) c.1800
7.2 x 5.6, watercolour on ivory
Transferred from the NMI, 1969 (where presented by Mrs G. Gorges, 1958)
NGI 7149
see Illus. 13 and 27.

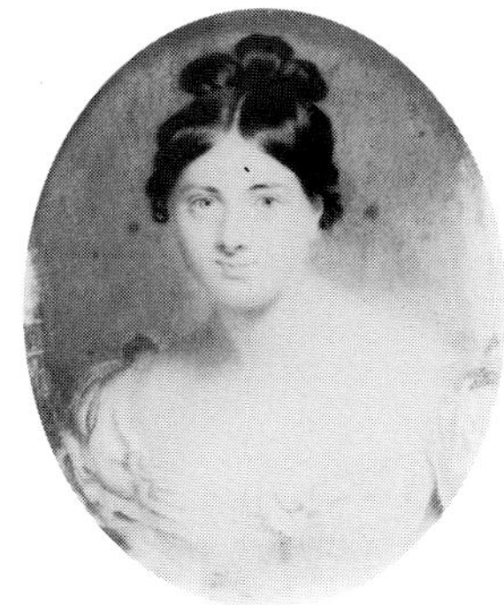

AFTER THOMAS LAWRENCE
Bristol 1769 – 1830 London
Margaret, Countess of Blessington, (born Power, 1789–1849), Writer, 1863. (after Lawrence exhibited 1822). Dated 23rd February 1863 on backing paper
7.5 x 7.8, watercolour on ivory
Purchased at Christie's, London, 1890. NGI 2141

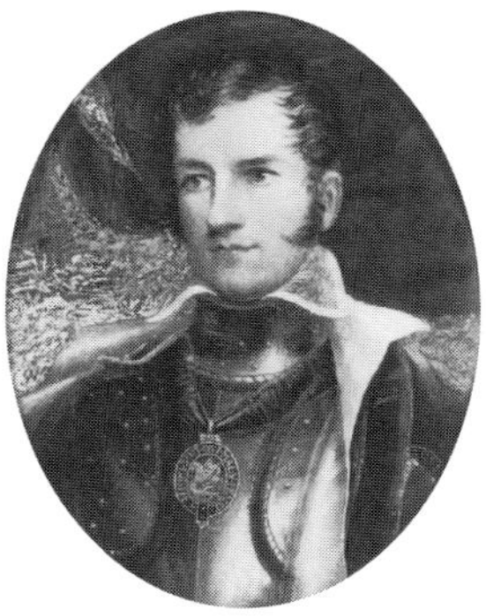

JOSEPH LEE
London 1780 – 1859 Gravesend, Essex
Prince Leopold, (1790–1865), later King of the Belgians, c.1820
Signed on reverse: *Lee*
7.3 x 6, enamel on copper
Presented by Sir Alfred Chester Beatty, 1951. NGI 3625

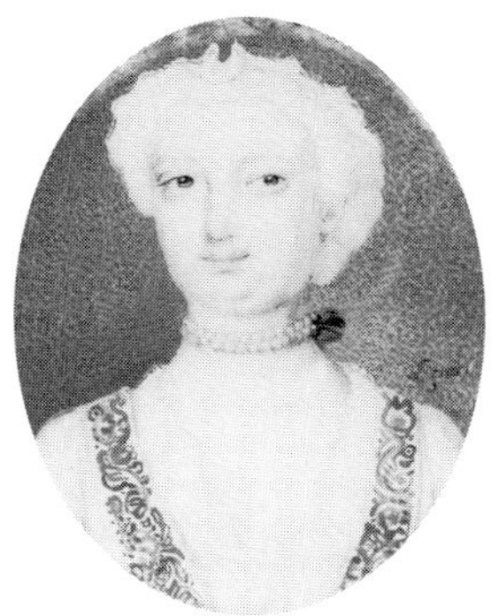

ATTRIBUTED TO ANDREW BENJAMIN LENS
active London c.1713 – after 1779
Amalie Sophie Marianne, Countess of Yarmouth, (born von Wallmoden, 1704–1765), mistress of King George II. Signed: *Lens*. 4 x 3.1, watercolour on ivory (damaged)
Transferred from the NMI, 1969 (where purchased from Mr A.B. Bennett, 1885). NGI 7063

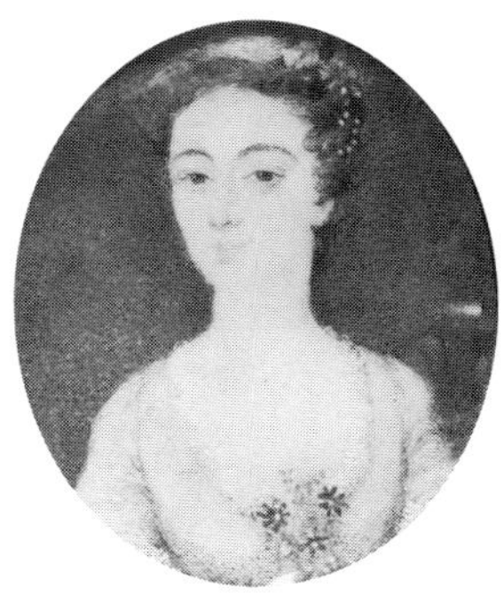

ATTRIBUTED TO ANDREW BENJAMIN LENS
Portrait of a lady in a pink dress
4.9 x 4.1, watercolour on card
Miss Mary A. McNeill Bequest, 1985
NGI 19247

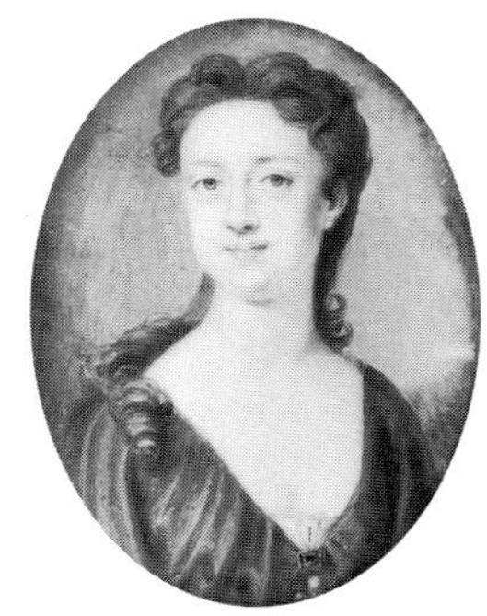

BERNARD LENS III
London 1682 – 1740 London
Portrait of a lady in a blue dress, c.1715. Signed: *BL*(in mono)
6.1 x 4.8, gouache and watercolour on ivory
Miss Mary A. McNeill Bequest, 1985
NGI 19246. see p. 46.

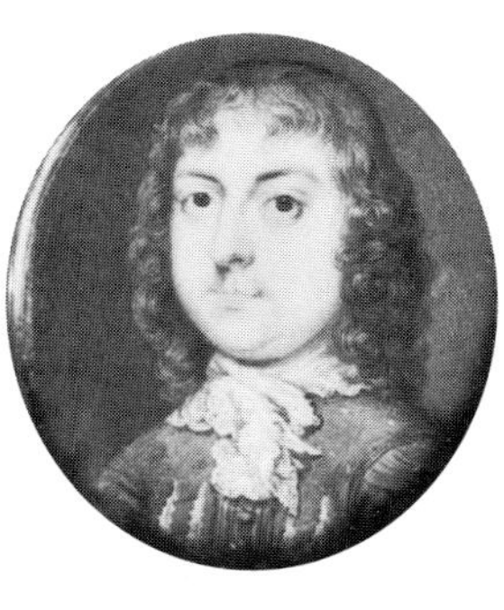

CIRCLE OF BERNARD LENS III
Portrait of a man in a blue coat
3.1 x 2.6, watercolour on ivory
Miss Mary A. McNeill Bequest, 1985
NGI 19249

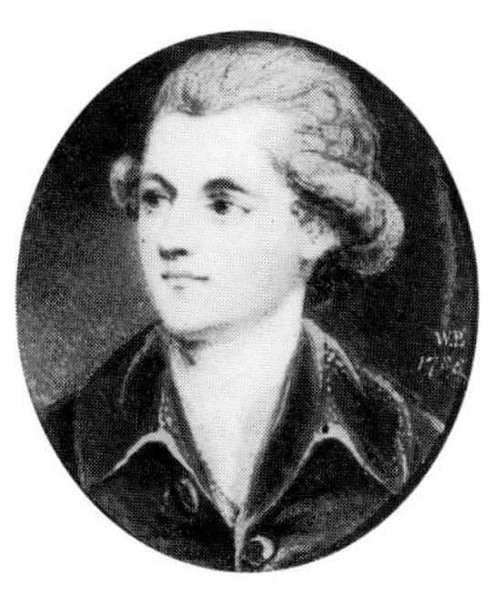

W.P. LONG
active England 1785 – 1800
Portrait of a man in a red velvet coat, 1785
Signed and dated: *W.PL*(in mono) *1785*. 2.9 x 2.5, enamel on copper
Presented by Sir Alfred Chester Beatty, 1951. NGI 3667

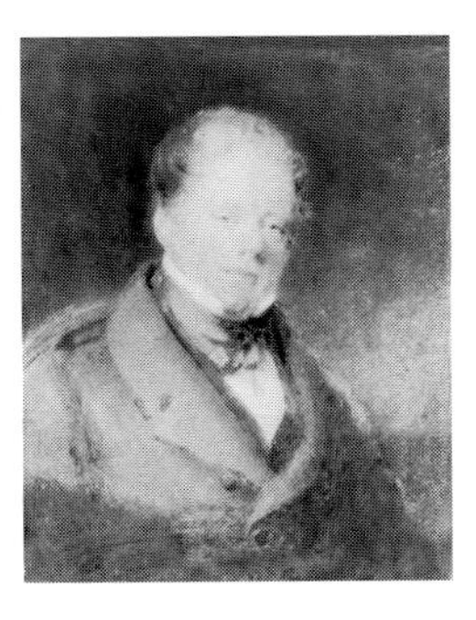

SAMUEL LOVER
Dublin 1797 – 1868 St Helier, Jersey
John Bennett of Blackstoops, Co. Wexford, 1830
10.3 x 8, watercolour on ivory
Purchased from Mrs E.L. McCann, 1898. NGI 2338

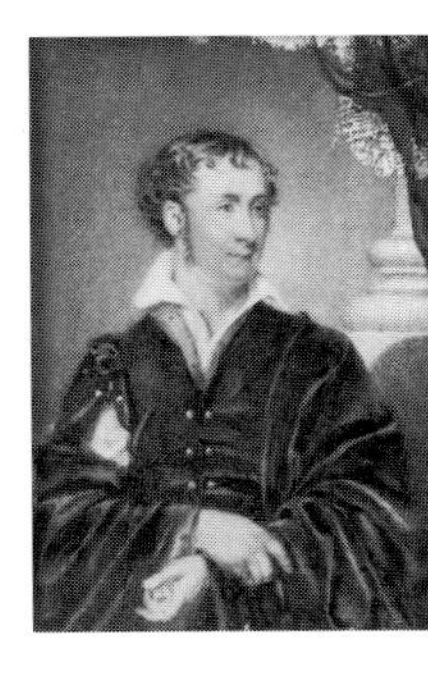

SAMUEL LOVER
Portrait of a man in theatrical costume, c.1830
Signed: *S. Lover. Pinx*
19.6 x 13.5, watercolour on ivory
Presented by Mr T.F. Tivy, 1953
NGI 3267

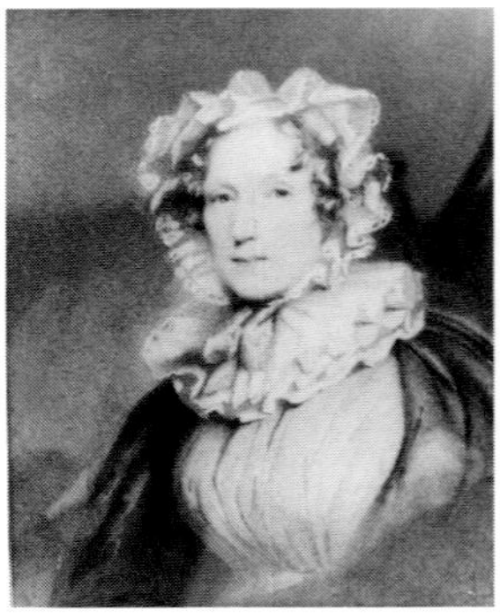

Samuel Lover
Mrs Daniel Lawrence of Ballard Park, Co. Wicklow, 1840
Signed: *S Lover R.HA.*
Inscribed, signed and dated on reverse: **Painted by S. Lover RHA Date 1840.* 9.9 x 8, watercolour with gouache on ivory. Transferred from the NMI, 1969 (where acquired 1914).
NGI 7210. see pp. 138–39.

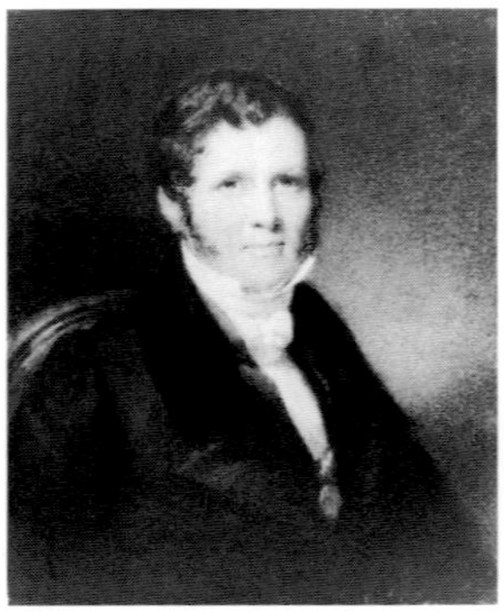

Samuel Lover
Daniel Lawrence of Ballard Park, Co. Wicklow, 1840
Inscribed, signed and dated on reverse: **Painted by S. Lover RHA 1840.* 9.9 x 8, watercolour with gouache on ivory. Transferred from the NMI, 1969 (where acquired 1914). NGI 7211.
see pp. 138–39.

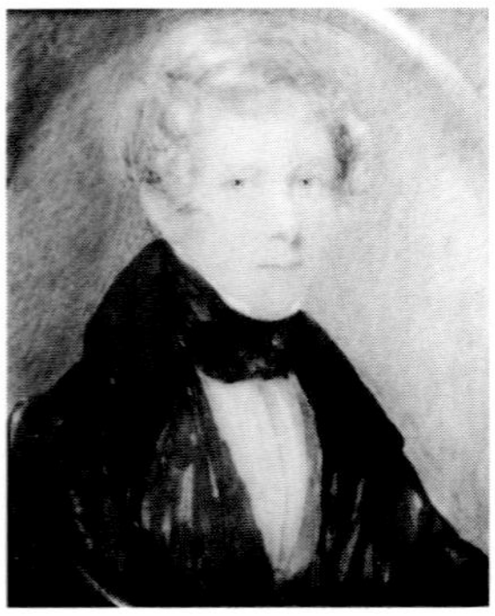

Samuel Lover
Self-Portrait, c.1830
6.6 x 5.5, watercolour on ivory
Purchased at B.F. Stevens and Brown, London, 1942
NGI 7340. see p. 137.

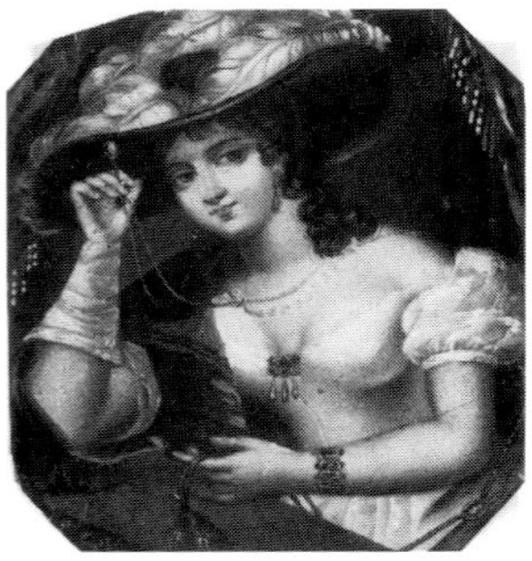

Samuel Lover
Imaginary portrait of Lady Morgan, (born Sydney Owenson, 1776–1859), Author, at the Opera in the Theatre Royal, Dublin, late 1820s. Signed: *S.L.* 5.3 x 5.2, oil on tin. Transferred from the NMI, 1969 (where presented by Mrs M. Sullivan, 1949)
NGI 7509. see p. 136.

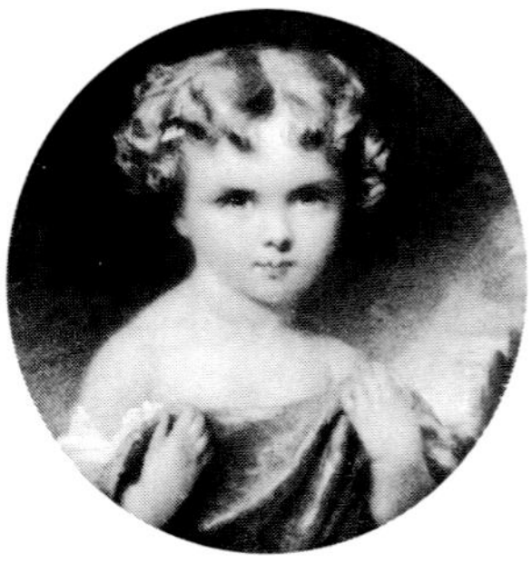

Samuel Lover
Portrait of a young girl
8.5 x 7.5, watercolour on ivory
Bequeathed by
Mrs E.H. Bartlett, 1974
NGI 7665

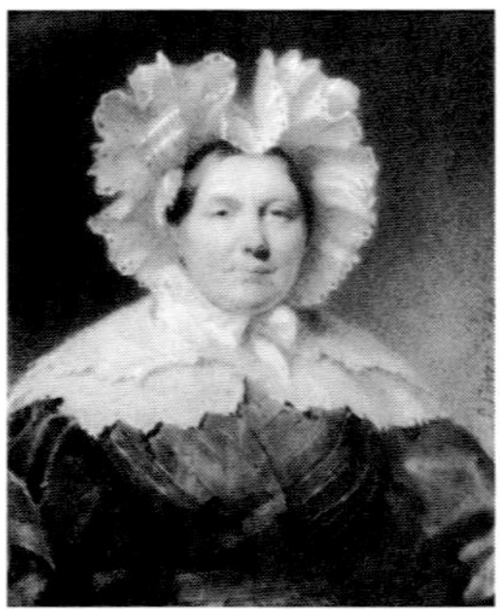

Samuel Lover
Portrait of a lady with white cap, c.1830
Signed: *S. Lover. R.H.A.*
11.2 x 8.5, watercolour on ivory
Bequeathed by
Mrs E.H. Bartlett, 1974
NGI 7666

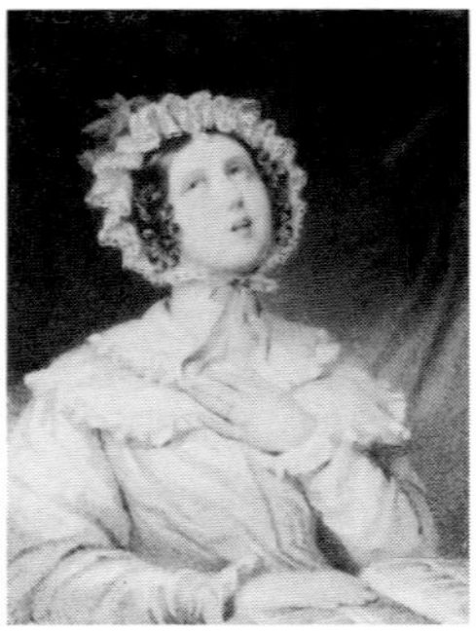

Samuel Lover
Portrait of a lady singing, c.1830
Signed: *S. Lover. R.H.A.*
11 x 8.3, watercolour on ivory
Bequeathed by
Mrs E.H. Bartlett, 1974
NGI 7667

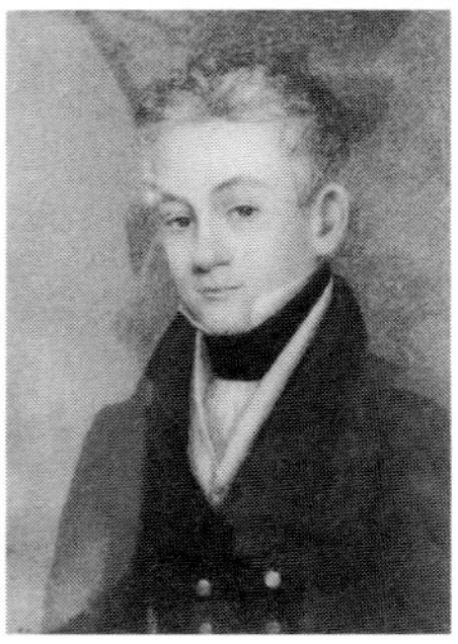

Samuel Lover
Portrait of a boy in a blue coat
Signed: *S. Lover pxt*
7.5 x 5.5, watercolour on ivory
Bequeathed by
Mrs E.H. Bartlett, 1974
NGI 7668. see p. 137.

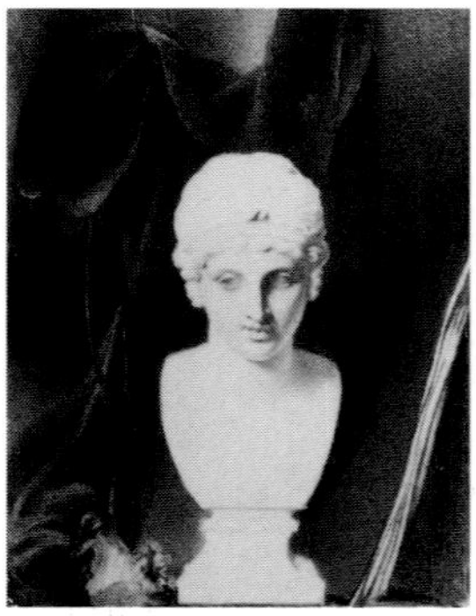

Attributed to Samuel Lover
A bust of Minerva and artist's folio
12.7 x 9.5, watercolour on ivory
Bequeathed by
Miss A. Callwell, 1904
NGI 6046

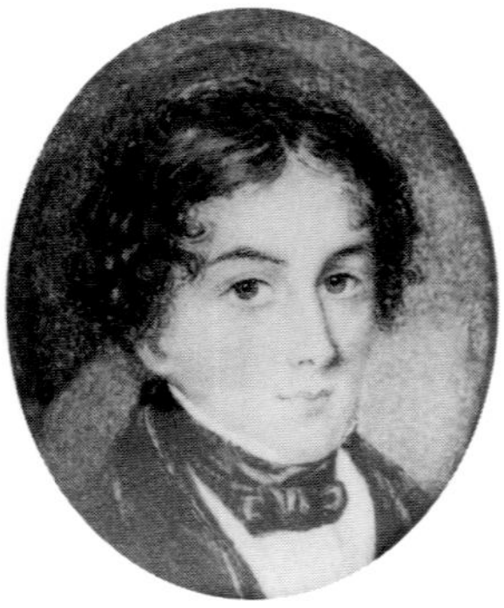

Attributed to Samuel Lover
Thomas Ellis, (d.1839)
6.3 x 5.7, watercolour on ivory
Transferred from the NMI, 1969
(where presented 1939)
NGI 7184

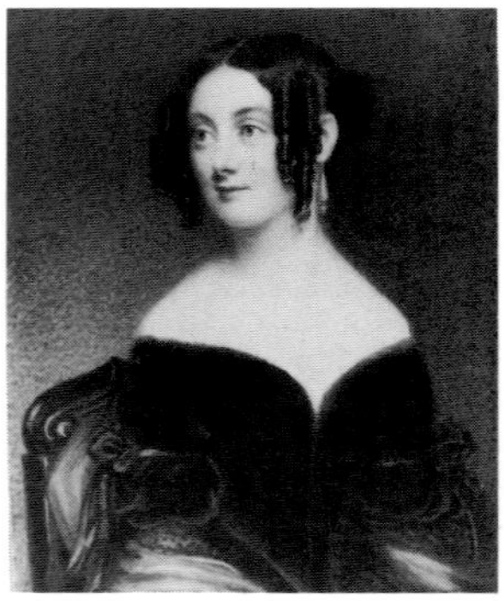

Attributed to Samuel Lover
Portrait of a lady in a black velvet dress
9.9 x 8, watercolour on ivory
Transferred from the NMI, 1969
(where bequeathed by
Miss A. Kinchela, 1948)
NGI 7232

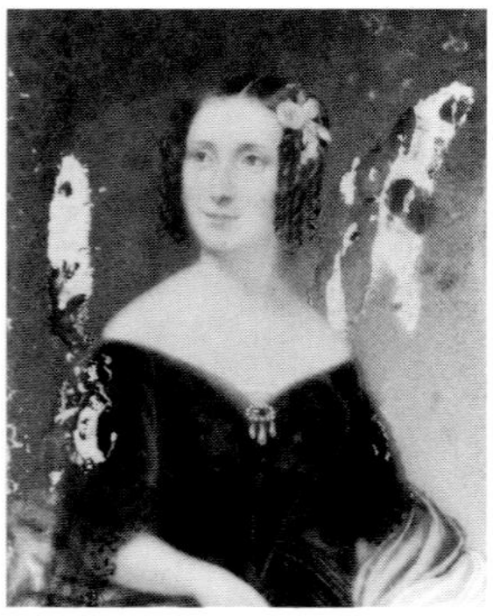

Attributed to Samuel Lover
Portrait of a lady in a black dress
12.7 x 10.2, watercolour on ivory
(damaged)
Provenance unknown
NGI 19319

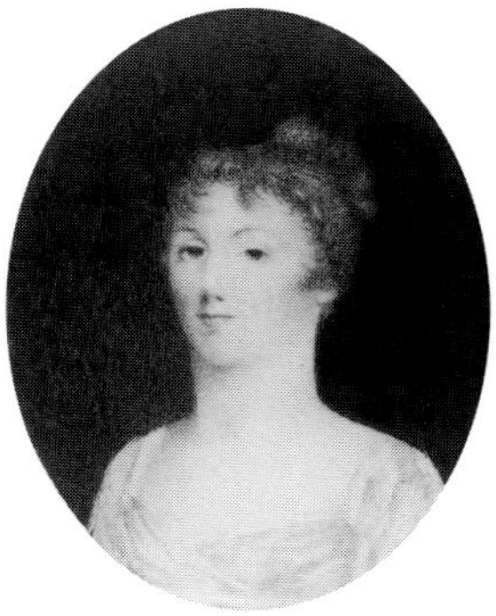

ELIZABETH MCCAUSLAND
active Ireland 1806 – 1807
Charlotte Edgeworth, (1783– 1807), 5th daughter of Richard Lovell Edgeworth, 1807. Inscribed, possibly signed and dated, on backing paper: **E. McCauseland* [sic] *1807.* 6.6 x 5.2, watercolour on ivory. Presented by Mrs C.E. Colvin, 1970. NGI 7549

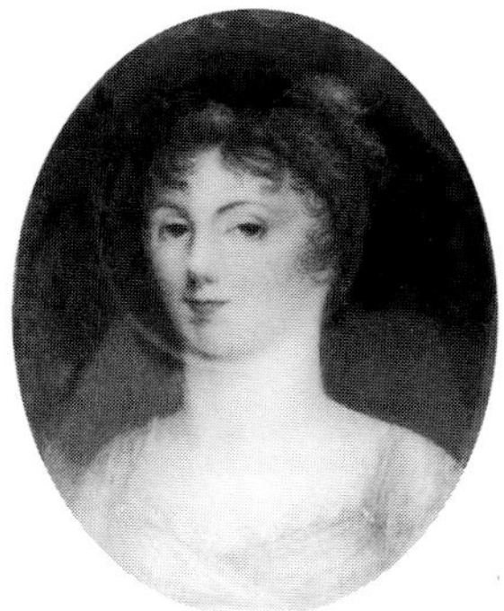

ELIZABETH MCCAUSLAND
Charlotte Edgeworth, (1783–1807), 5th daughter of Richard Lovell Edgeworth, c.1807
6.8 x 5.3, watercolour on ivory
Presented by Mrs C.E. Colvin, 1970
NGI 7550

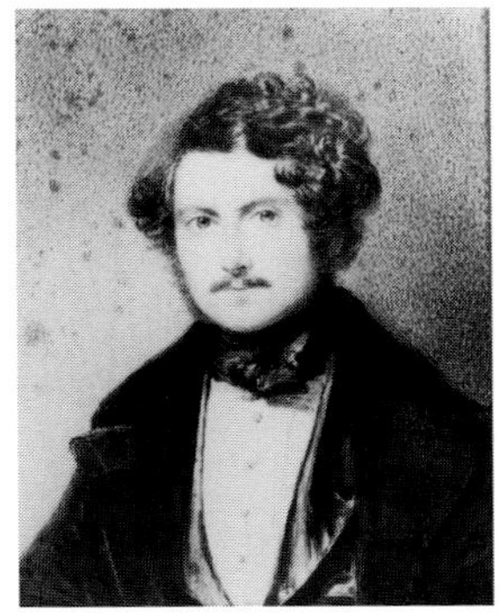

DANIEL MACLISE
Cork 1806 – 1870 London
Portrait of a man in a black coat
9.4 x 7.5, watercolour on ivory
Transferred from the NMI, 1969 (where purchased 1949)
NGI 7195

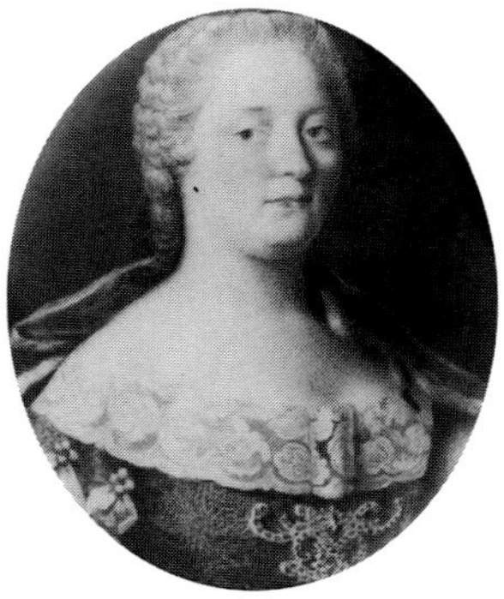

GIUSEPPE (JAMES OR JOSEPH) MACPHERSON.
Florence 1726 – after 1778 Florence,
Empress Maria Theresa, (1717–1780), Archduchess of Austria, Queen of Bohemia and Hungary, late 1740s (after J.-E. Liotard 1745 pastel, engraved 1747). Signed and dated on reverse: *Macpherson fecit 174...* 4.2 x 3.8, enamel on copper. Presented by Sir Alfred Chester Beatty, 1951. NGI 3624. see p. 61.

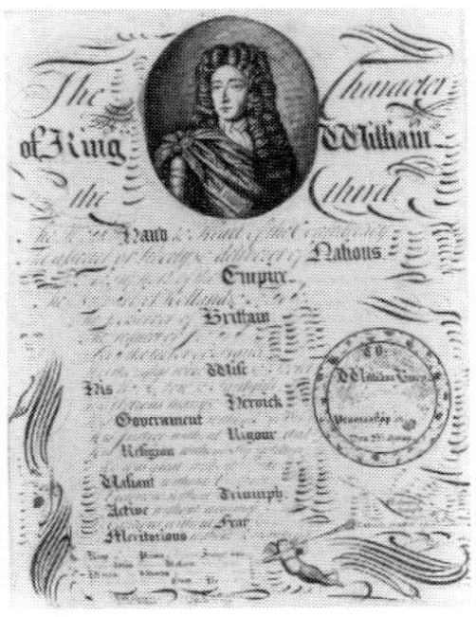

DANIEL MAHONY
active Ireland c.1738
A Testimonial to the Character of William III, King of England (1650–1702), 1738 (portrait after G. Kneller c.1690). Signed and dated: *Mahony Scripsit 1738.* 51 x 39.3, ink on vellum (miniature 16.6 x 14). Presented by Mr V. Newman, 1981. NGI 7927

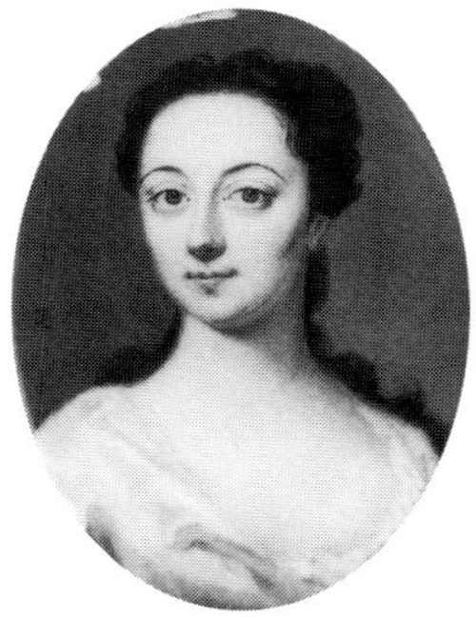

JEREMIAH MÈYER
Tübingen, Germany 1735 – 1789 Kew, Surrey
Portrait of a young lady in a pink dress, c.1760
Signed: *JM*(in mono)
4.3 x 3.5, enamel on copper
Presented by Sir Alfred Chester Beatty, 1951. NGI 3636. see p. 68.

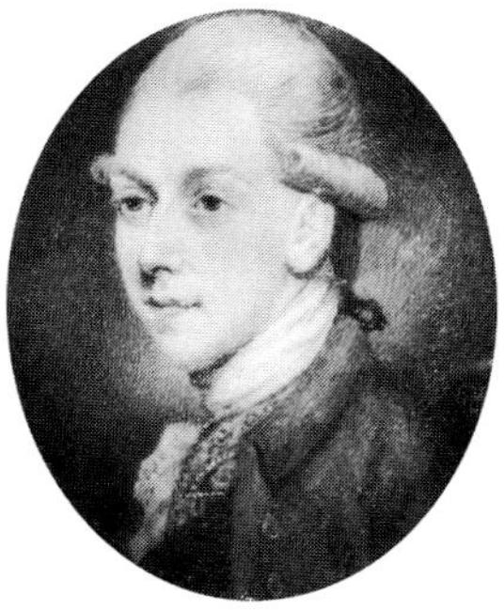

JEREMIAH MEYER
(?)Henry Frederick, Duke of Cumberland (1745–1790), c.1770
3.8 x 3.2, watercolour on ivory
Miss Mary A. McNeill Bequest, 1985
NGI 19258

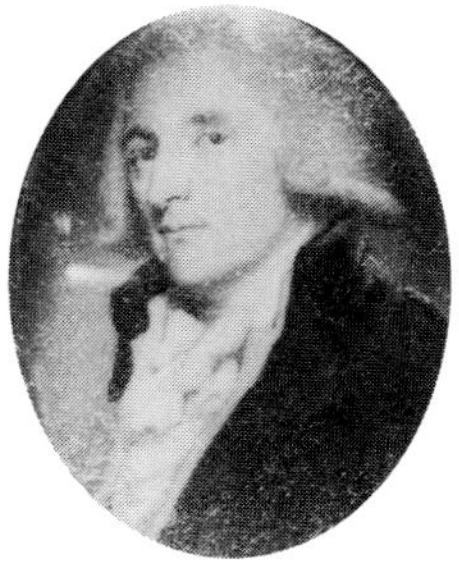

EDWARD MILES
Great Yarmouth 1752 – 1828 Philadelphia
George Augustus Chichester, 2nd Marquess of Donegall, (1769–1844), c.1795
4 x 2.8, watercolour on ivory
Miss Mary A. McNeill Bequest, 1985. NGI 19273. see pp. 81–82.

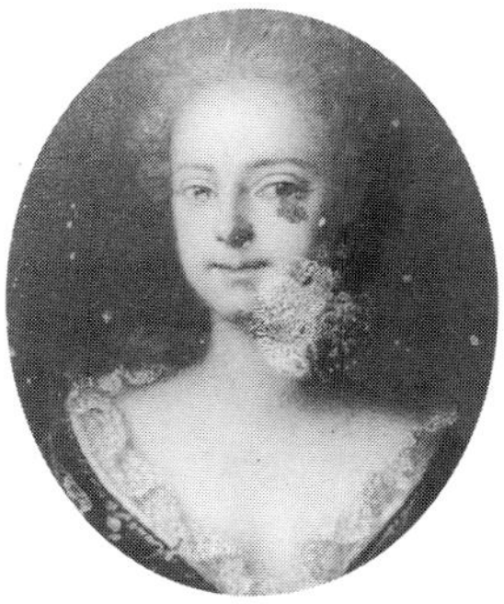

CIRCLE OF GARRET MORPHY
active Dublin 1673 – 1716 Dublin
Miss Chaimberlain, c.1690
7 x 5.8, oil on brass
Presented by Mrs C.E. Colvin, 1970
NGI 7551

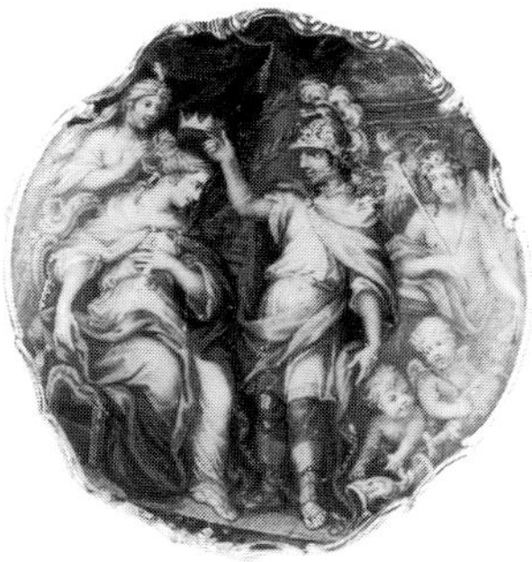

GEORGE MICHAEL MOSER
Schaffhausen, Switzerland 1706 – 1783 London
The Wedding of Alexander and Roxana, c.1730
Signed: *GM Moser fecit*
4.2 diam., enamel on gold
Presented by Sir Alfred Chester Beatty, 1951. NGI 3736. see p. 51.

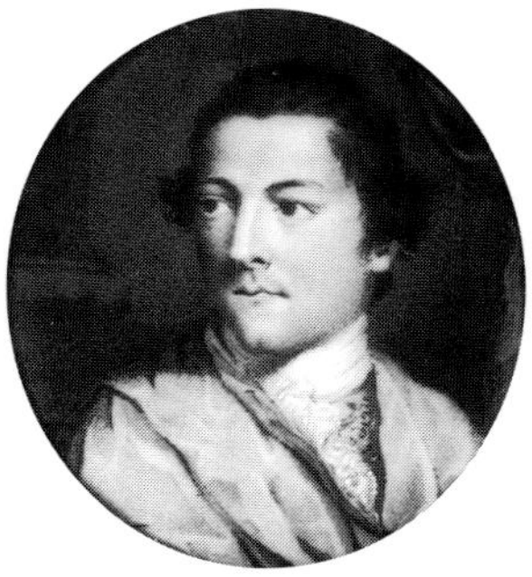

GEORGE MICHAEL MOSER
Portrait of a man in a blue cloak, c.1760
Signed: *GM Moser*
3.7 diam., enamel on metal
Presented by Sir Alfred Chester Beatty, 1951
NGI 3760. see p. 52.

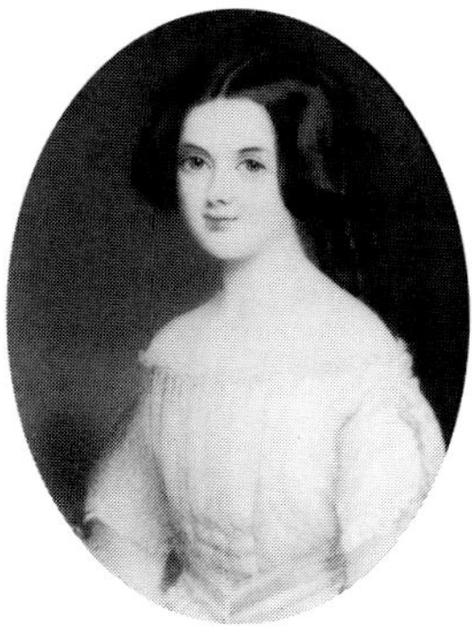

WILLIAM MULREADY
Ennis, Co. Clare 1786 – 1863 London
Mary Emily French of Riversdale, Co. Roscommon, (1839–1907), c.1855. 9.9 x 7.6, watercolour on ivory. Transferred from the NMI, 1969 (where presented by Mrs G. Gorges, 1958). NGI 7229

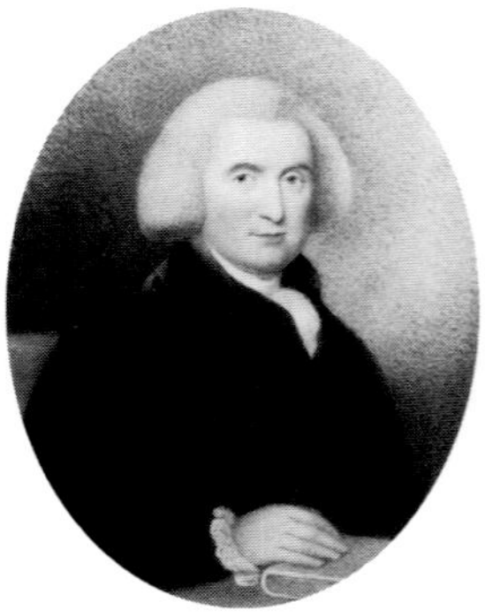

Bernard Mulrenin
Co. Sligo 1803 – 1868 Dublin
Charles O'Conor, (1710–1791), Historian and Antiquary
(after an oil)
25 x 20, watercolour on ivory
Provenance unknown
NGI 2196

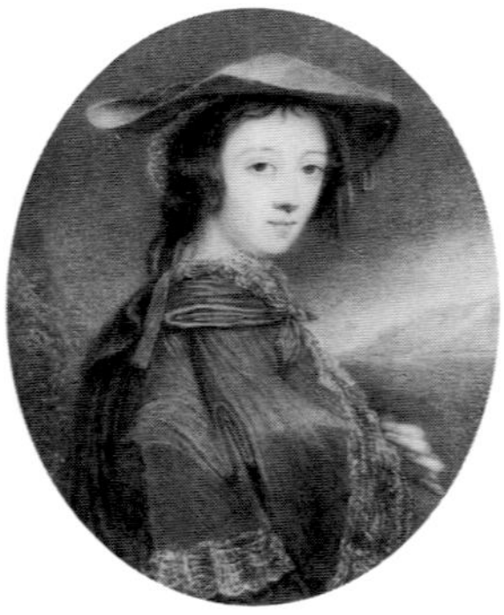

George Francis Mulvany
Dublin 1806 – 1869 Dublin
Margaret (Peg) Woffington, (1718–1760), Actress, 1865
(after Lewis NGI 579 of 1753)
Dated on backing paper. 8.7 x 7.1, watercolour on ivory. Transferred from the NMI, 1969 (where purchased 1911). NGI 7223

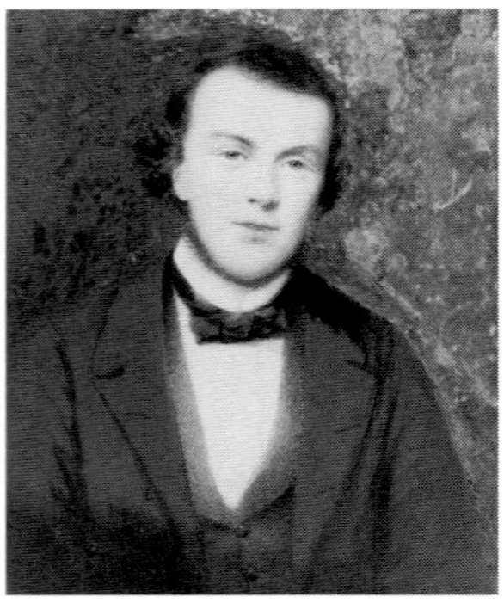

Attributed to John Skipton Mulvany
Booterstown, Co. Dublin 1817 – 1870 Dublin. *Sir John Gilbert, (1829–1898), Historian.* 11 x 9.5, watercolour on vellum. Inscribed on label on frame: *PAINTED BY John. S. Mulvany Esqre. M.R.H.A.*
Purchased from Mr R. Ussher, 1913. NGI 2949

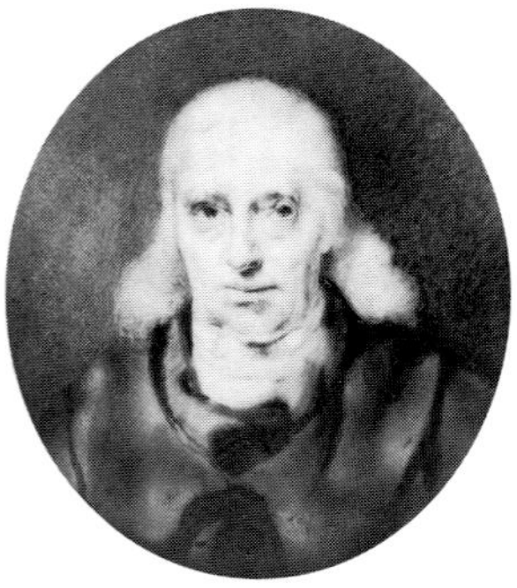

Thomas James Mulvany
Dublin 1779 – 1845
Booterstown, Co. Dublin
Portrait of an elderly man in a green coat, c.1800–03
Dated by inscription on backing card. 7.7 x 7.1, watercolour on ivory. Transferred from the NMI, 1969 (where purchased 1911)
NGI 7118

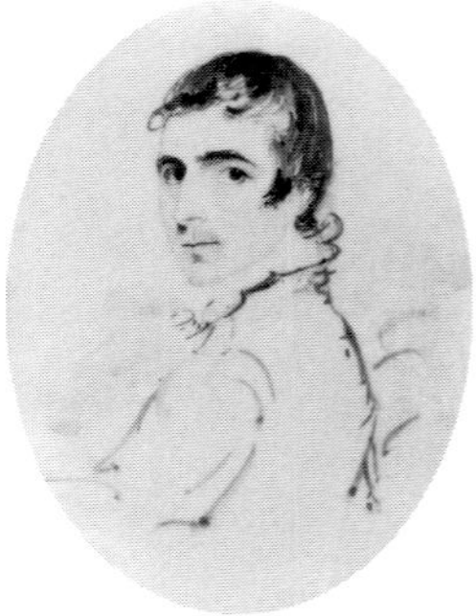

Denis Brownell Murphy
active Dublin 1763 – 1842 ?London
Portrait of a young man
12.8 x 9.5, watercolour on ivory
Purchased from
Lady Geraldine Mayo, 1937
NGI 2966

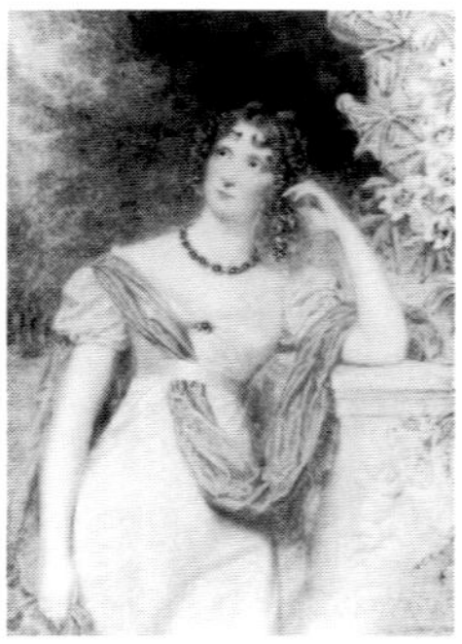

William John Newton
London 1785 – 1869 London
Eliza O'Neill, (1791–1872), Actress, Mrs, later Lady, Wrixon-Becher, 1826. Signed and dated: *W. J. Newton. 1826.* 18 x 13, watercolour on ivory. Purchased at Christie's, London, 1890
NGI 2206. see pp. 130–31.

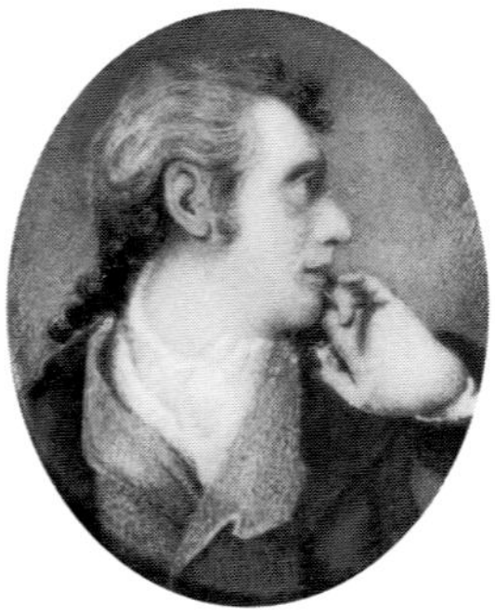

Daniel O'Keeffe
Dublin 1740 – 1787 London
John O'Keeffe, (1747–1833), Actor, Playwright and the artist's brother, 1776. Signed and dated on reverse of frame: *Daniel O'Keeffe pinxt. Dublin 1776.* 7.7 x 6.5, watercolour on ivory. Presented by Mrs F. Vickerman, 1977. NGI 7795. see p. 71.

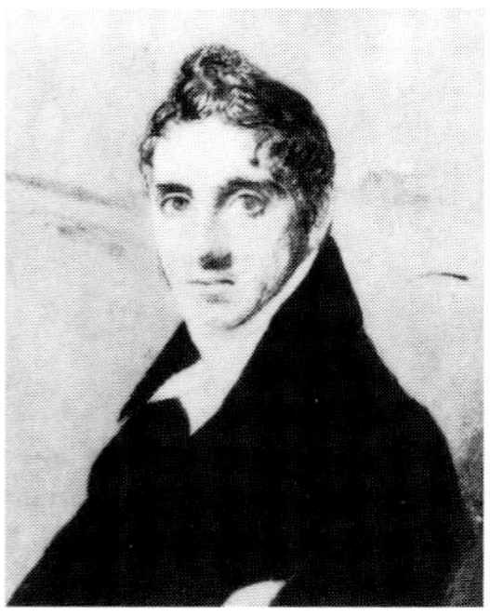

James Petrie
Aberdeen 1750 – 1819 Dublin
George Petrie, (1789–1866), Artist, Antiquary and the painter's son, c.1815
10.7 x 8.3, watercolour on ivory
Purchased from
Miss or Mrs J. Petrie, 1895
NGI 2231

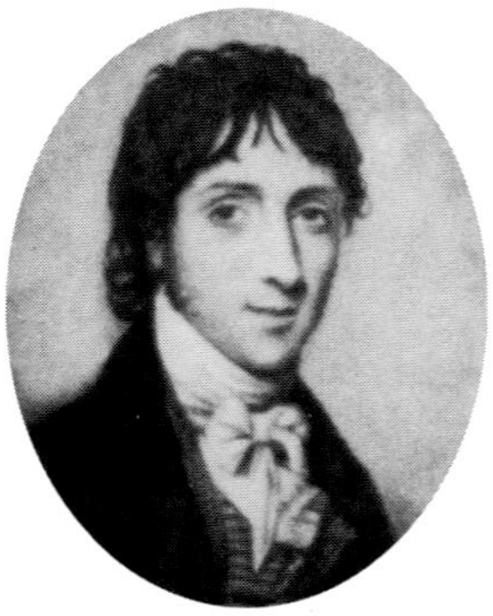

James Petrie
George Petrie, (1789–1866), Artist, Antiquary and the painter's son, c.1805
6.6 x 5.4, watercolour on ivory
Provenance unknown
NGI 3036

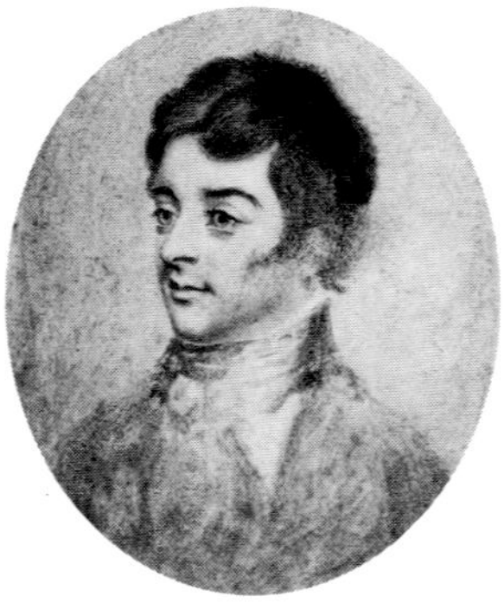

James Petrie
Lord Edward Fitzgerald, (1763–1798), Patriot, c.1800
10.5 x 8.6, watercolour on ivory
Bequeathed by
Miss M. Stokes, 1900
NGI 6323

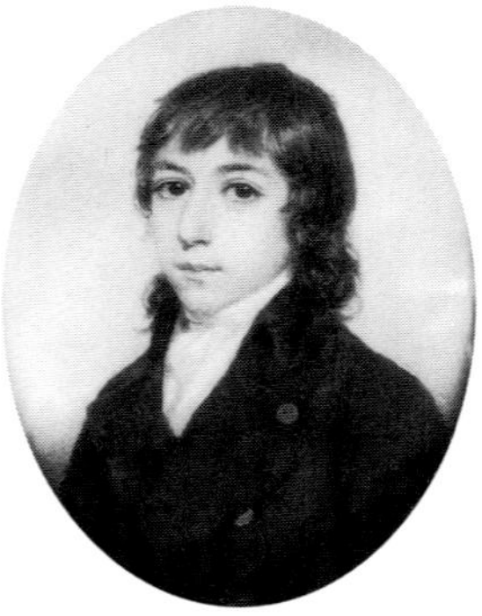

George Place
Dublin c.1763 – 1805 Lucknow, India
John F., c.1790
6.5 x 5, watercolour on ivory
Miss Mary A. McNeill Bequest, 1985
NGI 19280. see p. 113.

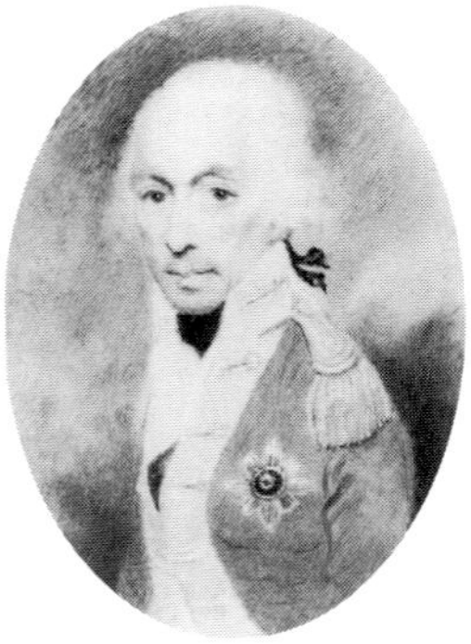

After George Place
Alexander Gordon, 4th Duke of Gordon, (1743–1827)
(after a miniature)
9.2 x 6.7, watercolour on ivory
Transferred from the NMI, 1969
(where bequeathed by
Miss Gardiner, 1929)
NGI 7219

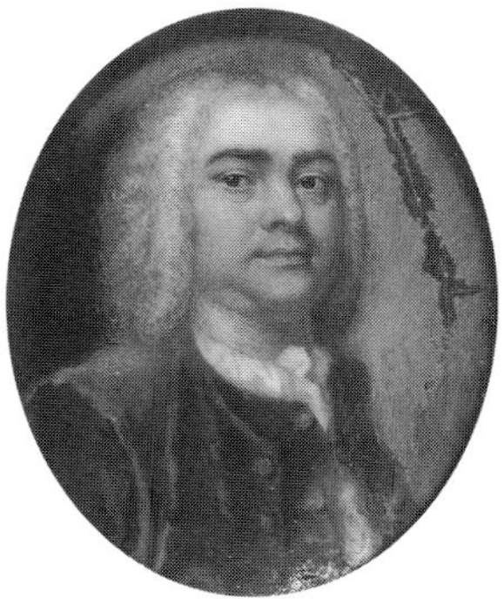

William Prewett
active London 1733 – 1755
Portrait of a man in a brown coat, c.1740
Signed: *W. Prewett pinx*
4.6 x 3.7, enamel on copper
Presented by Sir Alfred Chester Beatty, 1951
NGI 3610. see p. 50.

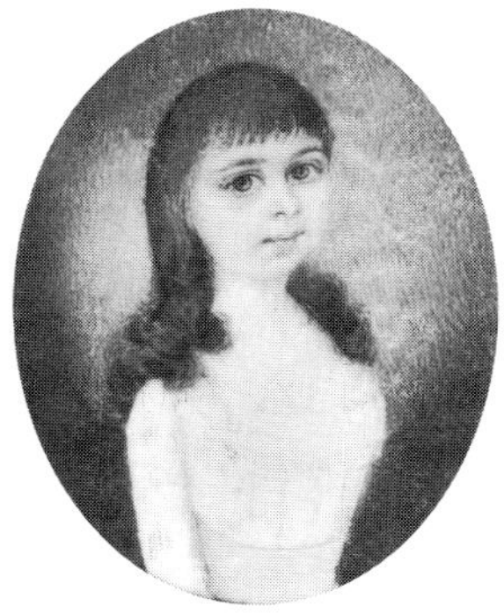

William Read
active London 1778 – 1796 (?) London
Portrait of a girl,(?) Miss L.F.
4.5 x 3.5, watercolour on ivory
Miss Mary A. McNeill Bequest, 1985
NGI 19286

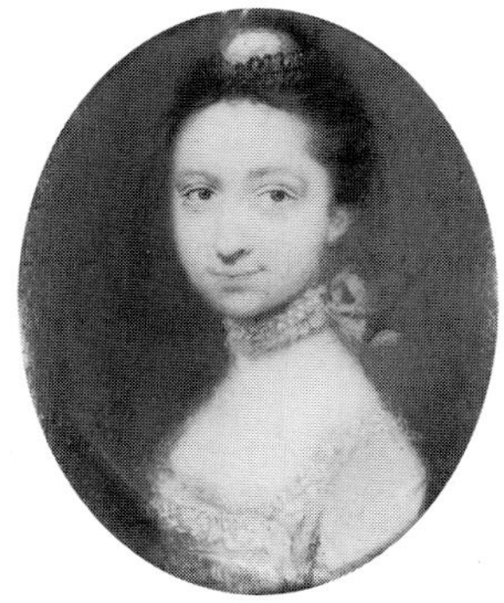

James Reily
active Dublin 1745 – 1780/88 Dublin
Portrait of a lady in a pink dress, 1764
Signed and dated: *I Reily 1764.*
3.8 x 3.2, watercolour on ivory
Transferred from the NMI, 1969 (where purchased 1908)
NGI 7086. see p. 70.

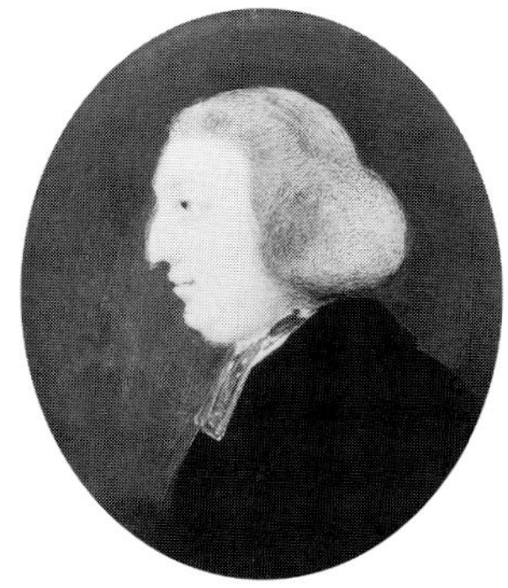

Attributed to James Reily
Revd. William Blachford, (1727–1773)
5.6 x 4.9, watercolour on ivory
Bequeathed by Miss M. Ashley, 1903
NGI 2533

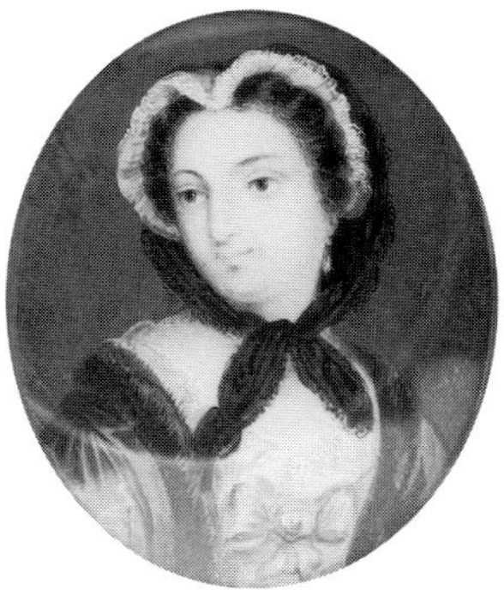

Attributed to James Reily
Portrait of a lady in a lace bonnet
5.4 x 4.5, watercolour on ivory, set in a brooch
Transferred from the NMI, 1969 (where bequeathed by Mr T. Mercer, 1924)
NGI 7090

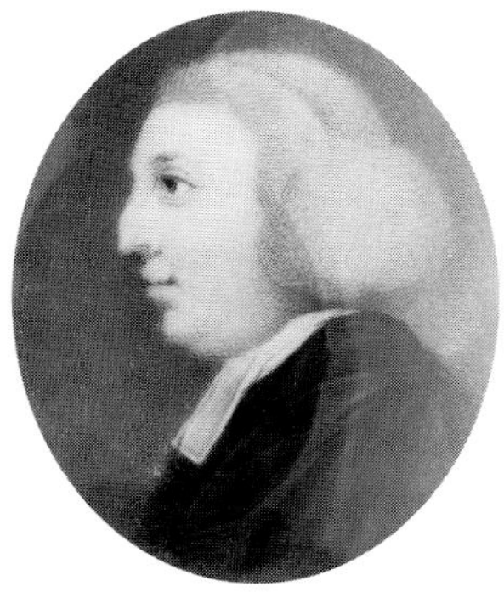

Attributed to James Reily
Revd. Robert Gorges, (d.1803)
3.6 x 3.1, watercolour on ivory
Transferred from the NMI, 1969 (where presented by Mrs G. Gorges, 1958)
NGI 7099

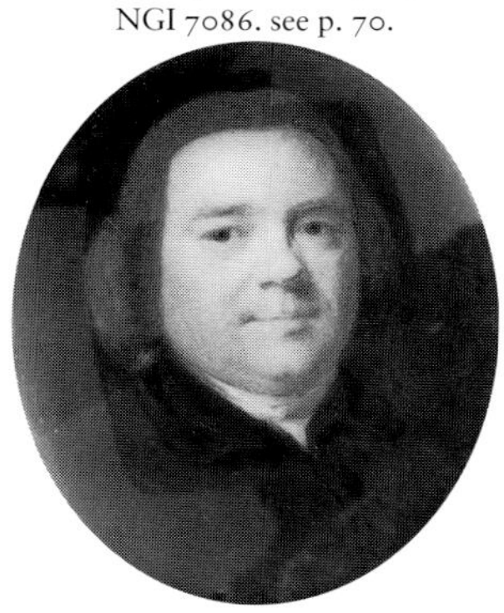

Attributed to James Reily
Portrait of an elderly man in a blue coat
3.7 x 3.3, watercolour on ivory
Transferred from the NMI, 1969 (where acquired 1953)
NGI 7100

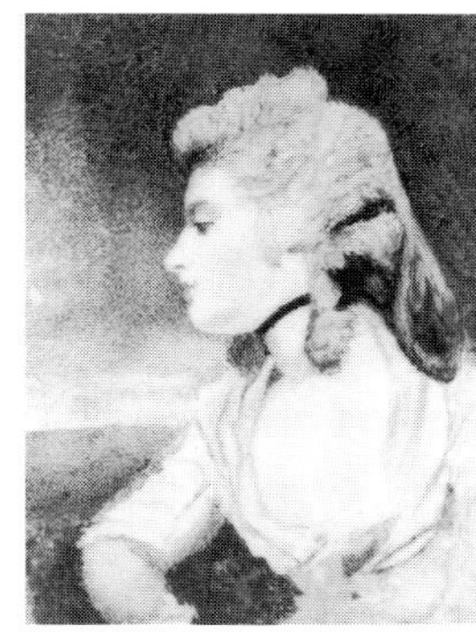

After Joshua Reynolds
Plympton, Devon 1723 – 1792 London
Mrs Robinson, (born Mary Darby, 1758–1800), Actress
(19th century after Reynolds of 1784, WCL). 8.9 x 7, watercolour on ivory. Transferred from the NMI, 1969 (where bequeathed by Miss Gardiner, 1929). NGI 7114

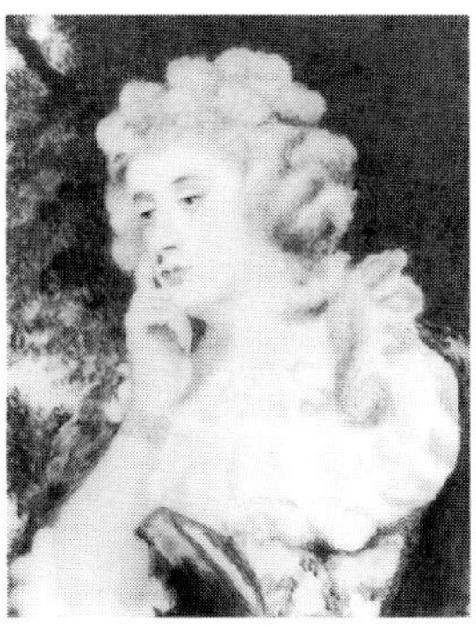

After Joshua Reynolds
Mrs Jane Bradyll, (born Gale, active 1776–1819)
(19th century after Reynolds of 1788, WCL)
9.1 x 7, watercolour on ivory
Transferred from the NMI, 1969 (where provenance unknown)
NGI 7188

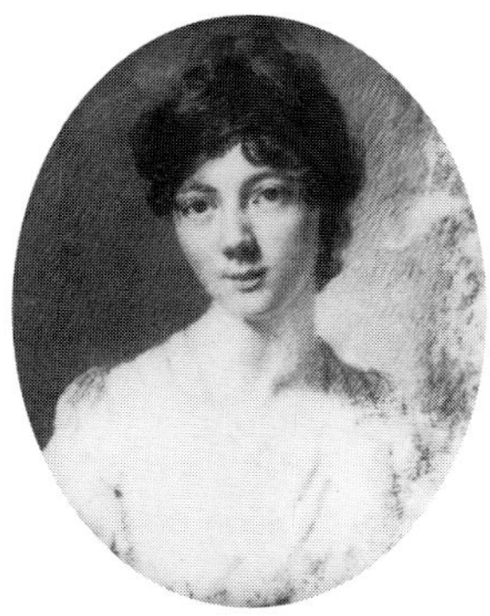

Charles Robertson
Dublin 1760 – 1821 Dublin
Christina Noletor, (born Jaffrey), the artist's wife
6.9 x 5.7, watercolour on ivory (unfinished)
Presented by Mr E.S. Robertson, great-grandson of the artist, 1901
NGI 2434

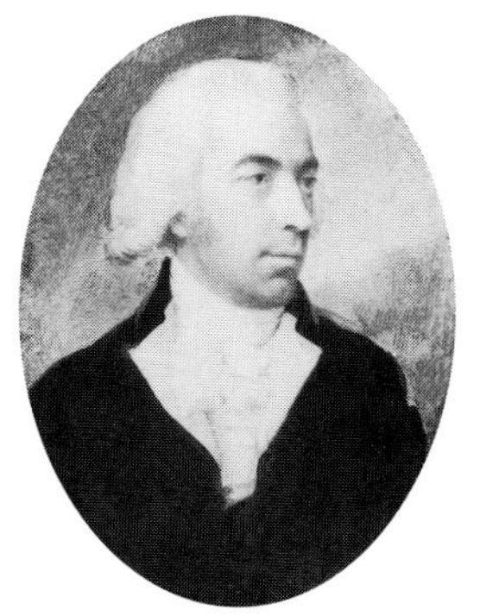

Charles Robertson
Walter Robertson, (c.1750–1801), Miniaturist and the artist's elder brother, c.1780
7.5 x 5.9, watercolour on ivory
Presented by Mr E.S. Robertson, great-grandson of the artist, 1901
NGI 2524. see pp. 109–10.

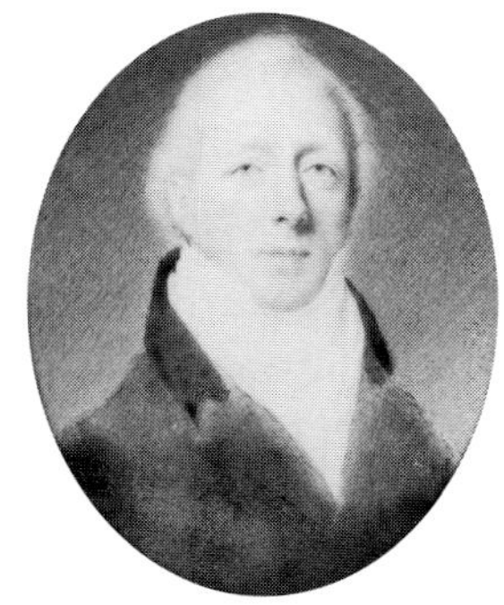

Charles Robertson
Portrait of a man in a blue coat
7 x 6, watercolour on ivory (unfinished)
Presented by Mr E.S. Robertson, great-grandson of the artist, 1901
NGI 2525

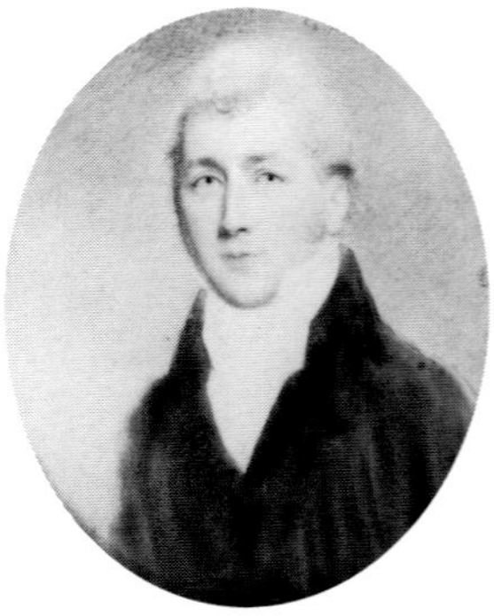

CHARLES ROBERTSON
Portrait of a man in a black coat
8.6 x 6.6, watercolour on ivory (unfinished)
Presented by Mr E.S. Robertson, great-grandson of the artist, 1901
NGI 6228

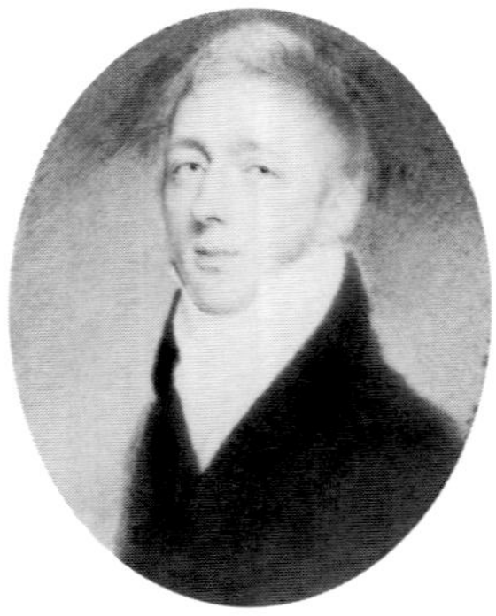

CHARLES ROBERTSON
Portrait of a man in an emerald green coat
6.7 x 5.5, watercolour on ivory
Presented by Mr E.S. Robertson, great-grandson of the artist, 1901
NGI 6229

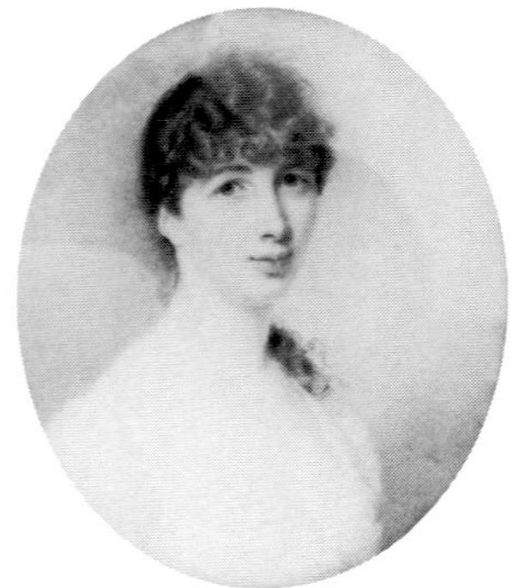

CHARLES ROBERTSON
Miss or Mrs P.P.
7 x 6, watercolour on ivory
Transferred from the NMI 1969 (where purchased 1949
NGI 7026

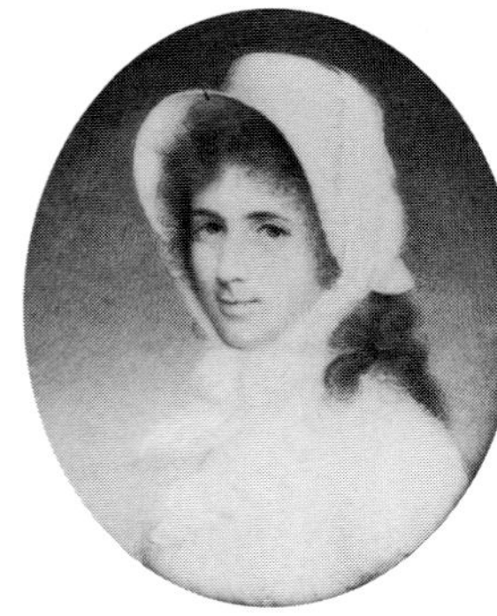

CHARLES ROBERTSON
Portrait of a lady in a white dress, c.1800
5.9 x 4.9, watercolour on ivory
Miss Mary A. McNeill Bequest, 1985
NGI 19276. see p. 110.

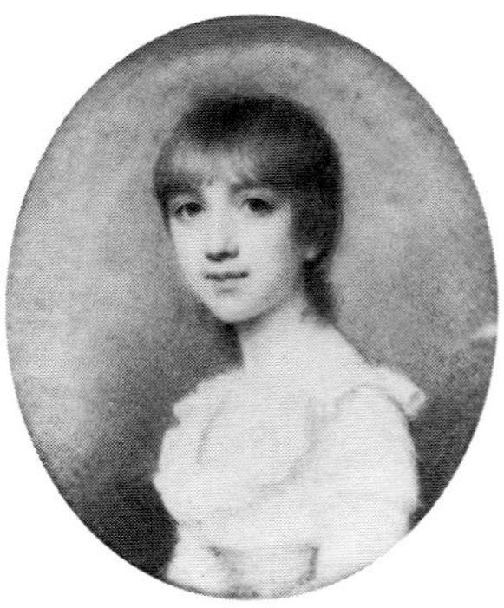

CHARLES ROBERTSON
Portrait of a young girl, c.1800
6.5 x 5.5, watercolour on ivory
Miss Mary A. McNeill Bequest, 1985
NGI 19277. see p. 111.

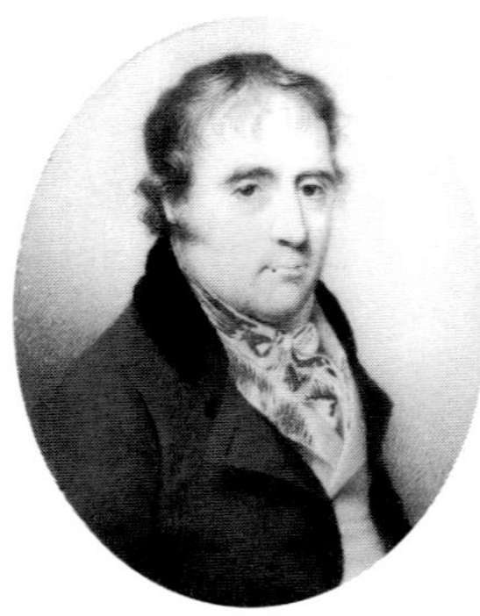

CHARLES ROBERTSON
Henry Joy Junior, (1754–1835), Belfast Newspaper owner and Political Reformer, c.1800
7.7 x 6.2, watercolour on ivory
Miss Mary A. McNeill Bequest, 1985
NGI 19278

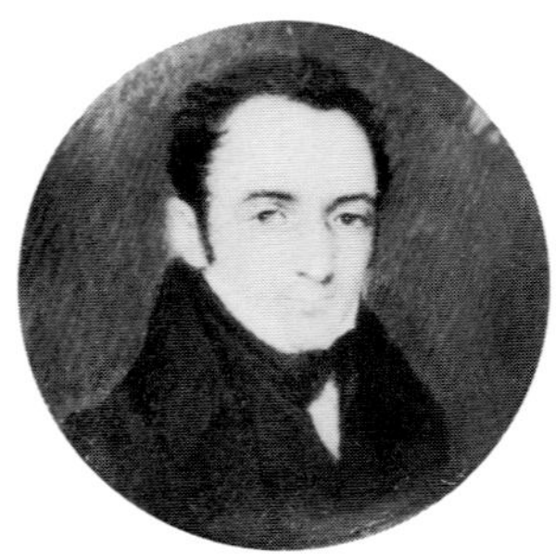

CLEMENTINA ROBERTSON (MRS SIREE)
Dublin 1795 – c.1853/58 Dublin
John Siree, (1800–1835), the artist's husband, c.1830
4 diam., watercolour on ivory
Presented by Mr E.S. Robertson, 1905. NGI 2529. see p 135.

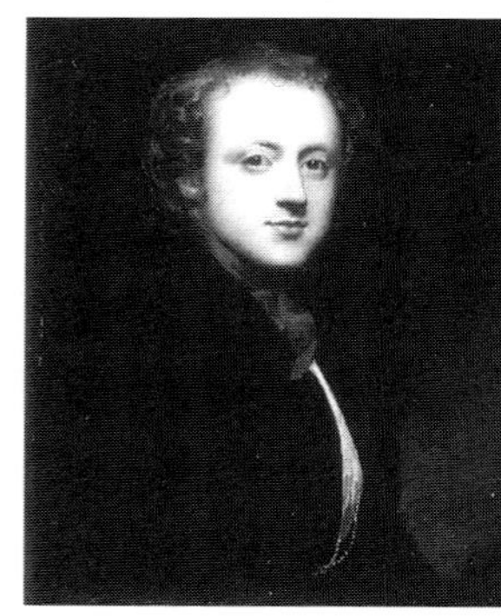

EDWARD ROBERTSON
(?) London 1809 – c. 1840(?) Dublin. *Self-Portrait,* 1831. Inscribed, signed and dated on backing paper: **Dublin 1831 Edwd Robertson.* 8.9 x 7.6, watercolour with varnish on card. Purchased at Sotheby's, London, 1974. NGI 7710. see Illus. 8.

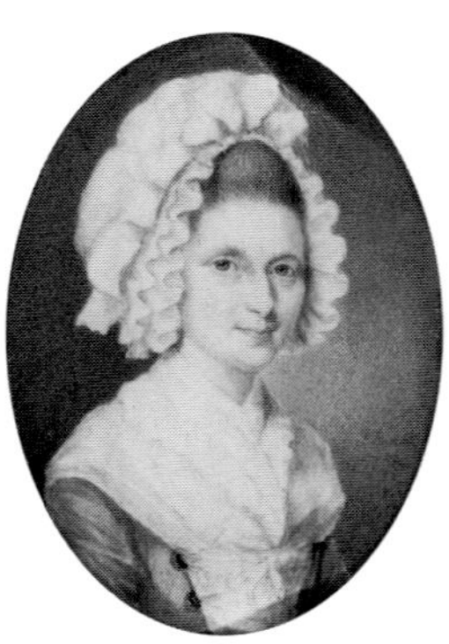

SAMPSON TOWGOOD ROCH
Youghal, Co. Cork 1757 – 1847 Ardmore, Co. Waterford
Mrs Mangan, (born Hoey), 1788
Signed and dated: *S Roch 1788*
6.7 x 5.1, watercolour on ivory
Purchased from Miss Langan, 1903. NGI 2532. see p. 103.

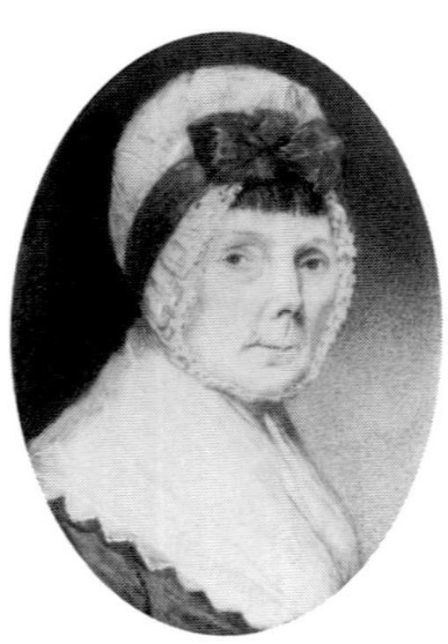

SAMPSON TOWGOOD ROCH
Mrs Thorp, c.1790
5.5 x 4, watercolour on ivory
Purchased from Miss L. Marks, 1912
NGI 2672

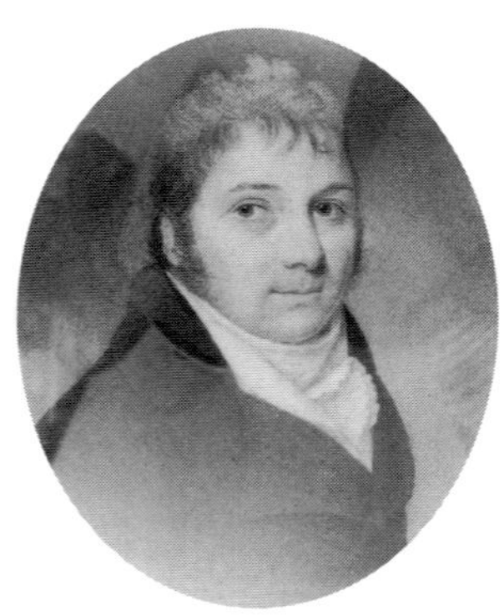

SAMPSON TOWGOOD ROCH
Mr R. James Tisdall of Rathcoole, Dunleer, Co. Louth, c.1800
7.5 x 6.1, watercolour on ivory
Transferred from the NMI, 1969 (where purchased 1914)
NGI 7087. see p. 104, Illus. 13.

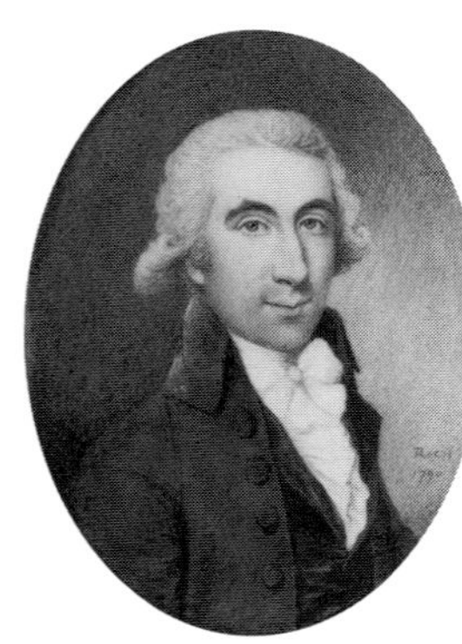

SAMPSON TOWGOOD ROCH
Portrait of a man in a grey-blue coat, 1790
Signed and dated: *ROCH 1790*
6.5 x 5, watercolour on ivory
Purchased from Hibernian Antiques, Dublin, 1971
NGI 7356. see p. 104.

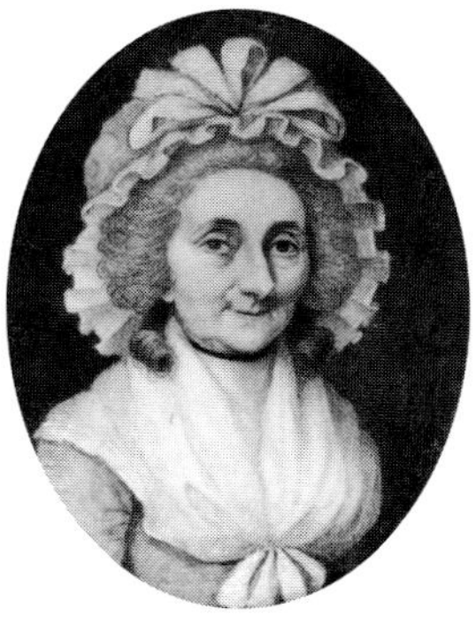

Sampson Towgood Roch
Portrait of a lady and her grandson (back to back), 1789
Both signed and dated: *ROCH 1789*
7 x 5.3, watercolour on ivory
Miss Mary A. McNeill Bequest, 1985
NGI 19284. Illus. 11.

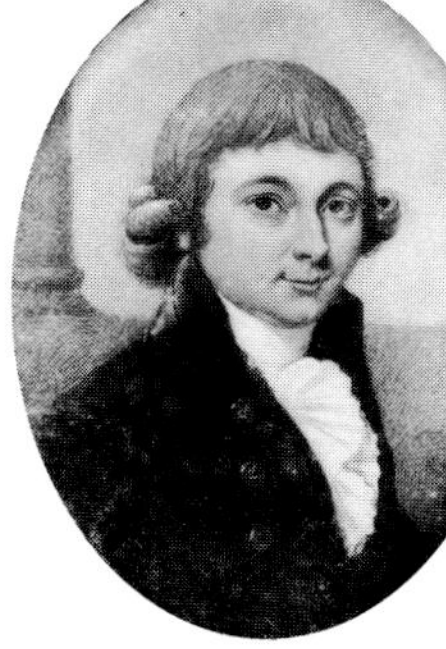

Reverse of NGI 19284

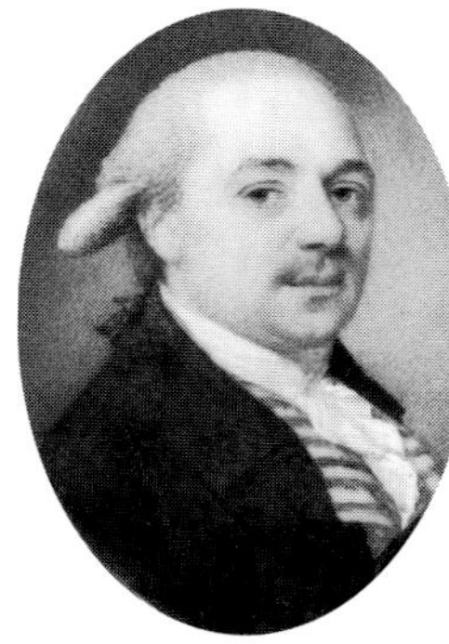

Sampson Towgood Roch
Gaspar Erck (d.1806)
4.5 x 3.5, watercolour on ivory
Bequeathed by Dr S.D. Oliver, 1989
NGI 19381. see Illus. 13.

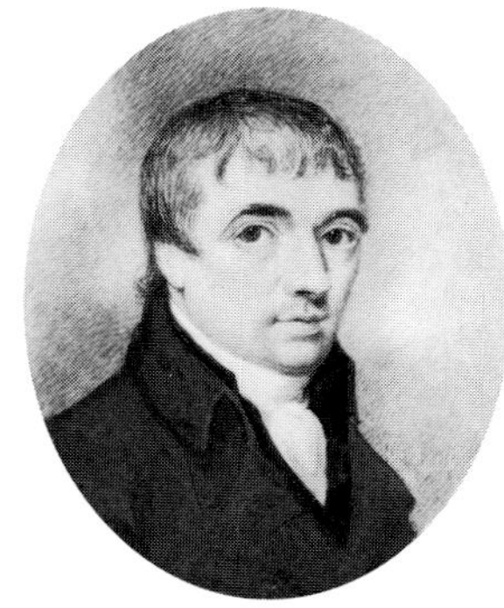

Attributed to Sampson Towgood Roch
Portrait of a man in a black coat, c.1795
6.3 x 5.2, watercolour on ivory
Miss Mary A. McNeill Bequest, 1985
NGI 19287

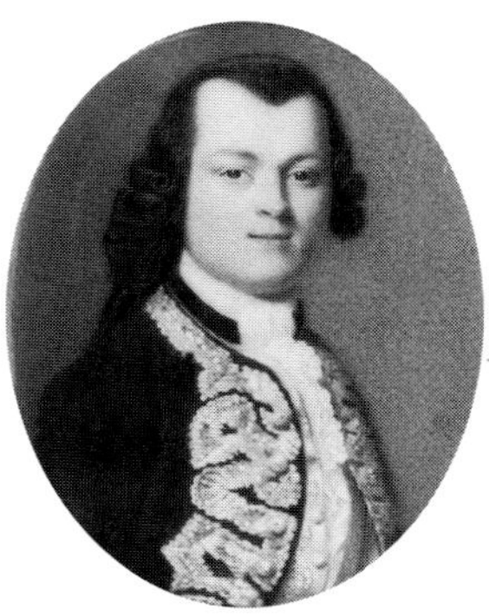

Jean André Rouquet
Geneva 1701 – 1758 Charenton, near Paris
Portrait of a man in a brown coat, c.1750. Signed: *R*
4.2 x 3.5, enamel on copper
Presented by Sir Alfred Chester Beatty, 1951
NGI 3601

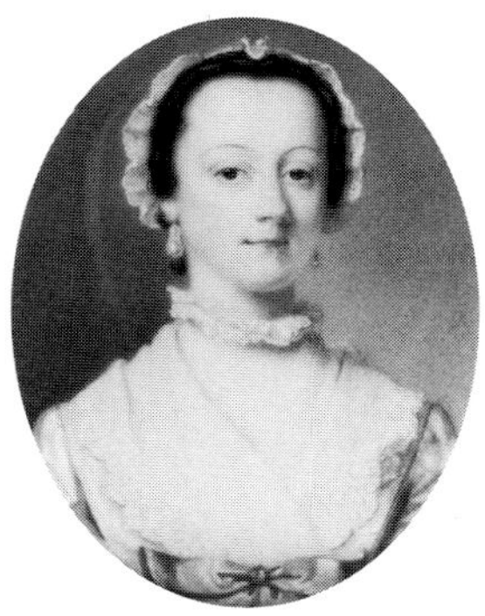

Jean André Rouquet
Portrait of a lady with a blue bow
Signed: *R*
4.2 x 3.5, enamel on copper
Presented by Sir Alfred Chester Beatty, 1951
NGI 3649. see p. 48.

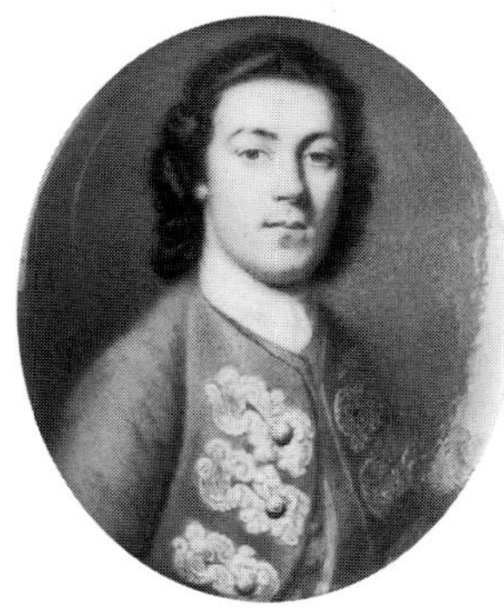

Jean André Rouquet
Portrait of a man in a blue coat
Signed: *R*
4.2 x 3.5, enamel on copper
Presented by Sir Alfred Chester Beatty, 1951
NGI 3656. see p. 48.

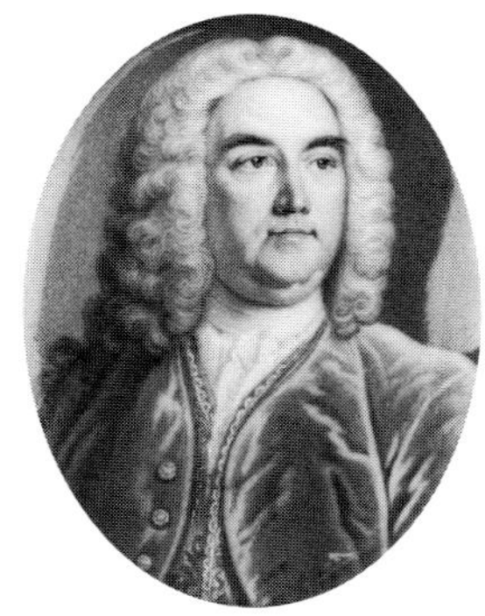

Attributed to Jean André Rouquet
Portrait of a Noble, 1741
Dated 8th September 1741 on reverse
4.9 x 3.9, enamel on copper
Presented by Sir Alfred Chester Beatty, 1951
NGI 3646

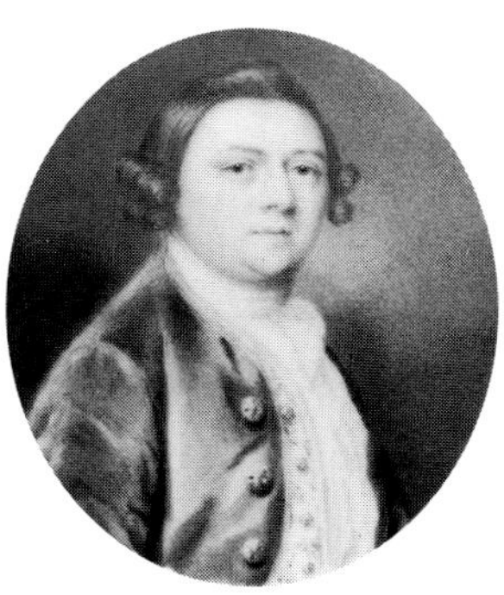

Circle of Jean André Rouquet
Portrait of a man in a grey coat
4.1 x 3.7, enamel on gold
Presented by Sir Alfred Chester Beatty, 1951
NGI 3741

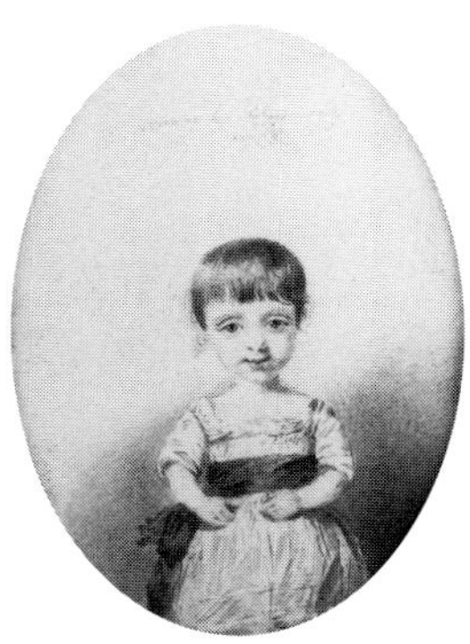

Andrew Rysmdyk
London 1754 – 1786 Bath
Reinaud Diedrich Jacob de Ginkel, 7th Earl of Athlone, (1773–1823), as a boy, 1783. Signed and dated: *Drawn by ARymsdyk 1783*
12.5 x 8.9, pencil and watercolour on paper. Transferred from the NMI, 1982 (Miss M. J. Alexander Coll.)
NGI 18993

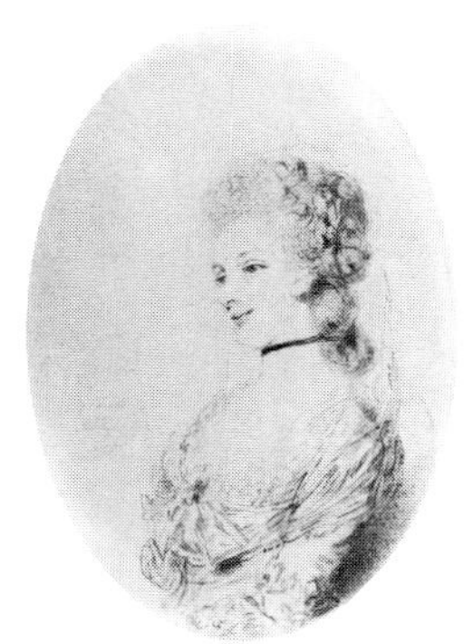

Andrew Rysmdyk
Supposed portrait of Mrs Sarah Siddons, (born Kemble, 1755–1831), Actress, 1783
Signed and dated: *Drawn by Andw Rymsdyk 1783.*
12.7 x 9.3, pencil and watercolour on paper. Transferred from the NMI, 1982 (Miss M. J. Alexander Coll.) NGI 18994

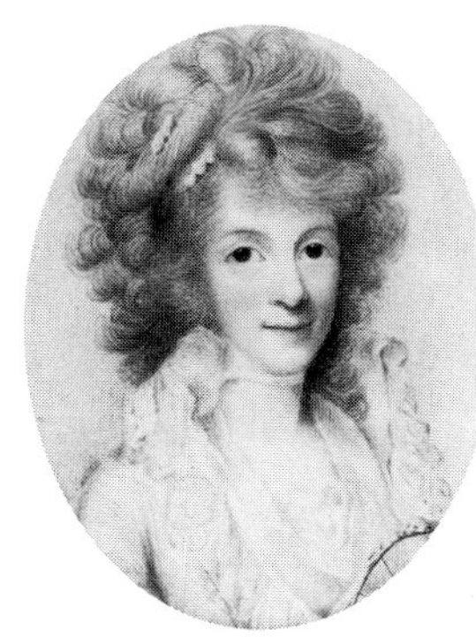

James Scouler
Edinburgh c.1740 – 1812 London
Miss J. Spicer, (active 1801–02), Enamelist, 1801
Dated 1801 on reverse
4.6 x 3.8, enamel on copper
Presented by Sir Alfred Chester Beatty, 1951
NGI 3653. see p. 74.

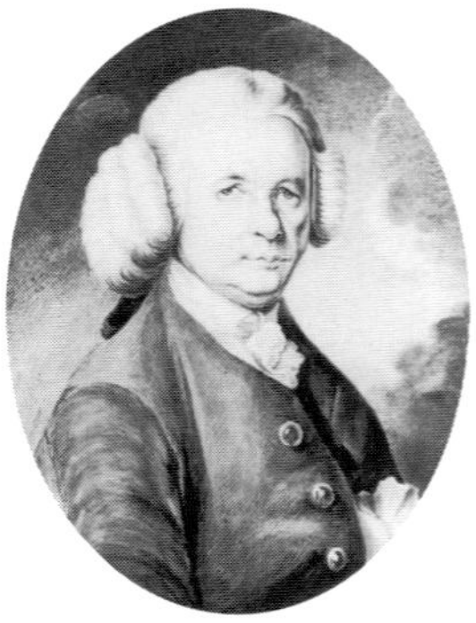

Noah Seaman
active England 1724 – 1741
Portrait of a man in a blue coat
7.3 x 5.6, enamel on metal
Presented by Sir Alfred Chester Beatty, 1951
NGI 3612

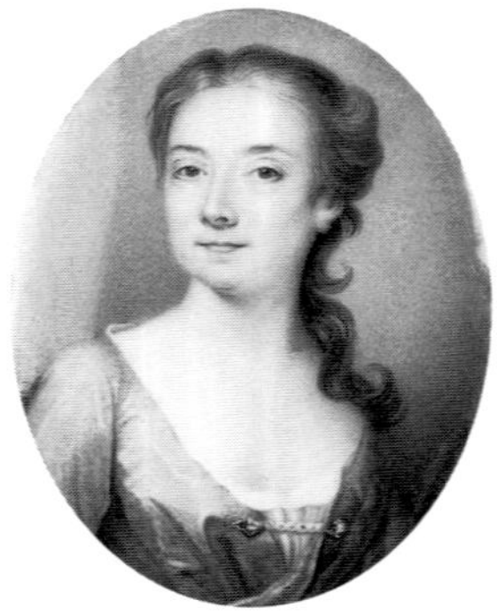

Noah Seaman
Portrait of a lady in a blue dress, 1728
Signed and dated on reverse: *Noah Seaman pinx. 1728*
4.9 x 3.9, enamel on copper
Transferred from the NMI, 1969 (where provenance unknown)
NGI 7330. see p. 49.

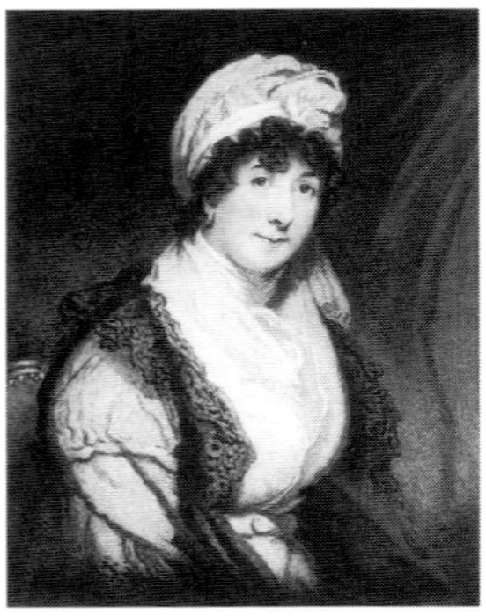

Anna (or Mary) Archer Shee
active 19th century
Mrs Dillon, great-aunt of the artist
13.6 x 10.9, watercolour on card
Purchased from Mrs S. Kelly, 1972
NGI 7473

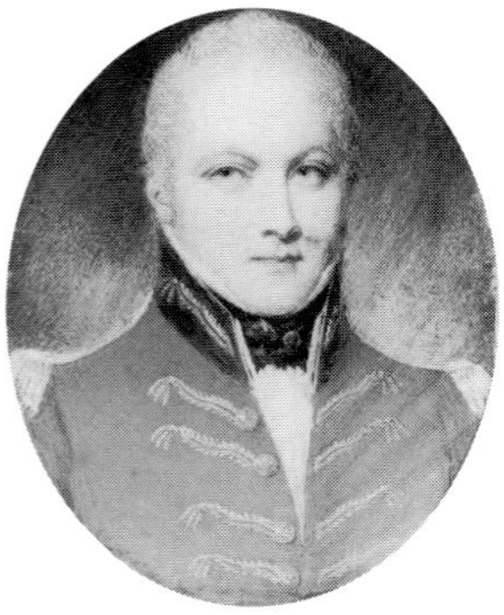

Samuel Shelley
London 1756 – 1808 London
General Duffield, Hanover Guards, c.1800
7.4 x 6, watercolour on ivory
Transferred from the NMI, 1969 (where bequeathed by Mr T. Mercer, 1924)
NGI 7014. see p. 93.

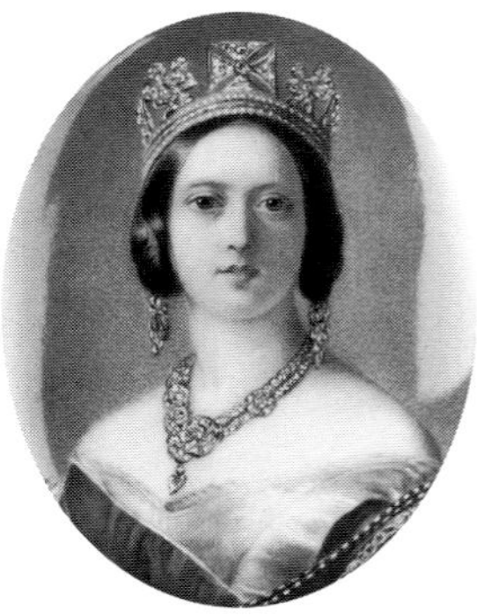

John Simpson
(?) Staffordshire 1811 – after 1871 London.
Queen Victoria, (1819–1901), 1847, (after Winterhalter 1843 wl, Royal Collection). Inscribed, signed and dated on reverse: **Simpson after Winterhalter 1847*. 5.6 x 4.5, enamel on copper. Presented by Sir Alfred Chester Beatty, 1951.
NGI 3613. see pp. 139–40.

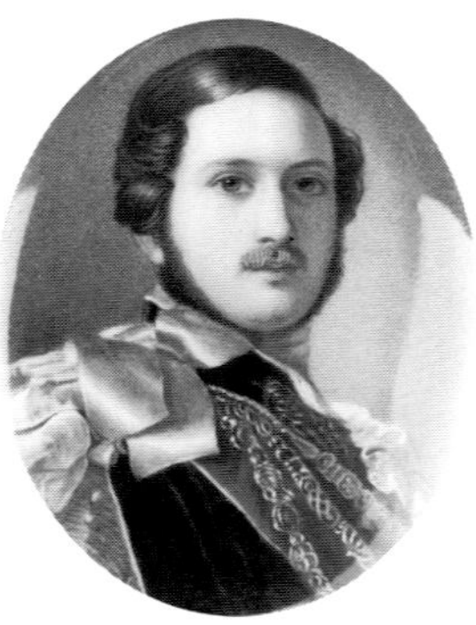

John Simpson
Prince Albert, (1819–1861), Consort of Queen Victoria, 1847
(after Winterhalter 1846 wl, Royal Collection). Inscribed, signed and dated on reverse:
**Simpson after Winterhalter 1847*
5.6 x 4.4, enamel on copper
Presented by Sir Alfred Chester Beatty, 1951.
NGI 3614. see p. 140.

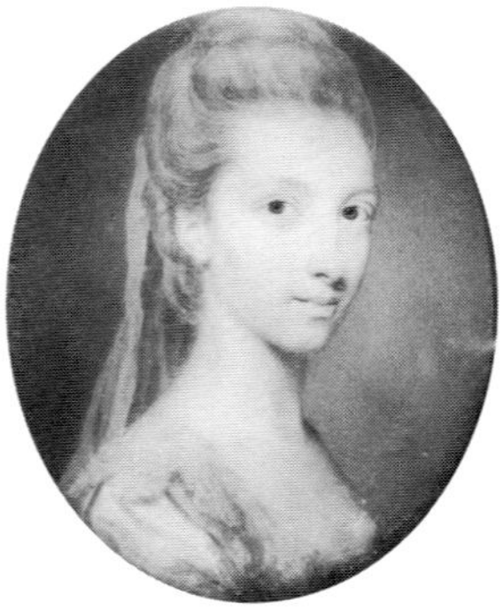

John Smart
near Norwich 1741/43 – 1811 London
Mary Cholmondeley, (d.1806), 1775
Signed and dated: *J.S. 1775*.
4 x 3.3, watercolour on ivory
Miss Mary A. McNeill Bequest, 1985. NGI 19260. see p. 72.

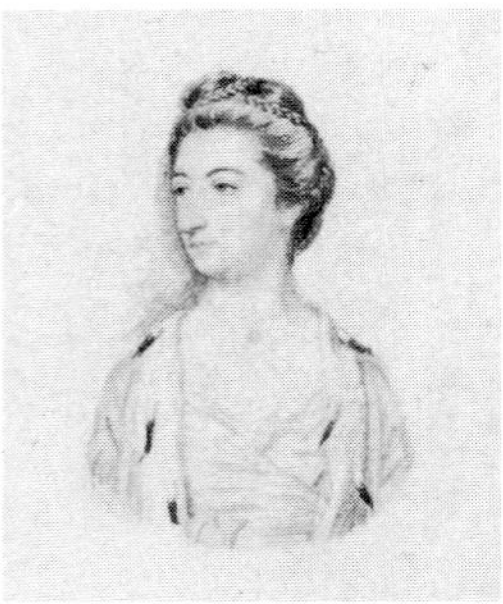

John Smart
Lady Margaret Clive, (born Maskelyne, 1733–1817), wife of 'Clive of India'
6.2 x 6.5, pencil and watercolour on board
Miss Mary A. McNeill Bequest, 1985
NGI 19261

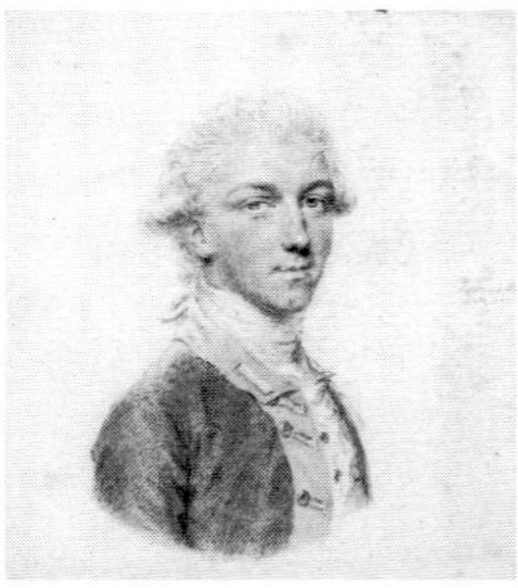

John Smart
Captain Cooke of the 'Blues', possibly Sir George Cooke, Bt., or Bryan Cooke
6.6 x 6, pencil and watercolour on board
Miss Mary A. McNeill Bequest, 1985
NGI 19262

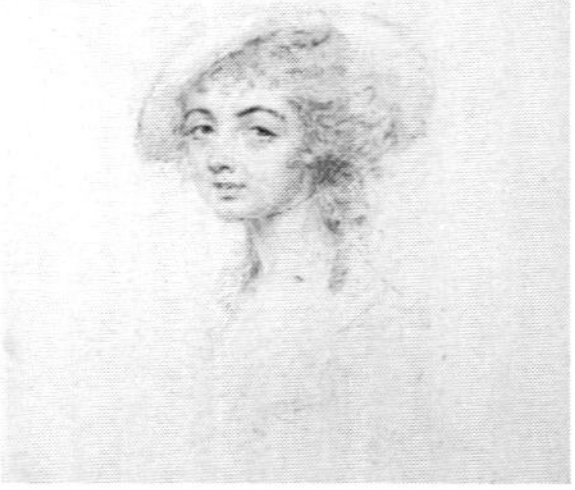

John Smart
Lady Helena Oakeley, (born Beatson, active 1777–1839)
6.3 x 7.2, pencil and wash on board
Miss Mary A. McNeill Bequest, 1985
NGI 19263

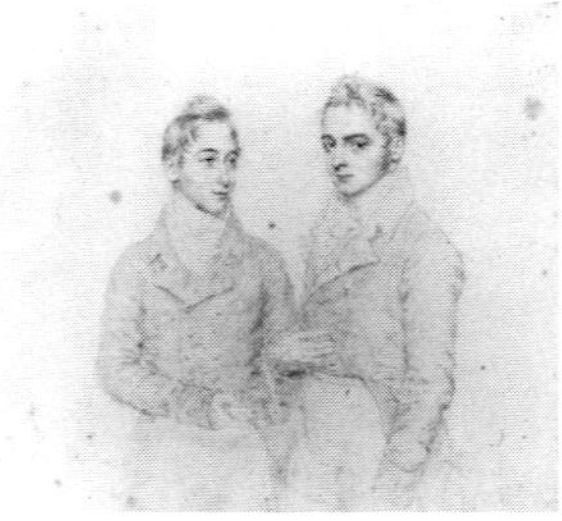

John Smart
(?) Henry Wigram,(1791–1866), and a brother, sons of Sir Robert Wigram, Bt., of Co. Wexford,
1805. 17.2 x 19.9, pencil on paper
Miss Mary A. McNeill Bequest, 1985
NGI 19265. see p. 73.

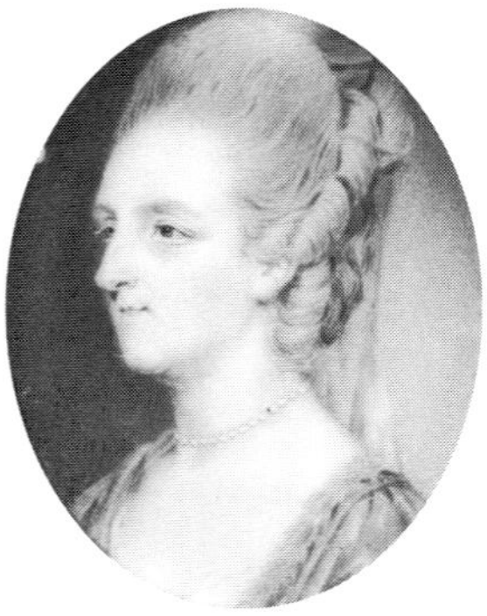

After John Smart
Countess Jane Macartney, (born Stuart, 1742–1828), wife of Earl Macartney
(copy of watercolour miniature)
4.1 x 3.3, enamel on copper
Miss Mary A. McNeill Bequest, 1985
NGI 19264

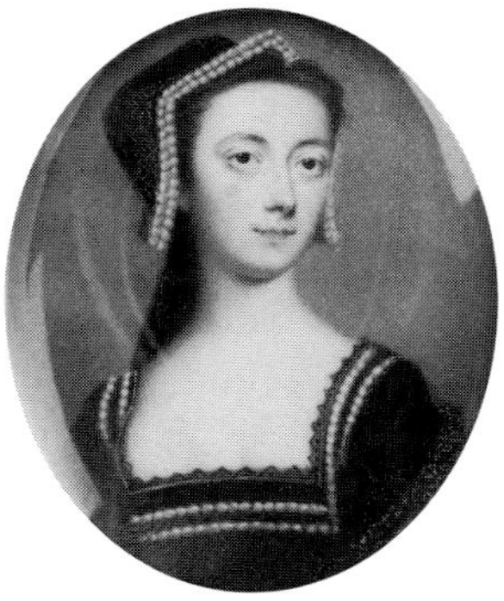

GERVASE SPENCER
England c.1715 – 1763 London
Portrait of a lady in Holbein dress, c.1750
Signed: *G S*
4.8 x 4.2, enamel on copper
Presented by Sir Alfred Chester Beatty, 1951.
NGI 3615. see p. 54.

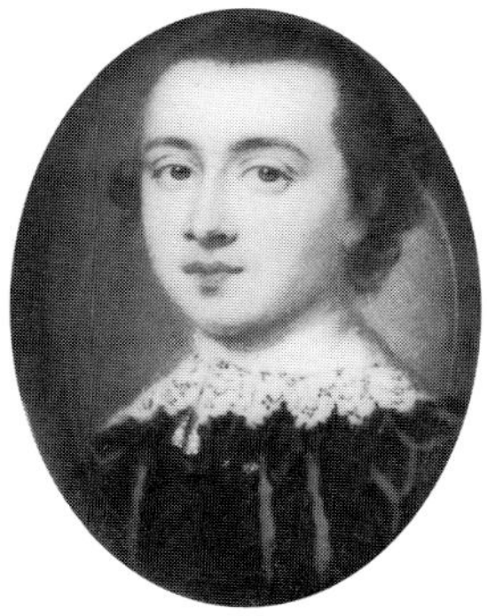

GERVASE SPENCER
Portrait of a youth in a Van Dyck costume, 1753
Signed and dated on reverse: *G. Spencer Pinxt. 1753*
2.9 x 2.3, enamel on gold
Presented by Sir Alfred Chester Beatty, 1951
NGI 3616. see p. 54.

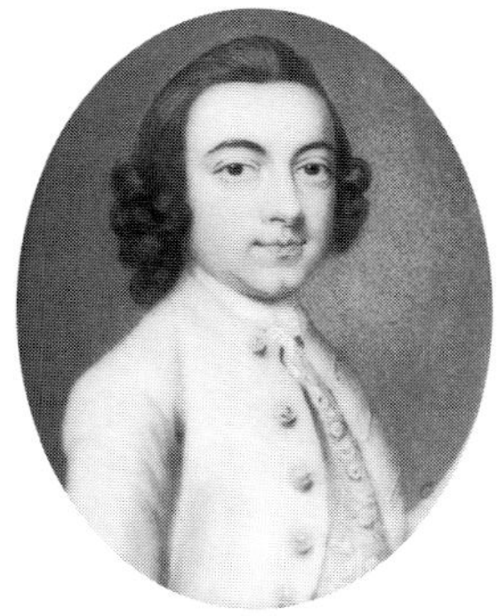

GERVASE SPENCER
Portrait of a man in a grey coat, 1749
Signed and dated: *G.S. 1749*
4.5 x 3.5, enamel on copper
Presented by Sir Alfred Chester Beatty, 1951
NGI 3632

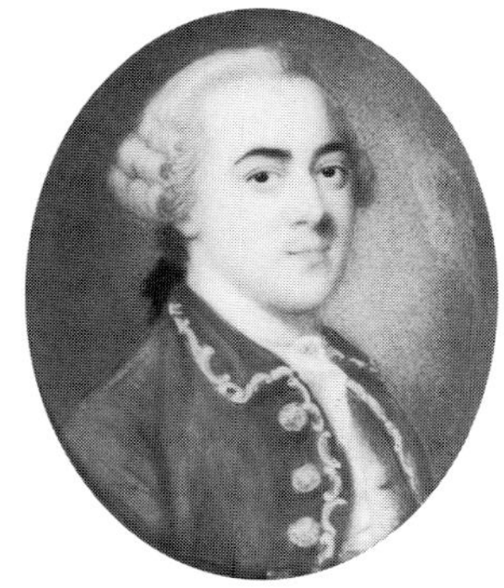

GERVASE SPENCER
Portrait of a man in a red coat, 1755
Signed and dated: *G S 1755*
2.8 x 2.4, enamel on gold
Presented by Sir Alfred Chester Beatty, 1951
NGI 3664. see pp. 54–55.

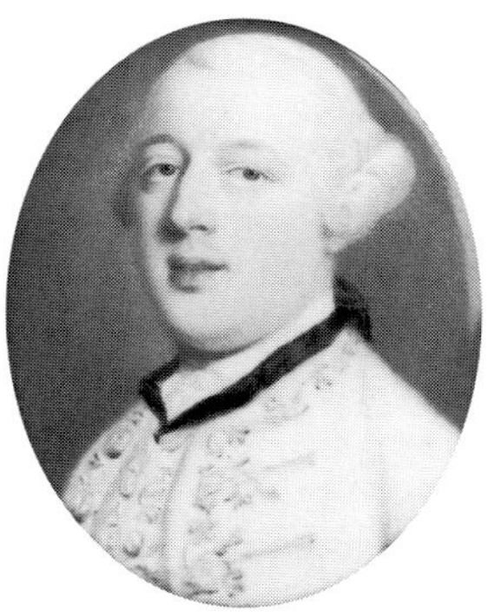

GERVASE SPENCER
Portrait of a man in a white coat, 1755
Signed and dated: *G S 1755*
2.8 x 2.3, enamel on gold
Presented by Sir Alfred Chester Beatty, 1951
NGI 3670

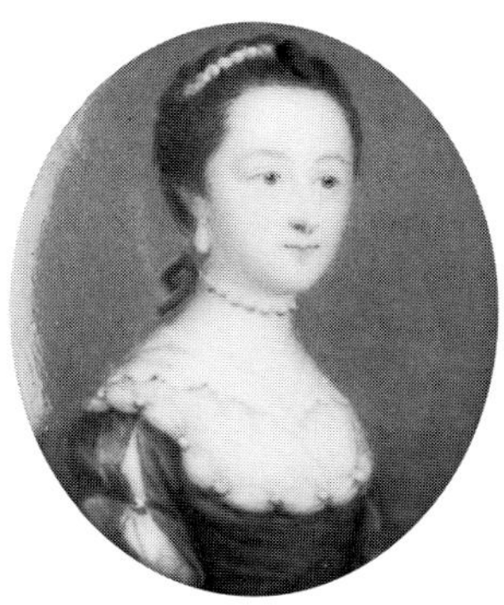

GERVASE SPENCER
Portrait of a young lady in a purple dress, c.1755
Signed: *G S*
3.4 x 2.9, enamel on copper
Presented by Sir Alfred Chester Beatty, 1951
NGI 3672. see p. 55.

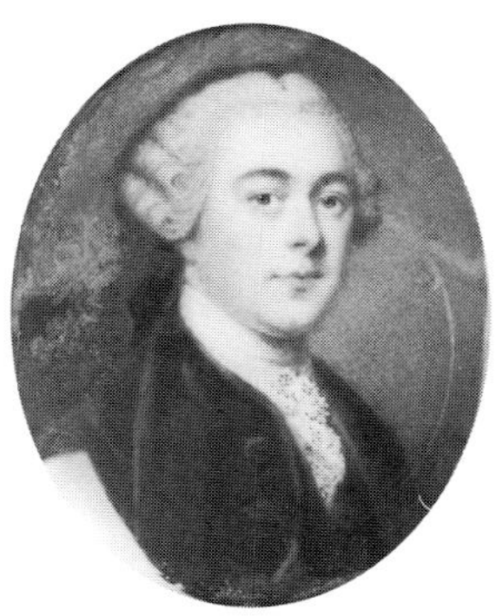

GERVASE SPENCER
(?)William Pitt, 1st Earl of Chatham, (1708–1778), British Prime Minister
Signed: *G.S.*
3.1 x 2.8, enamel on copper
Presented by Sir Alfred Chester Beatty, 1951
NGI 3674

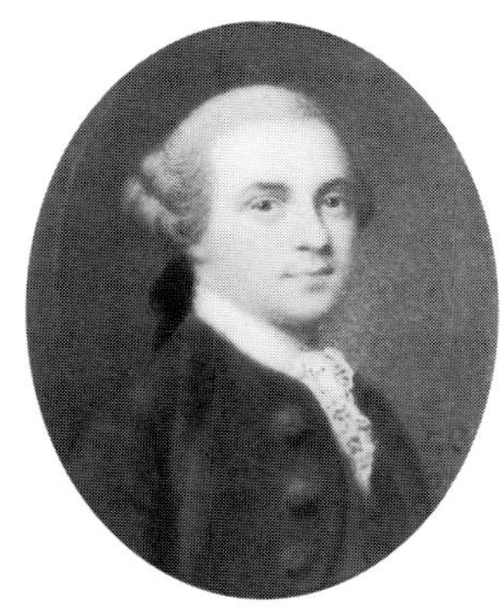

GERVASE SPENCER
Portrait of a man in a burgundy coat, 1757
Signed and dated: *GS 1757*
2.8 x 2.4, enamel on copper
Presented by Sir Alfred Chester Beatty, 1951
NGI 3681

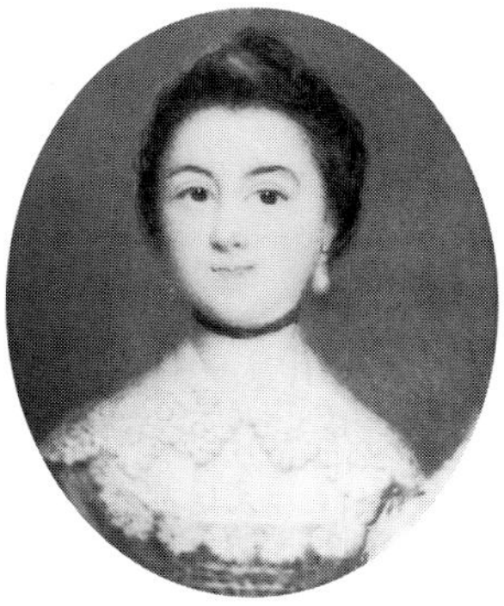

GERVASE SPENCER
Portrait of a young lady in a blue dress, 1760
Signed and dated: *G.S. 1760*
3.4 x 3, enamel on copper
Presented by Sir Alfred Chester Beatty, 1951
NGI 3685

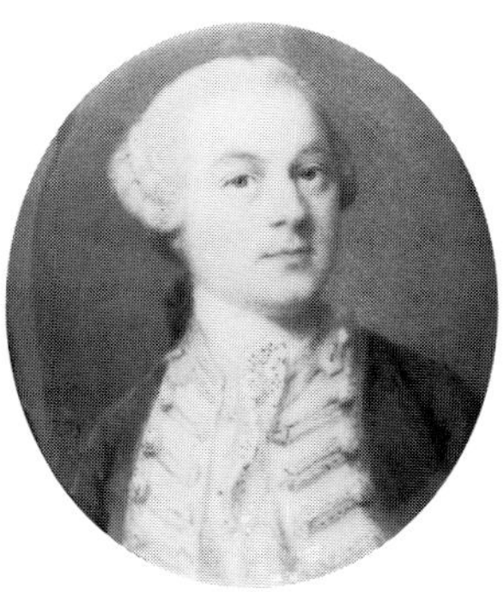

GERVASE SPENCER
Portrait of a man in a blue coat with gold braid, 1758
Signed and dated: *G S 1758*
3.3 x 2.8, enamel on copper
Presented by Sir Alfred Chester Beatty, 1951
NGI 3739

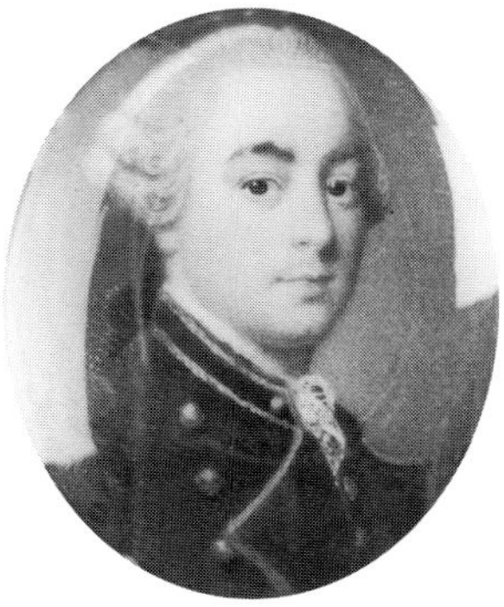

GERVASE SPENCER
Portrait of a man in a blue coat edged with gold, 1750
Signed and dated: *G.S. 1750*
3.1 x 2.8, enamel on copper
Presented by Sir Alfred Chester Beatty, 1951
NGI 3745

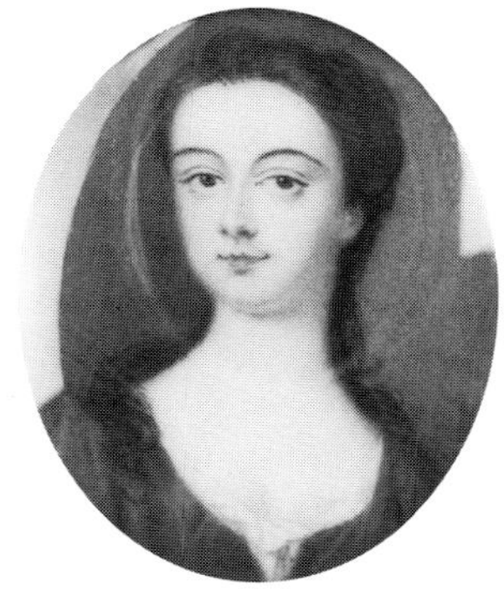

GERVASE SPENCER
Portrait of a lady in a blue dress with undressed hair
Signed: *G S*
3.5 x 3, enamel on copper
Presented by Sir Alfred Chester Beatty, 1951
NGI 3747

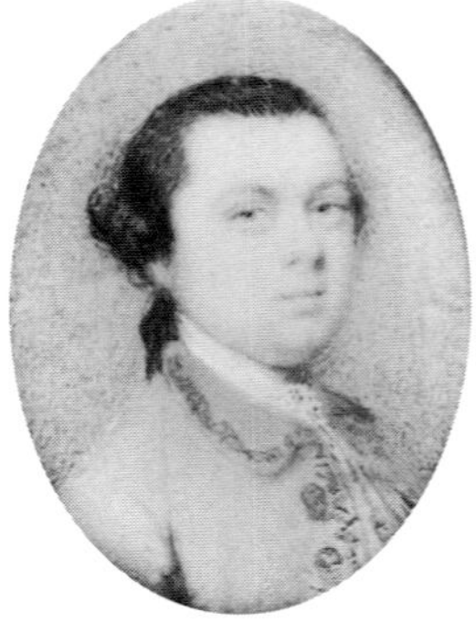

GERVASE SPENCER
Portrait of a man in a mauve coat
Signed and part dated: *GS 17...*
3 x 2.3, watercolour on ivory
Miss Mary A. McNeill Bequest, 1985
NGI 19250

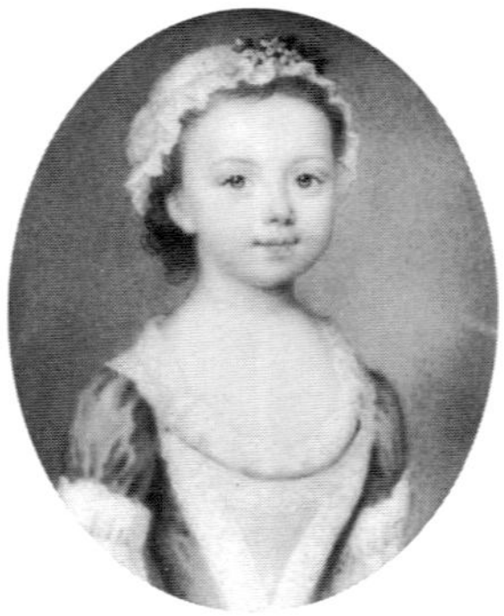

GERVASE SPENCER
Portrait of a young girl
4.3 x 3.6, enamel on copper
Miss Mary A. McNeill Bequest, 1985
NGI 19251

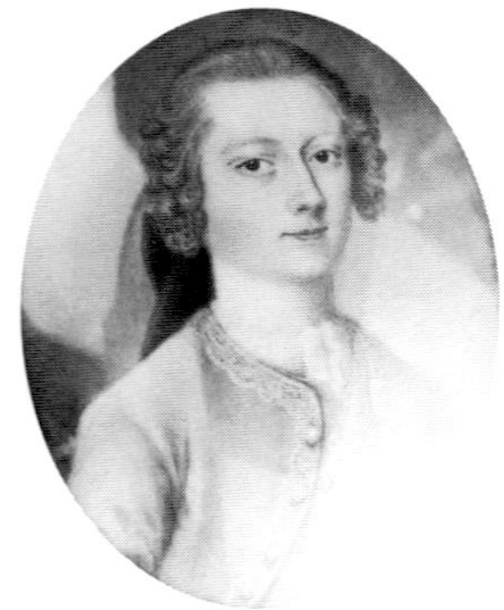

CIRCLE OF GERVASE SPENCER
Portrait of a young man in a pale violet coat
4.7 x 3.9, enamel on gold, set on a patch box
Transferred from the NMI, 1969 (where presented by Mrs M. Sullivan, 1949)
NGI 7103. see Illus. 8

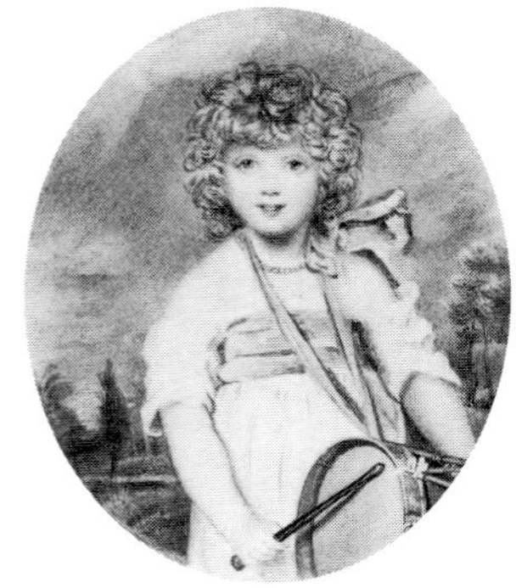

LADY ANNA MARIA STANHOPE (MARCHIONESS OF TAVISTOCK AND DUCHESS OF BEDFORD)
(?) London 1783 – 1857 London
Hon. Leicester Fitzgerald Charles Stanhope, (1784–1862), later 5th Earl of Harrington, the artist's brother, as a boy (after J. Reynolds oil, 1788, mezzotinted 1789)
8.7 x 7.5, watercolour on card
Milltown Gift, 1902. NGI 7324

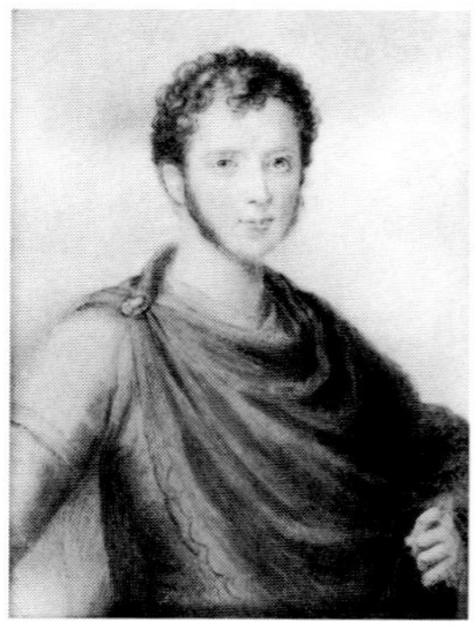

LADY ANNA MARIA STANHOPE
Leicester Fitzgerald Charles Stanhope, later 5th Earl of Harrington, (1784–1862), the artist's brother. 9.5 x 7.6, watercolour on ivory
Milltown Gift, 1902. NGI 7325

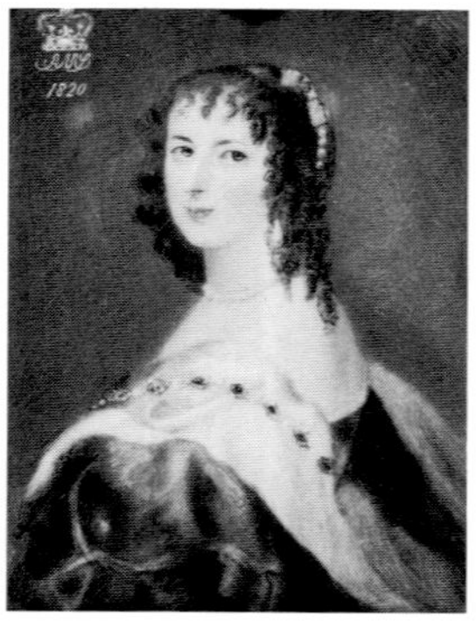

LADY ANNA MARIA STANHOPE
Self-Portrait, 1820
Signed and dated: *AMS*(in mono) *1820*
9.3 x 7.4, watercolour on ivory
Milltown Gift, 1902
NGI 7326

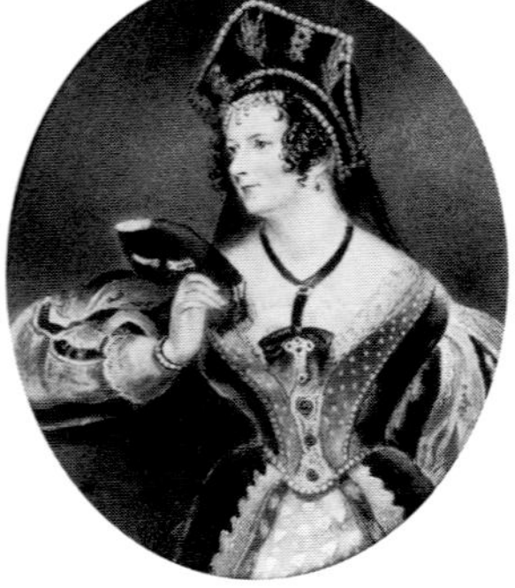

LADY ANNA MARIA STANHOPE
Self-Portrait in fancy dress holding a mask
12.5 x 10.1, watercolour on paper
Milltown Gift, 1902
NGI 7327

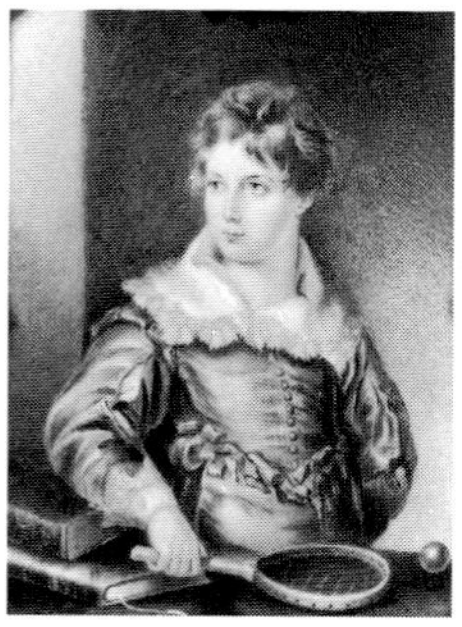

LADY ANNA MARIA STANHOPE
William Russell, Marquess of Tavistock, later 8th Duke of Bedford, (1809–1872), the artist's son, as a boy, 1820s. Signed and part dated: *AMS*(in mono) *182...*
15.9 x 11.7, watercolour on ivory
Milltown Gift, 1902. NGI 7328

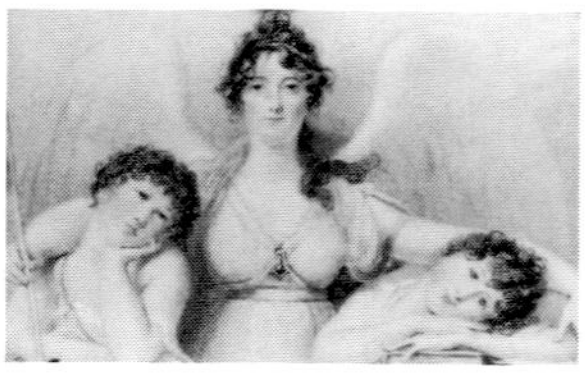

LADY ANNA MARIA STANHOPE
Self-Portrait with her sisters, (left) Lady Caroline Stanhope, (d.1853), (right) Lady Charlotte Stanhope, later Duchess of Leinster, (1793– 1859), c.1805. 7.8 x 12, watercolour on ivory. Milltown Gift, 1902. NGI 7329. see p. 127.

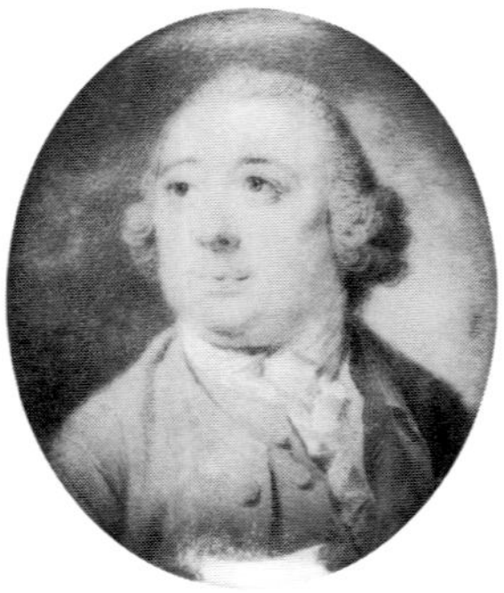

LUKE SULLIVAN
Co. Louth 1705 – 1771 London
Portrait of a man in mushroom coloured coat, c.1765
Signed: *LS*(in mono)
3.8 x 3.3, watercolour on ivory
Miss Mary A. McNeill Bequest, 1985. NGI 19248. see pp. 50–51.

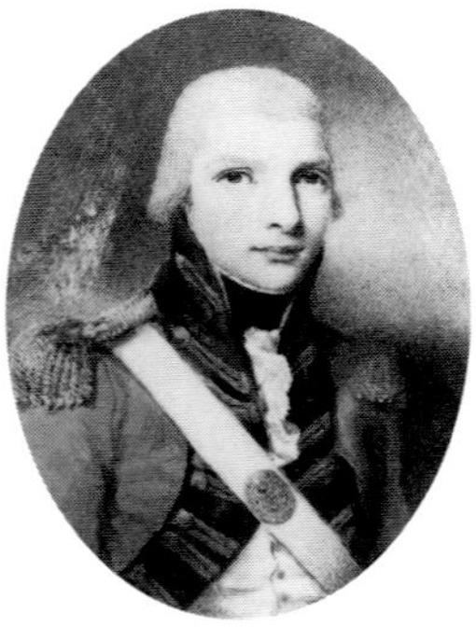

JOHN THOMASEN
active Ireland late 18th century
Richard Gorges of Kilbran, Co. Meath
Signed: *IT*. 7.3 x 5.6, watercolour on ivory. Transferred from the NMI, 1969 (where presented by Mrs G. Gorges, 1958)
NGI 7192

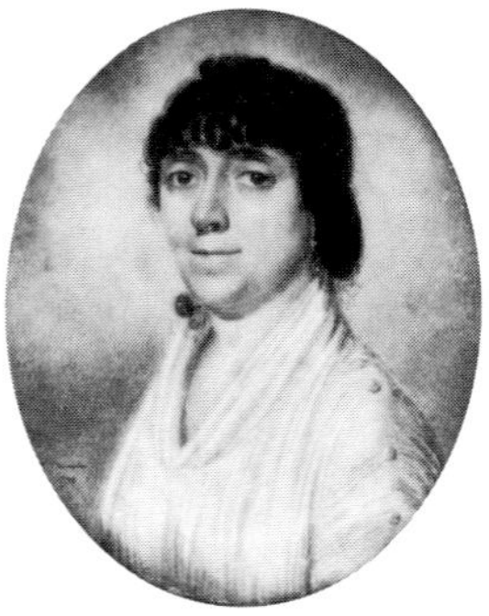

THOMAS CLEMENT THOMPSON
Belfast c.1778 – 1857 Cheltenham
Mrs Reid, wife of Captain Reid of Co. Tipperary, 1799
Signed and dated: *T Thompson 1799*. 6.8 x 5.6, watercolour on ivory. Transferred from the NMI, 1969 (where purchased 1911)
NGI 7084. see p. 123.

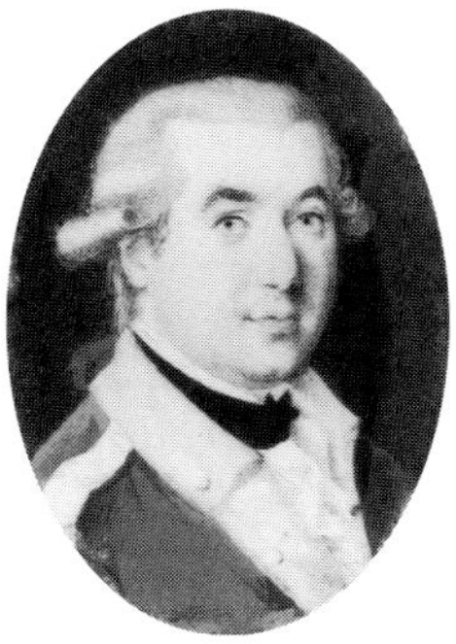

ROBERT WADE
active Dublin c.1765 – 1785 Dublin
Richard Ellis, (1744–1814), (husband of NGI 7185), c.1780
3 x 2.1, watercolour on ivory
Transferred from the NMI, 1969 (where purchased 1939)
NGI 7186. see p. 72.

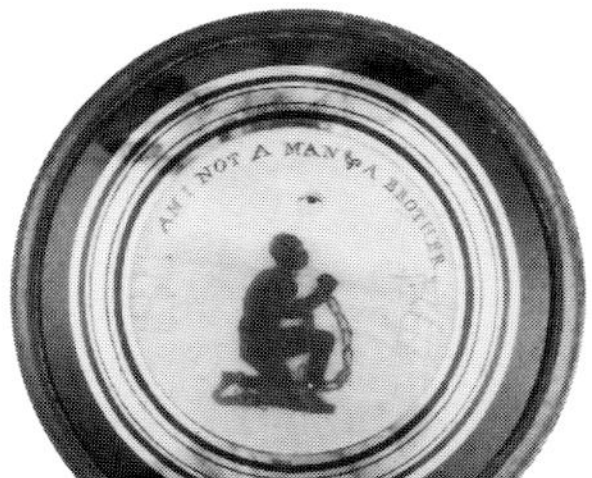

AFTER JOSIAH WEDGWOOD
Burslem, Staffordshire 1730 – 1795 Etruria, Staffordshire
Am I not a Man and a Brother, c.1790. 3.8 diam., ivory, metal and watercolour on ivory
Presented by Sir Alfred Chester Beatty, 1951
NGI 3722. see p. 63.

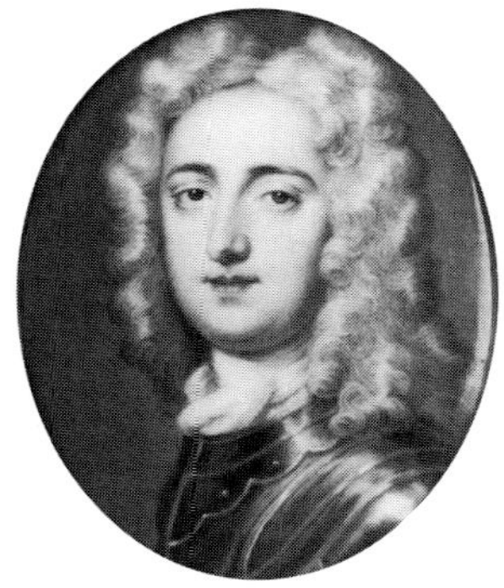

CHRISTIAN FRIEDRICH ZINCKE
Dresden 1683/85 – 1767 London
Portrait of a man in armour, 1715
Signed and dated on reverse: CF(in mono) *Zincke. Fecit 1715*
4.3 x 3.5, enamel on copper
Presented by Sir Alfred Chester Beatty, 1951
NGI 3593

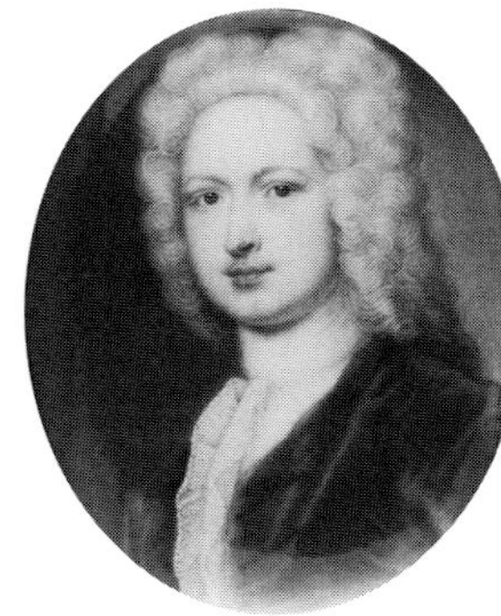

CHRISTIAN FRIEDRICH ZINCKE
The Hon. Thomas Foley, (d.1766), later 2nd Baron Foley of Kidderminster, 1723
Inscribed, signed and dated on reverse: **CF*(in mono) *Zincke fecit 1723*. 4.5 x 3.7, enamel on gold
Presented by Sir Alfred Chester Beatty, 1951. NGI 3594. see pp. 46–47.

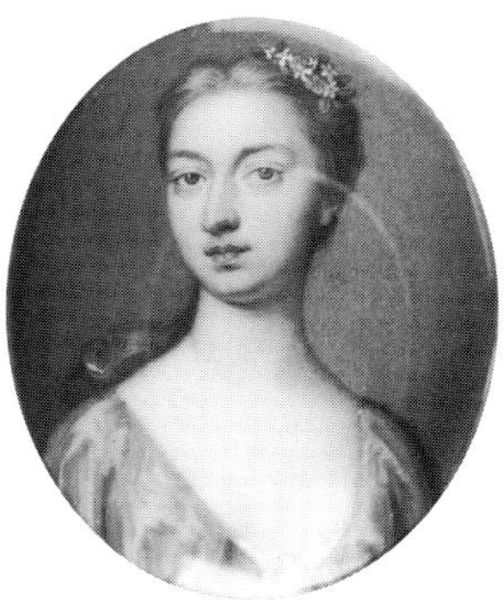

CHRISTIAN FRIEDRICH ZINCKE
Portrait of a lady in a blue dress, 1718
Signed and dated on reverse: *Zincke. fecit 1718*
4.6 x 3.8, enamel on copper
Presented by Sir Alfred Chester Beatty, 1951
NGI 3595

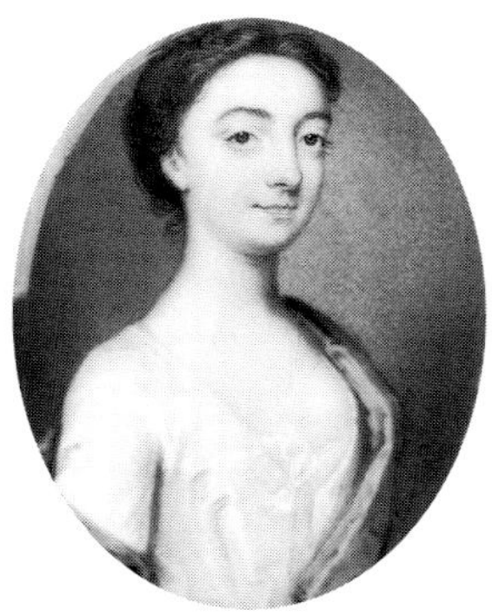

CHRISTIAN FRIEDRICH ZINCKE
Portrait of a lady in a white dress
4.5 x 3.7, enamel on copper
Presented by Sir Alfred Chester Beatty, 1951
NGI 3596

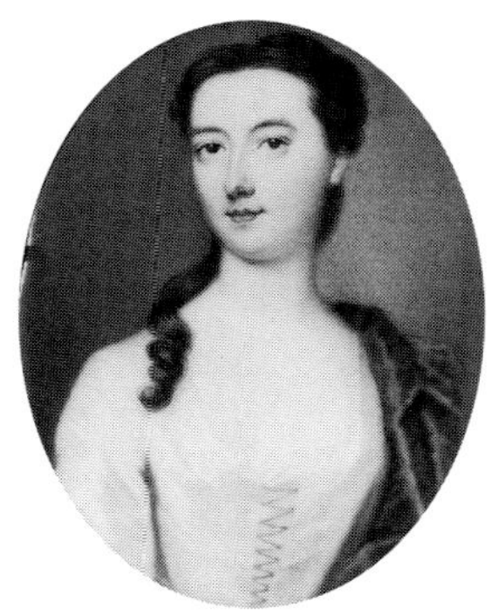

CHRISTIAN FRIEDRICH ZINCKE
Lady Dorothy Boyle, (1724–1742), daughter of the 4th Earl of Cork and 3rd Earl of Burlington, 1739. Inscribed, signed and dated on reverse: **CF*(in mono). *Zincke Fecit 1739*
4.4 x 3.6, enamel on copper
Presented by Sir Alfred Chester Beatty, 1951. NGI 3597. see p. 47.

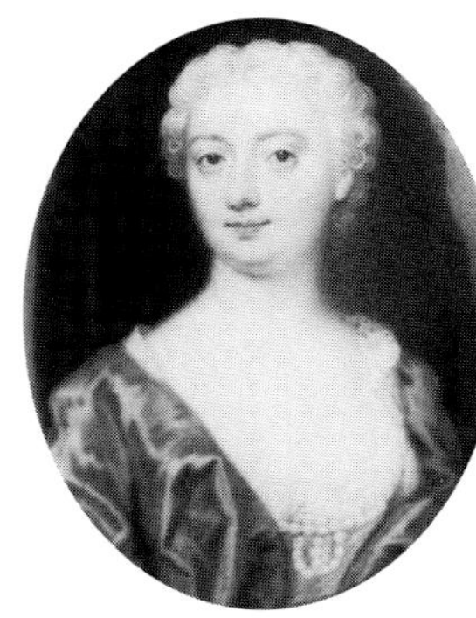

CHRISTIAN FRIEDRICH ZINCKE
Portrait of a lady in a blue dress
4.3 x 3.6, enamel on gold
Presented by Sir Alfred Chester Beatty, 1951
NGI 3648

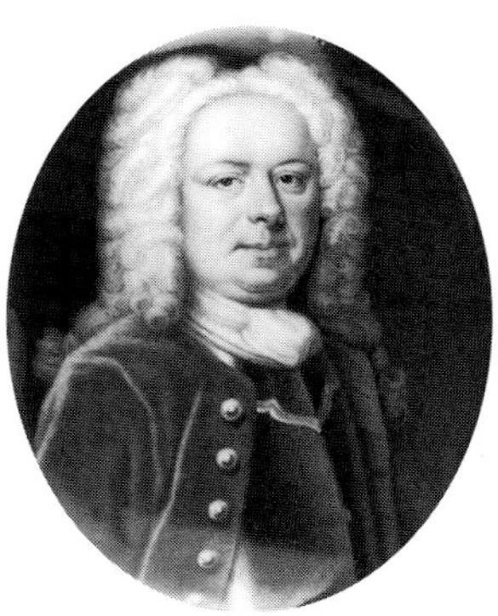

CHRISTIAN FRIEDRICH ZINCKE
Portrait of a man with a breastplate, 1736
Dated 1736 on reverse
6.7 x 5.4, enamel on copper
Presented by Sir Alfred Chester Beatty, 1951
NGI 3658

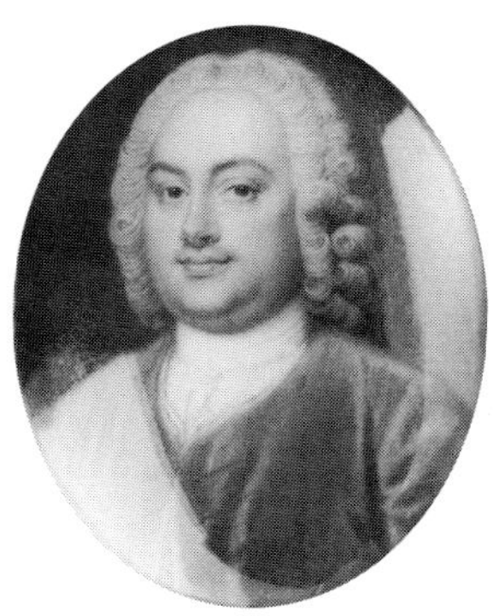

CHRISTIAN FRIEDRICH ZINCKE
Portrait of a man in a blue coat
4.3 x 3.7, enamel on copper
Presented by Sir Alfred Chester Beatty, 1951
NGI 3693

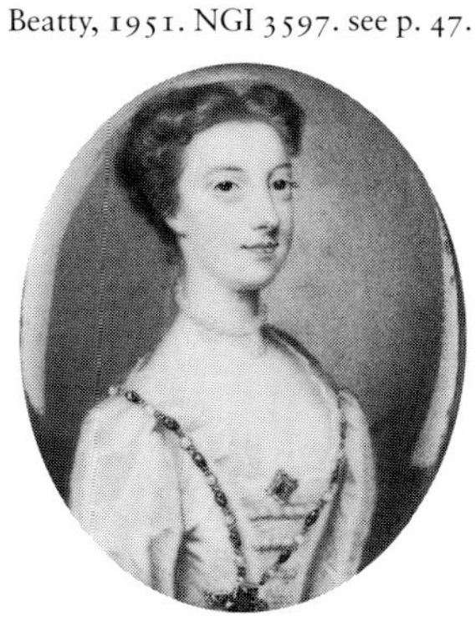

CHRISTIAN FRIEDRICH ZINCKE
Margaret Cavendish, Duchess of Portland, (born Harley, 1715–1785), Wife of the 2nd Duke, 1735. Inscribed, signed and dated on reverse: **CF*(in mono) *Zincke fect. 1735*. 4.5 x 3.7, enamel on copper. Presented by Sir Alfred Chester Beatty, 1951.
NGI 3744. see p. 47.

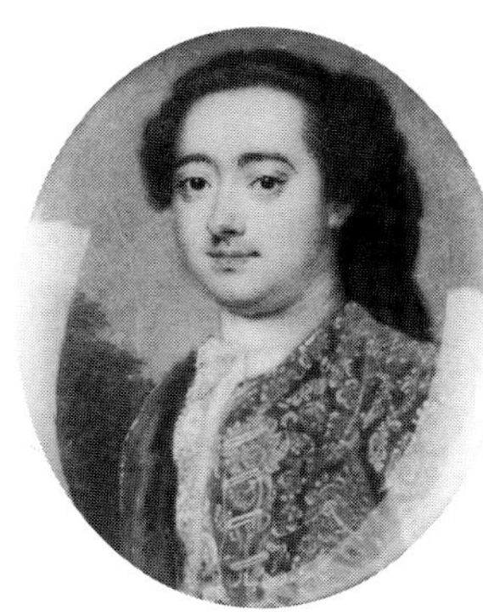

CHRISTIAN FRIEDRICH ZINCKE
So-called portrait of William Bentinck, 2nd Duke of Portland, (1709–1762)
3.5 x 2.3, enamel on copper
Presented by Sir Alfred Chester Beatty, 1951
NGI 3765. Illus. 8

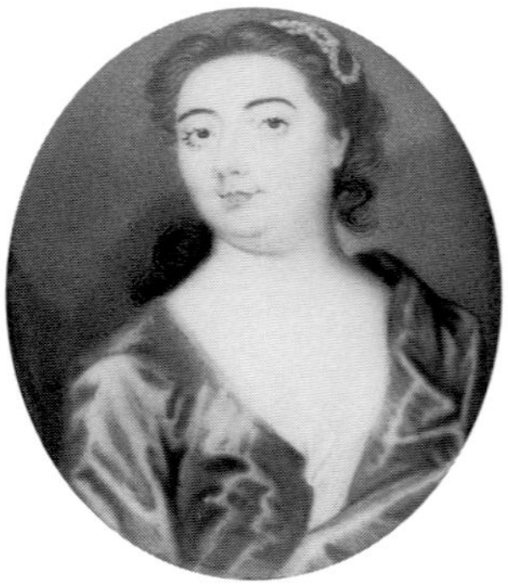

Christian Friedrich Zincke
Portrait of a lady in a blue dress
4.5 x 3.8, enamel on copper
Presented by Sir Alfred Chester Beatty, 1951
NGI 7042

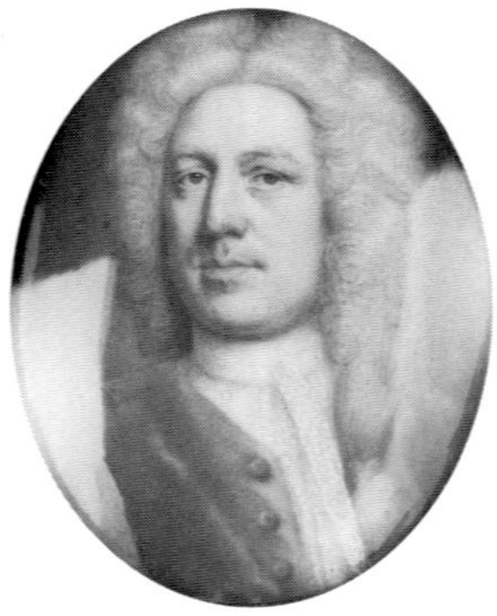

Attributed to Christian Friedrich Zincke
Portrait of a man in a purple coat
4.3 x 3.8, enamel on copper
Presented by Sir Alfred Chester Beatty, 1951
NGI 3638

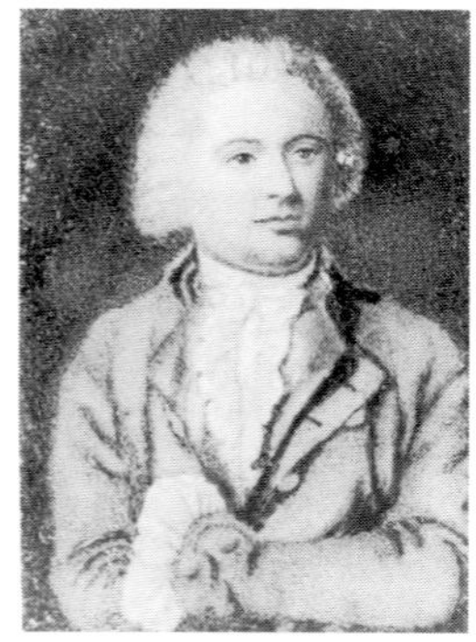

After Johann Zoffany
near Frankfurt-am-Main 1733 – 1810 Strand-on-the-Green, near London
David Garrick, (1717–1777), Actor (after NGI 530 of 1760s)
8.7 x 6.1, watercolour on ivory
Transferred from the NMI, 1969 (where provenance unknown)
NGI 7187

Use of initials and monograms^{M} in signatures by miniature painters

B	Lucius Barber (active 1746–1767)
AB^{M}	Adam Buck (1759–1833)
ABL^{M}	Andrew Benjamin Lens (active c.1713–after 1779)
AEC^{M}	Alfred Edward Chalon (1780–1860)
AMS	Lady Anna Maria Stanhope (1783–1857)
AP	Andrew Plimer (1763–1837)
AR	Andrew Robertson (1777–1845)
AR^{M}	Archibald Robertson (1765–1835)
BL^{M}	Bernard Lens III (1682–1740)
CB^{M}	Charles Boit (1662–1727)
CFZ^{M}	Christian Friedrich Zincke (1683/85–1767)
CR	Christian Richter (1678–1732)
DDG	David des Granges (1611/13– ?1675)
GE	George Engleheart (1750/53–1839)
GH	Gustavus Hamilton (c.1739–1775)
GL	George Lawrence (c.1758–1802)
GS	Gervase Spencer (c.1715–1763)
HB^{M}	Henry Bone (1755–1834)
HH^{M}	Horace Hone (1754/56–1825/27)
HJ^{M}	H. de Janvry (active 1793–1800)
HS/S	Henry Spicer (1743–1804)
IH	John Camillus Hone (1759–1836)
IT	John Thomasen (active late 18c)
JB	John Bogle (c.1746–1803)
JM^{M}	Jeremiah Meyer (1735–1789)
JR^{M}	Jean André Rouquet (1701–1758)
JS	James Scouler (c.1740–1812)
JS	John Smart (1741/43–1811)
LB^{M}	Lucius Barber (active 1746–1767)
LS^{M}	Luke Sullivan (1705–1771)
NH^{M}	Nathaniel Hone (1718–1784)
NS	Noah Seaman (active 1724–1741)
OH^{M}	Ozias Humphry (1742–1810)
PC	Peter Crosse (?1630–?1716)
PC	Penelope Carwardine (c.1730–1801)
R	Jean André Rouquet (1701–1758)
RC^{M}	Richard Cosway (1742–1821)
SC	Samuel Cooper (?1608–1672)
SC	Samuel Collins (1735–1768) – smooth strokes
SC	Samuel Cotes (1734–1818) – broken strokes
SE	Sarah, Countess of Essex (c.1761–1838)
SL	Samuel Lover (1797–1868)
SS	Samuel Shelley (1756–1808)
TD	Thomas Day (c.1732–1807)
TF^{M}	Thomas Flatman (1635–1688)
TH	Thomas Hazlehurst (c.1740–1821)
TT	Thomas Clement Thompson (c.1778–1857)
WB^{M}	William Bate (active 1799–1845)
WB	William Birch (1755–1834)
WB^{M}	William Bone, Senior (active 1815–1843)
WJN	William John Newton (1785–1869)

Irish and English Miniatures Numerical List

Former attribution in square brackets

NGI	ARTIST
2034	C. Byrne
2051	J. Comerford
2052	J. Comerford
2053	J. Comerford
2076	W. Denning
2116	T. Gainsborough
2141	After T. Lawrence
2143	J.P. Haverty
2156	H. Hone
2157	H. Hone
2158	H. Hone
2196	B. Mulrenin
2158	H. Hone
2206	W.J. Newton
2231	J. Petrie
2333	W. Bate
2338	S. Lover [Attrib. S. Lover]
2353	J. Comerford
2376	G. Jackson
2433	G. Lawrence [Attrib. G. Lawrence]
2434	Ch. Robertson
2524	Ch. Robertson
2525	Ch. Robertson
2529	Cl. Robertson
2530	F. Buck [Attrib. A. Buck]
2531	Irish School (early 19c)
2532	S.T. Roch
2533	Attributed to J. Reily
2552	J. Bogle
2553	A. Buck
2554	A. Buck
2555	A. Buck
2581	J. Cooke
2612	H. Hone
2657	H. Hone
2672	S.T. Roch
2673	Irish School (18c) [Attrib. J. Comerford]
2685	English School (c.1830) [G. Chinnery]
2686	T. Hazlehurst
2716	English School (18c) [Ascr. G. Chinnery]
2717	N. Hone
2718	J. Faber
2719	Follower of C. Jervas [Ascr. C. Jervas]
2726	R. Barber
2735	J. Comerford [Attrib. J. Comerford]
2739	J. Comerford
2745	Irish School (c.1810)
2924	J. Comerford
2926	Irish School (c.1800)
2949	Attributed to J.S. Mulvany
2951	A. E. Chalon
2952	A. E. Chalon
2966	D.B. Murphy
3023	R. Cosway
3024	R. Cosway
3034	Irish School (late 18c)
3036	J. Petrie
3195	J. Comerford
3196	J. Comerford
3197	J. Comerford
3198	J. Comerford
3199	J. Comerford
3200	J. Comerford
3201	J. Comerford
3202	J. Comerford
3211	T. Gainsborough
3267	S. Lover
3568	H.P. Bone
3569	H. Bone
3570	H. Bone
3571	H. Bone
3572	H. Bone
3573	W. Bone, Senior
3574	H. Bone
3575	H. Bone
3576	H. Bone
3577	H. Bone
3578	W. Bone, Senior
3579	W. Bone, Senior
3580	P.J. Bone
3581	Countess of Essex
3582	W. Craft
3583	J.H. Hurter
3584	W. R. Birch

NGI	ARTIST
3585	W. Craft
3588	W. Bone, Senior
3593	C.F. Zincke
3594	C.F. Zincke
3595	C.F. Zincke
3596	C.F. Zincke
3597	C.F. Zincke
3601	J. A. Rouquet
3607	Continental artist – G. M.... [as English artist]
3610	W. Prewett
3611	J.H. Hurter
3612	N. Seaman
3613	J. Simpson [W. Simpson]
3614	J. Simpson [W. Simpson]
3615	G. Spencer
3616	G. Spencer
3617	W. Essex
3618	H.P. Bone
3619	H. Bone
3620	H. Bone
3621	W. Bone, Senior
3622	W. Bone, Senior
3623	W. R. Birch
3624	G. Macpherson
3625	J. Lee
3626	W. Craft
3627	W.C. Bell
3628	W.C. Bell
3629	Countess of Essex
3632	G. Spencer
3634	French artist – S. Bernard [as English artist]
3635	N. Hone
3636	J. Meyer
3637	English School (17c)
3638	Attributed to C.F. Zincke [English School (18c)]
3640	Continental School (18c) [English School (18c)]
3641	Continental School (18c) [English School (18c)]
3646	Attributed to J. A. Rouquet [English School (1741)]

NGI	ARTIST
3648	C.F. Zincke [English School early 18c]
3649	J. A. Rouquet
3650	English School (late 18c)
3651	C. Boit
3652	Follower of C. Boit [C. Boit]
3653	J. Scouler
3654	W. R. Birch
3656	J. A. Rouquet
3657	French School – F. Adam [I. Adam]
3658	C.F. Zincke
3659	German artist – C.F. Ardin [Attrib. J.-A. Arlaud]
3660	German artist – C.F. Ardin [Attrib. J.-A. Arlaud]
3662	English School (c.1850) [English School (19c)]
3663	N. Hone
3664	G. Spencer
3665	Continental School (19c) [English School (19c)]
3666	N. Hone
3667	W.P. Long
3668	W. Craft
3670	G. Spencer
3672	G. Spencer
3674	G. Spencer
3679	English School (c.1750) [English School (18c)]
3681	G. Spencer
3685	G. Spencer
3693	C.F. Zincke
3695	M. Gunter
3696	M. Gunter
3697	M. Gunter
3698	M. Gunter
3699	M. Gunter
3700	M. Gunter
3701	M. Gunter
3702	Continental School (18c) [English School (18c)]
3705	L. Barber
3707	W. Bate
3708	W. Bate
3709	W. Bate

NGI	ARTIST
3720	Continental School (18c)
	[English School (18c)]
3722	After J. Wedgwood
3728	Attributed to R. Barber
	[Irish School c.1740]
3729	English School (c.1740)
3731	S. Collins [S. Cotes]
3736	G.M. Moser
3739	G. Spencer
3741	Circle of J. A. Rouquet
3744	C.F. Zincke
3745	G. Spencer
3747	G. Spencer
3749	English School (early 18c)
3751	English School (18c)
3752	C. Boit
3760	G.M. Moser
3761	English School (18c)
3765	C.F. Zincke [Attrib. C.F. Zincke]
3766	English School (early 18c)
3771	E. James
4015	W. Essex
6046	Attributed to S. Lover
6228	Ch. Robertson
6229	Ch. Robertson
6314	A. Dunn
6323	J. Petrie
7012	English School (early 19c)
7013	Continental School (19c)
	[English School (19c)]
7014	S. Shelley [English School (late 18c)]
7015	English School (early 18c)
7016	English School (19c)
7017	English School (late 18c)
7018	English School (early 18c)
7019	English School (18c)
7020	English School (late 18c)
7023	Circle of J. A. Arlaud
7024	Follower of G. Engleheart
	[G. Engleheart]
7026	Ch. Robertson [A. Buck]
7029	English School (18c)
7031	Swedish artist – M. de Meytens
	[J. Meyer]
7032	English School (18c)

NGI	ARTIST
7033	English School (18c)
7034	English School (18c)
7035	English School (18c)
7036	English School (18c) [Attrib. G. Smart]
7037	H. de Janvry [H. J....]
7038	English or Irish School (18c)
7039	English School (18c)
7040	Continental School (early 19c)
	[English School (early 19c)]
7041	English School (early 19c)
7042	C.F. Zincke
7043	English School (late 18c)
7044	Attributed to L. Barber [Attrib. H. Bone]
7045	S. Cooper
7046	H. Hone
7053	English School (c.1750)
7055	English School (late 18c)
7056	H. Hone
7057	Irish School (late 18c) [Attrib. H. Hone]
7059	French artist – Corbit [as English artist]
7061	English School (c.1770)
7062	English School (17c)
7063	Attributed to A.B. Lens [B. Lens III]
7065	English School (18c)
7066	English School (18c)
7067	English School (18c)
7068	English School (early 18c)
7070	J. Comerford
7071	Attributed to N. Hone
7072	G. Hamilton
7073	J. Ballard
7074	Irish School (early 19c)
7075	English School (18c)
	[English School (19c)]
7076	Irish School (18c)
	[Irish School (early 19c)]
7077	Irish School (early 19c)
7078	G. Lawrence
7079	Irish School (c.1810) [A. Buck]
7080	Irish School (late 18c)
7081	After R. Hunter [Irish School (18c)]
7082	N. Hone
7083	Irish School (late 18c)
7084	T.C. Thompson
7085	Irish School (early 19c) [A. Buck]

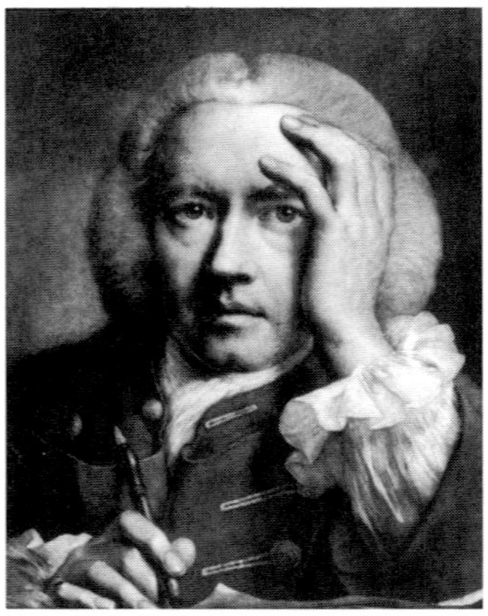

Illus. 51 *Self-Portrait*, 1760 mezzotint
THOMAS FRYE (c.1710–1762)
The dramatic lighting and sharpness of detail in the artist's late prints are in contrast to the powdery refinement of his miniatures (see Cats. 22–23).